AF605898

ONTARIO SINCE CONFEDERATION: A READER

Second Edition

Ontario since Confederation: A Reader

Second Edition

Edited by

Lori Chambers, Edgar-André Montigny,
James Onusko, and Dimitry Anastakis

UNIVERSITY OF TORONTO PRESS
Toronto Buffalo London

Toronto Buffalo London
utorontopress.com
Printed in the USA

ISBN 978-1-4875-3401-1 (cloth) ISBN 978-1-4875-3400-4 (EPUB)
ISBN 978-1-4875-2429-6 (paper) ISBN 978-1-4875-3399-1 (PDF)

Library and Archives Canada Cataloguing in Publication

Title: Ontario since Confederation : a reader / edited by Lori Chambers, Edgar-André Montigny, James Onusko, and Dimitry Anastakis.
Names: Chambers, Lori, 1965- editor. | Montigny, Edgar-André, editor. | Onusko, James A., 1972- editor. | Anastakis, Dimitry, 1970- editor.
Description: Second edition. | Includes bibliographical references and index.
Identifiers: Canadiana (print) 20240393600 | Canadiana (ebook) 20240393635 | ISBN 9781487524296 (paper) | ISBN 9781487534011 (cloth) | ISBN 9781487534004 (EPUB) | ISBN 9781487533991 (PDF)
Subjects: LCSH: Ontario–History. | CSH: Ontario–History–1867-
Classification: LCC FC3061 .O577 2024 | DDC 971.3/03–dc23

Cover design: John Beadle
Cover image: ilbusca / istockphoto.com

We wish to acknowledge the land on which the University of Toronto Press operates. This land is the traditional territory of the Wendat, the Anishnaabeg, the Haudenosaunee, the Métis, and the Mississaugas of the Credit First Nation.

University of Toronto Press acknowledges the financial support of the Government of Canada, the Canada Council for the Arts, and the Ontario Arts Council, an agency of the Government of Ontario, for its publishing activities.

Contents

PART II: CLASS, BUSINESS, AND POLITICS

PART III: FAMILY

PART IV: EPIDEMIOLOGIES AND ENVIRONMENTS

Tables and Figures

TABLES

FIGURES

Preface to the First Edition, 2000

Ontario since Confederation: A Reader is a collection of essays dealing with the history of Ontario. Although that may seem a straightforward statement of fact, it is by no means obvious what the subject matter of such a collection should be. There is considerable debate over what constitutes 'Ontario' history.

For some, Ontario history simply refers to the history of the province of Ontario. According to this definition, Ontario is but one region of the many that make up Canada. Many historians have found this 'limited' definition of Ontario history problematic. As Michael Piva puts it, while no one denies that Ontario is a region of sorts, it is a region that seems to defy description or analysis.[1] Firm portrayals of Ontario's distinctive regional character are rare. It becomes difficult to determine which topics would be included in a history of 'Ontario as a region' when few people are certain what defines Ontario as a region.

One of the main reasons why Ontario has not been clearly defined as a region is that, until recently, many Ontarians failed to regard Ontario as a region at all. Instead, any sense of regional pride was so closely associated with national pride that Ontario and Canada were almost blended into one entity, with many Ontarians assuming that what was best for Ontario was best for the nation.[2] Accordingly, most historians of Ontario did not see themselves as Ontario historians. As Peter Oliver argues, for most of the twentieth century 'there seems to have been a tacit, almost unthinking assumption that a regional approach to Ontario history was neither necessary nor appropriate.'[3] The one clear aspect of Ontario's historical identity that historians could agree on was a confident acceptance of the province's dominant role in Canadian Confederation. The fact that so many Ontario politicians played a leading role in defining and defending Canadian national ideals only helped to blur the distinction between the national identities and a sense of a specific Ontario identity.[4] For this reason, few of Ontario's historians felt that Ontario was merely a region. Instead, they treated their subject as a kind of provincial equivalent to Canada as whole.[5]

According to this definition, the subject matter of Ontario history was not the region of Ontario alone but of all Canada. This approach has made it extremely difficult for historians to decide where Ontario history ends and Canadian history begins. Therefore, any collection that purports to deal with Ontario history is bound to be criticized by some for being too local in scope, and by others for including too much 'national' history that does not focus on local Ontario issues. Recognizing this dilemma, *Ontario since Confederation* sidesteps the thorny question of whether Ontario is merely one region among the many that make up Canada, or whether it is more than a region, one tied closely to national activities and ideals. Rather, the purpose of this collection is simply to bring together a series of new essays and recently published articles that focus on Ontario. It showcases work from established scholars, promising young members of the profession, and graduate students, bringing together innovative writing on traditional topics and path-breaking work in new areas of inquiry.

For the purposes of this volume, any activity or event that occurred within Ontario, or had an impact on the development or character of the province, was recognized as being part of Ontario's history. In some cases the material is local in nature, dealing solely with provincial or even municipal activities; in others the actions of the federal government loom large. In this way, we hoped that the paradox of Ontario history could be addressed. Ontario is a region with its own local and even parochial history. At the same time, it is more than a region. The interaction between Ontario history and national history is clearly something that cannot be ignored. Only by blending the two approaches can a collection capture the dual nature of Ontario.

Despite the duality or diversity of this collection, the unifying theme of 'state and society' ensured that the articles shared a common concern with the interaction between social values and ideals on the one hand and political action and government bureaucracies on the other. From a wide range of perspectives, and exploring several superficially unrelated topics, the essays included in this collection all ask fundamental questions about the role, nature, and development of the modern bureaucratic state. How pervasive has the influence of the state been? Has the state determined or reflected social values? To what degree, and in what manner, has the power of the state been successfully resisted?

These essays are but a small example of the exciting new scholarship on the history of Ontario. Even if Ontario's status as a region is uncertain and its identifying characteristics remain undefined, interest in every aspect of Ontario's economic, social, and political history is high. Numerous scholars are now willing to call themselves Ontario historians.

This volume was a collaborative effort. The contributors donated their time, energy, and talent. The demands of work and family often intervened, and in some cases it would have been reasonable for authors to abandon this project in favour of more pressing priorities. Yet they carried on, sometimes under circumstances that were far from ideal, and we appreciate their commitment. As editors of the collection, the most exciting aspect of the project was being exposed to the wealth and breath of new research on the history of Ontario. Even more rewarding was the opportunity this project offered us to get to know the various scholars personally. The diversity of styles, personalities, and interests the authors represent attests to the diversity of Ontario and the rich fabric of its history.

We also wish to thank the many people who do not appear as contributors, but who were crucial in preparing the collection. They guided us to the historians who finally prepared the essays, advised us on topics to select, and counselled us on how best to avoid the many pitfalls that can befall a project of this scope. Special thanks are due to Emily Andrew, Jill McConkey, Frances Mundy, and senior editor Gerry Hallowell for offering us the opportunity to prepare this collection and for helping us to see it through to completion. Despite the many obstacles and frustrations involved in editing a collection of this size, it was a most worthwhile and enriching experience. We certainly learned much about Ontario in the process. We hope the collection proves as useful to others.

We dedicate this collection to 'our little ones,' Catherine and Geoffrey Chambers-Bedard and Maude Montigny-Gibbs.

NOTES

1 Michael Piva, ed., *A History of Ontario* (Toronto: Copp Clark Pitman, 1988), 1.
2 Peter Oliver, *Public and Private Persons: The Ontario Political Culture, 1914–34* (Toronto: Clark Irwin, 1975), 8.
3 Ibid., 8.
4 Allan Smith, 'Old Ontario and the Emergence of a National Frame of Mind,' in F.H. Armstrong, H.A. Stevenson, and D.J. Wilson, eds., *Aspects of Nineteenth-Century Ontario* (Toronto: University of Toronto Press, 1974), 194.
5 Sid Wise, 'Ontario's Political Culture,' in Donald C. MacDonald, ed., *Government and Politics of Ontario*, 3rd ed. (Scarborough, Ont.: Nelson, 1985), 160–1.

Acknowledgments

The editors would like to thank all the collection's contributors for their wonderful work and patience as we completed this project together. We would also like to thank the University of Toronto Press, including Len Husband, Stephanie Mazza, Christine Robertson, and Aidan Thompson. Thanks to our excellent copyeditor Matthew Kudelka, and the outside reviewers. The L.R. Wilson and R.J. Currie Chair in Canadian Business History at the University of Toronto supported publication of this collection.

Finally, James and Dimitry would like to thank the previous contributors and Lori Chambers and Edgar-André Montigny, editors of *Ontario since Confederation: A Reader* (2000), for allowing us to take on a dramatically revised version of this important collection. Perhaps, in a few decades, another set of editors may revise it yet again, resulting in an equally transformed collection, another reflection of this province and its ever-changing history.

ONTARIO SINCE CONFEDERATION: A READER

Second Edition

CHAPTER ONE

Introduction: Ontario since Confederation

In the more than two decades since *Ontario since Confederation: A Reader* first appeared, Ontario, Canada, North America, and the world have experienced a whirlwind of transformational change. In 2000, when this collection was first published, the province was in the midst of Progressive Conservative Mike Harris's tumultuous neoliberal "Common Sense Revolution," a movement that wrought dramatic change upon Ontario's social and cultural fabric. Many Ontarians, like others around the globe, had feared the Y2K threat as computer clocks tentatively scrolled towards the year 2000, yet the wholesale digitization of work, education, commerce, entertainment, and information itself was still to come. So, too, were the terrorist attacks of 9/11, with all their attendant economic and political consequences for race, religion, and geopolitics, including Canada–US relations. The Great Recession of 2008–9, which accelerated trends in inequality, precarity, and the financialization of the economy, was still a few years away. And, of course, the COVID-19 pandemic of 2020 had not yet reshaped so many people's lives, in both small and deeply profound ways.

Clearly, 2000, the year of the millennium, was not some sort of pre-dystopian paradise, as ordinary Ontarians grappled then – as they do today – with a host of difficult issues that continue to challenge the people and their province. While climate change was not as provocatively central to political and economic discourse as it is today, the environment was a growing theme in how Ontarians imagined their future. While demands for greater minority rights, particularly for women and Indigenous, racialized, LGBTQ, and disabled Canadians, had not yet exploded across the spectrum through the Me Too, Idle No More, Black Lives Matter, and other movements, intersectional demands for equality and recognition had unquestionably become increasingly prominent in Ontario's politics and policies since the end of the Second World War. And while the Ontario economy had not yet experienced the rapid deindustrialization that marked the decline of manufacturing in the province after 2003, worries about the province's future economic well-being were already being raised as longer-term post-war trends became impossible to ignore.

Many of these developing issues underpinned the chapters in *Ontario since Confederation*, a collection that explored a wide range of social, political, and economic themes. In the years since its publication, history has seemingly accelerated: Ontarians have experienced dramatic and unexpected developments; indeed, our very understanding of this history has been transformed as well. This revised collection is an effort to take into account the transformational events since it was first published, so as to reflect the equally dramatic changes in historical practice and understanding that have marked the past two decades.

In 2000, Ontario's role as Canada's keystone province was increasingly being questioned. Books like Tom Courchene's *From Heartland to North American Region State* (1997) and John Ibbitson's *Loyal No More* (2002) pondered whether the seismic changes that been unfolding since the 1980s had detached the province from its traditional role in Confederation. These changes were deep and foundational. Ontario's status as the central player within Canada's brokerage federalism had been destabilized by the fallout from more than two decades of mega-constitutional politics, which saw the province's power diminished as Quebec's and the West's demands crowded out Ontario's own challenges. Economically, the province had lost the 1980s battle against free trade, and the changes wrought by the 1989 and 1994 agreements with the US, and then with Mexico, had not only lessened the rest of the country's economic dependence on Ontario, but also significantly weakened Ontario's connections to the rest of Canada. Worse, the devastating 2008–9 recession had resulted in Ontario becoming, for the first time in its history, a "have not" province under the country's equalization schemes, a humbling reckoning that reflected Ontario's harsh new reality.

These constitutional and economic upheavals played themselves out in the political realm: between 1985 and 2003 Ontarians dizzyingly elected Liberal, New Democratic, Progressive Conservative, and then Liberal governments, a sharp contrast to the moderate Progressive Conservatism that had ruled the province steadily for forty-two years, from 1943 to 1985. Moreover, the province's inability to grapple with the long-standing demands of its Indigenous peoples for rights and recognition – reflected in conflicts from Ipperwash in 1995 to Caledonia in 2006 – meant that Ontario could no longer blissfully ignore the social and cultural problems the rest of the country had long faced. Added to these issues was the longer-term erosion of state's capacity to tackle social welfare, infrastructure, regulatory, and health challenges, from the 2000 Walkerton water crisis to the 2003 SARS outbreak, reflecting the impact of sharply neoliberal policies in a province that had once prided itself on its bland centrism.

Perhaps most destabilizing was the rapid onset of deindustrialization, which seemed to accelerate after 2002. In the automotive industry, Ontario's most important economic sector, cities and towns across the province were left reeling by plant closures that threw thousands of people out of work and disrupted communities large and small. All told, Ontario lost nearly 300,000 well-paying manufacturing jobs between 2000 and 2020, including in Oshawa, where more than a century of auto production came to a halt with the closure of General Motors' final plant in the city in 2019. Unimaginably, after five generations as the heart of Canada's auto sector, Oshawa, a city that had put much of Canada and North America on wheels, and home to junior hockey's "Generals," no longer produced cars.

All these convulsions led to some scholarly assessment of where Ontario was as a province. Greg Albo and Bryan Evans's important 2018 collection, *Divided Province: Ontario Politics in the Age of Neoliberalism*, is one of the few scholarly works that have tackled the dramatic changes between the 1990s and late 2010s. In many ways, that book serves as an economic and political companion to this revised edition of *Ontario since Confederation*. Albo and Evans focused mostly on the economy, the provincial state, politics, and political activism; the present book is aimed at history students and is less concerned with political economy and more attuned to utilizing a diverse range of historical case studies to tell a broader story about how the province has evolved. Our approach here is more wide-ranging; it is also more accessible for readers.

Moreover, this book does something that few works have done: it assesses Ontario as its own entity. Little work of this has been done in the past. Broader, survey assessments of Ontario using an historical frame are few and far between. Some of the available few include *Divided Province*; Ian Drummond's *Progress without Planning: The Economic History of Ontario from Confederation to the Second World War* (1987); Michael Piva's edited collection, *A History of Ontario* (1988); *Old Ontario: Essays in Honour of J.M.S. Careless* (1990), edited by David Keane and Colin Read with Frederick H. Armstrong; and Peter A. Baskerville's *Ontario: Image, Identity and Power* (2002). This relative paucity reflects Ontarians' tendency to identify less with their province and more with their nation-state (or with their specific locality, as many Torontonians tend to do, to the chagrin of other

Canadians). Ontario, in short, has not been an object of focused or sustained scholarly investigation.

This collection is a significant step towards rectifying the situation. Fifteen of its twenty-two chapters are entirely new or significantly revised. Even so, we are greatly indebted to the two editors of the original collection, Edgar-André Montigny and Lori Chambers. Their excellent work has made our task easier by providing a framework for us to supplement, and we thank them both for allowing us to do so.

Collections aimed at undergraduates generally bring together diverse perspectives, approaches, and frameworks. It is often a challenge to develop a central argument that binds all these diverse pieces together, and for a collection like this, which looks at Canada's most populous province across more than one and half centuries of historical change, it is especially daunting. Nonetheless, we feel that this collection does indeed tell a central story, about the constancy of relentless change over the last century and a half, and the resilience of Ontarians to adapt to that change.

Ontario's transformation from a relatively homogeneous, white, Protestant, English-speaking, rural, agricultural outpost of Victorian Britishness in the late nineteenth century into a multi-ethnic, urbanized, industrialized/deindustrialized, multilingual magnet for migrants anchored by a sprawling world city, Toronto, was neither seamless nor easy. The chapters in this book testify to the efforts of generations of Ontarians of all races, classes, languages, abilities, genders, and orientations to overcome the challenges of change, however reluctant some of them were. Despite so many obstacles and trials across a wide range of issues, these pages also show that Ontario has been relatively successful in navigating change. The province remains a magnet for people from across Canada and around the world, who see Ontario as a desirable place to live, work, and learn.

We contend that an edited collection can make valuable contributions to methodology, historiographical development, and interdisciplinarity. The British historian Peter Webster has written about the utility of edited collections and historiography in his *The Edited Collection: Pasts, Present, and Futures* (Cambridge University Press, 2020). He argues that edited collections have been unfairly criticized as being academically less valuable than scholarly journals, as inherently incoherent, and as difficult to access (since the pieces are embedded in larger texts). Furthermore, the critique goes, some of those in the academic world who make decisions about hiring, promotion, funding, and tenure believe there is something suspect about contributing to, or editing, an collection; which means that those who do so risk some sort of censure, or at least a penalty. We have been mindful of all of this as we have gathered chapters from our excellent contributors.

But we ourselves believe that undergraduates, especially in their earliest years of study, can only benefit from edited collections such as *Ontario since Confederation*. We agree with Webster that such volumes often serve as sites for the rich interplay that a variety of subjects and approaches can engender. Sometimes the emergent interplay can be unintentional, and at times this can yield insights never imagined beforehand by the authors or the readers. An edited collection can engage readers with the material it contains and, perhaps more importantly, synthesize with their everyday lives to allow for even greater depth of meaning. It may even lead to further learning, discovery, and engagement beyond the confines of the classroom. In other words, and as Webster so eloquently states, what emerges, in the grand scheme, is a "profoundly communal and conversational endeavour." An undertaking that is interdisciplinary in nature – in some instances within individual chapters, but more often than not interdisciplinary *across* chapters.

Thus, this edition of *Ontario since Confederation* includes new discussion questions for each chapter, which we believe will reinforce the best qualities of an edited collection. While most of the questions focus on individual chapters, some questions are intended to stimulate readers to make connections between the chapters. At other turns, we ask readers to connect the discussion, without the prompt of a certain chapter. We believe that when undergraduate students engage in such critical thinking, individually or collectively, this offers teachable moments of great value. We hope that adding these chapter questions to the collection adds an additional learning tool that will help instructors create more lively debates in the classroom, besides serving as a resource for creating lecture material.

We have each had the privilege of teaching various iterations of post-Confederation Ontario history to undergraduate students. The experience of using the first edition in many of those courses provided us valuable insights regarding which aspects of the collection would continue to work well for students and what would enhance an updated collection. We combined student feedback based on their interests, level of engagement, and relevance with our knowledge of pedagogical techniques and current historiography. We have retained some chapters in their original form, had some scholars revise their original chapters, and solicited new contributors to write original pieces. We believe that the end result offers something for everyone with an interest in Ontario's history.

This new collection thus builds on an excellent core to provide a wide range of stories that illustrate the diversity of Ontario's historical experience, which we think students will find inherently interesting. The five themes addressed in *Ontario since Confederation* – "Race and Gender," "Class, Business, and Politics," "Family," "Epidemiologies and Environments," and "The State and Welfare" – reflect a kaleidoscope of events, peoples, and places as well as long-standing issues that are rooted in Ontario's deeper past and more recent topics that illuminate emerging concerns and questions.

Part I, "Race and Gender," focuses on societal concerns that have been a constant in Ontario's demographic evolution. In chapter 2, Afua Cooper invites readers to consider women's history more expansively, by focusing on a nineteenth-century Black woman, Julia Turner. Cooper recounts how Turner, through her teaching and strength of personality, transcended class, racial, gender, and sexual oppression to become a successful, wealthy, and single property owner. Cooper's chapter forces readers to rethink preconceived notions about class, race, and gender not only in the late nineteenth century, but today as well. Similarly, in chapter 3, Rebecca Beauseart utilizes court records to explore conceptions of gender, criminality, and female agency in Oxford County at the end of the nineteenth century. Her chapter reveals some of the underlying gender, class, and rural/urban tensions that shaped responses to women's lawbreaking in Victorian Ontario.

Race played a key role in shaping social relations in the province in this period. In chapter 4, Margaret-Mona Pon revisits the scandalous case of Charles Lee Hing, a Woodstock shopowner who in 1909 was accused of luring, drugging, and raping an innocent white girl. In reconstructing a case that captured public attention, Pon brilliantly explores early twentieth-century beliefs and prejudices about race, class, sex, and patriarchy in Ontario. Indigeneity has emerged as a major aspect of how we understand race in Ontario and Canada, and in chapter 5, about the Six Nations of Brantford and how they managed education within provincial frameworks and during the Indian Residential Schools era, Alison Norman reveals a different side of the question of Indigenous education and agency. In chapter 6, the final chapter of this section, Carly Adams returns to the theme of gender, examining another aspect of female activity in the early —twentieth century – leisure.[1] In exploring women's participation in company-sponsored softball in interwar London, Ontario, Adams illustrates how different hierarchies of gender, work, and leisure shaped women's responses to important elements of their lives, from education to marriage to childbirth.

Part II of the collection, "Class, Business, and Politics," provides another departure point for understanding material and political tensions in the province, tensions that echo to this day across a host of issues and themes. In chapter 7, Bryan Palmer and Gaétan Héroux use Toronto as a "laboratory" for examining the lives of working people who, through no fault of their own, experienced the inherent crises of capitalism during the Age of Industry. Many workers protested, at different times, the social, economic, and political realities of a capitalist society that produced poverty, inequality, and marginalization. Many of them resisted the capitalist society in which they lived, one that ultimately criminalized poverty, often doing so under the flags of anarchy (black) and socialism (red).

In chapter 8, on Indigenous land and natural resources in Northern Ontario, Jean Manore reminds us that not all politics is local, nor is it confined to partisan electoral battles. Here, the fight over the terms of Treaty 9, which encompassed a huge swath of the province's north, reflects the ongoing conflict over how Ontario (and the federal government) have dealt with Aboriginal title, Indigenous rights, and questions about land and resources. Manore explains that readers must understand that there is a profound dissonance regarding what constitutes traditional "Indian" territories and the meanings of treaty lands in the province. These matters reach from the past to shape the present and future of Ontario's relations with Indigenous peoples.

An insight into Ontarians' business world is provided by Keith R. Fleming's analysis in chapter 9 of the firm of William Kennedy & Sons, an enterprise that spanned one and half centuries.[2] This study situates the role of manufacturing within the province's history but also engages in discussions about the nature of entrepreneurship and what constitutes success (and failure) in a dramatically shifting business and economic landscape. By exploring the fortunes of this industrial equipment supplier, readers will gain insight into the evolution of a family business and the challenges it faced.

The next three chapters in *Ontario since Confederation* focus on traditional political issues: federalism, leadership, and the civil service. In chapter 10, on the "Ontario–Quebec Axis," P.E. Bryden explores federal–provincial and intergovernmental relations in the post-war period, revealing the leading role that Ontario and its premiers played in reshaping federal–provincial relations across a host of fundamental matters, all of which had deep consequence for the functioning of the federation. Personalities, provincial priorities, and the dramatic pace of post-war change reordered the political economy of Canadian federalism, and Bryden's analysis provides a window into these dynamics, which continue to this day to shape how Canadians see themselves as provincial and "national" citizens.

An interesting counterpoint to Bryden's chapter can be found in chapter 11 by Patrice Dutil and Peter P. Constantinou, which examines the role of political staff in the highest echelons of political power, how premiers have utilized budgets and personnel to advance their goals within the power structure of Queen's Park, and how this has translated into different ideas about executive power. Then in chapter 12,

David Rapaport tackles the question of how neoliberal approaches to information technology within the Ontario Public Service reframed the delivery of services in a way that challenged the primacy of traditional civil servants. The longer-term implications of both issues illustrate the changing dynamics of governance in Ontario.

Families in the province have always been directly impacted by government policies. As everywhere else, the family remains the fundamental unit of society in Ontario, though its form has evolved over time. Part III considers how families have responded to changing legislative priorities, institutional shifts, and crises from the late nineteenth century until today. In analysing institutional change, the impact of the economic upheaval, and evolving policies towards adoption, chapters 13, 14, and 15 Edgar-André Montigny (families and institutional change, particularly around poor relief), Lara Campbell (families and the Great Depression), and Valerie Andrews and Lori Chambers (family and adoption) utilize a range of methodologies and sources that allow us to peer into the dynamics of families under strain, both economic and emotional.

Epidemiological and environmental stresses impact families, of course, but they also fundamentally reshape society. Pandemics have long had generational impacts, from smallpox in the late nineteenth century (for both settlers and Indigenous peoples), to flux and polio in the twentieth century, to SARS and COVID in the twenty-first. In chapter 16, James Onusko examines the impact of the 1918–20 influenza pandemic on Ontario children; that world event speaks to us across the century as we can connect the challenges of our own time with those that were experienced by a Great War generation scarred by trauma and dislocation. Chapters 17 and 18 delve into the question of environmental change and policy from local and provincial perspectives. Jennifer Bonnell's examination of how the Don River Valley environment was understood and shaped in Toronto is a case study in people, policies, and pollution across more than a century. She identifies competing visions based on values and beliefs that imagined this space to be many different things. Ultimately, Bonnell reveals how layers of human use have been inscribed on Ontario's landscapes, the Don Valley in particular. A broader view is offered by Mark Winfield and Colleen Kaiser, who assess the shifting provincial responses to environmental issues starting in the 1980s and consider the impact that politics and policy have had on Ontario's place in the global climate crisis.

Finally, Part V considers a key theme that binds together the previous four parts: the role of the state, particularly in terms of the development of the welfare state. In chapter 19, Cynthia R. Comacchio explores how the modern public health system in Canada was shaped by war and pandemic. Ontario led the way as the province's doctors and policy-makers developed progressive structures and programs for children's and maternal health that had a greater impact than any previous public health endeavours. The theme of children continues in chapter 20, in which Lisa Pasolli explores a critical juncture in Ontario's history related directly to families, women's rights, and child care advocacy. Having identified the 1970s battles over the "Birch proposals" for day care regulation as a key locus of social policy and activism, Pasolli concludes that the defeat of those proposals effectively halted the expansion of commercial and for-profit child care, with long-term repercussions in that ongoing battles in the province among various stakeholders.

Chapters 21 and 22 offer original and compelling insights into how other minority populations mobilized to demand rights and care. In chapter 21, Mathieu Arsenault and Marcel Martel examine how Franco-Ontarians, the province's oldest and largest linguistic minority, challenged provincial policies to ensure adequate health and educational services in their own language – a seemingly intractable and constant battle for French-speakers in the province. Then in chapter 22, Geoffrey Reaume shows us that, like the activist groups discussed in the Pasolli and Arsenault and Martel chapters, Ontarians with disabilities pursued their rights with determination and alacrity across multiple generations, forcing the province to listen to their voices. While this struggle continues, there is no question that the disability community has forced Ontario governments – both in the past and today – to recognize their concerns, listen to their demands, and respond to their needs.

Finally, in chapter 23, the collection's last, James Struthers focuses on Ontario's welfare state and its responses to citizens in need from the Great Depression until the present day. Struthers identifies previous cycles of welfare reform and dependency debates in the province. He closes with the basic income project, which was cancelled despite being lauded by many recipients, and which might have replaced welfare altogether, had it been deemed successful. Struthers views the 1990s and its heated political climate as the closest to what Ontarians experienced during the catastrophic Great Depression; this climate produced a system and corresponding policies that endured into the twenty-first century.

The chapters offered in *Ontario since Confederation: A Reader* are not meant to serve as a complete analysis of the province's past. Rather, they are snapshots or focused overviews of a range of topics that students and readers can connect with to understand not only Ontario's history but also its present, and its future.

The themes and issues explored here offer a way to understand the evolution of a province that stands at the centre of the Canadian experience by virtue of its large population, its place in Confederation, its historical role, and its continuing influence on the broader Canadian polity. As it grapples with change, Ontario's journey, and that of its people, continues.

NOTES

1 Chapter 6 was originally published as "'I Just Felt Like I Belonged to Them': Women's Industrial Softball, London, Ontario, 1923–1935," *Journal of Sport History* 38, no. 1 (2011): 75–94.

2 Chapter 9 was originally published as "The Rise and Fall of an Ontario Business Dynasty: William Kennedy & Sons and Its Successors, 1857–1997," *Ontario History* 104, no. 2 (2012): 63–89.

Part I

RACE AND GENDER

CHAPTER TWO

Putting Flesh on the Bones: Writing the History of Julia Turner

AFUA COOPER

Practitioners of the new women's history are producing accounts that articulate their subjects' oppression and victimization along with their agency and power as these women attempt to create meaningful lives for themselves. Such an approach enables historians to construct a more holistic view of women's historical experiences.[1] The case of Julia Turner, a Black woman who taught in Essex County, Ontario, during the middle and late nineteenth century, is instructive. Her life and work provide an opportunity to study the dialectical interplay of women's oppression, subordination, and agency as these aspects are informed by gender, class, race, family, and marital status and the world of paid employment.

Methodological Approaches in Constructing Black Women's History

The metaphor of the skeleton is apt not only in finding a methodology to construct a history of Julia Turner but also in allowing us to consider approaches for the study of Black women's history in Canada. Most of the sources for this chapter are archival: data came from school superintendents' reports, the manuscript censuses of 1851, 1861, 1871, 1881, and 1891, a probate document from the surrogate court in Sandwich, and the Sandwich assessor's rolls from 1870 to 1899, which detail Turner's tax contributions. Newspaper articles, specifically from *Voice of the Fugitive*, were used. The minute book of the trustees of the Amherstburg Black school (King Street school) was also invaluable in constructing Turner's history. A personal testimony, in the form of a letter to the American Missionary Association, came from Turner herself. In the probate document, Jordinia Turner, Julia's sister, gave a brief family history that also stands as a form of personal testimony.

Oral evidence was useful in helping me write this history. I conversed with Sylvia Jackson, Jordinia's granddaughter, about Turner's life and family background. Though I had no formal interview with Mrs. Jackson, the evidence she provided was useful in helping me anchor Turner in a poor, working-class family in the Black community of nineteenth-century Essex County. Secondary sources also helped. History texts about African Canadian women and men and about white women provided the historical, racial, and gender contexts in which to place Turner and helped elucidate her life.

Black Women in Canadian History

Most historians no longer bemoan the exclusion of "women" from history because, over the past twenty-five years, valiant "restoration" work has been done in white women's history. The same cannot be said, however, for Black women's history in Canada.[2] Until recent years, the focus in Canadian women's historical studies has been on white, middle-class women. And because this "whiteness" has not been broken down by race, an analysis of race is missing from the narratives. As a result, the history of Black women and other minorities has been mariginalized, if not made outright invisible, in Canadian historical writing. Sherry Edmunds Flett puts it well in her study of Black women in British Columbia: "The lives of African Canadian women have been reduced to being mere illustrations or 'add-ons' within feminist history."[3] For a truly inclusive women's history, we need a redefinition of the term *woman*. This new definition would have to consider the various factors that make up woman: gender, race, class, socio-economic stature, and sexuality in all their differences.[4]

Because Canadian women's history developed as a field of inquiry that focused on white women, there are few studies that centre on the experiences of Black women.[5] American historian Darlene Clark Hine states in her discussion of the development of African American women's history that Black women, belonging as they do to two subordinate groups in society, tend to "fall between the cracks" of Black history, with its male focus, and women's history, with its white women focus.[6] This situation was not rectified until Black female historians started to place Black women at the centre of historical inquiry. The same cannot be said of African Canadian women's history, for although there is a well-developed field of white women's history in Canada, African Canadian history as a branch of legitimate historical inquiry is virtually non-existent. Given this state of affairs, the conclusion that can be drawn for Black women's history is that it has dropped into a huge crater.[7]

Black feminist historians cannot wait for a field of Black Canadian women's history to come into being on its own; we must develop one. Numerous sources for Black women's history abound, and, with the recent explosion of white women's history in Canada and the development of African women's history, the historian of Black women's history in Canada has at her or his disposal a variety of methodologies, theories, and interpretive frameworks drawn from women's history, gender history, and social history. In addition, because the field of African Canadian women's history is relatively uncharted, we are in the process of developing our own theoretical approaches and methodologies.

This essay on Julia Turner, then, is an exploration in methodology, interpretive frameworks, and theoretical issues. It attempts to provide an integrated analysis of how race, gender, class, family, and marital status made their impact on the life, employment, and work choices of one woman. It is located, then, at the intersection of African Canadian history, women's history, and the history of teaching in Canada. As Gisela Bock notes in *Gender and History*: "Women's history holds the possibility of doing much more than recovering a history of women's past lives. It can shed light on gender relations and provide new understandings of general history."[8]

Family Origins

Julia Turner was the second child born to Henry and Rosina Turner in Ontario. Rosina and Henry fled from slavery in West Virginia and Kentucky, respectively, with two young daughters and arrived in Ontario in 1828. Their first child born in Ontario was a girl named Mary Jane Crawford.[9] Julia was born in 1831 and was followed by nine more children, two of whom died in infancy. The history of African Americans, both slave and free, leaving the US to settle in Ontario and Canada has been documented elsewhere, so it is not necessary to relate it here.[10] Suffice it to say that Rosina and Henry Turner were part of that group of Black Americans who created an American diaspora in Ontario, one that eventually became Canadianized.

The Turner family is listed in the 1861 census report for Amherstburg. It lists only four children: Julia, aged 30, Jordinia, 17 (spelt "Georgina" by the enumerator), Louisa, 13, and Henry, 22. The senior and junior Henry are listed as labourers, but no occupation was given for Rosina or any of her daughters. This lack of information on occupation for the women in the family was a common feature of the census records. Enumerators, in keeping with the prevailing gender ideology of man as breadwinner, tended not to note the occupations of women in a household considered to be male headed. Women and their work were thereby made invisible. In fact, Julia Turner had at this point been teaching school for a number of years.

The Turners were of "humble" background. According to the census, they lived in a half-storey frame house and had six pigs, two cows, and two horses. The real and personal value of Henry Turner's estate was $160. Because of the prevailing gender ideology, Julia's salary as a teacher would not have been included in the counting of the family's wealth by the census taker. The father of the family, Henry Turner, was listed as a labourer, which meant that his wages were low. Having several young children to support most probably meant that the family was struggling "to make ends meet." However, Sylvia Jackson related that when Henry and Rosina came to Ontario in 1828 they opened a grocery store and a rooming house in Amherstburg, and that they also made and sold carpets. She did not know for how long the couple operated these enterprises, but if they were still engaged in such activities in 1861, the enumerator did not report it.[11]

The census taker also reported that every one of the enumerated family members was born in the US, though research has indicated this was not the case. Since many, if not most, of the Black families in Ontario were of US origin, it was felt by the census takers that "anyone who was Black" must have been born in the US. This perception has served to deny African Canadians a Canadian identity, since members of the dominant group constantly saw them as newcomers. And because African Canadians were imagined as newcomers, their role in the making and shaping of Canadian history has been effectively denied.[12] Like many other Black Ontarians, the Turners were identified as Baptists.

The census is not the only source for uncovering the presence of the Turners in Amherstburg. The list for Captain Caldwell's Company of Coloured Volunteers at Amherstburg reveals that Henry Turner served as a sergeant in active duty during the Upper Canadian Rebellion from 27 December 1837 to 25 January 1838.[13] This information supports the oral evidence given by family members of the early arrival of Henry and Rosina into the province.

Having several young children to care for, Rosina and Henry Turner had to come up with various survival strategies. In nineteenth-century Ontario one such strategy was for older children to engage in some kind of paid employment, whether this meant working as an apprentice or labourer for boys, and, for girls, going into domestic service or, as the century matured, into teaching. Julia, being one of the senior children in her family, went out to work at an early age. By the time she was fourteen she was teaching at a Black separate school in Essex County.[14]

Gender, Race, and Work: Teaching in Nineteenth-Century Ontario

Julia Turner's presence in the teaching force at this early age is recorded in a letter she wrote to George Whipple, field secretary of the American Missionary Association, asking for financial help for a Black school in the town of Amherstburg.

Amherstburg Jan. 25th, 1853

Dear Sir,

I have forwarded this letter to you by recommendation to solicit aid in behalf of a school in Amherstburg. Their [*sic*] is a school in this place kept in Mr Rice's[15] mission house by a young man by the name of James Underwood. As to the teacher they are satisfied with his teaching but are dissatisfied with the course he has taken by going to the mission house.[16] As he was paid twenty dollars per month by the trustees of the incorporation, they feel dissatisfied under those circumstances and having known their disapproval of that course to the trustees, they [the trustees] refuse to hear them, being rather in favour of his course and partial to Mr Rice.

They [the parents] have requested me to apply for assistance in carrying on their school in the coloured Wesleyan Church which I shall teach and the number of scholars are from thirty-five to forty, which I shall take up if I can be supported. They will pay what they can, but having to their taxes to pay to the other school whither they send or not, but by not sending will be exempted from paying the rate bill which they will pay to their own teacher if they can get assistance from you.[17]

They say you would assist them if they would come under the AMA society. As for myself, I have been teaching in Canada for eight years and for some of them I have received twenty four dollars per year for two years and I had the promise [of] more but the people were too poor, I could not bear to distress them. I have taught five years ... in one settlement by the name of Mount Pleasant to which if I do not get support in town will teach.

It is a large settlement of coloured people and a large quantity has moved there within the two years time, to give you sir, an idea of the number that have [*sic*] gone in that settlement since the fugitive bill has passed.[18] I have received from them last year, for the first time $72 for the year so I can say thank God, times are getting better ... As to my assertions and character as

> a schoolteacher, you can inquire of Mr Peden, minister of the Presbyterian church, Mr A. Binga, pastor of the Baptist church …
>
> I am your humble servant,
>
> Julia Turner
>
> p.s. I will teach either place that you will support me in, Amherstburg or Mount Pleasant.[19]

Turner's letter makes for wonderful reading in aspects of African Canadian social history in Essex County in particular and Ontario in general. It highlights the tensions and the partisanship that plagued certain Black communities with special regard to education: the fight between parents and trustees, which for many Ontario communities became a constant theme, with the teacher caught in the middle; and the recurring tensions between missionaries and their congregations. It sheds light on the state of education for Black children in Essex, and it also reveals the poverty of many of the Black settlers, especially those newly arrived from the US. Much of this poverty was engendered by the dislocation and disruption that the Fugitive Slave Law caused for Black families. In the letter, Turner presents herself as a devoted and dedicated teacher who empathizes deeply with the parents. More important for our purpose is what Turner reveals about her long teaching experience in Canada. The letter was written at the beginning of 1853, so, if she had been teaching for eight years, she began in 1845, when she was fourteen years of age.

Schoolteaching is one of the richest areas of women's history in Canada and one of the most developed fields of women's history. By the last quarter of the nineteenth century in several provinces, teaching had become essentially a women's occupation. The entry of so many young women into teaching had to do with the limited job opportunities available to women at this time. Teaching was one of the few professions that courted and encouraged women, and, gradually, women became a majority among elementary school teachers. Canadian historians have documented and analysed this phenomenon well, even though the focus has been on white women teachers.[20]

Julia Turner was part of that initiative of women becoming teachers as the educational state expanded. Although teaching probably functioned as a survival strategy for her and her family, other forces were at work to propel her into the world of teaching. The growth of the Black population through natural increase and emigration from the US meant there was a rapid increase in the number of Black children for whom educational facilities had to be provided.[21] Turner points in her letter to the inadequacy of such facilities. Moreover, the real fact and persistence of separate schooling for Black children in much of the province exacerbated the educational difficulties they and their parents already faced.

Separate Schooling in Nineteenth-Century Ontario

As early as 1828 Black parents in Ontario protested against the lack of schooling for their children, and by 1838 Black children in Brantford, Amherstburg, and other places were attending separate schools.[22] This de facto segregation in education became a fact of life for many Black children, though their access to schooling varied. In Toronto and other towns and hamlets in the east, Black children attended school with white children, but not so in the western and southern portions of the province. In these regions, of which Essex County was a part, racial segregation in education was the norm.

Propelled by the vision of Egerton Ryerson, Canada West's energetic superintendent of education, public education expanded in the 1840s. During this period a series of laws recognized separate schooling for religious groups, and in 1850, the crowning piece of legislation enshrined in law separate schooling for Blacks.[23] Although Blacks were given permission to set up their own schools if they desired, whites often insisted that Blacks leave the common schools and set up their own separate schools. School segregation based on race was already a reality before 1850, but white school supporters used the separate school act as the most effective weapon in their fight to expel all Black children from the common schools. When Blacks declined, many whites began to prevent Black students from physically entering the public schools. White school trustees also began to gerrymander districts to prevent Black children from attending schools deemed to be white.[24] The combined action of these groups resulted in numerous Black children not receiving any kind of formal education.[25]

Black parents, teachers, and other supporters responded to this situation in a number of ways, primarily by setting up schools for their children.[26] In both Canada and the US, the Black community made a valiant effort in educating and attempting to educate the children. This effort fostered both pride and bitterness.[27] As a young female teacher, Julia Turner in Mount Pleasant and elsewhere was responding to the educational needs and demands of her community. A major part of this response was premised on the imperative of race uplift.

Race Uplift in Ontario

Race uplift, an ideology articulated by the Black middle class in the nineteenth century and one that most Blacks eventually subscribed to, entailed "acting for the good of the race" and thereby "elevating" it.'[28] Blacks who had the means were called upon to help their less fortunate fellows. Uplift was best expressed and manifested in the realm of education. Linda Perkins underscores the centrality of this ideology in Black educational efforts in her discussion of Black women and uplift: "Since the intellectual inferiority of the race was the primary justification for slavery... blacks sought as a central goal in their mission of uplift to improve their education to help dispel the widespread myth of the dull black intellect."[29]

Most Blacks, slave and free, felt that if the race were educated, the oppression it experienced from white society would lessen. Henry Bibb used classic uplift language when he wrote in *Voice of the Fugitive* that, with the acquisition of education, Black people would be "strengthened and elevated."[30] Uplift doctrine reigned full force in the Black teaching community, as most teachers expressed the view that one of their main desires was to elevate their oppressed brethren.[31] They still went into teaching with pragmatic aims and expected to be paid for their labours so that they could support themselves and their family members. But many times teachers were not paid, simply because the parents did not have the money or the aid that some of the schools received from the province was not adequate or not forthcoming.[32] Yet these teachers pressed on. What kept most of them in the school in spite of insufficient remuneration was the uplift ideology.

Since uplift was an ideology that most in the Black community subscribed to, it was not necessary to be a teacher to want to help fellow brothers and sisters. The Turners were farmers, or worked in agriculture, and most of the Black settlers pursued similar paths.[33] Other people, such as newspaper publishers, medical doctors, and Black intellectuals, all vigorously espoused the uplift doctrine.[34]

Thus, in the early stages of the establishment of the Black communities in the province, it did not seem to matter if the teachers were as young as fourteen. What mattered was that they knew more than their charges and had the necessary literacy and numeracy skills. For Julia Turner and her family, however, her entry into the workforce was perhaps first dictated by economic considerations rather than the impulse of race elevation. Would a young teenage girl have internalized the concept of uplift sufficiently to be inspired by it and incorporate it in her praxis? For much of the nineteenth century, children went out to work at an early age, and Turner was part of this momentum. Yet, given the fact of the racial oppression that Black people encountered in Canada, including the lack of educational opportunities, Turner was forced at an early age to consider uplift in both theory and practice.

Julia Turner, Teacher

There is no evidence that Turner received the aid she requested from the American Missionary Association. One year later, however, she assumed the position of teacher at the Amherstburg Black school for a salary of £50 per annum.[35] From this meagre salary she was responsible for providing the classroom space and the fuel. The teacher before Turner, James Underwood, taught the Black school in Isaac Rice's mission house, but, given the controversy with the parents, Turner did not continue the school there. Turner found an alternative space, but it was an uncomfortable structure, as Benjamin Drew, the Boston abolitionist who was touring "Black Ontario," discovered when he stopped in Amherstburg in 1855. Drew's description of the Amherstburg Black school says volumes about Turner's working conditions and the state of education for Black children in Canada West:

> A separate school has been established here, at their own request:[36] their request was given them, but leanness went with it ... There was an attendance of twenty-four – number on the list, thirty. The school-house is a small, low building and contains neither blackboard nor chair. Long benches extend on the sides of the room, with desks of corresponding length in front of them. The whole interior is comfortless, and repulsive. The teacher, a colored lady,[37] is much troubled by the frequent absences of the pupils, and the miserably tattered and worn-out conditions of the books ... The teacher appeared to bear up as well as she could under her many discouragements: but the whole school adds one more dreary chapter to the "pursuit of knowledge under difficulties."[38]

Turner's working conditions were not poor and dreary simply because she was a Black woman working in a Black school. Conditions were wretched in many of the province's fledgling schools, but there was hope of improvement as the educational enterprise expanded and as the state began to take education more seriously and to allot more money for the education of its young. However, race was a crucial factor in the process. White schools improved; most Black schools did not. Over time, primarily because of poor government funding, conditions worsened in many of the Black separate schools.[39]

Drew tells us that Turner was troubled by the difficulties she and her students encountered. Black children were taught in a facility that was dilapidated and lacked the necessary learning apparatus. The superintendent's reports of 1855 and 1856 confirmed some of Drew's observations. The 1856 report noted that the school lacked

> blackboards and maps. The school is described as "old" and "rented." In comparison, the white school had eight maps and a blackboard.[40] This report confirmed the low priority that the provincial government accorded the Black schools. By and large, the needs of the whites were given first priority.

The absence of relevant teaching apparatus in the Black school raises some important pedagogical questions. Since maps and blackboards were missing, how did Turner teach subjects that required the use of these things? On a personal level, did she continue living with her parents while she taught at the Amherstburg school? It is likely that she was still living at home, since she was teaching in her home town, receiving a pitiful salary, and remained unmarried. She had a number of young siblings, and it is feasible to assume that her earnings went a long way in helping her family out.[41]

At the time of her tenure at the Amherstburg school, Turner held a third-class county certificate. She did not attend the Normal School, so must have obtained her certificate from a county institute. These institutes held summer courses at various places in the county. Examinations were held at the courthouse in Sandwich, the seat of Essex County. Although in 1855 she held the lowest county certificate, which implied that her level of educational training was not extensive, she had been teaching for more than ten years. Turner continued at the Amherstburg school until the end of 1856, when she was forced out of the school by the parents, trustees, and other school supporters. According to the minutes of the school trustees, on 12 January 1856 "a petition was received from the coloured people on the subject of employing a male teacher instead of a female. It was agreed to call a meeting of the coloured people on Monday evening next to consider the matter. A balance of $167.00 being due to Miss Turner and it was agreed the same should be paid."[42] The trustees give no indication as to why parents and others wanted a male teacher instead of Julia Turner. Did they believe that a man would be a better teacher? Did they feel that Turner and other female teachers were incompetent? Did it have to do with a developing belief in the province that men were better managers of children? Some historians have noted that "rural authorities worried about the ability of women teachers, particularly if they were young, to manage schools attended by young men and about the ability of women to 'govern' children in general."[43] Those who favoured the "men as better managers" position felt that men could give more advanced training and discipline, especially to older boys. Since the minutes do not give the reason for the male preference, we can only assume and speculate. What is certain is that sexism was at the base of Turner's dismissal.

How does one explain this kind of sexism in the Black Amherstburg community? Was it reflective of the larger southwestern Ontario Black community? Mary Ann Shadd, while teaching school in Chatham, wrote to George Whipple of the American Missionary Association and expressed the view that Chatham Blacks had a preference for male teachers. She said that the Chathamites had a "prejudice" against female teachers.[44] This is a strange charge considering the crucial role Black women played in setting up schools in Ontario and the number of Black women teachers. How can this paradox be explained?[45] James Horton notes that many free Blacks, despite economic limitations and racial constraints, sought to model the gender conventions articulated by white society. Even though lack of employment opportunities for Black men dictated that most Black women would work for a wage, the preference, in subscription to the ideal espoused by separate sphere ideology, was for women to remain at home and be "model housewives." Male editors at Black newspapers were at the forefront of pushing the separate ideology ideal. However, Horton notes that these same men also exhorted Black women to undertake reform and uplift work.[46]

Turner continued on in the midst of the controversy until 18 December 1856. At the beginning of the new year a man, John B. Williams, replaced her at the Amherstburg school. It was not until 1869, thirteen years after the firing of Turner, that the Amherstburg separate school trustees hired another woman as a teacher, though they hired women as assistants.[47]

From the end of 1856 to 1861, Turner's name seems not to be listed in any of the superintendents' reports for separate schools in Essex County. What did she do in these years? Did she continue teaching? Did she leave the province? Did she change occupation? Seeking different employment was not an uncommon route for teachers. Some became seamstresses, some went to work full time on the farm, and some became domestics.[48] It is possible that Turner continued teaching. The schools' reports are not the most reliable sources for tracking down a teacher or following the activities of a separate school. Not all Black schools received government aid. Some were run solely by Black parents or with the help of missionary associations. These schools would not have made it into the government's report.

In 1862 Turner emerges as a teacher with a second-class certificate at the Black separate school in Anderdon. She may well, then, have continued in teaching during the years her name was absent from the superintendents' reports. She had upgraded her school certificate, and would most likely not have done so if she had not been in the education business.[49] Turner remained at Anderdon for only one year. In 1863 she started teaching at the Sandwich separate school, where she was to spend the rest of her teaching life.

The separate school at Sandwich had a troubled history. Mary Bibb, on arriving in Sandwich in 1850, started a school in her home for the Black children of the area because they were being driven from the common school by whites and had no access to schooling. Bibb's school later became "public" when she applied for and received a small subsidy from the province. However, the school floundered owing to a lack of financial resources. Sometime in 1853 the government reactivated the school, but it was closed again a year later.[50] The Black children of Sandwich went without a common school until 1859, when, after years of agitation by their parents, the trustees for the town opened a school for them. Turner was the third teacher to be appointed to the Sandwich school since its opening. She was paid $200 for her services that year. The Sandwich trustees, like those in several other places, did not spend much money on the separate school. Turner instructed her charges in the "coloured church." The province, then, did not fully support the school, and the community had to "pitch in" to make the school viable.

Turner again worked to upgrade her credentials, and in 1866 she was awarded a first-class certificate. In 1869, the last year that the superintendents' reports were filed, Julia Turner was still at Sandwich and the school was still being kept in the Black Methodist Church.[51]

Turner continued on at Sandwich until her retirement. In the 1871 and 1881 censuses, her name appeared in the town of Sandwich as "schoolteacher." In the latter year she was fifty years old and had taught Black children for more than thirty-five years. She is listed in the 1891 census, but no profession is given, so presumably she had retired. It is quite possible that Turner taught well after 1881, when she was last listed as a schoolteacher. If so, she may have taught for forty years or more – a phenomenal record, given that, in the mid- and late nineteenth century, most teachers did not spend more than four years in the occupation.[52] Turner devoted most of her life to teaching and became a "career woman" before the term was invented. Another point is instructive: she taught for her whole career in rural schools. Turner's story alerts us to the fact that the history of teaching in Ontario and Canada must be rewritten to include Black women, many of whom devoted decades to the occupation and helped to give it a professional "image" at a time when teaching was often seen as an interlude before marriage.

The bulk of Turner's teaching career occurred during the post-Confederation period, after 1867. In the new nation-state, the position of Black people was to be even more tenuous than under the old order. Blacks became even more marginalized. With the end of the American Civil War and the abolition of slavery, many white Canadians felt that the "Black" problem was over. Abolition was interpreted by many whites to mean that Blacks would no longer be seeking refuge on

Canadian soil. It never seemed to occur to Canadian whites that American Blacks would want to come to Canada as immigrants, in the same way that Europeans and white Americans were coming. Several hundred African Canadians of American stock went to the US during the Reconstruction to find lost relatives, pursue better opportunities, and help in the building of a new society, but the bulk of Black Ontarians, even those who were American-born, remained in Ontario. Their children and grandchildren were Canadians and saw Canada as home. This post-Confederation Black community became more and more invisible as a vibrant nationalism emerged that did not see Black people as part of the Canadian nation-building ethos. Blacks now faced extreme discrimination in employment, education, and other areas of life. A paradox of post-Confederation Canada is that, as European immigrants flooded to country to take up opportunities provided by an expanding agricultural and industrial sector, Black Canadians were denied these opportunities and many families sank into poverty.[53]

As a result, hundreds of Black Canadians from both the Maritimes and Ontario went south to the US to find work and other economic opportunities. In the US racial segregation was enshrined in law, and African Americans continued to feel the sting of racial oppression. Yet because of the size of the population and the Jim Crow laws, American Blacks were able to establish their own institutions and to provide employment for themselves along with educational, social, and other opportunities. In Canada there was no official colour bar, yet African Canadians were consistently denied the opportunity by white society to improve their lives. Many of the hundreds who migrated to the US in the post-Confederation era were able to find a "larger world" there.[54]

The post-Confederation era did not augur well for either Black women or Black men, in spite of the new economic opportunities that resulted from the industrialization of the country. Historian Jane Errington, in assessing the impact of this new mode of production on women, notes: "Between 1870 and 1920, as the Canadian economy became industrialized and urbanized, women were ... drawn to the growing towns and cities of the new nation, where factories, shops, and mills promised adventure, greater personal and economic independence."[55] But the "generic woman" Errington is talking about was white. Black and other racial minority women were not allowed in these factories, shops, or mills. Oral accounts from Black women about their life and work experiences, and those of their mothers in the first half of this century, attest to this discrimination. Their stories detail their exclusion from the new industrial opportunities right up to the outbreak of the Second World War. Not until then were Black women allowed in the factories. As Marjorie Lewsey, with stinging irony, testifies: "We weren't allowed to go into factory work until Hitler started the war."[56] It was the labour shortage occasioned by the war, not a civil rights impulse, that dictated the "integration" of the workforce in terms of race and sex.

In the post-Confederation era in which Julia Turner taught, Black women who worked outside the home were concentrated in the fields of teaching and domestic work. For Black men who were not farmers, or who did not pursue other independent work activities, a "racially split" labour market developed. Black men were primarily employed as railway porters. They found it almost impossible to find any other kind of public employment.[57]

Given the lack of job opportunities that existed for Blacks as a whole, and Black women in particular, the fact that Julia Turner was a consistent wage earner for more than thirty-five years was a stunning achievement. She fought sexual and racial oppression to live as best she could in the world. She must have been aware of how her race and sex were perceived by white society: that the most suitable employment for Black women was domestic work. She must also have been equally aware of her status as a consistent wage earner and of the difficulties Blacks faced in gaining viable paid employment. Turner did not conform to the stereotypes that were placed on her gender and her race in nineteenth-century North America. She created her own reality and, though she did not leave many written records behind, it is clear that her sense of self was quite developed. Her longevity in teaching must have created in her a tremendous amount of self-confidence, self-esteem, and pride.

The fact that Turner worked solely in separate schools points to the nature of racial oppression and race relations in Canada. In some places, Black teachers could be found teaching in white schools, but only in areas where there were few Black families and teachers were sorely needed.[58] Whites sometimes instructed in Black schools, but, by and large, Black teachers worked in Black schools and perhaps preferred it that way. Evidence shows that Black teachers clung tenaciously to their jobs in Black schools, for the Black school was one of the few places where permanent work was available to them.[59]

In addition, Black parents generally preferred Black teachers for their children.[60] The flip side was that white trustees and white-dominated school boards were unlikely to hire Black teachers to teach in largely white schools. The fact that it was only in 1913 that the Windsor School Board hired its first Black teacher, Ada Kelly, points to the racialized nature of teaching in Ontario, a situation that did not ease in the later period.[61] After the Second World War, Fern Shadd Shreve reported that when she graduated from Normal School, she taught in a school that for all intents and purposes was a Black school. After returning to work following the birth of her son, and with the dismantling of the Black school, she could not find a job in a white school. "Black teachers were not allowed to teach in white schools," she said.[62]

Turner gave most of her life to one of the very few professions open to women at that time. Women teachers were underpaid and overworked, but, as historians have pointed out, teaching was one of the few areas that "welcomed" women. Many women knew they were being exploited by the school officials; nonetheless, they used teaching as a vehicle to acquire independence and as a real and positive alternative to marriage. Teaching provides an excellent example of how women used an exploitative situation to acquire independence and power. For Turner it was a site where race, class, economic stature, and gender were inextricably linked.

Family and Marital Status

Turner did not marry. She started her work life as a "daughter in the house," and at some point moved out to establish her own hearth. According to the Sandwich assessor's roll for 1870, she was living by herself and paying the school tax for a property she had purchased on East Bedford Street. It would therefore be safe to conclude that Turner began living on her own when she took up the teaching position at the Sandwich school.

Once Turner began to live on her own, she had to continue working. Teaching for her was not a stopgap before marriage and motherhood. It would appear that the consistent manner in which she strove to upgrade her teaching credentials meant she saw teaching as a lifelong occupation. Her rejection of marriage also indicates that she realized she was capable of supporting herself. Clearly she saw teaching as a way to "make her way in the world," to support herself and live independently.

African diasporic scholar Filomina Chioma Steady, in her work on the historical experiences of African-descended women, identifies two dominant values – self-reliance and a survival imperative – that Black women resorted to in combating racial, gender, and class tyranny. These values, according to Steady, have become institutionalized in many African and African-descended communities. Given the multiple forms of oppression that Turner faced as a Black woman in the mid- and late nineteenth century, it becomes apparent that she articulated these two values in her quest to overcome social inequities and to live as fully human as possible.[63]

The fact that Turner did not marry does not mean that she missed out on love or sexual relationships. She may well have chosen to remain single. Historians of women teachers have chronicled the loss of independence and income that women teachers experienced when they married. The potential loss of income loomed large as a reason why many female teachers chose not to marry. Also, for women used to looking after themselves, even on a small salary, the thought of having to succumb to male authority within a marriage, and accepting the inherent inequalities in most heterosexual marriages, was something many found unappealing.

As was to be expected, Turner remained close to her family. The 1891 census revealed that her sister Jordinia (spelt "Georgina" in the census) was living with her. Jordinia was married at this time and had children, but her husband is not listed as being part of the household. According to the census, Jordinia was also working as a servant. Perhaps a dislocation in her immediate family situation necessitated her living with her sister and working to support herself and her children.[64]

For much of the 1870s, 1880s, and 1890s, children lived with Turner. They may have been family members, children of her siblings. It is also probable that they were Jordinia's children and that Turner helped support them both financially and emotionally.[65] Turner must also have had a circle of friends, some of whom may have come from her church community. Various records show that she was a Baptist. Given the religiosity of the period, especially among Black people, one can easily surmise that Turner was a practising Christian and a faithful Baptist and that she helped organize social activities for her church and participated in church affairs. Her uplift work would have extended beyond the classroom.

Julia Turner, A Wealthy Woman

On 10 November 1900, Julia Turner died at Amherstburg from heart failure and an enlarged thyroid.[66] She had died "intestate," that is, without leaving a will. Five weeks later an application was filed in the surrogate court at Sandwich by attorney Arthur St. George Ellis to administer Turner's estate. The persons named on the document as her heirs were two brothers, James and William, two sisters, Rosina Monroe and Jordinia Matthews, a niece, Estella Thomas, and a nephew, Walter Viney. Her real estate was valued at $4,200; her personal estate and effects at less than $1,800.[67] According to this document she owned property in Amherstburg, Sandwich, Malden, and Colchester.

The probate document, read along with the tax records, reveals that Turner invested and speculated in real estate. The assessment rolls for Sandwich show that in 1870, she began to acquire property in that town, and that by 1899, she owned at least five lots of varying size and value.[68] At the time of her death she owned only two properties in Sandwich, but several in at least three other townships, placing her among those who paid the highest taxes in Essex County. Family lore has it that, along with liquor magnate Hiram Walker, Turner was one of the county's leading taxpayers. Clearly, Turner not only saved the money she earned as a teacher but invested in property. The probate document speaks volumes about the kind of woman Turner was. She persisted in teaching for more than thirty-five years and used her exploitation and subordination to "raise herself in the world." Through teaching and the force of her own personality she was able to transcend in varying degrees racial, sexual, and class oppression. Here was a person who was born poor but died relatively well off. Perhaps that in itself is not so unusual, but when racial oppression and the sexist nature of the society are considered, Turner's accomplishment truly must be described as phenomenal.

QUESTIONS FOR CONSIDERATION:

1. Why does Cooper argue that Black Canadian women's history has not emerged on its own?
2. What was separate schooling? Why is it significant?
3. What was race uplift? Describe it in your own words.
4. Why did Julia Turner write to George Whipple?
5. Why is oral history vital in writing the history of Julia Turner?
6. Cooper explores some of what family and marriage may have meant to Turner. Offer some thoughts on her conclusions.

NOTES

1 See Linda Gordon's discussion, "U.S. Women's History," in *The New American History*, a pamphlet published by the American Historical Association in 1997.

2 The outpouring of works on white women's history, both in French and in English, over the past two decades has been staggering. Two examples will suffice: Veronica Strong-Boag, *The New Day Recalled: Lives of Girls and Women in English Canada, 1919–1939* (Toronto: Penguin, 1988); and the Clio Collective, *Quebec Women: A History* (Toronto: Women's Press, 1987). Recently, attention has shifted to include women of non-English- and non-French-speaking backgrounds. See Jean Burnet, *Looking into My Sister's Eyes* (Toronto: Multicultural History Society of Ontario, 1986); Barbara Latham and Roberta Pazdro, eds., *Not Just Pin Money: Selected Essays on the History of Women's Work in British Columbia* (Victoria: Camosun College, 1984); and Franca Iacovetta and Mariana Valverde, eds., *Gender Conflicts: New Essays in Women's History* (Toronto: University of Toronto Press, 1992). Although attention is paid in these studies to "immigrant women" and some women of colour, the main focus is still on white women. The authors have failed to develop adequately in their texts an analysis in which race is part of the consideration of gender. Gender is usually perceived as "something belonging" to white women.

3 Sherry Edmunds Flett, "'Abundant Faith': 19th Century African Canadian Women on Vancouver Island" (unpublished paper), 3.

4 Gail Cuthbert Brandt deals with some of these issues and the state of Canadian women's historiography in "Postmodern Patchwork: Some Recent Trends in the Writing of Women's History in Canada," *Canadian Historical Review* 62, no. 4 (1991): 441–70.

5 I am not suggesting that there be separate areas for each category of women or that white women's history be "decentred" to make the experiences of Black women and women of colour visible. The centre can be "constantly and appropriately" pivoted. See Elsa Barkley Brown, "African-American Women's Quilting: A Framework for Conceptualizing and Teaching African-American Women's History," *Signs* 14, no. 4 (1989): 921–2. Brown acknowledges Bettina Aptheker, *Tapestries of Life: Women's Work, Women's Consciousness, and the Meaning of Daily Life* (Amherst: University of Massachusetts Press, 1989), for this concept of looking at history from "numerous centers and thus to maintain the reality that all these centers exist simultaneously."

6 Darlene Clark Hine, *Hine Sight: Black Women and the Re-Construction of American History* (Bloomington: Indiana University Press, 1994), xxvi.

7 The following works, centring Black women's experiences, have been critical in making Canadian women's historical writing more inclusive. Sylvia Hamilton, "Our Mothers Grand and Great: Black Women of Nova Scotia,' *Canadian Woman Studies* 4, no. 2 (1982): 32–7; Adrienne Shadd, "300 Years of Black Women in Canadian History: Circa 1700–1980," *Tiger Lily* 1, no. 2 (1987): 4–13; Myriam Merlet, "Black Women Immigrants," in *Women: Isolation and Bonding: The Ecology of Gender*, ed. Kathleen Storrie (Toronto: Methuen, 1987), 159–75; Esmeralda Thornhill, "Focus on Black Women," *Socialist Studies* 5 (1989): 26–36; Agnes Calliste, "Canada's Immigration Policy and Domestics from the Caribbean: The Second Domestic Scheme," *Socialist Studies* 5 (1989): 133–65; Makeda Silvera, *Silenced: Talks with Working Class Caribbean Women about Their Lives and Struggles as Domestic Workers in Canada*, 2nd ed. (Toronto: Sister Vision Press, 1989); Dionne Brand, *No Burden to Carry: Narratives of Black Women Working in Ontario, 1920s to 1950s* (Toronto: Women's Press, 1991); Afua Cooper, '"The Search for Mary Bibb, Black Woman Teacher in Nineteenth-Century Canada West," *Ontario History* 83, no. 1 (1991): 39–54, reprinted in "*We specialize in the wholly Impossible*": *A Reader in Black Women's History*, ed. Darlene Clark Hine, Wilma King, and Linda Reed (Brooklyn: Carlson, 1995), 171–85; Peggy Bristow, Dionne Brand, Linda Carty, Afua Cooper, Sylvia Hamilton, and Adrienne Shadd, *"We're rooted here and they can't pull us up": Essays in African Canadian Women's History* (Toronto: University of Toronto Press, 1994/1999); Suzanne Morton, "Separate Spheres in a Separate World: African Nova Scotia Women in Late 19th-Century Halifax County," in *Separate Spheres: Women's World in the 19th-Century Maritimes*, ed. Janet Guilford, (Fredericton: Acadiensis Press, 1994), 185–210; Shirley J. Yee, "Gender Ideology and Black Women as Community-Builders in Ontario, 1850–1870," *Canadian Historical Review* 75, no. 1 (1994): 53–73; Judith Fingard, "From Sea to Rail: Black Transportation Workers and Their Families in Halifax, c. 1870–1916,' *Acadiensis* 24, no. 2 (1995): 49–64; Kenneth Donovan, "Slaves and Their Owners in Ile Royale, 1713– 1760," *Acadiensis* 25, no. 1 (1995): 3–32; Carol B. Duncan, "'Dey give me a house to gather in di chil'ren': Mothers and Daughters in the Spiritual Baptist Church," *Canadian Woman Studies* 18, nos. 2–3 (1998): 126–31.

8 Gisela Bock, "Women's History, Gender History," *Gender and History* (1989): 7.

9 See documents filed in the surrogate courts of Essex County regarding Julia Turner's property. Jordinia Turner relates a brief family history in these documents. Archives of Ontario (AO), probate documents, Julia Turner, GS1–741.

10 See Robin Winks, *The Blacks in Canada: A History* (1971; reprint, Montreal and Kingston: McGill–Queen's University Press, 1997).

11 Personal conversation with Mrs. Jackson, March 1991.

12 Colin Thomson, *Blacks in Deep Snow: Black Pioneers in Canada* (Toronto: J.M. Dent, 1979).

13 Metropolitan Toronto Reference Library, Black Canadian Militia file.

14 For a discussion on the extreme youthfulness of Ontario's early female teachers, see Marta Danylewycz, Beth Light, and Alison Prentice, "The Evolution of the Sexual Division of Labour in

Teaching: A Nineteenth-Century Ontario and Quebec Case Study," *Histoire sociale/Social History* 26, no. 31 (1983): 81–109, esp. 93, 96, 97.

15 Isaac Rice was a white missionary maintained by the American Missionary Association in Amherstburg. He started one of the first schools for Black children in that town. However, Rice soon came in conflict with some of the parents and members of his congregation. See Jason H. Silverman and Donna J. Gillie, "'The pursuit of knowledge under difficulties': Education and the Fugitive Slave in Canada,' *Ontario History* 74 (1982): 97.

16 Trustees developed a notorious reputation because of their parsimonious attitude with regard to spending money on schools and school programs. By having the Black school in Rice's mission house, they would avoid having to build or rent a suitable building for the school. The trustees must also have felt that the mission house was "ideal" since Rice had earlier started a school there for Black youths.

17 Schooling at this time was supported by the taxpayers. The rate bill was one kind of tax designed by school officials to help pay the teacher's salary. Turner hints at the dilemma that many Black parents faced in getting an education for their children: although they paid the school tax, their children were often chased from the common schools by whites who did not want their children to mix with Black children. Black parents could not withhold their taxes, but they could withhold the rate bill. Parents often sued the trustees or the government over the lack of educational opportunities for their children. See H.W. Arthur, "Civil Liberties – Public Schools – Segregation of Negro Students," *Canadian Bar Review* 41 (September 1963): 453–7; and Claudette Knight, "Black Parents Speak: Education in Mid-Nineteenth-Century Canada West," *Ontario History* 89, no. 4 (1997): 269–84.

18 The Fugitive Slave Bill became law in the US Congress in September 1850. It granted slave owners the power to hunt and capture slaves who, so they claimed, had run away from them. This right caused great panic and fear among Blacks in the northern states, many of whom were escaped slaves who had been living in freedom for a long time. Numerous families fled to Ontario because of this law. Alarmed at the proscriptive laws against them, many free families also left. Fred Landon, "The Negro Migration to Canada after the Passing of the Fugitive Slave Act," *Journal of Negro History* 5 (1920): 22–36.

19 Original copy of the letter is at the American Missionary Association's Archives, Amistad Research Center, Tulane University, Louisiana.

20 Bruce Curtis, *Building the Educational State in Canada West, 1836–1871* (London: Althouse Press, 1988); Alison Prentice, "The Feminization of Teaching in British North America and Canada, 1845–1875," *Histoire sociale/Social History* 8, no. 15 (1975): 5–20; Janet Guilford, "Separate Spheres: The Feminization of Public School Teaching in Nova Scotia, 1838–1880," in her *Separate Spheres*, 119–44.

21 Historian Michael Wayne notes that by 1861 at least 40 per cent of the Black children in Ontario were born in the province: "The Black Population of Canada West on the Eve of the American Civil War: A Reassessment Based on the Manuscript Census of 1861," in *A Nation of Immigrants: Women, Workers, and Communities in Canadian History, 1840–1960s*, ed. Franca Iacovetta, Paula Draper, and Robert Ventresca (Toronto: University of Toronto Press, 1998), 64, 65.

22 See William Riddell, "Petition of People of Colour of Ancaster," *Journal of Negro History* 15 (1930): 115–16; Alison Prentice and Susan Houston, *Schooling and Scholars in Nineteenth-Century Ontario* (Toronto: University of Toronto Press, 1988), 300; and Silverman and Gillie, "'The pursuit of knowledge under difficulties,'" 95–112.

23 For details of the Common School Act, which legislated separate schooling for Blacks, see J. George Hodgins, *Documentary History of Education in Upper Canada*, vol. 9: *1850–1851* (Toronto: L.K. Cameron, 1902), 24–5, 38–9.

24 "Petition of Black Residents of Euphemia against Boundary Changes to Exclude Them from the White School," AO, RG 2 C6c, Incoming General Correspondence to the Department of Education, 9 August 1853.
25 See Silverman and Gillie, "'The pursuit of knowledge under difficulties,'"; and Knight, "Black Parents Speak."
26 Afua Cooper, "Black Teachers in Canada West, 1850–1870: A History" (MA thesis, University of Toronto, 1991).
27 Carter G. Woodson, *Education of the Negro prior to 1860* (New York: Arno Press, 1968); Silverman and Gillie, "'The pursuit of knowledge under difficulties,'"; Cooper, "Black Teachers in Canada West"; and Yee, "Gender Ideology and Black Women."
28 Those who exhorted Blacks to uplift the race appealed to both women and men. Because of racial oppression, both sexes were convinced of the need for elevating the race. Most of the exhorters seem to have been men, but, owing to racial and sexual oppression, they had more access to the means of public expression and left more written records behind than women. The women who did leave records made it clear that they, too, supported and engaged in uplift activities. See Linda Perkins, "Black Women and Racial 'Uplift' prior to Emancipation," in *The Black Woman Cross-Culturally*, ed. F.C. Steady (Cambridge, MA: Schenkman, 1981), 317–34; and James Oliver Horton, "Freedom's Yoke: Gender Conventions among Antebellum Free Blacks," *Feminist Studies* 12, no. 1 (1986): 51–76.
29 Perkins, "Black Women and Racial 'Uplift,'" 323.
30 *Voice of the Fugitive*, 15 January 1851.
31 Cooper, "Black Teachers in Canada West," 95–6. Also, Ronald Butchart examines uplift in the work of some African American teachers he studied; see his "'We can best instruct our own people': New York African Americans in the Freedmen's Schools, 1861–1875," *Afro Americans in New York Life and History* (January 1988): 33.
32 For a discussion of several teachers who kept on teaching despite inadequate remuneration, see Cooper, "Black Teachers in Canada West," 81–98.
33 A large majority of the young female teachers in Ontario, Black and white, were the daughters of farmers. Prentice and Houston, *Schooling and Scholars*, 170.
34 One could argue that uplift was a middle-class ideology, given the push that came from the Black intelligentsia. This class privilege gave it access to print. Still, I maintain that, even though the Black middle class presented its opinions as *the* Black opinion, poor and working-class people, given the racist nature of the society, willingly supported and promoted uplift. For a Black intellectual position, see Martin Delany, *The Condition, Elevation, Emigration, and Destiny of the Colored People of the United States* (1852; reprint, New Hampshire: Ayers Co., 1988). Delany wrote this book before he came to live in Ontario, but residence in the province did not change his view, as his actions on behalf of Kent's Black community testified.
35 See AO, McCurdy Collection, King Street School, Amherstburg, Minutes of Public School Trustees, 1851–82.
36 In fact, Amherstburg's Blacks fought segregated schooling and refused to set up a separate school when Ryerson advised them to do so in 1846. They firmly believed in integrated education and desired to send their children to the local schools. But the whites would not agree. Finally, unable to "beat down white prejudice," Amherstburg's Blacks capitulated and set up a separate school by 1851. AO, RG 2 cbc, Robert Peden to Egerton Ryerson, 23 February 1846; RG 2 C1, Egerton Ryerson to Isaac Rice, 5 March 1846; see also Silverman and Gillie, "'The pursuit of knowledge under difficulties.'"
37 The minutes of the Amherstburg Trustees reveal that it was Julia Turner who was the "colored lady teacher" at the time of Drew's visit to the Amherstburg school. See AO, McCurdy Collection, Minutes of Public School Trustees.

38 Benjamin Drew, *Narratives of Fugitives Slaves in Canada* (Boston: Jewett & Co., 1856), 348.

39 For the poor condition of the province's schools as the educational state got into full gear, see Prentice and Houston, *Schooling and Scholars*, 210–12.

40 See AO, RG 2 17, superintendent's reports, 1855, 1856, Amherstburg, Essex County.

41 One study shows that, by 1881, well over half the female teachers in at least seven Ontario counties were daughters living at home. Danylewycz, Light, and Prentice, "The Evolution," 100.

42 See AO, McCurdy Collection, Minutes of Trustees.

43 Danylewycz, Light, and Prentice, "The Evolution," 85.

44 American Missionary Association, Shadd to Whipple, 6 August 1861.

45 The prejudice against women teachers in Western society can probably be traced back to Saul of Tarsus's injunction against the practice: "Let not a woman teach, nor to usurp authority over the man, but to be in silence," says the man who later became Saint Paul. In his view, patriarchal civilization would crumble if women stepped into the public realm and "uttered." Their silence ensured their subordination to male authority.

46 Horton, "Freedom's Yoke," 51–76.

47 The hiring of Black women as assistants after Turner's firing lends credence to my suspicion that Turner was fired because trustees and parents became "anxious" about a woman being in charge of their children. This fear probably derived from the belief that a woman could not instil the "proper discipline" in their children.

48 Mary Bibb, for example, became a dressmaker after her first school foundered in Sandwich. She advertised her business in *Voice of the Fugitive* from July to December 1852.

49 Another possibility is that Turner worked at home while at the same time studying to raise the level of her education. When she obtained a second-class certificate, she reapplied for work in the system.

50 For a history of Mary Bibb and the Sandwich school, see Afua Cooper, "Black Women and Work in 19th-Century Canada West: Black Woman Teacher Mary Bibb," in Bristow et al., "'*We're rooted here*,'" 143–70.

51 See AO, RG 2 17, Superintendent's Reports for Essex, 1863–69.

52 Danylewycz, Light, and Prentice, "The Evolution," 97.

53 Robin Winks calls this period, from 1865 to 1930, the "nadir" in the Black historical experiences in Canada. See his *Blacks in Canada*, 288–336.

54 See James Walker, *A History of Blacks in Canada* (Quebec: Government of Canada, 1980), 67–8.

55 Jane Errington, "Pioneers and Suffragists," in *Changing Patterns: Women in Canada*, ed. Sandra Burt, Lorraine Code, and Lindsay Dorney (Toronto: McClelland and Stewart, 1993), 70.

56 Dionne Brand, 'We weren't allowed to go into the factory until Hitler started the war': The 1920s to the 1940s,' in Bristow et al., "'*We're rooted here*,'" 179.

57 Agnes Calliste, "Sleeping Car Porters in Canada: An Ethnically Submerged Split Labour Market," in *Canadian Working-Class History*, ed. Laurel MacDowell and Ian Radforth (Toronto: Canadian Scholars' Press, 1992), 673–92.

58 For example, Emmaline Shadd taught in a Scottish Gaelic community in Peel County. The fact that Shadd was extremely light-skinned and did not have "Negroid" features perhaps helped her to gain acceptance by this community. Her photograph suggests that she could, if she wanted to, pass for white. Shadd stayed in Peel for a year, after which she left, married, and retired from teaching. The case of Walter Rolling bears on this point. Rolling, descended from Black pioneers who homesteaded in the Aurora area in the 1830s, became the principal of a white school in 1895. Aurora had few Black families, and perhaps whites there did not see someone like Rolling as a threat. Also, the school needed a teacher/principal. On Shadd, see Cooper, "Black Teachers in Canada West," 113; on Rolling, see Carl Finkle, 'Walter Rolling: Black School Principal,' *Akili: Journal of African Canadian Studies* (March 1995): 14–15.

59 Alfred Whipper and Aaron Highgate, two Black teachers, fought hard for their jobs in the Chatham separate school when the white trustees tried to oust them from it. See n60.

60 Black parents protested in 1859 when the Chatham school trustees fired the two Black teachers at the separate school, Aaron Highgate and Alfred Whipper, and hired a white teacher, Peter Nichol. The trustees justified their action by claiming that Nichol was the most qualified because he had a first-class teaching certificate. The Black parents objected angrily, arguing that their children needed Black teachers as they served as better role models. For them, a first-class certificate was not as important as having a Black person in charge. See Cooper, "Black Teachers in Canada West," 59–60.

61 See "Ada Kelly Whitney's Story," in the kit *Black Women in Canada: Past and Present*, compiled by Marguerite Alfred and Pat Staton (Toronto: Green Dragon Press, 1997).

62 Brand, *No Burden to Carry*, 272.

63 See Steady, *The Black Woman Cross-Culturally*, 22–4. Rosalyn Terborg-Penn elaborates on Steady's research and theory in her article, "Through an African Feminist Lens: Viewing Caribbean Women's History Cross-Culturally," in *Engendering History: Caribbean Women in Historical Perspective*, ed. Verene Shepherd, Bridget Brereton, and Barbara Bailey (Kingston: Ian Randle, 1995), 3–19.

64 Jordinia at some point in her life also taught school. It could be that after she married she left teaching, but had to continue in paid employment to help her family.

65 See AO, GS 976, Assessors' rolls for Sandwich from 1875 to 1899.

66 AO, MS 935, reel 96, Vital Statistics Records, Death Registration. The fact that Turner died in Amherstburg indicates that she may have been ill for some time and moved to her home town to be cared for by family members.

67 AO, GS 1, 741, application filed in the surrogate court of Essex County, 15 December 1900.

68 AO, GS 976, Assessors' rolls, Town of Sandwich, Essex County, 1870–99.

CHAPTER THREE

"Both silly and loose": Deconstructing Women's Criminal Behaviour in Late Nineteenth- and Early Twentieth-Century Oxford County, Ontario

REBECCA BEAUSAERT

On 10 October 1887, the *Woodstock Sentinel-Review* reported that "Mrs. Dalson and her two daughters, West end, were arrested on Saturday night coming out of J. & T. Grant's shoe store, charged with shop-lifting. They were remanded to jail for a couple of days, pending the forthcoming of some evidence."[1] This display of unlawful behaviour by local women, recounted from the Police Court proceedings, would not have surprised readers: females in and around Oxford County violated several civil and criminal codes in the later nineteenth and early twentieth centuries. Such stories were commonplace and remind us that women's conduct, and that of all citizens in a community, was intricately linked with the courts. According to Karen Dubinsky, "judges at assize court, for example, would congratulate or condemn an entire community, depending on the number of sexual crimes on the docket."[2] Rural communities often boasted in newspapers that local citizens were morally superior to their urban counterparts, yet when court cases and detailed press reports are examined, such righteous attitudes are dismantled.

For their unlawful actions, the Dalsons would have been considered antithetical to the Victorian womanly ideal. This further complicates myths about rural society, ones in which honourable women played an integral role. When we look at the women who acted (willingly or not) in a way defined as criminal or dishonourable, a new dimension of rural society comes to light. The types of crimes committed by rural women were analogous to those appearing before the urban courts, indicating that crime was neither a "rural" nor an "urban" phenomenon. When it came to crime, the rural–urban divide was less stark than often suggested at the time.

Using data from predominantly rural Oxford County in southwestern Ontario, this case study of women's criminal behaviour in the later nineteenth and early twentieth centuries addresses an important yet understudied aspect of the province's socio-legal history. In past analyses of rural crime, historians have privileged the actions of male criminals, with women largely portrayed as passive victims. A few works by legal and feminist historians have examined female criminals outside of Ontario's urban centres; missing, though, is a more inclusive study that details the particulars of rural and small-town women's incarceration and how they faced the courts in a small community. This chapter addresses this lacuna by examining a selection of the crimes committed in Oxford County and how they demonstrate the interplay between gender, crime, and place.

Investigating examples of female criminality also reveals the seedier side of rural and small-town life. Though the women examined here were only a small segment of Oxford's population, the ways that ostensibly personal and private matters (such as pregnancy and alcoholism) sometimes entered public discourse through the criminal justice system offer a window into the more intimate lives of rural and small-town people. How women became entangled with systems of authority, and the public's fascination with certain types of criminal behaviour, especially those associated with sex, reveals moral regulation's strong influence on the courts. Initially, imprudent behaviour in rural communities was managed by families, neighbours, and the clergy.[3] Though such regulators continued to participate in debates about citizens' conduct, and women's especially, by the later nineteenth century the growing judicial power of municipal councils and police constabularies had superseded much of this informal authority. Yet, despite knowing that law enforcement officials were closely watching them, some women continued to resist the gendered constraints imposed on them by acting in ways widely viewed as unwomanly and unlawful.

The complicated relationship between women and the judicial system poses several interpretive challenges for historians, particularly the murky nature of offences where women were coerced or victims of circumstance (such as infanticide or abortion). As historian Susan Sessions Rugh acknowledges, it is also difficult to measure whether patterns of female crime and delinquency were changing around the turn of the century.[4] Were women acting out more, or were their actions being scrutinized to a greater degree? Statistics about incarceration provide an idea of what sorts of behaviours were considered unseemly in the eyes of the law, but jailtime does not account for all instances of criminality in Oxford County, as many crimes went unreported or justice was administered informally. When women "acted out" they faced a gauntlet of regulatory systems, ranging from watchful community members and defamation by local reporters to interactions with the police and court systems. Some behaviour was codified under the Criminal Code of Canada and municipal by-laws; other bothersome "moral infractions"[5] fell outside the boundaries of legal authority.

This chapter also considers how women's increasing visibility in public spaces prompted concerns over their vulnerability, and whether publicly engaging in what was perceived to be inappropriate behaviour could impact a woman's reputation. Despite contemporaries' claims to the contrary, moral panic and fears of deviancy *were* present in rural areas and small towns. The increased regulation of women's activities and conduct indicates that the social reform movement had permeated remote locations, as well as the extent to which this discourse influenced locals' intolerance of women whose activities stepped outside the bounds of respectability and femininity. Evidence from Oxford County shows that factors such as race, class, and reputation also shaped how women were judged in their communities and beyond. Criminal or immoral behaviour, when exhibited by women who were white and/or from "good" families, tended to be scrutinized less by the courts and the local press than that of people who were racialized or of "poor character."

A Note on Sources

Pertinent information about female deviancy varies depending on region and period. Some county records are rich with archival materials from the courts, which can "provide a window into instances of personal life"[6] that historians may not otherwise be privy to. These sources can be useful in studying how female criminality was framed by lawmakers, but, as historian Steven Maynard reminds us in his study of urban males and sexual danger, "the view provided by court records is rarely clear and therefore must be wiped clean."[7] Historians must pay attention to the perspectives, objectives, and biases of the male judges and other court-appointed recorders who were responsible for mediating these sources as they contributed to socially constructed ideas about gender and "proper" behaviour.

Most of the surviving case files deal with serious criminal matters (such as murder) that were judicial anomalies in small communities. More common occurrences of women's criminal behaviour, such as public intoxication and prostitution, fell under the rubric of minor civil offences and were handled by the local police magistrate, justice of the peace, or biannual court of assize. Historian Constance Backhouse, in her work on Canadian women and the criminal justice system, concedes that researching female criminality, even in urban centres, is made difficult due to the lack of records from the lower courts. Evidence of the women from Oxford County who committed both serious and petty crimes is accordingly difficult to uncover because they, too, were tried primarily before the lower courts.[8]

When females committed more serious crimes in Oxford, detailed and descriptive texts of their trials have survived only sporadically. The county jail register and community newspapers, when paired with personal data in census returns, hold the richest information on female offenders, though they, too, have their limitations. The jail registers from urban centres like Toronto contain considerably more personal information about inmates, whereas Oxford's only state the detainee's name, date of admittance, why they were apprehended, the length of their stay, and occasionally a note about their fate. When compared to other legal records, however, the register provides the most comprehensive look at criminality, as many individuals who were arrested stayed in the county jail at some point in their legal journey. Although these records should be used with caution – an 1879 report of the jail noted that they were known "not to be properly kept"[9] – they still provide information not found elsewhere.

Another useful source for piecing together these women's lives is the Canadian census for this period. It, too, comes with its own set of challenges for historians, especially regarding employment, since women whose income was derived from criminal activity, such as running a gambling den or working in the sex trade, rarely admitted such wage-earning activities to enumerators. For example, twenty-three-year-old Clarissa Lambert was detained in the Oxford County jail for keeping a house of ill fame in 1900.[10] According to the 1901 census, Lambert was living in the town of Tillsonburg with her three-year-old daughter and making $700 as a charwoman.[11] This far exceeds the average earnings of a male head of household in 1901,[12] so Lambert probably lied to the census enumerators about her occupation, or the inflated wages included money she earned in the sex trade.

For the purposes of this study, evidence of women's criminality will be drawn mainly from the handwritten Oxford County jail register and municipal council minutes, surviving court documents, and newspapers. The print media provided the broadest range of information about female criminality in Oxford County due to the considerable attention paid to court cases. Stories were also printed about disreputable behaviour that fell outside the boundaries of the criminal justice system. Not surprisingly, the stories receiving the most coverage involved lewdness or private matters, a defendant who was a racialized person, or sexual violence. In this way, events involving personal business were pushed to the forefront of community commentary. The amount of attention paid to women's crimes in newspapers, and the pejorative ways in which "bad" women were usually described, served as cautions for other "wayward" women.

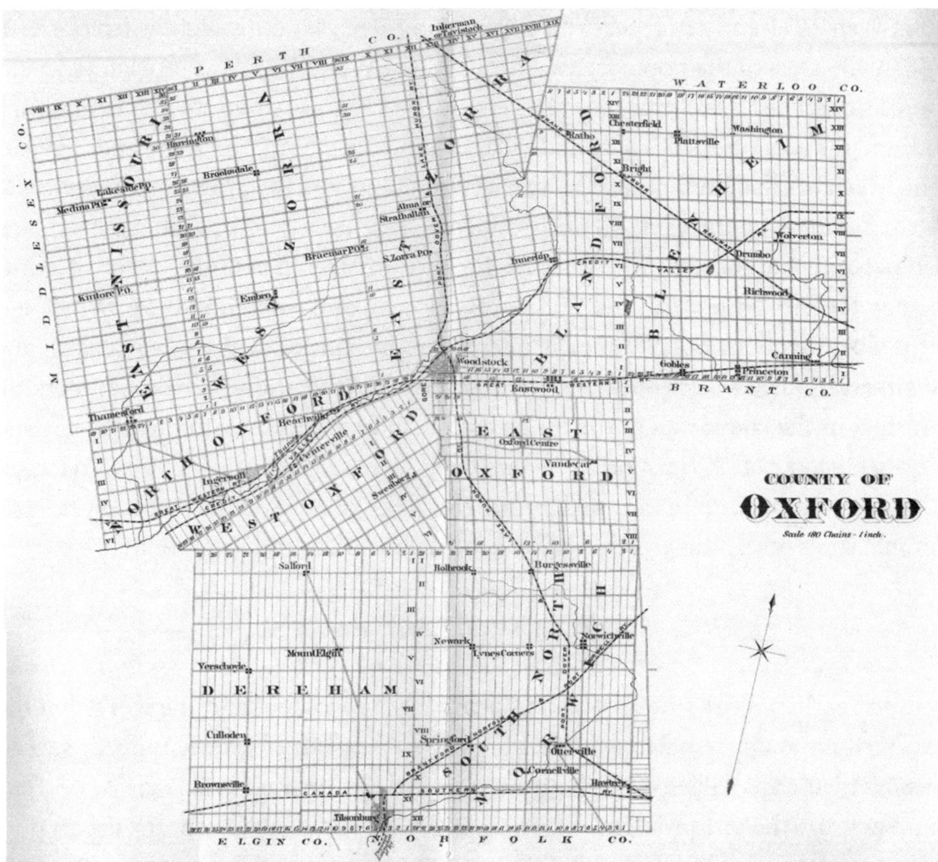

Figure 3.1. Map of Oxford County, 1876.
Source: Used with permission from County of Oxford Archives. Found in Wadsworth, Unwin & Brown, *Topographical and Historical Atlas of the County of Oxford, Ontario* (Toronto: Walker and Miles, 1876), 30-31.

A Brief History of Oxford County

Oxford County, in southwestern Ontario, was initially home to the Attawandaron, Anishinaabeg, Haudenosaunee, and the Mississaugas of the Credit First Nation, who were largely displaced. when the area received its first significant wave of immigrants after the American Revolution. Colonial administrators had great hopes for the area, and Anglo-Celtic settlement increased between the 1830s and the 1850s due to territory ceded in Treaty 3 (1792) and the abundance of waterways that aided the development of milling and lumber operations. The arrival of several half-pay British naval officers during that period led to the growth of Woodstock, which was named the county seat in 1839.

Between 1871 and 1911 Oxford's population increased only slightly, from 47,921 to 48,404.[13] Most of the populace was rural. When Woodstock was proclaimed a city in 1901, it had just 8,833 citizens.[14] The county was renowned for its rich agricultural land, and the economies of towns and villages like Tillsonburg, Norwich, and Ingersoll were driven by small milling and industrial operations and the provision of services to the surrounding countryside. Oxford's citizens were largely of English, Scottish, and Irish descent, and mostly Protestant. In the mid-nineteenth century, Oxford County also had the fifth largest concentration of Black men and women in the province due to the employment opportunities it offered, its proximity to the Great Lakes, and the sizeable Quaker settlement in Norwich Township.[15] Though their numbers diminished in the later years of the nineteenth century, according to the 1881 census, forty-two people of "African origin" were living in Woodstock alone.[16] Oxford largely reflected the broader religious and ethnic character of rural Ontario; however, local criminal trials reveal the presence of some racial diversity and class conflict.

Situating Rural "Bad Girls"

As noted earlier, most studies of rural crime ignore women, and the work that has been written about female crime tends to focus on *urban* crime. Indeed, several feminist historians[17] have described the perceived growth in female crime and delinquency, or "the girl problem," as primarily a late nineteenth-century urban phenomenon, defined as "the vulnerability and moral irresponsibility of young working women in the city."[18] For Ontario, Karen Dubinsky and Lynne Marks have shown that there *were* rural and small-town "bad girls";[19] even so, studies typically situate the "girl problem" within the confines of urban settings. This is unsurprising, given that most of these historians emphasize the rhetoric of the period's reformers, who believed that as women entered North America's urban centres seeking employment, adventure, or escape from the drudgery of rural life, their independence and separation from family made them susceptible to a seedy underbelly of sex, pleasure, and leisure. Whether coerced by potential seducers or acting independently, the women who "acted out" were sent to jails and reformatories for a variety of criminal acts – many of which were defined by society as "female" – such as prostitution, procuring an abortion, or committing infanticide. Because women's purity was so coveted, increasingly the "girl problem" came to represent women's "fall" as they rejected the moral precepts of domesticity by flagrantly walking city streets, earning an income, and engaging in dangerous and promiscuous sexual acts.

Historians point out that criminal women tended to share many of the same characteristics – they were young, single, immigrant, working-class urban dwellers.

In this sense, the "girl problem" fails to address the unique variances in class, age, race, and religion found among female deviants in rural settings like Oxford. Indeed, it is not surprising that when it came to female delinquency, rural and urban were juxtaposed in the eyes of reformers. In the nineteenth century a number of "bad girls" who had been convicted of crimes in urban centres such as Toronto and Hamilton were sent to rural southern Ontario to be reformed by the clean air and hard work of farm life. Notions of the countryside were consistently associated with morality and wholesomeness, while the crowded, dirty city was immoral and "bad." The countryside represented virtue, peace, happiness, health, and hard work; the city represented vice, danger, pleasure, deviance, and corruption. Nostalgic sentiments about rural society at the turn of the century judged its women and girls to be "pure, modest, affectionate. They made good wives" and "were the best and most thoughtful mothers that ever watched over the well-being of their children."[20]

In fact, there were rural women who drank publicly, committed violence against unwanted infants, and ran gambling dens. Some of these women served lengthy jail sentences or were sent to reformatories and asylums to receive instruction on "proper" female decorum. This reality conflicts with nineteenth-century assumptions that rural areas and small communities had developed effective systems of regulation that kept women and girls on the straight and narrow and protected them from dangerous situations.[21] Farmyards and sideroads could provoke and serve as backdrops for criminal acts just as easily as tenement stoops and alleyways. Despite this, female criminality was (and continues to be) associated with cities, so those living outside their parameters have largely been left out of the dialogue.

In this study, "crime" refers to actions codified by laws, and "bad" behaviour and deviancy refer to acts that do not necessarily fall under courts' jurisdiction. Absent are cases where women appeared in front of the courts as victims of sexual coercion or violence, including rape. Juvenile delinquents have also been left out of this discussion, for they were increasingly being treated as separate entities in the eyes of the law. The 1908 federal Juvenile Delinquents Act (JDA) identified juvenile delinquents as persons between the ages of seven and sixteen.[22] This discussion has adopted a similar definition by mainly examining women beyond sixteen years of age.

Rural Ontario Justice Systems

The administration of justice varied across Ontario. In smaller locales, it was overseen by a justice of the peace or a local police chief or constable. That police constabularies had recently been established – however inept they reputedly were – demonstrates that smaller communities needed greater protection from lawlessness, for the church

Figure 3.2 Last trial in the "old" courthouse, Woodstock, 1890.
Source: Woodstock Museum National Historic Site, 1989.7.8

and a tight-knit group of community members were no longer enough. Likely, the creation of formal policing systems in the later nineteenth century helped dissuade some citizens from engaging in criminal behaviour, especially in public. Oxford's jail register demonstrates this fact: rates of incarceration began to decline in the 1880s.[23] Even if a woman was not obviously committing an offence, her mere presence in public, especially at night, left her open to questioning. In the town of Tillsonburg, Police Chief Archie Pow was known for his strict stance on public lawbreakers, even vocalizing his displeasure over illegal acts in the *Tillsonburg Observer*.[24]

Crimes that occurred in public and that were considered minor, such as drunkenness or vagrancy, were straightforward in terms of the legal process. A woman would be witnessed committing a crime, or a citizen would request that a woman's actions be investigated; the suspect would be detained until a hearing could be convened with the justice of the peace or police court magistrate. It would there be decided whether the accused should remain in jail, be released, or pay a fine. More serious crimes, such as abortion and infanticide, also appeared before the police court. An accused who was committed for trial would be remanded in custody until the case could be heard by the judges' criminal court or the criminal assize court.

Figure 3.3 Courthouse Square, Woodstock, 1865. The "old" courthouse is in the foreground and the jail is in the background. The old courthouse was built in 1839, condemned in 1888, and a new one was built nearby in 1891.
Source: County of Oxford Archives, Photograph #3: Old Courthouse in Woodstock – 1865 – b/w photograph: & w; 20.3x25.3 cm

The latter was only held twice each year in Oxford County, so detainees could end up spending a considerable time behind bars.

The county courthouse in Woodstock was the location of the assizes, which began with evidence being presented against the accused. If the grand jury returned a "True Bill," the case went to trial. The execution of justice was swift; even the most serious of infractions were adjudicated within a few days. All presiding officials in the courtroom were white males, and the jury was drawn from local community members. Judges travelled on a circuit, so they did not intimately know the communities they visited. How the judiciary "applied and interpreted"[25] the law was undoubtedly influenced by race, class, and gender biases. Consequently, when women appeared in front of the courts, especially for crimes associated with sex, "prejudice, mistrust and outright misogyny were the order of the day."[26] Guilty verdicts usually resulted in jail time or relocation to a provincial insane asylum or reformatory. Acquittals freed women to return to their homes and families. Resuming a semblance of normalcy, however, was difficult due to a woman's experience in the jail, with the courts, and in the pages of local newspapers.

Doing Time: The Oxford County Jail

In the later nineteenth century, Ontario's prison system was divided into levels according to the severity of offences. In smaller communities, especially those that were "police villages,"[27] local deviants were usually held in cells constructed in the basements of public buildings, or a small, free-standing jail was constructed. Generally, incarceration in these jails was for "the Saturday night drunks, vagabonds, and, on occasion, wandering livestock."[28] The county jails were primarily for short-term stays and prisoners awaiting trial; penitentiaries held prisoners serving lengthy sentences for serious felonies.

Constructed in 1854 in Woodstock, Oxford County's jail held that city's lawbreakers as well as offenders and those awaiting trial from the surrounding towns and countryside. The jail was a multi-purpose facility, housing criminals as well as anyone incapable of caring for themselves or who were considered a danger to the community. At one point the town of Woodstock was accused of crowding the jail with non-criminal inmates for the purposes of turning a profit.[29] A small staff presided over the jail at all times, consisting of the gaoler, who managed the jail, the turnkey, who guarded the prisoners, the matron, who oversaw the needs and safety of female prisoners,[30] and a jail surgeon, who handled prisoners' health. Male and female prisoners were kept separated and had different responsibilities around the jail as part of their rehabilitation.

Upon their admittance, female prisoners were bathed and given a uniform consisting of an "over-dress and under-skirt, a pair of shoes and underclothing."[31] In an 1880 report by the Standing Committee on County Buildings and Property, it was suggested that female prisoners not wear uniforms as there were too few of them to warrant the cost.[32] All prisoners' hair was shorn for hygienic reasons, though women had to provide consent for this unless mandated by the jail surgeon. Each prisoner had their own cell with basic amenities, but overcrowding, especially during the winter months, was common. Female prisoners assisted with laundry, cleaning the premises, and growing the foodstuffs they consumed. Male prisoners also performed tasks such as "cutting wood" and "breaking stone."[33]

The Oxford County jail was by no means comfortable, but prisoners did have some conveniences at their disposal. The courtyard surrounding the jail was used for exercise and fresh air. Religious services and hymn books were available, as was a library and space for prisoners to write letters. The food offered to inmates was often described as wholesome, but a typical day offered little beyond gruel, bread, potatoes,

Figure 3.4 Oxford County jail, c. 1877. According to the description in the photo record, the insets are (left to right): "George Forbes Sr. Gaoler The County Gaol John Cameron Gov."
Source: Woodstock Museum National Historic Site, x1956.326.1

and boneless meat. The facility's sewage and plumbing systems needed constant maintenance. Outbreaks of infectious disease were rare – only a few isolated cases each year. Whatever its faults, the jail was often reported to be in "excellent order, and in a very commendable state of cleanliness."[34] The province closed the jail in 1977, and the building was repurposed for use by the Oxford County Board of Health. The present structure still has many of its original features, including the bars on the cells.[35]

Curtailing Criminality in Oxford County

By the mid- to late nineteenth century, politicians in Oxford County were aware that citizens, like their urban counterparts, needed to be shielded from the immorality that some evangelicals and reformers argued accompanied the vast socio-economic changes occurring in the province. As early as 1859, the Municipal Council of Oxford County had constructed and enforced its first "By-Law to enforce the observance of Public Morals," which attempted to prohibit the construction of venues, such as bowling alleys, thought to encourage inappropriate behaviour like gambling.[36] In 1874, another set of morality by-laws were passed that outlawed (among other indiscretions) drunk and disorderly conduct on streets and public spaces, the use of profane or blasphemous language, any "indecent or immoral behavior," and the "[keeping] of a bawdy house or house of ill fame or frequent[ing] the same."[37] That the first morality by-laws were passed at a time in the county's history when the population was still relatively small suggests the importance that was placed on establishing and maintaining, even this early on, a law-abiding and morally upstanding community. Prior to the creation of overarching federal laws, local decrees demonstrated an attempt to implement a stronger, formalized, and more rigid system of behavioural controls, in which regulatory powers were handed over to civic officials. Across the county, the passage of such by-laws continued into the late nineteenth century, pointing to the fact that immoral and criminal conduct had become a very real concern.

Indeed, by the later years of the nineteenth century, articles detailing anxieties about bad behaviour were appearing in rural periodicals and newspapers. While never explicitly stating that feminine conduct was a serious issue in Oxford, the cautionary tales and advice pieces appearing in the print media pointed to fears that being in the wrong places or partaking in "disreputable" activities might lead women down an immoral path of pleasure, danger, and ultimately criminality. In 1887, for instance, an item in the *Woodstock Sentinel-Review* stated simply, without elaboration: "Wherever you find dancing, you find kissing."[38] That same year, another story in the *Sentinel-Review* condemned "thoughtless young ladies" who indulged in "promiscuous correspondence with gentlemen."[39] When reports of women carousing with men or indulging in alcohol appeared, they were often framed within a cautionary discourse that associated women's engagement in unladylike activities, such as premarital sex, with the breakdown of home, family, and Victorian notions of respectability and femininity.

Sex Work

While unladylike behaviours were concerning, outright criminal activity – prostitution, for example – prompted immense anxiety among social purists across the province. Fears around prostitution were often concentrated in urban centres owing to the belief that young, unassuming females adrift in the "big city" were succumbing to immoral pleasures.[40] However, around the turn of the century, cities offered more plentiful employment opportunities for women, which provided alternatives to prostitution; in Oxford County, prospects for waged labour were limited, and in rural areas especially, opportunities were restricted to agricultural and domestic work. Between 1870 and 1914, around three dozen Oxford County women were incarcerated for crimes associated with sex work.[41] Historians have shown that prostitution could be an occasional gig, with women trading sexual favours for trinkets or a little pocket money. For others, it helped cover necessary expenses such as food and shelter. How many such liaisons took place cannot be calculated, but casual sex in exchange for compensation was a common occurrence in both rural and urban contexts.[42]

Regardless of location, engaging in any form of prostitution was widely perceived as a "fall" for women, who had thereby "transgressed the bounds of respectable womanhood" and were now considered "beyond the pale." Thus, they "could never be fully redeemed."[43] In Oxford County, some women were incarcerated multiple times for prostitution, indicating the importance of the compensation, prostitution's omnipresence, or possibly indifference to the "fallen" label. Between 1879 and 1880, Mary Ann Garner of Ingersoll was arrested four separate times for crimes associated with sex work.[44] Information culled from census returns may help explain Garner's struggles with the law. In 1871, fourteen-year-old Mary Ann lived with her parents James, aged thirty-nine, and Ann, aged fifty-two, and her brother, William, aged seventeen. The family was of Irish descent and belonged to the Church of England, and James worked as a labourer.[45] Ten years later, James was listed as a "Widower," and Mary Ann was the only other occupant in the home. Neither had an identified occupation.[46] Around this time, at the age of twenty-four, Mary Ann's legal troubles began. The grief of losing her mother, coupled with the lack of income in the household, likely accounts for Mary Ann's arrests. By 1891, James and Mary Ann were still living in the same household, though James was now employed again, working as a stonemason.[47]

When young women became entangled with the law, the reputation they acquired could affect matrimonial prospects, as these women had forsaken their virginity, considered one of the cardinal attributes of respectable womanhood. Ingersoll was a small community of just over 4,000 inhabitants, so undoubtedly the public was aware of Garner's criminal activities. But census returns indicate that Garner did go on to marry: in the 1901 census she is listed as the wife of Charles Smith, a forty-three-year-old machinist of Scottish ancestry.[48] Ten years later the couple was still living in Ingersoll, with Charles working as a blacksmith and earning a respectable yearly income of $550. Now in their fifties, Charles and Mary Ann had adopted a twelve-year-old girl named Lily, who was born in Ontario and of Irish descent. Two male boarders were also part of the household.[49] As Mary Ann Garner's experience suggests, economic struggles account for many women's engagement with sex work, but the stigma could be temporary or forgivable. Despite her multiple incarcerations and public knowledge of her actions, Garner appears to have redeemed herself by choosing the more respectable vocation of marriage and motherhood.

Vagrancy

Arrests for prostitution indicate that women in Oxford County were very much fixtures in their communities' public spaces. Contrary to popular belief, like women in urban areas, they "defied social convention and conducted their social lives in public."[50] Traversing these traditionally male-dominated spaces, however, was not always easy, uneventful, or safe. For example, as both rural and urban women increasingly took to the streets, arrests for vagrancy rose substantially, a phenomenon that historians argue was not a coincidence. In the late nineteenth century, vagrancy was defined by a multiplicity of "deviant acts," which meant that "the net of the criminal justice system" could be "cast over a large number of women who could be arrested for a variety of reasons."[51] The simple act of loitering "on any street, road, highway or public place" or "wander[ing] in the fields, public streets or highways, lanes or places of public meeting or gathering of people, and does not give a satisfactory account of herself" constituted vagrancy and called for a fine of upwards of fifty dollars or prison time.[52] Clearly, gendered meanings were embedded in vagrancy's many definitions, showcasing contemporaries' "social anxieties about women's sexuality, respectability, and increasingly public role."[53]

In Oxford County, vagrancy was the fourth most common reason for arrest among females.[54] In the jail registers, seventeen women were incarcerated for vagrancy between 1870 and 1914, which is likely only a fraction of the women traversing public spaces in ways that troubled authorities. Women were arrested individually and as part of groups, and their imprisonment varied from two days to two months. In 1873, four female members of the Fairbrother family were arrested for vagrancy and committed to the Oxford County jail from 30 September to 28–31 November. The accused included thirty-six-year-old Brigit and daughters Eliza, aged fourteen, Mary, aged nine, and Susan, aged three and a half, as well as another family member named Jane (age unknown). The Fairbrothers were of English descent, members of the Church of England, and the head of household, George, worked as a boiler maker. The 1871 census shows that the Fairbrothers lived in the nearby town of Brantford; it is unclear whether they had relocated to Oxford County at the time of their arrest or were simply visiting.[55]

Several other women in Oxford County were arrested for crimes analogous to vagrancy, including "walking the streets at night," "street walking," and "night walking." It is unclear how these transgressions differed from vagrancy, for descriptions in the register were often at the whim of the recorder. Vagrancy charges and the like tended to arise in conjunction with other petty crimes, such as prostitution and drinking; this was a deliberate move by authorities to punish women who had "stepped outside prescribed roles as private, domestic, and mannerly citizens."[56] In September 1882, Fanny Monk, age and address unknown, was arrested on both vagrancy and prostitution charges and spent three days in the county jail.[57] The increasing surveillance of women's behaviour in public, even in the smallest of towns, confirms that the Victorian ideology of separate spheres was more construct than reality, and clearly difficult to enforce, despite authorities' attempts to monitor women's actions in the public spaces of rural and small-town Ontario.

Race and the Criminal Justice System

When a serious crime against a woman occurred in a rural area (such as murder or sexual assault), the print media typically characterized this as out of women's control and as evidence that they required protection when in public. As rural areas underwent vast social and economic changes, and unfamiliar faces began constantly appearing – entertainers, peddlers, farm labourers, immigrants, and so on – local people were advised to be wary of them.[58] Rural communities were predominantly White and of Anglo-Celtic heritage, with the result that "otherness" was often pinpointed as the cause of reprehensible behaviour. A 1908 article in the *Farmer's Advocate*, a popular rural publication, suggested that mounting crime rates in rural areas were due to "hobos; the large importation of undesirable immigrants of the submerged and criminal classes; and … the increasing number of gangs of Italians and other foreigners employed by the railways and other public enterprises on construction work."[59] In Oxford, jail surgeon Andrew McKay remarked in 1913: "It is regrettable that the immigration officials are not able to check the entrance of so many undesirables into our country. Some of them are feeble-minded, others criminally disposed."[60]

In the Oxford County jail register between 1870 and 1914, very few women of colour appear. An exception is a formerly enslaved woman named Letitia Munson, who on two occasions, 26–30 August 1882 and 1 October 1882–16 January 1883, was imprisoned for "procuring an abortion."[61] The second occasion involved the death of a thirty-five-year-old white hotel waitress, Ellen Weingardner, in September 1882. The elderly Munson had discovered Weingardner's remains in the deceased woman's home in the township of Oxford West. The two were acquaintances as Munson had assisted Weingardner and her young daughter when they needed a home.[62] A post-mortem revealed the cause of death to be a botched abortion, and Munson, who had long "borne a very bad reputation"[63] in the community for performing abortions, was arrested for complicity. During the highly sensationalized trial, the Crown presented Munson as a bane to the local community for performing unlicensed and illegal medical services who for her actions should face the full brunt of the law. Much to the surprise of a packed courthouse, a verdict of not guilty was returned due to lack of evidence, and the case was dismissed.[64]

Throughout the court proceedings, the press painted Munson as a sinister Black "doctress" whose medical services to local women challenged popular notions of femininity and morality. Given that Weingardner was deceased and could not respond to the charge of unlawfully seeking an abortion, Munson's alleged involvement became the focus of the trial. Race undoubtedly played a role in how the press, local authorities, and the public judged the two women; the naive Weingardner was depicted as one of many victims of the deplorable Munson. The Black community in Oxford County was small in the 1880s; even so, its visibility spawned distrust and discomfort among the white citizenry. Instances of anti-Black racism were known to occur, and these attitudes were amplified when Black defendants appeared in court. In such cases, the courthouse became a theatre as local citizens vied for the opportunity to watch Black defendants answer for their crimes.[65]

The attention paid to a case was greater when it involved a serious transgression committed by a member of a marginalized group. In 1895, the Woodstock courtroom was packed with spectators who had gathered to hear a fifteen-year-old mixed-race girl describe her entire romantic history after her lover, a young Black man named Thomas Marshall, was charged with seduction. The "prepossessing mulatto"[66] girl, Beatrice "Maud" Anderson, told the court how she and Marshall engaged in consensual sex near the gate outside her home. She confirmed that she "never had anything to do with any man before then. Prisoner used caution with me." She then admitted that she was now "in the family way."[67] Both she and Marshall affirmed that they wished to marry but had been forbidden to do so by Anderson's father, who disapproved of the match. When called as a witness, Marshall Anderson (a respected watchman in the community) stated that prior to his daughter's relationship with the accused, he believed her to be of "pure character."[68] Though the jury rendered a verdict of guilty, mercy was recommended and the sentence postponed. Seduction cases were common in Oxford County, but the fact that the courtroom was crowded with spectators suggests that when illicit sex and miscegenation were the focus of a trial, the proceedings served as a spectacle for Oxford's white citizenry. In this case, both Beatrice and her father had to defend her actions and convince the audience of her "pure character." Divulging to the crowded courthouse that she had engaged in consensual premarital sex likely affirmed for many the popular stereotype that Black females had loose sexual morals.[69]

Drinking

Drinking was another public act that compromised women's "pure character." Generally, it was viewed as a low form of amusement when engaged in by members of the "lower orders," or by women, or to the point of overindulgence. Of the forty-two different criminal acts for which women were incarcerated in the Oxford County jail, "drunk and disorderly" was the second most common, according to the jail register. Gender played a central role in the construction of appropriate and inappropriate drinking practices. Working-class men often congregated in barrooms and hotels to grab a pint and socialize with other men after work; middle- and upper-class men enjoyed a glass of claret or port when assembled in one another's homes or at members-only clubs.[70] Setting aside teetotallers, as well as instances when excessive drinking provoked violence or immoral behaviour, alcohol was a customary means for men to foster social ties. In contrast, when women participated in this sort of disreputable leisure, they were viewed as "de-womanized" and as "exhibiting features of a 'bastardized masculinity.'"[71] Drinking, and other forms of vice with which it was associated (such as prostitution), sharply diverged from nineteenth-century ideals of the pious woman, especially as the temperance movement and its female supporters gained traction across the province.

Despite rising calls to criminalize drinking, the consumption of alcohol continued everywhere and throughout the year in rural and small-town Ontario. Holidays and celebrations of all kinds were popular occasions to drink, and these often led to arrests for public intoxication. Several local by-laws attempted to censure instances of overindulgence but never outright denounced drinking. As mentioned, an 1874 by-law in Oxford County stipulated that any person found drunk, or guilty of any disorderly conduct on any of the streets, highways, or public places of the county, could face a fifty-dollar fine, or jailtime if the fine was not paid.[72]

The number of women arrested for alcohol-related crimes pales in comparison to the number of men similarly charged because drinking was so closely aligned with rough masculinity. Still, arrest records indicate that, regardless of where they lived, women imbibed. In the Toronto Women's Court, public drunkenness accounted for one in four arrests.[73] The information gleaned about females accused of drunk and disorderly conduct in Oxford County indicates that their ages ranged from early twenties to late thirties and that most were Protestant and of Anglo-Celtic descent. In contrast, in Toronto, women thus charged tended to be over the age of thirty, Roman Catholic, and largely itinerant, occasionally employed as domestics or prostitutes.[74] In both places, several of the women accused of drunkenness were recidivists or had been charged with drunkenness and other offences besides, such as vagrancy or prostitution. These patterns reveal that drunkenness was commonplace within the justice system and that few woman, after being written up or arrested, "learnt their lesson." Mary Sommers, for instance, appears in the Oxford County jail register four times between 1876 and 1880 for drinking and vagrancy charges. Most alcohol-related arrests, such as Sommers's, amounted to little more than a few days' jailtime or the payment of a small fine.

When seeking information about female drinkers in Oxford County, except for what can be gleaned from records of incarceration (which are scanty, albeit semi-useful), little can be learned about how much (or how little) women actually imbibed. But in his 1913 year-end report of conditions, jail surgeon Andrew McKay noted that he was "sorry to have to report that all the females and many of the males became inmates of the Gaol owing to indulgence in strong drink."[75] The previous year, McKay made a similar comment in his report, when referencing cases of illness in the jail: "by the great majority needing attention were those committed to 'sober up' from an over-indulgence, too prolonged."[76]

Some cautionary reports did appear in local papers to deter women from drinking. In 1872, for instance, a brief notation appeared in the *Woodstock Sentinel-Review* about a local woman who had died from injuries sustained while severely intoxicated.[77] Despite the high proportion of women who led temperance crusades in their respective communities, women of all classes drank, though where and how they did so varied. Cocktails were customary at the soirées and dinner parties of the elite. Middle-class women discreetly purchased spirits or liquor-laced patent medicines from local shops under the guise of needing a medicinal tonic. Some women were also involved in the illegal sale of alcohol. Shopkeepers required a special permit to sell liquor in bulk (to limit its availability), and failure to secure a permit was a misdemeanour. In 1880, two women in Oxford County were arrested for "selling liquor without a license." Annie Gibbs was incarcerated from 21 September to 1 October, and Minnie Wright from 3 January to 4 February.[78]

Though rural and small-town women drank, they generally stayed away from public hang-outs lest they be "assumed to be prostitutes or gin-shop derelicts."[79] The traditional haunts of drinkers – barrooms, hotels, pool halls, and the like – were, in rural and small-town Ontario, almost completely populated by men. Small communities made for greater familiarity with neighbours, so women rarely entered these masculine domains lest they generate local gossip. Though they may not have consumed alcohol in the customary places, the record of drunk and disorderly arrests indicates that women did inhabit public spaces and were reluctant to curtail pleasurable activities that contravened laws.

Reproduction, Sex, and Criminal Behaviour

Many of the transgressions that led to women's arrests in Oxford County, such as drinking, were relatively minor infractions or lapses in moral judgment. When stronger repercussions such as jailtime were doled out, it was often for a crime associated with illicit sex. Notwithstanding the "simplicity, innocence, and solid family values" purportedly associated with small-town and rural life, "the farmhouse and farmyard could [also] serve as a setting for acts of sexual violence, seduction, and strife."[80] Popular and seemingly innocent turn-of-the-century social activities – skating, attending the theatre, going out walking, buggy rides, and the like – provided venues for couples to meet, flirt, and engage in sexual activity. Despite community censure, women in Oxford County did test the boundaries of Victorian womanhood by exploring sex for pleasure. While some were victims of unfortunate and horrific acts of sexual violence, most women who appeared in front of the local courts or were chastised for immoral behaviour in newspapers were there for offences involving consensual sex.

The *Tillsonburg Observer* reported on 9 April 1880 that according to data compiled by the Registrar General, one in every sixty-five children born in Oxford County in 1878 was illegitimate.[81] This statistic, while by no means alarming, does remind us that female sexuality was not always restricted to the marital bed. When intercourse resulted in an unwanted pregnancy, desperation pushed some women to seek an abortion or commit infanticide. In the later nineteenth and early twentieth centuries, both were illegal according to the Criminal Code of Canada, and guilty parties faced heavy financial penalties, life imprisonment, or even capital punishment.

In the courts and in the press, "abortion" was often synonymous with "murder." Not surprisingly, these cases received considerable public attention, demonstrating a misogynistic desire to regulate women's sexuality and control their reproduction.[82] Women who defied the law by ridding themselves of an unwanted pregnancy consulted "back door" abortion services provided by local midwives, herbalists, or quacks. These amateur healers were present in rural areas and small towns, their services advertised through hushed word of mouth. The necessary secrecy of abortions makes it impossible to calculate how many occurred; instances of safe, clean abortions have survived mainly through the notebooks of physicians who performed such procedures as a life-saving measure.[83] Gruesome, unhygienic, and painful "backdoor" abortions too often resulted in death or long-term injury. In many cases, the death of the mother was the only grounds on which to investigate an abortion case, and as trials conducted in Oxford County indicate, abortions were difficult to prosecute due to inconclusive evidence.

One notable case in Tillsonburg grappled with the problem of proof. In 1877, sixteen-year-old Theresa Collins was found deceased at the home of Edwin and Sarah Lutz, allegedly due to a botched abortion performed by her mother, Sarah Jane Collins. Sarah Lutz's son, John, would have been the father of Theresa's child. The autopsy led Dr. J.M. Ault to conclude that both Collins and Lutz were responsible for Theresa's abortion and subsequent death; even so, the jury rendered a verdict of not guilty.[84] In this case, due to inadequate evidence, the character and habits of the defendants and the victim became the basis for recommending condemnation or mercy. In the late nineteenth century, "the process of criminal prosecution gave wide latitude to lawyers, police and judges to investigate and make decisions based on the background and character of those suspected of contravening legal standards."[85] According to newspaper reports, the Collins and Lutz families were relatively well-respected in the community, and Theresa was not known to have any sort of reputation prior to her death. These facts likely contributed to the women's exoneration. As mentioned, in the Munson abortion case, the Crown relied on the defendant's supposedly dissolute reputation in their quest for a guilty verdict. Analyses of a woman's character and habits unquestionably played an important role during a trial in which sex or reproduction were front and centre.

At the turn of the century, "infanticide," "murder," "manslaughter," "child desertion," "child abandonment," and "concealing childbirth" were used interchangeably to describe crimes women committed against unwanted infants. Between 1870 and 1914, eight women in Oxford County were arrested for such crimes. Motivations typically included financial hardship, the desire to limit family size, or protection of reputation. In small rural communities, it was difficult if not impossible for a woman to hide an unwanted or illegitimate pregnancy. In 1877, a woman from West Zorra Township was committed to the Oxford County jail on a charge of vagrancy; upon further inspection, it was revealed that the true purpose of her incarceration was to "provide an asylum for the woman during her expected confinement." To save the county the costs of caring for the woman in the jail, a decision was made to move her to the Lying-In Hospital in Ottawa, where she could give birth more discreetly.[86]

In more desperate circumstances, women in Oxford County disposed of their babies in public places. In 1879, Oxford County Coroner J.M. Ault noted two instances of infanticide where corpses were found in public areas in Tillsonburg—one in a wooded area south of the town and the other in the closet of a railway station. In both cases, the mothers were believed to be culpable in the infant's death.[87] Such shocking acts made good copy for newspapers, besides serving as morality lessons. As legal scholar Elizabeth Rapaport notes, historically, infanticide "has been less about the protection of children than the regulation of women."[88]

Parents did not habitually turn their unmarried daughters out when they became entangled with the justice system; neighbours and other community members, however, may not have been as understanding of the circumstances, especially when it came to illicit or premarital sex. According to Peter Ward, "gossip there no doubt would be, and likely a woman's marriage prospects would be blackened as well." Premarital sex was scandalous enough, as the Anderson/Marshall case demonstrates, and cases of infanticide were further sensationalized due to the sensitive nature of the alleged offence. As evidenced by local news stories, public opinion of women accused of infanticide could be very cruel. Such was the experience of two women who received considerable attention for their alleged crimes: Fanny Hague and Nancy Legg.

Hague's problems with the law began around 1879 when she appeared in front of the fall assizes to answer to an abortion charge. The *Woodstock Sentinel-Review*, referring to Hague as "both silly and loose," reported that the accused had admitted guilt and received a six-month prison sentence.[89] Four years later, Hague spent nearly two months in the county jail on suspicion of manslaughter. She appeared before the spring assizes in 1883 to defend herself against claims that she had killed her newborn son. Woodstock police constable Thomas McKee testified at the inquest that upon hearing that a deceased child was in the accused's domicile, he visited Hague, who informed him that she had delivered the infant and that this was her seventh delivery. Its body was found in a box in a corner of the room. Hague's brother, John, testified that before the child's birth, Hague had informed him that she was unwell. After the birth she told John that the child had been born alive as she saw it move. Another witness, Mrs. Sarah Locke, recalled that she heard Hague say "she was glad this child was dead." A post-mortem convinced Drs. Archibald McKay and A.B. Welford that "the child was either/probably or entirely born alive – although we have no evidence that the child had breathed and had proper care been taken at birth life might have been retained."[90] Their testimony assisted the jury in returning a verdict of not guilty, and Hague, presumably, was released from custody.

According to court transcripts and newspaper reports, another local woman accused of infanticide, Nancy Legg,[91] was viewed as a nuisance by the community and the judiciary. According to the 1881 census, thirty-eight-year-old Legg worked as a domestic and lived with the Bell family in Dereham Township. Legg was born in Ontario, of English descent, and Methodist.[92] She first appears in the county jail register in 1882, when she was committed on 9 January for the murder of her newborn child; allegedly, she had driven a pin through its brain. Though found guilty, she was acquitted on the grounds of insanity and remanded to custody.

In 1887, Legg was still in custody, but the *Woodstock Sentinel-Review* reported that she displayed an obedient disposition and was helpful around the premises. County officials were appalled, however, when they heard that Legg had given birth in the jail in November 1887. This incident was branded "a disgrace to the county," and jail staff were blamed for their "great lapse of discipline and care."[93] This indiscretion received even more negative attention than Legg's first conviction of murder/infanticide in 1882–83. It was now recommended that Legg be removed from the jail.[94] The *Sentinel-Review* reported that Legg's conduct had "received such publicity" that the facts needed to be provided to the public. In response, Inspector of Prisons W.T. O'Reilly explained that Legg was "simply a silly creature, but not insane." Her lengthy incarceration permitted her a measure of freedom, and such liberty, O'Reilly notes, led to her association with the infant's father. O'Reilly's sense was that "Legg is not insane at all, she is simply an imbecile who got into similar trouble five years ago and killed her child … She is no sense a proper subject for a Lunatic Asylum; she is a harmless, simple creature." At the same time, however, O'Reilly believed "she is a woman who is quite unsafe to be at large and that is all that can be said about her, and that because she will become the victim of any man who chooses to approach her. When we have accommodation in the Orillia Asylum I shall have her sent there, but, at the same time, she is just as well in gaol."[95]

Two years after the scandal, Legg and the child were still languishing in the county jail. An 1889 report by Oxford's Standing Committee on County Buildings and Property revealed that a letter had been received from Legg's adult son Peter, a resident of Fayette, Michigan, requesting $50 to remove his young sibling from the jail. The county agreed to the request, with full payment granted "upon the certification of the Gaol that he has removed them from the Gaol."[96] "Them" indicates that both Nancy and the child may have been "bought" by Peter Legg and released from the jail. This case is unique in that most women did not spend several years in the Oxford County jail; clearly, local officials could not decide on a proper course of rehabilitation for Nancy Legg, or they were simply indifferent. Female prisoners had no agency or choice when it came to how and where they "did time"; such decisions were left to male juries, judges, and political councils.

Murder

Though capital punishment was carried out at the Oxford County jail, in its history only one woman was executed, for the murder of her husband in 1935. Women rarely faced murder charges in late nineteenth- and early twentieth-century Oxford County. According to the jail register, only four women were incarcerated on charges of murder that were separate from acts of infanticide or abortion. In 1913, several Ontario newspapers, including Toronto's *Globe*, published a story about the alleged killing of an Oxford County man by his wife. On 25 March, Frederick E. Beemer, a "highly-respected farmer" from Blenheim Township, was found dead after a short illness, "the circumstances in connection therewith being so suspicious that an inquest was ordered." During the inquest Beemer's stomach contents were examined and a grain of strychnine was found, suggesting poisoning. His wife Grace was accused of administering the poison. She denied doing so, explaining that the strychnine found on the property was for killing crows.[97]

Naturally, this event caused considerable uproar in the community, for it was not the first time that Grace Beemer had been the subject of rumour and gossip. The couple's marriage had provoked "considerable comment" within the community, as Grace was Frederick's niece.[98] At the time of Frederick's death, the couple had eight small children. On suspicion of murdering her husband, Grace was held in the county jail from 6 April to 7 November 1913. At some point during her incarceration, Grace gave birth to another child and was temporarily moved to a hospital for two weeks for her "accouchement."[99] During the preliminary hearings, John Mason, a farm labourer acquainted with the Beemers, claimed that he had witnessed Grace administering what she alleged to be medicine to her husband. The deceased's brother, Sylvester Beemer, testified that Frederick was in dire financial straits but still well and healthy. Others who testified asserted that the relationship between the Beemers "could not be better."[100] Despite testimony that contradicted Mason's claims, at the 30 June hearing, Grace was committed to stand trial during the fall assizes, and remanded to custody in the county jail. Before the pronouncement, "Mrs. Beemer sobbed and moaned throughout the entire hearing, and when the time came for her to say farewell to those who had come to attend the court became quite hysterical. Jail Surgeon McKay was called, and she gradually became more composed."[101]

The fall assizes began in early November 1913. Holding her infant daughter in the prisoner's box, Grace presented a composed appearance, despite a True Bill on the charge of murder being returned. On 6 November, Grace was cross-examined by the Crown, her "one hand resting on the rail for almost two hours, her position never varying except when she frequently applied a handkerchief to her face with the other hand. Occasionally her eyes would fill with tears when the name of her husband was mentioned."[102] Besides contradicting John Mason's testimony, Grace informed the court that her husband had presented signs of illness well before his death and that she had given him three doses of medicinal salts. The next day, after deliberating for one hour and ten minutes, the jury acquitted Grace due to conflicting evidence. At this announcement, the crowded courtroom, consisting mostly of women who had been present for the duration of the trial, "broke into a tremendous outburst of cheering and clapping of hands." During her incarceration, Grace had earned the sympathy of many in the community who believed her innocent. Upon her release, "when Mrs. Beemer reached the corridor she was surrounded by a group of sympathizers and escorted to one of the court offices, where she found her aged parents and the police matron with her nine-months-old baby girl awaiting her. The parents with tear-stained eyes embraced their daughter."[103] Grace indicated to a reporter from the *Globe* that she desired to seclude herself from public life and looked forward to going back to the farm and raising her children. She remarked that "it was an awful stain to be thrust upon my character and reputation in the neighboring settlement, but I am going to try like a faithful and honest woman to live the whole thing down."[104] Despite their inability to convict, after the trial the prosecution continued to condemn Grace as a "foxy woman," as "poison is a woman's weapon."[105] This invocation of the stereotype of the conniving female criminal demonstrates a desire to ensure that, exonerated or not, Grace Beemer would be perceived as guilty and would suffer the consequences.

Insanity

Of all the offences for which women were incarcerated, "insanity" accounts for the highest arrest rate in Oxford County. Such "crimes" could result in long jail sentences, transfer to a lunatic asylum, or removal to the Oxford County House of Refuge after it was constructed in 1893. In jail records and newspaper reports of criminal trials, insanity is often discussed in conjunction with serious crimes such as abortion, murder, and infanticide. In the criminal justice system, insanity was a catch-all description for variations of mental illness or problematic behaviour. Jails were often home to both the insane and the criminal insane; the "offence" of being insane was, in effect, being unable to care for oneself or posing a danger to society, whereas the criminal insane had committed unlawful acts owing to their affliction. As scholar Kathleen Kendall points out, the notion of criminal insanity posed a challenge for lawmakers. To be a criminal was to have knowledge of evildoings, whereas insanity was characterized by lack of such knowledge. Thus, the two contradicted each other, and gender complicated this even further.[106]

In the medical literature of the time, the insane woman was often described as suffering from hysteria, a sex-selective disorder rooted in the reproductive system that typically affected females between puberty and menopause. The sex organs were thought to impact the mind, leading to emotional, irrational, and uncontrollable behaviour. Though its pervasiveness is impossible to gauge, Wendy Mitchinson argues it was "one of the more frequently reported nervous disorders."[107] Medical professionals prescribed a variety of therapies, ranging from placebos to dangerous gynecological surgeries, in the hope of curing what seemed to be an incurable "disease."

By the later nineteenth century, insanity diagnoses and the criminal justice system were complexly linked. Characteristic behaviours of the insane – poverty, erratic behaviour, unlawfulness – became a problem for the courts, asylums, and prisons to handle when families chose not to care for loved ones. If taken at face value, jail records and other legal documents suggest that insanity was a serious health and legal issue in Oxford County in the later nineteenth and early twentieth centuries. So prevalent was it, in fact, that the Oxford County Municipal Council had a "Lunatic Account" to which money was regularly allocated for the management of local "lunatics." On 19 December 1876, $3.25 was paid out for furnishing straightjackets for the jail.[108] The fund was also spent on services such as medical examinations and the costs of transporting inmates from the county jail to nearby asylums.[109]

Judicial officials wrestled with how to treat the insane and what sorts of freedoms they should be allowed. Too much freedom, such as that given to Nancy Legg, could lead to dangerous or scandalous behaviour. At several points between 1870 and 1914, efforts were made to relocate prisoners to more "suitable" institutions as the Oxford County jail was improperly equipped to care for the insane. In December 1912, jail surgeon D.J. McKay remarked: "one feature which is much in need of improvement is the care of the insane. It is a common thing, yes, the usual thing, for an insane prisoner to be retained for weeks after commitment. There is now an insane prisoner who has been there since February 1912. It seems to me that if asylum treatment is to do any good at all, an immediate removal is a prime necessity."[110]

Insanity accounts for some of the longest confinements in the county jail. Like Nancy Legg, Margaret Copley[111] was a long-serving inmate in the Oxford County jail who had been committed for insanity. Because the small jail staff could not properly look after her, in 1871 a woman named Margaret Johnson was paid $40 "for taking care of Margaret Copley, a helpless person in Gaol."[112] In an October 1873 article in the *Woodstock Sentinel-Review*, a report was published about conditions in the jail; it mentions Copley, "an imbecile woman," who had been "confined for a number of years." The author maintained that the jail was "a most unfit place for a woman in her condition." It was requested that she be "removed to some suitable place, as her presence in gaol is a source of great trouble to the gaol officials." She was also described as having "filthy habits" and as a danger to other inmates.[113]

Over time, the burden on the county jail was lifted somewhat as suspected cases of insanity were sent to the newly constructed House of Refuge. County officials had long hoped to establish a poorhouse but had been deterred by its substantial cost. Finally, in 1891, a farm was purchased for the purpose of building a House of Refuge; two years later, its doors were opened. There was now a place where "people whose only 'crime' was indigence and/or the afflictions of age" could go.[114] Though most residents were elderly or destitute, several single and widowed women were also committed by doctors, family members, neighbours, or law enforcement officials.[115]

It was no coincidence that the building of the House of Refuge coincided with a significant decrease in the numbers of women confined to the county jail. But how different were the two institutions? Arguably, committal to the House of Refuge was akin to jailtime, if not worse, as many women were detained for the remainder of their lives with little hope of being rehabilitated or released. The House of Refuge also became a spectacle: its visitors' register indicates that people were allowed in to view the "unfortunates" in their cells. In March 1894, Elfie Raike of Woodstock commented in the register that she was "pleased with the cleanliness and babies," while Mrs. George Imes was "pleased to see the old lady indigents so well cared for and especially the pets, the babies."[116]

Conclusion: Rethinking the "Good" Rural Woman

When women "acted out" and exhibited "bad behaviour" in Oxford County, the criminal justice system was one of many regulatory bodies that censured activities deemed suspect and in need of regulation. Families, neighbours, community watchdogs, and newspapers exacted their own forms of influence when attempting to keep local women "good," but increasingly the enforcement of communal standards of morality, respectability, and feminine appropriateness had to be supplemented by the powers bestowed in local politicians and the criminal justice system. Incarcerations, sensationalized trials, and the print media all played a role in drawing attention to the fact that women were circumventing ideals of feminine behaviour. Analyses of women's arrests and unlawful activities show how various modes of authority were intolerant of actions that allowed women to step outside the bounds of respectability, femininity, and patriarchal control.

Previous studies have made some inroads towards debunking the myth that rural areas and small towns were morally superior and, thus, less prone than cities to inspiring criminal behaviour, but as this analysis of Oxford County has revealed, women's criminal actions indicate that moral panic and fears of deviancy *were* present in rural areas, as evidenced by the degree to which females were scrutinized. For the period examined here, the types of crimes for which women were arrested and the amount of attention paid to court trials was evidence of greater interest in the social and sexual activities of females; that attention often exposed the private areas of their lives and made them subject to public scrutiny. Through the criminal justice system, intimate and personal matters that contradicted legal and moral codes entered the public discourse, uncovering not only women's personal business but also the intimate details of rural people's lives more generally. The experiences of women like Letitia Munson, Nancy Legg, and Margaret Copley, for instance, show that factors such as race, reputation, and sound-mindedness played integral roles when determining wrongdoing; they also problematize the notion that Ontario's countryside was populated by women who abided by patriarchal notions of what a "good" woman should be.

QUESTIONS FOR CONSIDERATION:

1. What is the "seedier side of rural and small-town social life," according to Beausaert?
2. Why is the relationship between women and the judicial system complicated?
3. Comment on the sources used for this chapter. Why are they of particular note?
4. Describe Oxford County in your own words. Why does "place" matter in this chapter?
5. What was it like for women "doing time" in the Oxford County Jail in these times?
6. How did the print media characterize women's criminal acts, according to Beausaert?
7. How were insanity diagnoses and the criminal justice system interrelated in this period?

NOTES

1 "Police Court," *Woodstock Sentinel-Review*, 10 October 1887, 1.
2 Karen Dubinsky, *Improper Advances: Rape and Heterosexual Conflict in Ontario, 1880–1929* (Chicago: University of Chicago Press, 1993), 67–8.
3 See Lynne Marks, "No Double Standard?: Leisure, Sex, and Sin in Upper Canadian Church Discipline Records, 1800–1860" in *Gendered Pasts: Historical Essays in Femininity and Masculinity in Canada*, ed. Kathryn McPherson, Cecilia Morgan, and Nancy M. Forestell (Toronto: University of Toronto Press, 1999), 48–64.
4 Susan Sessions Rugh, "Civilizing the Countryside: Class, Gender, and Crime in Nineteenth-Century Rural Illinois," *Agricultural History* 76, no. 1 (Winter 2002): 64.
5 Dubinsky, *Improper Advances*, 125.
6 Karen Dubinsky, "'Maidenly Girls' or 'Designing Women'?: The Crime of Seduction in Turn-of-the-Century Ontario," in *Gender Conflicts: New Essays in Women's History*, ed. Franca Iacovetta and Mariana Valverde (Toronto: University of Toronto Press, 1992), 29.
7 Steven Maynard, "'Horrible Temptations': Sex, Men, and Working-Class Male Youth in Urban Ontario, 1890–1935," *Canadian Historical Review* 78, no. 2 (June 1997): 197.
8 Constance Backhouse, "Nineteenth-Century Canadian Prostitution Law: Reflections of a Discriminatory Society," *Histoire sociale/Social History* 18, no. 36 (November 1985): 396.
9 County of Oxford Archives (hereafter COA), RG 2, series 1, minutes – box 4 (1864–1908), Copy of Mr. Langmuir's Report of Inspection of County Gaol, on 24 October 1879.
10 COA, RG 2, series 6, treasurer box 2, subseries A, Administration of Justice, 1887–1907.
11 A charwoman was a cleaning lady, usually taking care of a larger building. See LAC, Census of Canada, 1901, Schedule 1 – Population, Ontario, Norfolk North, Tilsonburg, http://www.collectionscanada.gc.ca/databases/census-1901/index-e.html.
12 Peter Baskerville and Eric W. Sager, *Unwilling Idlers: The Urban Unemployed and Their Families in Late Victorian Canada* (Toronto: University of Toronto Press, 1998), 115.
13 *Fourth Census of Canada 1901, Volume I, Population* (Ottawa: S.E. Dawson, Printer to the King's Most Excellent Majesty, 1902), 3, https://archive.org/details/fourthcensusofca01cana/page/2/mode/2up?q=oxford; *Fifth Census of Canada 1911, Area and Population by Provinces Districts and Subdistricts, Volume I* (Ottawa: C.H. Parmelee, Printer to the King's Most Excellent Majesty, 1912), 524, https://archive.org/details/n00bsessionalpape47cana/page/524/mode/2up?q=oxford
14 *Fifth Census of Canada 1911, Areas and Population by Provinces Districts and Subdistricts, Volume I* (Ottawa: C.H. Parmelee, Printer to the King's Most Excellent Majesty, 1912), 540, https://archive.org/details/cu31924094333204/page/n565/mode/2up?q=woodstock
15 Michael Wayne, "The Black Population of Canada West on the Eve of the American Civil War: A Reassessment Based on the Manuscript Census of 1861," in *A Nation of Immigrants: Women, Workers, and Communities in Canadian History*, ed. Franca Iacovetta (Toronto: University of Toronto Press, 1998), 71–6.
16 Canada, *Census of Canada, 1881 – Population* (Dominion Bureau of Statistics, 1881), 286.
17 See, for example, Carolyn Strange, *Toronto's Girl Problem: The Perils and Pleasures of the City, 1880–1930* (Toronto: University of Toronto Press, 1995); Joan Sangster, *Girl Trouble: Female Delinquency in English Canada* (Toronto: Between the Lines, 2002); Tamara Myers, *Caught: Montreal's Modern Girls and the Law, 1869–1945* (Toronto: University of Toronto Press, 2006); Ruth Alexander, *The Girl Problem: Female Sexual Delinquency in New York, 1900–1930* (Ithaca: Cornell University Press, 1995); and Mary Odem, *Delinquent Daughters: Protecting and Policing*

Adolescent Female Sexuality in the United States, 1885–1920 (Chapel Hill: University of North Carolina Press, 1995).

18 Strange, *Toronto's Girl Problem*, 23.

19 Dubinsky, *Improper Advances*; Marks, "No Double Standard?"; Lynne Marks, *Revivals and Roller Rinks: Religion, Leisure, and Identity in Late-Nineteenth-Century Small-Town Ontario* (Toronto: University of Toronto Press, 1996), 16.

20 Canniff Haight, *Country Life in Canada with a new introduction by Arthur R.M. Lower* (Belleville: Mika, 1971), 48.

21 Dubinsky, *Improper Advances*, 122.

22 Sangster, *Girl Trouble*, 15.

23 COA, RG 2, series 6 treasurer box 1, subseries A, Administration of Justice, 1850–1887; box 2, subseries A, Administration of Justice, 1887–1907; box 3, subseries A, Administration of Justice, 1908–1925.

24 See, for example, *Tillsonburg Observer*, 22 April 1892, 1, and 20 April 1894, 1, when Pow chastises cyclists for disobeying by-laws and exhibiting reckless behaviour.

25 Dubinsky, *Improper Advances*, 22.

26 Dubinsky, *Improper Advances*, 23.

27 According to Ron Brown, "police villages were a form of municipal structure created by the county within which they were found. With limited powers, police villages had no municipal council nor could they collect taxes. They consisted only of a Board of Police whose sole responsibility was to pass local bylaws, and maintain public order." In Brown, *Behind Bars: Inside Ontario's Heritage Gaols* (Toronto: Natural Heritage Books, 2006), 121.

28 Brown, *Behind Bars*, 73.

29 "Oxford Assizes," *Woodstock Sentinel-Review*, 10 November 1887, 1.

30 City of Woodstock, "Oxford County Jail," https://www.cityofwoodstock.ca/en/live-and-play/resources/museum/Collections/Oxford-County-Jail.pdf.

31 COA, *Oxford County Old Gaol* (pamphlet).

32 COA, RG 2, series 1, minutes – box 4 (1864–1908), Second Report of the Standing Committee on County Buildings and Property, 17 December 1880.

33 COA, RG 2, series 1, minutes – box 4 (1864–1908), Gaol Inspector's Report, Copy of Mr. Langmuir's Report of Inspection of County Gaol, 21 April 1881.

34 "Just What Was Said: The Way It Was," *Globe and Mail*, 1 February 1977, 35.

35 Stephanie Johns, "County of Oxford Jail: A History of Change," https://www.youtube.com/watch?v=rhtZzenSj_Y

36 COA, series 2 – By laws (1850–1867), No. 59 By Law No. 2, By Law for the purpose of protecting and enforcing the observance of Public Morals within the County of Oxford, 1859.

37 COA, series 2, box 2, file 7#11, By-Law No. 189 – By-Law to enforce the observance of Public Morals in the County of Oxford, 1874.

38 "Dancing vs. Kissing," *Woodstock Sentinel-Review*, 24 March 1887, n.p.

39 "Promiscuous Correspondence," *Woodstock Sentinel-Review*, 27 October 1883, 3.

40 Lesley Erickson, *Westward Bound: Sex, Violence, the Law, and the Making of a Settler Society* (Vancouver: UBC Press, 2011), 93.

41 COA, RG 2, series 6, treasurer box 1, subseries A, Administration of Justice, 1850–1887; box 2 – RG 2, series 6, treasurer, subseries A, Administration of Justice, 1887–1907; box 3 – RG 2 – series 6, treasurer, subseries A – Administration of Justice, 1908–1925.

42 See Frances Swyripa, "Negotiating Sex and Gender in the Ukrainian Bloc Settlement: East-Central Alberta between the Wars," in *Home, Work, and Play: Situating Canadian Social*

History, 1840–1980, ed. James Opp and John C. Walsh (Toronto: Oxford University Press, 2006), 53.

43 Marks, *Revivals and Roller Rinks*, 90.

44 COA, RG 2, series 6, treasurer box 1, subseries A, Administration of Justice, 1850–1887; Garner was imprisoned 25–30 August 1879 for "frequenting a house of ill fame," 8–9 March 1880 for "keeping a house of ill fame," 13–20 August 1880 for "fighting on the street," and 3 November 1880–1 January 1881 for "being an inmate in a house of ill fame."

45 *Census of Canada*, 1871 – Population (Canada: Dominion Bureau of Statistics, 1871).

46 *Census of Canada*, 1881 – Population (Canada: Dominion Bureau of Statistics, 1881).

47 *Census of Canada*, 1891 – Population (Canada: Dominion Bureau of Statistics, 1891).

48 *Census of Canada*, 1901 – Population (Canada: Dominion Bureau of Statistics, 1901).

49 *Census of Canada*, 1911 – Areas and Populations by Provinces, Districts and Subdistricts (Canada: Dominion Bureau of Statistics, 1911).

50 Dubinsky, *Improper Advances*, 117.

51 Mary Anne Poutanen, "The Homeless, the Whore, the Drunkard, and the Disorderly: Contours of Female Vagrancy in the Montreal Courts, 1810–1842," in *Gendered Pasts*, ed. McPherson, Morgan, and Forestell, 46.

52 *The Criminal Code of Canada and the Canada Evidence Act, 1893 with an Extra Appendix ...* (Montreal: Whiteford & Theoret, Law Publishers, 1894), 126.

53 Amanda Glasbeek, *Feminized Justice: The Toronto Women's Court, 1913–1934* (Vancouver: UBC Press, 2009), 97.

54 This included arrests for vagrancy, walking the streets at night, prostitution and night walking, and prostitution and street walking.

55 *Census of Canada*, 1871 – Population (Canada: Dominion Bureau of Statistics, 1871).

56 Joan Sangster, "'Pardon Tales' from Magistrate's Court: Women, Crime, and the Court in Peterborough County, 1920–50," *Canadian Historical Review* 74, no. 2 (1993): 165.

57 COA, RG 2, series 6, treasurer box 1, subseries A, Administration of Justice, 1850–1887.

58 Rugh, "Civilizing the Countryside," 73.

59 "To Cope with Rural Crime," *Farmer's Advocate*, 43, no. 827 (30 July 1908): 1213.

60 COA, RG 2, series 1, minutes – box 5 (1904–1935), Report of Dr. Andrew McKay, Gaol Surgeon, 1 December 1913.

61 COA, RG 2, series 6, treasurer box 1, subseries A, Administration of Justice, 1850–1887.

62 "Found Dead," *Woodstock Sentinel-Review*, 22 September 1882, 1.

63 "Found Dead."

64 "Oxford Assizes," *Woodstock Sentinel-Review*, 24 November 1882, 4.

65 For a full account of the Munson abortion case, see Rebecca Beausaert, "Not Guilty, but Guilty: Race, Rumour, and Respectability in the 1882 Abortion Trial of Letitia Munson," *Ontario History* 106, no. 2 (Fall 2014): 165–90.

66 "A Young Couple of Color," *Woodstock Sentinel-Review*, 10 January 1895, 8.

67 Archives of Ontario (hereafter AO), MS 8496, RG 22-392, Supreme Court Criminal Indictment Files Oxford County, 1890–1907, Thomas Marshall Case.

68 "The Assize Court. The Seduction Case," *Woodstock Sentinel-Review*, 22 March 1895, 4.

69 For more on Black men and women in the criminal justice system, see Barrington Walker, *Race on Trial: Black Defendants in Ontario's Criminal Courts, 1858–1958* (Toronto: Osgoode Society for Canadian Legal History by University of Toronto Press, 2010), 145–57, which details a seduction case in the small Ontario community of Raleigh that involved a white woman and a Black man.

70 Craig Heron, *Booze: A Distilled History* (Toronto: Between the Lines, 2003), 126.
71 Glasbeek, *Feminized Justice*, 123.
72 COA, series 2 , box 2, file 7#11, By-Law No. 189 – By-Law to enforce the observance of Public Morals in the County of Oxford, 1874.
73 Glasbeek, *Feminized Justice*, 119.
74 Glasbeek, *Feminized Justice*, 120.
75 COA, RG 2, series 1, minutes – box 5 (1904–1935), Annual Report of the Gaol Surgeon, 1 December 1914.
76 COA, RG 2, series 1, minutes – box 5 (1904–1935), Annual Report of the Gaol Surgeon, 2 December 1912.
77 *Woodstock Sentinel-Review*, n.d., n.p.
78 COA, RG 2, series 6, treasurer box 1, subseries A, Administration of Justice, 1850–1887.
79 Cheryl Krasnick Warsh, "'Oh, lord, pour a cordial in her wounded heart': The Drinking Woman in Victorian and Edwardian Canada," in *Drink in Canada: Historical Essays*, ed. Cheryl Krasnick Warsh (Montreal and Kingston: McGill–Queen's University Press, 1993), 76.
80 Lesley Erickson, "'A Very Garden of the Lord'? Hired Hands, Farm Women, and Sex Crime Prosecutions on the Prairies, 1914–1929," *Journal of the Canadian Historical Association* 12, no. 1 (2001): 134.
81 *Tillsonburg Observer*, 9 April 1880, 1.
82 See Angus McLaren, "Illegal Operations: Women, Doctors, and Abortion, 1886–1939," *Journal of Social History* (Summer 1993): 798.
83 Constance Backhouse, "Desperate Women and Compassionate Courts: Infanticide in Nineteenth Century Canada," *University of Toronto Law Journal* 34 (1984): 448; Peter Ward, "Unwed Motherhood in Nineteenth-Century English Canada," *Canadian Historical Association Historical Papers* (1981): 44.
84 "Oxford Spring Assizes," *Woodstock Weekly Review*, 12 April 1878, 1.
85 Dubinsky, *Improper Advances*, 125.
86 COA, RG 2, series 1, minutes – box 4 (1864–1908), Second Report of the Standing Committee on County Buildings and Property, 1877.
87 COA, RG 2, series 6, treasurer box 1, subseries A, Administration of Justice 1850–1887.
88 Elizabeth Rapaport, "Mad Women and Desperate Girls: Infanticide and Child Murder in Law and Myth," *Fordham Urban Law Journal* 33, no. 2 (January 2006): 527–69.
89 "Oxford Assizes," *Woodstock Sentinel-Review*, 24 October 1879, n.p.
90 AO, MS 8495, RG 22-392, Supreme Court Criminal Indictment Files Oxford County 1881–1889, 1883 Oxford Spring Assezes [*sic*], Arranged Pleaded Not Guilty, 28 March 1883, *The Queen vs. Fanny Hague*.
91 In various documents the surname also appears as "Leg" or "Clegg."
92 *Census of Canada*, 1881 – Population (Canada: Dominion Bureau of Statistics, 1881).
93 "Oxford Assizes," *Woodstock Sentinel-Review*, 10 November 1887, 1.
94 "Oxford Assizes," *Woodstock Sentinel-Review*, 10 November 1887, 1
95 "The Gaol Case," *Woodstock Sentinel-Review*, 15 November 1887, 1.
96 COA, RG 2, series 1, minutes – box 4 (1864–1908), Second Report of the Standing Committee on County Buildings and Property for the Year 1890.
97 "Charged with Murder," *The News*, 13 June 1913, 2.
98 "Charged with Murder."
99 "Accouchement" is defined as the time or act of giving birth; COA, RG 2, series 1, minutes – box 5 (1904–1935), Report of Dr. Andrew McKay, Gaol Surgeon, 1 December 1913.

100 “Startling Testimony By Young Farm Hand: He Tells of Bottle Labelled ‘Poison’ at Beemer’s,” *The Globe*, 19 June 1913, 1.
101 “Mrs. Beemer to Stand Trial at Assizes: Magistrate Ball Commits Her on Murder Charge,” *The Globe*, 1 July 1913, 16.
102 “Mrs. Grace Beemer Tells Her Own Story: The Crown Fails to Shatter Her Evidence With Cross-examination,” *The Globe*, 7 November 1913, 1.
103 “Mrs. Beemer Acquitted by Jury at Woodstock: Crowd in Courtroom Could Not Restrain Cheer,” *The Globe*, 8 November 1913, 1.
104 “Mrs. Beemer Acquitted.”
105 “Mrs. Beemer Acquitted.”
106 Kathleen Kendall, "Criminal lunatic women in 19th century Canada," Correctional Service Canada, https://www.csc-scc.gc.ca/research/forum/e113/113l_e.pdf.
107 Wendy Mitchinson, "Hysteria and Insanity in Women: A Nineteenth-Century Canadian Perspective," *Journal of Canadian Studies* 21, no. 3 (Fall 1986): 89.
108 COA, RG 2, series 1, minutes – box 4 (1864–1908), Lunatic Account, 1877.
109 COA, RG 2, series 1, minutes – box 4 (1864–1908), Gaol Account, 1876.
110 COA, RG 2, series 1, minutes – box 5 (1904–1935), Annual Report of the Gaol Surgeon, 2 December 1912.
111 Surname also appears as Copeley in some documents.
112 COA, RG 2, series 1, minutes – box 4 (1864–1908), Gaol Account, 1871.
113 *Woodstock Sentinel-Review*, 17 October 1873, 5.
114 COA, House of Refuge (pamphlet).
115 COA, RG 2, 12B, House of Refuge Residential Residents’ Register 1893–1959 B.V. 109, County of Oxford Industrial Farm and House of Refuge Register of Names and Particulars.
116 COA, RG 2, 12B, House of Refuge Residential Residents’ Register 1893–1959 B.V. 109, County of Oxford Industrial Farm and House of Refuge Register of Names and Particulars.

CHAPTER FOUR

The Case of the "One Good Chinaman": *Rex v. Charles Lee Hing*, Stratford, Ontario, 1909

MONA-MARGARET PON

On 2 October 1909 the *Stratford Daily Herald* printed this eye-catching headline: "15-YEAR OLD STRATFORD GIRL ESCAPES FROM CHINESE JOINT." The story that followed was as gripping as its title promised:

> It appears that Charlie Lee Hing kept a laundry in Stratford [in 1907] where he employed a 13 year old orphan girl at large wages to help in the laundry. The girl ... alleges that a few days after she entered his employ the Chinaman assaulted her. Lately he has kept the "Gold Dollar" restaurant in Woodstock and by a letter to this child offering big wages and saying there were other girls in his employ she was induced to work for him again last Monday. On Wednesday last she claims that he again brutally assaulted her. The child returned to Stratford yesterday in a stupor. Two local doctors examined her and found she had been drugged.[1]

Although some readers in 1909 might have been shocked and appalled, most would not have found this story incredible or fantastic. Indeed, this scenario might have serviced many social reform projects popular at the time – confirming yellow perilist fears, fuelling anti-Chinese immigration campaigns, and vindicating concerns about the dangers confronted by working single women, especially those employed by Chinese men. At first glance this "little girl" and her horrific encounter with Hing seemed a perfect fit with the pattern of fiendish Chinese behaviour so often complained of in British Columbia and, more recently, in Toronto.

This story, as reported, ought to have played out according to a predictable script. A predatory Chinaman had lured, drugged, and raped an innocent white girl. Justice would be served. But what if the victim was not a "maidenly girl"[2] and the accused was not a "fiendish Chinaman"? The result, in this case, was an extraordinary criminal trial in which the main characters defied easy categorization and no one did what might have been expected. For the historian, the outcome offers a complex case study highlighting the unresolved tensions among race, class, and gender, complicated further by sex and sexuality. What becomes apparent in *Rex v. Charles Lee Hing* is that a discussion on race, sex, and interracial sex cannot be carried on without class analysis. As the array of social hierarchies come into play, everything is misaligned and turned around: the Chinaman goes free.

The criminal indictment case file for *Rex v. Charles Lee Hing* can be found among the court records housed at the Archives of Ontario. Researchers who have used these records will be familiar with the unpredictable nature of each individual file's contents. In this case, historians will be simultaneously elated and disappointed by their findings. An exhilarating discovery will be the twenty-one letters written between 1907 and 1909 by the complainant to the prisoner that were entered as evidence in Hing's defence. Unfortunately, the case file does not contain the preliminary testimonies sworn before the Stratford police magistrate or the trial transcripts. Nonetheless, the case file, and other court records such as the judge's benchbook and the court minute books, together with newspaper reports, contain important pieces to reconstruct this rape trial. The case provides a unique opportunity to explore the dynamics of early twentieth-century practices and attitudes surrounding racial hierarchies, class biases, and patriarchal privileges.

On 1 October 1909 a working-class white woman named Daisy Reid laid information against a Chinese man, Charles Lee Hing. Reid swore out that Hing first raped her in 1907 while she was ironing in his Stratford laundry. She alleged that he again assaulted her a few days later in Woodstock while she was working in his restaurant. Hing was arrested the next day in Woodstock and escorted to Stratford. On the 4 October, evidence was taken in camera before a police magistrate, Reid's letters to Hing were entered as defence evidence, and Hing was committed to stand trial at the upcoming assize courts. Hing's first application for bail was denied. The judge reportedly said that "in view of the difference between the Chinese and Canadian standards of morals, Chinamen should not be allowed to employ girls of the tender age of the complainant."[3] On 26 October, Hing was granted bail of $300 in cash and $3,000 in cash bonds. According to the *Toronto Globe*, "The Judge remarked that the fact of the girl being in the Chinaman's employ made the offence more serious," hence the steep bail.[4] At the trial, Hing was indicted on the charge of raping Daisy Reid in the year 1907. Based on the testimonies and evidence, the presiding judge instructed the jury that "the charge could not be substantiated under any statute and it would be absolutely unsafe to ... make a conviction."[5] Without leaving their seats, the jury acquiesced. At 9 p.m. on 17 November 1909, following a five-hour trial, the "Chinaman [was] a Free Man."[6]

This is the basic chronology derived from news accounts. An examination of how this case was reported in newspapers and a closer look at Reid's letters will add greater complexity and density to this narrative. At the time, the Crown attorney, stymied by the "peculiar" nature of the case, foresaw "a good deal of difficulty"[7] to come in the trial; a newspaper declared it "most curious";[8] and the trial judge described it as the most puzzling he had ever come across.[9] This case, which on the surface ought to have ignited great moral indignation on behalf of the victim, instead aroused widespread bewilderment. The source of puzzlement stemmed from an ill fit between the "predatory Chinaman" archetype and the evidence at hand – between what ought to have happened and the finer details. From beginning to end, Hing's behaviour and character would not be reconciled with the supposed perils wrought by his kind.

In news reports, Hing was described as a thirty-two-year-old Presbyterian widower.[10] As of 1909 he had been in Canada for almost sixteen years; according to the *Woodstock Sentinel-Review*, he was "looked upon by many of the Chinamen in the district as a friend [and an] advisor."[11] According to the *Toronto Daily Star*, Hing "was regarded as a very respectable Chinaman. His education appeared to be above the average of his class."[12] Educated or not, Charles Lee Hing would have made a striking physical presence in both Stratford and Woodstock. At the time of the trial, both cities were racially and ethnically homogenous, composed mostly of immigrants from the British Isles.[13]

In the early twentieth century the large majority of Chinese in Canada were still on the west coast.[14] In 1911 there were only 2,766 Chinese in all of Ontario, and they were scattered throughout the province.[15] According to the 1911 census data, Toronto's Chinese community was the largest in Ontario (1,036), with the next-largest enclaves in Ottawa (162) and Hamilton (160).[16] The 1901 census enumerated only five Chinese in Stratford and eight in Woodstock.[17] By 1911 these numbers had increased only slightly, to thirteen and sixteen, respectively.[18]

Despite the small numbers of Chinese in Stratford and Woodstock, neither city would have been immune to the various forms of anti-Chinese racism that were so virulent in British Columbia and often echoed in Toronto.[19] News reports taken "off the wire," intense lobbying in Ottawa to restrict Chinese immigration, and the vocal efforts of social and moral reform groups to curtail Chinese civil rights in Canada all served to diffuse the "yellow peril" myth. Relying heavily on rhetoric and *a priori* reasoning, anti-Chinese arguments held that *all* Chinamen were inherently prone towards immoral and criminal behaviour. The individual Chinese was subsumed within a larger collectivity, which, in turn, was invested with values and habits deemed inferior and repulsive.

By the time of Hing's trial, the alleged consequences of Chinese immigration into Canada had coalesced into a fatalistic paradigm, a predicted pattern of social, moral, and economic decline. This model interwove such themes as the fall of Canadian democratic institutions, the ruin of white labour, the Chinese inability to assimilate, and the debauching and degrading of decent white women. It was on this latter theme that the Stratford press initially based its story-telling, case-reporting strategy.[20] However, this storyline was thwarted by a nonconformist cast of characters.

From a legal standpoint, the situation seemed equally unclear. In the 1906 Criminal Code of Canada, under the heading "crimes against the person or reputation," three indictable unlawful carnal knowledge offences were listed.[21] The first was the charge of rape – that is, having carnal knowledge of a woman not being the accused's wife and without her consent. The second was attempted rape, and the third was committing rape on a woman, who was not a spouse, under the age of fourteen.[22] The point of contention between the prosecution and the defence was Reid's age in 1907, the year of the alleged assault.

According to Reid, she had turned fifteen on 18 September 1909.[23] If this claim were true or, more important, if it could be proven by the Crown attorney, the charge against Hing would have been statutory rape, since the age of sexual consent was fourteen. This charge not only carried a different punishment from rape but also omitted the need to address the issue of female consent.[24] Thus, if Reid was underage in 1907, and if Hing had sexual relations with her, he was liable for criminal indictment whether or not she gave her consent. Determining Reid's age, however, proved a difficult task for the Crown. She was adopted, and at the time of the trial, her foster mother was dead. Reid herself could not produce a birth certificate and could give only her word that she was underage. But this assertion was deemed insufficient by the prosecution. L.H. Bradford, King's counsel in this case, "thought it advisable to procure the evidence of some one other than Daisy Reid as to her age."[25] Inquiries into this matter turned up that Reid was seventeen years old in 1909 and thus of legal consenting age in 1907.[26]

Concern over verifying Reid's age and the Crown's reluctance to base its case on her word arose after preliminary testimonies had been sworn and the letters to Hing had been produced as defence evidence. Reid had initially tried to deny authorship of these letters,[27] but this lie proved to be a futile attempt at self-protection. Reid was wise beyond her years: she understood that the letters could, and would, be used against her in public and in a court of law. Scholars of Canadian legal, social, and women's history have shown that a woman's character is placed on trial even, or especially, when she is the complainant in a sexual assault case.[28] This convention has held true in different historical time periods and geographic settings. The rape trial held in Stratford was not an exception. Daisy Reid, her moral character, and her reputation did not stand up well under social and legal scrutiny. On many counts, social conventions were in a state of disarray.

The problem was that Hing would not conform to the behavioural expectations of the "predatory Chinaman," while Reid seemed repeatedly and unabashedly to breech the moral codes accorded to her race and sex. Race, class, gender, and sexual lines were crossed and criss-crossed. But these boundaries were fault lines, and, as this case pointed out, the spaces on either side were not as self-contained, stable, and well defined as had been assumed. News writers and editors employed their own strategies when dealing with these zigzagging lines and demarcated their own moral boundaries.

Soon after Hing's arrest an interesting competitive dynamic emerged between the Stratford and Woodstock newspapers. Stratford, home of the victim, quickly positioned Reid in the role of the underage, exploited, orphan child lured, drugged, and raped by a Chinese man.[29] Woodstock, current home of the accused, responded with articles recounting his side of the story.[30] The *Woodstock Sentinel-Review* did not deny that an assault may have occurred in 1907 in Stratford, but it was quick to point out that no evidence existed of "any misconduct upon the part of the Chinaman while she was working in Woodstock last week."[31] While Stratford may have housed a "terrible Chinese joint," Woodstock, at least, was free of such vice and crime. The two newspapers engaged in repartee. The *Sentinel-Review* claimed that the *Stratford Herald* was "considerably excited by the case" to the point that its journalistic judgment was clouded and its "version" of the story near ridiculous.[32] "*Et tu*," responded the *Herald*, claiming that the paper "there" could barely "disguise its sympathy with the accused."[33] Beneath this "professional" jostling is an example of what historian Karen Dubinsky has termed "moral boosterism," wherein sex-related crimes were used as a gauge to measure an area's general moral condition and the efficacy of the local police and citizenry as keepers of law and moral order.[34] The issue of debate was not *whether* an assault had occurred but *where* – in which city, which county –this transgression had taken place. From the onset, Reid's allegations and the relationship between this white woman and her Chinese employer were invested with broader social and moral implications. Aspects of anti-Chinese rhetoric were propounded by the *Herald* and conditionally endorsed by the *Sentinel-Review*. In the early days of October, however, the structural integrity of the yellow peril myth would begin to buckle under the internal contradictions of this particular case. Three days after Hing's arrest, Reid's letters had become public knowledge and property.

On 5 October the *Sentinel-Review* printed a long front-page story describing the "conflicting lot of evidence ... heard in the Stratford police court yesterday." "The evidence," continued the report, "showed that Hing had been most generous in his treatment of the girl." It recounted how Reid repeatedly wrote to the prisoner claiming she was "hard up" and asking for dresses, shoes, money, and employment at Hing's restaurant in Woodstock.[35] On 13 October the *Sentinel-Review* quoted directly from the letters:

> In one letter she thanked "Charlie" for a birthday present. Hing said he had sent her $1. In the same she proposed to come to him at Woodstock and said 'Don't tell anyone, but me and you will have a good time.'
>
> 'When I come to Woodstock I can get a coat, hat, and shoes and we will have a swell time, Charlie if you don't tell," is a quotation from another alleged letter.[36]

The Stratford paper printed, verbatim, the 5 October story run by the Sentinel-Review. However, the Herald tucked the report onto page 4 and cast editorial doubt on its accuracy with this preface: "His Side of It Spread Large by One of Woodstock's Papers."[37] Although the Stratford daily was more reticent in broadcasting the contents of Reid's letters, their existence could not be ignored. One week later, the Stratford paper reported: "The girl in her affidavits both admits and denies having written some letters put in as evidence."[38]

Reid's letters can be read from different angles and perspectives. In 1909 they were used by Hing's lawyer to exculpate his client and to blemish Reid's credibility as a Crown witness. For historians these letters are remarkable sources for many different reasons. They provide a partial glimpse into the life of one young, working-class woman in early twentieth-century small-town Ontario. Finding documentary evidence created by women, and especially those living on the economic fringes of society, is often a daunting task for historians. In this light, Reid, quite unintentionally, bequeathed to us a rare historical treasure. She often chatted about her days, recounting her leisure and wage-earning activities. She included tidbits on special events in Stratford and told anecdotes about her and Hing's common acquaintances. There was the time, for example, when Lee John was run over by a horse and rig, and another when the Avondale cemetery was decorated and the whole town turned out for a marching band parade.[39] We know that Reid attended Sunday school, enjoyed moving pictures, liked snowfalls and "good sleighing," and became tired when the weather turned "awful hot."[40] We know also that she continued working for Chinese men after Hing had moved away from Stratford in 1907. As an unskilled female worker, there were limited wage-earning options available to her. She worked long days – "from 7 or 7.30 till night" – and she worked sporadically.[41]

In the first letter, dated 4 June 1907, she told Hing that "Lee John and Bang have been kind to me so far."[42] Six months later, however, she wrote the following: "I came very near quitting work for Lee John but I could not get a good job last week. But I think the beginning of the New Year I may get a really good steady job and not far away from home and next Spring I am going to try get mother to come down ... and I will work for you[.] How would you like that?"[43] The new year came to pass, and Reid was still in Stratford. Only two of the letters on file were written in 1908, and it is unclear where, and by whom, Reid was employed. Then in February 1909 she wrote: "I am not working for Hong any more but I think I will try and go and learn the millinery business in a few days."[44] It does not appear that she acquired this new skill. Throughout 1909, Reid's life was undergoing some difficult changes, and her increasing anxiety was reflected in her correspondence to Hing.

Written over three years, Reid's letters help us trace her relationship with a Chinese man. What becomes increasingly clear as one reads through these twenty-one pieces of correspondence is that Hing was considered to be a friend of the Reid family. He was constantly urged to visit their home in Stratford and was made to feel welcome over holidays such as Christmas and New Year's. Many of the notes opened with this salutation: "We received your ever welcome letter and was glad to hear from you," implying that his correspondence was shared with her foster mother and brother, Charles Reid. Once, in 1907, when the post office mislaid one of Hing's letters, Daisy Reid wrote: "I am very sorry I did not get it before. Mother thought it was strange you did not [*sic*] write before this."[45] Thus, at least in the earlier years, their letter-writing relationship was not carried on in any covert or devious fashion. The clandestine tone of her writing began to emerge in the letters written from June 1909 through to the end of September, just before Hing's arrest.

Daisy Reid's foster mother, who had been ill for some time, died on 9 June 1909.[46] Daisy and her foster brother were then moved to Greenville, Michigan, to live with other siblings. Throughout this period, as Reid's life became less predictable and increasingly out of her control, she turned to Hing for assistance. Letters written to him in these months grew increasingly demanding, conspiratorial, and even desperate. The press focused on these letters and, indeed, they posed the most damage to the Crown's case and to Reid's moral character. Part of Reid's difficulty was that she had to stop working for wages in order to care for her mother and the house. Without her own income, she started asking Hing to send her things. Such requests were not uncommon, but while she was working she had usually asked for trivial items such as fancy chocolate boxes or picture postcards to add to her collection.[47] When her mother became unable to eat, Reid asked Hing to send a roast chicken. She explained to him: "The doctor told us to get a nice chicken & I tried but couldnot [*sic*] get one ... it is bad to bother you Charlie but I couldnot get one anywhere."[48] Given the long-term relationship between Hing and the Reid family, he may have seemed a natural supporter to whom Daisy Reid could turn.

On 5 June 1909, Reid wrote to Hing from Stratford: "Mother has been very sick and she can not live but a few hours more. My sister and two brothers are home. I will try and come down and see you because [we] will go to Greenville about next Saturday. Charlie would you be kind enough to send me a little money as I want a new dress. I have not been able to work much. When you answer this letter you must register it and do not sign your name."[49]

One day before her foster mother's death, Reid responded to a letter from him: "Charlie I would love to come and work for you but I half [*sic*] to go to Greenville with my brother and sister but when I get a new dress I will come and see you a day before we go away. Well will you try and give me a little money at once and I will try my best to work for you. Answer at once and don't sign your name."[50] Then from Greenville, Reid wrote: "Mother died last Wednesday ... at 7 o'clock and we all came with the body to Greenville Michigan. They are going to bury her this afternoon at 3 o'clock. We received the chicken very safely. I came here to live with my sister and I think I will try and go back to Stratford as soon as I can."[51] On 10 September 1909, Reid began to plan her escape. She wrote to Hing:

> I will have to go to school in January and all the time after then and this is my only chance to come & work for you and see you for a while. I am feeling better now ... My sister does not want me to go but I told her I knew a girl down in Woodstock ... But if I come I will half [*sic*] to be very careful of myself as I will have an operation in my stomach at Stratford Hospital in December ... Don't tell anyone I am coming because then there will be terrible trouble if my brother finds out & do not sign your name to the letter. (Be sure) ... Answer so I get it Wednes. morning as I am afraid she might get it.[52]

On 16 September she wrote again: "Received your letter. Thanks for birthday present. I will leave here a week from next Tuesday for Woodstock to work ["to work" is crossed out] don't tell anyone but me & you will have a good time. Am feeling better now ... Do not write any more now."[53]

The last letter in Hing's case file is undated but appears to accompany an envelope post-dated 22 September 1909. In it Reid wrote:

> Got in with my sister today noon. If you send me the $6.00 for fare for my sister she goes home on Monday and send me a ticket and I will come & work for a while answer at once for sure. Answer at once
>
> Address Daisy R
> Stratford Ont.[54]

She told friends she was going to Port Dover but instead took the train to Woodstock. She was with Hing for two days before, suddenly, she returned to Stratford. There she was examined by doctors, told she had been drugged, and became a ward of the Children's Aid Society. Under the guidance of a Reverend W.A. Gunton, she swore to the rape. Until this time she had never told anyone of Hing's "mistreatment." Thus, concluded the *Sentinel-Review*, the alleged assault was a "case of his word against hers."[55] Unfortunately for Reid, the defence and the press had three years' worth of her written words. In court, each of her twenty-one letters was read aloud and Reid was subjected to a two-hour cross-examination.[56] Shortly thereafter, Hing was acquitted.[57] But had he, at some time, coerced Daisy Reid into sexual relations?

In this case of he said/she said, Daisy Reid inadvertently said a lot, and she often said the wrong things. Under oath, she tried to deny writing the letters to Hing, and in the process she perjured herself. These letters were damning pieces of evidence. They were read as being overly familiar, intimately confidential, and even "couched in affection." Once these letters became public property, the Stratford press retreated from her defence. Had the letters not existed or had they not been produced as evidence, the original storyline crafted by the *Herald* – the young girl rescued from Chinese joint scenario – might have held water. But in her writings Reid revealed what was considered to be a terrible moral flaw: she yearned for pretty things, things she could not afford to buy for herself. Then she asked a Chinese man to provide her with these fineries. It was all too easy, really, to see Daisy Reid not as the victim of a horrific sexual crime, but as a "good times girl." She had either consented to perform sexual acts with a Chinese man in exchange for presents and promises, or she had willingly placed herself at peril.

Had Reid told someone about the 1907 rape, the Crown's case would not have rested solely on her word. The grand jury, remarking on the case and the final verdict, highlighted the uncorroborated nature of the prosecutorial evidence.[58] In its final report on the case the *Herald* hypothesized that if Reid had made complaints to a friend or to her foster mother, the outcome might have been different.[59] Thus, according to this paper, even the testimony of a woman from her grave might have undermined the credibility of Charles Lee Hing. But Reid had never told on Hing, and there was no one to speak on her behalf, to lend credence to her claims. Hing, on the other side, was able to gather impressive resources to his defence, drawing from both the Chinese and the English-speaking communities in southern Ontario. The Stratford and Woodstock papers referred to Hing's wide assortment of supporters, who were ready to fund a vigorous defence.[60] And the *Herald* cautioned Reid supporters to be on the alert. Hing's $3,000 bond had been paid by a Jim Lee, who lived in Toronto.[61] Hing's brother and nephew, harking from Brantford and Hamilton respectively, were in constant attendance to lend support.[62] On the day of Hing's trial the courtroom was packed with curious spectators and crowded with Hing's advocates. According to the *Sentinel-Review*, many prominent professional and business men were on hand to testify for the prisoner, but most were never even summoned to the stand.[63] Hing's lawyer called only three witnesses. Hing testified on his own behalf, and the other two, Woodstock's police chief and a Presbyterian church minister, were character witnesses.[64] Law and moral order fell on the side of the defendant – the Chinese man.

If Hing were white, he would have been on level standing with any of Stratford's and Woodstock's white middle class. He was, after all, a self-made Christian man. But he was Chinese. He had worked past the economic constraints that so oppressed most Chinese immigrants. He had crossed into the economic class of men who had power and authority, as the employer, over a white woman. Charles Lee Hing had accomplished something that Chinese immigrants were mythically incapable of – he had assimilated. Hing became the beneficiary of what Barrington Walker has termed the "residual benefits of white patriarchy."[65] By virtue of his sex, but compromised by his race, Hing was given partial access to white male prerogatives. The patriarchal circle had closed, leaving Daisy Reid, a white woman, on the outside.

Against the odds, Charles Lee Hing had become a respectable Chinese in Canada. This one man's seemingly exemplary life history flew in the face of a predicted pattern of Chinese behaviour. How could he be explained within the yellow peril paradigm? Hing was a frontal assault on a belief system based on the assumption that Chinese immigrants were a single predictable entity. How could it now be maintained that Hing and other Chinamen like him were few and far between and that stringent immigration policies were necessary? To remain effective, anti-Chinese rhetoric would need to somehow reconcile Hing and the "predatory Chinaman" stereotype. Towards this end, the One Good Chinaman theory served as a conceptual loophole, a means to evade the structural rigidity of the yellow peril paradigm. This loophole made it possible, within a race-conscious and racially organized culture, to deal with those like Hing: the anomalies, the blips inside the pattern. And the cunning of the theory was that it left the paradigm intact. In this, Daisy Reid played a strategic role. She was the escape out of the loophole and back into the paradigm. She embodied the dangers and the consequences of interracial liaisons. Reid was a fallen woman, and a Chinese man, albeit an exceptional one, had been the cause of her ruination. Physically, with her body and her outrageous sex, Reid formed a bridge between the theory and the paradigm, connecting Hing to the rest of the yellow race. In her ruined state, she protected and proved the paradigm's validity. In juxtaposition to the exceptional Hing, there was Daisy Reid – "Yet Another Bad Girl."[66] Operating in tandem, the existence of one archetype made the other viable.

The idea of the One Good Chinaman made it possible for the *Sentinel-Review* to alternate between stories defending Hing's (and hence Woodstock's) good reputation and stories describing loathsome Chinamen in Montreal who held innocent white girls as captive sex slaves.[67] There was no contradiction, and the truth of the latter story need not be questioned because Hing was a rare exception to the Chinese rule. Even the *Herald* contributed to the construction of the exceptional Charlie Lee Hing, describing the accused as "rather a fine looking Oriental, well-dressed in American style, and indeed [he] is a splendid specimen of the well-to-do Americanized Chinese."[68] The *Toronto Daily Star* condescendingly, and ironically, given the charges against him, described Hing as a "superior Celestial" and a "good Christian boy."[69]

Then there was Daisy Reid – a white woman who worked for a Chinaman. The sympathies Reid may have garnered because of her struggling working-class background were offset by her having worked in a Chinese business. This choice of occupation, and her tenacious pursuit of it, placed her among the lowest of working-class women. By becoming affectionate with her Chinese employer, by transgressing racial boundaries, she also forsook her white racial privileges. For all these reasons, she was excluded from the "maidenly girl" category. Thus, in the multifarious social hierarchies brought to bear on the case, Reid retained no leverage, no claim to credibility or respectability. She left the space wide open for Hing to stake his claims to class and gender superiority. But what of his race? What happened was a reverse ricochet effect whereby Hing's Chineseness rebounded onto Reid and damaged her case and her reputation. In the end it was Reid, in her proximity to Hing, who suffered the consequences of anti-Chinese racism. She was the casualty, the object lesson, in this conceptual deployment of the One Good Chinaman theory.

But this is not the end of the story. In the Charles Lee Hing criminal case file there is one small clue pointing towards a tragic aftermath. On file is a letter dated

11 October 1910, almost one year after Hing's acquittal, in which G.G. McPherson, the Stratford Crown attorney, had the following request made to the registrar at Osgoode Hall in Toronto:

> *Rex vs. Charles Lee Hing*
> This case was I understand tried last November at Stratford and certain exhibits were put in. There is now an enquiry to be held at Stratford in connection with an inquest and Mr. McPherson the Crown Attorney wishes to have the exhibits forwarded to him. Will you please have them sent accordingly to Mr. McPherson.[70]

A handwritten notation tells us that this request was fulfilled. Another letter dated 19 October indicates that all exhibits were being returned from Stratford to Toronto. Newspaper reports help fill in some of the gaps concerning an inquest held in 1910 that somehow involved Daisy Reid, Charles Lee Hing, and the letters she had begun writing to him years before:

> On 22 September 1910 the Stratford *Daily Herald* printed the following story:
> Body of Infant Found in Attic of Ontario St[reet] House ... The remains are those of a new-born or a few days' old baby ... From a cursory examination coroner J.P. Rankin, who was called in could not tell whether the babe had been still-born or how it had come to its death. He estimated that it had been there about a year or a considerable number of months.[71]

The finder of the body, a young man named Harry Dockerill, had been in the attic searching for some lost pigeons and accidentally placed his hand on the infant's skull. The Dockerills, who lived directly beneath the attic, had been bothered by a "faintly apparent but inexplicable odor" for some time. This mystery was solved. It now remained to determine the cause of death and those who were responsible for the infant's birth and death.

In its first report the *Herald* constructed a general scenario of this "gruesome discovery." There was no floor in the attic, and the body was found lying, unclothed and uncovered, in between two joists. The Dockerill family had been in the house for only the past three months. Before their occupancy, the house had been vacant. A year previously, however, "at the time when the body is supposed to have been put there, an old lady, who has since died, was living in the lower apartments, Mrs. Reid by name. Since, however, the body was found in the attic, it could have been put there without her being any the wiser, as there is a stair-case up the outside, to the second storey."[72] Beyond this information, the *Herald* could speculate no further. A coroner's hearing into the matter could not be called until the Crown attorney, who was away on business, returned to Stratford.

The initial inquest was held on 4 October, and a dozen witnesses were called forth, including previous and current tenants, the owner, an architect, a coroner, a health inspector, and a police officer. The following information came to light. The remains were of a fully formed infant so decomposed that it was impossible to determine its sex. It was estimated that the body had been there from at least one year up to a year and a half. Next to the remains were an old valise, which was closed but unclasped, and also an edition of the *Stratford Daily Herald* dated 10 September 1909. The architect described the building's layout, explaining that the attic could only be accessed by the apartment in the west end of the house. The owner and previous tenants helped to reconstruct the history of occupancy and to account for the children born to tenants over the past two years. It came out that an elderly Mrs. Reid had lived in the west end of the house and that she had an adopted daughter. One witness had known Daisy Reid and stated: "Daisy had worked in a Chinese laundry." The inquest was then adjourned until 18 October, at which time important documentary evidence would be produced and out-of-town people contacted.[73]

The out-of-towners were Reid and Hing. The important documents were Reid's letters, which once again became pivotal evidence in a criminal investigation. Details on the inquest hearings are sketchy. The Stratford paper ran only three stories, while the *Woodstock Sentinel-Review* never reported on the inquest. The paper and the city no longer had a vested interest in Hing, for he had moved on. The attorney general's efforts to track him down as a witness led to uncertain ends. Hing's lawyer from 1909 thought he was in Toronto, while other sources claimed he might be in Brantford.[74] Daisy Reid was still a ward of the Children's Aid Society and living with a family in Niagara Falls. CAS officials recommended that an officer be sent to bring her to Stratford. Although a CAS representative was present at the second inquest, it is unclear whether Hing or Reid was in attendance. Reid's letters did, however, make it to the hearing. But once again the letters failed to secure a criminal conviction, this time in Daisy Reid's favour. The inquest was held in camera, and insufficient evidence existed to place responsibility for the infant's death. The coroner's jury returned an "open verdict" to the effect that "an unknown child came to its death by means unknown."[75] A few days later, Reid's letters were returned to Toronto and replaced in the *Rex v. Charles Lee Hing* criminal case file.

Although it is not unreasonable or impossible to believe that Daisy Reid gave birth, it is difficult to determine the date of the infant's birth and the identity of the biological father. Was the child born in the spring of 1909, before her foster mother died and Daisy moved from Stratford to Michigan? Was Daisy referring to her pregnancy when she wrote about a stomach operation scheduled for December 1909?[76] If this was so, and if she was accurate in calculating the date of conception, she would have been seven or eight months pregnant in November, at the time of Hing's rape trial. Perhaps, however, this operation was unrelated to a pregnancy.

Another possibility is that Daisy Reid gave birth in September 1909. Given that a newspaper dated 10 September 1909 was found next to the body, it is likely that the infant was placed in the attic sometime after its publication. On the 10th, Reid had written to Hing from Greenville, Michigan, planning and plotting her departure. In this letter she mentioned the operation, but told Hing, "I am feeling better now."[77] In the next letter, she reiterated the exact same message.[78] If the infant was born in September, Reid would have conceived at the beginning of 1909. In a letter written in February, Reid had said: "I am not working for Hong anymore."[79] Then, two months later, she wrote to Hing: "Charlie Hong is going to move in a couple of weeks." This letter, which contained little else of obvious significance, was entered as Exhibit 1 for the defence case.[80] Had she told Charles Lee Hing she was pregnant? In June 1909, when her letters became secretive and desperate, she would have been five or six months pregnant. Was her changing body becoming more difficult to hide as she was asking Hing for a new dress, and for a place to which she could escape? It is unclear whether the trial lawyers and presiding judge were aware that she had been pregnant. There is no mention of a child in the judge's notes or in the newspapers. She might, however, have confessed to the birth while she swore out her preliminary testimony, which was taken in closed court. Had Daisy Reid been coerced into sexual intercourse and impregnated by this other Chinese man, Charlie Hong? Where did Charles Lee Hing fit into these affairs?

Despite all the research historians can do, there are some fundamental questions we may never answer. Did Reid and Hing have sexual contact? Let us say they did and that it was consensual sex. Why did Reid accuse him of rape? Did the rape charge stem from Reid's resentment, guilt, shame, or anger at having to go through the motions of sexual intercourse in order to acquire things – the dress, shoes, hat, the money, and the employment – things she needed and desired? Consent, as a legal category and construct, absolved the judge and jurors from considering why Reid may have complied sexually against her deeper wishes. Or was the accusation of rape the most expedient and socially accepted explanation for making love with a Chinese man? Was Reid "found out," and was her rape charge an instinctive response to being caught in a socially despised relationship?

What if Hing was guilty of the crime, and Reid had felt too frightened, too helpless, to report his assault? Would the "not guilty" verdict have been passed if Hing had not been an "Americanized Chinaman," a prominent, respected, Christian businessman with the economic resources to launch a strong defence? What if Reid had come from a solid middle-class family, rather than being of "unknown parentage"[81] and residing in tenement housing? Recall that Reid was identified by a witness at the 1910 coroner's inquest by the words, "Daisy worked in a Chinese laundry." Through elliptical thinking, this phrase not only encapsulated her employment record but alluded to her sexual history and questioned her moral character. What if Reid had kept and produced the letters she had received from Hing? To what words, hints, subtle pleas, or threats was Reid responding when she promised never to forget him?[82]

Who would have thought that things would turn out as they did? How could a Chinese man accused of raping a white teenager go free? Perhaps, however, the outcome should not be such a surprise. Daisy Reid was no match for Charles Lee Hing, the One Good Chinaman.

QUESTIONS FOR CONSIDERATION:

1. Why would the *Stratford Daily Herald* story about this case not have been "fantastic" or "incredible" to southwestern Ontario readers in 1909?
2. Why are letters such a valuable resource for many historians? Think about how other historians have used them in this collection.
3. Why was Charles Lee Hing on trial?
4. Describe the "yellow peril" in your own words.
5. What was the "One Good Chinaman" theory?
6. What was the tragic aftermath following the end of the criminal case?
7. How does Pon's narrative fit with the popular one that both Ontario and Canada have always been welcoming, tolerant, and multicultural?

NOTES

I would like to thank several grant agencies that funded my work: the Social Sciences and Humanities Research Council, Toronto Chinese Businessmen's Association, Federation of Chinese-Canadian Professionals (Ontario), Canadian Federation of University Women, and Robert F. Harney Memorial Trust Fund. I am grateful to Phillip Bird for taking the time and having the enthusiasm to talk and work through historical "conundrums."

1 *Stratford Daily Herald*, 2 October 1909, 1.
2 For a discussion of this concept of the "maidenly girl" and its diametric opposite, the "designing woman," see Karen Dubinsky, *Improper Advances: Rape and Heterosexual Conflict in Ontario, 1880–1929* (Chicago: University of Chicago Press, 1993).
3 *Woodstock Daily Sentinel*, 13 October 1909, 1; also in *Toronto Globe*, 13 October 1909, 5.
4 *Toronto Globe*, 27 October 1909, 7.
5 *Stratford Daily Herald*, 18 November 1909, 1.

6 *Woodstock Daily Sentinel*, 17 November 1909, 1.
7 Archives of Ontario (hereafter AO), RG 22 unprocessed files, County of Perth, miscellaneous correspondence, 1903–11, box 4, L.H. Bradford to G.G. McPherson, 11 November 1909.
8 *Woodstock Daily Sentinel*, 2 October 1909, 1.
9 *Woodstock Daily Sentinel*, 17 November 1909, 1.
10 *Woodstock Daily Sentinel*, 13 October 1909, 1; *Toronto Daily Star*, 4 October 1909, 1; *Toronto Globe*, 13 October 1909, 5; *Stratford Daily Herald*, 12 October 1909, 1.
11 *Woodstock Daily Sentinel*, 5 October 1909, 1.
12 *Toronto Daily Star*, 4 October 1909, 1.
13 In 1901 there were 113 "Negroes" in Woodstock; this number had dropped to 60 by 1911. The African-descent population in Stratford was much smaller; however, that city had a slightly larger Eastern European population than did Woodstock. *Census of Canada*, 1901, vol. 1, table 11: Origins of the People, 338–9.
14 For general histories of Chinese immigration and settlement in Canada, see Anthony Chan, *Gold Mountain* (Vancouver: New Star Books, 1983); David Chuenyan Lai, *Chinatowns: Towns within Cities in Canada* (Vancouver: UBC Press, 1988); Peter S. Li, *The Chinese in Canada* (Toronto: Oxford University Press, 1988); and Edgar Wickberg et al., *From China to Canada: A History of Chinese in Canada* (Toronto: McClelland and Stewart, 1982).
15 *Census of Canada*, 1911, vol. 2, table 7: Origins of the People by Sub-districts, 204–5. In Northern Ontario, for example, there were 165 Chinese in the District of Thunder Bay and Rainy River, and 149 in the Nipissing District. *Census of Canada*, 1911, vol. 2, table 8: Origins of the People by District, 336–7.
16 *Census of Canada*, 1911, vol. 2, table 7: Origins of the People by Sub-districts, 248–9, 234–5, 218–19.
17 *Census of Canada*, 1901, vol. 1, table 11: Origins of the People, 338–9. In the 1901 census, Chinese and Japanese were enumerated under a single category. It is safe, however, to assume that these numbers for Stratford and Woodstock refer to Chinese immigrants. In 1911, when the two groups were categorically distinguished, there was one Japanese person in Woodstock and none in Stratford. *Census of Canada*, 1911, vol. 2, table 7: Origins of the People by Sub-district, 234–5, 238–9.
18 In 1911 the total population of Stratford was 12,946, and in Woodstock, 9,320. *Census of Canada*, vol. 2, table 7: Origins of the People by Sub-districts, 9, 234–5.
19 For discussions of attitudes towards Chinese in Canada, see Kay J. Anderson, *Vancouver's Chinatown: Racial Discourse in Canada* (Montreal and Kingston: McGill–Queen's University Press, 1990); Gillian Creese, "Exclusion or Solidarity? Vancouver Workers Confront the 'Oriental Problem,'" *BC Studies* 80 (1988–89): 24–51; M. Pon, 'Like a Chinese Puzzle: The Construction of Chinese Masculinity in *Jack Canuck*,' in *Gender and History in Canada*, ed. Joy Parr and Mark Rosenfeld (Toronto: Copp Clark, 1996), 88–100; Patricia Roy, *A White Man's Province: British Columbia Politicians and Chinese and Japanese Immigrants, 1858–1914* (Vancouver: UBC Press, 1989); and Peter Ward, *White Canada Forever: Popular Attitudes and Public Policy toward Orientals in British Columbia* (Montreal and Kingston: McGill–Queen's University Press, 1978).
20 For studies on the moral panic surrounding relations between white women and Chinese, and the various ways in which this panic was manipulated to instigate anti-Chinese policies and laws, see Constance Backhouse, "White Women's Labour Laws: Anti-Chinese Racism in Early 20th Century Canada," *Law and History Review* 14 (1996): 315–68; Carolyn Strange, *Toronto's Girl Problem: The Perils and Pleasures of the City, 1880–1930* (Toronto: University of Toronto Press, 1995); Mariana Valverde, *The Age of Light, Soap, and Water: Moral Reform in English Canada,*

1885–1925 (Toronto: McClelland and Stewart, 1991); and James W.St.G. Walker, *"Race," Rights and the Law in the Supreme Court of Canada: Historical Case Studies* (Toronto: Osgoode Society for Canadian Legal History and Wilfrid Laurier University Press, 1996).

21 For a concise description and analysis of the history of Canadian sexual assault laws, see Constance Backhouse, 'Nineteenth-Century Canadian Rape Law, 1800–92,' in *Essays in the History of Canadian Law*, vol. 2, ed. David H. Flaherty (Toronto: University of Toronto Press, 1983), 200–47.

22 *Selected Chapters of the Revised Statutes of Canada, 1906, and Amendments, 1907– 1909, Relating to the Criminal Law* (Ottawa 1909), 72–3.

23 AO, Judges' Benchbooks, RG 22-491-1-13, Justice Teetzel, 22 June 1909–March 1910, box 2, 171. In a letter to Hing dated 10 September 1909, Reid wrote, "my birthday is Saturday week," but made no reference to her age. AO, Criminal Assize Indictment Case Files, RG 22-392-0-5107, box 122 (hereafter Case Files).

24 In 1909 the punishment for committing rape on a woman was death or life imprisonment, and for statutory rape it was life imprisonment with the lash. Canadian Criminal Code, section 301, chapter 146.

25 AO, RG 22 unprocessed files, County of Perth, miscellaneous correspondence, 1903–11, box 4, L.H. Bradford to G.G. McPherson, 11 November 1909.

26 AO, RG 22 unprocessed files, County of Perth, miscellaneous correspondence, 1903–11, box 4, Chief of Police, Greenville, Michigan, to Bradford, 1 November 1910.

27 *Woodstock Daily Sentinel*, 13 October 1909, 1; *Toronto Globe*, 13 October 1909, 5.

28 See, for example, Backhouse, "Nineteenth-Century Canadian Rape Law"; Dubinsky, *Improper Advances*; and Strange, *Toronto's Girl Problem*.

29 *Stratford Daily Herald*, 2 October 1909, 1.

30 *Woodstock Daily Sentinel*, 5 October 1909, 1.

31 *Woodstock Daily Sentinel*, 5 October 1909, 1.

32 *Woodstock Daily Sentinel*, 4 October 1909, 1.

33 *Stratford Daily Herald*, 6 October 1909, 4.

34 Dubinsky, *Improper Advances*, 67–8.

35 *Woodstock Daily Sentinel*, 5 October 1909, 1.

36 *Woodstock Daily Sentinel*, 13 October 1909, 1.

37 *Stratford Daily Herald*, 6 October 1909, 4.

38 *Stratford Daily Herald*, 12 October 1909, 1.

39 Case Files, letters dated 4 June, 19 July, 4 August 1907.

40 See, for example, Case Files, letters dated 11 July, 18 September, 18 November, 19 June, 11 August 1907.

41 Case Files, letter dated 27 October 1908.

42 Case Files, letter dated 4 June 1907.

43 Case Files, letter dated 18 November 1907.

44 Case Files, letter dated 10 February 1909.

45 Case Files, letter dated 7 November 1907.

46 In her letters, Reid had referred to her mother's bouts of ill health since 1907.

47 Case Files, letters dated 11 August and 7 November 1907, 27 November 1908.

48 Case Files, letter dated 27 May 1909.

49 Case Files, letter dated 5 June 1909.

50 Case Files, 8 June 1909.

51 Case Files, letter dated 15 June 1909.

52 Case Files, letter dated 10 September 1909.

53 Case Files, letter dated 16 September 1909.
54 Case Files, letter dated 22 September 1909.
55 *Woodstock Daily Sentinel*, 5 October 1909, 1.
56 *Woodstock Daily Sentinel*, 17 November 1909, 1.
57 *Woodstock Daily Sentinel*, 17 November 1909, 1; *Stratford Daily Herald*, 18 November 1909, 1; AO, Judges' Benchbooks, RG 22-491-1-13, box 2, Justice Teetzel, 22 June 1909–March 1910, 171–3.
58 AO, Supreme Court of Ontario Criminal Assize Clerk Reports, County of Perth, RG 22-391, 15–18 November 1909.
59 *Stratford Daily Herald*, 18 November 1909, 1.
60 Woodstock *Daily Sentinel*, 7 October 1909, 1; Stratford *Daily Herald*, 8 October 1909, 1.
61 AO, RG 22 unprocessed files, County of Perth, miscellaneous correspondence, 1903–11, box 4, 24 November 1909.
62 Stratford *Daily Herald*, 5 October 1909, 4.
63 Woodstock *Daily Herald*, 17 November 1909, 1.
64 AO, Judges' Benchbooks, RG 22-491-1-13, Justice Teetzel, 22 June 1909–March 1910, box 2, 173.
65 Barrington Walker, "Sexual Conflict, Black Patriarchy, and the Law: Reading the Story of George and Eliza Ross in Ontario's Criminal Case Files, Essex County, Ontario, 1882," paper presented at Canadian Historical Association, Ottawa, June 1998.
66 I am indebted to Carolyn Strange for pointing out the codependence of these two social constructs.
67 *Woodstock Daily Sentinel*, 15 November 1909, 1.
68 *Stratford Daily Herald*, 4 October 1909, 1.
69 *Toronto Daily Star*, 4 October 1909, 1.
70 Case Files, G.G. McPherson to A.F. McLean, 11 October 1910.
71 *Stratford Daily Herald*, 22 September 1910, 1.
72 *Stratford Daily Herald*, 22 September 1910, 1.
73 *Stratford Daily Herald*, 5 October 1910, 1.
74 AO, RG 22 unprocessed files, County of Perth, miscellaneous correspondence, 1903–11, box 4.
75 *Stratford Daily Herald*, 19 October 1910, 1.
76 Case Files, letter dated 10 September 1909.
77 Case Files, letter dated 10 September 1909.
78 Case Files, letter dated 16 September 1909.
79 Case Files, letter dated 10 February 1909.
80 Reid's letter, entered as Exhibit 1, reads as follows:

Stratford Ont April 21st [1909]

Dear Friend Charlie

We recieved your ever welcome letter and was glad to hear from you. We are all well hoping to find you the same. I should of [*sic*] answered your letter sooner but have been busy and did not get time. How is you business now. did you get many presents for Easter I got quite a few Charlie Hong is going to move in a couple of weeks.

Well I guess I must close for now as I am making some blouse waists answer soon

Yours Truly D.

For a list of exhibits, see Case Files, 'List of Exhibits filed on the trial of this action 16th day of November 1909.'

81 *Daily Sentinel*, 13 October 1909, 1.
82 Case Files *Woodstock*, letter dated 19 July 1907.

CHAPTER FIVE

The History of Education at Six Nations of the Grand River, 1828–1939

ALISON NORMAN

The Six Nations of the Grand River Reserve in southwestern Ontario is unique in a variety of ways. Six Nations is the largest reserve in the country, and the community has a special relationship with the Crown, including the gift of a large grant of land in the late eighteenth century that brought them into Ontario from New York. The education system on the reserve is also unique: Six Nations people were involved in colonial, Christian, Western-based education at Grand River from the beginning. The first residential school in the province, the Mohawk Institute, was established there in 1828, along with a number of day schools for local children. Missionary societies supported the schools in the nineteenth century, and later, the Six Nations School Board was founded to manage the local day schools; half of the board's members were Six Nations chiefs. The Mohawk Institute, known for a period as the Indian Normal School, produced many Indigenous teachers who went on to teach in local day schools, the residential school itself, and schools on reserves elsewhere in the province. This chapter will examine how the colonial education system at Six Nations grew and evolved over time; the policies and curriculum that children who attended these schools were subject to; the important role that Haudenosaunee[1] teachers and community leaders played in the education of the community's children; and the experiences of children who attended both the residential school and the day schools.

The early adoption of the Anglican faith and an interest in Western education on the part of Six Nations leadership, especially among the Mohawk, resulted in a unique history of education on the reserve, one that is different from that of most other First Nations in the province. This chapter complicates the history of Indigenous education in Canada, given the unique situation at Grand River. It was home to the first and longest-lasting residential school in the province, as well as to the largest number of day schools on a single reserve. Moreover, Haudenosaunee leadership was involved in the local school board, and numerous Haudenosaunee teachers were employed in local schools. All of this was unlike the situation faced by all other Ontario First Nations. Unlike most other First Nations in the province, the Six Nations had some limited control over the education of their community's children – certainly not full control, but enough to have a positive educational impact on the children in their own community, especially because they were able to employ their own teachers in the reserve's day schools. All of this contrasts with the broader history of Indigenous education in Canada, which has had an almost entirely negative impact.

The schools at Six Nations were part of a broader project in Canada to educate and convert Indigenous children to Christianity and to assimilate them to Western culture. Scholars (both Indigenous and non-Indigenous) and First Nations community historians are increasingly researching and publishing the history of education at both residential schools and on-reserve day schools across the country. Several broad studies of the residential school system exist;[2] there are also the reports of the Truth and Reconciliation Commission, which focused its attention on residential schools.[3] It is clear from this research that residential schools in Canada were places of abuse, neglect, hunger, and even death.[4] For these reasons, former students and graduates are often called survivors. The schools operated within a culture of systemic racism, and as Senator Murray Sinclair noted, "what took place in residential schools amounts to nothing short of cultural genocide – a systematic and concerted attempt to extinguish the spirit of Aboriginal peoples."[5] Evidence of cultural genocide is apparent in the descriptions of children's experiences at the Mohawk Institute in this chapter.

Regarding the history of reserve day schools, the published research tends to focus on specific schools and communities. In addition to more studies of reserve day schools in local communities, what is needed is a broad overview of the history of day schools in Ontario and Canada that examines the larger system and that makes comparisons and connections between regions and across the country.[6] There has also been research conducted and published specifically on the Mohawk Institute,[7] though little on the Six Nations day schools.[8] Several Haudenosaunee community historians have written about education at Six Nations over the past decades. After her retirement in the 1940s, Julia Jamieson (Mohawk), a long-time teacher on the reserve, wrote a short history, *Echoes of the Past: A History of Education from the Time of the Six Nations Settlement on the Banks of the Grand River in 1784 to 1924*.[9] Given her decades of personal experience as a teacher, and the experiences of her siblings as teachers, as well as her role as a founding member of the Six Nations Teachers' Organization, *Echoes of the Past* is a valuable resource.[10] Second, Mohawk knowledge keeper Keith Jamieson wrote a *History of Six Nations Education* (1987), a short but detailed history of the first century of education that tapped into missionary society and government records. The same booklet contains an appendix setting out the 1906 federal government regulations for the management of "Indian schools."[11] Lastly, three former teachers, Olive Moses, Doris Henhawk, and Lloyd King (King was from the Mississaugas of New Credit, the neighbouring Anishnaabe community), researched and wrote a longer piece, *History of Education on the Six Nations Reserve*, with the help of a federal grant.[12] This 1987 study relies on records from the Six Nations Council and Six Nations School Board, as well as memories of community members, and includes much detail on the twentieth century, including some reminiscences of former students. All three are useful studies produced by community members, Indigenous educators themselves, that tell the story of education in their own community. Numerous interviews with survivors of the Mohawk Institute are also available. While most available interviews are from the post-war period, they are a valuable resource for learning about how children experienced education in the residential school on the edge of their community.[13]

This chapter provides an overview of the history of the various forms of education that existed in the community, with a focus on both the Mohawk Institute, but also the day schools, where most children went to school. As much as possible, it relies on what women and men from Six Nations themselves wrote decades ago, on interviews conducted with community members in the past, and on other sources written at the time, including school board records, records of the Department of Indian Affairs, policy documents, newspaper articles, and letters. For various reasons, including the early introduction of English to the Six Nations in the eighteenth century, the influence of the Christian missionaries, and the success of Western education, the community itself produced many written records in the nineteenth and early twentieth centuries, which is not the case for most Indigenous communities in Canada, whose oral traditions remained the dominant method of communicating the community's history and knowledge for a longer time. Fortunately, the voices of Six Nations people exist in writing in a wide variety of sources, including letters to government officials, the school board, and newspapers; published histories of churches and the education system; and interviews conducted with community members and published in newspapers, held in community repositories, or published in the decades after the closing of the residential school.

Background History: Indigenous Education and the Six Nations

The Six Nations of Grand River are Haudenosaunee people, and their traditional territory is in upstate New York. The original Five Nations of the Confederacy were the Mohawk, Onondaga, Seneca, Oneida, and Cayuga; they were joined by the Tuscarora in the early eighteenth century to make the Six Nations, as they are now known. Each nation has its own language (all of which belong to the Iroquoian language family), and each occupied its own territory in New York. Each had chiefs that represented its members within the confederacy, and women acted as clan mothers in a political structure in which both men and women played important roles. Clan mothers held leadership positions within each of the clans for each nation, and descent was matrilineal, following the female line. The Haudenosaunee had long-held spiritual values, and their communities were guided by the Great Law of Peace.[14]

Before Western systems of education were introduced, Haudenosaunee children learned in unstructured and non-coercive ways, through participation, and studying their environment, and from instruction provided by older members of their communities.[15] For instance, young girls worked with their mother, aunts, and other women to make clothing; and children of both sexes learned about plants while gathering herbs with women for medicinal, ceremonial, and other needs. The women also taught them the skills they needed to survive and to fulfil their community obligations. At an early age, children were trained to carry small bundles of sticks and to fetch small pots of water for cooking and washing, for instance, as part of the process of developing the knowledge and skills to equip them to contribute to everyone's well-being as they grew up.[16] Once children were a bit older, men would spend some time teaching boys to make tools and weapons; even so, it was women who were central to the education of Haudenosaunee children: "the mother-child relationship in tandem with all the women of the Longhouse, shared in the task of developing in the child, an appreciation for the home and family, language, values and beliefs."[17] Ideas about cooperation, competence, coexistence, and individuality were the basis of education, and learning took place through observing and engaging in quotidian life: it was not normally separated from day-to-day activities.

Families brought with them to Six Nations their traditional familial methods of educating their young. But by the eighteenth century, there were also leaders who believed it would be useful to provide Haudenosaunee children with Western forms of education. To that end, some chiefs and leaders developed relationships with missionary societies, and schools were built in the late eighteenth century that would have a significant impact on the community. Some members of the community practised their traditional faith, but many others were Christian, including much of the Mohawk leadership, who were Anglican. Mohawk Chief Joseph Brant (aka Thayendanega, 1743–1807) had been baptized as a child and attended a missionary school, and had helped recruit other Haudenosaunee boys to the school.[18] Brant later sent his sons (including John Brant) to be educated at some of the same institutions he had attended, all before the move from New York to Grand River. Other young Haudenosaunee men, and other Indigenous young men from the northeastern US and Canada, converted to Christianity and attended Western schools during this period, but the numbers were small.[19]

After Britain lost its American colonies in the War of Independence (1776–89), it offered lands in British North America (what later became Canada) to its allies who had fought on their side, including their Indigenous allies. About 1,800 Haudenosaunee people chose to follow Chief Joseph Brant and move west across the Niagara River into British territory (what later became Ontario); on arrival, they were granted a tract of land by Governor Sir Frederick Haldimand as compensation for their losses in upper New York state. The Six Nations established national villages, which spread out along the length of the Grand River, with the Mohawk settling where Brantford is today, and with Onondaga, Cayuga, Tuscarora, and other villages established along the river south towards Lake Erie. People worked to clear land for agriculture, to build homes, and to erect schools and churches; these efforts reflected an attempt to rebuild the familiar structure they had left behind in New York.[20]

The Day Schools

Chief Joseph Brant and other Mohawk Anglican leaders were concerned with promoting Christianity at Grand River; they also desired to create opportunities for Haudenosaunee children to acquire a Western education.[21] Governor Haldimand had promised that the new settlement at Grand River would have a sawmill, a grist mill, a church, and a school and that an annual sum of £25 would be provided for the schoolteacher's salary.[22] The first Anglican Church built in Upper Canada was the Mohawk Chapel, on the banks of the Grand River in 1785, soon after their arrival from New York state.[23] With the help of the New England Company (NEC), a Protestant missionary society, the number of schools and churches grew over time. Missionaries were crucial to the spread of Christianity among Indigenous people in Canada, both for the funds they raised and spent in the mission field and for the groundwork of the missionaries themselves. At Grand River, the first school building opened in 1786 at the Mohawk Village, and Mohawk teachers used prayer books, scriptures, and primers in their own language to teach the children. Some of the schools were short-lived due to inconsistent funding.[24] John Brant, Joseph's youngest son, worked to acquire permanent support for the schools at Grand River, travelling to England in 1822 to meet with the New England Company. Brant asked them to provide funding to pay a teacher, "preferably an Indian competent to teach 'plain reading and writing'" to the Mohawk community at Grand River.[25] Brant was successful; the NEC gave him £200 for the school, of which £25 was allocated for the teacher's salary.

Over the next decade, the NEC contributed several hundred more pounds towards the construction of schools and the appointment of missionaries and teachers in their Canadian mission field, including at Grand River. Funding for Indigenous schools was a priority for the NEC, and as the number of Christians grew during the nineteenth century, their efforts enjoyed some support within the communities. Some community leaders and parents believed there would be benefits to their children learning to read and write in English. They saw schooling not as assimilation but as a useful tool for navigating the colonial world that was encroaching upon them. In response to demand, additional schools were built along the Grand River during the 1830s in the communities of the Oneida, then the Tuscarora, and then the Cayuga.[26]

After the reserve was consolidated in 1847, more day schools were built, so that by 1900 there were twelve at Grand River (eleven controlled by the Six Nations School Board and one controlled by the Six Nations Council, called the Thomas School).[27] School No. 2 was the largest, located in the central village of Ohsweken on the reserve. No other First Nation in Ontario had so many day schools. There was no high school on the reserve, so students who passed the entrance examination generally attended either Brantford Collegiate or the nearby Caledonia High School. The expansion of the number of schools at Grand River is evidence not only of attempts by government and church officials to "civilize" and Christianize Haudenosaunee people, but also of a demand for these Western institutions among at least some Haudenosaunee leaders who were supportive of the initiatives for their own purposes. The curriculum at the schools included subjects that Haudenosaunee leaders thought might be useful for children growing up in a changing world, surrounded by English-speaking settlers.

The NEC hoped to hire local Haudenosaunee teachers in their day schools during the nineteenth century, in part because they believed it was useful to have teachers who could speak to the children in one of their own Haudenosaunee languages, as well as in English. A number of Mohawk women in particular were hired at these local schools, and they worked to build careers as educators, despite various challenges.[28] Jemima Loft Beaver (b. 1833) was likely the first Indigenous woman to teach at the Grand River in the 1860s, had previously travelled in New York and elsewhere as a performer and Gospel singer in order to raise funds for publishing Mohawk translations of the Bible. As a teacher at two schools on the reserve (No. 6 and No. 9), Beaver struggled with low attendance and a lack of supplies (including desks, ink, and pens) while teaching in an upper room in her own home.[29] Another Mohawk woman, Elizabeth Martin Powless (1837–1916, and Beaver's first cousin once removed), also faced material barriers while teaching in Grand River schools, including at No. 4 and No. 6. She later resigned over a conflict with the NEC, and her son George Powless took over her position.[30] By 1882, seven of the eight teachers in day schools on the reserve were Haudenosaunee.[31] Despite the challenges they faced because they were women, their efforts and careers teaching in missionary-funded schools continued the Haudenosaunee tradition of female educators and provided an important cultural link for Haudenosaunee children in local day schools.

Another important factor in education at Grand River was the central role played by the first and only Indigenous school board in Canada at the time, the Six Nations School Board (SNSB).[32] The board, which functioned between 1878 and 1933, was comprised of local missionaries, several chiefs, and a representative from the Department of Indian Affairs (DIA).[33] The board often hired Indigenous teachers and generally gave preference to them.[34] While the local Indian agent often chaired the school board meetings, men from the community held positions on the board and made the hiring decisions, as well as decisions about salaries, curriculum, and the construction of new schools. The board worked to ensure that their buildings were comparable to schools built for non-Indigenous children in neighbouring counties.[35] The board also wanted its teachers to use the Ontario Curriculum of Studies with their students, not the separate curriculum designed for "Indian Schools," produced by the DIA, because its members thought the provincial curriculum was academically stronger. In 1908, after several years of lobbying, the board adopted the Ontario Programme of Studies.[36] The board continued to hire local Haudenosaunee teachers throughout the first decades of the twentieth century until the DIA dissolved the Board in 1934 after disagreements over the hiring of Haudenosaunee teachers. However, community members continued to be hired as teachers in the decades that followed. With much of the education system in the hands of the community itself through the board and the teachers at these schools, it is understandable that there was support for the day schools in the community even though the schools did contribute to the loss of language and tradition in the community. The community's confidence in the schools was likely due in part to the fact that so many of the teachers were Six Nations people.

Twentieth-Century Day Schools

The experience of attending a day school at Grand River in the early twentieth century was in many ways similar to that of non-Indigenous children in rural Ontario schools at the time. Most of the day schools on the reserve were one-room schoolhouses with one teacher; they were heated by a wood stove and had two outhouses outside for boys and girls. Children from ages seven to thirteen would attend for several years before possibly taking an entrance examination for high school. The younger children would attend school until 2 p.m., and older children would stay until 4 p.m.[37] The day schools at Six Nations used the regular Ontario Programme of Studies after 1908, and the teacher would be responsible for teaching groups of students at different levels throughout the day. By the twentieth century, children were being taught in English in day schools; it is unlikely that any of the Haudenosaunee languages were being used in the classroom, although it is impossible to know for certain. While it was common for rural teachers in one-room schoolhouses to focus on reading and writing,[38] teachers at Six Nations schools went far beyond that in their lessons.

It is difficult to know exactly what teachers taught in the classroom; there is evidence, though, that it was a priority for Haudenosaunee teachers to teach history and culture from a Haudenosaunee perspective, along with the regular curriculum. The Six Nations School Board was supportive of these sorts of efforts. In 1915 they ordered Mohawk poet Pauline Johnson's book of poems for all eleven schools on the reserve.[39] Certainly, for Haudenosaunee teachers like Emily General (1908–1991) and Julia Jamieson (1889–1975), instilling pride in Haudenosaunee heritage was one of their goals in the classroom.[40] Emily General used traditional stories and customs to "bring to life for her students the heritage of their people," according to one of her biographies.[41] She had a strong belief that it was necessary to instil pride in the children of Six Nations by teaching them about their culture – so strong that she founded the Six Nations Reserve Forest Theatre after her teaching career ended. Julia Jamieson was similarly passionate. After her retirement from teaching, she worked to create Mohawk language resources and helped create a community museum exhibit about Pauline Johnson.[42] In the late 1930s, Julia's sister Nora Jamieson also worked to incorporate learning about Haudenosaunee culture into her classroom:

> As S. S. No. 5 I did concentrate on the study of Indian culture. My class there was small and we had some time to do extra work. We decorated our classroom with

> Indian artefacts, made booklets of Indian stories and legends, made scrap books of Indian articles which appeared in newspapers and magazines including pictures. Our art work consisted of the drawing of masked Iroquois ways of living, longhouses, corn pounders, turtle rattles. After everything was in readiness we had an open house for a couple of days including Saturday. Pupils were to welcome the visitors and escort them around telling them about the different displays.[43]

So she taught her students about Haudenosaunee culture and history, and in turn the students shared their cultural knowledge with the community through the work they did at school.[44] These teachers were proud Six Nations women with a passion for teaching, who believed that traditional language, culture, and history had to be preserved and taught to the younger generations and, via the children, to the larger community as well.

Along with aspects of traditional culture and Haudenosaunee history, children in day schools were taught content from the standard Ontario curriculum, which included lessons about the history and geography of the British Empire, and teachers would have focused on the place of their community within it. The Six Nations have a long history of alliance with England going back to the Covenant Chain of the seventeenth century, as well as a proud military tradition of their own. During the First World War, from 1914 to 1918, several teachers from the day schools enlisted, and many graduates of both the day schools and the Mohawk Institute enlisted as well. In total, the Mohawk Institute had ninety-five graduates enlist, and the No. 2 School in Ohsweken had sixty-five.[45] These high enlistment rates were in part the result of the education they received, the warrior tradition in Haudenosaunee culture, and the long history of alliance to the United Kingdom, and directly to the Crown.

Throughout much of the twentieth century, Christianity remained another important component of the education provided by the day schools, though it was not as central as it was at the church-run Mohawk Institute. This could be seen in the schools and the curriculum in various ways. And while the specifics are unclear, classes in religion were taught in the day schools, often by the teachers themselves; all the teachers in the day schools were Christian. As part of the Christian education mandated by the province, both the Mohawk Institute and the day schools made an effort to teach "manners and morals," including the virtues of "purity, health, nobility, self-control, self-reliance, generosity, truthfulness, good taste in dress, cultivation of will power, economy, moral value of work, etc.," according to Ontario's "Public School Courses of Study, Duties of Teachers and Pupils" (1909).[46] Exactly how these virtues were to be communicated is unclear, but individual teachers apparently attempted to teach morality. Traditionally, the Haudenosaunee held many of the same values in their own Longhouse faith, but they were not recognized by the school board or teachers as such.[47]

Lastly, children were taught some gender-specific skills in the day schools, though these were not as integral to the curriculum as at the Mohawk Institute. Girls in the day schools learned domestic science, but somewhat sporadically, as it was generally not part of the curriculum. While agriculture wasn't central to the running of the day schools (as it was at the Mohawk Institute), day school children did learn about farming. Most importantly, the school board held an annual Agricultural Fair at the No. 2 School in Ohsweken, a day apart from the larger Six Nations Agricultural Society Fair, in which children competed in a variety of contests. One student remembered how exhibits were placed in the two classrooms, art and writing were hung on the walls, and exhibits in sewing, baking, and woodworking were set out on the tables. Students made collections of seeds and dried plants, which were mounted and labelled. And the Six Nations Council supplied children with packages of vegetable seeds, which could be planted at school or at home, and in the fall, the students showed their vegetables at the school fair, much as their parents did at the SNAS Fair.[48] Agricultural education was important to both the parents and the day school teachers at Grand River, though perhaps for different reasons. The DIA was trying to use agricultural education as a "civilizing" influence on the children; at the same time, parents and community members were taking an active part in improving farming on the reserve. The DIA saw prosperous farms as leading to assimilation, whereas Six Nations people saw them as a way of maintaining identity and independence.

The Mohawk Institute

At the time of Confederation in 1867, there were only two residential schools in the four provinces of Canada, the Mohawk Institute and Mount Elgin, outside London.[49] The Mohawk Institute, which was the oldest continuously operating Anglican residential school in Canada, was founded by the Rev. Robert Lugger (1793–1837) and the New England Company in 1828 as a Mechanics Institute. It was built across the road from the Mohawk Chapel on land granted to the company by the Six Nations chiefs and the colonial government. At first, the school was a day school for boys, but after several years, boys began boarding there, and in 1834, girls were also admitted.[50] A central goal of the school throughout this period was conversion of the children to Christianity, as well as "civilizing" the children by teaching them skills deemed useful by the NEC. In 1837, the Rev. Abraham Nelles (1805–1884) became principal and changed the school's focus, from industrial training to farming. In the early decades, the children all came from Six Nations, most of them were Mohawk, and many of the chiefs and leaders of the community sent their children there. In the 1840s, the Six Nations chiefs supported the institute, and they asked that 200 acres be set aside near the Mohawk Chapel in Brantford for an agricultural institute to teach boys farming skills.[51] In 1854, a new, larger building was raised, set farther back from the Grand River. When this building was destroyed by fire in 1903, the school was quickly rebuilt nearby; that building still stands today. The missionary society paid all the school's costs until 1885, when the federal government began to contribute to its operation.[52]

Most Haudenosaunee children from the Six Nations attended local day schools rather than the Mohawk Institute. For example, in 1900, there were 125 children living at the Mohawk Institute (including some from other First Nations), and 520 children attending the nine local day schools. In 1920, there were 134 students living at the Mohawk Institute and 546 attending the eleven local day schools.[53] In the 1890s, residential school policy changed, and the Mohawk Institute began to take in children the DIA considered "orphaned or destitute." It would continue to do so throughout the early decades of the twentieth century. Vulnerable and orphaned children from other First Nations in southern Ontario were sent to the residential school, along with some Six Nations children from similar kinds of family situations. Many of the students came from other reserves, such as neighbouring Mississaugas of the New Credit and more distant Moraviantown, Sarnia, Walpole Island, Muncey, Scugog, Stoney Point, Saugeen, Bay of Quinte, and Kahnawake.[54] At times, there was a waiting list of children whose parents hoped to get them into the school. Elizabeth Graham, in her study of the Mohawk Institute and Mount Elgin residential schools, notes that these schools both had waiting lists "at first because parents wanted to send their children to the schools, and latterly because of the number of needy children as determined by the Indian Agents."[55] In 1844, for instance, enrolment at the Mohawk Institute was fifty, and there were fifty more names on a waiting list.[56] The waiting list is not evidence, however, that the school was a force for good.

Within a few decades of its founding, the Mohawk Institute became an important site for the education and training of Indigenous teachers. In 1859, it employed four of its own graduates as staff.[57] By the 1870s, it had become the institute's stated aim "to impart such an education as shall fit its pupils for teachers amongst their own people, at the same time training them in the arts and practices of civilized nations."[58] The school played a central role as a teacher's college in the nineteenth and into the early twentieth centuries, so much so that in 1885 it was known as the Indian Normal School. (Normal schools were colleges for training teachers, prior to the present-day university training process.)[59] The missionaries and officials at the school realized that the most promising students should have the opportunity for further education and training for a variety of careers, but teaching seems to have been the most popular choice. From about the 1870s onwards, almost every year the institute requested funds from the New England Company for a select number of students to further their education at various colleges in southern Ontario, including Huron College and Hellmuth College, both in London, Ontario, and the Toronto Normal School. Isaac Barefoot, an Onondaga man, was perhaps the best known among these teachers. A graduate of the Mohawk Institute, he taught in a local day school; he was the first Indigenous person to teach at the Mohawk Institute, where he remained for many years before attending Huron College for further education and training. He later became the school inspector at Six Nations and an ordained Anglican priest. In the 1880s, principal Robert Ashton created a teacher training program and a teaching certificate for graduates in what was likely the first and only teacher education program in a residential school in Canada.[60] By the 1890s, the Mohawk Institute had graduated twenty-five girls and twenty boys who went on to become schoolteachers in reserve day schools and other residential schools.[61]

Throughout much of the nineteenth century, there was a shortage of teachers in the land that makes up today's Ontario, and this had an impact on the reserve schools. Increasingly, women were hired to work in the rapidly growing public school system, in part because there were not enough qualified male teachers.[62] This was also the case at the Mohawk Institute and the day schools at Grand River. The institute began training teachers for Indigenous schools by offering a six-month course for teachers who had completed junior matriculation – four years of high school.[63] As one teacher remembers about the Thomas School, "once the school was established it was easy to find children to attend but school-teachers were not secured so easily. The Mohawk Institute graduates came to the rescue."[64] In 1884, all of the day schools under the control of the Six Nations School Board had teachers trained and qualified from the Mohawk Institute.[65] This was relatively uncommon; at other reserve day schools in Canada, the teachers were "with rare exceptions untrained."[66] Both the New England Company, who ran the Mohawk Institute, and the chiefs, however, were concerned that the quality of the teaching was inadequate, and surmised that action needed to be taken. Over time, the school board began to require all teachers to have a Normal School Certificate (the provincial standard), and by 1923 every teacher in Grand River had one.[67] Mohawk Institute students, particularly girls, spent time working as assistants and teachers at the school after graduation to gain experience before going to teach at a day school or another residential school. For example, Mildred Thomas (later Mrs. Franklin Lickers) attended the Mohawk Institute and after graduation taught there for two years.[68]

There were implications for teachers who were trained at the Mohawk Institute. If they still spoke their Indigenous language on entering the school, it is likely that they lost some of their language skills over their time there, as English was the language of instruction and children could be punished for speaking their own language. Students of the institute also experienced a particular type of upbringing, removed from their family, separated from students of the opposite gender, and taught that their traditional culture had little value. With the advent of Western schools (both the day schools and the residential school), the pattern of the community raising the child, and of women educating the young, was broken. Not all teachers at Six Nations were from the Mohawk Institute, and not all students at the institute were from the Six Nations (in the twentieth century, most were not). Many came from other First Nations communities in Ontario, and some of these students, too, became teachers. However, it is important to consider how the school affected the students who then became teachers. Those who spent much of their youth at the institute likely lost some or most of their connections to Haudenosaunee culture.

The Mohawk Institute in the Twentieth Century

Children who attended the Mohawk Institute in the early twentieth century would have experienced a similar sort of residential school experience as children in other such schools in Canada, one that was likely marked by hunger, sorrow, hard work, and sometimes by abuse. The school used a half-day system, in which children attended school for half the day and did chores and "instructive labour" for the other half. This fit the goal of training students to be productive and self-sufficient adults after graduation; it also meant free labour for the school. One former student suggested that "they had built-in servants" in the students, made necessary at least in part because of the inadequate funding provided to residential schools by the DIA.[69] While the curriculum boys and girls learned was the same, children received gender-specific training to prepare them for their future role either as mothers and homemakers, or husbands, fathers, and farmers, again as was common in the broader North American world.[70] Indigenous girls studied domestic science and clerical skills to help them get jobs in these areas, as well as in teaching and later in nursing. At times, boys learned carpentry and other manual training, but because boys usually stayed in school for a shorter period, they received less schooling; girls typically received more schooling and acquired more useful and marketable skills. Especially in the interwar period, senior girls were sometimes taught stenography, typing, and telegraphy in the hope that they would be prepared for business college and clerical jobs after they graduated. During that time, principal Alice Boyce worked to secure funding for girls who wanted to attend business college. This type of work was considered appropriate by the DIA and by some Indigenous women themselves. More than a few graduates were able to go on to clerical and administrative jobs after leaving the school.[71] While the Mohawk Institute went up to grade eight, some staff at the school did work to help students prepare for the high school entrance exam, just as teachers at the local day schools did. Children who passed the exam could attend high school in Brantford or Caledonia. Teenagers sometimes boarded with families in those non-Indigenous towns, and sometimes with Indigenous families. Some teenagers boarded at the Mohawk Institute while they attended Brantford Collegiate, including graduates of the institute itself. Long-time teacher Susan Hardie (1867–1961), a Mohawk woman and former student herself, was known for her work in preparing children for the test and helping students achieve their higher education goals.[72]

Religion was a more important part of the curriculum at the Mohawk Institute than it was at the day schools. Children participated in prayers as part of the daily routine; there were also weekly visits to the Mohawk Chapel for church services and Sunday school, and the children participated in the Christian sacraments. Children were segregated by sex, with most of their activities and living spaces divided between boys and girls. They sat on separate sides of the classroom, slept in separate dormitories, and played in separate schoolyards. One Mohawk Institute student in the 1910s remembered how "the girls played with the girls over here, and the boys played with the boys. The only time you might say we mixed together was when we went into church, because there wasn't enough seats and we had to mix. But even our dining rooms – our dining room was here – the boys' dining room over there."[73] This segregation often kept siblings apart, a devastating arrangement that had a negative impact on sibling relationships.

Another important point is that the Mohawk Institute was a militarized environment, especially during the first decades of the twentieth century. The children were meant to learn obedience, discipline, and order. A cadet corps was formed at the institute in 1895 and, in March 1907, it was formalized as the Royal Canadian Army Cadet Corps No. 161.[74] They did well in competitions, and many of the Mohawk Institute boys who were cadets went on to enlist in the First World War. This military training, combined with their historic alliance with the Crown and their learning about British and Canadian history in reserve schools, led to the high enlistment rates of Six Nations men in the Great War, and in later wars.

It is important to note that children, parents, and community leaders protested the ill treatment of children and the poor conditions at the Mohawk Institute and tried to effect change. Children frequently ran away from the school; most often, they were brought back and punished. Several boys burned down the school building in 1903 and, after confessing, were sent to the Mimico Industrial School for several years, and the oldest boy, aged sixteen, was sent to the Kingston Penitentiary.[75] Many parents wrote letters of complaint to the DIA about the treatment of their children, and other community members wrote letters to national newspapers to try to draw attention to the conditions at the institute. In 1913, several girls ran away and, on being caught, were punished with beatings, short haircuts, and solitary confinement. They ran away again, and this time, the father of two of the girls sued principal Nelles Ashton in Brantford's High Court. After a day-long trial, the student who had been most severely punished, Ruth Miller, was awarded $400.[76] This was an extraordinary case, but it is clear that while children were victims of abuse, violence, and poor living conditions, they did not lack agency and used their voices where they could to try to improve their situations.

While there was likely abuse at the Mohawk Institute throughout its history, evidence and reporting of abuse is much higher in the postwar period. The National Centre for Truth and Reconciliation's narrative on the school describes multiple incidences of physical and sexual abuse in the twentieth century, and of course, many more cases likely went unreported.[77] There are many more complaints about abuse related to Rev. John Zimmerman's tenure as principal from 1945 to the school's closing in 1970. As at other such schools, the experience of individual children depended largely on the staff and teachers; some (a minority) formed positive relationships with their students and encouraged them in their education and careers, but many others were incompetent, intolerant, violent, and abusive. The TRC's recent report, *They Came for the Children: Canada, Aboriginal Peoples, and Residential Schools*, argues that "the individual student's ability to succeed within the residential school system, and the positive difference that individual teachers and school staff made in some students' lives, are important parts of the history and legacy of the schools and deserve recognition."[78] Despite the mental, emotional, physical, and sexual abuse endured by children, a significant number of Mohawk Institute survivors were able to go on to pursue further education, become leaders in their own communities, and enjoy successful lives. Yet tragically, others never escaped the traumas of their time in these institutions. Experiences of children varied, depending on the staff, funding, and numerous other factors. It seems that during the 1920s, and with Alice Boyce as principal and then lady principal, for instance, conditions were somewhat better for students, compared to after the Second World War, when they were much harsher. Regardless, damaging cultural disruption occurred for all children who were educated in the residential school.

Conclusion

This chapter has aimed to show that the history of education at the Six Nations of Grand River reserve was not simple, straightforward, uniform, or uncomplicated. Instead, because of a variety of factors, the situation was very complex. When they came to the lands that became Ontario, the Six Nations brought with them both a tradition of Haudenosaunee education by the community, as well as newer traditions of Christian missionary schooling they had adopted in New York. There were a variety of perspectives on the value of Christian schooling, with some leaders supporting the establishment of missionary schools on the reserve, and others wishing to maintain traditional forms of education and rejecting the idea of Western schools.

Six Nations people themselves were very much involved in the education of children in their own community, especially in the important role of teacher. While the community did not have control over the schools (either the residential school or the day schools), their work at the front of the classroom had an impact on the children, whom they taught in a variety of ways. Teachers in the day schools were able to pass on some knowledge and traditions – which would not have been possible with non-Indigenous teachers at the front of the room – and they provided students with an example of a career that children from the community could aspire to. Haudenosaunee teachers in the day schools and, to a certain extent, the residential school also educated children and prepared them for high school, and for some, for higher education. For instance, long-time teacher Susan Hardie was generally considered a successful teacher and role model by the school and community. She took great pride in the fact that all the students she had trained for the high school entrance exam passed and went on to attend high school.[79] The community boasts a high number of members who built significant careers as leaders, educators, authors, nurses, doctors, lawyers, and business people, and this success has been in spite of the damaging effects of the colonial education system, a system intent on destroying the languages, religion, and culture of the Haudenosaunee people.[80] The Six Nations of the Grand River are still today a community with a strong sense of their culture, history, and tradition.

QUESTIONS FOR CONSIDERATION:

1. Describe some Indigenous people's learning prior to the introduction of Western systems of education.
2. Who were some of the early teachers at the day schools described by Norman? Why were they important?

3. Describe the early twentieth-century experiences for Indigenous students attending school.
4. What was the Mohawk Institute? Why was it important?
5. How did some people resist and contest practices and policies at the Mohawk Institute?
6. Discuss Norman's use of sources written by Six Nations people. What do these sources contribute to the chapter?

NOTES

1 The term "Haudenosaunee" refers to people who belong to a confederacy of nations; in the past they were referred to as the Iroquois, or the Iroquois Confederacy. "Haudenosaunee" means "the people of the longhouse" – this was the type of housing they lived in, which set them apart from their other Indigenous neighbours, like the Anishnaabe. The longhouse is also a metaphor for the political confederacy that unites the nations within it.

2 J.R. Miller, *Shingwauk's Vision: A History of Native Residential Schools* (Toronto: University of Toronto Press, 1996); John S. Milloy, *A National Crime: The Canadian Government and the Residential School System, 1879–1896* (Winnipeg: University of Manitoba Press, 1999). Milloy's book built on the research of the Royal Commission on Aboriginal Peoples (1996) which examined multiple issues related to Indigenous people in Canada and included a section on the history and impact of residential schools. See Canada, *The Report of the Royal Commission on Aboriginal Peoples*, 1996.

3 Truth and Reconciliation Commission of Canada (hereafter TRC), *Canada's Residential Schools: The History*, pt. 1: *Origins to 1939*; pt. 2: *1939 to 2000* (Montreal and Kingston: McGill-Queen's University Press, 2015). See also Brian Gettler, "Historical Research at the Truth and Reconciliation Commission of Canada," *Canadian Historical Review* 98, no. 4 (2017): 641–74.

4 I have discussed the issue of food and hunger at the Mohawk Institute in Norman, "'Our strength comes from the land': The Hybrid Culinary Traditions of the Six Nations of Grand River," *Cuizine: The Journal of Canadian Food Cultures* 6, no. 2 (Fall) 2015. http://cuizine.mcgill.ca.

5 "For the record: Justice Murray Sinclair on residential schools," *Maclean's*, 2 June 2015. https://www.macleans.ca/politics/for-the-record-justice-murray-sinclair-on-residential-schools.

6 Eileen Antone, "The Educational History of the Onyote'a:ka Nation of the Thames," *Ontario History* 85 (December 1993): 309–20; Jean Barman, "Revisiting the Histories of Indigenous Schooling and Literacies, *Historical Studies in Education* (Spring 2017), 29, no. 1; Sean Carleton, "Settler Anxiety and State Support for Missionary Schooling in Colonial British Columbia, 1849–1871," *Historical Studies in Education/Revue d'histoire De l'éducation* 29, no. 1: 57–76; Ken Coates, "A Very Imperfect Means of Education: Indian Day Schools in the Yukon Territory," in *Indian Education in Canada*, vol. 1: *The Legacy*, ed. Jean Barman, Yvonne Hébert, and Don McCaskill (Vancouver: UBC Press, 1986), 132–49; Susan Elaine Dueck, "Methodist Indian Day Schools and Indian Communities in Northern Manitoba, 1890–1925," *Manitoba History* 30 (1995): 2–16; T. Fleming, L. Smith, and H. Raptis, "An Accidental Teacher: Anthony Walsh and the Aboriginal Day Schools at Six Mile Creek and Inkameep, British Columbia, 1929–1942," *Historical Studies in Education* 19, no. 1 (Spring 2007): 1–24; Crystal Fraser, "T'aih k'ìighe' tth'aih zhit dìidìch'ùh (By Strength, We Are Still Here): Indigenous Northerners Confronting Hierarchies of Power at Day and Residential Schools in Nanhkak Thak (the Inuvik Region, Northwest Territories), 1959–1982,"

PhD diss., University of Alberta, 2019; W.D. Hamilton, *Federal Indian Day Schools in the Maritimes* (Fredericton: University of New Brunswick Press, 1986); Brittany Luby and Kathryn Labelle, "Cooperative Education at the Day School on Dalles 38C Indian Reserve, 1890–1910," *Ontario History* 107, no. 1 (Spring 2015): 88–110; Hope MacLean, "A Positive Experiment in Aboriginal Education: The Methodist Ojibwa Day Schools in Upper Canada, 1824–1833," *Canadian Journal of Native Studies* 22, no. 1 (2002): 23–63; Alison Norman, "'Teachers amongst their own people': Kanyen'kehá:Ka (Mohawk) Women Teachers in Nineteenth-Century Tyendinaga and Grand River, Ontario," *Historical Studies in Education/Revue d'histoire De l'éducation* (Spring 2017) 29, no. 1: 32–56; Norman, "'True to my own noble race': Six Nations Women Teachers at Grand River in the Early Twentieth Century," *Ontario History* 107, no. 1 (Spring 2015): 5–34; Thomas Peace, "Borderlands, Primary Sources, and the Longue Durée: Contextualizing Colonial Schooling at Odanak, Lorette, and Kahnawake, 1600–1850," *Historical Studies in Education/Revue d'histoire De l'éducation* 29, no. 1 (Spring 2017): 8–31; Helen Raptis et al., *What We Learned: Two Generations Reflect on Tsimshian Education and the Day Schools* (Vancouver: UBC Press, 2016); Braden Paora Te Hiwi, 2017. "'Unlike their playmates of civilization, the Indian children's recreation must be cultivated and developed': The Administration of Physical Education at Pelican Lake Indian Residential School, 1926–1944," *Historical Studies in Education/Revue d'histoire De l'éducation* 29, no. 1 (2017): 99–118; Martha Walls, "'The teacher that cannot understand their language should not be allowed': Colonialism, Resistance, and Female Mi'kmaw Teachers in New Brunswick Day Schools, 1900–1923," *Journal of the Canadian Historical Association* 22, no. 1 (2011): 35–68.

7 Elizabeth Graham, *The Mush Hole: Life at Two Indian Residential Schools* (Waterloo: Heffle, 1997); Jennifer Pettitte, "From Longhouse to Schoolhouse: The Mohawk Institute, 1834–1970," MA thesis, University of Western Ontario, 1992; National Centre for Truth and Reconciliation, "Mohawk Institute Indian Residential School IAP Narrative" (2013). http://nctr.ca/School%20narratives/EAST/ON/MOHAWK%20INSTITUTE.pdf. See also our forthcoming book, *Behind the Bricks: The Life and Times of the Mohawk Institute, Canada's Longest Running Residential School*, edited by Rick Hill, Alison Norman, Thomas Peace, and Jennifer Pettit (Calgary: University of Calgary Press, forthcoming 2025).

8 This has been an area of my own research. See Alison Norman, "'True to my own noble race': Six Nations Women Teachers at Grand River in the Early Twentieth Century," *Ontario History* 107, no. 1 (Spring 2015): 5–35; Norman, "'Teachers amongst their own people': Kanyen'kehá:ka (Mohawk) Women Teachers in 19th Century Tyendinaga and Grand River, Ontario," *Historical Studies in Education* 29, no. 1 (Spring 2017): 32–56.

9 Julia L. Jamieson, *Echoes of the Past: A History of Education from the Time of the Six Nations Settlement on the Banks of the Grand River in 1784 to 1924*. Brantford: n.p., n.d.

10 See Norman, "True to my own noble race," 22–4.

11 Keith Jamieson, *History of Six Nations Education* (Brantford: Woodland Indian Cultural Educational Centre, 1987).

12 Olive Moses, Doris Henhawk, and Lloyd King, *History of Education on the Six Nations Reserve* (Ohsweken, 1987, n.p.).

13 Interviews have been published in Elizabeth Graham's *The Mush Hole: Life at Two Indian Residential Schools* (Waterloo: Heffle, 1997). See also TRC, *Canada's Residential Schools: The History*, pt. 1: *Origins to 1939*; pt. 2: *1939 to 2000* (Montreal and Kingston: McGill–Queen's University Press, 2015). The Woodland Cultural Centre Library also holds interviews done with survivors.

14 The Great Law of Peace was given to the Haudenosaunee by the prophet many centuries ago, at the time the confederacy was created. It is the basis of the Haudenosaunee political structure as well as the guiding text for how people should live within the community. See Kayanesenh Paul Williams, *Kayanerenkó:wa: The Great Law of Peace*. (Winnipeg: University of Manitoba Press, 2018).

15 Jamieson, *History of Six Nations Education*, 3.

16 Jan Noel, "Power Mothering: The Haudenosaunee Model," in *Until Our Hearts Are on the Ground: Aboriginal Mothering, Oppression, Resistance, and Rebirth*, ed. D. Memee Lavell-Harvard and Jeannette Corbiere Lavell (Toronto: Demeter Press, 2006), 80–1.

17 Noel, "Power Mothering."

18 Barbara Graymont, "Thayendanegea," in *Dictionary of Canadian Biography*, vol. 5, (University of Toronto/Université Laval, 2003–). http://www.biographi.ca/en/bio/thayendanegea_5E.html.

19 See work being done by Thomas Peace on Indigenous education in the St. Lawrence Valley and the northeastern United States: "Dartmouth College and Canada: The Problem of National Historiographies," 14 March 2016, https://earlycanadianhistory.ca/2016/03/14/dartmouth-college-and-canada-the-problem-of-national-historiographies; and "Borderlands, Primary Sources, and the Longue Durée: Contextualizing Colonial Schooling at Odanak, Lorette, and Kahnawake, 1600–1850" *Historical Studies in Education* 29, no. 1 (Spring 2017): 8–31.

20 Charles M. Johnston, *The Valley of the Six Nations: A Collection of Documents on the Indian Lands of the Grand River* (Toronto: Champlain Society for the Government of Ontario, by the University of Toronto, 1964), 170; Elizabeth Elbourne, "Managing Alliance, Negotiating Christianity: Haudenosaunee Uses of Anglicanism in Northeastern North America, 1760s–1800s," in *Mixed Blessings: Indigenous Encounters with Christianity in Canada*, ed. Tolly Bradford and Chelsea Horton (Vancouver: UBC Press, 2016): 38–60.

21 See Elbourne, "Managing Alliance." On Brant himself, see Harvey Chalmers and Ethel Brant Monture, *Joseph Brant, Mohawk* (East Lansing: Michigan State University Press, 1955); and Isabel Thompson Kelsay, *Joseph Brant, 1743–1807, Man of Two Worlds*, (Syracuse: Syracuse University Press, 1984).

22 Frederick Reville, *The History of the County of Brant* (Brantford: Hurley Print Co., 1920), 37.

23 W. Barry Hill, *The Chapel's Place in Six Nations History, 1710–2016* (Brantford: 2016, n.p.).

24 At one point, an apparently inexperienced Indigenous man was hired to teach, "for want of a white teacher," but according to missionary Robert Lugger, he was soon dismissed, and the school ceased to function for a period. Johnston, *The Valley of the Six Nations*, lxxxv.

25 Sir John Winnifrith, Robert Murray Collins, and Gerald Anthony Charrington, *The New England Company, 1870–1992: A Charity for the Propagation of the Gospel in New England and the Parts Adjacent to America* (Colchester: New England Company, 1993), 11.

26 Winnifrith, Collins, and Charrington, *The New England Company*, 15. Four or five teachers were employed at Grand River in these years, generally non-Indigenous men and women.

27 The Six Nations Council, comprised of hereditary chiefs, controlled the Thomas School. By contrast, the Six Nations School Board, consisting of the Indian Agent, missionaries, and chiefs, was funded by the Indian Department.

28 Norman, "'Teachers amongst their own people,'" 39.

29 Norman, "'Teachers amongst their own people,'" 44.

30 Norman, "'Teachers amongst their own people,'" 47.

31 Moses, Henhawk, and King, *History of Education on the Six Nations Reserve*, 2.

32 In a memorandum written after the board was dissolved by the Department of Indian Affairs, the Deputy Superintendent General noted that "there is not a school board at any other reserve in Canada." 29 June 1936, 3. Six Nations School Board, 1936. RG 10, vol. 2012, file 782-4B.

33 The missionaries were moved from the board in 1921, after a motion from the Six Nations Council that was approved by the Department of Indian Affairs. Moses, Henhawk, and King, *History of Education on the Six Nations Reserve*, 12.

34 Letter from Deputy Superintendent General to the Superintendent General, 22 August 1936. LAC, Indian Affairs, RG 10, vol. 2012, file 7825-4B, page 2.

35 Jamieson, *Echoes of the Past*, 15.

36 Jamieson, *Echoes of the Past*, 13.

37 Moses, Henhawk, and King, *History of Education on the Six Nations Reserve*, 51–2.

38 R.D. Gidney and W.P.J. Millar, *How Schools Worked: Public Education in English Canada, 1900–1940* (Montreal and Kingston: McGill–Queen's University Press, 2012), 277.

39 Minutes of the Meeting, 16 December 1915. LAC, RG 10, vol. 2010, file 7825-3, Six Nations Reserve – Minutes of the School Board, 1908-1913.

40 See Norman, "'True to my own noble race.'"

41 The University Women's Club of Brantford, "Emily General: Six Nations Teacher, Activist," 113.

42 See Norman, "'True to my own noble race,'" 22–6.

43 "Miss Nora Jamieson, interviewed by Joanne McNaughton Linda Hunks and Jim Hill." 1977. Six Nations Education File, Woodland Cultural Centre Library. Jamieson began teaching at No. 5 in the fall of 1938 and stayed at the school for five years.

44 Nora's last comment in the interview was this: "Had Indians been educated earlier, the Federal and Provincial Government would not be having the problems they have today, especially in the matter of land settlement, now that the Indians are able to read and understand the treaties that were made in the past." Ibid, 16.

45 "The Honour Roll of the Mohawk Institute, Brantford, Ontario, Canada, in the Great War" (The Woodland Cultural Centre); Douglas F. Reville, *History of the County of Brant*, vol. 2, Brantford: Brant Historical Society, The Hurley Printing Company, Limited, 1920), 616.

46 *Public School Courses of Study, Duties of Teachers and Pupils. For the use of the Teachers-in-Training in the Faculties of Education and the Normal and Model Schools of Ontario* (Toronto: Legislative Assembly of Ontario, 1909).

47 And in fact, historically the Longhouse people at Grand River looked down on the morality of the Christian converts, as Susan Hill discusses in *The Clay We Are Made Of: Haudenosaunee Land Tenure on the Grand River* (Winnipeg: University of Manitoba Press, 2017), 172.

48 Moses, Henhawk, and King, *History of Education on the Six Nations Reserve*, 57.

49 TRC, *Canada's Residential Schools: The History*, pt. 1: *Origins to* 1939, 63.

50 "The Mohawk Institute – Brantford, ON," Anglican Church of Canada. https://www.anglican.ca/tr/histories/mohawk-institute.

51 Six Nations Council Minutes, 1844. LAC, RG 10, vol. 144, pages 286–300 [83269-83287]).

52 Graham, *The Mush Hole*, 9.

53 For 1900, see "Report of Six Nations school Board" and Report from R. Ashton, 13 August 1900, both in the Dominion of Canada Annual Report of the Department of Indian Affairs for the year ended 30 June 1900 (Ottawa: Queen's Printer, 1901). For 1920, see the "Statement of Indian Day Schools in the Dominion (from which returns have been received) for the Fiscal Year ending March 31, 1920" and "Statement of Indian Industrial Schools in the Dominion" in the Annual Report of the Department of Indian Affairs for the year ended March 31, 1920 (Ottawa: King's Printer, 1921).

54 "The Mohawk Institute – Brantford, ON," Anglican Church of Canada. https://www.anglican.ca/tr/histories/mohawk-institute.

55 Graham, *The Mush Hole*, 17.

56 Jamieson, *History of Six Nations Education*, 7.

57 Graham, *The Mush Hole*, 64.

58 *Six Years' Summary of the Proceedings of the New England Company for the Civilization and Conversion of Indians, Blacks, and Pagans in the Dominion of Canada and the West Indies, 1873–1878* (London: Gilbert and Rivington, 1879), 136.

59 Jamieson, *Echoes of the Past*, 12. In the 1885 Kelly Report by the Brant County School Inspector, the school was referred to as the "Mohawk Institution and Indian Normal School." Graham, *The Mush Hole*, 84.

60 Alison Norman, "The Indian Normal School: The Role of the Mohawk Institute in the Training of Indigenous Teachers in the Late 19th Century," in *Behind the Bricks: The Life and Times of the Mohawk Institute, Canada's Longest Running Residential School*, edited by Rick Hill, Alison Norman, Thomas Peace, and Jennifer Pettit (Calgary: University of Calgary Press, forthcoming 2025). See also Norman, "'An excellent young Indian': Isaac Bearfoot and the Education of the Six Nations of Grand River," paper presented at The House that Isaac Built: The Architecture of Cultures and Identities in Canada, Huron University College, London, Ontario, 13–15 May 2013. His name is spelled both Barefoot and Bearfoot, but in his own writings, he used the Bearfoot spelling.

61 Russell T. Ferrier, "History of the Mohawk Institute, Successful Graduates." LAC, RG 10, vol. 6200, file 466-1, pt. 2.

62 Paul Axelrod, *The Promise of Schooling: Education in Canada, 1800–1914* (Toronto: University of Toronto Press, 1997), 50. See also Alison Prentice, "The Feminization of Teaching in British North America and Canada, 1845–1875," *Histoire social/Social History* 8 (1975): 5–15.

63 Abate Wori Abate, *Iroquois Control of Iroquois Education: A Case Study of the Iroquois of the Grand River Valley in Ontario, Canada* (PhD diss., University of Toronto, 1984), 137.

64 Jamieson, *Echoes of the Past*, 5. Jamieson herself taught at the Thomas School, as did George E. Bomberry. The last teacher there was John Miller from Onondaga, who spent more than twenty-five years there.

65 Abate, *Iroquois Control of Iroquois Education*.

66 Jean Barman, "Schooled for Inequality: The Education of British Columbia Aboriginal Children," in *Children, Teachers, and Schools in the History of British Columbia*, ed. Jean Barman, Neil Sutherland, and J.D. Wilson (Calgary: Detselig, 1995), 65.

67 Jamieson, *Echoes of the Past*, 19.

68 Interview with Gladys Lickers Hill, about her parents, Mildred Thomas and Franklin Lickers, file 17, box 471, accession 89/55, Sally Weaver Collection, Canadian Museum of History.

69 Interview with Marjorie Groat (née Smith); Graham, *The Mush Hole*, 363.

70 Additional information about the education that boys received can be found in Alison Norman, "Race, Gender, and Colonialism: Public Life among the Six Nations of Grand River, 1899–1939," PhD thesis, University of Toronto, 2010, in chapter 2, esp. 125–30.

71 See Norman, "Race, Gender, and Colonialism," 122–5.

72 See Norman, "'True to my own noble race," 17–22.

73 Interview with Martha Hill, resident at the Institute from 1912 to 1918. Graham, *The Mush Hole*, 355.

74 Report on the Mohawk Institute and Six Nations Boarding Schools by Martin Benson, 1895. LAC, RG 10, vol. 2006, file 7825-1A; Army Cadet League of Canada History and Heritage Committee, "The Official History Website of the Royal Canadian Army Cadets," http://www.armycadethistory.com.

75 Graham, *The Mush Hole*, 102–4.

76 "Damages for Plaintiff in Miller vs Ashton Case – Girls Too Severely Punished," *Brantford Expositor*, 1 April 1914.

77 National Centre for Truth and Reconciliation, “Mohawk Institute Indian Residential School IAP Narrative” (2013). http://nctr.ca/School%20narratives/EAST/ON/MOHAWK%20INSTITUTE.pdf, 13–14.

78 TRC, *They Came for the Children: Canada, Aboriginal Peoples and Residential Schools*, Winnipeg, 2012. http://www.myrobust.com/websites/trcinstitution/File/2039_T&R_eng_web[1].pdf.

79 See Norman, “‘True to my own noble race,’ 18.

80 For example, the “Indian Hall of Fame,” an Indigenous initiative set up during the Canadian National Exhibition beginning in the 1960s, featured many high-achieving citizens of Six Nations: Joseph Brant, Dr. Peter Martin (Oronhyatekha), Elmer Jamieson, Pauline Jamieson, Cameron D. Brant, Oliver Milton Martin, Dr. Gilbert C. Monture, Tom Longboat, and Ethel Brant Monture.

CHAPTER SIX

"I just felt like I belonged to them": Women's Industrial Softball, London, Ontario, 1923–35

CARLY ADAMS[1]

By the mid-1920s, company-sponsored sport leagues for women were well established in Canadian cities such as London, Ontario, Canada. As both an act of welfarism and convenient brand-identification advertising, London companies such as Kellogg's, Silverwood Dairy, Smallman & Ingram, and Gorman Eckerts sponsored, and in some cases organized, women's industrial softball teams for workers from 1923 until 1935. As a part of corporate welfarism, employers viewed team sports as activities that would encourage and develop a sense of co-operation, team spirit, and loyalty among employees – characteristics that employers hoped would transfer to the production line. From the narratives of three women who worked and played for various London companies, I consider the constructions of meaning that shape our understanding of the leisure time pursuits of working women in the city and the meaning it has for them decades later. The narratives and industrial sport experiences of these three women suggest that gender hierarchies and competing (sometimes conflicting) loyalties were at the foundation of how they negotiated belonging to company sports teams, related work and educational opportunities, and the eventual changes in their recreation practices that came with marriage and childbirth.

During the 1920s, record numbers of Canadian women, predominantly those aged fifteen to thirty-four, were moving to cities and taking up paid work in the labour force.[2] Most of these women were single, filling positions in the growing clerical and service-oriented job market, and were supporting themselves or contributing to a family wage.[3] Coinciding with this increase of women in the workforce was a growing concern for employee welfare, especially as it affected productivity. Among the programs that were adopted, leisure-time activities such as sport and recreation emerged as important parts of companies' efforts to increase employee welfare and by extension employee productivity, with a focus on fostering loyalty and discouraging unionism. Historian Elizabeth Fones-Wolf suggests, "Manufacturers hoped that recreation . . . might offset the monotony of factory work."[4] Sponsoring women's teams specifically was a brilliant public relations tool. Historian Lynne Emery suggests it was about positive product identification: "Identifying a product with a women's team was excellent advertising and projected a clean, caring image."[5] By the mid-1920s, company-sponsored sport leagues for women were well established in Canadian cities such as London, Ontario. As both an act of welfarism and convenient brand-identification advertising, London companies such as Kellogg's, Silverwood Dairy, Smallman & Ingram, and Gorman Eckerts sponsored, and in some cases organized, women's industrial softball teams for workers from 1923 until 1935. This was a part of corporate welfarism: employers viewed team sports as activities that would encourage and develop a sense of cooperation, team spirit, and loyalty among employees – characteristics that employers hoped would transfer to the production line.

Most studies of industrial recreation as corporate welfarism look at recreation through the lens of services provided and company policies and not from the perspective of the employees and participants.[6] One notable exception is historian Joan Sangster's study of industrial paternalism at Westclox, a clock factory in Peterborough, Ontario, from 1923 to 1960. Sangster argues that "women's own memories of work at Westclox illuminate the way in which workers understood, utilized, negotiated, and repudiated paternalism."[7] Reinforcing the importance of women's experience, this chapter explores women's paid work and recreational opportunities in the context of corporate welfarism through a case study of industrial softball in London, Ontario. From the narratives of three women who worked and played for various London companies, I consider the constructions of meaning that shape our understanding of the leisure time pursuits of working women in the city and the meaning it has for them decades later.[8] Women's memories of their experiences playing softball during this era illuminate the way these athletes understood and negotiated sport and work and the associated familial and social tensions. An exploration of the ways meaning was, and is, constructed by and through women's sport experiences suggests that the industrial diamond was a space where the physical skills and abilities of women were practised, developed, and celebrated. However, this case study of women's industrial sport in London, Ontario, also suggests that how women negotiated paternalistic practices, and how they made sense of them as part of corporate welfarism, is central to the choices they made and their experiences.

By focusing on these three women, my intent is not to privilege their "voices" over those of the other women who participated on industrial sport teams during this era; rather my intent is to expand further our understanding of women's industrial softball experiences from the perspective of the women themselves. As historian Paul Thompson explains, oral narratives serve as a link between the personal experiences of the athlete and the wider social history of which she was a part.[9] The narratives and industrial sport experiences of these three women suggest that gender hierarchies and competing (sometimes conflicting) loyalties were at the foundation of how they negotiated belonging to company sports teams, related work and educational opportunities, and the eventual changes in their recreation practices that came with marriage and childbirth.

Women's Industrial Softball in London

By the 1920s, London, Ontario, was taking the form of a modern city. Surrounded by thriving agricultural land and with a growing population that had reached 69,742 by 1929, London was the commercial centre of southwestern Ontario. [10] Manufacturers were increasingly interested in capturing a spot in this growing commercial landscape. For example, W.K. Kellogg, the founder of the US-based Kellogg Company, established the company's first plant outside of the US in London, Ontario, in 1924. By the 1920s, employee welfare was becoming an important part of that company's business plan as it sought ways to increase productivity and maintain employee loyalty.

Defined as "any service provided for the comfort or improvement of employees which was neither a necessity of the industry nor required by law," corporate welfarism in the 1920s included many practical initiatives, from a library within the factory, or a picnic area or softball diamond outside, to medical facilities and comprehensive insurance in the event of disability or death.[11] Sangster suggests that historians "have explored the way in which an employer, playing a visible role on the factory premises, tried to create the feeling of an 'organic community,' often by equating the factory with an actual or imagined family."[12] By offering employees something more than a wage for their labour, employers hoped to create a sense of family, belonging, and community among workers as a way of encouraging loyalty and discouraging unionism and strife. Historian Monys Ann Hagen found that employers in the US repeatedly cited decreased employee turnover and strengthened company loyalty as two of the main advantages of company-sponsored recreation programs.[13]

Concern with employee welfare was not new during the interwar period. Historian Margaret McCallum suggests that by the 1920s corporate welfarism was a "curious amalgam of the old and the new."[14] A 1927 Ontario government study investigating the physical, recreational, and financial benefits offered by companies revealed that "many companies offered cheaper benefits like recreation and cafeterias, while fewer offered more costly employer-paid vacations, sickness insurance, pension plans and so on."[15] Most companies in London offered less expensive but highly visible benefits such as picnic areas and industrial softball teams. For example, similar to other companies in London, the Kellogg Canada manufacturing plant – as an extension of its parent plant in Battle Creek, Michigan – was committed to the welfare of its employees as a means of increasing productivity and employee loyalty. Providing opportunities for recreation outside of business hours as a means of better living and, by extension, better working conditions was an important part of the company's corporate welfare philosophy.[16] In London, Kellogg sponsored a team in the YWCA Girls' Softball League from 1925 until 1929 and in the Major Intercity Girls' Softball League from 1930 until 1934. Similarly, Silverwood Dairy supported employee welfare initiatives such as company picnics and softball teams.[17] Silverwood sponsored women's softball teams from 1927 until 1935.

As early as 1922, the *London Free Press* was reporting briefly on women's exhibition games between company-sponsored teams such as Smallman and Ingram and Woolworths.[18] In August 1923, the *Free Press* reported on a softball tournament in Woodstock involving nine teams from London, Brantford, and Oxford County. Community teams such as Dunn's Corner and the Stratford Rattans joined company-sponsored teams such as McCormick's Molly-O's to compete in what the *Free Press* labelled "one of the most successful girls' softball tournaments ever held in Western Ontario."[19] That same year, the *Free Press* offered sporadic coverage of the London YWCA Girls' Softball League, which had at least three teams: the London Brownies, Smallman & Ingram Thistles, and Woolworths.[20] By 1924, organized softball was thriving in the city, with two leagues and eighteen teams.[21] The Manufacturing and Intercity Leagues were comprised solely of industry-sponsored teams; the YWCA league included church, business, and educational teams as well.[22] The number of teams and the news coverage of women's softball in the pages of the *Free Press* during the 1920s suggests that by this time, softball for girls and women was popular in London, industrial sponsorship was widespread, and women's softball was a serious competitive sport in the city.

News reports also indicate that international exhibition games between London and US industrial teams were common practice in the 1920s and 1930s. For example, in July 1924 the Cleveland Favorite Knits played the London Brownies before a reported 5,000 people in Port Stanley as part of Dominion Day celebrations.[23]

Indeed, the Cleveland teams seemed to visit London regularly, perhaps because of a lack of competition at home. [24] In 1929, while in London with his team for an exhibition game, Carl Barth, coach of the Cleveland Barth Gems, was quoted in the *Free Press* as saying, "Canadian girls' softball is superior to that played in the United States." The article went on to suggest: "Lack of competition handicaps the American teams. There are but two clubs in Cleveland and the teams only play once a week."[25] It was also common for teams from London to hold exhibition games against teams from industrial-sponsored leagues in other cities such as Toronto and Hamilton. For example, the Hamilton Zimmerknits and teams from the Toronto Major Girls' Sunnyside League, such as the Supremes and the Patricias, were regular visitors to London.[26]

Until the mid-1930s, the industrial sport leagues in London were controlled by men. Company managers or men appointed by the company organized the teams, recruited players, and operated the leagues.[27] In 1925, the Major Girls' Softball League was run by Honorary President William Gorman (owner of Gorman, Eckert & Co.), President Tom Munro, Vice-President Fred Goulding, Acting Secretary Fred Parsons (replaced by Percy Ferguson in June 1925), Acting Treasurer Charles E. Speiran (manager of Smallman & Ingram Department Store), Frank McCormick (owner of McCormick Manufacturing Company), and Major Gordon Ingram (past president of the London Chamber of Commerce and owner of the Smallman & Ingram Department Store).[28] These were influential London businessmen and city leaders who owned or were involved with the companies for which the women worked.[29] As historian Andrew Holman suggests about women's hockey in the US during the 1920s, male managers and coaches "cultivated and controlled the women's game from top to bottom."[30] During the same period in which other governing bodies for women's sport in Ontario such as the Ladies Ontario Hockey Association and the Women's Amateur Athletic Federation sought to establish organizations run by women for women, industrial softball for women in London was completely under the control of men.[31] Male administrators went so far as to operate the league under the Ontario Amateur Soft Ball Association, the men's provincial governing body, instead of the Ontario Women's Softball Association (OWSA), also established in 1925.[32]

The OWSA from the first had an executive comprised entirely of women. According to historian Bruce Kidd, "the new constitution denied males the right to 'take part' in meetings, though they retained their right to vote."[33] The OWSA, like other organizations of the time, was an organization *for* women run *by* women. Perhaps the decision of the London women's industrial-sponsored softball league to operate under the men's provincial body was not surprising given the male-controlled and male-operated orientation. It was women who played the sport, but for the most part they were not involved in the league's organization. Six years later, in 1931, the *Free Press* reported that the London Intercity Girls' Softball League had affiliated with the newly established Provincial Women's Softball Union, which was formed out of the OWSA.[34] Ann Spalding was elected president of this new governing body, but all the other positions on the executive were held by men.[35] In 1935, the *Free Press* reported that the presidency of the London Intercity Girls' Softball league had been taken over by player Hazel Aiken, marking a shift in organizational control.[36] Incidentally, it was also in that year that industrial softball ceased to operate in the city. With the debilitating economic depression of the 1930s, companies no longer had the financial resources to devote to leisure activities such as the women's industrial softball leagues.[37] Women attempted to take over the organizational aspects of the game, but without financial resources at their disposal, they were unsuccessful.

Hazel Shackleton, Gladys Oliver, and Olive Campbell

The women who played for the industrial teams were often recruited from smaller neighbouring towns – their skills on the field made them attractive prospects for the industrial team scouts – and were offered employment or financial support for educational endeavours in exchange, as was the case with Hazel Shackleton, Gladys Oliver, and Olive Campbell. These women often moved to London and with the help of their employer found places to live near their workplace. Oliver and Shackleton lived in boarding houses near where they worked and played; Oliver remembers paying $7 a week for her own room and board.[38] Campbell lived in the home of Charles Speiran, the manager of Smallman & Ingram.[39]

Before examining their industrial softball stories in more detail, it is important to understand how these three women became involved in sport and the role the men in their lives played. Shackleton, Oliver, and Campbell all credit their interest in softball to men in their lives. Hazel Shackleton was born on 6 August 1911 on her family's farm near the village of Lyons, Ontario (near Aylmer). The daughter of George Lorne Shackleton and Margaret Mae Abbott, Hazel grew up in a family of ten children – six boys and four girls – a family that had to milk cows, wash milk barrels and milk cans, and care for the horses as part of the farm's daily operations. In addition to running a dairy and horse farm, the Shackletons operated a country store that offered a variety of essential supplies such as food, clothing, and household items. Shackleton learned to play ball from her brothers, who organized informal games on the nearby fields. She recalls, "We skated and we played ball. We made our own softballs. We didn't have money to buy softballs. We took stuff and sewed and kneaded."[40]

Gladys Oliver was born on 2 February 1911. Part of a family of six children, three girls and three boys, Oliver grew up on a 175-acre dairy farm near Beachville, Ontario. She recalls her love of working on the farm alongside her father: "There was plenty of work. I worked outside. I was my Dad's companion. His right hand man." Like Shackleton, Oliver credits her interest in softball to a man in her life: "My Dad was my biggest supporter all my life, through all the games I ever played."[41] Oliver began playing softball with the Dunn's Corner team in 1922, when she was eleven years old. She recalls that although there was not a league, the teams played in regular tournaments and in exhibition matches against neighbouring towns such as Drury.

Olive Campbell was born on 8 April 1913, in Alvinston, Ontario, in Brook Township. She was raised by her mother after her father passed away, the victim of a farming accident when Campbell was a child. Campbell was born on the family farm and then moved with her mother to Alvinston when, for financial reasons, they were forced to sell the farm. Campbell learned to play ball from her high school principal and coach Carmen Powell at Alvinston High School. Noting her potential, Powell taught Campbell to pitch.[42]

Having joined industrial sport teams in the 1920s, Shackleton, Oliver, and Campbell had to deal with the related tensions and challenges. For some, that meant changing or ceasing altogether their recreation practices because of marriage or childbirth. This investigation of three women's remembrances of industrial recreation highlights the life choices the women made as they negotiated paternalistic practices and gender hierarchies, both familial and work-related.

Recruitment to a Company-Sponsored Team

By the mid-1920s, companies in London were beginning to recruit and hire women specifically for their athletic skills, among them Shackleton, Oliver, and Campbell. The companies frequently offered employment or educational support to women who agreed to play.[43] These women's stories suggest that industrial team coaches were often more concerned about the success of the team than about the employment needs of the factory.[44] Obviously, sponsoring a softball team provided companies with visibility and advertising, but employers believed that having the best players would also result in team excellence and city championships. They hoped this excellence would in turn be equated with company and product excellence among local consumers, besides fostering qualities of teamwork, loyalty, and excellence among workers.[45]

Figure 6.1. Silverwood Women's Softball Team, League Champions, 1930. Top (left to right): I. Bates, I. Hudson, H. Shackleton, M. Dodds, L. Horlick, G. Johnson, E. Kennedy, V. Cunningham. Middle left to right: Gord Southcott, Mr. A. E. Silverwood, Mr. H. Gillies, G. Proctor. Bottom left to right: E. Garside, E. Saunders, H. Barclay, D. Gardiner.
Source: Courtesy of Hazel (Shackleton) Ferguson.

In 1926, at the age of fifteen, Hazel Shackleton was recruited to play for the Silverwood Dairy softball team. Figure 6.1 shows the Silverwood 1930s championship team in their uniforms, with shorts, team shirts, long socks to protect their legs, hats, and identical running shoes. Photographs such as this as well as Figure 6.2 (showing the Kellogg's team) suggest that a complete uniform was provided to each woman on the industrial teams. Shackleton recalls the day she was recruited:

> These men came to Dorchester and saw me hit two home runs and Carrie Hunter pitched . . . and they came to school the next day . . . and they knocked on the door and they wanted Carrie and Hazel and they wanted to know if we would play ball in London that night. So my father had a store and my brother was running the store that day. And I got all excited and I said well let's go down to the store, or go to my house to see if my mother and Dad were home. And we went to the home and mother and Dad weren't there. So we went to the store, and Stewart [Shackleton's brother] says ah, well, I'll tell you what I'll do. I will say that she can go tonight but that doesn't

Figure 6.2. Kellogg's Ladies Softball Team, 1930, The *London* (Ontario) *Free Press*, 25 June 1930, p. 14. Gladys Oliver kneels on the far left of the front row.
Source: Courtesy of the *London Free Press* Negative Collection, Regional Collection, the University of Western Ontario, London, Ontario.

> mean she'll ever be able to go again. So we went away to London and practised for the game that night.[46]

Because Shackleton was not employed by Silverwood Dairy, the company offered her paid work if she agreed to play for the team – a practice familiar to other women on industrial teams in London.[47] Similarly, Gladys Oliver was recruited by the Kellogg's team in 1927.[48] In her home in Woodstock, Ontario, Oliver proudly displays a photograph of herself in the Kellogg's uniform (Figure 6.3): a cherished memento of her time playing softball. She recalls playing with other teams, such as St. Thomas, for select tournaments in the late 1920s: "I used to hit home runs and I was a heavy hitter, and that's what they scouted me for."[49] Oliver recalls that Mr. Neilson and Mr. Stanley, the managers of Kellogg's, came to speak to her parents about the job opportunity that came with agreeing to play ball for the Kellogg's team: "They came down and talked to my Dad and mother. They said they had a job that I could go to. To start out I was supposed to work in the office, but at that time it didn't [work out] and he explained working in the factory and at that time it was good money then."[50] It was a tough decision

Figure 6.3. Gladys Oliver, member of the Kellogg's team, 1927–32.
Source: Courtesy of Gladys (Oliver) Porter.

for Oliver to leave the farm in search of paid employment and softball. Referring to her father, she recalls, "He said he lost his right arm. That was the last decision him and I had to make. Did I want to go? The money was enticing." At Kellogg's, Oliver was given a job on a box assembly line. She recalls: "I was on the box maker. I did do a little bookkeeping in the off time but I liked the money in the factory."[51]

Unlike Shackleton and Oliver, who were recruited to play and work in London, Olive Campbell credits her high school principal, Powell, with making this happen for her. The photographs she has of this time in her life (see Figure 6.4) are prominently displayed in her home in St. Jacob's, Ontario. She shares them proudly and relates many stories about how she came to play in London. She recalls that around the time she graduated, Principal Powell arranged a place for her in London playing for the Smallman & Ingram department store: "He said, if I can get you on a ball team in London, which I think you're capable of, would you be willing? And I said yes, 'cause I had no plans for when I was through school."[52] Campbell began playing with the Smallman & Ingram Burroughes Thistles in the summer of 1930.[53]

Figure 6.4. Smallman & Ingram Burroughes Thistles team. Top (left to right): C. Kennedy (coach), G. Gramlick, B. Richards, F. Tilley, M. Meleash, G. Middleholt, C. Speiran (manager). Middle (left to right): E. Middleholt, Olive Campbell, A. Munro, Mary Grassick. Bottom (left to right): P. Tulcit, H. Wade (bat boy), H. Middleholt. 1933.
Source: Courtesy of Olive (Campbell) Mahon.

That companies during this time encouraged team managers and coaches to scout for softball talent in neighbouring villages and towns and to offer employment in the city in exchange for skills on the field suggests that women's softball was taken very seriously at the time. Women's softball was a part of corporate welfare strategies, but it was also convenient brand-identification advertising for the London companies. Shackleton recalls that she was treated really well by the owner of Silverwood Dairy: "Mr. Silverwood would treat us like royalty. He would take us into restaurants and feed us all."[54] She recalls that the team was good advertising for the company. Some companies, like Gorman Eckerts, went so far as to sponsor a team specifically in the name of a product (see Figure 6.5). Named after the governor general's residence in Ottawa, Rideau Hall was a brand of coffee produced by Gorman Eckerts.[55] Gorman Eckerts's Rideau Hall team competed in the Manufacturer's Girls' Softball League Teams from 1924 to 1929, winning the league championship in 1928. It was

Figure 6.5. Gorman Eckerts's Rideau Hall women's softball team, 1929. Left to right: Gord Southcott, Lil Horlick, Hazel Brown, M. Boyer, G. Johnson, Ivey Capsey, Gladys Oliver, M. Blakely, Hazel Shackleton, Gladys Proctor, Elsie Saunders, Dorothy Gardiner, Sadie Watson, Lenore Chappelle. Source: Courtesy of Mary Cammaert.

important for companies to have a winning team. The more successful a team was, the more newspaper coverage and fan support it would receive and, of course, the more advertising a company would receive for its products.

For a young woman, joining an industrial softball team in the 1920s often meant discussing the opportunity and gaining permission from their family. In essence, the women were negotiating the substitution of one paternal figure (father) for another (an employer and/or coach). Choosing to play for a team and move away from home and the security of one's family (and the duties that entailed) was a difficult decision to make. Yet being recruited to play softball also had its advantages. It presented women with an opportunity to continue playing a sport they loved and to receive something in exchange for their physical skills. This exchange often came in the form of employment or, in the case of Olive Campbell, paid tuition to business school.

Family and Company Loyalties

The narratives of Shackleton, Oliver, and Campbell suggest that competing and sometimes conflicting loyalties to family and company were an important part of how they negotiated playing for an industrial team. Hazel Shackleton, for example, recalls that her parents were not eager for her to move to the city at the young age of fifteen. When she was recruited to play for Silverwood Dairy, she was offered a permanent position in the milk bar at the store on King Street in London. As a compromise, alternative arrangements were made for a Silverwood coach or manager to pick Shackleton up for practices and games and return her home at their conclusion – an arrangement that led to a relationship and eventual marriage with one of the drivers, Gord Ferguson (see Figure 6.6). Shackleton worked and played ball for Silverwood Dairy in 1926 and 1927, and again in 1930 and 1931 (see Figure 6.1). In 1928 and 1929 she worked and played for Gorman Eckerts's Rideau Hall (see Figure 6.5).[56] As she got older, Shackleton, with the approval of her parents, made the decision to move to London. She remembers the familial tensions around her brief position at Labatt's Brewery: her parents objected to her working in a brewery. She recalls having to leave her job there at the insistence of her father, who thought she should have a more respectable position:

> So then I'm sitting at the desk one day and my mother and father come into Labatt's and said we're sorry. My father said "Hazel cannot work here because we have a grocery store and we have a church, Baptist church one side and two miles down the road we have our own church, the United church in Harrietsville." So he said, "They're going to ask where's Hazel? And we cannot say working at Labatt's." Because my Dad didn't drink. He was very strict. So I had to leave.[57]

Working in the city was acceptable under certain conditions. In this case, employment at a brewery as a young female violated unofficial familial codes of conduct. With prohibition not officially ending until 1927 in Ontario, many people associated alcohol with spaces and activities such as taverns and gambling, which were considered inappropriate for women.[58]

Gladys Oliver also recalls negotiating familial obligations and tensions. When she moved away from home to work and play ball for Kellogg's, Oliver's life did not revolve solely around work and the leisure pursuits the city offered. Many women enjoyed increased independence living away from home in the city, though they also often had what Sangster calls a "double burden of responsibility."[59] Through their employment they could contribute to their family's livelihood. Oliver, for example,

Figure 6.6. Hazel Shackleton and Gord Ferguson, coach of the Silverwood team.
Source: Courtesy of Hazel (Shackleton) Ferguson.

still maintained close ties to her family, offering financial support through her weekly paycheques and travelling home most weekends to help with farm chores. She recalls:

> Well, I paid board in London, and I bought things for home and helped out. I missed one weekend coming home to Beachville where my Dad and mother lived. But I worked when I got home too. The one woman I was working with . . . she says "Gladys, what do you do when you go home for the weekend?" And I said, "Why I help either outside my Dad driving horses doing whatever I can to help" and she said "you come back here a lot tireder [*sic*] than when you leave." I said "Yeah, I suppose I do."[60]

Having grown up on a farm, Oliver found moving to the city a difficult transition: "I was born and raised in the country. Never lived in the city and that was a transaction [*sic*] for me too. At night I could go home and walk up a street to a store. But lo and behold when I lived at home . . . why I couldn't do that, I was out helping my Dad."[61] Moving to the city forced Oliver to negotiate familial obligations, which meant working for Kellogg's during the week and travelling home on Friday evening to help on the family farm over the weekend. At the same time she provided financial support to her parents, thus playing a more vital role in supporting her family.

Oliver remained loyal to Kellogg's while living and working in London, although this work/sport relationship and her continued loyalty to her employer were tested at times. She had a hard time saying no if the opportunity presented itself to play additional games with other teams in other city leagues. For example, in the early 1930s she played several games for Gorman Eckerts's Rideau Hall (see Figure 6.5) – a decision that caused some controversy among her coaches and employer when it was discovered:

> This was kind of funny. Of course I wasn't told anything at all. But they got in touch with me and wanted to know if I'd come and play a certain night so I [thought I was] going to help a team. I'd go and play ball any place those days. So I went and we won as far as I can remember. And then the next week or so, they wanted me again. And I didn't have a game with Kellogg's, so I thought well they're good to me to come and pick you up and bring you home, give you a good time, feed you if you want anything to eat. So anyway after the second time, I went into work at Kellogg's and Mr. Neilson called me into the office and I got in a lot of [trouble]. He'd been in touch with the manager of this team and told him he could not have me and he told me, he said, "If you go back and play another game with them you're disqualified." I thought it's a ball game, I'll go and play, but that was the wrong thing to do so I couldn't go back and play with them. But they offered me a job in their plant, their spice plant. I could have had one there if I wanted to have left Kellogg's.[62]

Oliver stayed with Kellogg's out of a sense of obligation, because they were the first team to recruit her to play softball in the city. Like many other working women, Oliver felt she owed her employers loyalty since they had provided her with a job opportunity. [63] She reminisces:

> I figured I owed Kellogg's because they came and got me in the first place and I had a good job, I had my boarding house, I was set up and I got home every weekend back to Beachville. So I just felt like I belonged to them. I couldn't see being mean, 'cause I thought it would be mean to leave a team that had treated me as well as they did. So I stayed with Kellogg's.[64]

Similar to Sangster's findings about women at the Westclox factory in Peterborough, Oliver remained a loyal worker and player at Kellogg's despite playing one or two games for Gorman Eckerts.[65]

Olive Campbell did not face as much family tension when she decided to move to London to play ball. She wanted to continue her education after high school, and moving to the city to play softball was the only way she could do this. Her mother, as a single parent, had little financial means and could not pay for Campbell to live in London and go to school. In exchange for agreeing to play for the Smallman & Ingram team, she was offered room and board and tuition to business school. While living in London and playing for the team, Campbell lived in the home of the manager of Smallman & Ingram, Charles Speiran. Reminiscing that "they were determined to keep me for the ball team," she recalls that Speiran covered all of her educational expenses, as well as room and board, in exchange for her performance on the softball field.[66] Unlike Shackleton and Oliver, Campbell did not receive employment in exchange for her skills on the field. Campbell's mother was very supportive of this opportunity for her daughter – one she would not have had otherwise.

Campbell was a loyal player on the Smallman & Ingram Burroughs Thistles softball team. As demonstrated by the company paying her educational expenses, they were determined to keep her. The company continually expressed their satisfaction with her performance as a pitcher, and did so publicly. For example, the company's head office frequently sent telegrams recognizing Campbell's achievements. Referring to a telegram that was sent from the Smallman & Ingram head office in Toronto to the Smallman & Ingram branch in London, Campbell recalls that a message was read over the loudspeaker during a regular season game in London: "Toronto Ont AUG 11-710P Miss Olive Campbell, Care Burroughes Thistles Tecumseh Park London Ont Congratulations on your fine performance in pitching no hit game against St. Thomas last evening. C A Burroughes 730PM" (see Figure 6.7). [67] Public recognition of this sort seemed to be one way a company fostered loyalty among its most successful athletes.

Conclusion

Most working women in the 1920s and 1930s left waged labour when they married or had children.[68] This was also the accepted norm for women playing sports. Marriage and childbirth were prioritized over leisure activities such as softball. For example, Hazel Shackleton met her husband, Gord Ferguson, while playing for the Silverwood softball team – he was one of the coaches (See Figure 6.6).[69] While softball for Shackleton was associated with this positive memory of meeting her husband, marriage also marked the end of her softball experience. Shackleton did not continue playing softball once she got married and moved to Toronto in 1935.

CANADIAN PACIFIC TELEGRAPHS

CANADIAN PACIFIC COMMUNICATIONS

DIRECT COMMUNICATION WITH

THE INTERNATIONAL SYSTEM - POSTAL TELEGRAPH - MACKAY RADIO
COMMERCIAL CABLES - ALL AMERICA CABLES
MONEY TRANSFERRED BY TELEGRAPH

IMPERIAL AND INTERNATIONAL COMMUNICATIONS LIMITED -
IMPERIAL CABLES - BRITISH PACIFIC CABLE
HALIFAX AND BERMUDA CABLE CO.

DL	DAY LET
NL	NIGHT L
NM	NIGHT T
LCO	DEFERRE
NLT	CABLE L
WLT	WEEK E

STANDARD TIME

21RNRO 14

TORONTO ONT AUG 11-710P

MISS OLIVE CAMPBELL

CARE BURROUGHES THISTLES TECUMSEH PARK LONDON ONT

CONGRATULATIONS ON YOUR FINE PERFORMANCE IN PITCHING NO HIT GAME AGAINST ST THOMAS LAST EVENING.

C R BURROUGHES

730PM

Figure 6.7. Canadian Pacific Telegram, c. 1932.
Source: Courtesy of Olive (Campbell) Mahon.

Similarly, Gladys Oliver quit playing ball and working at Kellogg's when she married in 1933. She recalls: "Around Christmas time, we were off for a month and it was then I decided I wasn't going back to Kellogg's, I had other things to do at that time. I worked yeah but not away from the house."[70] Marriage was a life-altering experience for these women. Olive Campbell explains that she lost touch with most of the women she played ball with over time, "We all got married. We did as much as we can. 'cause when you get married and get here and go there, you lose track as time moves on."[71] For these women, giving up sport and giving up the female friendships they had fostered on the baseball diamond in exchange for marriage seemed to be a part of becoming an adult.

With as many as three women's industrial softball leagues operating in London, there were many opportunities for women to play the sport from 1923 until 1935. However, softball programs for women had disappeared altogether in the city by the mid-1930s and were not revived again until 1942, when the London Public Utilities Commission organized a community league for women aged sixteen to twenty-one.[72] For the individuals involved, such as Hazel Shackleton, Gladys Oliver, and Olive Campbell, company-sponsored softball was an important part of their life experience. Sociologists Barbara Laslett and Barrie Thorne suggest that life histories "bring forth 'experience' and 'voice'; they link the personal and the political, the private and the public."[73] Shackleton, Oliver, and Campbell's memories of playing industrial softball during this era illuminate the way they understood and negotiated their recruitment to industrial softball teams, work (education, in Campbell's case), and the related familial and company loyalties and tensions. Gender hierarchies and competing (sometimes conflicting) loyalties were at the foundation of how they negotiated belonging to company sports teams. The employers created a supportive environment – steady work, privileges, and in some cases tuition. The women felt obligated to stay with the company that had hired them and that offered them these opportunities. To some extent these women understood themselves as company commodities. They were hired and "bought" for a specific purpose: to win softball games. This case study of women's industrial sport in London, Ontario, suggests, much like Sangster does, that at the core of the women's experiences were paternalistic practices in the guise of corporate welfarism. But this was only one part of their stories.

Softball for these women meant more than corporate welfarism and family obligation. The stories of Shackleton, Oliver, and Campbell suggest that when negotiating joining a team and navigating the related family and company loyalties, they did not simply let the paternal figures in their lives dictate their sport involvement. They were continually weighing options and figuring out what made sense for them, committing themselves to their team or their family based on their personal values and pleasures. For example, some women continued to play ball after marriage. Campbell played ball in London until she married Thomas Mahon. In their first year of marriage, Mahon, who had difficulty at the time finding a job in his tool and dye trade, sought work in Sudbury with International Nickel, and Campbell moved there with her husband. Not ready to give up something she loved, Campbell sought out opportunities to play ball in the new city. During the 1937–38 season she pitched for a team sponsored by the local brewery. Campbell helped her new team, the Sudbury Silver Foamettes, win the OWSA intermediate championship in 1938.

Ultimately, by entrusting me with their stories and reminiscences, these three women have given me the responsibility of presenting and interpreting their lives in a public forum to which they have little access.[74] Shackleton, Oliver, and Campbell's stories, in the context of industrial sport and corporate welfare strategies, remind us that silences in historical scholarship do not mean absences. Historian Carolyn Strange suggests that "because the 'working girl' was not a career woman, was only rarely a unionized worker, and was never involved in the power structures of urban life, she has fallen between the cracks of conventional historical enquiry."[75] This pattern of historical silence is especially evident in sport history, for rarely are working women and their sport and leisure activities the centre of scholarly investigation. Women's industrial sport in London during this period was a unique social space for the women themselves, a space often sponsored for the purposes of corporate welfare and advertising. The stories of Hazel Shackleton, Gladys Oliver, and Olive Campbell offer insight into women's experiences beyond the win/loss records and team rosters, and place women's experiences and "women's words" as central to our understanding of women's industrial sport.[76]

QUESTIONS FOR CONSIDERATION:

1. Why did local companies sponsor women's softball teams in the 1920s?
2. In your own words, how do you define corporate welfarism?
3. According to Adams, who controlled these leagues until the mid-1930s? Why is this significant?
4. How did the three interviewees for this chapter become involved with softball?
5. Describe some of the familial tensions that grew from these young women moving to work and play softball.
6. What opportunities arose for these women when they moved to London to live, play, and work?
7. What do you believe was lost when women stopped playing softball?

NOTES

1 Correspondence to carly.adams@uleth.ca. The quotation in the title is from Gladys (Oliver) Porter, interview with author, 12 April 2006, Woodstock, Ontario, notes in possession of author.

2 Veronica Strong-Boag, "The Girl of the New Day: Canadian Working Women in the 1920s," *Labour/Le Travail* 4 (1979): 132. For more on working women in Canada during this period see Joan Sangster, *Earning Respect: The Lives of Working Women in Small-Town Ontario, 1920–1960* (Toronto: University of Toronto Press, 1995).

3 See Raelene Frances, Linda Kealey, and John Sangster, "Women and Wage Labour in Australia and Canada, 1880–1980," *Labour/Le Travail* 38 (1996): 55.

4 Elizabeth Fones-Wolf, "Industrial Recreation, the Second World War, and the Revival of Welfare Capitalism, 1934–1960," *Business History Review* 60 (1986): 234.

5 Lynne Emery, "From Lowell Mills to the Halls of Fame: Industrial League Sport for Women," in *Women and Sport: Interdisciplinary Perspectives*, ed. D. Margaret Costa and Sharon Ruth Guthrie (Champaign: Human Kinetics, 1994), 108.

6 See, for example, Leonard J. Diehl and Floyd R. Eastwood, *Industrial Recreation: Its Development and Present Status* (Lafayette: Purdue University Press, 1940); W.H. Kilby, "Industrial Recreation in Canada," *Recreation* 25 (1932): 554–5; John R. Schleppi, "'It Pays': John H. Patterson and Industrial Recreation at the National Cash Register Company," *Journal of Sport History* 6 (1979): 20–8; Fones-Wolf, "Industrial Recreation," 232–57; Emery, "From Lowell Mills," 107; Monys Ann Hagen, "Industrial Harmony through Sports: The Industrial Recreation Movement and Women's Sports" (PhD diss., University of Wisconsin–Madison, 1990); Gerald R. Gems, "Welfare Capitalism and Blue-Collar Sport: The Legacy of Labour Unrest," *Rethinking History* 5 (2001): 43–58; and, in the

Canadian context, Susan L Forbes, "Gendering Corporate Welfare Practices: Female Sports and Recreation at Eaton's during the Depression," *Rethinking History* 5 (2001): 59–74.

7 Joan Sangster, "The Softball Solution: Female Workers, Male Managers, and the Operation of Paternalism at Westclox, 1923–60," *Labour/Le Travail* 32 (1993): 168.

8 A note on methods: This article is part of a larger study of recreation and sport in London, Ontario, from 1920 to 1951. Although organizational documents, newspapers, and secondary source materials were used in this research, oral histories of women who participated in various leagues are central to this study and my conclusions. As part of my data collection for this part of the study on industrial recreation, an advertisement was published in the reader-to-reader section of the local newspaper, the *London Free Press*, in March 2006, indicating that I was interested in speaking to women who played industrial softball during the 1920s and 1930s. As a result of this ad, I received dozens of phone calls from people living in London and the surrounding areas offering photographs and anecdotes of mothers, aunts, friends, and sisters who competed in the industrial leagues. Through these exchanges, I was able to identify and contact Hazel (Shackleton) Ferguson, Gladys (Oliver) Porter, and Olive (Campbell) Mahon – three women who played on various London industrial-sponsored teams during the 1920s and 1930s. The interviews with these women were two to three hours in length and were sometimes followed up with telephone calls to clarify issues.

9 See Paul Thompson, *The Voice of the Past: Oral History* (New York: Oxford University Press, 2000), 25–81, 118–89. On oral history as a methodology, see also Sherna Gluck and Daphne Patai, eds., *Women's Words: The Feminist Practice of Oral History* (New York: Routledge, 1991).

10 For more on the history of London, see Frederick H. Armstrong, *The Forest City: An Illustrated History of London, Ontario* (Northridge: Windsor, 1986); and Orlo Miller, *A Century of Western Ontario* (Toronto: Ryerson Press, 1949).

11 Stuart D. Brandes, *American Welfare Capitalism, 1880–1940* (Chicago: University of Chicago Press, 1976), 5–6.

12 Sangster, "The Softball Solution," 169. For examples, see Donald Reid, "Industrial Paternalism: Discourse and Practice in Nineteenth-Century French Mining and Metallurgy," *Comparative Studies in Society and History* 27 (1985): 579–607; Stephen Meyer, *The Five Dollar Day: Labor Management and Social Control in the Ford Motor Company, 1908–21* (New York: SUNY Press, 1981); and Gerald Zahavi, *Workers, Managers, and Welfare Capitalism* (Urbana: University of Illinois Press, 1998). More recently, see Alexander Hicks and Lane Kenworthy, "Varieties of Welfare Capitalism," *Socio-Economic Review* 1 (2003): 27–61; and Shakila Yacob, "Model of Welfare Capitalism? The United States Rubber Company in Southeast Asia, 1910–1942," *Enterprise and Society* 8 (2008): 136–74.

13 Hagen, "Industrial Harmony," 233.

14 Margaret E. McCallum, "Corporate Welfarism in Canada, 1919–39," *Canadian Historical Review* 71 (1990): 47.

15 Sangster, "The Softball Solution," 180.

16 One of the most notable corporate welfare strategies of Kellogg's was the transition from the eight-hour workday to the six-hour workday. Benjamin Kline Hunnicutt argues that the six-hour day "represented the company's latest effort to 'share the benefits' of mechanization and increased productivity with workers and the community." See Hunnicutt, "Kellogg's Six-Hour Day: A Capitalist Vision of Liberation through Managed Work Reduction," *Business History Review* 66 (1992): 481. For more on Kellogg's corporate welfare philosophy, see also Hunnicutt, *Kellogg's Six-Hour Day* (Philadelphia: Temple University Press, 1996).

17 James E. Girvin, "A Study of Personnel Administration as Practised at Silverwood Dairies" (MA thesis, University of Western Ontario, 1946), 127–31.

18 See "Woolworths Win," *London Free Press* (hereafter *LFP*), 22 August 1922, p. 11; and "Woolworth Girls Win," *LFP*, 31 August 1922, p. 17. Some studies of women's industrial recreation and women's sport broadly suggest that newspapers rarely reported on working-class women's sport, leading to a dearth of information. In London, this was not the case: there was plenty of coverage in the *London Free Press* throughout the 1920s and 1930s. The *Free Press* was the most widely circulated local newspaper in London, and had been since the late 1800s. Today it is an important source of information about of women's sport participation in the city. For discussions of the newspaper as a source for historical research, see Roberto Franzosi, "The Press as a Source of Socio-Historical Data: Issues in the Methodology of Data Collection from Newspapers," *Historical Methods* 20 (1987): 5–16. From a sport history perspective, see Jeffrey Hill, "Anecdotal Evidence: Sport, the Newspaper Press, and History," in *Deconstructing Sport History: A Postmodern Analysis*, ed. Murray G. Phillips (Albany: SUNY Press, 2006), 117–129.

19 "Duns Corners' Girls Win Tournament," *TFP*, 13 August 1923, p. 10. See also "Keen Interest in Softball Tourney," *TFP*, 3 August 1923, p. 16.

20 See, for example, "Brownies Play Thistles Crucial Game To-night," *TFP*, 17 August 1923, page 14. The YWCA Girls' Softball League existed from 1923 until 1929. There were as many as ten and as few as three teams competing in the league in various years. In 1925 the Brownies and the Thistles left the league and joined the Manufacturer's Girls' Softball League, which also existed in London from 1924 to 1929. Between 1930 to 1935, the two leagues merged to form the Major Intercity Girls' Softball League.

21 See "Jackies Beat Thistles," *TFP*, 19 August 1924, p. 11; and "M'Cormick Molly O's Win Second Series," *TFP*, 27 August 27, p. 10.

22 For example, the Church of Latter Day Saints entered a team in the 1924 season, Wells Academy business school entered a team for three seasons from 1927 to 1929, and throughout those seasons many businesses were represented, including McCormick's, Bell Telephone, and Kellogg's. In 1924, the *Free Press* sports pages also reported leagues in London, Oxford County, Bruce County, and Grey County. See "Bruce County Girls Have Softball League," *TFP*, 7 May 1924, p. 12; "Ladies Softball Dates," *TFP*, 26 May 1926, p. 12; "Grey & Bruce Ladies Soft Ball Dates," *TFP*, 17 June 1924, p. 14; "Beachville Tigers Win," *TFP*, 27 June 1924, p. 15; "Drury Girls Beat Hickson," *TFP*, 27 June 1924, p. 15; and "Wiarton Girls Win," *TFP*, 5 August 1924, p. 8.

23 See "Favorite Knits Beat Brownies, 26–10," *TFP*, 2 July 1924, pp. 8, 9.

24 See, for example, "M'Cormicks Defeat Cleveland Girls," *TFP*, 4 August 1925, p. 12; "London Girls Outplay Cleveland Barth Gems," *TFP*, 26 August 1929, p. 17; and "Cleveland Girls Drop First Games," *TFP*, 26 July 1930, p. 17.

25 "London Girls Outplay Cleveland Barth Gems," *TFP*, 26 August 1929, p. 17.

26 See, for example, "Toronto K and S. Girls Nine at Pt. Stanley On-Dominion Day," *TFP*, 10 June 1925, p. 12; "Toronto Supremes Defeat McCormicks," *TFP*, 5 August 1926, p. 11; "McCormick Girls Beat Zimmerknits," *TFP*, 30 August 1926, p. 10; "London Girls Whip Toronto Patricias," *TFP*, 3 May 1927, p. 13; "Thistles Drop Two To Toronto Girls," *TFP*, 2 August 1927, p. 14; "Brownies and McCormick's Defeat Toronto Patricias," *TFP*, 2 August 1927, p. 15; "Supremes Well Beaten by London," *Toronto Globe*, 8 September 1927, p. 8; "London Girls Whip Toronto Patricias," *TFP*, 25 May 1928, p. 18; "Seiberling Girls Divide Softball Exhibitions Here," *TFP*, 7 August 1928, p. 13; "London Girls Beat Zimmerknits' Nine, *TFP*, 27 August 1928, p. 11; "Softball Chatter," *TFP*, 3 July 1930, p. 15; "Girls Divide Two with Otis-Fensom," *TFP*, 14 July 1930, p. 10; "Toronto Girls Play Winning Softball," *TFP*, 4 August 1930, p. 8; "Kelloggs Again Whip Toronto,"

TFP, 4 August 1931, p. 11; "London Thistles Divide Twin Bill," *TFP*, 2 August 1932, p. 12; "Kelloggs In Smart Win," *TFP*, 6 August 1934, p. 12; and "Kelloggs Again Whip Supremes," *TFP*, 7 August 1934, p. 16.

27 This is consistent with industrial women's sport in the United States during this period. See Emery, "From Lowell Mills," 108.

28 "Girls' Softball Season Opens To-Morrow Here," *TFP*, 11 May 1925, p. 10.

29 The league also had the support of local politicians. For example, MP Frank White donated the league trophy in 1927; see "Girls Soft Ball Stars Monday," *TFP*, 7 May 1927, p. 14. In 1925, Mayor George Albert Weinge threw the first pitch to open the season and City Treasurer James Bell caught the ball behind the plate; see "Girls' Soft Ball Season Opens Tomorrow Here," *TFP*, 11 May 1925, p. 10.

30 Andrew C. Holman, "Stops and Starts: Ideology, Commercialism, and the Fall of American Women's Hockey in the 1920s," *Journal of Sport History* 32 (2005): 341.

31 For more information on the Ladies Ontario Hockey Association see Carly Adams, "Organizing Hockey for Women: The Ladies Ontario Hockey Association and the Fight for Legitimacy, 1922–1940," in *Coast to Coast: Hockey in Canada to the Second World War*, ed. John Chi-Kit Wong (Toronto: University of Toronto Press, 2009), 132–59. For more information on the Women's Amateur Athletic Federation see Bruce Kidd, *The Struggle for Canadian Sport* (Toronto: University of Toronto Press, 1996), 122–30; and M. Ann Hall, *The Girl and the Game* (Peterborough: Broadview Press, 2002), 50–4.

32 For the 1925 season, there were four teams in the league: Gorman-Eckerts' Rideau Hall, Smallman & Ingram Thistles, Brownies, and McCormick's. For a complete list of registered players for the 1925 season see "Percy Ferguson Has a New Job," *TFP*, 2 June 1925, p. 19. According to Hall, among the more than one hundred individuals who attended the inaugural organizational meeting for the Ontario Women's Softball Association, there were no representatives from London. See Hall, *The Girl and The Game*, 61.

33 Kidd, *The Struggle for Canadian Sport*, 109.

34 See "Girls Softball Loop Season Opens," *TFP*, 14 May 1931, p. 16.

35 See Kidd, *The Struggle for Canadian Sport*, 137–8.

36 See "Girls Get Busy on Civic Holiday," *TFP*, 3 August 1935, p. 16.

37 For more on the effects of the Depression in Canada in the early 1930s, see John Herd Thompson, *Canada 1929–1939: Decades of Discord* (Toronto: Mclelland and Stewart, 1985); and Michiel Horn, *The Depression in Canada: Responses to Economic Crisis* (Toronto: Copp Clark Pitman, 1988).

38 Gladys (Oliver) Porter, interview with author, 12 April 2006, Woodstock, Ontario, notes in possession of author.

39 Olive (Campbell) Mahon, interview with author, 26 April 2006, St. Jacobs, Ontario, notes in possession of author.

40 Hazel (Shackleton) Ferguson, interview with author, 14 March 2006, Toronto, Ontario, notes in possession of author.

41 Porter interview.

42 Mahon interview.

43 The recruitment of players suggests that skilled female athletes were enticed through offers of employment to play for industrial teams, thus suggesting in turn that the demarcation between amateur values and professional ideologies in women's sport during this era was unclear. For more on the amateur/professional debate in women's sport see Carly Adams, "Softball and the Female Community: Pauline Perron, Pro Ball Player, Outsider, 1926–1951," *Journal of Sport History* 33 (2006): 323–43.

44 Sangster also found this in relation to the Westclox Company; see Sangster, "The Softball Solution," 190.

45 Gems suggests much the same in the United States in the 1930s. Many American cities had industrial leagues for men and women. Employers sought skilled athletes for their teams in the hope that they would help win championships and thereby increase the visibility of the company's products. See Gems, "Welfare Capitalism," 50.

46 Ferguson interview.

47 There is evidence that Silverwood Dairy also sponsored a women's hockey team in the early 1930s. Unlike in softball, there was no women's hockey league in the city. The Silverwood team represented the city of London in the Ladies Ontario Hockey Association senior league in 1933. See Carly Adams, "'Queens of the Ice Lanes': The Preston Rivulettes and Women's Hockey in Canada, 1931–1940," *Sport History Review* 29 (2008): 6.

48 See "Kelloggs Score Twenty-Nine Runs," *TFP*, 4 August 1927, p. 12.

49 Porter interview. In 1927, The *Free Press* reported that Oliver hit a home run during a game between her team the London Imps and the COF. See "C.O.F. Girls Beat London Imps 19–11," *TFP*, 18 August 1927, p. 24.

50 "C.O.F. Girls Beat London Imps.". The *Free Press* lists Oliver as part of the Kellogg's roster in the position of third base in August 1927. See, for example, "Kelloggs Score Twenty-Nine Runs," *TFP*, 4 August 1927, p. 12.

51 "Kelloggs Score Twenty-Nine Runs."

52 "Kelloggs Score Twenty-Nine Runs."

53 See "Girls Divide Two With Otis-Fensom," *TFP*, 14 July 1930, p. 10.

54 Ferguson interview.

55 See "Founders made $9.63 a week club house began with $750," *Canadian Grocer*, November 1986, p. 160.

56 This is supported by team rosters found in the *Free Press* from 1926 until 1931.

57 Ferguson interview.

58 See Lynne Marks, *Revivals and Roller Rinks* (Toronto: University of Toronto Press, 1996), 81–106.

59 Sangster, "The Softball Solution," 133.

60 Porter interview.

61 Porter interview.

62 Porter interview. The *Free Press* reported Oliver playing for Gorman Eckert Rideau Hall for a game against Cleveland. She scored a reported two home runs during this game. See "London Girls Outplay Cleveland Barth Gems," *TFP*, 26 August 1929, p. 17. News reports suggest that Oliver played for other teams as well, including the London Imps in 1927. See "Wells Academy Outplay Imps in Exciting Game," *TFP*, 6 August 1927, p. 19.

63 Both Sangster, "The Softball Solution," 176, and Joy Parr, *The Gender of Breadwinners* (Toronto: University of Toronto Press, 1998), 35, argue that women often developed a sense of debt to their employers – they felt that they owed them loyalty in exchange for their job.

64 Porter interview.

65 See Sangster, "The Softball Solution," 192.

66 Mahon interview.

67 Mahon interview.

68 See Strong-Boag, *The New Day Recalled* (Toronto: Copp Clark Pittman, 1998), 41; and Strong-Boag, "The Girl of the New Day," 132.

69 Gord Ferguson was not an employee of Silverwood Dairy. During the time he coached the team he worked at Dunlop Rubber in London.

70 Porter interview.

71 Mahon interview.

72 Some of the women who played in the 1920s and 1930s industrial softball leagues in London were recruited to join teams in this new league. The new league was sponsored by the city and had no direct affiliation to industry and companies in the city. See Adams, "Softball and the Female Community," 323–43.

73 Barbara Laslett and Barrie Thorne, eds., *Feminist Sociology: Life Histories of a Movement* (New Brunswick: Rutgers University Press, 1997), 2.

74 Oslon and Shopes suggest that "acting on this responsibility conscientiously challenges many of the conventions of normal academic practice" (p. 198). For further discussion on doing oral histories with working-class men and women, see Karen Oslon and Linda Shopes, "Crossing Boundaries and Building Bridges: Doing Oral History among Working-Class Women and Men," in *Women's Words: The Feminist Practice of Oral History*, ed. Sherna Berger Gluck and Daphne Patai (New York: Routledge, 1991), 189–204. Olson and Shopes's notion of women's stories as "commodities of privilege" is an idea I am exploring elsewhere. It is important to note here, but a more detailed discussion goes beyond the scope of this chapter.

75 Carolyn Strange, *Toronto's Girl Problem: The Perils and Pleasures of the City* (Toronto: University of Toronto Press, 1995), 3.

76 Taken from Berger Gluck and Patai, eds., *Women's Words.*

Part II
CLASS, BUSINESS, AND POLITICS

CHAPTER SEVEN

"Cracking the Stone" and Marching under Flags Black and Red: Toronto's Dispossessed in the Age of Industry, 1880–1925

BRYAN D. PALMER AND GAÉTAN HÉROUX

The Poor and Historical Development

For much of history poor people have been portrayed as the architects of their own misery. They are poor because they lack the ability to plan their lives adequately and govern themselves according to "rules" of comportment that ensure personal well-being and social advancement. If they lack good and secure jobs, *the* foundation of material success in our society, they are blamed because they squandered opportunities to be educated; because they have been indulgent in the use of drugs or alcohol; because they cannot defer gratification; and because (in particularly racialized misrepresentations) they lack stable family structures and have opted for lifestyles of profligacy and promiscuity.[1]

This chapter refuses to assign personal guilt to the poor in this easy displacement of responsibility onto individuals. As much as private decision-making can, of course, play a role in determining how people's lives unfold, it is the social, economic, and political conditions of society itself that must be interrogated, understood, and changed if poverty, inequality, and marginality are to be challenged and overcome. We approach these problems, not as consequences of individual and personal deficiencies, but as integral parts of the collective experience of a socio-economic order, in which who has power and who does not matters profoundly. These relations are historical, which is to say that they came about because of a process of development and are, and were, subject to change.

Toronto in the Age of Industry, reaching from the late nineteenth into the early twentieth century, is a fitting laboratory in which to study the social transformations of a new society and the dislocations that the transition to it produced.[2] The city's growth captured much of how Canada moved from a largely rural, agriculturally oriented network of communities, in which productions of goods and services was small-scale and the population was concentrated in the countryside, to an urban-based industrial-capitalist society, in which cities and factories became increasingly prominent. As this happened, social relations grew more impersonal and inequality and poverty became more visible. This had pronounced consequences for large swaths of the population, who found themselves displaced from direct ownership of resources essential to self-sufficiency and to the acquisition of cash. Money, for the privileged few, grew into fortunes, becoming *capital*. Savings were invested in the establishment of ever-larger enterprises, often family-owned, which, by the opening decades of the twentieth century, through mergers of specific businesses and the buying out of smaller companies by their larger competitors, resulted in the formation of vast corporations, headed by boards of directors linked to financial institutions, governments, and national and international markets. This regime of accumulation, based on the private ownership of varied instruments of production, widening spheres of production and exchange, and the concentration of wealth in fewer and fewer hands, consolidated a new, modern political economy.[3] *Capital* gave rise to capital*ism*.

Routinely presented as a natural evolution, in which the hidden hand of the market prodded those with ambition and the talents of innovation to orchestrate new efficiencies of production, capitalism was heralded as liberating humankind. More was being produced, and this abundance would be available to more and more people. Innovations in transportation and communication – steamships, railways, and telegraphs – opened the globe to capital and facilitated movements of resources, commodities, and people like never before. New kinds of goods and services, from automobiles to hydroelectric power, from mass-produced clothing and foodstuffs to the steel that girded new high-rise buildings, enhanced life in the new capitalist order. But all of this depended on securing a labour force that was divorced from the land of the family farm or the skills and small-scale tools of earlier craft production, on display in the local wheelwright's or blacksmith's or shoemaker's shop of past times. Capital*ism* could not function without thousands and thousands of these workers, whose labour was required to attend to the machines or bring the natural assets of forests and mines to the marketplaces of Canada and the world, where they would be converted to capital. These workers were capitalism's dispossessed. Just as colonialism (not unrelated to capitalism's global expansion) needed to subject indigenous peoples to varied processes of dispossession so that it could sink deeper its roots of control in a particular territorial base, capitalist

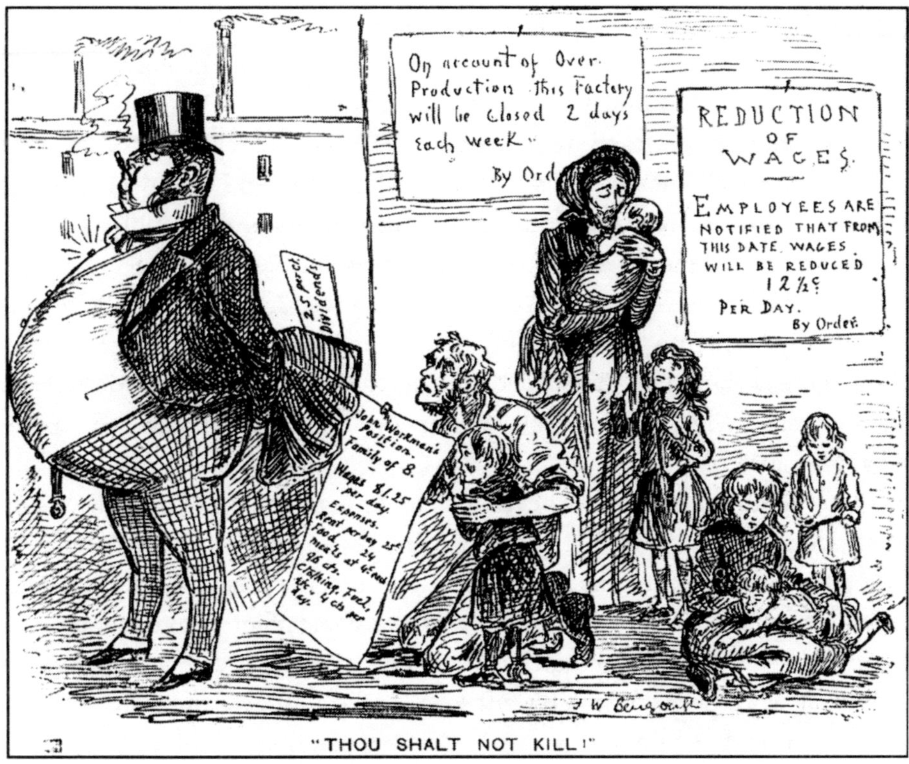

Figure 7.1. J.W. Bengough, *Grip*, 3 November 1883.

production depended on creating a ready supply of dispossessed wage labourers on whom it could depend to do the work necessary to feed its voracious appetite for accumulation.[4]

This chapter takes as its starting point the trials and tribulations that were lived by people who were being made into workers in Toronto between the years 1880 to 1925. It does so by looking at how workers who could not find work fared. How did they cope with Toronto's Age of Industry when they were, through no fault of their own, unable to be "industrious," in the conventional sense of working for a wage? Starting from this vantage point, the history of Toronto looks markedly different than its usual representation. Our chapter explores how capitalism was punctuated by crises of economic downturn and dislocation, at which times those without jobs were forced to rely on the charitable impulse of a society that did not always look kindly on those without jobs and the means to sustain themselves. Before the Second World War, in the decades before the welfare state consolidated, the poor were provided with public relief only when they were able to undertake demeaning labour, which their judgmental superiors demanded they do as proof that they were actually willing to work. That many would take up such tasks is not surprising. That others would protest, and march under the flags of anarchy (black) and socialism (red), is less well known, yet is central to what we intend to show in the pages that follow. Furthermore, pernicious nineteenth-century understandings of "eligibility" that restricted public assistance to the "deserving" poor did not end with the establishment of the welfare state. As Frances Fox Piven has argued forcefully, such ideas continued well into the late twentieth and early twenty-first centuries, gaining traction as the welfare state was eroded and increasingly conservative ideas came to dominate social policy in a political economy ordered by the dictates of a modern penchant for austerity.[5]

In adopting this approach, we begin with an understanding of capitalism somewhat at odds with conventional wisdom. We stress, not capitalism's benevolence and progressive essence, but its routine descent into crises, during which Toronto's workers were often thrown out of work, and the archaic relief system that pressured workers to the point that it generated resentments and protests, including uprisings of the out-of-work, some of which went so far as to question capitalism itself.

These protests structure our narrative. They break our chapter into three distinct albeit related periods: first, an initial series of protests that demanded "Work or Bread," occasionally mobilized under the black flag of anarchism (1873–96); second, an increasingly organized unemployed movement that rose and fell on the crests of economic boom and bust in the decades preceding the First World War (1900-1918), animated by a rising socialist movement; and third, a continuation of Toronto's campaigns of the workless as the red flag of resistance unfurled first by socialists was hoisted high by the newly established Communist Party and its militant activists (1918–25). All of this was background to the unemployed protests that would take centre stage in Toronto and across Canada during the Great Depression of the 1930s.

This was a history of the criminalization of poverty. Ostensibly charitable structures like the House of Industry took on the trappings of penal institutions, and policies towards the poor were shaped according to punitive understandings of who was eligible for relief and who was not. The vilification of tramps, commonplace in the depressions of the 1870s and 1890s, gave way to antagonism towards protests, whoever led them – anarchists, socialists, or communists. Those who sought food and shelter amidst the routine crises of capitalism were subject to "labour tests," such as cutting wood or breaking rocks. If they complained or refused they were made to suffer deprivation, even jailed. The much-vaunted freedom of the capitalist marketplace was, for many, an illusion.

Capitalism and Crisis

When capitalism is understood not merely as a political economy of development, advance, and progress, but also as a social order that routinely descends into economic downturns, depressions, and recessions, how we view its history necessarily changes. Capitalism is a regime of accumulation governed by complex and contradictory characteristics: the ostensible freedom to pursue employment according to choice exists alongside the undermining of freedom as work is routinely unavailable. Engaging with this contradiction forces us to consider how crises are integral to capitalism, as is abundantly evident in the history of the present.[6]

Appreciating capitalism *as* crisis and accumulation *as* at least partly about destruction of weak producers in a competitive marketplace entails looking at labour differently. Michael Denning has recently advocated reconceptualizing life under capitalism in ways that "decentre wage labour" and replace a "fetishism of the wage" and the "employment contract" with attention to "dispossession and expropriation." Karl Marx, after all, did not invent the term "proletarian," but adapted it from its common usage in antiquity, when, within the Roman Empire, the word designated the uncertain social stratum, divorced from property and without regular access to wages, reproducing recklessly. J.C.L. Simonde de Sismondi drew on this understanding in an 1819 work of political economy that chronicled the "threat to public order" posed by a "miserable and suffering population," dependent as it was on public charity. "Those who had no property," Sismondi wrote, "were called to have children: *ad prolem generandum.*" Max Weber commented similarly: "As early as the sixteenth century the proletarianising of the rural population created such an army of unemployed that England had to deal with the problem of poor relief." Three centuries later, across the Atlantic, transient common labourers were being described in a discourse seemingly impervious to change: "a dangerous class, inadequately fed, clothed, and housed, they threaten the health of the community." As Denning concludes, "unemployment precedes employment, and the informal economy precedes the formal, both historically and conceptually. We must insist that 'proletarian' is not a synonym for 'wage labourer' but for dispossession, expropriation and radical dependence on the market."[7]

Yet a dichotomization of wageless life and working for wages is not an adequate way of approaching the history of the 99 per cent. It clarifies the importance of workers who are experiencing dispossession – who have been cut out of ownership of land, tools, and decision-making affecting their working lives – but it also obscures the extent to which this fundamental aspect of daily life is meaningless outside of the existence of the (often distant) wage. Waged work is both an enduring if universally unpleasant end and a decisive means of survival within modern capitalist relations. David Montgomery captures the link between waged and unwaged in his rich discussion of common labourers: "Whether they were working flat out, sleeping behind a furnace or inside a boxcar, getting 'quitting mad,' enjoying the conviviality of the saloon, or being thrown back into the ranks of the unemployed ... one thing was clear: For common laborers, work was the biblical curse. It was unavoidable, undependable, and unrewarding. But they had urgent need for money."[8] Wagelessness and waged employment are not oppositions, then, but gradations on a spectrum traversing desire and necessity that encompasses many possibilities for the masses of people existing within capitalism's social and economic relations.

Unemployed Protests under the Black Flag, 1873–1896

By the time Toronto embarked on its Age of Industry in the 1870s and 1880s, the city's major enterprises employed almost 13,000 workers out of a population of roughly 85,000. The Queen City's material development rested on decades of socio-economic differentiation and dislocation. Economic crises, devastating in their human toll, punctuated the 1830s, the 1850s, and the 1870s and would close the century in the 1890s. Pauper immigration, epidemics, and growing class conflict all struck daggers of fear in the bosom of an emerging bourgeois society.[9] Beginning in the 1830s, a number of carceral institutions, the most prominent of which was the House of Industry, were established, which criminalized the poor and marked them with the stigma of dependency.[10] The boundaries separating the "rough" and the "respectable" in working-class Toronto were often porous. These distinctions were socially constructed in the ideology of the times and often reinforced materially. "Unemployment" emerged as a derogatory designation.[11]

Toronto's nineteenth-century industrial-capitalist revolution spurred the growth of workers' organizations. Over the course of the 1880s, of a national total of 425 political mobilizations and protests, including strikes, fully 122 erupted in Toronto. Labour newspapers like the *Ontario Workman* and *Palladium of Labor* anchored themselves in Toronto. The Nine-Hour League and the Canadian Labour Union in the 1870s and the Knights of Labor and the Trades and Labor Congress of Canada played significant roles in the now bustling capital of Canadian manufacturing, which boasted a population approaching 200,000 by the end of the nineteenth century. The working class was emphatically making its presence known and was challenging the hegemony of both employers and their often servile state.[12]

The entrenched ideologies reflected in British Poor Law discourse proved remarkably resilient in nineteenth-century Canada. The "undeserving poor" were

Figure 7.2. "The Charity Season," *Grip*, 1 January 1881.

to be subject to the laws of "less eligibility," which stipulated that relief would be made available only to those among the wageless who *would* work for their aid, which would only be dispensed in ways that made it even less attractive than what could be secured by the worst-paid unskilled labour. Toronto's *Globe* made all of this abundantly clear in an 1877 manifesto-like declaration on the wageless: "we do not advocate a system which could leave them to starve, but we do say that if they are ever to be taught economical and saving habits, they must understand that the public have no idea of making them entirely comfortable in the midst of their improvidence and dissipation. If they wish to secure that they must work for it and save and plan. Such comfort is not to be had by loafing around the tavern door, or fleeing to charity at every pinch."[13]

A floating mass of workless males generated increasing panic as the depression of 1873 deepened into 1877–78. Hordes of migrant labourers, ostensibly travelling to secure elusive waged employment, became the scourge of small towns and large cities alike. Welcomed with the lock-up and with public derision in the press, tramps were criminalized, socially constructed as thieves, and vilified as "pests," "voracious monsters," "outrageously impertinent," an "irrepressible stampede" deserving of "a well-aimed dose of buckshot rubbed in well with salt-petre." In Lindsay, Ontario, ninety miles east of Toronto, the local newspaper the *Canadian Post* ran more than one hundred news items relating to tramps between 1874 and 1878. Tramps were depicted as an outcast stratum rarely interested in finding employment, and as poor because they were "work-shy and degenerate." Many were riding the rails en route to Toronto, where police stations, in 1877 and 1878, reported sheltering more than 1,200 "waifs" annually.[14]

The 1880s saw the economy struggle out of its 1870s doldrums, but the recovery was anything but robust, and the migratory wageless continued to unsettle respectable society. Toronto's newspapers competed against one another, pushing their denunciations of the "loafing aristocracy" to new extremes and calling for the expulsion of tramps from the city, judicious use of the lash against those for whom work was an aversion, and vigilant police monitoring of peripatetic vagrants, who were given to "murders, burglaries, incendiaries, and highway robberies." A little "hard labour," suggested the *Globe*, would do this "dissipated" and "shiftless" element good. The House of Industry had supposedly become increasingly lax in enforcing earlier expectations that those seeking a meal and a bed for the night would chop wood for them. Some called for a more rigorous "labour test," such as stone-breaking. The House of Industry focused instead on establishing an expanded wayfarer's lodge in 1884–85, where large numbers of indigent men could be put up for the night in a "casual" ward, their bodies soaked in a hot bath, their heads doused with vermin-killing liquid solution, and their clothes fumigated ("cleansed and classified," in the vernacular of poor relief officialdom). The growing number of habitual tramps furnished with temporary board and lodging by the de facto Poor House in the mid-1880s necessitated adoption of a modified "labour test," if only to deter the ostensibly shiftless and physically weak from staying too long in its expanded "casual" ward. Making inmates saw a quarter-cord of wood, a job that took the able-bodied and reasonably dexterous approximately three hours before they were allowed to lunch on a watery bowl of soup and a hunk of stale bread, had its effect. The numbers of men checking into the wayfarer's lodge declined from 730 in 1886 to 548 in 1889.

The worsening economic climate of the 1890s saw an expanded need for the House of Industry's relief, however, and the "casual" ward was opened for the summer as well as winter months. The number of "casuals" staying at the enlarged lodge now soared, climbing to highs of 1,700 in 1891 and 1,500 in 1895 and 1897, rarely falling below 1,200. The average contingent sleeping at the house per night never dipped below 60 between 1890 and 1897, when a high of 100 was reached (a comparable figure for 1880–85 had been roughly 26). In 1891, 832 "casuals" stayed in the wayfarer's lodge of Toronto's House of Industry for two or three nights, while 415 put up in the poor house for more than three days; 24 hard-core recidivists spent more than 100 nights in the refuge.[15] Increased use of the House of Industry's relief facilities and provisions generated a backlash. Reverend Arthur H. Baldwin, rector of Toronto's All Saints Church and one of the House of Industry's most outspoken trustees, provided advance notice that Toronto's premier institution of poor relief was not interested in coddling itinerant idlers. "It seems a great pity," he pontificated, "that these people should be allowed to go in and dwell [in the casual ward] and do nothing but cut a little wood, as we insist upon their doing."[16] A new labour regime was clearly in the offing.

"Until the vagrant is offered some alternative that even he will recognize as more unpleasant and disagreeable than work," claimed the Board of the House of Industry in 1891–92, "the tramp trouble will never be cured." Cutting wood wasn't cutting it: relatively few refused this "labour test." Between 1891 and 1895, according to James Pitsula's calculations from the *Annual Reports of the House of Industry*, 29,652 requests of the indigent to cut wood were complied with, while a bare 432 refusals were registered. In 1896 the House of Industry abandoned wood cutting, replacing it with the more onerous discipline of stone-breaking. Almost immediately the new regime met with resistance: only 792 completed the required task of stone-breaking, compared to 1,202 who balked at undertaking the new, and more stringent, "labour test." As indicated by the vagrancy convictions of John Curry and Thomas Wilson in January 1896, those who refused stone-breaking assignments at the House of Industry were soon subject to confinement. Magistrate Denison sentenced this duo, who said they preferred jail to the new "labour test," to a three month-term in the refuge of their choice. One month later, upping the ante, City Alderman Jolliffe introduced a motion making it mandatory for all able-bodied applicants for relief in Toronto applying for outdoor assistance to break a yard of stone in return for their coal subsidy, doubling the amount of work required to receive winter fuel. "The stonepile," as Pitsula concludes, had become "an emblem for the work ethic."[17]

Clearly, an offensive against the tramps was being waged in the name of morality and the disciplining power of relief.[18] This class war was not waged one-sidedly. Not only was stone-breaking unpopular, but it also occasioned organized protests by the poor. The rush of refusals in 1896 could not have happened without discussions and deliberations on the part of the wageless. The consequences of their recalcitrance were quite severe. For the single unemployed men, the tramps, of whom 65 to 75 per cent came from outside Toronto,[19] refusal to break stone left them homeless, without visible means of support and sustenance, possibly confined to a cell. Family men seeking outdoor relief in the form of food and fuel put themselves and their wives and children at risk with their oppositional stands. Yet "casuals" and domestic providers in need bolted from stone-breaking, and some of the indigent gathered outside City Hall to protest Jolliffe's motion. An unidentified spokesman, described as "a strong hulk fellow," spoke for his wageless counterparts: "And they calls that charity, do they? Got to crack a heap o' stones for what yer get. Ain't no charity in that es' I can see."[20]

The rebellion against stone-breaking in the 1890s was, to be sure, a minor event, but it signalled a shift in the activities of the workless, which had taken a more organized and collective turn during the depression of 1873–77 and in its immediate aftermath. With industrialists acknowledging that "fifty percent of the manufacturing population of the country are out of work," and fledgling newspapers of the organized working class addressing unemployment and its evils, it was but a short step to deputations of the jobless marching to demand some kind of redress.[21] Ottawa became a centre of this 1870s agitation, a natural enough development given parliament's proximity and the possibility that federal politicians might vote funds for expanded public works.[22] Over the course of the winter of 1879–80, Ottawa newspapers bristled with accounts of petitions, marches, torchlit processions, and other gatherings of hundreds of "unemployed workingmen." Editorials chastened those who were described as looking "needy and seemed determined to get work or fight," claiming that the government could not be expected to provide for them. Canada was not a land of "State Socialism."[23]

To be sure, the unemployed protests of 1873–80 were seldom unambiguous expressions of solidarity between the waged and the wageless. Racism obviously kept workers divided, and native-born Canadians and English-speaking immigrants resented deeply the suggestion that they could cure the disease of wagelessness by moving west to take advantage of the booming resource and railway frontier. The unemployed of 1880 protested the fairness of suggesting that mechanics in Canada's capital "leave the city" of Ottawa when they had contributed so much to "building it up." They buttressed this legitimate argument with angry statements far less salutary: "It was nonsense to ask residents of the city to go away west and live with Indians and half-breeds, and to work upon the railway in British Columbia, competing with Chinese cheap labour."[24]

Nonetheless, the trajectory of labour in the 1880s *was* towards greater unity: it was becoming clearer that the skilled and the unskilled had common interests and that the struggles of the waged and the plight of the wageless both needed to be addressed. This demanded organization, which the Knights of Labor promoted through its call for "one big union" of all workers. Labour reform intellectuals of the 1880s, such as Toronto's Phillips Thompson, were acutely aware of the ongoing capitalist crisis and that acquisitive individualism was feeding on labour's contributions and despoiling the working class. "Capitalism has created a monster which threatens to destroy the classes, if not the system, that gave it life," Thompson wrote. "The number of men and women who cannot get work on any terms implies a far larger class whose pay has become a mere pittance." Thompson's *The Politics of Labor* (1886) sought to break down the separation between the skilled and the unskilled, and to erase – at least somewhat – the barriers to working-class solidarity erected by gendered and racialized prejudice, not to mention craft exclusion. "Where is the advantage of cheapness of production to the army of the unemployed and half-employed, or to those whose labor has been so cheapened by competition that their purchasing power is correspondingly lessened?" he asked. The half-employed, the cheapeningly employed, and the unemployed -- for Thompson this was the army that would march against capital, the beginning of a union of the dispossessed.[25]

As this union struggled, against all odds, to organize itself in the 1880s, evidence of how the lives of the waged and the wageless shaded into each other surfaced in many quarters. Toronto workers surveyed by the Bureau of Industries at the end of the decade averaged only 44 weeks of employment a year. That was in the best of times. For many workers, being out of work for a good part of every year was the norm. Testimony before the Royal Commission on the Relations of Labor and Capital in the late 1880s, from both employers and workers, made it abundantly clear that few industrial establishments, building projects, and transportation endeavours paid workers for more than eight to ten months annually. The Toronto House of Industry accommodated tramps, to be sure, but to the extent that the migratory wageless who depended on its shelter and subsistence fare can be classified occupationally, skilled workers were not far behind unskilled labourers in lining up for relief. Toronto printers claimed that 30 per cent of them were without work in the 1890s. "I am not alone in my trouble," declared one Toronto unemployed father of six in 1891. "There are two hundred members of the union to which I belong in the same position as myself." If the organizing of the wageless had not made great strides in this period, it had nonetheless started and was making particular kinds of statements. In Ottawa in 1880, at a demonstration of the unemployed, a black flag was unfurled. Those responsible thought they "would be clubbed by the Police and shot down like dogs." The anarchist banner was a fitting signal, for it signified for the angry workers who marched under it the possibility of death. This was the wages of the war on the dispossessed. Those out of work understood that their own demise by starvation might well be imminent, and they shook their fists defiantly in the face of authority, vowing "death to the government" that they claimed was responsible for their destitution.[26]

In February 1891, two Toronto protests of 300 to 1,000 out-of-work labourers marched under the black flag, this one emblazoned with the words "Work or Bread." "There are many others hungry," declared one of the unemployed, most of whom were reluctant to admit that they had appealed to "the charities" for the first time in their lives. The crowd had been angry from the start and grew more so as Mayor Clarke told the protesters that there were no more public works projects to fund. Threatening disorder, one man shouted, "Necessity knows no law," and that his need was for immediate work to feed a "dependant [*sic*] family." Many of those demonstrating were craft "breadwinners" – building tradesmen, transportation workers, printers – and were noticeably angered that they had not been not privileged over the single unemployed when the city hired workers for sewer construction.[27] This kind of division mirrored the House of Industry's labelling of "casuals" and recipients of outdoor relief. It suggested that divisions among the waged and the wageless might survive the breaking down of the material walls keeping these two halves of proletarianization apart. Nonetheless, a new page had been turned in the late nineteenth century as workers began to address dispossession as an experience that brought together long-separated contingents of the working-class. This organized protest, however, also hinted at the decisive role that left politics would play in future mobilizations of what had now come to be referred to as "the unemployed."

The black flag that flew at demonstrations of the wageless in the late nineteenth century proclaimed the presence of the left among the jobless, for that was the anarchists' banner. It was associated with the Haymarket martyrs. In May 1886, during a labour protest in Chicago's Haymarket Square, a bomb was thrown into a group of policemen, killing seven of them. In the ensuing melee, the police fired recklessly into the agitated crowd; further injuries and deaths resulted. Memories of the black flag associated with such events and with jobless protests in Ontario's capital would haunt Toronto's community of relief professionals for some time. In 1908, Superintendent Arthur Laughlan of Toronto's House of Industry explained how it had come to pass that the "labour test" of breaking stone, so exemplary in its disciplining capacities, had been charitably reduced from two yards to half a yard, which still constituted a crate weighing over 600 pounds:

> We were the victims of considerable imposition during the depression about 14 years ago, when the unemployed were carrying the black flag. … We then decided to establish a stone-yard, and before we would give relief each able-bodied man had to break two yards of stone. This innovation was pronounced a success, and the applications for relief began to fall off at a rapid rate, until we had very few families to talk of. We found, however, that two yards of stone was too much for a man to break, and at my suggestion the Board reduced it to one yard. It was afterwards reduced to half, and today they only have to break a quarter of a yard.

"The labour test" of "cracking the stone," it turns out, was born under the black flag.[28]

Crisis and Escalating Protest in the Pre-First World War Era

To be sure, the left would fly other flags, including, between 1890 and 1925, those of "deepest red" that were associated with socialism and communism. And some in the often fragmented left would disparage the wageless as little more than capitalism's refuse and would denounce the poor as parasites. In Lindsay, Ontario, echoes of the earlier 1870s tramp panic could be heard in a Socialist Party of Canada publication, *Gems of Socialism* (1916), which declared confidently that "the tramp and the millionaire are brothers under the skin. They both live without labor, or rather, live on the labor of others." This was, however, far more jaundiced than the left's more inclusive norm. "Revolts of the unemployed" erupted across Canada in the early decades of the twentieth century, fuelled as often as not by the crisis of capitalism. With the revolutionary left's involvement in and support of these uprisings, a more expansive understanding of the complex reciprocity that joined the employed and the out of work under capitalism emerged.[29]

Toronto had helped nurture the Canadian socialist left in the 1880s and 1890s, becoming a haven for bohemian radicalism and dissident thought. It was a centre of the Canadian Socialist League, the country's first popularly based socialist organization, founded in 1899. The long capitalist crisis of 1873–96 had convinced many Toronto radicals, nascent socialists, and developing Marxists that chronic unemployment, among other afflictions plaguing the working class, could only be resolved through a root-and-branch overhaul of the entire capitalist system. Many such critics were Christian socialists, and they found themselves locking horns with more conservative voices in the eclectic Social Problems Conferences that often addressed issues of poverty in the 1890s. As early as 1889, more radical activists clashed in the Toronto Labour Council, with one of Canada's leading public intellectuals, Goldwin Smith, who had a penchant for denouncing William Morris, John Ruskin, the British Fabians, and other "poverty destroyers." As this broad left coalesced, it articulated increasingly radical views on how capitalism, recurring economic crises, the mechanization of industry, and the concentration of wealth and ownership of productive forces were widening the domain of wagelessness.[30]

Between 1900 and 1925 Toronto was transformed. The largest manufacturing centre in Ontario, and the heartland of Canadian industrial capitalism, the city grew by leaps and bounds. Fed by a massive influx of immigrants, Toronto's population soared by 75 per cent between 1901 and 1911, when it surpassed 375,000. Annexation gobbled up new land, which was needed for developing industries and working-class suburbs. The capital invested in manufacturing increased by 618 per cent between 1900 and 1921, while the gross value of production, indexed at 100 in 1900, climbed to 148 in 1905, to 255 in 1910, and to 847 in 1919. Changes in the lives of working-class Torontonians abounded. White-collar jobs expanded as the offices and financial institutions facilitating the new economic order proliferated. Work opportunities for women, who now had alternatives to domestic service and sweated work in the garment trades, increased significantly. But for all the change experienced by Toronto's expanding working class, the continuity in capitalism as crisis was perhaps most decisive. Boom years never lasted long enough; bust inevitably followed. Panics and severe depressions occurred in 1907–8, 1911–15, and again in the post-war climate of 1919–21. Wagelessness, for a time, became the lot of "all but a relatively small number of wage earners."[31]

The left perspective on capitalism, crisis, and unemployment may not have resonated that well in Toronto's boom years of expansion (1896–1906) that followed the late nineteenth-century economic malaise. Claims were made that the Trades and Labor Congress of Canada had grown from a membership of 8,000 in 1900 to 100,000 in 1914, and much of this affiliation would have been in unions under the umbrella of the often conservative, craft conscious, job-protecting American Federation of Labor (AFL). These bodies, with little use for the wageless, numbered only sixteen in Toronto in the 1880s, but totalled 106 by 1902. No other city came even close to rivalling this AFL presence. When the voice of the unemployed was heard early in the century, it sometimes spoke in the idiom of the rights of the skilled to be protected from competition in the labour market.[32]

In December 1903, a "meeting of the unemployed of the city of Toronto," undoubtedly spurred to action by the winter's coming layoffs, adopted a resolution deploring the misrepresentation of industrial conditions in Canada and the resulting "encouragement of indiscriminate immigration." By January 1908, with the economy slowed to a snail's pace and the ranks of the out-of-work reaching crisis proportions, Toronto was forced to open a Civic Bureau to register the names of those in need of work. Three thousand workers promptly signed up, and those 300 fortunate enough to secure work at snow removal received $2 daily for a maximum three-day stint. The following December, with winter again threatening, another Free Employment Bureau was opened, and within three months 5,500 jobless workers had registered. City of Toronto disbursements for the House of Industry's outdoor relief jumped from an average of around $10,000 annually between 1904 and 1907 to over $26,000 in the depressed years 1908 and 1909. At the height of the 1908 economic crisis, 240 so-called tramps were being sheltered in Toronto's House of Industry, with fully 90 of them forced to sleep on concrete floors for want of beds. Those who refused to "crack the stone" for those accommodations faced criminal charges and incarceration. Vagrancy arrests, never above 975 in any two-year period between 1901 and 1906, ballooned to over 800 annually between 1908 and 1910. In such a climate, with the wageless driven to destitution and marked out for a variety of coercions, the left critique of capitalist crisis undoubtedly registered more forcefully among Toronto's dispossessed.[33]

Organized protests reflected this. March 1908 saw 1,000 unemployed converge on Toronto's City Hall, demanding work. Rebuffed by the mayor, who stated clearly that temporary employment would never be provided solely as a means of relief, the wageless retreated. Nine months later they were back in force, a contingent of socialists at their head. The unemployed rebellion in Toronto in January 1909 was led by two well-known agitators, Ernest Drury and Wilfred Gribble. More militant than their 1908 predecessors, 1,000 of the out of work surrounded City Hall and spilled over onto an adjacent street, blocking the road. Drury had barely begun to address the crowd when the police intervened, forcing the protest to reassemble in Bayside Park, a kilometre from the downtown core. Ankle-deep in mud, the jobless listened to a parade of revolutionaries, whose speeches scaled the heights of political denunciation of capitalism besides addressing more immediate prosaic demands. There was talk of the forcible seizure of property to provide for the poor. Socialist Party of Canada soap-boxer Wilfred Gribble told those assembled that "it goes hard with me to have to stand here in three or four inches of mud when we want to hold a meeting. You men built these great buildings … you built these railways, you built the big halls in this city, but when you want to meet you can't have one of them." A petition was soon placed with the City's Board of Control, demanding a hall at which the unemployed could assemble.[34]

A few days later, the wageless again convened at City Hall, their mood described as "dangerous." Albert Hill climbed atop a wagon to address the throng, which had again spilled over into streets, prompting the police to disperse the gathering. He pointed out, as had Gribble earlier, that while the "big guns and important people" received warm welcomes at the municipal seat of power, the unemployed could not find a place to meet. Making their way again to Bayside Park, the body promptly appointed a committee of twelve to return to City Hall and demand access to St. Andrews Hall as a place where the out of work could gather. Five hundred demonstrators trailed the delegation and, upon arriving at their destination, swarmed the front and side entrances, seeking out the top-floor meeting rooms of the Board of Control. Told to depart by the police, the unemployed offered no resistance, but determined to return.[35]

As several hundred of the unemployed milled about City Hall the next day, their movements watched closely by the police, Drury led a delegation into the building, where the Board of Control was addressed. The board was beseeched to let out St. Andrews Hall for regular meetings of the unemployed. Mayor Oliver remarked that Drury had led "every unemployed deputation" that had crossed his threshold over the course of the past year and a half. When Drury detailed the suffering of those unable to find paid employment, the mayor told him that the House of Industry was always available to the destitute, which drew heckles from the crowd. Controller Geary demanded to know whether the protesters were socialists. Three of the contingent acknowledged that they were indeed advocates of a radical overhaul of capitalist institutions. This unleashed a flury of concern that St. Andrews Hall would be used to "preach a doctrine of discontent."[36]

Over the next few days the nascent unemployed movement enlisted the support of sympathetic clergy, often associated with the emerging Social Gospel movement. Pre-eminent among them was Dr. G.S. Eby of the College Street People's Church, aka The Church of the Revolution. The travails of the outdoor relief system were now being complained about by religious figures and elected municipal officials, who criticized the long delays experienced by destitute families applying for emergency aid from the House of Industry. Meanwhile, an organized group of eighty-five refused the "labour test" at the Poor House two days running in what was obviously a direct action protest, albeit one that left the single unemployed "casuals" homeless in the dead of winter.[37] More than 1,000 unemployed gathered at St. Andrew's Hall on 21 January 1909 to hear a rousing Social Gospel address from Reverend Eby. "The day has come when men are tired of talking of hell and heaven," he thundered. "There are multitudes of people in the churches who want to bring heaven to earth." Drury's speech was even more provocative. Urging the wageless to refuse both the symbolism and the substance of "cracking the stone," he railed against the quality of the House of Industry's provisions and urged relief recipients to steal what provisions they could from the Poor House pantry. "I wouldn't give a pig the provisions I got there," he snorted.[38]

Out of this initial St. Andrew's Hall meeting came an extraordinary set of recommendations, quite unlike anything before articulated by those seeking relief. The six demands generated by the mobilization of January 1909 amounted to an unambiguous indictment of decades of Toronto's treatment of the dispossessed, governed as it was by routines of "labour tests" and procedures of "cleansing and classifying." Those demands also united the interests of the "casual" single unemployed men who stayed overnight in the House of Industry, recipients of indoor relief, and resident families drawing on outdoor dispensations. The wageless, whatever their station, wanted the civic relief department to be abolished; "running baths" for workmen; daily fare composed of more than cheap servings of adulterated soup and hard bread; provision of adequate winter clothing; investigation of the bread depots so that there was monitoring of their activities and assurances that distressed families would not suffer; and, finally, and most strikingly, control of the distribution of relief, taking it out of the hands of the Associated Charities of Toronto and vesting it in a committee of the unemployed. Not yet ready to demand the abolition of "cracking the stone," the socialist-led wageless had, in 1909, nonetheless mobilized their ranks, broadened their struggle, and crystallized a fundamental challenge to their dispossession.[39]

Mayor Oliver made threatening noises that trouble-making advocates of the right of the out of work to control the relief system could be deported. Meanwhile, a letter to the editor of the Toronto *Star* bemoaned the "Brutal Treatment of the Unemployed." It suggested that resistance to "cracking the stone" had unleashed an ideological counter-assault on property and propriety, described as "savage":

> When a man goes to a place like the House of Industry, it is plain that he is half starved already. There he gets bread and some warm water called tea, at night, and in the morning. Most likely he will not get a bed the first three nights, but will sleep on a floor, with hardly any room to turn. When he gets up in the morning, after what little sleep he had been able to get, he is required to break a lot of stones. The quantity of stones to be broken will take a man used to it three hours, but a man not used to that kind of work will take from four to six hours. Six hours hard work for a bit of dry bread and a rest on the floor. And we sing "Britons Never Shall be Slaves." Let the people of Toronto reflect a little on the conditions in this city and cease casting slurs upon those who are for the time being in bad circumstances.

The letter, signed simply "Out of Work," was a reflection of what the dispossessed were up against in their daily struggle to survive, as well as in their organized effort to resist.[40]

A year later, in February 1910, seven members of the non-stone-breaking brotherhood refused the House of Industry "labour test" and found themselves before Magistrate Ellis, charged with vagrancy. Amidst growing animosity to the Ontario workless flooding into Toronto from parts unknown, turning the city into an "Eldorado of the tramp fraternity," the men became scapegoats in an age-old ideological assault on the "undeserving poor." Unimpressed with the lot before him, the Magistrate sentenced the group to jail terms of from thirty days to three months, promising them "a chance to do real work." Meanwhile, the House of Industry, pleading economies, doubled the quantity of stone it required from all "casuals" receiving bread, water, and a place to lay their heads.[41]

The criminalization of the dispossessed proceeded apace as the crisis of worklessness deepened in 1911–12, worsening still further during a severe 1913–15 depression. National in scope, the economic downturn generated what one historian has termed a "Canadian unemployed revolt," in which prods to action often came from the Industrial Workers of the World on the prairies or the Social Democratic Party in Ontario. Toronto's wageless were hit particularly hard. The municipal relief system sagged under the pressure of more and more applications for aid. In the winter of 1914–15 more than 5,000 families, representing more than 25,000 people, were applying for relief to the beleaguered House of Industry. Long queues of men, "two and three deep, lined up outside the … building waiting for shelter for the night." One official commented that he "had never before seen anything like it." The usual recourse to a series of start-up/close- down Civic Employment Bureaux did little to ease the situation. Maladministered and overwhelmed by applications, such ad hoc agencies competed with corrupt private employment enterprises and managed, for the most part, only to secure temporary work, in limited amounts, for the growing army of the unemployed. Calls for "able-bodied vagrants" to be "made to work for their living until they have acquired the habit of self-support" continued to be heard. Ontario's Commission on Unemployment reported:

> The vagrant thrives on Soup Kitchens, Houses of Industry, Salvation Army Shelters and similar institutions maintained for the purpose of rendering temporary assistance to a worthier class … .Men are coming into Toronto from the mining camps and smaller places, spending their money in drink, and complaining of not being able to get work. A lot of them don't want it and wouldn't take it if they had a chance. This class of men augment the already too numerous criminal class.

Decimating the trade unions, whose membership numbers in Ontario dropped 25 per cent, and straining the disciplinary order of relief to the breaking point, the crisis of 1913–14 left the waged and the wageless in the same sinking boat of capitalist crisis.

In September 1914, 600 delegates to the Toronto Trades and Labour Council gathered in an effort to compile information on the unemployment crisis. They set up a committee system with captains appointed for each ward, tasked with assembling in-depth statistics on the dimensions of joblessness in the city. A labour movement–funded Trades Industrial Toy Association was set up to give work to unemployed mechanics in the manufacture of children's playthings. Joseph T. Marks, whose *Industrial Banner* was something of a beachhead of Toronto trade union labourite radicalism, spearheaded a "Provincial Publicity Campaign on Unemployment," but his efforts apparently led to little. The situation for working women was particularly dire; they were being driven to accept "situations in the country, glad to be able to rely thereby upon board and lodging at least." Claims were being made that the unemployment crisis of 1913–14 was the most severe in Canada's history. The *Labour Gazette* routinely reported on the worsening conditions in Toronto.[42]

Toronto's wageless thus faced an uphill battle in the crisis of 1911–15. Many refused the labour discipline of "cracking the stone." "I'd lay down on the street and die before I'd go to the House of Industry or any such place. The jail's the place for me," declared one malcontent who had been hauled before the court. He was sentenced to four months. In February 1915, "casuals" spending nights in the wayfarer's lodge ward of the House of Industry were again refusing to break stone for their keep. George Bust and Nick Melasel were charged with vagrancy for their insubordinate behaviour. Described as sullen, his court testimony defiant and unrepentant, Bust got as good as he gave. Stands of combativeness before constituted authority had a way of being repaid in kind. "I think you need looking after," concluded His Worship Squire Ellis, "it'll be $20 and costs or 90 days." Other shelters faced similar resistance to the "labour test." At the Fred Victor Mission, which housed upwards of seventy homeless people a night, the unemployed organized a protest against what they considered "unfair practice." The mission was of the view that the agitation was the work of socialists.[43]

The outbreak of the First World War ended the 1911–15 crisis of capitalism. Wartime production eased wagelessness. This happened, for the most part, in the aftermath of military enlistment, be it coerced or voluntary. The pressure put on the relief system both by the sheer numbers of unemployed requiring assistance and by the growing resistance to relief discipline, often orchestrated by left agitators, lessened. One measure of this is the statistics regarding the poor's utilization of police jail cells as lodging. In 1915 in Toronto, more than 10,500 people had been sheltered at various police stations across the city. One year later, in 1916, with the war drive and its recruitment campaigns in full swing, fewer than 375 had availed themselves of the jail's beds. The Canadian Patriotic Fund, privately financed and administered, provided the families of unemployed men who enlisted a "reasonable standard of comfort," and tens of thousands of single men joined the armed forces to extricate themselves from wagelessness. Roughly 600,000 served in the Canadian Expeditionary Force, with 250,000 joining between June 1915 and May 1916. Sixty thousand families benefited from the Patriotic Fund's largesse, which totalled almost $40 million between 1914 and 1919. The unemployed had been vanquished, as it were; capitalism had found something of a solution to its economic and political crises with the breakout of hostilities in Europe. Inducements to patriotic duty were everywhere and often overrode class solidarity. In a January 1915 fundraising entertainment at Massey Hall, organized by the Toronto District Labour Council on behalf of the jobless, the message of fighting against unemployment was drowned out in dutiful renditions of "The Death of Nelson" and "We'll Never Let the Old Flag Down." The evening was capped off by a recitation of "The Empire Flag," the address delivered by a speaker wrapped in the Union Jack.[44] No black flags few at this unemployed rally.

Preparing the Offensive of the Outcasts: The Red Flag Unfurled, 1918–1925

The war ended. The capitalist crisis continued. But the years 1914 to 1918 had mobilized the state to harness the productive enterprise and energy of the nation, refining a new apparatus of the regulatory state, and in doing so it had galvanized initiatives aimed at monitoring and addressing unemployment. By war's end, amidst the winding down of specialized industrial pursuits and the return of veterans, it was feared that unemployment nationally would swell to 250,000 in 1918 alone. Labour, having tasted the possibilities of full employment during wartime, and having provided waged and wageless men for battle, both in the war and on the homefront, was in a combative mood. Class-based criticisms of war and of the conscription of labour, but not wealth, was commonplace. Tensions were exacerbated by a growing left-wing presence in the unions and among the unorganized and unwaged working class. Talk of the revolution in Soviet Russia and ideas about production for use rather than for profit grew more menacing. Sir Robert Borden, who led Canada's coalition government, was warned by one high-ranking adviser in 1918: "People are not … in a normal condition. There is less respect for law and authority than we probably have ever had in the country. If … Canada faces acute conditions of unemployment without any adequate programme to meet the situation, no one can foresee just what might happen." Setting up the Employment Service of Canada, a national network of labour exchanges funded and operated jointly by the federal and provincial governments, was one component of the state response. Unemployment insurance systems were studied, and drew a surprisingly strong consensus of favourable opinion among government officials, mainstream trade union leaders, and progressive employers. But the political will to implement such a system evaporated in the Red Scare climate of 1919. Clampdowns on working-class militancy, suppression of a wave of strikes in 1919, the deportation of "alien" radicals, and the use of state trials of socialist agitators to establish decisively that the red flag, Soviets, and workers' control of production would not become part of the Canadian way of life trumped a forceful state program that would have decisively addressed unemployment in new ways.[45]

Toronto had contributed more recruits to the Canadian war effort than any other city. Now it would see the return of more soldiers, all of them looking for work. Besides that, no city in Canada had been harder hit than Toronto by the closure of wartime's munitions industries. Amidst the labour revolt of 1919, there was a push not only for sympathetic and general strikes but also for a cash bonus to be paid to war veterans. One commentator described the proposed $2,000 gratuity as "one grand solution for virtually all the troubles due to unrest, unemployment, discontent and Bolshevism." Many Toronto veterans agreed, and rallied on the legislative grounds at Queen's Park to demand action. But no bonus would be granted in 1919. Instead, out-of-work veterans were advised to head to the hinterlands. A "back to the land" movement, said many employers and not a few farmers, would allow rural producers to "get labour more cheaply." At this, the Toronto Great War Veterans Association took considerable umbrage, arguing that those who had served overseas for four years, separated from their loved ones, would not now be told they could "take employment mucking in the bush," far from the family hearth.[46] Toronto-headquartered Frontier College put a novel spin on the idea that movement to the country could alleviate unemployment, suggesting that municipalities purchase homesteads and employ the jobless in clearing 160 acres and building a house and barn on each improved lot, which could then be sold for a profit.[47]

The crisis of wagelessness that afflicted veterans and non-soldiers alike deepened until, in the fall of 1920, the economy took another turn for the worse, plunging into depression. Toronto employers reduced work hours in order to stave off mass layoffs, but such band-aid solutions were of little help. Veterans who had managed to secure work now lost their jobs, with estimates being that one in five able-bodied ex-soldiers had been forced out of work. National unemployment rates soared to over 10 per cent (214,000 jobless, in raw numbers), and the situation in Toronto taxed the public employment bureaux to the breaking point. More than 3,000 of those registered with the bureaux, which favoured veterans, were "unplaced"; at the height of the crisis, in the winter of 1921, the number skyrocketed to 15,000. Federal payments to the Municipality of Toronto for emergency relief for the unemployed between December 1920 and April 1921 totalled $134,128 – almost 40 per cent of the total distributed across the country. Toronto police cells, which had provided a "home" to so many destitute in 1915, but were largely empty of these patrons by 1916, began to fill again. By 1925, a record 16,500 people were being housed in city jails, many of them ex-servicemen who had joined the army of the unemployed.[48]

At the Toronto House of Industry, the number of complaints rose. A nurse who regularly visited homes of the Toronto indigent saw children going hungry and concluded that it was "impossible for human beings to live at all on what the city supplies." The plight of the workless, claimed these critics, was reminiscent of the "Dark Ages."[49] Such allegations were met with the usual arsenal of denial. Officially constituted and often church-affiliated Neighbourhood Workers' Associations and the superintendant at the House of Industry maintained as always that "everyone should know that no man needs to sleep in the parks or walk the streets in Toronto. There is shelter for him. When we encourage begging on the street – which is against the law in the first place – you are encouraging something at the same time that is most deadly for the man."[50]

When jobless veterans sought help making rental payments in order to stave off eviction, they found themselves "chasing around from one place to another … for … three weeks," unable to find any agency to lend them a hand. Seeking loans that they committed to pay back, the ex-servicemen formed a delegation and went to City Hall to seek out Mayor Maguire. Finance Commissioner Ross curtly dismissed the group: "Anybody who thinks that we are going to liquidate his arrears of rent is in error." The former soldiers who decided to organize a Toronto-to-Ottawa trek in protest of inaction on unemployment fared no better. They hoofed it the 220 miles to the nation's capital, only to be sent back empty-handed on the train.[51] Liberal reformers like Bryce Stewart looked disdainfully on the tendency of those in power to pass the buck of unemployment to the next generation. "If we wait long enough," he wrote in 1921, "the bread lines and out-of-work doles will cease, unemployment will be gone, men and women will rise out of dull inaction and find joy again in the work of head and hands." Then, all would pass out of mind: "The present time will be referred to as the 'hard times of 1920–1921' an unfortunate experience to be forgotten if possible." Bryce had seen it all before, having written about the 1913–15 crisis, and he was convinced that "the divine right of unpreparedness" was not going to stave off the next, inevitable downturn: "Men will pursue their usual ways and in 1925, or 26 or 27 or some other year, the dark ogre of unemployment will again thrust his long arm into the factories and mines and shops and offices, tear the workers from their tasks, bank the fires, hang out the 'No Help Wanted' signs and shut the doors against them."[52]

The economy improved somewhat after 1921; even so, unemployment was far from extinguished in the 1920s. Between 1922 and 1929, the annual average unemployment rate was 11 per cent, and 30 per cent of all workers found themselves jobless at some point in the year, usually for around eighteen weeks.[53] By 1925, the presence of beggars on city streets and the influx of the wageless into Toronto from other municipalities had precipitated yet another round of ideological and material attacks on the poor. Toronto's chief medical officer, Dr. Charles Hastings, campaigned to rid the city of beggars, whom he considered a variant of the age-old "undeserving poor." Known as an aggressive advocate of improved public health and an enemy of slum conditions, Hastings was also capable of sounding the tocsin of vigilance against vagrants. He suggested that Toronto civic officials publicize "through the local papers and the Canadian press generally" their intention next winter to terminate "relief to non-residents, or anyone unable to prove their residence, and that, in addition to this, citizens of Toronto be urged not to give promiscuously to men soliciting help at private houses, or to those accosting individuals on the streets, but that they be asked to refer all such persons to the House of Industry, where their case can be properly investigated and where those deserving will receive the necessary food and shelter." Hastings launched his harangue at a time when George Hamilton, who worked for a government employment bureau, noted that every day between 1,500 and 2,500 men were applying for jobs of any kind. For every 100, there was work for one. Malnutrition and exposure incapacitated many of those seeking work, and according to Frank Fleming, a representative of the unemployed, 75 per cent of them were veterans. A moderate in his views, Fleming still emphasized that for all its efforts to relieve the poor, the House of Industry was unable to keep up with the rising pressures on its resources. Hundreds of the unemployed spent their nights huddled in "cold box cars and [on] cement floors." The vast majority of the unemployed were genuinely wanting, Fleming insisted, and they were actively looking for work and should receive sympathy from Toronto residents. "Misery and suffering," he claimed, were widespread. If there was indeed unrest among these poor folk, he suggested, it was the work of "Reds" and "Communists," who were prodding the army of the unemployed to vocalize its discontent and mobilize its ranks.[54]

The red flag had by now been unfurled among the wageless. The Workers Party of Canada, a new communist organization born amidst the post-war downturn, had from its inception been working to form "large and militant" Unemployed Associations in Toronto and Hamilton. Capitalism was assailed as the cause of the crisis of wagelessness, and among these advocates of a Soviet Canada the demand among the jobless was for "work or full maintenance." The communists viewed unemployment as central to the class struggle, on a par with wage reductions and the open shop, as an issue around which to organize and cultivate resistance. "Moscow Jack" MacDonald, a Toronto patternmaker who would emerge in the 1920s as one of Canadian communism's leaders, toured the country in the hard winter of 1921, making speeches to fellow militants about the scourge of unemployment.

Even so, the communist presence in Canadian working-class circles was weak, and faced red-baiting in the mainstream press as well as the sharp hostility of employers. Communism also roused the ire of reactionaries entrenched in conservative corners of trade union officialdom. Since 1919, this part of the labour bureaucracy had taken direct aim at revolutionaries in the workers' movement. Two Toronto District Labour Council figures, W.J. Hevey and Arthur O'Leary, were representative figures in this trend, launching a newspaper, the *Labor Leader*, as a strident voice of the most entrepreneurial wing of business unionism. It railed against the Industrial Workers of the World as well as One Big Unionism and Bolshevism; the unemployed found little support within its pages.

As the economic downturn of the early 1920s sapped the strength of the waged and threw more and more of the wageless into the trough of material despondency, conservatizing tendencies could be discerned among the Toronto dispossessed. Tim Buck, a Toronto machinist and perennial Communist candidate for the presidency of the Trades and Labor Congress of Canada, polled 25 per cent of the delegates at the 1923–24 annual convention. Thereafter it was downhill: as the capitalist crisis of the early 1920s abated in 1925–26, the workless, their numbers declining, had a brief reprieve. The red flag, flying listlessly over the thinning ranks of the unemployed, readied itself for the next capitalist crisis. It would not be long in coming. A reinvigorated offensive of the outcasts would break out during the Great Depression of the 1930s. The reception of the red flag, unfurled in the agitations of the wageless between 1920 and 1925, would prove unprecedented.[55]

QUESTIONS FOR CONSIDERATION:

1. Palmer and Héroux argue that wagelessness and waged employment are not opposites. Explain what they mean.
2. Why were "workless males" so feared in Ontario in the 1870s? Was this justified?
3. Describe stone-breaking in your own words. Why was it important?

4. What did the "black flag" symbolize? Was it an effective tool? Compare and contrast it with the "red flag."
5. How did the wageless, the unemployed, and the underemployed mobilize in Toronto in the early twentieth century?
6. Why did wageless people refuse "cracking the stone?" Do you feel this was justified?
7. How do Palmer and Héroux describe the situation for workers and the unemployed in Toronto in the 1920s?

NOTES

1 See the broad discussion in Bryan D. Palmer and Gaétan Héroux, *Toronto's Poor: A Rebellious History* (Toronto: Between the Lines, 2016); and for the persistence of this stereotyping of the poor into modern times, Sylvia Bashevikin, *Welfare Hot Buttons: Women, Work, and Social Policy Reform* (Toronto: University of Toronto Press, 2002).

2 See for a useful introduction Peter Goheen, *Victorian Toronto, 1850–1900: Pattern and Process of Growth* (Chicago: Department of Geography, 1970).

3 Still valuable in terms of a general statement on Canada's transformation in these years is Robert Craig Brown and Ramsay Cook, *Canada, 1896–1921: A Nation Transformed* (Toronto: McClelland and Stewart, 1974). A useful collection of articles outlining the social consequences of this consolidation of capitalism is Michael S. Cross and Gregory S. Kealey, eds., *The Consolidation of Capitalism, 1896–1929 – Readings in Canadian Social History*, vol. 4 (Toronto: McClelland and Stewart, 1983).

4 As an introduction to the historical processes outlined above see, for instance, H.V. Nelles, *The Politics of Development: Forests, Mines, and Hydro-Electric Power in Ontario, 1849–1941* (Toronto: Macmillan, 1974); Tom Traves, *The State and Enterprise: Canadian Manufacturers and the Federal Government, 1917–1931* (Toronto: University of Toronto Press, 1979); and Gregory S. Kealey, *Toronto Workers Respond to Industrial Capitalism, 1867–1892* (Toronto: University of Toronto Press, 1980).

5 For a brief statement only see Frances Fox Piven, "Foreword," in Palmer and Héroux, *Toronto's Poor*, xi–xiii.

6 For an introduction to modern capitalist crises see Ernest Mandel, *The Second Slump: A Marxist Analysis of Recession in the Seventies* (London: New Left Books, 1978); and for different approaches to the ongoing nature of crises, reaching destructively into our own times, see Robert Brenner, *The Economics of Global Turbulence: The Advanced Capitalist Economies from Long Boom to Long Downturn, 1945–2005* (New York and London: Verso, 2006); Murray E.G. Smith, *Global Capitalism in Crisis: Karl Marx and the Decay of the Profit System* (Halifax and Winnipeg: Fernwood, 2010); and Greg Albo, Sam Gindin, and Leo Panitch, *In and Out of Crisis: The Global Financial Meltdown and Left Alternatives* (Oakland: PM Press, 2010). As we prepare this text for publication the COVID 19–induced economic crisis of 2020 is unfolding, taxing the health care system to the breaking point, pushing unemployment levels to their highest points since the Great Depression of the 1930s, and necessitating massive government intervention unprecedented in the history of Canada in the post-war era.

7 Michael Denning, "Wageless Life," *New Left Review* 66 (November–December 2010), 79–81; J.C.L. Simonde de Sismondi, *Nouveaux principes d'économie politique ou de la richesse dans ses*

rapports avec la population, 2 vols. (Paris, 1819), II: 262, 305, I: 146, quoted in Gareth Stedman Jones, *An End to Poverty? A Historical Debate* (London : Profile Books, 2004), 151; Max Weber, *General Economic History*, trans. F.H. Knight (New York, 1961), quoted in G.E.M. de Ste. Croix, *The Class Struggle in the Ancient Greek World* (London: Duckworth, 1981), 262; Edith Abbott, "The Wages of Unskilled Labor in the United States," *Journal of Political Economy* 13 (June 1905): 324; and Catharina Lis and Hugo Soly, "Policing the Early Modern Proletariat, 1450–1850," in *Proletarianization and Family History*, ed. David Levine (Orlando: Academic Press, 1984), 163–228.

8 David Montgomery, *The Fall of the House of Labor: The Workplace, the State, and American Labor Activism, 1865–1925* (New York: Cambridge University Press, 1987), 91. See also Peter Way, *Common Labor: Workers and the Digging of North American Canals, 1780–1860* (Baltimore: Johns Hopkins University Press, 1993); and Andrea Graziosi, "Common Laborers, Unskilled Workers, 1880–1915," *Labor History* 22 (Fall 1981), 512–44.

9 As an introduction only to Toronto in the years 1830 to 1890, see Albert Schrauwers, "The Gentlemanly Order and the Politics of Production in the Transition to Capitalism in Upper Canada," *Labour/le Travail* 65 (Spring 2010): 9–46; Lisa Chilton, "Managing Migrants: Toronto, 1820–1880," *Canadian Historical Review* 92 (June 2011): 231–62; Stephen A. Speisman, "Munificent Parsons and Municipal Parsimony: Voluntary vs Public Poor Relief in Nineteenth-Century Toronto," *Ontario History* 65 (March 1973): 32–46; and Kealey, *Toronto Workers Respond to Industrial Capitalism*.

10 See, for instance, Albert Sschrauwers, *"Union Is Strength": W.L. Mackenzie, the Children of Peace, and the Emergence of Joint Stock Democracy in Upper Canada* (Toronto: University of Toronto Press, 2009), esp. 56–65; and for a useful general statement, Michael B. Katz, "The Origins of the Institutional State," *Marxist Perspectives* 4 (Winter 1978): 6–23. We offer an extended discussion of this early history in Bryan D. Palmer and Gaétan Héroux, "'Cracking the Stone': The Long History of the Toronto Dispossessed," *Labour/Le Travail* 69 (Spring 2012): 9–62.

11 See, for instance, Peter Baskerville and Eric W. Sager, *Unwilling Idlers: The Urban Unemployed and Their Families in Late Victorian Canada* (Toronto: University of Toronto Press, 1998). For statements on unemployment's recognition in the nineteenth century see also John Garraty, *Unemployment in History: Economic Thought and Public Policy* (New York: Harper and Row, 1978), esp. 4, 109–28; and Alexander Keyssar, *Out of Work: the First Century of Unemployment in Massachusetts* (New York and Cambridge: Cambridge University Press, 1986).

12 Kealey, *Toronto Workers Respond to Industrial Capitalism;* Bryan D. Palmer, "Labour Protest and Organization in Nineteenth-Century Canada, 1820–1890," *Labour/Le Travail* 20 (Fall 1987): 73; Gregory S. Kealey and Bryan D. Palmer, *Dreaming of What Might Be: The Knights of Labor in Ontario, 1880–1900* (Cambridge and New York: Cambridge University Press, 1982).

13 *Globe*, 26 January 1877, as cited in Michael Cross, ed., *The Workingman in Nineteenth Century Canada* (Toronto: Oxford University Press, 1974), 196.

14 Richard Anderson, "'The Irrepressible Stampede': Tramps in Ontario, 1870–1880," *Ontario History* 84 (March 1992): 33–56. This period saw repeated concern expressed by trustees of the House of Industry that other Ontario municipalities were dumping their poor on Toronto, especially in the depths of winter. See *Annual Report of the House of Industry, City of Toronto, 1877*, 3; *Annual Report of the House of Industry, City of Toronto, 1879*, 6.

15 James M. Pitsula, "The Treatment of Tramps in Late Nineteenth-Century Toronto," Canadian Historical Association, *Historical Papers* (1980), 116–32; "The support of the poor," *The Canada Presbyterian*, 7 January 1881; "Tramps and Waifs," *Globe*, 22 March 1887. One part of the inner history of woodcutting as a "labour test" involved the board of the House of Industry

subcontracting the delivery of cordwood and the transportation of cut wood sold to clients of the Rogers Coal Company. The owner of this enterprise, Elias Rogers, was involved in a price-fixing ring in the coal industry in the late 1880s. See J.M.S. Careless, *Toronto to 1918: An Illustrated History* (Toronto: James Lorimer, 1984), 143.

16 *Report of the Commissioners Appointed to enquire into the Prison and Reformatory System of the Province of Ontario*, 8 April 1891, 682–5. See also the comments on "work tests" in *All Saints Church Parish Magazine*, vol. V (December 1895), 138.

17 *Fifty-Fifth Annual Report of the House of Industry, City of Toronto, 1891–1892*, 9; Pitsula, "The Treatment of Tramps in Toronto," 131–2; "Talking of the Law," *Toronto Evening Star*, 10 January 1896; "House of Industry Still in a Bad Way Financially," *Toronto Evening Star*, 19 February 1896; *Report of the Commissioners Appointed to Inquire into Prison and Reformatory System in the Province of Ontario*, 8 April 1891, 684.

18 "The Labor Test," *Toronto Evening* Star, 16 May 1896; Thomas Conant, *Upper Canada Sketches* (Toronto: William Briggs, 1898), 195.

19 Pitsula, "The Treatment of Tramps in Toronto," 130.

20 "Around a Stove. Daily Gathering of Queer People at City Hall. Men out of Employment and Those Seeking Charity. How They View Officials and How Officials View Them," *Toronto Evening Star*, 22 February 1896. See also "Stone Test Scares Them. Tramps Object to Work for Food and Lodging," *Toronto Evening Star*, 21 December 1897.

21 B. Rosamund, *House of Commons Journals* (1876), App. 3, 200, quoted in Steven Langdon, "The Emergence of the Canadian Working Class Movement, 1845-1875," Part II, *Journal of Canadian Studies*, 8 August 1973), 21. For relevant discussions in the Toronto-based *Ontario Workman* see "Number and Condition of the Unemployed," 18 December 1873; "The Unemployed," 5 February 1874.

22 Debi Wells, "'The Hardest Lines of the Sternest School': Working-Class Ottawa in the Depression of the 1870s," MA thesis, Carleton University, 1982. Much of the discussion of unemployed demonstrations in this thesis is summarized in Baskerville and Sager, *Unwilling Idlers*, 30–33. For political context see as well Bernard Ostry, "Conservatives, Liberals, and Labour in the 1870s," *Canadian Historical Review* 61 (June 1960): 93–127; and for 1878 Quebec City public works protests demanding "work and bread," see Jean-Philip Mathieu, "'C'est le people qui est maître; nous sommes les maîtres a Québec': La grève des ouvriers des travaux publics, juin 1878," *Labour/Le Travail* 70 (Fall 2012):133–57.

23 See, for instance, *Ottawa Herald*, 23 February 1880; *Ottawa Daily Free Press*, 23 February 1880, among dozens of other newspaper accounts that might be cited.

24 Quoted in Wells, "'The Hardest Lines,'" 98; and cited in Baskerville and Sager, *Unwilling Idlers*, 33. Note the wider discussion in David Goutor, *Guarding the Gates: The Canadian Labour Movement and Immigration, 1872–1934* (Vancouver: UBC Press, 2007).

25 Phillips Thompson, *The Politics of Labor* (New York and Chicago: Belford, Clarke, 1987), 186–88; Russell Hann, "Brainworkers and the Knights of Labor: E.E. Sheppard, Phillips Thompson and the Toronto *News*, 1883–1887," in *Essays in Canadian Working-Class History*, ed. Gregory S. Kealey and Peter Warrian (Toronto: McClelland and Stewart, 1976), 35–57.

26 Bettina Bradbury, "The Home as Workplace," in Craven, ed., *Labouring Lives*, 417, citing *Bureau of Industries*, 1888, 42; Greg Kealey, ed., *Canada Investigates Industrialism: The Royal Commission on the Relations of Labor and Capital, 1889* (Toronto: University of Toronto Press, 1973), for a small sampling of the testimony; Charles Lipton, *The Trade Union Movement of Canada, 1827–1959* (Toronto: NC Press, 1973), 90; *Ottawa Free Press*, 27 February 1880; Wells, "'The Hardest Lines,'" 95; Baskerville and Sager, *Unwilling Idlers*, 33 and 40, quoting *Globe*, 21 February 1891.

27 The *Globe's* 19 February 1891 image of a black flag, "Work or Bread" demonstration adorns the cover of Baskerville and Sager, *Unwilling Idlers*, where the event of 11 February 1891 is discussed, 39–40, citing and quoting "Work or Bread," *Globe*, 12 February 1891; *Globe*, 13 February 1891; *Labor Advocate*, 20 February 1891; 27 February 1891. See also Lipton, *Trade Union Movement of Canada*, 90; Russell G. Hann, Gregory S. Kealey, Linda Kealey, and Peter Warrian, *Primary Sources in Canadian Working Class History* (Kitchener: Dumont, 1973), 9–10.

28 "Need Not Hunger If They'll Work. Superintendant Laughlan of House of Industry Willingly Feeds the Industrious. He Has a Work Test – It's Work … Soup, Fuel and Grocery Orders Result," *Toronto Daily Star*, 28 January 1908. On the amount of stone that had to be broken and its weight see Dennis Guest, *The Emergence of Social Security in Canada* (Vancouver: UBC Press, 1980), 37. Haymarket's story is told in two important studies: Paul Avrich, *The Haymarket Tragedy* (Princeton: Princeton University Press, 1986); and James Green, *Death in the Haymarket: The Story of Chicago, the First Labor Movement, and the Bombing That Divided Gilded Age America* (New York: Pantheon, 2007). The unemployed who carried the black flag in Toronto's 1891 protest did so a mere four years after the execution of the Haymarket anarchists. Phillips Thompson recorded his sense of the climate surrounding this first North American Red Scare, condemning "the hideous brutality which found in the death sentence of the … convicted Anarchists a subject for ghoulish rejoicing and heartless jests." Thompson, *Politics of Labor*, 167.

29 Ian McKay, *Reasoning Otherwise: Leftists and the People's Enlightenment in Canada, 1890–1920* (Toronto: Between the Lines, 2008), 208–11.

30 Note Gene Homel, "'Fading Beams of the Nineteenth Century': Radicalism and Early Socialism in Canada's 1890s," *Labour/Le Travailleur* 5 (Spring 1980): 7–32; Ian McKay, ed., *For a Working-Class Culture in Canada: A Selection of Colin McKay's Writings on Sociology and Political Economy, 1897–1939* (St. John's: Canadian Committee on Labour History, 1996), esp. 34–9, 47–52.

31 Michael J. Piva, *The Condition of the Working Class in Toronto – 1900–1921* (Ottawa: University of Ottawa Press, 1979); Leonard C. Marsh, "The Problem of Seasonal Unemployment: A Quantitative and Comparative Survey of Seasonal Fluctuations in Canadian Employment," MA thesis, McGill University, 1933, 134–5; and for women workers Marsh, *Canadians In and Out of Work: A Survey of Economic Classes and Their Relation to the Labour Market* (Oxford: Oxford University Press, 1940), 273–9.

32 Robert H. Babcock, *Gompers in Canada: A Study of American Continentalism before the First World War* (Toronto: University of Toronto Press, 1974), esp. 44, 53; Palmer, "Labour Protest and Organization in Nineteenth-Century Canada," 82.

33 Martin Robin, *Radical Politics and Canadian Labour* (Kingston: Queen's University Industrial Relations Centre, 1968), 117; Piva, *Condition of the Working Class in Toronto*, 69, 71–4; *Labour Gazette* IV (July 1903–June 1904), 614; VIII (July 1907–June 1908), 962–3; "Toronto Free Employment Bureau," IX (July 1908–June 1909), 1343; "Need Not Hunger If They'll Work," *Daily Star*, 28 January 1908.

34 *Globe*, 17 March 1908, cited in Piva, *Condition of the Working Class in Toronto*, 74; "Hot Talk in Muddy Park. Orators of the Soap-Box Order Harangue a Crowd on the Waterfront. And Talk of Taking Forcible Possession of Contents of Warehouse," *Toronto Daily Star*, 5 January 1909.

35 "Ugly Temper of Idle Men. The Unemployed Gathered Swiftly This Morning into Army at City Hall. Blocked Street but Had to Move On," *Toronto Daily Star*, 13 January 1909.

36 "To Get Work for Idle Men. Heard Deputation Today. The Speaker Dropped the Violent Tone When They Entered City Hall. A Large Force of Police on Hand to Guard Against Any Disturbance," *Toronto Daily Star*, 14 January 1909.

37 "Stuck a Pin in Ald. J.J. Graham," *Toronto Daily Star*, 18 January 1909.

38 "'A Preacher to the Unemployed. Rev. Dr. Eby Roused the Crowd to Very High Pitch of Enthusiasm. Then Speaker Got Hot and Proceeded to Abuse the Civic Authorities in Angry Terms," Toronto *Daily Star*, 21 January 1909. On the social gospel see Richard Allen, *The Social Passion: Religion and Social Reform in Canada, 1914–1928* (Toronto: University of Toronto Press, 1973). McKay, *Reasoning Otherwise*, 472, refers to Eby's 1909 Church of the Revolution, noting its connection to the Social Democratic Party and the encouragement of early socialist feminism.

39 "A Preacher to the Unemployed," *Toronto Daily Star*, 15 February 1909.

40 "Brutal Treatment of the Unemployed," *Toronto Daily Star*, 15 February 1909.

41 "Vagrants Sent Where They'll Have to Work. House of Industry Too Easy for Them and They Go to Prison – Early," *Toronto Daily Star*, 8 February 1910; "More Stone Breaking. Casuals at House of Industry Must Crack Double Quantity," *Toronto Daily Star*, 25 January 1910; "Toronto a Mecca of Tired Tramps. Tramps Flock Here, and the Associated Charities Want Steps Taken to Keep Them Working. Also Asks That Province Make a Grant to the House of Industry," *Toronto Daily Star*, 21 December 1910.

42 The above paragraphs draw on many sources. Piva, *Condition of the Working Class in Toronto*, 75–86, presents a good summary of the Toronto situation and provides the quote from Ontario, *Report of the Ontario Commission on Unemployment* (Toronto 1916), 77–8, 201–2. Note as well, McKay, *Reasoning Otherwise*, 209; James Naylor, *The New Democracy: Challenging the Social Order in Industrial Ontario, 1914–1925* (Toronto: University of Toronto Press, 1991), 18–19, 80; Baskerville and Sager, *Unwilling Idlers*, 176–84; *Labour Gazette*, XV (July 1914 to June 1915): 464–5, 666–7; *Eighty-Fourth Annual Report of the House of Industry, City of Toronto, 1920–1921*, 7, 10; "100,000 Jobless: The Forgotten Depressions of 1908–1916," in *The Canadian Worker in the Twentieth Century*, ed. Irving Abella and David Millar (Toronto: Oxford University Press, 1978), 73–6; James Struthers, *No Fault of Their Own: Unemployment and the Canadian Welfare State* (Toronto: University of Toronto Press, 1983), 12–16; and Bryce Stewart, "Unemployment and Organization of the Labour Market," American Academy of Political and Social Science, "Social and Economic Conditions in the Dominion of Canada," *The Annals* 107 (May 1923): 286–93.

43 "Preferred the Jail to Any Other Place. Aged Vagrant Insisted on Being Sent Across the Don, and He was Obliged," Toronto *Daily Star*, 18 December 1912; ""Refused to Work, But Took Meals – Jailed. George Bust was Defiant in Police Court – Received a Lesson. Couldn't Find Work. Wouldn't Crack Stone at the House of Industry for His Breakfast," Toronto *Daily Star*, 5 February 1915; Cary Fagan, *The Fred Victor Mission Story: From Charity to Social Justice* (Winfield, BC: Wood Lake Books, 1993), 62.

44 *Toronto Police Report, 1915*, 20; *Toronto Police Report, 1916*, 20; Phillip Morris, ed., *The Canadian Patriotic Fund: A Record of Its Activities from 1914 to 1919* (No Place, No Date), 23, 271, cited in Struthers, *No Fault of Their Own*, 14; Desmond Morton and Glenn Wright, *Winning the Second Battle: Canadian Veterans and the Return to Civilian Life, 1915–1930* (Toronto: University of Toronto Press, 1987), ix, 24; Naylor, *New Democracy*, 23.

45 Struthers, *No Fault of Their Own*, 14–27; *Report of the Ontario Commission on Unemployment* (Toronto, 1916); Udo Sauter, "The Origins of the Employment Service of Canada," *Labour/Le Travail* 6 (Autumn 1980): 89–112; Morton and Wright, *Winning the Second Battle*, 108. On the climate of this era see Gregory S. Kealey, "1919: The Labor Revolt," *Labour/Le Travail* 13 (Spring 1984): 11–44; McKay, *Reasoning Otherwise*, 417–530; Reinhold Kramer and Tom Mitchell, *When the State Trembled: How A.J. Andres and the Citizens' Committee Broke the Winnipeg General Strike* (Toronto: University of Toronto Press, 2010); and Craig Heron, ed., *The Workers' Revolt in Canada, 1917–1925* (Toronto: University of Toronto Press, 1998).

46 Morton and Wright, *Winning the Second Battle*, 124–9; Struthers, *No Fault of Their Own*, 28.

47 "Work of the Frontier College, Toronto: Proposal for Reduction of Unemployment," *Labour Gazette*, XXI (1921), 1289.

48 G.D. Robertson to Walter Rollo, 15 December 1921, in *Labour Gazette*, XXI (1921), 46; Morton and Wright, *Winning the Second Battle*, 142; Struthers, *No Fault of Their Own*, 29; Piva, *Condition of the Working Class in Toronto*, 83–4; "Emergency Relief for Unemployed in Canada," *Labour Gazette*, XXI (1921), 999; *Toronto Police Report, 1925*, 24; Marsh, *Canadians In and Out of Work*, 257–70.

49 "Can't Keep Wolf from Door with Doles from City. Families Would Starve If They Had to Depend on Civic Help Alone. Tales of Sufferers. Work of Other Institutions Hampered by Parsimony of the City," *Toronto Daily Star*, 27 August 1921.

50 "No Man Needs to Beg on Streets Though Destitute in Toronto. Your Response to Appeal of Furtive Individuals Is Likely to Be Tribute to the Professional 'Pan-Handler,'" *Toronto Daily Star*, 14 January 1922.

51 "Where to Get Relief, Many Still in Doubt," *Toronto Daily Star*, 7 February 1922; *Report of the Commissioner of the Ontario Provincial Police, 1922*, in *Ontario Sessional Papers*, 84 (1923), 29–31, cited in Morton and Wright, *Winning the Second Battle*, 142.

52 Bryce Stewart, "The Problem of Unemployment," *Social Welfare* (March 1921), 170, quoted in Struthers, *No Fault of Their Own*, 43.

53 Struthers, *No Fault of Their Own*, 4.

54 On Hastings, see Piva's repeated accounts of his aggressiveness as a public health official in Piva, *Condition of the Working Class in Toronto;* "Is Appointed to Study Single Man's Problem. Dr. Hastings Also Warns Non-Residents Not to Expect Aid During Winter," *Toronto Daily Star*, 17 September 1925; "Women Pledge to Help Unemployed Men," *Toronto Daily Star*, 3 February 1925.

55 The above paragraphs draw on Naylor, *New Democracy;* 118–21, 248; Walter Rodney, *Soldiers of the International: A History of the Communist Party of Canada, 1919–1929* (Toronto: University of Toronto Press, 1968), 47–8; and Bryan D. Palmer, *Working-Class Experience: Rethinking the History of Canadian Labour, 1800–1991* (Toronto: McClelland and Stewart, 1992), 227. On early Canadian communism see Ian Angus, *Canadian Bolsheviks: The Early Years of the Communist Party of Canada* (Victoria: Trafford, 2004).

CHAPTER EIGHT

Indian Reserves versus Indigenous Lands: Reserves, Crown Lands, and Natural Resource Use in Northeastern Ontario

JEAN L. MANORE

Today, settler Canadians generally believe that "Indian lands" are synonymous with Indian reserves.[1] This, however, is not the Indigenous view of Indian lands. For many First Nations, the lands they claim are the lands that were used by their ancestors. Even those First Nations that have signed treaties in which land surrenders supposedly took place still claim rights of access and use, if not ownership, to their traditional territories. This view of the treaties stands in stark contrast to those of the federal and provincial governments. They argue that the Indigenous signatories surrendered all their title and rights to the land covered by the treaty, except for their reserved areas.

In addition to this profound dissonance between Indigenous and non-Indigenous perceptions of what constitutes Indian lands and of the proper interpretation of treaties is a disagreement over where Indigenous and non-Indigenous activities are to be allowed. Historically, Indigenous economic activities were strictly defined by settler governments as hunting, fishing, and trapping. They were to take place only in areas where there were no non-Indigenous activities – especially industrial ones. In effect, Indigenous activities were to be segregated from non-Indigenous activities and were to take place ideally only on Indian reserves. Any Indigenous activities off reserve would be limited and subject to the same legislative authority and regulation as non-Indigenous activities. Many First Nations, however, wanted to include employment opportunities that were offered within the industrial economy into their traditional way of life. Reserves were places they could completely call their own, while the rest of the land was to be shared.

Historians and others have commented on these dissonant views, mostly in an effort to explain settler government policies towards Indigenous lands and peoples. Many have concluded that restricting First Nations lands and activities to Indian reserves has been unjust and, by implication, wrong. They have grounded their conclusions of injustice on the federal and provincial governments' ethnocentric interpretations of Aboriginal rights and title. This difference of opinion, however, goes beyond simple political narrow-mindedness.

First Nations experience the land in a different way than settler governments. The former largely experience the land through use – for example, through harvesting the living resources; the latter experience it through control – through claiming ownership of the land and administering it. Thus, more than ethnocentrism or a "cultural" dissonance is at work here; there is also a "cognitive" dissonance, as each group knows or experiences the land differently.[2] Despite attempts by the settler governments to eliminate the Indigenous idea of land and their use of it, it is clear from an examination of the historical record of treaties and their applications in Canada that each of these cognitive conceptualizations of the land continues largely intact to the present day.

When the Ontario and federal governments negotiated Treaty 9 with the Northern Cree and Anishnabe[3] in 1905–6 and 1929–30, for example, they agreed to set aside certain parcels of land for each of the signatory First Nations. According to the federal and provincial understanding of the treaty, each First Nation was to choose its own reserve and "settle" within its boundaries. Yet despite the establishment of the reserves, the northern First Nations continued to use or harvest the resources of the land and waters over a much broader area; they continued to live, work, and camp "off-reserve" on a regular basis. Even today, this level of activity remains largely intact, despite the sporadic attempts of the federal and provincial governments to restrict First Nations movements and activities off-reserve in the northeast and elsewhere. Consequently, the Treaty 9 First Nations can and do argue that the treaty did not limit their use of the land to the reserve areas. They are not alone. Other First Nations, treaty and non-treaty, make the same argument. Hence, First Nations' understanding of "Indian lands" is, on a practical level at the very least, much broader than that delimited by reserves. As a result, one could argue that reserves are in essence settler constructions superimposed on a landscape of more ancient custom and usage.

Thus, First Nations' continued use of the resources of a vast stretch of territory points to a weakness in the limited conceptualization of "Indian lands" as strictly Indian reserves – a weakness the federal and provincial governments are slowly recognizing in their current negotiations with First Nations for land and resource management agreements. Yet because the "non-Indigenous" orthodox view of Indian lands as reserves persists, there is significant resistance within government, and among large sectors of the non-Indigenous public, to these initiatives. An examination of the causes and history of these conflicting views of "Indian" land, using Treaty 9 and northeastern Ontario as a representative example, will provide a timely context for these negotiations and perhaps lead to a greater understanding of the historic relationship between Indigenous and non-Indigenous peoples and the land.

The First Nations peoples who inhabit northeastern Ontario are Cree and Anishnabe. In early contact times, these First Nations relied on hunting, fishing, and gathering for their food supplies. The seasonal availability of these living resources contributed to the mobile existence of the bands, as they travelled to their traditional lakes and rivers to fish in the warmer months of the year, and inland to their traditional lands to hunt for game in winter.[4] By the late eighteenth century, fur traders from the North West Company and the Hudson's Bay Company were trading regularly with Indigenous people in the Moose–Mattagami drainage basin. It has been argued that the intense competition between the two fur-trading companies placed pressure on the Indigenous peoples to increase their trapping activities.[5] Certainly, during this time, many Indigenous individuals and families did develop some dependency on European traders and their goods and began to settle near or adjacent to trading posts, as occurred around Fort Matawagamingue (Mattagami).[6] They did not, however, abandon their traditional pursuits, and they continued to depend on the land and resources for their survival. This way of life is amply illustrated by a quotation from an Ontario survey report written in 1901:

> There was good soil around Fort Mattagami and northwards and over to the east along the Grassy River there were many cabins belonging to Indians who made their summer homes there and were attempting to grow their own supplies. They were not too successful at this because they had to delay planting until the finish of their hunting season in June. But they did well with fish. Whitefish spawned in the river just before the Indians went out again to their hunting grounds for the winter and they caught great quantities in nets.[7]

When settler industrial activities such as mining, lumbering, and generating hydroelectricity spread into Northern Ontario, they conflicted with and disrupted the traditional lifestyles of the northern First Nations, to a far greater degree than had the post-contact fur trade. The Cree and Anishnabe consequently complained to government officials, pointing out that the resource developers were trespassing on their lands. As a result, the federal and Ontario governments realized that an agreement with the First Nations for land-use rights needed to be negotiated. The mechanism adopted by all the parties to reach agreement was the treaty.

Treaty 9, initially signed during the summers of 1905 and 1906, contained three key clauses that set the framework for future confusion over First Nations and settler rights to lands and resources within the treaty area. Within these clauses, the ambiguous wording allowed for both the Indingenous and non-Indigenous view of "Indian lands."

The first of these clauses stipulated that reserves should be laid aside for each of the signatory bands,

> the same not to exceed in all one square mile for each family of five or in like proportion for larger or smaller families, and the location of the said reserves was arranged between His Majesty's Commissioner and the chiefs and head men, as was described in the schedule of reserves, the boundaries to be hereafter surveyed and defined.

Furthermore,

> such portions of the reserves as may at any time be required for public works, buildings, railways or roads of whatsoever nature may be appropriated for that purpose by His Majesty's Government of the Dominion of Canada, due compensation being made to the Indians for any improvements thereon.

In addition to the reserve lands, the First Nations were to have

> the right to pursue their usual vocations of hunting, trapping and fishing throughout the tract surrendered ... subject to such regulations as may from time to time be made by the governments of the country, acting under the authority of His Majesty, and saving and excepting such tracts as may be required or taken up from time to time for settlement, mining, lumbering, trading or other purposes.[8]

These three clauses are the linchpin on which rests the cognitive dissonance of the Indigenous and non-Indigenous societies. According to the federal government, the lands occupied by the First Nations were to be surrendered for the purposes of opening up the territory for settlement and resource development when required. Those lands that remained in First Nations' hands – the reserves – were to be the only remaining Indigenous lands: the only ones to which they had a continuing claim.

Behind this simple division of land between Indigenous and non-Indigenous constituencies lay numerous cultural assumptions on the part of the settler governments about "Indians" and "Indian" land. After the treaty was signed, the federal and provincial governments viewed "Indian" lands solely as Indian reserves, and any lands that were to be used for industrial development or state-building purposes became non-"Indian" lands. Further proof of this distinction comes from another clause in Treaty 9 which stipulated that no reserves were to contain water power sites capable of generating energy over 500 horsepower. What is of paramount importance in interpreting the treaty, however, is not that the Treaty 9 territory could be divided neatly into Indigenous and non-Indigenous areas, but that much of the Treaty 9 area remained in an undeveloped state – as "Crown land" – and therefore remained outside this seemingly straightforward dichotomy. As long as the land remained undeveloped, then, according to the third clause of the treaty noted above, the First Nations could continue to pursue their traditional activities – that is, they could continue to exercise their Aboriginal hunting and fishing rights off the reserves. In this way, their way of knowing the land continued intact, including knowing the land beyond a reserve's boundaries.

Even today this perception is valid because large areas of Treaty 9 continue to be free of industrial development. To illustrate how this cognitive dissonance manifested itself in the Treaty 9 territory, we can look at two issues that continue to be of great importance to Indigenous and non-Indigenous people: reserves and hunting and fishing activities.

Before Treaty 9 Indian reserves could be "officially" recognized, they had to be surveyed and confirmed by the federal and Ontario governments. In most cases, the surveys were readily confirmed, but there were several instances in which the provincial government disputed the surveyor's suggested boundaries. In each case, the objections arose because projected reserves contained within them areas compatible for development activities.

Abitibi Indian Reserve 70, for example, was confirmed by Order in Council in 1907, with an addition confirmed in December 1910. Confirmation, however, was not automatic. Abitibi was a reserve in which mining claims had been allotted before the survey of the reserve. In May 1908, J.D. McLean of the Department of Indian Affairs wrote to Aubrey White of the Ontario Department of Lands and Forests informing him that the surveyor of Indian Reserve 70 noted that he "found a number of mining claims staked out and in one case preparations were being made apparently for active work."[9] McLean, uncertain how to deal with these claims, asked White for direction.[10] As a result, discussion took place between officials in Indian Affairs and their counterparts in Lands and Forests. By July 1909 it was agreed that the First Nations of Abitibi would receive another tract of land at the northwest corner of their reserve in exchange for the mining locations situated within their original reserve boundaries.[11] Thus, the provincial government sought to ensure that the Abitibi reserve and others were separated from development areas, maintaining the dichotomy of First Nations/settler lands as established by Treaty 9.

The Mattagami Indian Reserve also involved considerable negotiations between the federal and provincial governments. In the Schedule of Reserves appended to the original Treaty 9 document, Mattagami Indian Reserve 71 was described as being on the west side of Mattagami Lake.[12] Before the reserve was surveyed, however, a disagreement arose between the Mattagami First Nation and the federal and Ontario governments. In a letter dated 5 January 1908, James Miller, the Hudson's Bay Company agent at Fort Mattagami, who was writing on behalf of the First Nations signators of the Mattagami Band, explained the problem to the Treaty 9 commissioner, D.C. Scott:

> On reading the report of the transactions at Metagami [*sic*] to the men of the tribe, I found them unanimous in disgust and indignation at the reserve laid aside for them within the boundaries mentioned in the report. I myself was as certain as they that this was not the tract of land promised and to convince myself I communicated with three of the witnesses of the Treaty ... and found them all of our opinion here ... Their reserve promised lies East of the Metagami River immediately north of the [Hudson's Bay Company] Post.[13]

Scott and the other treaty commissioners, Samuel Stewart and Daniel MacMartin, attributed the confusion to a "clerical error," and in their letter to Frank Pedley, deputy superintendent general of Indian affairs, wrote: "We beg to submit that no clerical error should operate to deprive the Indians of the land which they themselves chose and which was confirmed by the Commissioners and promised them on the spot as the consideration under which they gave their adherence to the terms of the Treaty."[14]

The Department of Indian Affairs complied with the request of the Mattagami people and the Treaty 9 commissioners to have the Indian reserve at Mattagami changed to the east side of the Mattagami River. The Ontario government also agreed to this change, but only after securing the rights to all timber over eight inches in diameter on those lands for a period of ten years, effective from 1907.[15]

In approving the new description of Indian Reserve 71, the provincial government had succeeded in exerting its control over a valuable resource even within a reserve. Although the Mattagami negotiation was an unusual situation, it demonstrates that when natural resources were found within Indian reserves, the province would try to separate them from First Nations to ensure their development. Thus the province was acting as if development activities would or could only be undertaken non-Indigenous people on non-Indigenous land. Perhaps it was in this policy that the seeds of the "welfare Indian" were planted. There was no recognition on the part of settler governments that Indigenous culture might include developing an industrial economy, despite the knowledge that Indigenous people did take employment as construction workers, lumberers, and transporters.

This point needs further elaboration. To be Indigenous as defined by settler governments meant, among other things, to pursue an economic lifestyle of hunting game, trapping furs, and fishing for subsistence rather than commercial purposes. An Indigenous person who participated in the industrial economy was viewed as someone assimilating into, rather than adapting to, the settler "mainstream." In other words, to settler officials, an Indigenous construction worker was less "Indian" than an Indigenous trapper. "Indigeneity" was something frozen in time: there could be no change without a concurrent loss of Indigenous identity. An examination of the confirmation process provides us a clear record of Treaty 9 fulfilling its purpose of dividing the land into Indigenous and non-Indigenous areas, just as the federal and provincial governments intended it to do. In the examples provided, the provincial government insisted, and the federal government concurred, that areas of development, potential or real, be excluded from Indian reserves. Yet even though the land was ostensibly categorized neatly as either Indigenous or non-Indigenous, the First Nations in the area continued to pursue their usual harvesting activities both on and off reserve. Thus Indigenous and non-Indigenous activities seemingly were not as easily divided as into Indigenous and non-Indigenous lands. This point can be demonstrated by looking at the activities of the northeastern First Nations after the signing of Treaty 9.

According to Jim Morrison, the boundary separating the traditional territories of the Cree and Anishnabe in the Moose/Mattagami watershed was located in the Smoky Falls area near the Kapuskasing and Groundhog River junctions.[16] After the treaty, these two groups continued to traverse much the same area harvesting fish, fur, and game, but also seeking seasonal employment with the Hudson's Bay Company, Revillon Frères, the railways, and the pulp and paper industries. People from the Matachewan Band continued to trap in the eastern portions of the Porcupine, while members of the Mattagami Band trapped northwest of Timmins and along the Northern Transcontinental Line at Driftwood, Hunta, and Smooth Rock Falls. Others spent most of their time in newly established communities at Mattice and Smoky Falls. From Mattice, many spread out to traplines north of Kapuskasing. In the Abitibi area, trapping and other harvesting activities continued along the Abitibi and Mehkwanegon rivers. Certainly, there was some movement of families and of traplines from 1906 onwards because of hydroelectric generation, mining, and pulp and paper activities, yet, despite these site-specific developments that destroyed various wildlife habitats or drove wildlife away, the harvesting activities of the northern First Nations continued, in combination with industrial employment.

Oral testimonies taken from elders in the late 1980s portray not only the variety of activities pursued by the First Nations but also their extensive use of the resources of the land and the vast territory they covered in order to do so. Consider the testimony of Jane Louttit of the Moose Factory First Nation, who was born in 1922.[17] She spent all her childhood summers in the bush, frequenting areas such as Kesagami River, Hannah Bay River, Missinaibi River, and Kapuskasing. She wintered in Moose Factory. Her father's trapline was located at Wash-Ush-Gaw, or South Bluff Creek, which is twelve miles south of Moosonee. Her father caught fish and sold them at Wetabohigan River to the Ontario Northern Railway cookery. She also remembers:

> We used to stay all together and set nets in an area known as Niskinneau, which is two or three miles down river from Moose Factory. There would be a lot of tents. We would catch fish and salt them in barrels. We could smoke them until they would turn dry and crisp ... Another place that we caught fish was located directly down the river from Moose Factory. That place we called Muncie ... We would leave Moose Factory in August and get to Kapuskasing in September. We would go up the Mattagami River and then up the Kapuskasing River. I did this three times in the 1930s. I would walk most of the way.[18]

Louttit also mentioned that her father trapped at a place called Big Stone, halfway between Moose Factory Island and the Harricinaw River.[19]

George Cheena, who was born in 1928 and was also a member of the Moose Factory First Nation, testified that he moved his traplines from the Moose River to Fraserdale because the dams lowered the waters and the area became too dry. Cheena's father trapped "all over the place including at James and Hannah Bays ... He used to spend eight months in the bush and four months in Moose Factory."[20]

James Roderique, who was born in Hearst in 1924, grew up in Mattice with his parents until 1943, when he went to live with his grandparents along the Smoky Line, a railway that used to run from Kapuskasing to the Smoky Falls Dam. He, too, was a member of the Moose Factory First Nation. James's experiences following the traditional way of life were extensive. He reported:

> I lived in the bush from 1943 to the 1960s, trapping along both sides of the Smoky Line, going north along the Kapuskasing River to about 15 miles from Smoky [*sic*] Falls ... I spent the winters in the bush, and also parts of the summer ...
>
> The Becks, a Cree family ... had their trapping grounds close to our family, on the east side of the Mattagami River near to where the Harmon and Kipling dams

> are located now. The Becks and the Cheenas trapped around Smoky Falls and up to Mileage 35 on the Smoky Line.[21]

His testimony also revealed that the traditional activities of berry picking, hunting, and fishing continued to be important economic activities for him and his extended family. They caught fish in abundance, including sturgeon, whitefish, and trout along the Kapuskasing River and on many creeks that flowed into that river. Another gathering place for him and other Cree families was at Remi Lake in what is now René Brunelle Provincial Park. They would meet there during the summer as their forebears had done for "hundreds and hundreds of years."[22]

Peter Sutherland, a member of New Post First Nation, had his trapping territory east of Fraserdale. It used to stretch from the mouth of the New Post Creek right up to the dam at Island Falls. He reminisced:

> Our ground was around the lake across the Little Abitibi River and the head waters of New Post Creek ... During the 1930s and 1940s my foster father Thomas Sutherland and I trapped to the east of Island Falls and worked as labourers on the railway in the summer ... I trapped there until 1956 when I moved to Moosonee.[23]

The above examples amply illustrate that First Nations people continued to hunt and fish, to exercise their Aboriginal rights, both on and off reserve. They also illustrate the interaction between the Indigenous and non-Indigenous economies, an interaction that complemented, rather than replaced, the Aboriginal practice of hunting and fishing. For Indigenous people, Indian lands were, in a practical sense at least, not limited to Indian reserves.

There are even instances where bands never settled on their allotted reserves or where they left them for long periods of time. It appears from the historical record that the Moose Band never lived on the original reserve set aside for it under the treaty. In fact, by 1912, with the assistance of the Rt Rev. John G. Anderson, Anglican bishop of the diocese of Moosonee, the Moose Band requested a different reserve. In a letter to the secretary of the Department of Indian Affairs, the chief and councillors explained their request:

> When the treaty was made with us, a reserve on French Creek was given us, about seven miles south of Moose Fort. We find on examination that the above reserve is a poor one, not suitable for wood or farming. The wood has been largely cut down or destroyed and the land is too stony for agricultural purposes. Besides there is very poor hunting there. The arrangements were too hurriedly made and did not give us

> time to investigate. We much prefer and do hereby apply for a reserve extending from North Bluff to Navy Creek about nine miles N.W. from Moose Fort along the coast towards Albany. This is most suitable for all purposes – for farming and hunting and wood supply. Though rather swampy further back, it is far ahead of the French Creek Reserve. The hunting is especially good and we could leave our old and infirm there while the hunters are away in the winter, and they would be comfortable – there being also good fishing in the various creeks and streams.[24]

On 7 October 1912, J.D. McLean referred the petition to Aubrey White. McLean stated that his department had no trouble agreeing to the First Nation's request and asked White if the provincial government would agree to the change.[25] White's initial reaction was unfavourable; he stated in a letter to McLean that the province was not given sufficient reasons to make the change.[26] Apparently, the Band Council's petition had not been forwarded to White along with the letter of 7 October 1912.[27]

The matter of getting suitable reserve land for the Moose Band was still an issue in 1930. W.C. Cain, White's successor, informed A.F. MacKenzie, McLean's assistant, that his department would be glad to give the matter further consideration, although, he noted:

> While the Department is always glad to co-operate with the Indian Department in matters pertaining to the Indians, I do feel that after a Reserve has been duly established and laid out in accordance with the terms of Treaty, some hesitation should be shown in undertaking to make any substitution therefor.[28]

The provincial department's hesitation continued until 25 January 1956. On that date, Factory Island 1 was confirmed as a reserve for the Moose Band by Order in Council. During all this time and beyond, the Moose Band Cree had continued to visit their usual fishing spots and traplines, most of which were off reserve. Thus, when we examine the administrative history of reserves and contrast it with Indigenous off-reserve activities, it is apparent that there is an administrative history that supports the government goal of opening up land for development. Yet despite this development agenda, there is also a history of use by the First Nations in the Treaty 9 territory, with continued visits to family hunting grounds and seasonal migrations.

The other area of significant cognitive dissonance over the meaning of Treaty 9 is illustrated by the history of Brunswick House Indian Reserve 76. For the provincial and, at times, the federal government, Treaty 9 extinguished Aboriginal rights to hunt and fish off reserve except on Crown lands on which there was no industrial development. However, the province also believed it had the responsibility to protect fish and game species from depletion. Part of this responsibility arose from the knowledge that many non-Indigenous people also engaged in hunting and fishing activities, further blurring the distinction between Indigenous and non-Indigenous pursuits. Consequently, the province passed legislation for the conservation of these living resources not only over areas that were settled or developed but also over those that were undeveloped. As long as these living resources were plentiful – which generally meant there was little or no non-Indigenous activity – then Indigenous people could harvest them. When they became scarce, however, the province felt obliged to restrict Aboriginal rights to hunt and fish on unsettled portions of the Treaty 9 territory.

Wildlife scarcity had become a concern by the time the Department of Game and Fisheries made its annual report in 1919. The department noted that "great inroads have been made upon the fur-bearing animals, as well as the game and birds of the province during the past few years, and more attention must be given by the Department to the existing conditions."[29] In particular, the Ontario deputy minister of game and fisheries strongly recommended in this report that "one or more suitable areas of considerable extent be set aside by the Government for the establishment of a Game Sanctuary or Sanctuaries which, in my opinion, should be located somewhere in the north or western part of the province where arrangements could be readily made for such purposes and which are suitable for natural conditions."[30] Towards that end, the Chapleau Game Preserve was established by a provincial Order in Council effective 1 June 1925. The preserve comprised about 2,600 square miles and completely surrounded New Brunswick House Indian Reserve 76.[31]

While Game and Fisheries staff fretted over declining wildlife resources, members of the New Brunswick House First Nation continued to hunt, trap, and fish, even though they also appeared to hold waged employment off the reserve, at least on a seasonal basis.[32] Once the preserve was established, however, Ontario game wardens administered it as if Indian Reserve 76 were part of the game preserve. All persons, whether Indigenous or not, found hunting or trapping within the boundaries of the game preserve were either removed or charged under the Game and Fisheries Act.[33] The Reverend George Prewer reported to D.C. Scott, deputy superintendent general of Indian affairs, that the "Indians," when attempting to enter their trapping areas within the Game Preserve, were "halted at these game preserve boundaries and either turned back or stripped of their guns, traps and other paraphanalia [*sic*] which goes to make up their necessary equipment."[34]

On 12 November 1925, Scott wrote to W.C. Cain stating that the New Brunswick House Band was "rightly entitled to some reasonable compensation" because the province had "barred them from enjoyment of the privileges accorded them under the terms of Treaty No. 9, by including within the closed area [game preserve], the New Brunswick House Reserve."[35] Scott suggested that the band surrender the reserve for sale to the province and that money from the sale be used for the band's benefit.[36] The province agreed.[37]

The DIA obtained a surrender of Indian Reserve 76 from the New Brunswick House Band on 18 June 1926. In submitting the surrender documents to the DIA, T.J. Godfrey, the Indian agent at Chapleau, reported that he

> did not find one objection in the whole band but rather a feeling that they were anxious to dispose of it as the placing of their reserve within the limits of the game sanctuary has imposed a hardship on this band of Indians as they have not only lost the use of their reserve, but all good hunting and trapping grounds which were located all around their reserve, and the action of the Provincial Government in creating this sanctuary has imposed great hardship and distress on this band and many of them are having a hard time to find a place to hunt and trap and are having much difficulty in making a living.[38]

In this instance, it appears that the province's right to conserve wildlife prevailed over Aboriginal rights to hunt and fish. However, statements from several band members of other reserves in the northern portion of Treaty 9 illustrate that the enforcement of the province's conservation laws was at best spotty and in many instances completely unsuccessful. Examining these oral testimonies enables us to comprehend that a different history of the Treaty 9 area also exists from the one found in the provincial documented history. The oral testimonies illustrate that, once again, a history of use by First Nations peoples was maintained despite legislative restrictions.

James Davey was born at Me-tito-Bostik (Grand Rapids) on the Mattagami River in 1922 and was a member of the Moose Band. He stated in his testimony that he was born in the bush on his family's trapping grounds and that Moose Factory was the family base camp where he and his family spent the summers. When trapping was no longer economically viable because the price of furs had fallen and/or the animals had become scarce, he worked at the Moose Factory hospital power house. "Even in my lifetime," he noted, "Native people did not need the whiteman to tell them where and when to hunt. We did not require permission from the government, such as licences. Whenever we needed food, we simply went into the bush and hunted, or went to the rivers to fish. Today there are too many rules and regulations."[39]

Peter Sutherland had this to say about provincial government regulations:

> Some of the game wardens bothered us a lot. I recall one time when a game warden took away my net when I had it set in a lake while I was trapping. I had set it in the lake, not the river, so I would not be seen, but the warden was spying on me with binoculars. When he came to get the net, he asked me what I had a gun for, and who had caught the pike ... I told him I knew I had a right to do that, but he took my net. I told him I was going to keep on fighting to know more about my rights for hunting and fishing. Four days after he took my net, I got word from him saying he was sorry, they had made a mistake in taking my net, and then they shipped it back to me. This incident made me feel very hurt, because I was being stopped from living as an Indian.[40]

Bert Jeffries, who was born in 1924, remembered

> people being upset by the government's plans to build the bird sanctuary on Ship Sands Island in the 1940s at the mouth of the river. That was a very big issue. The people were worried that they would not be able to go to Ship Sands Island any more. When the document was signed, the game warden, Aleck Hunter, told us that native people would be allowed to hunt on the sanctuary, that it would be closed only to white hunters. We found out later that anybody caught hunting in the sanctuary would be taken to court by the Ministry of Natural Resources. The document was signed around 1949, but the sanctuary was not officially in use until ten years later. Once it was in use, Daniel Wesley was arrested after shooting a moose on Ship Sands Island. The moose and his equipment were confiscated and were later returned to him.[41]

The experiences of these individuals illustrate that the provincial government did on occasion attempt to prevent Indigenous people from hunting and fishing off reserve, but was often unsuccessful in doing so. Additionally, within the past twenty years, First Nations have increasingly asserted their rights to hunt and fish. At the same time, the ambiguous status of Aboriginal rights and title within Canadian law has made the issue of land use and access a lot more cloudy for the provincial and federal governments.

In this century, several cases involving charges laid against Indigenous people for hunting illegally have reached the Supreme Court of Canada. Often, if the charges were laid by provincial authorities in the name of conservation, the court rejected their ability to deny Aboriginal rights to hunt and fish. If, on the other hand, federal authorities laid the charges, usually under the Migratory Birds Convention Act, the Supreme Court acknowledged the federal authority to deny these rights in situations where conservation of a particular species was deemed necessary.[42]

Other Supreme Court cases involving more than hunting or fishing rights have also tended to support the First Nations view of land and resource use. In *Sioui v. R*, 1990, the Supreme Court recognized that treaties need not be limited to agreements over land; they could also include a recognition of political or cultural rights.[43] Thus, First Nations who were hunting to carry out a religious ceremony, for example, could have the right to do so even in off-reserve areas.

The *Sparrow* case, heard in late 1990, elaborated on the findings of the *Sioui* case to give recognition to the new status of Aboriginal rights as stipulated in the Constitution Act of 1982. In *Sparrow*, the court ruled that Aboriginal fishing rights were not traditional property rights. They were rights held by a collective and were in keeping with the culture and existence of that group.[44] Also, Aboriginal rights were not frozen in time, but could evolve with "the changing needs, customs and lifestyles of Aboriginal Peoples." Aboriginal peoples were to be given first priority in the allocation of renewable natural resources.[45] Although not every court case in recent years has ruled in a manner that supported or enlarged Aboriginal rights, many have reinforced the idea that the First Nations continue to enjoy Aboriginal hunting and fishing rights off reserve, despite a history of legislative rules and regulations that have tried to eliminate them.

In conclusion, there are many ways in which people "know" the land. In the examples given above, varying interpretations over the concept of "Indian" lands stem not only from cultural dissonance or ethnocentrism but also from a variety of other factors: the ability of the First Nations to continue to use the land according to their ancient customs, and the ability of the federal government and, more especially, the provincial government to control or administer the land through legislation. Although Indigenous and non-Indigenous ways of knowing the land are disparate, clashes between the two views occurred only where non-settler activities destroyed natural habitats or depleted the living resources of fish and game. In recent years, these clashes have at times been mediated by the court system, with considerable, though not unanimous, support being given to the First Nations' interpretation of what their treaty and Aboriginal rights mean.

Today, with self-government negotiations taking place at the highest levels, co-management agreements being negotiated, and the Supreme Court of Canada reversing some of the ethnocentric decisions of the nineteenth century, the opposing ways of knowing the land are better shared and understood. It is interesting to note that through these various processes, the Indigenous political leaders are now negotiating for administrative powers or control of the land, while the federal and provincial governments are recognizing Indigenous uses of the land. This historic coming together of Indigenous and settler viewpoints is always threatened by a public backlash, by citizens who feel threatened by the monetary cost of these negotiations, or by the loss of access and privileges to selected areas of what they know as Crown land. Many non-Indigenous citizens feel that their way of knowing the land has not been adequately considered by the politicians. Their opposition to this coming together has resurfaced particularly in Ontario and British Columbia,[46] where provincial politicians are once again expressing sympathy with the concerns of these citizens, thereby threatening a process of reconciliation that has taken more than a century to develop.

QUESTIONS FOR CONSIDERATION:

1. How is land viewed through a First Nations lens according to Manore?
2. How did mining, lumbering, and greater hydroelectricity collide with First Nations' lives?
3. What do the oral testimonies reveal about First Nations' everyday activities?
4. What are the major benefits to using these oral testimonies? What do they add to Manore's chapter?
5. What is the significance of the *Sparrow* case?
6. In recent years, why have many interpretations of treaty sided with the First Nations' views? Do you see this trend continuing?

NOTES

1 The phrase "Indian" lands is used here as a juxtaposition to Indian reserves, a historic term given to areas set aside for First Nations, usually arising out of treaty negotiations.

2 For the purposes of this chapter, cognitive dissonance occurs when individuals or groups have different knowledge and understandings about a given subject as a result of their experiences, training, or culture.

3 Anishnabe is the preferred appellation among those in northern Ontario who have been known historically as Ojibwa.

4 E.S. Rogers, "Southeastern Ojibwa," *Handbook of North American Indians*, vol. 15: *Northeast*, ed. Bruce G. Trigger (Washington, D.C.: Smithsonian Institution, 1978), 760–2.

5 E.A. Mitchell, *Fort Temiskaming and the Fur Trade* (Toronto: University of Toronto Press, 1977), 94.

6 E.E. Rich, *The History of the Hudson's Bay Company* (Toronto: 1960), 888; Ontario, Department of Lands and Forests, District History Series, "A History of Gogama District, No. 11," 1964, 29–30.

7 S.A. Pain, *The Way North: Men, Mines and Minerals, Being an Account of the Curious History of the Ancient Route between North Bay and Hudson Bay in Ontario* (Toronto: Ryerson Press, 1964), 99.

8 Canada, *Treaty 9, James Bay Treaty*, Report by the Treaty Commissioners, 5 October 1906 (reprinted 1962).

9 Ontario Native Affairs Secretariat (ONAS), Ministry of Natural Resources (MNR), Indian Land File 91551, Abitibi Indian Reserve 7, J.D. McLean, secretary, Department of Indian Affairs, to Aubrey White, deputy minister, Lands, Mines and Forests, 29 May 1908.

10 ONAS, MacLean to White, 29 May 1908.

11 ONAS, Abitibi Indian Reserve 70, J.D. McLean, assistant deputy superintendent general, to T.W. Gibson, deputy minister of mines, 13 July 1909.

12 ONAS, MNR Indian Land File 39414, Mattagami Indian Reserve 71, "Schedule of Reserves," 1906.

13 ONAS, James Miller, Hudson's Bay Company (HBC) agent, Fort Mattagami, to D.C. Scott, acting deputy superintendent general of Indian Affairs, 5 January 1908.

14 ONAS, MNR Indian Land File 39414, Treaty 9 Commissioners Scott, Stewart and MacMartin to Frank Pedley, deputy superintendent general, Indian Affairs, 22 January 1908.

15 ONAS, Treaty 9 Commissioners Scott, Stewart, and MacMartin to Frank Pedley, deputy superintendent general, Indian Affairs, 22 January 1908.

16 ONAS, Ontario Order in Council 3291/09, dated 20 January 1909. Ironically, the Mattagami Indian Band had chosen this eastern location with the intention of harvesting the timber themselves. See James Morrison, *Treaty 9: The James Bay Treaty* (Ottawa: DIAND, 1986), 56. The ten-year time limit elapsed before Ontario was able to remove the timber. Ontario requested an extension, but was turned down by the Department of Indian Affairs at the request of the Mattagami Indian Band. ONAS, MNR Indian Land File 91551, memorandum re Indian Reserves Treaty No. 9, 17 October 1919, from L.V. Rorke, director of surveys, Department of Lands, Forests, and Mines, to Albert Grigg, deputy minister of lands, forests and mines, 4.

17 James Morrison, "Colonization, Resource Extraction and Hydroelectric Development in the Moose River Basin: A Preliminary History of the Implications for Aboriginal People," Report for Moose River/James Bay Coalition, Environmental Assessment, Ontario Hydro Demand Supply Plan (OH/DSP), November 1992.

18 Ontario Hydro Public Information Centre (OH/PIC), OH/DSP, witness statement of Jane Louttit.

19 OH/PIC, OH/DSP, witness statement of Jane Louttit.

20 OH/PIC, OH/DSP, witness statement of Jane Louttit.

21 OH/PIC, OH/DSP, witness statement of George Cheena.

22 OH/PIC, OH/DSP, witness statement of James Roderique.

23 OH/PIC, OH/DSP, witness statement of James Roderique.

24 OH/PIC, OH/DSP, witness statement of Peter Sutherland.

25 ONAS, MNR Indian land File 185901, Indian Reserve 68, Moose Factory, Chief and Councillors of Moose Factory Band to Secretary of the Indian Department, 2 October 1912.

26 ONAS, J.D. McLean, assistant deputy and secretary, to Aubrey White, deputy minister of lands, 7 October 1912.

27 ONAS, Deputy Minister to J.D. McLean, assistant deputy minister of Indian affairs, 10 October 1912.

28 ONAS, S. Stewart, assistant secretary, Department of Indian Affairs, to Aubrey White, deputy minister, Department of Lands, Forests and Mines, 14 October 1912.
29 ONAS, Deputy Minister to A.F. MacKenzie, acting assistant deputy and secretary, Department of Indian Affairs, 12 March 1930.
30 Mary-Lynn Murphy, "Brunswick House Indian Band Land Claim with respect to the Chapleau Game Preserve and Brunswick House Indian Reserve 76, Treaty 9," ONAS Research Report, 1987, 13.
31 Murphy, "Brunswick House Indian Band Land Claim."
32 Ontario, Sessional Papers vol. LXIV, no. 36, Department of Game and Fisheries, 1930.
33 Murphy, 'Brunswick House Indian Band Land Claim,' 14, 17.
34 Murphy, "Brunswick House Indian Band Land Claim."
35 LAC, RG 10, vol. 6745, file 420-8A, D.C. Scott, deputy superintendent general of Indian affairs, to W.C. Cain, deputy minister, Department of Lands and Forests, 12 November 1925.
36 LAC, RG 10, vol. 6745, file 420-8A, 12 November 1925.
37 LAC, RG 10, vol. 6745, file 420–8A, D. McDonald, deputy minister of game and fisheries, to D.C. Scott, deputy superintendent general of Indian affairs, 27 November 1925.
38 David T. McNab, "Research Report on the Chapleau Game Preserve and New Brunswick House Indian Reserve 76, Treaty 9," ONAS Research Report, 1980, 6.
39 OH/PIC, OH/DSP, witness statement of James Davey.
40 OH/PIC, OH/DSP, witness statement of Peter Sutherland.
41 OH/PIC, OH/DSP, witness statement of Bert Jeffries.
42 Peter Cumming and Neil Mickenberg, eds., *Native Rights in Canada* (Toronto: Indian-Eskimo Association of Canada/General, 1972), 209.
43 Brian Slattery, "Understanding Aboriginal Rights," unpublished paper, 1986, 58.
44 Slattery, "Understanding Aboriginal Rights," 19.
45 Larry Chartrand, "R. v. Van der Peet: A Legal Leap Backward for Aboriginal Peoples," unpublished paper, Ottawa 1996, 7.
46 Since writing this chapter, tensions between Indigenous and non-Indigenous people have also increased in New Brunswick, following the Supreme Court ruling on *R v. Marshall*. Some people interpreted this ruling as a recognition of a Mi'kmaq right to fish anywhere at any time. The Supreme Court, in its response to a motion for a rehearing and stay of their judgment, denied that this was the meaning of their ruling and reasserted the authority of the federal government to regulate fisheries for the purpose of, among other things, conservation.

CHAPTER NINE

The Rise and Fall of an Ontario Business Dynasty: William Kennedy & Sons and Its Successors, 1857–1997

KEITH R. FLEMING

At the William Kennedy & Sons, Ltd., apprenticeship graduation banquet held in Owen Sound, Ontario in September 1947, T. Dowsley Kennedy, the president of the ninety-year-old-foundry and metal works, announced that "so far as is known" his was "the oldest firm in the nation still controlled by the same family which founded it."[1] This was an unverifiable but not improbable claim, particularly if Kennedy was comparing his company's longevity to that of other Canadian manufacturers specifically. Between its humble origins in 1857 and its acquisition by a foreign multinational corporation in 1951, three successive generations of the Kennedy family transformed William Kennedy & Sons into an Ontario business dynasty by consistently adhering to a strategy of product development and diversification made possible by ongoing and often in-house technological innovations. As a supplier of industrial equipment to the agricultural, milling, mining, railway, marine, hydroelectric, and pulp and paper sectors across Canada and internationally, "Kennedy's," as the company was known locally and abroad, became a model of entrepreneurialism despite challenging the conventional wisdom that competitiveness, profitability, and longevity in manufacturing depended upon economies of scale generated by product specialization. In marked contrast, not long after Kennedy's became a branch plant of British and American multinational corporations and was forced by its foreign owners to focus increasingly on a single product line – paper-making machinery – the firm commenced a protracted and ignominious slide ending in bankruptcy in 1997. The history of the rise and fall of William Kennedy & Sons is a rare account of how a medium-sized Ontario manufacturer conducted business over a span of 140 years. It is also a revealing chapter in the larger story of how fortunes shifted within the Canadian manufacturing sector generally between the 1850s and the 1990s.[2]

Given the modest scale of Kennedy's capitalization, revenues, workforce, and organizational structure relative to the giants of industrial mass production and distribution that were emerging in the US and to a lesser extent Canada by the final quarter of the nineteenth century, the company might seem undeserving of the lofty appellation "dynasty." But if we apply to Kennedy's the same definition of dynasty – "a succession of at least three generations of a family business, marked by continuity of identity and interest"– that the historian and economist David Landes uses in his study of the "fortunes and misfortunes of the world's great family businesses," then the Owen Sound firm certainly qualifies. Moreover, Landes stressed the dynastic family's role as "a nursery of knowledge and skill, an embodiment of trust, and a store of capital." Those functions were no less consequential to Kennedy's long-term success, albeit on a far more modest scale than was the case for the Fords, Rockefellers, Guggenheims, and other business titans Landes studied. Finally, taxation and inheritance laws – Landes called them "the institutions that help determine whether you can keep the money you earn" – significantly impacted succession opportunities within family dynasties great and small, and would prove instrumental in Kennedy's demise as a family-owned and -controlled enterprise.[3]

William Kennedy, the firm's founder, was born in 1808 or 1809 in Dalton, Dumfriesshire, Scotland. Trained as a millwright, he apprenticed in the River Clyde's famous shipbuilding industry before immigrating to Upper Canada in 1831. After many years plying his trade in Smiths Falls, Prescott, Port Hope, and elsewhere in the colony, William travelled in 1856 to Sydenham (incorporated and renamed Owen Sound in 1857), a port community of 2,000 residents on southern Georgian Bay, to install machinery at the Harrison Woolen and Grist Mill.[4] Encouraged by the business potential of Sydenham's bustling harbour and expanding agricultural hinterland, William opted to sink permanent roots at last. In competition with the two local foundries, he opened the Sydenham Foundry and Planing-mills in October 1857. Operating out of a ramshackle wooden building, William performed general repairs and manufactured iron castings, water wheels, ploughs, and cook stoves. His modest objective, according to the newspaper advertisement he placed announcing the new venture, was to earn "a share of the public patronage" through "strict attention to his business, good work, and moderate charges."[5]

After three years, William relocated his flourishing business to a 316m^2 two-storey frame building housing a machine shop on the upper level and equipment for wood planing and sash and door manufacturing on the ground floor.[6] He renamed the firm William Kennedy & Sons when Thomas (b. 1842) and Matthew (b. 1845) joined their father as partners in the enterprise. By the early 1870s Kennedy's had largely discontinued its woodworking and agricultural implement lines. Its dozen employees concentrated instead on manufacturing cast-iron propellers and sundry marine equipment, turbine water wheels for hydroelectric power and pumping facilities, and heavy shafting, gears, and pulleys for the province's proliferating saw, grist, flour, and woollen mills.[7]

When fire partly destroyed his building in 1880, William moved the business to its permanent location on the west shore of Owen Sound's harbour. With a workforce of thirty, Kennedy's commenced operations in January 1885 in an 818m^2 two-storey stone building complete with grey iron foundry, machine shop, and pattern shop. The new waterfront location, in addition to improving the firm's access to marine and railway facilities essential for transporting its bulky products to customers across Canada and to Australia, England, Ireland, and the West Indies, facilitated Kennedy's servicing of the growing commercial fleets plying the Great Lakes.[8] When William died later that year, the company he had founded twenty-eight years before was poised to become the pre-eminent manufacturer in the southern Georgian Bay region. An unassuming obituary in the local *Advertiser* described William as "a Reformer in politics," a community leader who served several terms on the town council, and an ardent Baptist and "advocate of temperance principles." Having "embarked in the foundry business in a small way," he had converted his entrepreneurial talents into "a large and prosperous business" by virtue of "close attention and a through [*sic*] knowledge of the requirements of the trade."[9]

During the ensuing fifty-year presidency of William's fourth son, Matthew, the company developed into a fully integrated foundry and industrial equipment manufacturer serving local, national, and international markets. Matthew had joined the firm at the age of fifteen, training as a machinist. While at its helm he followed the course his father had set of building the business through ongoing product diversification and adopting increasingly sophisticated fabrication techniques developed on-site. Kennedy's also actively marketed its growing international reputation for quality workmanship, which received a boost in 1894 when its propellers and water wheels won awards at industrial exhibitions in Paris, Philadelphia, and London, England.[10] Throughout his presidency Matthew displayed what Mark Casson, a leading historian of entrepreneurship, called "the paternalism associated with the dynastic motive," whereby business owners fulfil a "commitment to participate (as social superiors) in the life of the community to which their workers belong."[11] In keeping with his status as head of Owen Sound's largest and most important manufactory, Matthew served four terms as mayor and held executive positions on the local board of trade, the Manufacturers' Association, and the Imperial Cement Co. Ltd. Having inherited his father's prohibitionist proclivities, Matthew was a vocal critic of Owen Sound's lax liquor licensing, arguing that it harmed local trade, reduced property values, and "injured the moral well-being of very many." During Matthew's tenure, on 6 May 1896, the firm was incorporated as The William Kennedy & Sons, Limited. All $98,000 of the stock was held by Kennedy family members.[12]

Between its incorporation and the outbreak of the First World War, Kennedy's took on contracts of increasing scale and complexity. In 1900, for example, it manufactured several large iron bridges for the City of Montreal and designed water pumping systems for a number of Ontario municipalities. The foundry also diversified into steel production with the acquisition of a Bessemer converter that had a two-ton capacity. By 1911, Kennedy's workforce of 150 was producing castings and finished goods valued at $350,000 annually. Wartime contracts with the Imperial Munitions Board boosted the company's prospects. In March 1915, when Kennedy's received an initial order for 25,000 shrapnel shells, the equivalent of three months' production, Matthew was reluctant to expand the foundry and machine shop and purchase the requisite specialized machinery without first receiving government assurances that additional contracts would follow. Only after repeat orders for high-explosive shell casings started appearing in 1916 did he authorize the new investment in physical plant. Kennedy's further increased its productive capacity at that time by acquiring the facilities of the Owen Sound Iron Works (renamed the East Machine Shop) and purchasing the open-hearth steel plant and rolling mills of the Northern Iron & Steel Company, located 58 kilometres to the east in Collingwood. The two furnaces in the Collingwood plant – they had a combined daily capacity of seventy-five tons – required a complete rebuild to become operational. Kennedy's cited the need to protect its market share in munitions as justification for the expense. This proved to be a shrewd decision, particularly once supplies of the expensive low-phosphorous pig iron on which the Owen Sound plant's Bessemer converter depended grew increasingly scarce. Thus, when munitions production at Owen Sound began to slip in 1917, the Collingwood foundry made up the difference, aided by Kennedy's installation there of its first electric furnace, capable of producing fifteen tons of pig iron daily.[13]

Anticipating the return to peacetime, after which orders for munitions could no longer be relied upon to maintain its facilities at capacity, Kennedy's set out to expand its marine trade. In 1917 it redesigned and expanded the iron foundry to accommodate the manufacture of large propellers, an investment that bore fruit immediately when Kennedy's supplied the Montreal shipbuilder Canadian

Vickers Ltd. with four 17'6" diameter propellers, each weighing ten tons and believed to be the largest constructed in North America up to that point.[14] As soon as the Armistice was signed in November 1918, the company spent $25,000 adding a 465m^2 extension and twenty-ton electric travelling crane to the Owen Sound plant.[15] Soon thereafter it was advertising an extensive line of anchor windlasses, chain stoppers, steering engines, cargo winches, ash hoists, and solid and sectional propellers made of steel, iron, and bronze. Kennedy's innovative craftsmen also improved the efficiency of the firm's largest water turbines – they built several 4,500 horsepower units for the Ottawa and Hull Power Manufacturing Company plant at Chaudière Falls – and began producing heavy transmission gears, high-capacity (35-ton) winches and hoisting machines, and a reversible dipper tooth for dredges and steam shovels designed and patented by Matthew's brother, the renowned engineer Sir John Kennedy.[16]

At war's end Kennedy's cancelled all production at its Collingwood foundry, an investment valued at approximately $500,000, and abruptly dismissed the 350 workers employed there, a significant economic loss to the community.[17] At the same time, the firm augmented its Owen Sound operation by acquiring the neighbouring Canadian Malleable Iron Works plant. Kennedy's strategy throughout the 1920s of offering increasingly diversified products and services, which it advertised extensively in trade journals nationwide, was rewarded with a steady growth in orders once the economy had shaken off the torpor of the immediate post-war years. Sales rose from a low of $336,413 in 1921 to a high of $957,584 in 1929, and averaged $583,223 annually across the entire decade. The company's gross trading profits also exhibited a healthy upward trend, rising from $70,897 in 1922 to $229,567 in 1929, and averaging $126,637 annually.[18]

A 1922 advertisement in *Canadian Mining Journal* describing an array of Kennedy's products was typical: it mentioned ball mill feeders, boilers, buckets, cages, cam shafts, ore cars, car wheels and axles, cement machinery, crusher balls, assorted gears, hydraulic machinery, pulleys, pumps, smokestacks, and steel tanks.[19] An inventory assembled by Kennedy's sales staff around the same time added to the list castings (steel, chrome steel, manganese steel, grey iron, malleable iron, aluminum, and brass), patterns, structural steel, steering engines, tube mills, winches, propellers, and all manner of mining, milling, marine, and hydraulic power machinery.[20] Trading on its ability to engineer and manufacture an expansive range of custom projects, the company boldly pledged to fill all orders "no matter of what material or for what purpose … with accuracy and dispatch," using either the customer's pattern or one designed by Kennedy's.[21] New investments in sales and marketing further enhanced Kennedy's business profile nationwide. By 1927 it was operating branch offices in Halifax, Toronto, Montreal, and Cobalt – each one overseen by a "competent engineer" – and maintaining sales agents in Vancouver and Winnipeg.[22] One notable failure was Kennedy's sole attempt at manufacturing outside Ontario. In 1923, after just three years of operation, the company shuttered the open-hearth steel plant it had acquired in Medicine Hat, Alberta, when local demand fell well short of expectations.

During the interwar period, Kennedy's made substantial enhancements to its core products while also taking on new and operationally complex projects. For instance, when Owen Sound revitalized its harbour in 1925 by constructing a million-bushel grain elevator to replace one destroyed by fire in 1911, Kennedy's designed and manufactured the conveying and transmission machinery, a job unlike any it had undertaken previously. At the same time the company's reputation as Canada's premier propeller manufacturer received a boost in 1924 when it was the first to adopt manganese bronze as a primary construction material. Resistant to saltwater corrosion and as strong as high-grade carbon steel, yet easier to repair, propellers made from manganese bronze were prized for maintaining accurate pitch under load. By 1927 around 90 per cent of all propellers installed on Great Lakes commercial vessels had been cast, machined, and polished by Kennedy's.[23]

During the Great Depression of the 1930s, as demand for industrial products plummeted at home and abroad, Matthew Kennedy took special measures to protect the jobs of his 250 employees.[24] He thereby demonstrated what Mark Casson maintains is an attribute of dynastic leaders – a willingness to treat workers "as a part of the 'extended family' of the firm" during business slumps. Casson cites the accumulation of excess inventories and the reassignment of skilled production workers to unskilled maintenance tasks as strategies for stabilizing employment and enabling employees to continue supporting their families.[25] Kennedy's did both, and also introduced a shortened workweek. A less benevolent reason for the company's protectiveness was that it found it difficult to hire skilled labourers, given Owen Sound's distance from larger industrial centres. University-educated engineers needed to be recruited from outside the community; to train the foundry's moulders, core makers, and patternmakers, as well as the engineering division's machinists and draftsmen, Kennedy's typically relied upon its own apprenticeship programs.[26] Kay McKie, whose father T.D. Kennedy was company vice-president during the Depression, recalls management trying "really hard not to mothball things temporarily" by constantly searching for new products to build.[27] One such innovation was a propeller made from high-tension metals such as nickel cast suitable for high-speed pleasure boats, a market previously dominated by US firms.[28] Kennedy's also began producing the prized manganese-bronze alloy that prior to

1930 had been available exclusively from England. Other products the company introduced to fend off the worst effects of the economic downturn included a patented stop-log winch that Sir John Kennedy designed for hydroelectric dams[29] and a portable "Jack Nutt" grinding machine in demand by the gold-mining industry.[30]

Kennedy's sound financial position at the outset of the Depression was crucial to its survival. With a pecuniary strength in 1929 of between $200,000 and $300,000 (Dun & Bradstreet estimate), rising to between $300,000 and $500,000 in 1932, and assets valued at approximately $530,000 on average between 1930 and 1939, the company according to Kay McKie "never owed any money so there was no question of losing the plant."[31] In 1937, with its workforce expanded by one third and payroll up 50 per cent, Kennedy's reported its most successful year since the Crash of 1929, although persistent heavy competition prevented prices and profit margins from keeping pace with rising demand. All told the company survived the Depression by determinedly pursuing a risk-averse strategy of developing a diverse product and customer base disbursed across the mining, cement, rubber tire, pulp and paper, shipping, hydroelectric, and highway construction sectors.[32]

Kennedy's satisfied Landes's definition of a business dynasty in 1935 when Matthew's sixty-six-year-old son David John (b. 1869), a third-generation family member, assumed the presidency. Like his father, David was a machinist by training. He had begun working at Kennedy's as a boy of fifteen. He later attended Vanderbilt University in Tennessee and worked in several machine shops throughout Ohio before returning to Owen Sound in 1892 to organize Kennedy's new steel foundry. David followed his family's practice of exhibiting "the paternalism associated with the dynastic motive" by serving multiple terms as a city and county councillor, Board of Trade member, chair of the Owen Sound benevolence committee, hospital trustee, and director of the Owen Sound Transportation Company. When the city decided in 1924 to construct a new grain elevator, David took the lead by pledging $50,000 of his own money as security until funding for the half-million-dollar project could be finalized. The following year he became president of the Great Lakes Elevator Company.[33] By that point other third-generation Kennedys in the firm's employ were David's brothers, T. Dowsley (known as T.D.) and Matthew Jr., both vice-presidents. Several fourth-generation family members had also begun to ascend the company hierarchy, most notably David's son Albert, a salesman, and Matthew Jr.'s sons Arthur, a department superintendent, Neil, the foundry superintendent and chief metallurgist, and Roger, a patternmaker and moulder.

The only hint of dissension surrounding company succession that emerged across the generations is rumoured to have developed during 1938, one year after Matthew Sr. died and left his stock in William Kennedy & Sons to his four children:

David, Matthew Jr., T.D., and Marjorie. Although it is no longer possible to confirm the details, a foreman in the machine shop reportedly overheard Arthur and Neil Kennedy hatching a plot to displace their uncle T.D., who although nominally company vice-president had largely taken over presidential duties from an ailing David. When Ruth Bellamy, Kennedy's secretary-treasurer and a T.D. loyalist, was informed by the eavesdropping foreman of the intended coup, she dutifully alerted T.D., who quickly and without fanfare purchased David's shares, thus acquiring financial control of the firm.[34] When David died soon afterwards in December 1940, T.D. officially became president. Fourth-generation members of the Kennedy family would never command the company.

T.D. (b. 1885) had joined Kennedy's in 1910 after studying hydromechanical engineering at the University of Munich and was swiftly promoted to company director and manager of the iron foundries and machine shops. His greatest challenge as president would be overseeing the firm's dramatic expansion during the Second World War. When officials with the Department of National Defence inspected Kennedy's in 1938 to assess its potential contributions to Canada's rearmament program, they described it as "established over 80 years without reorganization" and "financially fully responsible." In addition,the company possessed an "excellent engineering department," an impressive inventory of heavy manufacturing equipment, strategic access to rail and water transportation, and extensive munitions experience from the previous war.[35] Ironically, T.D.'s willingness to relinquish temporarily his firm's diversified products and markets in order to support Canada's war effort ultimately dealt Kennedy's a competitive blow from which it never fully recovered.

Shortly after Canada entered the war in September 1939, T.D. asked the Owen Sound City Council to freeze Kennedy's property assessment for a ten-year period to ensure that any plant expansions the company made to meet wartime demand did not become tax liabilities once peace returned. Reminding councillors that his company had dismantled its Collingwood plant at the end of the previous war to avoid paying taxes on an idle facility, T.D. explained rather pessimistically that "'we want to be sure we are not penalized after the war is over and business is poor.'"[36] The local newspaper, in urging ratepayers to "give their unstinted support" to the resulting by-law allowing Kennedy's main west-side plant to retain an assessment of $47,900 for ten years commencing 1 January 1941, pointed out that the company had neither asked for nor received "any bonus, loan or fixed assessment from the city" in the eighty-three years of its existence.[37] It was a compelling case, and ratepayers responded generously on New Year's Day 1941, voting 1,346 to 147 in favour of the by-law.[38]

Kennedy's first agreement with the Department of Munitions and Supply, approved in June 1941, permitted expenditures of up to $496,900 for a plant expansion and improvements to the machine shop, foundry, laboratory, pattern shop, and powerhouse, plus $347,100 to purchase machine tools, cranes, compressors, and foundry equipment. The company conveyed to the federal government for one dollar the land on which the addition was built, and Kennedy's received (and eventually exercised) the right to purchase these government-financed assets at war's end. The first manufacturing contract, signed the same month, was for sixty-seven 18'6" manganese bronze propellers for 10,000-ton cargo vessels at a price of $7,150 apiece, as well as sixty-seven cast-iron propellers (each cargo ship carried a spare) and propeller cones costing $2,376 and $165 apiece respectively. Fabrication was to begin by 1 September 1941, and maximum production of ten propellers per month reached by 1 January 1942.[39]

Additional government orders soon streamed into Kennedy's, eventually accounting for 95 per cent of the firm's wartime production. Propellers for a variety of Canadian and Allied naval vessels – corvettes, minesweepers, destroyers, frigates, landing barges, cargo boats, and tenders – comprised the bulk of the manufacturing. Incomplete data prevent a comprehensive accounting of Kennedy's wartime business, but orders for at least 813 cargo-class (4,700 to 10,000 ton vessel) propellers were received.[40] Other marine equipment produced for the military included steam and electric steering engines, anchor windlasses, mooring winches, bronze liners for tail shafts, engine castings, struts, and stern bearings and tubes.[41] To accommodate this dramatic growth in activity the federal government financed several expansions and improvements to Kennedy's physical plant during the war, including a $1 million addition in the fall of 1941 that doubled the factory's size, an eight-ton electric melting furnace that doubled steel casting output, an office building to centralize administrative staff, and a $60,000 machine shop for manufacturing marine steering engines.[42] As a result, by 1945 the company's foundries and machine shops were among the most advanced in Canada. Unfortunately, wartime production levels would prove impossible to sustain when post-war markets weakened substantially.

In the meantime, Kennedy's continued to excel at equipment design. When commercial-grade mechanical planers proved too imprecise to finish the curvilinear surfaces of propeller blades to the required pitch, Kennedy's engineers designed a machine to do the job. Similarly, the company installed in its bronze foundry centrifugal casting equipment accurate to a thousandth of an inch, an unprecedented level of precision.[43] Early in the war T.D. had rallied his employees with assurances their work was "important" if "not spectacular," and urged them to "be justly proud" when reading "of the daring exploits and the gallant part being played in the Battle of the Atlantic."[44] Such efforts at fostering workplace *esprit de corps* were ongoing throughout the war. Kennedy's hosted a company dance to celebrate the completion of the one hundredth wartime propeller, and workers regularly assembled in group photographs next to their finished handiwork.[45] A point of special pride the company publicized extensively was news that "CT-72," the sixty-four-foot tug that was lead vessel in the 6 June 1944 D-Day invasion, was driven by a Kennedy propeller.[46]

Notwithstanding management's efforts to instil a "family" feeling among the rapidly expanding workforce – it peaked at 840 employees in May 1942 before falling to 538 by August 1945 – production workers unionized as Local 2469 of the United Steel Workers of America in the fall of 1941. Tangible benefits followed: Ontario's Regional War Labour Board granted Kennedy's employees a temporary exemption from the nationwide wage freeze; a company pension plan was introduced; employees were given the option to join an Ontario Hospital Association hospitalization scheme; and the union would be represented on the company's Employer–Employee Production Committee tasked with identifying workplace efficiencies.[47] Despite these gains, labour relations reached a nadir in July 1944 when a one-day walkout by approximately 520 workers halted production. Employees were already aggrieved that negotiations to renew their collective agreement had been stalled since the preceding October; their animosity only increased when the regional and national war labour boards disallowed their requested ten-cent per hour wage increase to fifty-five cents after granting a sixty-cent wage to workers performing comparable jobs elsewhere.[48] Charles Addison Eberle, Kennedy's assistant general manager, tried to calm dissent by explaining to union representatives that the company's business had fallen 27 per cent in volume over the past year alone. He emphasized that none of Kennedy's government contracts included the "cost plus" financial cushion some firms enjoyed, but were based on preset prices just as in peacetime. Consequently the company lost money whenever shoddy workmanship inflated foundry costs. Eberle urged the union membership to cooperate with management in correcting the recent rise in defective castings, since ultimately it was the firm's reputation for quality workmanship at competitive pricing that enabled the sales force to attract the "orders necessary to provide plenty of work at good wages."[49] The appeal temporarily ended labour strife at Kennedy's, but another ten months passed before the second collective agreement, which permitted workers to opt for a revocable check-off of union dues, was reached.

With the return of peace in August 1945, Kennedy's faced a double burden: it needed to regain the traditional markets and clientele it had forfeited when it shifted its focus to military contracts, and it had to find ways to sustain the much enlarged physical plant and workforce it had amassed during wartime. One response was to diversify internationally, and by 1947 around 40 per cent of company sales were overseas, in countries like Venezuela, Colombia, Brazil, Cuba, China, the US, India, and Palestine.[50] Kennedy's management nevertheless admitted in 1948 to harbouring "a great deal of anxiety" over the firm's ability to transition to peacetime markets. The tensions surfaced that November, when T.D. engaged Owen Sound's firebrand mayor, E.C. "Eddie" Sargent, in a public spat over increases in municipal tax assessments. T.D. warned that higher taxes would "drive industry out of this town" and claimed that only the prohibitive costs of moving its heavy equipment prevented Kennedy's from relocating to cheaper real estate outside the city. He blamed high municipal taxes for his recent decision to cancel renovations to the factory, declaring that "we're not interested in any further expansion as far as Owen Sound is concerned." When T.D. stated that Kennedy's added over $1.3 million to the local economy annually without receiving any benefit from the city, the mayor retorted that no company in Owen Sound's history had "received such concessions" as Kennedy's, citing as evidence its current fixed municipal assessment of just 42 per cent the normal rate. Sargent then accused the community's most substantial ratepayer of having no interest in "the boys and girls, working men and women, and the everyday folk of this city" beyond feathering his own nest. It was, as T.D.'s lawyer chided, an insensitive public attack on a "man whose family is one of the pioneer families of this city."[51]

The unsettled business conditions were also reflected in Kennedy's uneasy relations with its 500 employees, 74 per cent of whom were union members when negotiations broke down in February 1949 over renewal of the collective agreement that had expired the previous May. Central to the dispute was T.D.'s objection to a union demand that in place of the existing voluntary and revocable check-off, the Rand Formula, requiring all employees regardless of their union membership status to pay union dues, be included in the agreement. T.D. proposed depositing non-members' dues into a separate trust fund designated solely for benevolent purposes such as subsidizing workers' medical bills; this would prevent the union from spending that money on political or religious causes.[52] The conciliation board appointed by Ontario's Minister of Labour Charles Daley recommended that the removable check-off remain in place while the two sides continued to negotiate. The board's majority report reasoned that Kennedy's export business was already vulnerable, in large part because importing nations were struggling with dollar shortages stemming from the US Marshall Plan for financing Europe's post-war recovery. David Lewis, the National Secretary of the Co-operative Commonwealth

Federation and author of the conciliation board's minority report, dismissed as "improper and impertinent" T.D.'s rejection of a fundamental principle of "free, democratic trade unionism," namely that management not interfere with "the direction and administration of unions and union funds." Lewis's remonstrations notwithstanding, the majority report recommendation that the status quo be maintained was eventually incorporated into the collective agreement reached in May 1949.[53]

As predicted, concerns about union security soon paled next to worries over Kennedy's slackening export markets. In November 1949, the executive of Local 2469 wrote Colin Bennett, the Liberal Member of Parliament for Grey North, about the desperate employment situation at Kennedy's, the largest and "most severely hit" industrial enterprise in his riding. The missive described a workforce that had shrunk from 730 to 370 in the past year alone, with more than one third of those who remained being placed on reduced hours, a situation that threatened "the security and welfare of the community as a whole." The union blamed the rapid reversal in fortune on two factors: the company's slowness in reclaiming domestic markets lost when it shifted to military production during the war, and the negative impact of recent "monetary and exchange problems" on Kennedy's exports. Responding to rumours that the federal government was planning "increased naval commitments," the union executive urged Bennett "to use your influence in having an adequate channeling of marine and general engineering, as well as the production of steel castings, to our factory." Unfortunately, Bennett's response was purely perfunctory.[54]

A few days later, the company's recently appointed vice-president, Arthur McCorvie Kennedy (b. 1899), Matthew Jr.'s son and a fourth-generation member of the dynasty, offered the union a blunt but modestly encouraging assessment of what lay ahead. He stressed that given Canada's oversupply of foundry and engineering capacity, Kennedy's current production of one-third pre-war levels compared favourably with its largest competitors' average rate of just 20 per cent, due largely to the ability of Kennedy's sales force "to dig up new business." Consequently, despite growing complaints about staff reductions in other sections of the company, Kennedy's planned to enlarge the estimating, planning, and design departments to ensure that its sales representatives possessed the "accurate and detailed information" they required "to offer attractive deliveries, and to quote prices which, while low enough to secure business, will not result in loss of money on the order." Meanwhile, work-sharing on alternate weeks would be implemented throughout the plant as "the fairest and most equitable method of meeting the situation," even if it was "not the most economical way" for the company.[55]

Arthur's confidence initially appeared vindicated by the slight uptick in new orders during the first half of 1950, as well as by hints that Korean War defence contracts might be coming Kennedy's way.[56] Then disaster struck. A fire in the main machine shop on 12 May 1950 caused almost $1.3 million in damage, temporarily halting company efforts to regain lost production.[57] The fire, however, was a minor distraction next to the bombshell T.D. dropped ten months later.

On 1 March 1951, T.D. announced the sale of his family's ninety-four-year-old business to Had-Mils (Canada) Ltd., a sales and holding company of the Millspaugh Group subsidiary of Hadfields Ltd. based in Sheffield, England. T.D. assured his employees that the new owners had experience manufacturing products similar to Kennedy's and that they would "maintain the tradition of the Britisher." In addition to offering Kennedy's existing product line, Had-Mils planned to bring to Owen Sound its "very valuable know-how" manufacturing specialized paper-making machinery. Moreover, Had-Mils was certain to divert a share of its global export business to Owen Sound, provided Kennedy's "can keep our costs down." The company's name and top management were to be retained, including T.D. as president and C.A. Eberle as general manager. In short, T.D. promised, the sale of William Kennedy & Sons offered "more security of employment for all of us, through good times and bad."[58]

Had-Mils and Kennedy's seemed well-matched. Founded in 1872, the Hadfields Steel Foundry Company had grown to 15,000 employees by the time it became Hadfields Limited in 1913. A major producer of armaments during both world wars, it normally specialized in hardened steel rolls, crushers, dredge buckets, and colliery equipment. In 1946, Hadfields purchased Millspaugh Limited, a manufacturer of paper-making machinery, centrifugal castings, and propeller shaft liners based in Sandusky, Ohio, since 1933. When the British government nationalized Hadfields in 1950, Millspaugh was excluded from the takeover since its specialty was paper mill machinery rather than iron and steel production. In its burst of expansion that followed, the Millspaugh Group grew to eight firms by 1954, including five in Great Britain, two in Canada, and one in France.[59]

T.D. did not divulge his reasons for selling the company. Rumours abounded locally that none of the fourth generation of Kennedys involved in the business possessed either the will or aptitude to succeed T.D., but that is too sweeping a critique. A likelier explanation is provided by Kay McKie, who claimed that the federal government's wartime decision to tax estates – previously only provinces collected succession duties – had compelled her sixty-six-year-old father to dispose of the company that was his primary asset.[60] When J.L. Ilsley, the Minister of Finance, had announced in his 1941 budget the Mackenzie King government's intention to collect succession duties on estates valued at over $25,000, he predicted Canadians would not object, since they, unlike the British, felt "children should stand on their own feet and make their own living, rather than rely on inherited property."[61] T.D. would have disagreed, as did R.B. Hanson, the Conservative Leader of the Opposition, who warned in the House of Commons that the tax would force privately owned family businesses to liquidate. The rate of "business mortality in Canada," he observed, was already "exceedingly high," as few companies survived "into the third, fourth and fifth generations." To illustrate his point, Hanson raised a hypothetical scenario closely resembling the one T.D. must have considered as he calculated whether his future beneficiaries would need to sell the company in order to pay succession duties. According to Hanson, when assets of $1.5 million were invested in a private business "which the deceased owned and controlled" (a realistic estimate of Kennedy's selling price is between $1.6 and $2 million), the combined federal and Ontario provincial succession duties owed by a hypothetical spouse and six children would total $601,875. Hanson claimed that in the event that a majority of the deceased's assets were invested in the business – as were T.D.'s – with no other provision such as life insurance having been made to pay the death tax, liquidation would ensue, with a detrimental "effect upon the community life that may depend upon that business."[62]

T.D. was no longer in control of Kennedy's; has influence was now strictly managerial. The company's first years under foreign ownership produced mixed results. After an initial flurry of new business in 1951, when Millspaugh redirected manufacturing contracts and engineering staff from its British operations to Owen Sound, 1952 brought falling orders and rising layoffs. More positively, the recent purchase of the former Corbet Foundry and Machine Co. Ltd., which was located next to Kennedy's and would be used as a steel fabricating shop, seemed a harbinger of future expansion.[63] Indeed, when J.B. Thomas, the chair of Millspaugh's board, visited Owen Sound in September 1952, he dubbed Kennedy's "one of the jewels in our Crown" and promised that "considerable sums of money," possibly as much as $4 million, would be spent updating the plant and machine tools. He reiterated T.D.'s earlier assurances that Kennedy's established product lines would continue to be manufactured unless doing so proved "unremunerative," and that the highest priority remained operational diversification to ensure "there will be greater opportunities for increased employment in all branches old and new." A case in point was Millspaugh's recent $1 million contract to manufacture paper-making machinery. Thomas anticipated redirecting a "considerable amount" of this work to Kennedy's.[64]

Although Millspaugh professed to value Kennedy's manufacturing versatility and demonstrated aptitude for product diversification, it soon became evident that the Owen Sound firm had been acquired primarily to support Millspaugh's North

American paper machinery business.[65] An early indication was Millspaugh's purchase in 1954 of the Sault Ste. Marie–based Northern Foundry & Machine Company Limited, a supplier of northern Ontario's pulp and paper industry since 1907. The plan was to divert $500,000 of Northern's manufacturing trade to Kennedy's annually. Certainly, a boost was needed. Millspaugh's sales that year increased 15 per cent over 1953 levels, resulting in the highest net profit (£162,433) in its history, yet annual sales at Kennedy's declined by £294,000 ($801,000).[66] In their annual report to shareholders, the company's directors candidly admitted that "it may take us some time before [Kennedy's] is in a position to meet the competitive period which we now face, especially on the Canadian home market."[67] However, when Millspaugh's profits slipped the following year, blame was attributed to "a continuing recession in Canada." In response, Kennedy's was promptly reorganized, and engineering was made a higher priority than foundry work for the first time in the company's long history.[68]

Further proof of Kennedy's rapidly waning fortunes in traditionally core areas of its business was disclosed in its 1955 submission to the Royal Commission on Coasting Trade, which investigated the impact of foreign-owned shipping on Great Lakes commercial traffic. Between 1949 and 1954, the company's orders for marine-related products had plummeted from approximately $700,000 to $190,000 annually, and deliveries of steel castings for the shipbuilding industry had fallen from an average of 300 tons to just 90 tons, representing an additional annual loss of $126,000 in sales. As a result, Kennedy's was giving "serious consideration … to the economic advisability of abandoning these lines of endeavour and using the floor space for other more profitable products."[69] It was a candid admission that an important chapter in Ontario's manufacturing history was closing.

The return of Hadfields to private ownership in July 1955 and prompt reacquisition of the Millspaugh Group did not staunch the bleeding at the Owen Sound plant.[70] After authorizing an expansion of the machine shop in 1957, the English directors halted a planned addition to the foundry in 1959 and considered closing it completely when it posted a loss of $170,000 in just nine months. That drastic recourse was circumvented by local management's persuasive argument that the engineering division was only viable if its castings were manufactured on-site. The British owners' opinion of Kennedy's prospects dimmed further when workers there – they numbered 370 in 1959 – demanded contract enhancements at the same time as depressed market conditions were forcing the company to bid on jobs below cost just to keep the plant operational. Management reminded employees that they already received the highest industrial wages in the community, and suggested they be satisfied with their seniority protection, company pension plan, hospitalization coverage, group life and accident insurance, vacation eligibility, and forty-hour work week. The appeals went unheeded, however, and an Ontario Labour Relations Board conciliator was needed to settle the long list of unresolved differences separating the two sides before a collective agreement was reached in June 1959.[71]

A precipitous 20 per cent decline in Hadfields's earnings between 1955 and 1960, largely attributable to weak returns by its Millspaugh paper machinery subsidiary, heightened impatience with the Canadian branch.[72] When Hadfields's pre-tax profits fell £119,842 to £366,694 in 1961 and the Millspaugh Group again generated most of the declines, fingers were pointed at Kennedy's lacklustre performance.[73] The final straw, as Hadfields's chair Sir Peter G. Roberts later explained to the 1962 annual general meeting, was Kennedy's 1960 deficit of approximately £138,000 ($374,700), which included a £28,000 ($76,000) exchange rate shortfall. It was feared that unless preventive measures were taken, Kennedy's would drag the Millspaugh Group into a £77,000 deficit in 1961, with commensurate damage to Hadfields's bottom line. Thus the decision was made to sell 60 per cent of Millspaugh ordinary stock to the Swiss firm Escher Wyss Ltd. for £1,200,000. Then, on 7 November 1961, William Kennedy & Sons was sold to The Black Clawson Company of Hamilton, Ohio, for just £250,000 ($709,000).[74] It was almost one year to the day since the Kennedy dynasty had officially and quietly ended; T.D., who had stepped down as chair of William Kennedy & Sons in 1958, died on 9 November 1960.

The company that William, Matthew, David, and T.D. had led successfully and with entrepreneurial verve for almost a century would continue for another thirty-eight years under its second foreign owner, but with a dire result. As the eighth piece in Black Clawson's multinational web, Kennedy's joined five other manufacturers in the US and one each in England and Brazil. In an announcement reminiscent of the promises made by Had-Mils's executives ten years earlier, Carl C. Landegger, the son of Black Clawson chair Karl F. Landegger, reassured Kennedy's 400 employees that they would continue to produce marine and specialty castings at Owen Sound, that the local management team would stay intact, and that the company name would be retained. Soon enough, however, Black Clawson was utilizing Kennedy's principally as a specialized manufacturer of paper-making machinery. Black Clawson had previously subcontracted with Kennedy's to produce paper equipment for the Canadian market, but now was positioned to offer its entire product line from Owen Sound.[75]

Established in Hamilton, Ohio, in 1875, Black Clawson was the largest manufacturer of paper-making equipment in the US by the end of the Second World War. In 1961 its principal stockholder was Karl Landegger, an Austrian-born American who owned or controlled thirty-two paper companies with gross annual revenues of $90 million in fifteen countries. With a 24 per cent interest in Millspaugh Ltd., Landegger was well-versed in Kennedy's history, and he pledged publicly not to repeat the mistakes of its previous owners. He was particularly critical of T.D.'s decision after the war to focus on exports instead of capitalizing on the "immediate opportunity in the domestic market which beckoned enticingly."[76] The folly of this strategy had been revealed when a "lack of exchange currency left Kennedy's with [foreign] customers having needs but no money," while its long-established domestic "markets were all but lost." According to Landegger, management at Had-Mils subsequently squandered "ample markets for pulp, paper and industrial machinery" by breaking its promise to expand Kennedy's product lines, resulting in "exaggerated peaks and valleys of orders necessitating incessant lay-offs and recalls."[77]

Initially it seemed that a promising new era had dawned for Black Clawson-Kennedy (BC-K) – the company name was changed in December 1962 – with the brash Americans in charge. By 1963 order books were filling and the workforce again numbered 450 despite aggressive foreign and domestic competitors placing stiff downward pressure on prices and profits. Product innovation – Kennedy's traditional strength – was again encouraged. A wood pulp grinder and stainless steel pressure headbox for paper machines were just two of several new designs the firm marketed during the 1960s. The foundry revived its stellar reputation for marine products by manufacturing three of the largest four-blade bronze propellers ever made in Canada, each one 19'5" in diameter and weighing 48,000 pounds. Meanwhile, BC-K's engineers, in conjunction with the Canadian National Research Council, set a new international standard when it designed fourteen noise-reducing propellers for the Royal Canadian Navy.[78] Other initiatives included fabricating sluice gates for municipal water systems and experimenting with high-powered industrial pumps.[79] In 1968, BC-K constructed the world's first Verti-Forma paper machine, heralded as "one of the most revolutionary developments" in the paper industry since the early nineteenth century. Priced at $10 million apiece and the length of a city block when fully assembled, they were the largest newsprint machines ever manufactured in Canada. BC-K made a $1.25 million upgrade to the factory just to accommodate them.[80]

After criticizing Had-Mils's failure to diversify Kennedy's operations during the 1950s, followed by its own significant efforts at new product development in the 1960s, BC-K by the 1970s increasingly restricted the Owen Sound operation to manufacturing paper-making machinery. Several exogenous factors would eventually turn this heightened dependency on a single specialization into BC-K's Achilles' heel. First, the strengthening environmental movement pressured Canadian pulp and paper producers into making expensive pollution control modifications to their existing facilities, which deferred their investment in new equipment. In addition, a stronger Canadian currency was accentuating an already sagging US demand for paper-making machinery. BC-K therefore turned to export markets to revive its fortunes, and successfully secured orders for paper machines in Sweden, Iran, Peru, Turkey, and Bulgaria.[81] After its annual sales rebounded from just $11.4 million in 1978 to almost $21 million in 1980 and $27.2 million in 1981, the company defied prognostications that the resurgence in pulp and paper was temporary by adding a $2 million, 1,115m^2 extension to its factory in 1982. By mid-decade fully 85 per cent of BC-K's production was devoted solely to the paper machinery industry.[82]

This burst of business optimism immediately preceded the firm's final erratic slide into bankruptcy. Between 1982 and Black Clawson's historic 1992 decision to discontinue all manufacturing at Owen Sound – the plant was thereafter reduced to assembling prefabricated components acquired from subcontractors – BC-K's sales dropped from $42.1 million to $25.9 million, albeit fluctuating wildly between a high of $45.3 million in 1990 and a low of $15.6 million in 1984. The company's after-tax income for the same period tells an even more dismal tale: it plummeted from $1.4 million (1982) to $176,000 (1993), while recording annual losses of between $120,000 (1992) and $2.7 million (1987). A confluence of factors contributed to BC-K's woes, most notably reduced investment within the pulp and paper industry internationally and the rise of aggressive foreign competitors (from Scandinavia in particular) along with small-job manufacturers whose low overheads enabled them to drive profit margins below what BC-K could sustain. Convinced that its survival depended on even greater specialization, BC-K spent its final decade as a manufacturer attempting to develop niche markets within the paper industry. It promoted machinery upgrades for older inefficient paper mills, including retrofitting them to use recycled paper fibres. Other initiatives included designing de-inking machines used in newsprint recycling, experimenting with municipal waste separation systems, and targeting China's largely untapped market for paper-making machinery.[83] But to no avail.

Reduced to a shadow of its former self, the company that once employed more than 800 workers had just 165 on its payroll by 1990 and 30 in 1993. With little warning, what remained of BC-K was dismembered early in 1996, ending the 140-year Kennedy connection to manufacturing in Owen Sound. Black Clawson sold the Kennedy name and paper machine side of its business, along with Black Clawson's Watertown, New York, facilities, to Groupe Laperrière & Verreault Inc. of Trois-Rivières, Quebec, for $9.9 million. The corporate remnant in Owen Sound was named Black Clawson Canada.[84] Barely a year later, in March 1997, Black

Clawson Canada was bankrupt, and its remaining assembly operations were transferred from Owen Sound to the Canada Fibre Processing plant in Montreal, another Black Clawson branch. In April 1997 just four employees remained at the Owen Sound office, the smallest number since 1857, when William Kennedy opened the doors to his Sydenham Foundry and Planing-mills. Within days they too were laid off and the buildings permanently shuttered.[85]

Business historians sometimes refer to the "Buddenbrooks effect" or "three-generations paradigm" when explaining why some family firms fail after only a couple of generations of successful operation. The theory, simply put, posits that third-generation family members rarely inherit the entrepreneurial genius and drive of the company's founders. As David Landes explains, once "the firm develops power and prestige, the heirs find many interesting and amusing things to do rather than run the business … Rather than wear the shirtsleeves of their forefathers, they finish in silks and velvets, and focus on politics, culture, or the unabashed pursuit of the good life."[86] As Mark Casson describes in *Entrepreneurship: Theory, Networks, History*, a family company's handling of succession after the death or retirement of its head is a critical determinant of longevity. Even "very able entrepreneurs," he notes, can "groom unsuitable successors" and sacrifice "dynamism and innovation" by insisting upon "'insider succession'" rather than recruiting externally.[87]

The Kennedy manufacturing dynasty did not fall victim to flawed succession decisions. Indeed, to the extent that market conditions allowed, each generation of family members to succeed William, Sr. as company head maintained and expanded on his core business strategy, which entailed relying on ongoing product diversification and innovation to fuel steady if cautious corporate expansion. Ultimately it was the federal government's decision to tax estates that made it financially untenable for the Kennedy dynasty to continue into the next generation, causing T.D. to cede control of his company to investors beyond the family circle. Once operational decisions were consigned to strategists at multinational headquarters in England and the US, the Owen Sound plant was forced to follow a path of ever greater specialization, which increased with fatal consequences its vulnerability to market fluctuations.

The dramatic decline in Ontario's formerly diverse and dominant manufacturing sector by the 1980s suggests a possible inevitability to Kennedy's failure.[88] Certainly the company experienced difficulty after 1945 reclaiming the long-established markets it had lost as a consequence of dedicating most of its manufacturing capacity to wartime production. Moreover, given that Kennedy's own fortunes depended on its ability to service an array of industrial customers, the firm might not have escaped the province's general deindustrialization even had it remained under family control. Yet such a conclusion could also be too fatalistic by half. Prior to its acquisition by foreign interests and being forced to confine its manufacturing to a few highly specialized product lines, Kennedy's chief strength across the generations had been its entrepreneurial owners' determination to harness their craftsmen's ingenuity in designing and manufacturing a plethora of continually changing industrial products that were in demand domestically and abroad. One can only speculate as to whether that same genius, had it been permitted to continue, would have sustained Kennedy's within the dramatically restructured and rationalized Ontario, Canadian, and global manufacturing sectors of the 1990s and beyond. Among the wider pantheon of business dynasties, the Owen Sound family that built William Kennedy & Sons is among the less conspicuous. But the circumstances of its rise and fall nevertheless provide a useful glimpse into the entrepreneurial spirit behind the creation of a once imposing, but now much diminished, industrial Ontario.

QUESTIONS FOR CONSIDERATION:

1. What was the basis for the initial and longer-term success of this family firm?
2. What unique circumstances of the Ontario economy impacted the company in the period that it operated?
3. Was this family firm's failure inevitable?
4. What do you think is the legacy of William Kennedy & Sons? Are there other Ontario family firms that you know of that you can compare it to?

NOTES

This research was funded by a DanCap Private Equity Faculty Research Award, Faculty of Social Sciences, University of Western Ontario. The author thanks Joan Chandler, Artistic Director of the "Sheatre" community arts company, for generously sharing with him the research she compiled as background to her 2001 production "The Ballad of Kennedy's." He also gratefully acknowledges assistance by the staff of Grey Roots Museum and Archives, whose description of the William Kennedy & Sons collection published in the "Archival Sources" section of *Ontario History* (Autumn 2005) inspired this project.

1 *Owen Sound Sun-Times*, 16 September 1947.

2 Most histories of family-owned businesses in Canada and elsewhere have focused on large rather than small- or medium-sized firms such as Kennedy's. A succinct introduction to the history of family firms in Canada is Graham D. Taylor, *The Rise of Canadian Business* (Toronto: Oxford University Press, 2009), 215–22. The challenges of defining and analysing family businesses internationally since the nineteenth century are addressed in Andrea

Colli and Mary Rose, "Family Business," in *The Oxford Handbook of Business History*, ed. Geoffrey Jones and Jonathan Zeitlin (Toronto: Oxford University Press, 2009), 194–218. An excellent historical overview of factors contributing to either the decline or the persistence of family firms is Andrea Colli, *The History of Family Business, 1850–2000* (Cambridge: Cambridge University Press, 2003). Stereotypes of family-owned and -managed businesses as conservative and inefficient are tested in Geoffrey Jones and Mary B. Rose, eds., *Family Capitalism* (London: Frank Cass, 1993). See in particular Roy Church, "The Family Firm in Industrial Capitalism: International Perspectives on Hypotheses and History," which documents the positive performance of family firms vis-à-vis managerial enterprises (doi: org/10.1080/0007679930000127). Harold C. Livesay demonstrates the correlation between aggressive entrepreneurial management and firm success in "Entrepreneurial Dominance in Businesses Large and Small, Past and Present," *Business History Review* 63 (Spring 1989): 1–21. The largely overlooked significance of smaller companies to business history is explored in Jonathan Boswell's *The Rise and Decline of Small Firms* (London: George Allen & Unwin, 1972). The expansive theme of historical entrepreneurship is synthesized in Geoffrey Jones and R. Daniel Wadhwani, "Entrepreneurship," in *The Oxford Handbook of Business History*, ed. Jones and Zeitlin, (Oxford: Oxford University Press), 501–28. Mark Casson develops an interdisciplinary theory of entrepreneurial practice in *Entrepreneurship: Theory, Networks, History* (Cheltenham: Edward Elgar, 2010). Similarly, Jonathan Brown and Mary B. Rose, eds., *Entrepreneurship, Networks, and Modern Business* (Manchester: Manchester University Press, 1993) and two edited collections by Youssef Cassis and Ioanna Pepelasis Minoglou, *Entrepreneurship in Theory and History* (London: Palgrave Macmillan, 2005) and *Country Studies in Entrepreneurship: A Historical Perspective* (London : Palgrave Macmillan, 2006) utilize nation-based case studies to examine historical entrepreneurship theoretically and empirically. Other works useful for drawing comparisons to the Canadian experience include Andrew Godley and Mark Casson, "History of Entrepreneurship: Britain, 1900–2000," and Margaret B.W. Graham, "Entrepreneurship in the United States, 1920–2000," in *The Invention of Enterprise: Entrepreneurship from Ancient Mesopotamia to Modern Times*, ed. David S. Landes, Joel Mokyr, and William J. Baumol (Princeton: Princeton University Press, 2010), 243–72 and 401–42. An older but still significant collection of case studies is William Miller, ed., *Men in Business: Essays on the Historical Role of the Entrepreneur* (New York: Harper and Row, 1962). In "Understanding the Strategies and Dynamics of Long-lived Family Firms," *Business and Economic History* 21 (1992), 219–27, Philip Scranton considers the longevity of family-owned manufacturers based in the US throughout the nineteenth and twentieth centuries. Tom Nicholas tracks multigenerational predictors of entrepreneurial performance in "Clogs to Clogs in Three Generations?: Explaining Entrepreneurial Performance in Britain Since 1850," *Journal of Economic History* 59 (September 1999): 688–713. Obstacles to dynastic formation are the subject of Peter Dobkin Hall, "A Historical Overview of Family Firms in the United States," *Family Business Review* 1 (Spring 1988): 51–68. *Generation to Generation: Life Cycles of the Family Business* (Cambridge, MA: Harvard Business School Press, 1997) by Kelin E. Gersick and colleagues, is less historical but provides an insightful developmental model for describing changes to the business fortunes of family firms of various sizes. Philip Scranton's *Endless Novelty: Specialty Production and American Industrialization, 1865–1925* (Princeton: Princeton University Press, 1997), which details contributions by sundry specialty manufacturers to the Second Industrial Revolution, complements particularly well the early history of William Kennedy & Sons, Ltd.

3 David S. Landes, *Dynasties: Fortunes and Misfortunes of the World's Great Family Businesses* (New York: Viking, 2006), 291, 294, 302.
4 *Industrial Canada*, July 1927, 238.
5 *Owen Sound Comet*, 23 October 1857; Melba Croft, *The People of Owen Sound* (Owen Sound: M.M. Croft, 1979), 21, 25.
6 *Owen Sound Sun*, 16 March 1917.
7 *Owen Sound Advertiser*, 10 January 1867.
8 *Owen Sound Sun-Times*, 1 March 1951; Grey Roots Museum and Archives (hereafter GRMA), William Kennedy & Sons (hereafter WKS) Collection, box 40, "Historical Forward," 26 November 1952. Patterns are precise wooden replicas of pieces of machinery into which the molten metal is poured.
9 *Owen Sound Advertiser*, 27 August 1885.
10 *Owen Sound Advertiser*, 5 October 1894.
11 Mark Casson, *Enterprise and Leadership: Studies on Firms, Markets, and Networks* (Cheltenham: Edward Elgar, 2000), 212.
12 Alexander Fraser, *A History of Ontario: Its Resources and Development* (Toronto: Canada History Co., 1907), 1124. Unfortunately, financial data for much of the company's history is sporadic and not amenable to a sustained and systematic analysis. Only for the period since the early 1980s do relatively comprehensive financial reports exist.
13 GRMA, WKS Collection, box 44, scrapbook 1943–1961, PF11S1F8I10, article for *Canadian Machinery*, December 1917.
14 *Owen Sound Sun*, 12 October 1917.
15 *Owen Sound Sun-Times*, 10 December 1918.
16 GRMA, WKS Collection, box 44, scrapbook 1943–1961, PF11S1F8I10, article for *Canadian Machinery*, December 1917; box 40, "Wm. Kennedy & Sons Limited, Owen Sound, Ontario"; *Owen Sound Sun*, 4 January 1916, 4 February 1916. Sir John Kennedy (b. 1838) was employed with WKS from 1868 to 1872. Thereafter he was chief engineer of the Great Western Railway and the Montreal Harbour Commission. He was knighted in 1916 by King George V for "his devoted service to marine and rail transportation in Canada." Upon his death in 1921 he was dubbed the "Dean of the engineering profession in Canada" by the Engineering Institute of Canada. See Rod Millard, ed., *Biographical Dictionary of Canadian Engineers*, http://history.uwo.ca/cdneng/kennedy.html.
17 *Owen Sound Sun-Times*, 10 December 1918.
18 GRMA, WKS Collection, box 14, Ledger Financial Statements, December 1917–December 1938.
19 GRMA, WKS Collection, box 38, scrapbook 1922–1923, PF11S1F8I1, WK&Sons Ltd. to *Canadian Mining Journal*, 11 February 1922.
20 GRMA, WKS Collection, box 38, scrapbook 1922–1938, PF11S1F8I1, "Products of The William Kennedy and Sons, Limited," *c.* 1922.
21 *Canadian Mining Journal*, 23 November 1923.
22 *Industrial Canada*, July 1927.
23 *Northern Miner*, 19 April 1924; *Canadian Boating*, July–August 1935; *Industrial Canada*, July 1927.
24 GRMA, WKS Collection, box 14, Ledger Financial Statements, December 1917–December 1938. Kennedy's sales fell to $244,686 in 1932 before climbing to a high of $731,430 in 1937 and averaging approximately $507,000 annually across the decade. Average annual gross trading profits of approximately $95,000 represented a 25 per cent decline from the 1920s.
25 Mark Casson, *Enterprise and Leadership*, 211.
26 *Industrial Canada*, July 1931.

27 Private collection of Joan Chandler, interview with Kay McKie, n.d.
28 *Canadian Boating and Cottagers' Magazine*, April 1934; *Canadian Boating*, July–August 1935.
29 US Patent Office, 22 December 1931, patent no. 1,837,909; 5 July 1932, patent no. 1,866,350; *Industrial Canada*, July 1927.
30 *The Northern Miner*, 16 November 1933.
31 GRMA, WKS Collection, box 14, Ledger Financial Statements, December 1917–December 1938; private collection of Joan Chandler, interview with Kay McKie, n.d.
32 *Owen Sound Sun-Times*, 8 January 1938.
33 *Owen Sound Sun-Times*, 4 February 1933, 23 December 1940.
34 Private collection of Joan Chandler, interview with Tac Agnew, n.d.
35 LAC, RG 24, series C-1, reel C-8336, file 7439, "Secret and Confidential Subject Files, Army – William Kennedy and Sons Ltd., Owen Sound, Ontario," notes for Col. G. Ogilvie, 3 May 1938.
36 *Owen Sound Sun-Times*, 11 December 1940.
37 *Owen Sound Sun-Times*, 27 December 1940, 28 December 1940, 31 December 1940.
38 *Owen Sound Sun-Times*, 2 January 1941, 21 January 1941.
39 GRMA, WKS Collection, box 40, PF11S3F1I24, memo from T.D. Kennedy, 2 June 1941; LAC, RG 28, vol. 508, The William Kennedy & Sons Limited. Owen Sound. Ontario. Formal Agreement, file 51-K-3, "Memorandum of Agreement," 19 June 1941; vol. 364, The William Kennedy & Sons Limited. Owen Sound. Ontario. Formal Agreement, file 4-4-1-123, "Memorandum of Agreement," 28 June 1941.
40 *Owen Sound Sun-Times*, 23 January 1942; *Shipping Register and Shipbuilder*, September 1944; LAC, RG 28, vol. 370, The William Kennedy & Sons Limited. Owen Sound. Ontario. Formal Agreement, no. 4-4-1-123, "Memorandum of Agreement," 31 January 1942; vol. 364, The William Kennedy & Sons Limited. Owen Sound. Ontario. Formal Agreement, no. 4-4-1-123, "Memorandum of Agreement," 20 February 1943 and 27 July 1944; vol. 370, The William Kennedy & Sons Limited. Owen Sound. Ontario. Formal Agreement, no. 4-4-1-123, "Memorandum of Agreement," 27 May 1943.
41 LAC, RG 28, vol. 364, The William Kennedy & Sons Limited. Owen Sound. Ontario. Formal Agreement, file 4-4-1-123, "Memorandum of Agreement," 29 July 1941; vol. 566, The William Kennedy & Sons Limited. Owen Sound. Ontario. File 200-612 Formal Agreement," 23 September 1944; *Owen Sound Sun-Times*, 23 January 1942; *Shipping Register and Shipbuilder*, September 1944.
42 *Owen Sound Sun-Times*, 27 January 1943; LAC, RG 28, vol. 508, The William Kennedy & Sons Limited. Owen Sound. Ontario. File 51-K-3. Formal Agreement, "Contract for Capital Expenditure to Manufacture Steering Engines for Vessels," 29 May 1942; The William Kennedy & Sons Limited. Owen Sound. Ontario. file 51-K-3 PC 888 F.E 1987-A, Formal Agreement, "Contract for Capital Expenditure to Increase the Manufacture of Propellers and Auxiliary Naval Equipment," 8 February 1943; file 51-K-3. Formal Agreement, "Contract for Capital Expenditure for New Plant at Owen Sound, Ontario," 3 July 1943; Formal Agreement, "Contract for Capital Expenditure for Production of Steel Castings," 16 February 1944; Formal Agreement, "Contract for Amendment No. 1 to Contract Dated February 16, 1944," 31 March 1944.
43 *Shipping Register and Shipbuilder*, September 1943, September 1944; *Owen Sound Sun-Times*, 28 January 1944.
44 GRMA, WKS Collection, box 40, PF11S3F1I24, memo from T.D. Kennedy, 2 June 1941.
45 http://www.greyroots.com/exhibitions/virtual-exhibits/kennedy/?search=kennedy. LAC, RG 28, series A, vol. 123, file 3-C2-1-293, Censorship Co-ordination Committee, William Kennedy & Sons Limited, n.d.

46 GRMA, WKS Collection, box 40, J.R. Thompson to T.D. Kennedy, 22 November 1944.
47 GRMA, WKS Collection, box 40, PF11S1F61S7-58, "Kennedy Can Cast It," *c.* 1944.
48 LAC, RG 27, Labour Canada, vol. 437, reel T-3039, file 123, "Metal Factory Workers – Owen Sound, Ontario;" *Owen Sound Sun-Times*, 11 July 1944; *London Free Press*, 13 July 1944; *Globe and Mail*, 11 July 1944.
49 GRMA, WKS Collection, box 40, memorandum of meeting with Union Committee, by C.A. Eberle, 19 July 1944.
50 *Owen Sound Sun-Times*, 16 September 1947, 28 January 1948; GRMA, WKS Collection, box 40, C.C. Agnew, "The Repair and Reconditioning of Ships' Propellers," n.d.
51 *Owen Sound Sun-Times*, 14 November 1948; 15 November 1948, 16 November 1948.
52 Archives of Ontario (AO), RG 7-30, B384917, "William Kennedy & Sons Ltd., Owen Sound, 1948," Jas. Hutcheon to Charles Daley, 30 October 1948; Jas. Hutcheon to Charles Daley, 13 November 1948; D.T. Cowan to Charles Daley, February 1949.
53 AO, RG 7-30, B384917, "William Kennedy & Sons Ltd., Owen Sound, 1948," David Lewis to Charles Daley, n.d.
54 GRMA, WKS Collection, box 40, Earl Farley and Archie J. Hayward to Colin Bennett, 4 November 1949; Colin Bennett to Archie J. Hayward, 16 November 1949.
55 GRMA, WKS Collection, box 40, A.M. Kennedy to employees, 21 November 1949.
56 *Owen Sound Sun-Times*, 31 January 1951.
57 GRMA, WKS Collection, box 40, C.A. Eberle to customers, 17 May 1950; C.A. Eberle to customers, 19 June 1950; A.M. Kennedy to employees, 20 June 1950; *Owen Sound Sun-Times*, 24 July 1950, 31 July 1950.
58 GRMA, WKS Collection, box 40, T.D. Kennedy, "Official Announcement," 1 March 1951; *Owen Sound Sun-Times*, 1 March 1951.
59 *The Times* (London), 4 April 1946, 17 April 1946, 12 March 1949, 28 April 1950, 13 October 1950, 11 January 1951, 11 July 1951, 21 July 1955; GRMA, WKS Collection, box 40, "A Brief History of the Millspaugh Group," *c.* 1954.
60 *Owen Sound Sun-Times*, 13 July 2001.
61 *Globe and Mail*, 16 January 1941, 30 April 1941, 20 May 1941; *Owen Sound Sun-Times*, 30 May 1941.
62 Canada, *House of Commons Debates*, 28 May 1941, 3224–6. The estimate of William Kennedy & Sons, Ltd.'s selling price was provided by Tac Agnew, a long-time employee and former bookkeeper of the company, who had access to internal financial information during the 1950s. Agnew calculated that Neil Kennedy received approximately $168,000 for his shares; Arthur Kennedy, $190,000; Roger Kennedy, $45,000; Marjorie (Kennedy) McMurtrie, $140,000; and Thomas Dowsely Kennedy, at least $1 million. The information is found in the private collection of Joan Chandler, interview with Tac Agnew, n.d.
63 *Owen Sound Sun-Times*, 11 September 1951, 31 January 1952, 28 January 1953.
64 GRMA, WKS Collection, box 40, memo of luncheon with J.B. Thomas, 17 September 1952.
65 *The Times*, 22 April 1953. Millspaugh's manufacturing activities in the early 1950s were allocated among six key sectors: pulp and paper, 40 per cent; shipbuilding, 20 per cent; general engineering, 10 per cent; iron and steel castings, 15 per cent; plastic and textile trades, 7.5 per cent; and cement industry, 7.5 per cent.
66 See http://fx.sauder.ubc.ca/etc/GBPpages.pdf for all currency conversion rates.
67 *Owen Sound Sun-Times*, 20 January 1954; *Financial Post*, 25 January 1954; *The Times*, 25 February 1954. The best estimate of Kennedy's sales at this time is $7–8 million annually.
68 *The Times*, 23 March 1955.

69 *Submission to the Royal Commission on Coasting Trade, Volume* One (1955), C.A. Eberle to G.G. McLeod, 20 April 1955.

70 *The Times*, 2 December 1955, 12 January 1956, 17 January 1956, 5 April 1956.

71 *Owen Sound Sun-Times*, 31 January 1958; GRMA, WKS Collection, box 40, "History of the William Kennedy & Sons, Limited," 1959; AO, RG 7-31, B383375, file RG-7-31-0-542, "The William Kennedy & Sons Limited, Owen Sound," G.W. Reed to Charles Daley, 5 May 1959; Louis Fine to Charles Daley, 15 May 1959; "Report of the Conciliation Board," July 1959.

72 *The Times*, 20 April 1961.

73 *The Times*, 1 April 1959, 1February 1961, 11 February 1961, 27 March 1961.

74 *The Times*, 11 December 1961, 2 April 1962, 18 February 1963.

75 *Owen Sound Sun-Times*, 8 November 1961.

76 http://www.paperhall.org/inductees/bios/2003/carl_landegger.php.

77 GRMA, WKS Collection, box 40, PF11S3F1I5, "Black Clawson Today: A reservoir of technical knowledge," 1967; "A History of Black Clawson-Kennedy Ltd.," 6 July 1966.

78 *Owen Sound Sun-Times*, 30 January 1964, 29 January 1965.

79 GRMA, WKS Collection, box 37, PF11S1F213, pt. 2, "1970 Business Outlook – Black Clawson-Kennedy Ltd., 23 January 1970; R. Warburton to L. Blue, 15 January 1970; "The Business Outlook for *Owen Sound Sun-Times*," n.d.

80 *Owen Sound Herald*, 16 November 1967; GRMA, WKS Collection, box 37, PF11S1F212, pt. 2, "For release in the 1969 *Owen Sound Sun-Times* annual Business Outlook edition," n.d. Operating on a horizontal plane, the Fourdrinier uses gravity to drain water from a slurry of pulp fibres, whereas the Verti-Forma produces a sheet of paper between two drainage wires operating in a vertical plane. When gravity was allowed to drain water from both sides of the sheet, a higher quality of paper could be formed at faster speeds than was possible with the Fourdrinier.

81 GRMA, WKS Collection, box 37, PF11S1F213, pt. 2, "Business Outlook 1972," 23 February 1972, "*Owen Sound Sun-Times* Business Review," 16 February 1973; "*Owen Sound Sun-Times* Business Review," 16 February 1974; untitled press release, 24 January 1978; "Business Outlook," 7 February 1980; *Owen Sound Sun-Times*, 25 February 1975.

82 *Pulp and Paper Canada*, 83, no. 3 (1982).

83 *Owen Sound Sun-Times*, 25 February 1988, 22 February 1990, 26 February 1991, 22 February 199, 25 February 1993, 8 April 1997.

84 *Owen Sound Sun-Times*, 8 April 1997; *Financial Post*, 5 March 1996, 6 March 1996; *Pulp & Paper Canada*, 4 April 1996; *Canadian Papermaker*, April 1996. Groupe Laperrière & Verreault Inc., with annual revenues in excess of $133 million in 1995, specialized in refurbishing equipment for the pulp and paper industry.

85 *Owen Sound Sun-Times*, 8 April 1997. In February 1997, the assets of the parent company Black Clawson were purchased for $110 million in cash and assumed debt by Thermo Fibertek of Waltham, Massachusetts, a subsidiary of the Thermo Electron Corporation and manufacturer of papermaking and paper-recycling equipment. Thermo Fibertek Inc.was renamed Kadant, Inc., in 2001.

86 Landes, *Dynasties*, xiv; Andrea Colli, *The History of Family Business, 1850–2000* (Cambridge: Cambridge University Press, 2003), 9.

87 Mark Casson, *Entrepreneurship: Theory, Networks, History* (Cheltenham: Edward Elgar, 2010), 33; Colli, *Family Business*, 71.

88 The indicators of provincial decline after 1980 are many and varied. To cite but a few examples, total manufacturing employment in Ontario fell from 1,034,000 to 837,000 (from

24.8 to 17.5 per cent of total employment) between 1981 and 1993. Between 1989 and 1996 more than 10 per cent of manufacturing establishments in the province closed. The trend continues, with almost one in five manufacturing jobs disappearing between 2004 and 2008. See Meric S. Gertler, "Groping Towards Reflexivity: Responding to Industrial Change in Ontario," in *The Rise of the Rustbelt*, ed. Philip Cooke (Taylor & Francis e-Library, 2006), 103–25; David A. Wolfe and Meric S. Gertler, "Globalization and Economic Restructuring in Ontario: From Industrial Heartland to Learning Region?," http://www.utoronto.ca/progris/pdf_files/WolfeNECSTS-RICTES99.pdf; and André Bernard, "Trends in Manufacturing Employment," *Perspectives* (Statistics Canada cat. no. 75-001-X), February 2009, 5–13.

CHAPTER TEN

The Ontario–Quebec Axis: Post-War Strategies in Intergovernmental Negotiations

P.E. BRYDEN

In the years between Confederation and the Second World War, Ontario developed a fairly consistent pattern in its dealings with Ottawa. Under the early leadership of Oliver Mowat, Ontario positioned itself as the guardian of provincial rights and the first line of defence against the enormous powers the British North America Act granted to the central government. By challenging the extent of federal powers in the courts and by broadening the force of provincial jurisdiction through the careful development of patronage networks, Mowat solidified the position of Ontario in relation to the federal government and more than earned the title of "father of provincial rights." The confrontations between the two levels of government were acrimonious, but they played out in the relatively sterile environment of the courtroom and hinged on the sometimes arcane interpretation of constitutional law.

By the 1930s, however, the battle had turned more personal. Although Premier Mitch Hepburn resolutely defended the Mowat position that provincial jurisdiction needed to be extended, the context of depression and war served only to heighten the level of antipathy between the two governments. Convinced that Prime Minister William Lyon Mackenzie King was dealing ineffectively with both the massive unemployment of the Great Depression and the need for full-scale deployment of resources during the Second World War, Hepburn engaged in an all-out war of his own against the federal government in general and King in particular. It seems, then, that Ontario's strategy in dealing with Ottawa was remarkably well established: using confrontational tactics to defend and extend the power of the province at all costs.[1]

As enduring as this approach seemed from the vantage point of mid-century, Ontario's relationship with Ottawa in the years since the end of the Second World War has been characterized by a surprising level of cooperation and compromise. In areas of social policy, economic arrangements, and constitutional renewal, Ontario politicians have generally supported the national interest. By no means, however, did Ontario become merely a puppet of the central government, nor did it support Ottawa's initiatives at the expense of clear provincial priorities. Instead, Ontario began to pursue a strategy of articulating a "national" position on issues of contest between the two levels of government – a position that was sometimes in harmony with that being taken in Ottawa but more often was in contrast to the federal position or in advance of it. This approach, which in many ways saw Ontario attempting to usurp the role of national government from Ottawa, demanded the development of alliances at the provincial level. Without support for their proposals on social, economic, or constitutional change, Ontario politicians could not hope to have them adopted on the national stage. The development of close relationships across provincial boundaries became far more important to Ontario's overall intergovernmental strategy in the post-war years than it ever had been before.[2]

The relationship Ontario enjoyed with Quebec, disparagingly referred to as the Ontario–Quebec Axis, was by far the most important of those links forged in the post-war years, and it was to have its most lasting significance on issues of constitutional reform. Growing out of the unlikely alliance that had developed between Ontario's George Drew and Quebec's Maurice Duplessis at the Dominion–Provincial Conference on Reconstruction in 1945 and 1946, the axis reached its apotheosis in the late 1960s. Currying favour with Quebec had two important effects on Ontario's intergovernmental strategy. First, it allowed Ontario to put some added weight behind its constitutional proposals and thereby offer serious alternatives to the federal position. Second, Ontario was forced to modify its own position in light of the relative strength or weakness of the connection with Quebec. The implications of this alliance for Canadian federalism more generally were profound. By taking the initiative for constitutional negotiation away from Ottawa in the 1960s, Ontario was responsible for opening a discussion that has continued, virtually unabated, for more than thirty years.

The election of George Drew as premier of Ontario in 1943, replacing the Liberal dynasty of Mitch Hepburn, was not in itself an event that suggested a sea change in the relationship the province experienced with Ottawa. While far less erratic in both life and politics than the hard-living Hepburn, Drew shared his predecessor's view of King. By the time Drew became premier of Ontario, he had long since reached the conclusion that the prime minister was duplicitous. He denied the existence of a "feud," but noted: "It is essential that we assert ourselves in provincial matters."[3]

Conventional wisdom on the Dominion–Provincial Conference on Reconstruction of 1945–46 holds that it was the last gasp of the old rivalry between Ontario and Ottawa. The conference, called to discuss the Dominion proposals for post-war reconstruction, ended in the spring of 1946 without any agreement being reached. The blame for the failure of the two levels of government to reach any conclusions on fiscal arrangements, social policies, and a system of equalization grants has generally been placed squarely on Drew's shoulders.[4] Although some revisionist scholarship has contended that the federal government's refusal to separate the social and equalization policies from the continuation of unpleasant wartime tax rental agreements, in conjunction with King's ideological resistance to an active central state, was really to blame for the conference's failure, no one has suggested that Drew was anything other than difficult.[5]

A closer examination of the conference suggests that, rather than being the final chapter in intergovernmental acrimony, it was instead the first verse of a new approach on the part of Ontario to dealing with Ottawa. Drew played a pivotal role in ensuring that there would be an intergovernmental discussion over the shape of post-war Canada. He first broached the subject of holding a conference devoted to considering post-war planning in early January 1944, when the tide had begun to turn in favour of the Allied powers, but "before the Dominion and Provincial Governments committed themselves to post-war legislation." A copy of this letter was sent by the Prime Minister's Office to all provincial premiers, whereupon it became "the basis for a proposal for a conference" and Drew began to deal more directly with his provincial colleagues.[6] What followed was an eighteen-month period of delay, obfuscation, blame casting, and general confusion. Drew repeatedly called for a conference to be convened; King repeatedly delayed. Federal officials asked for provincial statistical material to be forwarded to Ottawa to assist in the preparation of their reconstruction proposals; Ontario officials insisted on knowing to what end it would be used and ended up being accused of impeding the work towards opening a conference.[7] According to Leslie Frost, the provincial treasurer, King was "beating over some old straw and missing the real point."[8] Between the time Drew first raised the possibility of intergovernmental discussion on reconstruction in January 1944 and the start of the conference in August 1945, the tenor of Ontario's correspondence shifted from that of polite requests to barely contained fury, but, more than merely becoming enraged, Drew began also to establish a distinctly provincial strategy.

King's reluctance to act in what Drew considered a timely fashion encouraged the provincial leader to propose an alternative means by which agreement could be reached on some sort of plan to deal with the multitude of anticipated post-war challenges. The first tactic Ontario politicians employed in attempting to force King to call the leaders together in conference was soliciting support from the other provincial premiers. He sent copies of his voluminous correspondence to King to the provincial capitals and urged the premiers to contribute to the pressure he was exerting on the prime minister.[9] For months, such efforts resulted only in continued federal stalling. Drew also suggested to the other provincial premiers that they "might well hold a separate conference of their own after the preliminary conference to determine the measure of unanimity there is as to the general plan submitted to them."[10] But the failure even to call a preliminary meeting scuttled plans, for the time being at least, for any purely provincial gathering. Neither Drew nor his officials were deterred, however, and continued to develop the Ontario position for the post-war period.

It was absolutely vital for the Ontario representatives that "Dominion–Provincial relations be clarified before the post-war period is upon us." The most important issues that needed to be considered were the termination schedule of the Wartime Tax Rental Agreements and a more equitable rearrangement of the tax fields between the federal and provincial governments. To this end, "it is of the first importance," declared Ontario's preliminary draft discussion paper on dominion–provincial relations, "that Ontario and Quebec, representing about two-thirds of our population and resources, should agree upon certain principles and so far as possible present a united front. This would probably carry with it the other provincial governments and would have a tremendous influence on the Dominion Government."[11] To achieve that united front, however, it would be necessary for talks to open between the governments of the two provinces. This prospect might seem likely, given the similarity of Ontario and Quebec positions in regard to the current fiscal arrangements, but it posed enormous problems owing to the disposition of the premiers of the neighbouring provinces. Drew was a staunch proponent of conscription, and pointed to the anti-conscription sentiment in Quebec as undermining both the war effort and national unity. Duplessis, who returned to power in the fall of 1944 on the crest of popular opposition to the federal government's about-face on conscription, had never been a favourite of Drew. In fact, while Drew thought that "much can be done in the way of practical cooperation between the two Provinces" with Adélard Godbout at the helm, he despaired of an "Anti-British Government headed by either Duplessis or Raymond."[12] For his part, Duplessis would surely have disagreed with Drew's views on the nature of political community. "It seems to me," Drew wrote to a friend in Alberta,

> that every nation must have some clear central purpose. Ours must clearly be declared. Unity can only be based upon the acceptance of that purpose. I think the longer we appease the isolationists in Quebec, the surer we are of civil war. I think if we act now and leave no doubt about the determination of the English speaking part of Canada, whether of Anglo-Saxon stock or otherwise, to preserve British traditions and maintain the British connection, then we will have laid the foundation of unity, and if it is clear that we are determined in our course I am inclined to think it may not be long before Quebec itself will be offering us some support. Anything else simply means a steady trend toward a Quebec-dominated Canada. That I for one am not prepared to accept. I believe in the British connection and all it means. And I would much rather see my children grow up as citizens of the United States than to be citizens of a Canada which was reduced to the low ethical and moral standard of the people of Quebec.[13]

His flag-waving imperialism and his clear contempt for Quebecers in general made Drew an unlikely ally for the nationalist Duplessis.

Antagonism towards the federal government, however, can make strange bedfellows. Neither Ontario nor Quebec wanted to see the continuation of "unjust" federal incursions into provincial tax bases, and neither welcomed the possibility of Ottawa spending money in fields that were irrefutably provincial jurisdiction. While the two provinces might disagree on specific legislation, they were in complete accord on the principle of provincial autonomy. The introduction of a system of family allowances, for example, was widely regarded in Ontario as a means of appeasing Quebec. According to the Ontario civil servants charged with preparing the provincial position on dominion–provincial relations,

> when the Federal Government uses revenue from general taxation to finance services specially beneficial to non-Ontario provinces, the matter does not end with taking money from Ontario individuals and corporations and paying it out to the inhabitants of other provinces. Transfers of this nature reduce incomes and spending in Ontario. There is Dominion taxation but no compensatory Dominion expenditure, and the productiveness of the Government of Ontario's own taxes is reduced and its fiscal position impaired.

Despite this concern about the equalization component inherent in the system of universal family allowances, Drew's real opposition was to Ottawa's assumption of responsibility over an aspect of social policy where "experience shows that ... the more localized the supervision is, the more humane and also the more carefully supervised it is."[14] Politicians from Ontario and Quebec might disagree over the specifics of family allowances, but they could agree on the general principle that provincial powers were being eroded. Attempts on the part of others to refute Ontario's position on the need for intergovernmental reform usually ended up lumping Ontario and Quebec together and served to smooth over some of the specific areas of disagreement between the two provinces. Premier Stuart Garson of Manitoba was among the most vocal critics of the Ontario position, reputedly arguing that "Ontario and Quebec are credited with corporation income tax which is accumulated on commodities sold in the Prairies and other non-Ontario and Quebec provinces." Already sharing a fundamental distrust of the federal government and a desire to protect provincial jurisdiction, Ontario and Quebec, now jointly labelled the beneficiaries or spoiled children of Confederation, found common cause at the Conference on Reconstruction.

The better part of the five days of discussion was occupied with opening statements from the various government leaders, photo opportunities, and elegant meals. Most important, the meeting gave the federal government a chance to table its proposals for post-war reconstruction, contained in a document widely referred to as the Green Book. Now that the federal proposals had been made public, it was possible for each of the provinces to begin the real work of determining the acceptability of those reconstruction plans and, if necessary, developing counter-proposals. The question of whether to endorse the Green Book proposals was not a difficult one for Ontario or Quebec: the federal document outlined a plan for the continued right of the central government to occupy the corporate, income, and succession tax fields in return for introducing social policies and a system of equalization grants. It would mean a significant centralization of power and taxing abilities in the hands of the federal government, and a parallel reduction in the fiscal and administrative powers of the provinces. The proposals were clearly anathema to what Drew and Duplessis imagined for the post-war world, and, despite other areas of difference, the two became allies during the course of the August meeting. Provincial treasurer Leslie Frost had earlier visited other provincial capitals, to personalize the connections Drew had established through his correspondence with his colleagues, and was able to introduce his premier to Duplessis at the conference. This association, which became known as the "Drew-Duplessis axis,"[15] began auspiciously. Duplessis reiterated many of the points Drew had made, and the two were regarded with equal suspicion by King.[16] As the Ontario ministers and officials designed their response to the Green Book, they attempted not only to present an alternative national vision also but to ensure that it included proposals that would keep Quebec firmly in their camp.

Ontario's approach to dealing with the federal proposals was at odds with its traditional course of action. Rather than respond to the Green Book through confrontation or outright dismissal, the Ontario officials designed a completely different set of solutions to the problems facing the federation in the post-war years. There were clear problems with the division of tax powers, for the two levels of government shared rights to the lucrative direct tax fields. Ontario opposed leaving Ottawa with sole jurisdiction, as the Green Book proposed, and instead advocated a fiscal structure in which corporate and personal tax fields would be allotted to the federal government and succession duties to the provinces. In addition, the provinces would take over complete control of the "nuisance" taxes – gas, amusement, racetrack taxes, and the like. In response to the clear regional inequality, Ontario proposed a system of adjustment grants that would bring the poorer regions a level of income impossible to achieve simply through provincial taxation. The experience of the Depression had left little doubt in anyone's mind that new social welfare programs were necessary to combat the exigencies of old age, unemployment, and poor health, but all these areas fell under the constitutional authority of the provinces. Ontario's reconstruction plan anticipated a system of social security that would see Ottawa footing most of the bill and the provinces retaining administrative control, in line with Drew's thinking that such projects were best left to local authorities.[17]

An alternative to the federal proposal for constitutional change and economic renewal was of little use without some assurances that it met not only the concerns of the Ontario delegation but also those of other provinces. The most important opportunity for developing these relationships arose during the *in camera* sessions of the coordinating committee and the meetings of the various subcommittees of the Reconstruction Conference. Although each of the provinces was required to make submissions elaborating its particular financial situation and the "effects of the Dominion proposals on the budgetary position of the provinces," Ontario's submission went considerably further in outlining alternative arrangements. As a result, it became as much a topic of debate as the proposals outlined by the federal delegation. By taking Ontario's position as a starting point, the provincial alliances became more clear. Certain components of the plan were enthusiastically received: the British Columbia representatives called Ontario's "a well-proportioned scheme," and Nova Scotia's Angus L. Macdonald agreed with Drew that the provinces must have "certain definite fields of taxation" reserved for them.[18] Still, for one participant, the only clear alliance that had developed was the one between Drew and Duplessis. Although the federal "experts seem to think that Drew will have to yield his point of view" on the necessity of some provincial taxation autonomy, Prime

Minister King remained convinced that he "will follow Duplessis in opposing the other provinces."[19]

King probably overstated the degree to which Drew and Duplessis were positioned in opposition to the other seven premiers. During the closed meetings of the coordinating committee at the end of January 1946, premiers from both the West and the Maritimes supported elements of Ontario's proposal and repeatedly pressed for serious consideration of them.[20] However, he was not underestimating the degree to which the premiers of Ontario and Quebec were of one mind. Although Drew was prepared to make some concessions to Ottawa, particularly with respect to the vacating of personal income and corporation taxes, when "Duplessis came out strongly against allowing the Dominion to have the succession duties ... Drew took a similar stand."[21] He argued "that the B.N.A. Act in spirit, if not on strict legal grounds, provided for exclusive provincial jurisdiction in the direct tax fields, and he argued that the cause of the breakdown of every federation in history had been the abandonment of provincial rights of direct taxation."[22] When it became "quite apparent that neither Ontario nor Quebec [would] give up this field," King commented privately that he did "not blame them."[23] He later postulated that the unwillingness to give up the field of succession duties was based on a fear that "if a socialist government came in [in Ottawa] that would make it impossible for the people to leave much for their children."[24] While agreeing in principle with the stance taken by Ontario and Quebec, King seemed to believe that his civil servants were forcing the issue and making it impossible for him to say anything publicly.

Under pressure from Drew that the closed meetings of the coordinating committee be replaced by open sessions, to eliminate the possibility of views being misrepresented in the press, the full conference reconvened at the end of April 1946.[25] There could not have been much hope for success: neither of the architects of the two main proposals, Ontario and Ottawa, had been able to convince enough of the others of the utility of its position to ensure victory. Drew and Duplessis consistently backed each other up in their arguments against excessive centralization, although the Ontario premier accompanied his denunciations of the Green Book with solid counterproposals. When the conference concluded on 3 May with vitriol and acrimony, and without agreement, the public portrayal of the central Canadian premiers as the primary impediments to consensus was unfair. Garson seemed to strike an appealing chord when he declared, "it is calamitous for Canada that the Ontario and Quebec governments could not have continued with those of the other seven provinces in the negotiation of a compromise of the small area of disagreement which still remains between the seven provinces and the Dominion."[26] The characterization of the evil Drew–Duplessis axis thwarting the efforts of the

Dominion–Provincial Conference was created at the time and, to a large extent, has remained in the historical literature. This view masks some of the more complex features of the negotiation process and paints an inaccurate picture of both the role Ontario was attempting to play and the nature of the relationship between Ontario and Quebec.

Instead of asserting a provincial rights agenda, as had been the tactic of several generations of Ontario premiers before him, Drew sought to articulate an alternative to the Green Book proposals. While this alternative protected provincial taxation jurisdiction to a much greater degree than the federal position, it also included elements designed to address the specific concerns of other regions. The Ontario proposal recognized the need for equalization to redress regional imbalance, allowed federal occupancy of both income and corporate taxes, and included an expanded welfare system. It was not, then, a purely pro-Ontario position, but a first step in the direction of a national plan for reconstruction. The prime minister himself recognized the efforts Drew was making towards establishing a viable alternative and ultimately blamed his own civil servants for the conference's failure. He believed that the federal hard line "might cost the Liberal party power. We were simply allowing Drew to take the Liberal position and to get the support of [Nova Scotia's] Macdonald and others and that we could not hope to win with provinces against us one after the other."[27] When all was said and done, he lambasted his colleagues by reminding them, "I had said all along we were taking the wrong course in handing to the provinces an excuse for an attack on us on the score of centralization and not allowing certain tax fields to the provinces."[28] In the months that followed, Drew's repeated efforts to force the federal government to reconvene the federal–provincial conference attested to his commitment to reach agreement rather than merely scuttle the proceedings.[29] In the end, Drew was left feeling "convinced that King never had any expectation from the very beginning of reaching agreement and that his main purpose was to make generous promises to the public which would gain favour and then leave the responsibility on Ontario particularly, and Quebec as well if possible, for having prevented them from carrying out their generous intentions."[30]

The association that was forged with Quebec during the course of the Reconstruction Conference was only the most visible of the numerous relationships the Ontario government attempted to develop with its sister provincial administrations. Far from being an unholy alliance devoted to derailing the federal plans for post-war Canada, it was a natural partnership between two similar provinces and two premiers who distrusted centralization. Ontario and Quebec shared a position within Confederation that necessarily threw them together, and Ontario at least had a vision of how the federation should continue. The condemnation of the pair as the spoilers at the Reconstruction Conference, and Drew's and Duplessis's mutual dislike of Mackenzie King, kept them together.[31] The association would remain an important one if Ontario were ever to claim success in articulating a national vision and if Quebec were to gain a more widely shared understanding of its particular concerns with the Canadian federation.

Although Leslie Frost, who became premier of Ontario in 1948, had cordial relations with Duplessis, the increasing insistence of the Quebec premier in his final decade in office that Ottawa stay out of provincial jurisdiction left little room for alliance between the two premiers. There simply were few occasions in which the Quebec premier even entertained the idea of "federal–provincial relations," let alone the need for provincial allies in dealing with Ottawa. But new premiers in both the provinces in the early 1960s opened up the opportunity for a different sort of relationship. In the beginning, Conservative John Robarts and Liberal Jean Lesage forged an association that had all the appearances of being cast in the traditional mould: an axis designed to thwart federal policy. But by establishing linkages between the two provinces and solidifying both friendships and strategies, Ontario and Quebec in the 1960s were able to articulate alternatives to the national policies conceived in Ottawa much more effectively than had been possible in the 1940s. Their role was not simply that of federal antagonist, but a more sophisticated one that envisaged educating the federal government on the appropriate manner of governing. At first this alliance could most clearly be seen in attempts in the social policy field to pressure Ottawa to respect the traditional constitutional jurisdiction; ultimately, Ontario and Quebec dealt with the very heart of the matter by forcing a complete examination and overhaul of the British North America Act.

The decade of the 1960s opened with enthusiasm across Canada, nowhere more obviously than in the two largest provinces. Years of careful economic policies in Ontario had left the province in a strong financial situation and able to contemplate a more generous sharing of the wealth within the province. In Quebec the flurry of government activity soon to be known as the Quiet Revolution was under way, and there was cause for optimism in a province too long dominated by the conservative and isolationist policies of Duplessis. Politicians in both provinces were examining new roles for government, and their paths not surprisingly crossed. When in 1960 Premier Leslie Frost appointed a commission to examine the pension plans that currently existed in Ontario, with an eye to identifying ways in which the government could offer a portable pensions scheme, Quebec looked on with interest.[32] The first ministers of the two provinces shared thoughts on pension policy at the 1961 Inter-Provincial Conference in Charlottetown, and after Ontario introduced its Pensions Benefits Act, Lesage informed the Ontario premier that he intended to introduce his own portable pension system modelled after it.[33] Such a degree of harmony between the two provinces gave credence to Ontario's largely unspoken wish: that Ottawa would see the wisdom of the Ontario scheme, as Quebec had done, and introduce a similar system that would be in force nationwide. The Chartered Trust Company seemed to speak for many in the government when it predicted that the Ontario legislation "should have far reaching social significance not only in this province but all across Canada."[34]

At first, the question of pension reform and the desire on the part of both Ontario and Quebec to introduce legislation that would create provincially based systems of compulsory, contributory, and portable pensions seemed to have little to do with either federal–provincial relations or with the utility of the existing constitutional framework. Even the election of Lester Pearson as prime minister in the spring of 1963, armed with a policy package that included national pension reform, suggested little in the way of intergovernmental conflict. Earlier, new Ontario premier John Robarts had been so disgusted with the ineptitude of Prime Minister John Diefenbaker that he had confided to Liberal leader Pearson in 1962 "that the government of Ontario would concur in and facilitate proper and reasonable plans by your government resulting in a contributory social insurance program becoming a reality."[35] But the accord was not long-lasting, for, soon after his own election, Pearson indicated that he intended to force the provinces into accepting a pension scheme of national design.[36] The proposed incursion into what was clearly provincial jurisdiction was enough to sound the alarm, and the old Ontario–Quebec axis sprang back into action.

The occasion for the rekindling of the flame of cooperation between the two provinces was a visit to Quebec City from an Ontario parliamentary and press delegation in June 1963. The visitors included the leaders of the three Ontario political parties, Cabinet ministers, and members of the press corps. They were given the red-carpet treatment throughout their several days in the Quebec capital, but nothing was more gratifying than the appearance of agreement on a variety of issues between the two premiers.[37] In welcoming the group, and in outlining Quebec's current constitutional concerns, Lesage remarked on the history of interprovincial relations and his hopes for continued positive relations in the future:

> The evolution of our constitutional regime so far has not given to Quebec the possibility of playing its full role as the political expression of French Canada. We know that we are undertaking a very delicate task, which may require time, but mostly a spirit of understanding and co-operation from the English- Canadian nation ... In

> our eyes, the province of Ontario is probably the Canadian province that is in the best position to understand our situation ... I am sure that Ontario and English-speaking Canada will help us to do our part, the way we feel this part should be done ... Not only do you have to understand the deep motives lying behind the changes you are witnessing, but you have to help us bring it about, so that Canada will become a country in which two nations can live side by side in peace, freedom and security.[38]

For his part, Robarts gave every indication of being a strong ally of the Quebec government. The "cracks and crevices" in Confederation, he claimed, "should not cause us to flee and panic and abandon our century-old home." Instead, Robarts continued, "let us proceed as good craftsmen and overcome these defects and make it a durable dwelling. For I am certain that we are capable of better political leadership and I am equally certain that the two great peoples who first established our Confederation are ready to make a greater effort to make it work and succeed."[39]

Ottawa would not see first-hand the effects of the renewed Ontario–Quebec commitment to enforcing the constitutional division of powers until discussions over pension policy were well under way. Robarts attended the first meeting called to discuss the national proposals in order to present the Ontario scheme as it had been laid out in the Pension Benefits Act and state the case for provincial control over any pension plan, whether operating on a national level or not. Although it was clear that "Ontario had dominated the conference," the "observers" who attended from Quebec "left little doubt that, if pushed, [Quebec] was more than prepared to fight the legislation on constitutional grounds."[40] But if Ontario was the first to attack Ottawa's conception of national pension policy, it was Quebec that dealt the death blow. At a federal–provincial conference called, fittingly, for 1 April 1964, Lesage announced his province's intention to introduce its own pension legislation. The differences between the Canada Pension Plan, as Pearson's government outlined it, and the Quebec Pension Plan, as Lesage explained it, were relatively minor but enormously significant. The Quebec scheme would cover all employed and self-employed persons compulsorily, begin paying benefits at age sixty-five, and be based on a larger proportion of a person's income than Ottawa had envisioned. More important, the fund of contributions would be at the complete disposal of the provincial government. This was the key to the Quebec plan: not only did a provincially sponsored plan fit the letter of the constitution, but the Lesage scheme also benefited the province by establishing a significant fund with which to finance some of the governmental initiatives of the Quiet Revolution. When the contours of the Quebec plan were elaborated, "the response at the conference was electric ... and [there was] just no question at that moment the Canada Pension Plan was dead."[41]

The fact that all the premiers were more attracted to the Quebec scheme than they were to the national plan had important ramifications for federal–provincial relations as well as for the shape of the Ontario–Quebec axis.[42] First, in an effort to save the conference, the national pension proposals, and face, Ottawa made two major concessions that were to change the shape of intergovernmental relations. Key Ottawa bureaucrats came up with the idea of striking a tax structure committee that would be a continuing body, composed of representatives of both levels of government, charged with reviewing the entire fiscal structure. While Lesage publicly considered the suggestion nothing more than another federal stalling tactic, it was generally viewed as the first step towards a tax realignment more favourable to the provinces.[43] Some weeks later, the same group of officials met with their counterparts in Quebec City and essentially agreed on a rewriting of the Canada Pension Plan that would have it conform to the Quebec Pension Plan. Ottawa would have its national pension system, Quebec would opt out in favour of its own virtually identical plan, and a system of asymmetrical federalism was born – a key component of Pearson's "cooperative" approach to federal–provincial relations.

Ontario and Quebec had both entered into negotiations with the federal government with the same goal – respect for their prior constitutional rights in the pension field – and both had used the same body of information to combat federal incursions into provincial jurisdiction. Yet despite Pearson's efforts to keep Robarts apprised of the state of negotiations with Quebec, there was still a sense that Ontario had been outmanoeuvred.[44] But Quebec's decision to opt out, and Ontario's decision to opt in, merely reoriented the axis rather than severing it. On one level, Quebec's actions in 1964 represented a watershed in intergovernmental relations that paved the way for a new role for Ontario. One participant recalled that

> after extensive bilateral discussion between Ottawa and Quebec, the Quebec plan was virtually adopted for Canada. Whatever the political reasons behind the decisions, the result was a veritable landmark in federal–provincial financial relations. A province suddenly moved to centre stage on a very complex national issue, and the so-called mysteries of government finance – previously the exclusive domain of the federal civil servants – could be understood by a province with the will to do so. The lesson was not lost on other provinces.[45]

Ontario certainly learned the lesson and took Quebec's position as a legitimation of the role of the provinces in articulating a national vision. On another level, however, the acceptance of the Quebec Pension Plan represented a step towards the isolation of Quebec. It was the only province to opt out of the pension scheme, a decision open to all provinces but taken only by one. The result was the appearance of a special arrangement for Quebec. For Robarts, whose 1963 visit to Quebec had been well received in part because it emphasized that Quebec was not alone, the work of the axis was far from over.

By the end of 1966 much had changed, but the fact that so much remained the same left Canada even closer to crisis. Lesage's fortunes had taken a turn for the worse, in part because of his acceptance of the constitutional amending formula proposed by federal ministers Davie Fulton and Guy Favreau. Work on a means to alter the BNA Act domestically had begun under Diefenbaker, continued through the first years of the Pearson administration, and resulted in a proposal by which each province had to agree to any changes that affected provincial jurisdiction. Lesage had been personally in favour of adopting the Fulton–Favreau formula because it recognized Quebec's right to a veto, but the Quebec public was strongly opposed. This divergence between elite and grassroots sentiment left the provincial Liberals wounded and, despite an impressive record of Quiet Revolution reforms, the Union Nationale under Daniel Johnson was able to step into the breach and assume power in the provincial election of 1966. The new government was equally committed to the spirit of *mâitre chez nous*, but replaced it with a more aggressive strategy of *indépendence ou égalité*. Thus, despite a new government, its aspirations were essentially the same as those of the Lesage regime, and the rejection of the Fulton–Favreau formula had again set Quebec at odds with Ottawa.[46] The province remained isolated, and insisted on a new relationship with the federal government.

The concerns in Quebec did not go unnoticed. At a federal–provincial conference deadlocked over issues of higher education and the fiscal structure, Robarts reportedly "astonished" everyone present by calling for a full-blown meeting to discuss the very nature of Confederation.[47] He made clear his intention to spearhead such a discussion some months later during a visit to Montreal, and confirmed in the Speech from the Throne in early 1967 that a conference of first ministers would be convened in Ontario to discuss the future of Confederation.[48] While the prime minister objected to an apparent federal–provincial conference being called at the initiative of a province, Robarts clearly saw it as something much greater.[49] What would become known as the Confederation of Tomorrow Conference was designed not only to end the isolation of Quebec but to restore some prestige to the province of Ontario.

Publicly, Robarts stressed the importance of this conference for the state of the federation, particularly for reaching a pan-Canadian understanding of the situation in Quebec. In the face of suspicions "that Ontario and Quebec are joining together in some sort of power play to bring about changes in the terms of our Confederation,"

Robarts maintained that "there is no Ontario–Quebec axis." Ontario had called the conference to facilitate open discussion "in the widest possible context" and to reduce the sense that "Canadians are not particularly well-acquainted with the problems of the regions of the country other than those in which they live." He saw certain advantages to a conference with such purposes being called by a province, rather than by the federal government, because that genesis might "diminish the friction" that all too often developed at the more traditional federally chaired intergovernmental conferences. Moreover, Ontario was, in Robarts's mind, the obvious province to initiate a public discussion of the future of Confederation because it "has a special role to play as an outstanding and an understanding interpreter of the view of Quebec to some of the other parts of Canada."[50]

But if the conference was publicly portrayed as a generous and selfless initiative on Ontario's part towards greater national unity, privately Robarts seemed to regard the Confederation of Tomorrow Conference as an opportunity to reassert the power of the provinces. Although he assured a somewhat wary Pearson that he had not intended "to infringe upon the jurisdictional authority of the federal Government," it was absolutely clear that Robarts did intend to insert the compact theory of Confederation back into the political consciousness.[51] This theory of origin, while having little or no basis in reality, holds that either the two founding nations, English Canada and French Canada, or the provinces themselves created the federal government as a result of a compact undertaken in 1864. It was only as a result of agreement between the originators that changes could be made to the union.[52] This theory found its voice in the first Interprovincial Conference of 1887, and was used thereafter as an argument on the part of French Canada to repudiate the extension of federal power or a call for the acceptance of a provincial veto over constitutional change. But Ontario also endorsed the compact theory. Robarts's letter to Pearson explaining his reasons for calling the Confederation of Tomorrow Conference makes clear that this particular Ontario premier was willing to haul out the appealing rhetoric of the compact theory:

> It is well to remind ourselves that one hundred or more years ago, only because the provinces existing came together, by conference and finally through legal union, did it become possible to bring about the establishment and creation of the Dominion of Canada ... Today the problems which beset the body politics of Canada cry out for solution. We are in a new era. With the expansion and growth of Canada and its economy, the powers of the Provinces, which created the Canadian Federation, have naturally increased, as have those of the Federal Government. There must be flexibility and understanding if this country of ours is to survive. The one objective I have in mind for this Conference is that it will serve the interests of the Canadian people and

> their nation which the Provinces created and in whose continued existence, unity and strength, the Provinces are vitally concerned.[53]

It was a sentiment that would have made the ghosts of Oliver Mowat and Honoré Mercier smile, but, interestingly, it was not one that Robarts was willing to express too publicly. When, during the debate over the motion to host the Confederation of Tomorrow Conference, the Ontario attorney general suggested that "the provinces originally created Confederation. It is the provinces who must come together and say 'this is the type of federation we shall have,'" the premier apparently sat 'red-faced through the speech.' It was certainly a sentiment he shared, but not one he wanted to expose to open debate.[54]

In using the language of the compact theory, Robarts extended the significance of an Ontario–Quebec axis. In his public statement, he made clear that discomfort in Quebec with the existing constitution had been the impetus to calling the Confederation of Tomorrow Conference in the first place. As he stated, "because our problems are very similar ... we have much in common with the province of Quebec."[55] The meeting would provide a forum for the discussion of problems most keenly felt by the axis. In his private statements, Robarts underscored the commonalities between the two provinces in a more subtle manner: by using the language of the compact theory, traditionally the preserve of Quebec, he was drawing Pearson's attention to the continued and powerful alliance of the two provinces. The message was not lost on the prime minister, whose initial anxieties about Ontario hosting a dialogue on the future of Confederation did not dissipate. As the conference drew closer, Pearson first refused to participate, then forced Robarts to call it an interprovincial rather than a federal–provincial conference, and finally "persist[ed] in downgrading [it] by sending along as observers (not participants) four advisors or civil servants."[56] But the combination of inaction and hostility on the part of the federal government was not enough to derail the conference plans.

In fact, Ottawa's decision to dissociate itself from the conference left open the possibility, probably always imagined, of the provinces, and especially Ontario and Quebec, articulating a "national" vision in the absence of any contribution from the federal government. The Ontario provincial election just six weeks before the conference opened gave some indication of the role Ontario politicians saw themselves playing in the future of the country. In an election campaign that was devoid of much grassroots participation and instead "operated on a high level," Robarts drove home his case for constitutional renewal and a new era of cooperation between English Canada and French Canada.[57] As one observer noted, without Ottawa's presence the conference's two "principal participants" – Robarts and Johnson

– could reach a "deal between Ontario and Quebec which would have far-reaching implication." Moreover, the "provincial premiers would be speaking together for the 'national' interest, while Ottawa would become the voice of the 'federal' interest, and the two would no longer be the same."[58] But if the public statements of the two provincial premiers and the media opinion in Ontario and Quebec seemed to support the existence of close ties between the two provinces, the position papers prepared by the Ontario Advisory Committee on Confederation suggested a certain disparity between their constitutional policies. The committee, whose members included historians, legal scholars, political scientists, and opinion makers, had been struck years earlier to spearhead investigations into the nature of Confederation and to propose changes that were deemed necessary.[59] It was natural to assume that the position papers, the first volume of which appeared in the April prior to the Confederation of Tomorrow Conference, would form the basis of the Ontario constitutional position. If this were to be the case, however, there was cause for concern. The collection was immediately described as a "remarkably negative and reactionary report" with "scarcely a positive or constructive idea in it."[60] The contributions dealing specifically with issues anticipated to be part of the discussion at the interprovincial conference were especially unsettling. Eugene Forsey's three pieces on the legislatures, the Crown, and associate states systematically denounced key components of Quebec's position on necessary changes to the constitution. His colleague W.R. Lederman endorsed the already rejected Fulton–Favreau formula and concluded that "we do not need a major re-writing of the Canadian Constitution at all."[61] Yet, apart from the pre-conference public posturing of the various participants, the report of the advisory committee remained the only glimpse into an Ontario position until the opening of the Confederation of Tomorrow Conference. Its reactive rather than progressive tone left more than one Quebec spokesman wondering, "Doesn't Ontario have any ideas of its own?"[62]

Despite evidence that agreement between the premiers would be difficult to achieve, the days leading up to the opening of the conference were filled with optimistic anticipation.[63] The spirit that had motivated the idea of the meeting was positive, so there was no reason that the results should not be too. It was fortunate that the conference was scheduled to last three days, as accord was not immediately apparent. In his opening remarks, Johnson indicated that profound constitutional change was necessary to accommodate Quebec. "Our present constitution still contains elements which are valid for organizing Canada as a partnership of ten," he stated, but "we are forced to conclude that much of this other two-partner Canada remains to be invented."[64] One again, the rhetoric of the compact theory was being used to underscore the importance of constitutional change: Johnson's "partnership of ten" was an association of provinces, his "two- partner Canada" an alliance of the English-speaking Canada and the French-speaking nation. The process of "invention" that Johnson mentioned would demand a thorough constitutional overhaul, and the line was drawn. Interestingly, it was a line that for the most part had already been drawn in 1867: the original provinces in Confederation tended to agree that constitutional change was necessary, while the "newcomers" held firm that "adjustments could be made within the framework of the existing Constitution."[65]

The second day of the conference opened with an even more serious rift: Robarts and Johnson disagreed over whether amendment to the constitution was sufficient or whether a complete rewriting was necessary. Robarts's statement that Ontario "was not necessarily anxious for a complete revision" aligned him with Ernest Manning from Alberta and Joey Smallwood from Newfoundland and threatened to break the axis. Yet the relaxation of Johnson's "hard line" policy went further than mending relations with Ontario. By insisting that a solution could be achieved through a series of amendments that "could later be consolidated," Johnson was essentially stating that rewriting the constitution was unnecessary; when he offered a metaphor, the tension broke with laughter. "Some people in Quebec want to divorce Canada and then remarry the same woman with a new marriage contract," he declared. "I want to see if we can't amend the marriage contract, rather than take the chance of a divorce and having the woman meet someone else."[66]

Any division between Robarts and Johnson was perhaps more apparent to the reporters who were covering the conference than to the principal players. They had been in near constant contact in the days leading up to the opening of the conference and seemed to be in "collusion" on how to handle a number of issues that arose during the discussions.[67] In any real sense, the axis was far from the breaking point. But the step that Johnson took towards compromise at the end of the conference was a key moment in transforming the alliance from one of two central Canadian provinces to an alliance of almost all the provinces.[68] It had been clear to observers that the provinces had similar problems with the federal government and were, for example, unanimous in "deploring the imposition of Medicare on them when they need money for other things";[69] but the conference called to discuss the constitution more generally resulted in a significant agreement to band together in the face of Ottawa's reluctance to initiate a constitutional review process. The conference was a major coup for Robarts, who received congratulations for his "expert handling" of the "risky venture." If it were followed by "goodwill and continued effort, Confederation may yet be saved."[70] The conference was also a major coup for the "axis powers," who found supporters for their attempt to force the national agenda and assert a national vision.

In a sense, Ontario had already forced the federal government's hand. The decision to hold the Confederation of Tomorrow Conference, and the positive reception that decision received, had already convinced Ottawa of the necessity of convening a full-blown federal–provincial conference to discuss the future of the constitution. Robarts had not imagined that the provinces would have the last say on the issue: as he declared after the fact, "we believe that our decision to call the Confederation of Tomorrow Conference made it possible for the federal government, if it chose to, to resume its primary role in these matters, and I think that events have proved us to be correct."[71] In January 1968 Pearson, who had already been accused too often of inaction, convened what was to be the first of a series of seven first-minister constitutional conferences in Ottawa.

In his opening statements, the prime minister attempted to recreate something of the tone of the previous interprovincial conference, and, to establish that this new series of discussions would be conciliatory in nature, he acknowledged:

> We all know that French Canada today feels a deep dissatisfaction with its place in Confederation. The reasons for that are complex and of varying significance. I have said in the past, and I repeat now, that I believe most of those reasons to be valid and justified. But this is not the occasion either to try to analyze why there is discontent in French Canada, to assess the responsibility or weigh judiciously everything that has contributed to produce that result. What is far more important is to admit that this dissatisfaction is a fact and recognize that, if it is allowed to continue without remedy, it could lead to separation and the end of Confederation.[72]

Despite the good intentions, the presence of the federal government at this conference, as distinct from the Robarts-convened conference, seemed to loosen the alliances that had formed in Toronto. Provincial premiers, led by Joey Smallwood, seemed more ready to question the validity of Quebec's position. Even the partnership between Ontario and Quebec was strained, not because their positions had changed but because Quebec was lured into a head-on confrontation with the federal government. The debate between Daniel Johnson and federal justice minister Pierre Trudeau, the main federal spokesperson, ended as a public and aggressive declaration of Trudeau's vision of Canada. The nationalist agenda was rejected out of hand, and the future of the French language was to be secured through individual participation in the federal system rather than collective autonomy within it.[73] The clash was the turning point: not only did it help propel Trudeau into the Prime Minister's Office two months later but, as Robarts said at the time, "that's the end of Ontario's role as a helpful middle man. From here on in, it is going to be a battle between two varieties of French-speaking Quebeckers."[74]

Over the next three years, first ministers, departmental chiefs, and continuing committees of officials engaged in a near-constant debate over the constitutional changes necessary. The agenda had shifted from addressing Quebec's concerns, which had been the original impetus to open up the discussions, to debating a broad range of issues including a bill of rights, taxing powers, equalization payments, social policy jurisdiction, and the amending formula. In the eyes of some, the federal government was "exploiting the English-speaking backlash" and ignoring the Ontario lesson – that "an ounce of negotiation is worth a pound of confrontation."[75] The Ontario–Quebec axis seemed to fade into the background.

Although an alliance continued between the two central provinces, circumstances had changed so rapidly after the first constitutional conference that a public axis was difficult to maintain. As one commentator put it, "it is easy to recall how the first blush of constitutional revision seemed so exciting. It was all a bit lyrical and apocalyptic, like Expo '67 which had just closed its gates."[76] As the lustre faded, reality set in. While Ontario politicians accepted that the "real root of the Quebec situation" was "encroachments and interference of Ottawa," it became increasingly difficult to acknowledge the commonalities between the two provinces.[77] Despite calls to convene a second Confederation of Tomorrow Conference, to undescore that "Canada is a working partnership, not a 'king and his subjects,'" Robarts was "running into a good deal of opposition" to his constitutional position and found it necessary to "reassure the people of this province that we are not selling out to Quebec."[78] The public concerns rested mainly with the extension of French-language rights, which Trudeau had turned into the real issue in the Quebec–Ottawa dialogue.[79]

In the absence of public statements of an alliance with Quebec, which Ontario officials had always been loath to make, there was still evidence of a working association. Ontario's constitutional proposals, for example, meshed easily with those of Quebec and reiterated suggestions that had been made by Quebec premiers at previous constitutional discussions. In addition to stating bluntly that "Canada should have a new constitution," a firmer commitment than Ontario had yet made, the proposals included a call for a form of asymmetrical federalism. In putting forward the resolution that "provinces in Canada should have separately or severally a variety of relationships with the federal government," Ontario was endorsing Johnson's earlier proposition that powers be "delegated" to the federal government as individual provinces see fit.[80] As the final conference approached, Quebec politicians and commentators could point to a common cause with Ontario, if not an overt alliance.[81]

Sympathetic proposals from Ontario were not enough to secure agreement on changes to the constitution, however. The final episode in this first round of what Peter Russell has termed "mega-constitutional politics" was held in Victoria amid much fanfare but limited expectations.[82] The new key players had their own concerns that in part prohibited any likelihood of national consensus. John Robarts had been replaced as premier by William Davis, a man who had fewer personal connections to Quebec and who was more wary of the anti-French sentiment growing in Ontario. Daniel Johnson had retired from public life shortly after the 1968 constitutional conference and died soon after, leaving something of a leadership void in Quebec when it came to confrontations with Ottawa. Prime Minister Trudeau had to protect his reputation in English Canada of being able to "settle the Quebec questions."[83] And Quebec premier Robert Bourassa was clearly under pressure at home "not to agree to the partition and amending formulae ... unless he has a solid promise on the question of income social-security welfare jurisdiction."[84] It was not surprising, then, that Bourassa issued a press statement on 23 June 1971 indicating that the Quebec government could not accept the Victoria Charter, the constitutional proposal agreed to by the first ministers. The sticking point was the lack of clarity on the issue of jurisdiction over social policy.

Ontario's relationship with Quebec has remained the same over much of the last twenty-five years of constitutional negotiation, and the results of the almost constant discussion have varied little from those witnessed after the Confederation of Tomorrow Conference. While there have been numerous points of common cause, especially over the need for constitutional reform and a greater degree of decentralization, there has been little mention of an Ontario–Quebec axis. The agreements between the provinces have been less obvious than the alliance that formed in the 1960s through personal friendships, the acceptance of the compact theory, and a shared commitment to a new national vision. The result has been the increasing isolation of Quebec, the very situation that prompted Robarts's initiatives in the first place. It has been all too easy in English Canada to regard Quebec's constitutional demands as particular to one geographic area, unwarranted, or excessive. Perhaps the reassertion of the Ontario–Quebec axis is a precondition to constitutional reform that addresses the concerns of all parts of the country.

QUESTIONS FOR CONSIDERATION:

1. Create and answer your own set of questions for consideration for this chapter. Be creative!

NOTES

This project has been funded by the Social Sciences and Humanities Research Council of Canada. An earlier version of the article was delivered to the Department of History faculty seminar at Dalhousie University in March 1998. I would like to thank the participants for their helpful comments, and Jennifer Bottos, Andrew Clark, and Christine Clayton for their assistance with the research.

1 On the Mowat legacy, see A. Margaret Evans, *Sir Oliver Mowat* (Toronto: University of Toronto Press, 1992), ch. 6; Christopher Armstrong, *The Politics of Federalism: Ontario's Relations with the Federal Government, 1867–1942* (Toronto: University of Toronto Press, 1981), ch. 1; Christopher Armstrong, "The Mowat Heritage in Federal–Provincial Relations," in *Oliver Mowat's Ontario*, ed. Donald Swainson (Toronto: Macmillan, 1972), 93–118; Robert Vipond, *Liberty and Community: Canadian Federalism and the Failure of the Constitution* (Albany: SUNY Press, 1991), esp. ch. 6; and Garth Stevenson, *Ex uno Plures: Federal–Provincial Relations in Canada, 1867–1896* (Montreal and Kingston: McGill–Queen's University Press, 1993), chs. 3 and 11. On Hepburn's feuds with Mackenzie King, see John T. Saywell, *"Just Call Me Mitch": The Life of Mitchell F. Hepburn* (Toronto: University of Toronto Press, 1990).

2 Thomas Courchene argues that Ontario's post-war interest in maintaining a strong central government, the identification of the population with "Canada" rather than "Ontario," and the shift away from defending "provincial rights" are all characteristic of a "heartland." See Thomas Courchene with Colin R. Telman, *From Heartland to North American Region State: The Social, Fiscal, and Federal Evolution of Ontario* (Toronto: University of Toronto, Centre for Public Management, 1998), 10–17.

3 Archives of Ontario (AO), George Drew Papers, RG 3-18, box 5, letterbook 10, 12 September to 7 November 1944, Drew to Stanley Hall, MPP, 27 October 1944; box 3, letterbook 6, 18 March to 17 April 1944, Drew to J.H. Cranston, *Midland Free Press*, 31 March 1944.

4 The clearest example of this interpretation can be found in Marc J. Gotlieb, "George Drew and the Dominion–Provincial Conference on Reconstruction of 1945–46," *Canadian Historical Review* 66, no. 1 (March 1985): 27–47.

5 Alvin Finkel, "Paradise Postponed: A Re-examination of the Green Book Proposals of 1945," *Journal of the Canadian Historical Association* (1993): 120–42.

6 Library and Archives Canada (LAC), Drew Papers, reel M-8990, draft letter to *Financial Post*, 2 August 1944; AO, RG 6-41, Department of Finance Papers, Dominion–Provincial Conferences, 1935–55, vol. 3, file: Interprovincial Conference, 1945, Drew to King, 6 January 1944.

7 See, for example, AO, Drew Papers, box 3, letterbook 5, 16 February to 17 March 1944, Drew to King, 14 and 16 March 1944; letterbook 6, 18 March to 17 April 1944, Drew to King, 13 April 1944; box 4, letterbook 8, June 1 to July 31, 1944, Drew to King, 20 June 1944; box 5, letterbook 9, 1 August to 11 September 1944, Drew to King, 10 and 21 August 1944.

8 AO, Department of Finance, Dominion–Provincial Conferences, 1935–55, vol. UJ 3-4, file: Interprovincial Conference, 1945, Frost to Drew, 21 August 1944.

9 LAC, Drew Papers, vol. 62, file: 556, Drew to Adelard Godbout, 14 April 1944.

10 AO, Drew Papers, box 3, letterbook 5, 16 February to 17 March 1944, Drew to Ernest Manning, 13 March 1944.

11 LAC, Drew Papers, vol. 118, file: 1187, memo, "Dominion–Provincial Relations," n.d.

12 AO, Drew Papers, box 1, letterbook, 16 August to 30 September 1943, Drew to Horace Hunter, 21 September 1943.

13 AO, Drew Papers, box 5, letterbook 9, 1 August to 11 September 1944, Drew to Hugh C. Farthing, 21 August 1944. See also letterbook 10, 12 September to 7 November 1944, Drew to Norman Dawes, 31 October 1944; Drew to Thornton Purkis, 7 November 1944; Drew to Cecil Birchard, 7 November 1944.
14 AO, RG 6-44, Department of Finance, Policy Division Subject Files, box UF 22, file: Dominion–Provincial Relations, Ontario Bureau of Statistics and Research, "Facts Pertinent to Dominion–Provincial Relations," 16 July 1945, 41; AO, Drew Papers, box 5, letterbook 9, 1 August to 11 September 1944, Drew to John Diefenbaker, 24 August 1944.
15 AO, RG 3, box 3, "Dominion–Provincial Conferences on Various Subjects, 1943– 45," memorandum by Frost, May 1963. Quoted in Roger Graham, *Old Man Ontario: Leslie M. Frost* (Toronto: University of Toronto Press, 1990), 111.
16 King Diaries, 6 and 8 August 1945; Robert Rumilly, *Maurice Duplessis et son temps*, vol. 2 (Montreal: Fides, 1973), 84–9; Conrad Black, *Duplessis* (Toronto: McClelland and Stewart, 1977), 457.
17 AO, Department of Finance Papers, Dominion–Provincial Conferences, 1935– 55, vol. 7, file: From PMs "red book"; vol. 2, "Summary of the Minutes of the Dominion–Provincial Economic Committee, 4–14 December 1945 and 8–17 January 1946," 1–6.
18 Vol. 2, 'Summary,' 1–6; King Diaries, 31 January 1946.
19 King Diaries, 23 January 1946.
20 AO, Department of Finance Papers, Dominion–Provincial Conferences, 1935– 55, vol. 7, file: From PMs "red book"; vol. 2, 'Statements by the Ontario Premier at Co-ordinating Committee Meeting January 28 to February 1, 1946."
21 King Diaries, 31 January 1946.
22 AO, Department of Finance Papers, Dominion–Provincial Conferences, 1935– 55, vol. 7, file: From PMs "red book"; vol. 2, 'Statements by the Ontario Premier at Co-ordinating Committee Meeting January 28 to February 1, 1946."
23 King Diaries, 31 January 1946.
24 King Diaries, 1 February 1946.
25 AO, Department of Finance Papers, Dominion–Provincial Conferences, 1935– 55, box 3, file: Dominion-Provincial Conference, 1945 – original letters, Drew to King, 16 April 1946.
26 AO, Policy Division Subject Files, box UF 22, file: 6 "S" Speeches: G.A. Drew, "Speech by Premier George Drew to Progressive Conservative Business Men's Club, Tuesday, May 14, 1946."
27 King Diaries, 27 April 1946.
28 King Diaries, 6 May 1946.
29 AO, Department of Finance Papers, Dominion–Provincial Conferences, 1935– 55, box UJ 3-4, file: Dominion–Provincial Conference, original letters to and from Mr. King and Col. G.A. Drew, 1945, Drew to King, 7 September and 2 October 1946. See also LAC, Drew Papers, reel M-9018, Drew to Louis St. Laurent, 6 November 1947.
30 LAC, Drew Papers, reel M-8956, Drew to John Bassett, 9 May 1946.
31 LAC, Drew Papers, reel M-8976, Duplessis to Drew, 8 and 14 April 1947, and Drew to Duplessis, 10 April 1947.
32 AO, George Gathercole Papers, MU 5330, file: Source Papers, Charles E. Hendry to Gathercole, 25 February 1960.
33 AO, George Gathercole Papers, MU 5332, file: Portable Pension Correspondence, Gathercole to J.J. Connolly, 1 May 1963.
34 *The Counsellor*, published by Chartered Trust, May 1963, The Ontario government had paid considerable attention to the insurance industry in drafting its pension benefits legislation. By

allowing the administration of a compulsory pension system to remain firmly in the hands of private business, the government earned the support of the insurance sector, so it is not surprising that Chartered Trust and others heralded the Ontario scheme as a blueprint for the rest of the nation.

35 Queen's University Archives, Tom Kent Papers, vol. 2, file: Correspondence, June 1963, Robarts to Pearson, 6 February 1962.

36 House of Commons, *Debates*, 21 June 1963.

37 The personal friendships and the festive atmosphere seemed to be equally gratifying. Those people who participated, and those who heard tales later, commented on the "good time" enjoyed in Quebec City – a better time than staid Ontario was able to provide when a Quebec delegation paid a courtesy call on Toronto. Interviews, Donald Stevenson, 17 July 1996; Rendell Dick, 15 December 1997.

38 Quoted in *Globe and Mail*, 15 June 1963.

39 Quoted in *Montreal Star*, 17 June 1963.

40 LAC, Privy Council Office Papers, RG 2, Cabinet minutes, 12 September 1963, 2; P.E. Bryden, *Planners and Politicians: Liberal Politics and Social Policy, 1957–1968* (Kingston and Montreal: McGill–Queen's University Press, 1997), 97.

41 LAC, Peter Stursburg Papers, MG 31, D78, vol. 33, file: Kent, Tom, 1977 interview. On the announcement of the Quebec Pension Plan and the April conference more generally, see John Saywell, ed., *The Canadian Annual Review for 1964* (Toronto: University of Toronto Press, 1965), 64–8; Claude Morin, *Quebec versus Ottawa: The Struggle for Self-Government* (Toronto: University of Toronto Press, 1976); and Richard Simeon, *Federal-Provincial Diplomacy: The Making of Recent Policy in Canada* (Toronto: University of Toronto Press, 1972), 54–60.

42 LAC, Department of National Health and Welfare Papers, vol. 2114, file: 23-3-6, draft minutes, "Canada Pension Plan, Federal-Provincial Conference, Quebec, April 1, 1964," 3–4.

43 Tom Kent, *A Public Purpose: An Experience of Liberal Opposition and Canadian Government* (Kingston and Montreal: McGill–Queen's University PRess, 1988), 276.

44 Kent Papers, vol. 3, file: Correspondence, April 1964, telegram to Robarts, 15 April 1964; Gathercole Papers, MU 5334, file: Pensions, 1964, Gathercole to John Bassett, 17 April 1964; A.K. McDougall, *John Robarts: His Life and Government* (Toronto: University of Toronto Press, 1986), 133; Wayne Austin Hunt, "The Federal–Provincial Conference of First Ministers, 1960–1976" (PhD diss., University of Toronto, 1982); Hunt's interview with Robarts, 25 September 1978; Bruce G. Pollard, *Managing the Interface: Intergovernmental Affairs Agencies in Canada* (Kingston: Institute of Intergovernmental Affairs, 1986), 11.

45 AO, Department of Treasury, Economics and Intergovernmental Affairs, RG 75-21-0-20, box 3, file: Role of Ontario in National Policy Formations, H.I. Macdonald, "The Role of Ontario in the Formation of National Policy," address delivered at Carleton University, 8 March 1974.

46 On the Fulton Favreau formula, see Gérard Bergeron, "The Quebecois State under Canadian Federalism," in *Quebec Since 1945: Selected Readings*, ed. Michael Behiels (Toronto: Copp Clark Pitman, 1987), 178–84; Peter Russell, *Constitutional Odyssey: Can Canadians Become a Sovereign People?*, 2nd ed. (Toronto: University of Toronto Press, 1993), 72–4.

47 John Saywell, ed., *Canadian Annual Review for 1966* (Toronto: University of Toronto Press, 1967), 76.

48 Private collection, *Canadian Annual Review* Papers, unorganized material, "Remarks by the Honourable John Robarts, Prime Minister of Ontario, to the Advertising and Sales Executives' Club in Montreal, Wednesday, November 23rd, 1966"; Ontario, *Legislative Debates*, 18 May 1967, 3566; Speech from the Throne, 25 January 1967.

49 Gathercole Papers, MU 5311, file: Corresondence, 1965–71, Pearson to Robarts, 26 January 1967.
50 Ontario, *Legislative Debates*, 18 May 1967, 3570.
51 Gathercole Papers, MU 5311, file: Correspondence, 1965–71, Robarts to Pearson, 1 February 1967.
52 Ramsay Cook, *Provincial Autonomy, Minority Rights, and the Compact Theory, 1867–1921* (Ottawa: Queen's Printer, 1969); Russell, *Constitutional Odyssey*, 17–18, 48–50; Robert Vipond, "Whatever Became of the Compact Theory? Meech Lake and the Politics of Constitutional Amendment in Canada," *Queen's Quarterly* 96 (1989).
53 Gathercole Papers, MU 5311, file: Correspondence, 1965–71, Robarts to Pearson, 1 February 1967.
54 John Saywell, ed., *The Canadian Annual Review for 1967* (Toronto: University of Toronto Press, 1968), 86; "PM cites Wishart statement to oppose conference,' *Globe and Mail*, 25 May 1967.
55 Ontario, *Legislative Debates*, 18 May 1967, 3570.
56 "An Unbecoming Shyness," *Globe and Mail*, 25 September 1967; "Mr Pearson Avoids Confederation Action," *Globe and Mail*, 31 October 1967.
57 "Mr Robarts and Confederation," *Winnipeg Free Press*, 16 October 1967. The election was waged on such a high level, in fact, that this western newspaper characterized it as "inaudible to people more accustomed to, say, a Saskatchewan type of election."
58 Peter C. Newman, "The Great Discussion about Canada's Future," *Montreal Star*, 25 November 1967.
59 The members of the Ontario Advisory Committee on Confederation were H. Ian Macdonald, Alexander Brady, John Conway, Donald Creighton, Richard Dillon, Eugene Forsey, Paul Fox, George Gathercole, Bora Laskin, W.R. Lederman, Clifford Magone, Lucien Matee, John Meisel, R. Craig McIvor, Edward McWhinney, J. Harvey Perry, Roger Séguin, and T.H.B. Symons.
60 Harold Greer, "Ontario Accentuates the Negative," *Montreal Star*, 18 April 1967.
61 Eugene Forsey, "The Legislatures and Executives of the Federation," 161–73; Forsey, "Constitutional Monarchy and the Provinces," 176–86; Forsey, "Memorandum on the Associate States," 189–92; W.R. Lederman, "The Process of Constitutional Amendment in Canada," 86, all in *Ontario Advisory Committee on Confederation: Background Papers and Reports* (Toronto: Queen's Printer of Ontario, 1967).
62 Federal forestry minister Maurice Sauvé, quoted in Harold Greer, "Ontario Radicalism Clearly out of Fashion," *Montreal Star*, 25 November 1967.
63 Interview, H. Ian Macdonald, 18 December 1996.
64 *Canadian Annual Review* Papers, press releases, "Opening Statement by the Honourable Daniel Johnson, Prime Minister of Quebec, to the Confederation of Tomorrow Conference," 27 November 1967.
65 Gordon Pape, "Confederation Conference: Premiers Badly Divided,' *Montreal Gazette*, 28 November 1967. Of the three original provinces, Ontario was the least firm in its commitment to major constitutional change, a position in keeping with that advanced by the Ontario Advisory Committee on Confederation. See Robarts's opening statement in Government of Ontario, *Preliminary Statement*, Confederation of Tomorrow Conference, Toronto, 27–30 November 1967. New Brunswick premier Louis Robichaud was "the most emotional voice heard in pleading with the rest of Canada to take action before it's too late to stem the separatist tide in Quebec." *Montreal Gazette*, 1 December 1967.
66 *Canadian Annual Review* Papers, notes on the minutes of the Confederation of Tomorrow Conference, 29 November 1967; Gordon Pape, "Johnson Relaxes Hard Line Policy," *Montreal Gazette*, 30 November 1967.
67 *Montreal Star*, 2 December 1967.

68 Newfoundland premier Joey Smallwood remained, at the end, the only premier unwilling to accommodate Quebec's need for major constitutional reform.

69 Trent University Archives, Leslie Frost Papers, 77-024, box 76, file: 8 (Political Correspondence, 1967), Frost to Robert Stanfield, 1 December 1967.

70 AO, John Robarts Papers, series F-15-4-3, MU 7998, box 2, file: Goldenberg, Carl, 1967–9, Goldenberg to Robarts, 4 December 1967.

71 Ontario, *Legislative Debates*, 27 February 1968, 263.

72 *Constitutional Conference: Proceedings*, first meeting, 5–7 February 1968 (Ottawa: Queen's Printer, 1968), 5.

73 Russell, *Constitutional Odyssey*, 79; Kenneth McRoberts, *Misconceiving Canada: The Struggle for National Unity* (Toronto: Oxford University Press, 1997), esp. ch. 3.

74 Private collection, Donald W. Stevenson Papers, "Notes for use by Don Stevenson at the Federal–Provincial Conference simulation, University of Waterloo, December 12, 1988."

75 LAC, Tommy Douglas Papers, MG 32, C28, vol. 7, file: general correspondence, pt. 23, Douglas to Frost, 1 July 1968.

76 John Gray, "Confederation '71," *Montreal Star*, 12 June 1971.

77 Frost Papers, box 83, file: 5, Frost to Joe Sullivan, 26 February 1968.

78 Robarts Papers, series F-14-4-3, box 4, MU 8000, file: MacLeod, A.A., 1967–9, W.A. Rathburn to Robarts, 4 October 1968; box 2, MU 7998, file: Goldenberg, Carl. Robarts to Goldenberg, 1 March 1968.

79 Peter Oliver, "Ontario,'" In John Saywell, ed., *The Canadian Annual Review for 1969* (Toronto: University of Toronto Press, 1970), 81–3.

80 Gathercole Papers, MU 5318, file: Source papers – conferences, Continuing Committee of Officials, 1968–70, Drafts of Ontario's Proposals, 24 June 1968; Private collection, *Canadian Annual Review* Papers, "The Ontario Position on the Spending Power Presented by the Government of Ontario," 3 June 1969, and "A Briefing Paper on Constitutional Review Activities and Discussions with the Continuing Committee of Officials," December 1969. At the Confederation of Tomorrow Conference, Johnson had suggested the possibility that areas of provincial jurisdiction, such as health care, could be given to Ottawa by those provinces that were not prepared to legislate effectively in those areas.

81 "L'Ontario s'oppose à la centralisation fédérale," *Le Devoir*, 29 April 1971; "M. Davis continue de critiquer la politique centralisatrice d'Ottawa," *Le Devoir*, 10 May 1971. In what appeared to be an attempt to distinguish himself from Robarts, the new Ontario premier, William Davis, "lashed out at feds and fed policy as Robarts never did," and was not predisposed to make the federal position any easier, "as Mr. Robarts might have done." *Canadian Annual Review* Papers, "The Victoria Conference – notes"; Maxwell Cohen, "The constitution – it's a priority," *Montreal Gazette*, 1 June 1971.

82 Russell, *Constitutional Odyssey*, 74–6.

83 Gray, "Confederation '71"; Dominique Clift, "Quebec"; Harold Greer, "Ontario" – all in *Montreal Star*, 12 June 1971.

84 Cohen, "The Constitution – it's a priority."

CHAPTER ELEVEN

Power at the Centre: The Evolution of the Premier's Office in Ontario since 1945

PATRICE DUTIL AND PETER P. CONSTANTINOU

For over fifty years, many observers of the Westminster system of government have lamented the growth in influence of prime ministers and their advisers. Members of Parliament have decried the increase in the number of prime ministerial advisers, claiming that they rob backbenchers of their ability to make government responsive. The growth at the centre has also been perceived as a threat to the independence of the bureaucracy. Senior members of the public service are often heard accusing brash young advisers of being abusive and presumptive in claiming to speak on behalf of "the power" and in holding that their "experience" is more important than bureaucratic expertise. In the United Kingdom as much as in the antipodes, from the provincial capitals of St. John's to Victoria, many have concluded that the strength of the prime minister's advisers is indicative of a push to "steer from the centre."[1]

Ontario has not been spared. One of Premier Dalton McGuinty's chiefs of staff was handed a four-month prison term (he served one quarter of it) for destroying vitally important documents. More recently, Premier Doug Ford's first principal secretary resigned after only six months in order to take a part-time position on the Ontario Energy Board. The premier was accused of doling out a highly paid sinecure to someone who lacked qualifications for the position.[2] Six months later, Ford's chief of staff was forced to resign over allegations that he had facilitated the appointment of uniquely unqualified friends and family members to lucrative government positions.[3]

Long before this, close advisers had been arousing the Ontario public's curiosity. Questions about the power "at the centre" endure, but to what degree is this the new reality? Graham White came to the compelling conclusion that while "the individuals in the centre – the premier's senior officials and personal advisers – have collectively become more powerful" and while "the premier's role within government has become more institutionalized … those at the centre probably enjoy less power than did their predecessors."[4]

This chapter reopens the question and seeks to answer it using a historical, institutionalist approach; such a research method emphasizes how an organization evolves. At the core of this analysis are relatively simple but revealing indicators: first, the expenditures attributed in the Public Accounts to the Premier's Office, and, second, staffing levels in terms of numbers, function, and evolution. The 1945–2020 period was chosen to yield insights on change, encompassing phases before and after the intensive period of "province building," as well as periods of economic growth and recession.[5] Given the difficulty of gauging the influence of individual advisers to the premiers, a structural approach can be helpful in capturing the reality of political staff influence. We posit that the close study of those who worked directly for the Prime Minister of Ontario – officially known as "the Premier" after 1972 – can indicate how power centres evolved. The hypothesis is that the number of advisers and their placement in the decision-making hierarchy should have a material impact on the quantity and quality of the advice being received by the premier.

The evidence indicates a number of trends. First, that the classic policy/administration gap was not clearly defined in Ontario. Indeed, succeeding premiers smudged the dividing line while trying to find and maintain an administrative structure that would respect it. In other words, the divide between political and administrative advice was constantly moved on a "complementarity" continuum.[6] The reality was an approach of "muddling through," a back-and-forth habit of experimentation that depended on the personality of the premier, the capacities of political and bureaucratic advisers, and the stages of the governmental cycle. The evolution also shows that there have been trends in the hiring of political staff and in the growth of expenditures indicating that the Premier's Office is much more concerned with messaging with the public, campaign preparations, and externalities that it is in expanding its bureaucratic or parliamentary influence. In Ottawa, the structures of the Prime Minister's Office and the Privy Council Office have become far more distinct since the 1940s; the Ontario experience, by contrast, has been one of constant experimentation.

Political Advisers in Question

Ontario's premiers have always required political advice. Over time, depending on circumstance and their own character and needs, they found counsel among a series of concentric circles: family members, old and trusted friends, political allies within their party, ministers, key deputy ministers in the public service, Members of Parliament, business magnates, labour leaders, interest group representatives, and local authorities (both political and grassroots). As premiers faced more complicated questions brought about by the economic, social, and environmental consequences of infrastructure building, and by the vast expansion of government services and state regulation, they required more and better briefings to face down oppositions that were well prepared, knowledgeable, and well connected to civil society, so they turned to political advisers.[7]

They found ad hoc advice in the usual places but clearly felt a need to surround themselves with individuals possessed of enough political passion to sustain endless hours of work and dedication. Advisers' tasks were divided depending on their abilities and on the premier's needs. Many were hired as propagandists to inform various constituencies of the government's plans and intentions. Others were used as funnels, that is, as liaison officers who would make sense of information regarding what stakeholders thought about about the government's priorities and actions. Most advisers performed both functions and functioned as processors of information. Few advisers were expected to generate political counsel on policy proposals or policy advice. They simply lacked the experience to provide dependable advice. But they were specialists in amassing the views of a wide range of actors and presenting them in a package that could be absorbed by busy political executives. At the same time, those political operatives could be relied upon to proffer the views and instincts of the premier to any and all who would listen to them. The dual role of political staffers made them young ambassadors of sorts for the reborn "court."[8]

In Ontario, a tradition persisted where a substantial number of the individuals named to work closely with the premier have been public servants. This model suited many premiers. Gradually, individuals with little or no government experience were appointed to the Premier's Office. The bureaucracy now had to compete for attention. Over time, and depending on the premier and their political outlook, the value of a politically sensitive staff was affirmed. That staff could be relied upon to make recommendations based on shared values and assumptions, of the sort that the public service could not be expected to provide. Their advice was more tactical and strategic than operational and programmatic, more dependable in "hot" situations because they were more likely than public servants to have a solid reading of the political field and public opinion, as well as more likely to have a network of outside contacts and relationships that could be engaged. In the increasingly mediatized political environment, in which nuances often become the subject of debate as hungry "24/7" news cycles demand more controversy, those skills (which largely are absent from the public service) can prove critical in securing support for the government.

The Evolving Structure

In the immediate post-war years, the "Office of the Prime Minister" was fit easily into the east wing of the Queen's Park legislative palace. George Drew, premier of Ontario from August 1943 to October 1948, had a small staff. The top-ranked public servants reported formally to the Provincial Secretary, a cabinet position. In 1945, the first year examined in this study, $127,798 was spent on the Office of the Prime Minister ($1,911,352 in 2020 dollars). Over the next two years, expenditures more than doubled, to $292,900 per year. Drew clearly spent a colossal sum of money (even by 2020 standards) on staff and travel to cope with the rising tide of the social democratic Co-operative Commonwealth Federation (CCF), led by Ted Joliffe (see chart 1). The election of 1948, which saw the CCF rise to Official Opposition status, marked the high tide of spending (in real dollars). Though his party was re-elected to government, Drew was defeated in his own riding, and he resigned as premier to join the race for the leadership of the federal Progressive Conservatives.

Thomas Kennedy's short stay in power marked a clear change in the structure: a formal "Cabinet Office" was created within the Provincial Secretary's Department, and Lorne R. McDonald was named Deputy Minister and Secretary of the Cabinet. Technically, McDonald (official title: Assistant to the Provincial Secretary) reported to Dana Porter, the Provincial Secretary. Note well here that titles, while important, have always been subject to manipulation and can be misleading. What clearly mattered was the individual giving advice, not the title being occupied.[9] McDonald's central task was to advise the premier.

Leslie Frost assumed the premiership in 1951 and significantly expanded his office, tripling the number of employees and adding to its budget (until 1955), so as to receive better advice systematically. McDonald was formally recognized as "Deputy Minister to the Prime Minister and Secretary of Cabinet"; it was now clear that he reported directly to the premier. The earlier post of "Clerk of the Executive Council" (H.A. Stewart), which was part of the Provincial Secretary's Office, was also integrated into the Office of the Prime Minister. In effect, that bureau had become the Cabinet Secretariat, signalling a desire to centre cabinet decision-making in Queen's Park's east wing. Frost added the Ontario Racing Commission to his office in 1952–54, in order to deal with those issues himself.[10] In 1954, William M. McIntyre replaced McDonald as Secretary to Cabinet, but he did not inherit the title of Deputy Minister to the Prime Minister. Instead, Frost added a new "Executive Officer" to his office, Don J. Collins, in 1955. In 1958 Frost himself formally took the title "President of the Council."

During the twelve years Frost was prime minister (1949–1961), the composition of the office fluctuated from year to year, but typically the staff positions were listed clearly as including an Executive Assistant to the Prime Minister, the Deputy Minister and Secretary of Cabinet, the Clerk of the Executive Council, a Solicitor, an Inquiry Clerk, an Accountant, and the Personal Secretary to the Prime Minister. There was no hint of political advisers in that office. The premier, according to Allan Grossman, a minister without portfolio in the last year of the Frost government, "ran a one-man show."[11]

Frost used his budgets to do more than pay salaries. As the election year of 1951 approached, expenditures in the Prime Minister's Office grew to $399,142 ($3,994,354 in 2020 dollars), with a staff of only seven people. Most of that public money went to defray the travel costs for the premier and his key cabinet ministers and staff and for political advice of all kinds. For the government, the money was well spent: the Frost PCs erased the results of the disastrous 1948 election, wiping out the left and increasing its number of seats by 50 per cent. Over the following years the expenditures were reduced until the election in 1955, when they grew again, to $371,511. Frost brought about many changes in 1956, a year after his electoral triumph in 1955. He slashed the budget for his office by getting rid of most non-personnel expenses, but he also increased the number of people who reported to him. The office continued to expand. In 1958 two more positions were established, vaguely designated as "Executive Officers"; these new "extra hands" were assigned a range of increasingly political functions, including communications, coordination, caucus relations, legislative support, policy formulation, and touring. One of these people, Ray Farrell, had been seconded from the Department of Economics.[12] In 1959 an "Economist" was hired (T.C. Clark), but that position disappeared the following year, never to again be located in the Office of the Prime Minister. (Frost evidently was quite comfortable in reaching into the talent pool of the Treasury Department or the Economics Department to get the help he needed.) In 1960 an Assistant Secretary of the Cabinet was added, and in 1961 an adjustment was made to the title of the most senior civil servant – W.M. McIntyre became Secretary of the Cabinet and Director, Executive Council Office.

Frost undoubtedly used financial tricks to fund his ever-growing office. In 1956 the PO's expenditures dropped dramatically to $121,576 ($1,173,510 in 2020 dollars) and remained around that low until the election of 1959, when they were raised to $192,917. After Frost was elected for the last time in 1960, expenditures were reduced slightly to $160,248 and $178,694 in 1961, his final year in office. This was reflective of his administrative style. Frost insisted on detailed knowledge of what was going on in his government, and from his earliest days as a minister he had cultivated a devout following in the bureaucratic and party ranks.[13] He did not hesitate to reach out for advice to the middle ranks of the bureaucracy that served him, and would ask public servants to write draft speeches for him and to handle sensitive correspondence. According to one of his own ministers, "it was common knowledge that senior civil servants in the departments often reported directly to him and not to their ministers."[14] In other words, most of the advice Frost sought and received was from the bureaucracy, not political advisers.

John Robarts became premier in 1961 and continued the Frost tradition, at least for a time. Upon assuming office, he asked Don Collins, the chairman of the Civil Service Commission, to review the organization of his office and to suggest improvements. Collins recommended an immediate increase in clerical staff; after that, he prepared a more extensive reorganization plan that Robarts could implement between sessions.[15] Robarts's response was slow, but some capacity was added. In 1963, McIntyre was formally recognized as wearing three hats: Secretary to the Cabinet, Deputy Minister, and Director of the Executive Council Office. A year later, a new Department of the Prime Minister was established, which would formally divide the Cabinet Office and the Prime Minister's Office. McIntyre, as Senior Deputy Minister, would be its administrative head, but he would focus on his duties as Secretary of the Cabinet. In 1963 a "Files Office" was created and the Inquiry function was remodelled, becoming an "Appointment and Inquiry Secretary in Charge" office. The most telling change was the hiring in 1963 of a journalist – an explicit attempt to master "communications" as a way of better positioning the government in the eyes of the public.[16] Robarts now had only two "executive officers" reporting to McIntyre, but they now included William Kinmond, a former *Globe and Mail* China correspondent and *Toronto Star* reporter, who now worked as press secretary. This recognition that the media were changing and needed to be "managed" was an important development. Until that time, the office had served mostly as an interlocutor as individual inquiries arrived from the bureaucracy and members of the public. As the government of Ontario grew, so did the Office of the

Prime Minister. The addition of a Director of Communications indicated that he required a more sustained approach to media inquiries, but more importantly, it showed that he wanted to manage his own communications.

In 1965, a new position was created: Chief Executive Officer (CEO). Keith Reynolds, a biologist by training and a career public servant, was hired to fill it. He would in effect lead the prime minister's personal and advisory staff. In particular, he would coordinate the flow of demands on the prime minister, "in such a way to ensure a minimum demand on the Prime Minister with a maximum result."[17] The new system was severely tested within a few months when Attorney General Frederick Cass decided to act promptly on a commissioned report in March 1964. Judge Bruce Macdonald had recommended that the Police Act be amended to give law enforcement agencies more latitude and discretion in battling organized crime, including the authority to suspend normal civil liberties. In tabling the bill, Cass admitted that the new measures were "drastic," "dangerous," and nothing less than "terrible legislation in an English common law country," but he felt comfortable in going forward. It took little time for the media to attack the legislation and for the opposition to denounce the government. The reaction spread to the government's own backbenchers and, soon afterwards, to leading cabinet ministers. The bill was withdrawn, Cass resigned as attorney general, and Robarts had learned a hard lesson. As his biographer A.K. McDougall noted:

> He [Robarts] could no longer be just a relaxed chairman of the board. He had to know more about what his ministers were doing, to take responsibility for the whole range of government actions. The buck stopped at the premier's office. Demonstrably, the office was not adequately staffed to process difficult bucks. A new political style and a new organization to suit that style would eventually emerge. In the meantime, to avoid further embarrassment, the premier spent many hours personally reviewing all the legislative proposals that were awaiting introduction to the legislature.[18]

McDougall observed that Robarts's "policy network extended beyond the cabinet to include his political group as well as his personal office staff. Whereas Frost had had a few advisers and many acquaintances, Robarts tended to cast his net more widely, having a larger circle of advisers over whom he exercised much less control."[19] As a result, the PO was kept at consistent levels in terms of full-time employees, with the office's budget showing increases that did not go much beyond inflation.

Within the Prime Minister's Office, Robarts would select his own political advisers, as well as his appointments secretary, press officer, and accountant. Robarts in effect had started to separate the political from the administrative, but only to a degree. The creation of the CEO position created some tension as Reynolds became the "go to" person to handle political issues. He acquired a great deal of influence with the premier, even if he technically reported to McIntyre. When the latter retired in 1969, Robarts promoted Reynolds to Secretary to Cabinet and abolished the CEO position, thus ending the experiment of having two key advisers in his office. Reynolds was now listed as "Principal Assistant" and veered towards political decision-making. By the spring of 1970, he was discussing cabinet postings directly with cabinet ministers.[20]

As his government progressed through two elections, including the election of 1967 in which the government lost seven seats and six points in popular vote, Robarts worried that the bureaucracy was not responding effectively to demands for efficiency. As McDougall noted, "he worried that the organizations and offices created in the new administrative state would foreclose his own personal need to communicate with and respond to Ontarians and the Ontario community. The rising bureaucracy was placing a policy filter between Robarts and the citizens the government was supposed to serve."[21] In February 1968, Robarts commented on the new political environment in a way that presaged the need for a new approach to governance. "We in government today find ourselves in a virtual maze of interrelated decisions – and I think this is true of any government you wish to look at in any part of the world," he told the Legislative Assembly. "We are confronted by multiple demands and by many complex considerations. We have discussed this in the House on other occasions, in terms of the vertical organization of government, in departments, and the increasing characteristic of our problems" to be horizontal in nature."[22] A cabinet minister complained that it had become "impossible to read the public opinion."[23] A year later, in February 1969, the government announced the creation of the "Productivity Improvement Project," a review of "the overall structure of government led by John Cronyn, a director of the Labatt Brewing Company. [24]

The Committee on Government Productivity had little to say about the Premier's Office except that its purpose was to serve the CEO in his three roles: as "first minister of cabinet," as "leader of the government and its chief legislative spokesman," and as "the elected representative of his constituents." The report emphasized that the Premier's Office was concerned mainly with the latter two functions. The key adviser to the premier was the Deputy Minister of the Office of the Premier.

The role of serving the "first minister of cabinet" belonged to the Cabinet Office, which was headed by the same individual who served as Deputy Minister of the Office of the Premier. "This merging of responsibilities into a single position facilitates the functional relationship between the Cabinet Office and the Premier's Office." The functions of the Premier's Office were clearly laid out:

> The Office of the Premier provides advisory support on policy matters and administrative support service to the Premier.
>
> The principal advisory functions are:
>
> - To provide the principal link between the Premier and all ministries and the major policy committees;
> - To coordinate government processes consequent to the establishment of policy (for example, by maintaining a primary role in the areas of intergovernmental relations, information policy and the nomination of key public servants and agency heads); and
> - To provide input to the Government's legislative program, long-term strategy, and program priorities
>
> The principal service functions are:
>
> - To budget the premier's time
> - To schedule and complete travelling arrangements
> - To maintain relations with the communications media
> - To write speeches and statements
> - To brief the premier daily on legislative matters
> - To receive and keep a record of mail, and prepare replies
> - To handle invitations and appointment requests
> - To assist with constituency matters
> - To maintain liaison with caucus members
> - To deal with inquiries from the public and from special interest groups; and
> - To receive delegations and unscheduled visitors.[25]

It was clear from this list that overwhelmingly, the Premier's Office's task was to deal with political priorities, not state demands. At the time this was written, the Premier's office counted twenty-one employees and was spending about $500,000 ($3,287,439 in 2020 dollars). From 1956 to 1971, the expenses of the office increased at roughly the same rate as the number of employees (see figure 11.1). That soon changed.

When Robarts retired in 1971, his office's structure was very similar to the one he had acquired in 1961; the only real innovation was the creation of the communications function. In 1971, W.A. Rathbun was listed as Director of Communications.

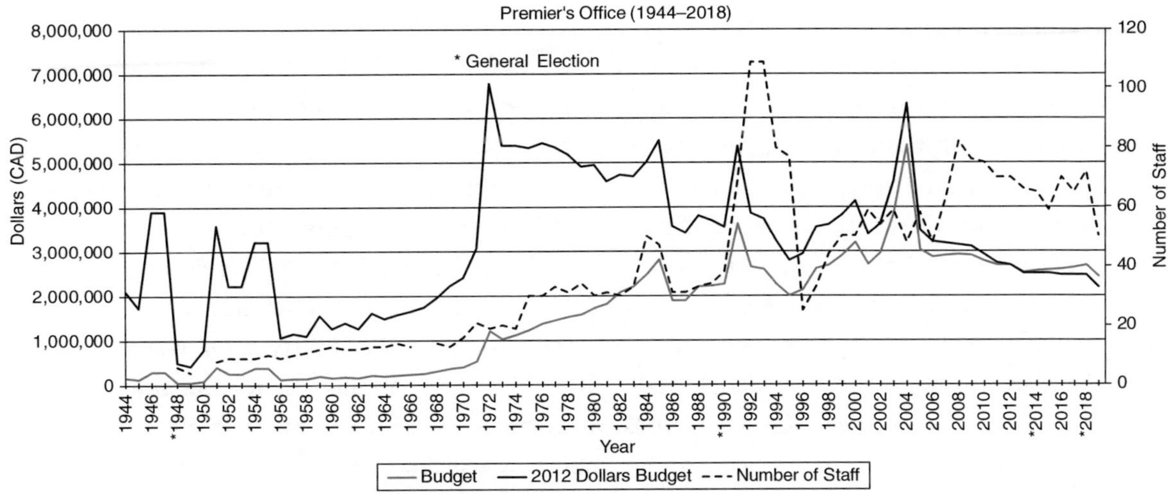

Figure 11.1. Premier's Office budget versus number of staff, 1944–2018

The Premier's Office was nothing more than an extension of the Cabinet Office, a trend that would continue for another fifteen years. The structure convinced many that because the Cabinet Office was staffed mostly by public servants, even the political appointees to that body were providing dispassionate, politically neutral advice. Still, Robarts grew weary of the bureaucracy's counsel. In 1970, when a new, more rigorous Treasury Board was planned, so that it more resembled the federal government's counterpart, Robarts hesitated. The legislation had been drafted and office space had been allocated, but in the end, he instructed that the bill be sidelined, surmising that the project was "being pushed by empire builders, meaning obviously [Carl] Brannan [Secretary to Cabinet], even perhaps JKR [Reynolds]."[26] For Robarts, the bureaucratization of the Premier's Office had gone too far.

The inheritor of the first report of the "Committee on Government Productivity" (COGP) was Robarts's successor, Bill Davis, who assumed the premiership in 1971. Davis insisted on adding strength to his office in order to bolster its policy capacity and its ability to respond both to the public and to the federal government. He started his premiership by setting aside the recommendation of the public service to extend the Spadina Expressway into downtown Toronto – an initiative promoted by the bureaucracy that had provoked a vigorous grassroots reaction. There were a number of other reasons for strengthening his office. First, earlier methods of collecting political advice were now clearly being outrun by the realities of an increasingly complex government. Second, in the run-up to the Victoria Conference called by the Trudeau government in the winter of 1971, it became clear that the Ontario delegation would have to be ready to explain itself in terms of government operations but also in political terms, both to the electorate and to the Ontario legislature. Third, the Davis government was encountering harsh economic headwinds, the sort of fiscal environment the province had not faced since the end of the Second World War. Finally, the Tories were preparing for an election – which they would win that October, with a substantial increase in seats and share of the popular vote.

Davis took a dramatic new approach to the Office of the Premier. Upon his election in 1971, he immediately doubled the budget for his office and set it on a course of continuous expansion (staff would double from twenty-one in 1971 to forty-seven when he retired in 1985). He immediately added three "Special Assistants"; there were now five "Executive Officers." Keith Reynolds was retained as deputy minister to ensure the transition, but the job of Secretary to Cabinet was given a separate function and occupied by C.E. [Carl] Brannan. Indeed, a formal "Cabinet Office" was recognized for the first time, though it was still formally part of the Office of the Premier. James Fleck, a York University professor and the key architect of the COGP, was brought into the Premier's Office in 1972 as CEO (the title of Deputy Minister to the Prime Minister having been abolished) and ordered his office to vet all speeches by cabinet ministers before they were delivered (a requirement that was largely ignored).[27]

The Office of the Prime Minister, now twenty people strong, including eight executive officers, was renamed the "Premier's Office" in 1972. Clare Westcott was named Executive Director and Executive Assistant to the Premier, and "special assistants" changed their titles to "special assignments," suggesting a deliberate application of resources to what could be deemed partisan activities. The Appointments function also doubled, to four employees, in part to cope with the growing number of jobs to be filled, but the significance of this function in the Premier's Office was not lost. The Big Blue Machine functioned well because it was organized, disciplined, and strategic and knew how to reward. Davis stuck to a very limited definition of the "Premier's Office" as nothing more than the few individuals who literally shared his office. The apparatus seemed very comfortable in bringing together capable young men and women who were as talented as they were unabashedly partisan. These people had deep roots in the Progressive Conservative Party and had cultivated long-standing friendships and loyalties to senior party officials and the premier.

To further harmonize horizontal collaboration between ministries, Edward E. Stewart, a former Deputy Minister of Education who knew Davis intimately, assumed the position of Deputy Minister to the Premier in the summer of 1974, while Fleck was named Secretary to Cabinet. By 1975, thirty people were working in the Premier's Office as the government readied itself for an election. Davis felt a need to receive policy advice that would counterweigh the civil service's monopoly on advice. Within the government, the role of the expanded office in terms of policy and political advice was grudgingly recognized. Certainly, he relied on the Progressive Conservative caucus to provide him with political intelligence, but increasingly he felt the need to have their input digested, organized, and acted upon coherently.

For all its strengths, the 1975 election went badly for Davis's Big Blue Machine; the government lost 27 seats and its majority (it now held only 51 of 125 seats). The prospect of a resurgent NDP under Stephen Lewis in the Official Opposition created an urgent need for more coordination at the centre (the 1967 election had shaken the Robarts administration in much the same way). As Edward Stewart noted, "the Premier began to broaden the consultative process on other fronts ... In many respects this was consistent with the changing times in which the government found itself and, in some ways, reflected an attempt at least to move in the direction of the wider participation which activist students in Ontario and elsewhere had brought so forcibly to the attention of university officials in the late 1960s."[28]

Davis retooled the office. First, he renamed it "the Office of the Premier and Cabinet Office." Fleck, who had little patience for politicians, was removed after numerous complaints from the caucus. Davis turned to his former Deputy Minister of Education, Ed Stewart, naming him Deputy Minister and Secretary to Cabinet. Ed Stewart then hired Hugh Segal, Davis's campaign secretary in the recent election, because he had worked in Robert Stanfield's office in Ottawa and had experience navigating a parliamentary minority. Segal was placed in the Cabinet Office, reporting to Stewart, not Clare Westcott. Notwithstanding his posting, Segal was hired as exempt staff (though an employee of the Crown, he had not been hired as a civil servant). Wescott, for his part, reorganized his office, hiring Sally Barnes as Director of Communications as well as seven "public liaison" and four "special assignment" officers. Stewart was an anomaly. Though viewed by many as a stalwart, non-partisan public servant,[29] he was entirely devoted to the personal success of Bill Davis and the PCs.[30] As Hugh Segal put it, "When Ed Stewart replaced Fleck as deputy in the premier's office and, subsequently, as secretary to the cabinet, the stage for real repositioning and pragmatic, hands-on political decision-making was set."[31]

Davis called an election in June 1977, and increased the government's number of seats in the legislature, but still fell five seats short of a majority. The premier now made more changes to tighten the coordination of his team. Stewart was named Deputy Minister to the Premier and Secretary to Cabinet and Clerk of the Executive Council in 1978, with the result, as he himself pointed out, that "the two operations were linked once again." He proceeded to build capacity: ironically, it was the head of the public service that was building up the structures necessary to provide political advice.[32] As Edward Stewart noted later, the PO's operation "was thought to be another serious problem area, particularly as it related to the Premier's availability to those who wanted or needed to see him."[33] More than a decade later, Stewart could still justify this reuniting of the political and administrative:

> To me, the notion that you can keep administrative responsibilities and political considerations in distinct compartments at the highest levels of decision-making, including many of the responsibilities which involve the deputy (and I use the term in a general sense here) is naïve and non-productive. I acknowledge that there are those who will disagree, and I expect to hear arguments about the matter with increasing frequency in the years ahead. But a deputy who claims that political considerations never influence his or her thinking, or the advice he or she is giving to the government, is either trying to deceive the public or is of limited value to the Premier and Ministers who he or she serves. After all, it is possible to be political without being partisan.[34]

New positions in the Office of the Premier and Cabinet were added, including a researcher, seven people in a "Public Liaison" unit, four people doing "Special Assignments," one person devoted to "Administration and Personnel," one person doing "Lieutenant Governor-in-Council Appointments," and three people in "Appointments and Public Engagement." Segal left the Davis team in 1977 but returned in 1979 as Associate Secretary to Cabinet, responsible for the Policy and Priorities Board of Cabinet, a position he held until 1982, when he assumed the position of Associate Secretary of Cabinet for Federal–Provincial Relations (again under the category of exempt staff). He was unabashedly political, yet he held a position in a central agency dominated by civil servants: "My rule was always to ask, 'are we doing this because as Progressive Conservatives we believe in this? Are we doing this because it corresponds to the Progressive Conservative notion of what is in the public interest?'"[35] Segal was also Secretary of the Progressive Conservative Policy Committee. In ensuring that his principal assistants were fixtures in the Cabinet Office, Davis had effectively hardwired the central agency of his government so it would work harmoniously with his personal office.

The March 1981 election finally gave the PCs the majority they had sought since 1975. Davis took advantage of the situation to make more changes. He created two senior positions to assist in the streaming of political advice. He kept Clare Westcott as Executive Director and appointed John Tory as Principal Secretary to the Premier (a title borrowed from Ottawa). Davis created a new model that would persist for the next thirty years by appointing two leading political advisers with a variety of titles: Executive Director, Principal Secretary, or Chief of Staff. The division of labour between the two positions depended entirely on the skills and background of the individuals. While some were more focused on party affairs, others favoured policy issues, and both emphases would change as electoral mandates approaches their limits. The number of staffers remained relatively stable until 1984; by the time of the 1985 election, there were fifty. By that year, the budget of the PO amounted to nearly $3 million ($6,100,525 in 2020 dollars).

In 1985, David Peterson, heading the new Liberal government, made significant changes to the Office of the Premier and Cabinet Office. He reduced the number of employees by one third (thirty-one people), and he abandoned the practice of giving the position of Secretary to Cabinet and Deputy to the Premier to a single person. The Cabinet Office would be led by the Secretary to Cabinet, Robert Carman, a career public servant. The Premier's Office would be led by the Principal Secretary to the Premier, Hershell Ezrin. Ezrin was a former federal public servant who oversaw formal departments of policy, legislation, and communications (he would be succeeded by Vince Borg, a long-trusted aide to Peterson, in 1988; and then by Daniel Gagnier, who took the title of Chief of Staff in 1989). Peterson added two new directors to his office: a Policy Director (with two staffers), as well as a Press Secretary (who oversaw three staff). The "Public Liaison" office was renamed the "Correspondence and Public Inquiries" unit and expanded to ten people (within six months, the correspondence unit would be transferred to the Cabinet Office). Finally, the Office of the Premier housed the Ontario Representative to Quebec and the Federal Government, Don Stevenson, until 1989.

By 1990, the "Policy" unit had grown to seven people and the "Communications" unit had grown to five. A third position was created: Executive Director, occupied by Gordon Ashworth, a political operative. That office would be responsible for community liaison, Order-in-Council appointments, correspondence, caucus relations, travel arrangements, and managing the premier's constituency affairs. The number of staffers was reduced to pre-election levels, but the budget was not slashed in the same measure, hovering around the $2 million mark for most of the mandate. In 1986 there were thirty-one staff; the staff complement would grow each year of the mandate until it reached thirty-eight staff in 1990, with expenditures of $2,251,132 ($3,932,979 in 2020 dollars).

The strongest growth in the Premier's Office occurred under the premiership of Bob Rae, who was deeply suspicious of the public service and who had no faith that it would carry out his government's wishes.[36] "From everything I saw over the years, it was already very political, though this was expressed in the inevitable code of options, warnings, and the sideways murmurings that were eventually fed full bore to the outside world," remembered Rae.[37] Under Rae, the number of staff in the Premier's Office increased from 69 in 1991, to 102 in 1992, to 109 in 1993. Every existing unit in the Premier's Office grew in numbers, and new units were created: "Public Appointments Secretariat," "Special Adviser, Projects," "Research and Policy" (this was essentially the "Policy and Issues" unit, which had been retained from the previous administrations). Rae also integrated into his office structures that had been created by Peterson to support the "Premier's Council on Health, Well-Being and Social Justice"; and he added a new division named "Partnership Development and Services." The budget rose from $2,251,132 to $3,611,438. (PO operations would not cost this much again until 2004, when the Liberals returned to power and $5,392,121 was spent.) Within a year there were 109 staff – a 63 per cent increase in one year – although the budget did not follow. Indeed, the budget fell as staff numbers increased, indicating again that the government, as in Frost's day, was seconding staffers who were being paid by other departments. A measure of equilibrium was re-established as the government tried to reduce expenditures in the final year of its mandate: the number of employees was reduced to eighty in 1994 and to seventy-seven in 1995, although expenditures were still more than $2 million.

Rae abandoned the "Chief of Staff" designation for his chief political adviser. He named his long-time aide David Agnew as Principal Secretary and also appointed an executive director. Rae, albeit reluctantly, kept Peter Barnes, the cabinet secretary appointed by David Peterson, for two years.[38] In 1992, borrowing from the practice of NDP governments in Saskatchewan and Manitoba, Rae appointed Agnew as Secretary to Cabinet and Clerk of the Executive Council, hoping to ensure more compliance from the bureaucracy. "The Conservatives solved the problem of 'asserting control and authority' by combining the roles of principal secretary to the premier and cabinet secretary," wrote Rae.[39] The Agnew appointment hardwired the political to the administrative, as had been the case in the Robarts and Davis years, but in reverse. PC governments since Frost had used the bureaucracy to bolster the Office of the Premier; Rae HAD inverted the Ontario tradition and appointed his closest political adviser to direct the bureaucracy.[40] Agnew ended his membership in the NDP at that point.

The tide was again reversed three years later. Elected in 1995, the Mike Harris government aimed at reducing the size of government and government spending, and the PO did not escape the cutbacks. The budget for the office fell into line with the number of employees, indicating that the practice of hiring secondments who stayed on the payroll of their home departments had ended.

In the first full year of the first term of the Harris government, the Premier's Office staff complement was cut by two thirds, matching the levels of the early years of the Davis government.[41] This Premier's Office focused on policy, issue management, and controlling and coordinating the agenda. All other functions that had been created by the NDP were either eliminated or removed from the Premier's Office. As Harris settled into government, however, the number of staff in the Premier's Office grew by ten people each year until the 1999 election (thirty-three in 1997, forty-four in 1998, fifty in 1999). During this period, growth took place in the policy, communication, and media relations functions. After Harris's re-election in 1999, there was marginal growth in numbers in the Premier's Office, peaking at fifty-nine. Harris announced his retirement in 2002 and was succeeded by Ernie Eves. Not much changed in Eves's seven-month tenure prior to the election in 2003; his staff in the Premier's Office grew by only five, to 59 in 2003.

In 2003, after the Liberals under Dalton McGuinty were elected, the number of staff remained relatively steady. The "Director of Communications" position would celebrate its fortieth birthday, but its functions had been carved into a number of roles (press secretary, speech writer, communications advisors, strategic communications planner, media relations). In 2006 the creation of a formal position responsible for "new media" communications acknowledged the importance of alternative forms of online communications. In his first year in office, McGuinty reduced the staff complement in his office to forty-eight, but expenditures went from $3,831,077 to $5,392,121, a dramatic and unprecedented explosion that went far beyond staff salaries. That practice ended in 2005, and a new spending pattern set in: budgets would decline steadily while the gap between full-time employees and expenditures remained high (repeating the trend of the Rae government).

Staff numbers grew to sixty-three prior to the election of 2006, and grew again in 2007 to eighty-two – a 30 per cent increase in time for the election – before settling to a complement of seventy-five. Far more significantly, McGuinty adopted a highly formalized process to extend the premier's latitude in making hires in ministerial offices, a strategy that had been attempted by the Rae government, but with little success, for ministers insisted on hiring their own staff. The McGuinty administration's approach brought more discipline to the procedure, but it proved to be time consuming, delaying many offices from being fully staffed, briefed, and operational for up to a year. The numbers in his own office may have grown only moderately, but its reach extended to an unparalleled degree. The impact of this change, however, is beyond the scope of this chapter. The creation and evolution of the Cabinet Office will also have to await further study.

The re-elected Liberals were full of ambition, but its plans were curtailed by the dramatic recession caused by a financial crisis in the US that eventually engulfed the entire world. The Ontario economy was not spared, and the McGuinty government (which had run budgetary surpluses in the mid-2000s) began to take on massive annual deficits. The election of October 2011 was hard-fought as both the Progressive Conservatives and the New Democrats had new leaders. The campaign was marked by one particular policy from the Liberals: it pledged to relent to public opinion and abandon plans to build new gas-burning power plants in Mississauga and Oakville. The Liberals lost 18 seats, ending up with 53 of the 107 seats in the legislature, just one seat shy of an outright majority. It was poorly equipped to deal with a rash of controversies, including misspent monies to reform the Ontario Air Ambulance Corporation as a federally incorporated charity, controversial revisions to teacher contracts (essentially a wage freeze, with a dramatically reduced sick-leave plan), and a partial privatization of the Ontario electricity grid.

The most prominent controversy was the revelation that the government would be absorbing massive costs to compensate a number of companies as a result of the cancellation of plans to build power plants in Mississauga and Oakville. The government was soon caught in allegations that it had wasted between $500 million and $1 billion in taxpayer dollars to win one or two seats. The range of controversies proved very difficult to handle, to the point that the government's legitimacy, especially in a minority situation, was questioned. Premier McGuinty decided to retire, and Kathleen Wynne, the Minister of Transportation, won the succession race. She immediately brought in new staff.

The Premier's Office saw a number of changes at this time. In 2012, the position of Social Media Coordinator was created in the Communications Branch, a full five years after Facebook and Twitter were launched. Two years later, the Wynne administration split the Communications and Operations branches and created a Strategic Messaging Unit (SMU). A year later, the Social Media coordinator was attached to the SMU, an indication that social media had become pivotal. To bring more unity to the office, the positions of Chief of Staff and Principal Secretary were combined in 2016.

The gas plant controversy continued to swirl around the government, with allegations of a Liberal cover-up and revelations of deleted emails. The Commissioner for Information and Privacy was called in to investigate reports that the Liberals were covering up their decision to scrap both power plants. In June 2013, she released *Deleting Accountability: Records Management Practices of Political Staff*, a report in which David Livingston, McGuinty's Chief of Staff, was accused of failing to keep records. She found that staff in the Premier's Office had illegally deleted emails tied to the gas plant scandal, but she also dangled the hope that they could be retrieved.[42] When it emerged that summer that the deletions were irretrievable, she released a second report as an addendum to her initial findings.[43]

The government was mired in controversy: it now emerged that the Liberals had tried to cover up a controversial decision to cancel two gas plants in Mississauga and Oakville. On 20 February 2014, the Ontario Provincial Police executed a search warrant on a Mississauga data storage company during their investigation into the power plant emails that had been deleted by the office of former Premier McGuinty.[44] A parliamentary committee started to examine the issue, hearing more than 117 hours of testimony from 77 witnesses, and consulting 311,000 documents and emails related to the gas plants, including 30,000 directly from the Premier's Office.[45]

The Ontario Provincial Police launched an investigation against Livingston in March 2014 for breach of trust for allegedly "arranging for someone outside government to access computers in the premier's office."[46] It was eventually revealed that the premier's Chief of Staff had given an outside consultant unrestricted access to the office computers of twenty-four employees before Kathleen Wynne became premier.[47] Livingston, and Laura Miller, another PO employee, were charged by the OPP in December 2015. Livingston was tried, found guilty, and and sentenced to a short term in jail.

It is not clear whether the gas plant controversy caused the downfall of the Liberal government in 2018, but the punishment was certainly grave. The Liberals were reduced to a handful of seats, and the Progressive Conservatives were returned to power after a fifteen-year absence. The number of staff was reduced, the Office of Policy and Research was renamed the Office of Policy, and in 2019 the Bureau of Digital Communications was assigned a Director-level manager.

Conclusion

The history of political governance in Ontario since the mid-1940s until the onset of the pandemic in 2020 reveals, first, that the office structure was malleable and that each premier changed titles, functions, and organizational charts to suit his own management style. Second, it reveals growth in the Premier's Office in terms of both staffing and budgets. Over the seventy-five years under study, budgeting and staffing figures were mostly correlated. In some years, governments played loosely with budget allocations, seconding staff to the Premier's Office but paying them out of departmental budgets, or spending money on non-staff items (e.g., polls, consultations, travel).

Also, staffing of the Premier's Office grew in a manner consistent with government growth, but not in a direct correlation. When the government's budget hit the $1 billion mark in 1960, fewer than ten people worked in the Prime Minister's Office. Forty years later, the government's budget hovered around $120 billion (a near 12,000 per cent increase), but the premier's staff had grown by only 650 per cent. By the time the number of provincial employees reached 90,000 in the early 1990s, 110 people worked for the premier directly: only 0.0012 per cent of the government's workforce. In 2010, there were roughly 60,000 people on the government payroll (not counting employees of the 635 government agencies, boards, commissions, and foundations), and seventy-five people working in the Premier's Office: again, around 0.0012 per cent. By 2019, when the Ontario Public Service counted 60,000 on its payroll, the ratio had been reduced to 0.0008%. If a centralization of power took place during these years, one has to look beyond structures and numbers.

The numbers of staff in the Premier's Office have been small, and except for the dramatic, if short-lived, staff increases in Premier Rae's office and the equally dramatic and short-lived growth in the budget of the Premier's Office in early 2000s, the growth has been steady, undramatic, and in line with general government expansion.

Judging from the data, it is clear that the budgets of the Premier's Office almost always increased in the final two years of a mandate, indicating that a key priority of the Premier's Office was to communicate externally at a time when the electorate was most responsive. One limitation of these data is that it is difficult to determine whether this occurred in the portion of the year prior to the election, or afterwards to reflect transition costs. Transitions were also important. Frost, Robarts, Davis, Peterson, and Rae all increased the number of employees as they assumed power, mostly temporarily. In contrast, Harris, Eves, McGuinty, Wynne, and Ford cut the staff contingents when they assumed office. It is worth emphasizing that, in terms of real dollars, the Premier's Office spent in 2020 roughly the equivalent of what was spent in 1944.

Even if numbers only go so far in explaining the realities of personal influence, they challenge theories that rely solely on anecdotes for proof. The numbers show that the "new political management" and its centralization of power in the Premier's Office is not a recent phenomenon; neither are the complaints made by those who resent the intrusion of the democratically elected in the affairs of the bureaucracy. The model of the new political management that posits that power is now more than ever concentrated in the hands of the premier and a small group of political advisers and senior public servants needs to be modified. Also, the argument that there has been an increase in premiers' attention to the appointment of senior public servants seems to lack validity. The issue of increased pressure on public servants to employ a "pro-government spin" with respect to government communications also hardly begs comparison to the days when the government of Ontario under the Progressive Conservative governments from Drew to Davis counted explicitly on their public servants to deliver messages that were coherent with government policy and that ensured that both the political and the administrative concerns were united in a person who reported directly to the premier. The same could be said about public servants showing enthusiasm for government plans and priorities.

Our final argument is that Ontario followed international trends in terms of building up the office of the chief political executive; in many ways this paralleled and sometimes anticipated the centralization of power in Ottawa that has been identified by others in the 1970s and 1980s.[48] The Premier's Office started to change in the 1960s as it increasingly hired professional political aides to deal with communications demand and electoral preparedness.

The public service could be counted upon up until the 1960s to provide reliable material, but its advice was always counterbalanced by efforts to seek out the views of the business community and, no less, labour. For the public service in Ontario, serving the premier (or ministers) with briefings about the political consequences of government policy was seen as legitimate. Indeed, the very structure of a combined Deputy Minister (Premier's Office) and Secretary to Cabinet facilitated the combination of advice. Political advice also came in the form of "kitchen cabinets," interviews with individual MPPs, and caucus meetings. But the combination of public service and informal political advice was insufficient. Government was becoming more important as well as more complex, and increasingly under the gaze of more inquiring, more impatient, and better-educated media.

The Ontario experience also revealed a few traits in the political style of the province. First, the Ottawa model was only slowly applied. It was Bill Davis who, in the 1980s – forty years after Ottawa – created structures to distinguish political from bureaucratic advice, even though that line has been blurred very often since. In terms of real dollars, it is important to note that while the Premier's Office expenditures have fluctuated, they are, at the timing of writing, equivalent to what was spent in 1945.

Do political staffers inside the Premier's Office make a difference? The question can only be answered by analysing case studies of policy and political questions, an approach that falls outside the scope of this chapter but that may have a better chance of discerning the boundaries of complementarity. For premiers, political staffs have played a critical structural role; they have been useful in receiving and evaluating the policy ideas put forward by competing ministers, social and economic interests, and the bureaucracy. Very few could be relied upon to actually

Table 11.1. Ontario Prime Ministerial Advisers, 1945–2019

Premier	Deputy Minister	Clerk of Executive Council	Secretary to Cabinet	Director, Executive Office	Chief Executive Officer	Principal Assistant	Executive Director	Principal Secretary	Chief of Staff
George Drew		H.A. Stewart							
Thomas Kennedy	Lorne R. McDonald		Lorne R. McDonald						
Leslie Frost	Lorne R. McDonald		Lorne R. McDonald						
			William M. McIntyre	William M. McIntyre	D.J. Collins				
John Robarts	William M. McIntyre		William M. McIntyre	William M. McIntyre	John Keith Reynolds				
	William M. McIntyre		John Keith Reynolds			Keith Reynolds			
William Davis	Keith Reynolds		Carl E. Brannan		James Fleck				
			James Fleck						
	Ed Stewart		Ed Stewart				Clare Westcott	John Tory	
David Peterson			Robert Carman Peter Barnes				Gordon Ashworth	Herschell Ezrin Vince Borg Daniel Gagnier	
Bob Rae			Peter Barnes David Agnew				Richard McLelland	David Agnew Melody Morrison	
Mike Harris			Rita Burak Andromache Karakatsanis					David Lindsay John Weir	Ron McLaughlin Guy Giorno
Ernie Eves			Andromache Karakatsanis					Jeff Bangs	Steve Pengelly
Dalton McGuinty			Tony Dean Shelly Jamieson Peter Wallace					David McNaughton Gerald Butts Jamison Steeve	Don Guy Peter Wilkinson Chris Morley David Livingston
Kathleen Wynne			Steve Orsini					Andrew Bevan	Thomas Teahen Andrew Bevan
Doug Ford			Steven Davidson					Jenni Byrne	Dean French

generate policy advice on their own, and few actually had enough influence to veto initiatives, but they could be depended upon to provide a political filter to ideas and advice advanced by others and ensure there were "no surprises." It is an error to assume that the number of advisers is, in and of itself, a sign of influence or of centralizing. The growth in the Premier's Office over the decades was necessary to ensure the level of comfort necessary for premiers to exercise their powers and prerogatives with a distinct "Ontario style."

QUESTIONS FOR CONSIDERATION:

1. The authors argue that the structuring of the Premier's Office has been marked by experimentation since the 1940s. Is this advantageous in any way?
2. How important is it for premiers to have qualified advisers? Has this changed over time?
3. Leslie Frost greatly expanded the Office of the Premier. Why did he do this?
4. How has communication by the Premier's Office with the public changed since the early post-war years?
5. According to Dutil and Constantinou, why did the Premier's Office grow to such an extent under Premier Bob Rae?
6. Has the growth and cost of the Premier's Office matched overall budget expenditures in the period covered? Why is this important?

NOTES

1 This is the first study of its kind in Canada. For a comparative study of the evolution of ministerial advisers over time, see Maria Maley, "Too Many or Too Few? The Increase in Federal Ministerial Advisers 1972–1999," *Australian Journal of Public Administration* 59 (2000): 48–53. Studies on the Ontario situation use much shorter frameworks. See Ted Glenn, "Politics, Personality, and History in Ontario's Administrative Style," in *Executive Styles in Canada: Cabinet Structures and Leadership Practices in Canadian Government*, ed. Luc Bernier, Keith Brownsey and Michael Howlett (IPAC and University of Toronto Press, 2005), Anna Lennox Esselment, "Birds of a Feather? The Role of Partisanship in the 2003 Ontario Government Transition," *Canadian Public Administration* 54, no. 4 (December2011); Anna Lennox Esselment, "An Inside Look at the Ontario Liberals in Power" in *The Politics of Ontario*, ed. Cheryl N. Collier and Jonathan Malloy (Toronto: University of Toronto Press, 2016); and Bryan Evans, "The Commanding Heights of Power and Politics in Ontario," in *The Politics of Ontario*, ed. Collier and Malloy.

The study of ministerial advisers has grown exponentially over the past two decades. To cite but a few titles, see Donald Savoie, *Governing from the Centre* (Toronto: University of Toronto Press, 1999) and *Court Government and the Collapse of Accountability in Canada and the United* Kingdom (Toronto: University of Toronto Press, 2008). See also Jonathan Craft, *Backrooms and Beyond: Partisan Advisers and the Politics of Policy Work in Canada* (Toronto: University of Toronto Press, 2016).

2 Robert Benzie, "Key Ford aide leaving for OEB," *Toronto Star*, 12 January 2019.
3 K. Rushowy and R. Benzie, "Ford chief of staff quits amid patronage flap: Move comes after Premier forced to revoke appointments of two with ties to French," *Toronto Star*, 22 June 2019.
4 Graham White, "Governing from Queen's Park: The Ontario Premiership," in *Prime Minister and Premiers: Political Leadership and Public Policy in Canada*, ed. Leslie A. Pal and David Taras (Toronto: Prentice-Hall, 1998), 130.
5 Background interviews were also conducted with key informants whose experience stretches back to the 1950s. We thank Ian MacDonald, Don Stevenson, Hugh Segal, and David Lindsay in particular.
6 See James H. Svara, "Complementarity of Politics and Administration as a Legitimate Alternative to the Dichotomy Model," *Administration and Society* 30, no. 6 (1999): 676–705; as well as his "The Myth of the Dichotomy: Complementarity of Politics and Administration in the Past and Future of Public Administration," *Public Administration Review* 61, no. 2 (2001): 176–83.
7 John Halligan, "Policy Advice and the Public Service," in *Governance in a Changing Environment*, ed. B.G. Peters and Donald Savoie (Montreal and Kingston: McGill–Queen's University Press, 1995).
8 Halligan, "Policy Advice and the Public Service."
9 F.F. Schindeler, *Responsible Government in Ontario* (Toronto: University of Toronto Press, 1969), 45.
10 Schindeler, *Responsible Government in Ontario*.
11 Roger Graham, *Old Man Ontario: Leslie Frost* (Toronto: University of Toronto Press, 1990), 173.
12 Graham, *Old Man Ontario*, 354.
13 Keith Brownsey, "The House That Frost Built," in *The Guardian: Perspectives on the Ontario Ministry of Finance*, ed. Patrice Dutil (Toronto: University of Toronto Press, 2011).
14 White, "Governing from Queen's Park," 166.
15 A.K. McDougall, *John P. Robarts: His Life and Government* (Toronto: University of Toronto Press, 1994), 77.
16 McDougall, *John P. Robarts*, 78.
17 McDougall, *John P. Robarts*, 133–4.
18 McDougall, *John P. Robarts*, 126–37.
19 McDougall, *John P. Robarts*, 88.
20 Peter Oliver, *Unlikely Tory: The Life and Politics of Alan Grossman* (Toronto: Lester and Orpen Dennys, 1985), 236.
21 McDougall, *John P. Robarts*, 231.
22 Edward E. Stewart, *Cabinet Government in Ontario: A View from Inside* (Montreal: Institute for Research on Public Policy, 1989), 11.
23 Oliver, *Unlikely Tory*, 294.
24 The Labatt Brewing Company seems to have entertained solid relations with the Progressive Conservative governments over the years. See Matthew Bellamy, *Brewed in the North: A History of Labatt's* (Montreal and Kingston: McGill–Queen's University Press, 2019)
25 Committee on Government Productivity, 1971, 100.
26 McDougall, *John P. Robarts*, 239–40.
27 Oliver, *Unlikely Tory*, 222.
28 Stewart, *Cabinet Government in Ontario*, 55.
29 Hugh Segal, *No Surrender: Reflections of a Happy Warrior in the Tory Crusade* (Toronto: HarperCollins, 1996), 64–5.
30 Ian Scott (with Neil McCormick), *To Make a Difference: A Memoir* (Toronto: Stoddart, 2001) 119.
31 Segal, *No Surrender*, 57.

32 Stewart, *Cabinet Government in Ontario*, 41.
33 Stewart, *Cabinet Government in Ontario*, 20.
34 Stewart, *Cabinet Government in Ontario*, 49.
35 Segal, *No Surrender*, 66.
36 Bob Rae, *From Protest to Power: Personal Reflections on a Life in Politics* (Toronto: Viking, 1996) 133.
37 Rae, *From Protest to Power*, 130.
38 Rae, *From Protest to Power*, 236.
39 Rae, *From Protest to Power*, 237.
40 Patrick Monahan, *Storming the Pink Palace: The NDP in Power: A Cautionary Tale* (Toronto: Lester, 1995); Thomas Walkom, *Rae Days: The Rise and Follies of the NDP* (Toronto: Key Porter, 2002); Randall White, *Ontario Since 1985* (Toronto: Eastendbooks, 1998)
41 David Cameron and Graham White, *Cycling into Saigon: The Conservative Transition in Ontario* (Vancouver: UBC Press, 2000), 112.
42 R. Ferguson, "Liberals illegally deleted emails," *Toronto Star*, 6 June 2013.
43 R. Ferguson and R. Brennan, "Privacy boss blasts Liberals again: Cavoukian says she was 'misled' into believing emails on gas plants irretrievable," *Toronto Star*, 31 August 2013.
44 R. Ferguson and R. Benzie, "OPP search data storage company in probe of deleted power plant emails: Critics say Mississauga operation 'no surprise,' as police silent on details," *Toronto Star*, 20 February 2014.
45 Ferguson and Benzie, "OPP search data storage company."
46 R. Ferguson, "Police suspect computers 'wiped,'" *Toronto Star*, 28 March 2014.
47 Ferguson, "Police suspect computers 'wiped.'"
48 See Marc Lalonde, "The Changing Role of the Prime Minister's Office," *Public Administration of Canada* 14, no. 4 (December 1971): 509–537. Patrice Dutil challenged the notion that the centralization of power in Ottawa was new by focusing on the first fifty years of Confederation. See Dutil, *Prime Ministerial Power in Canada: Its Origins under Macdonald, Laurier, and Borden* (Vancouver: UBC Press, 2017).

CHAPTER TWELVE

New Public Management – New Technology – Who Foots the Bill? Information Infrastructure Renewal in Ontario, 1997–2003

DAVID RAPAPORT[1]

Since the 1980s, the Ontario government has significantly altered its approach to designing and developing large-scale information technology (IT) systems for its vast administrative and policy apparatus, the Ontario Public Service (OPS).[2] There has been a shift from the development and deployment of in-house skills and expertise to the practice of procuring external skills, frequently from high-priced global IT-service-providing corporations such as Accenture and IBM. This practice often results in cost overruns, dependency, the depletion of skills and capacity within its own organization, and periodic public embarrassment (as happened with e-Health and the Integrated Justice Project in Ontario). The Business Transformation Project (BTP) in Ontario in 1997 was intended to "modernize" the software for social assistance programs and to align it with the recently implemented workfare policy of the neoliberal Mike Harris government. This chapter examines why high-level managers in the OPS contract out these skills and projects and why they continue with a process that frequently results in organizational inefficiencies and dysfunctions. This examination of the ideological and management frameworks that encourage the privatization of IT skills procurement is a construction of several themes.

This chapter begins by describing the neoliberal-informed public sector governance model, New Public Management (NPM), which encourages and facilitates the commercialization of public sector processes and goods. A brief history of computer technology in the OPS follows, with a focus on its growth in the 1980s, its expanding labour market, and the need for new technologies and new technical skills. In the 1980s, the OPS required information and communications technologies for its operational and decision-making processes. At the same time, the OPS was actively developing a costly dependency on external skills providers to build information systems. A case study of the BTP and its "partnership" with Andersen/Accenture,[3] a large corporate information services provider, is at the centre of this study. The case study provides the details for the remainder of the chapter, which analyses the mystification and misuse of technology and the triumph of neoliberal thinking in the ranks of high-level civil servants, politicians, and public policy scholars.

New Technologies, New Public Management

Two separate transformations, one technological and one ideological, informed the "modernization"[4] of the OPS in the 1980s and 1990s. Rapid IT innovation during those decades confronted management with the mammoth task of integrating administration, operations, and planning with new telecommunication, database, and digital technologies. At the same time, the OPS as a public institution was experiencing an ideological shift regarding its managerial and operational practices. Neoliberal politicians, policy analysts, and theorists viewed the privatization of government processes as an opportunity to inject "market efficiencies" into what they saw as wasteful bureaucracies. In a "reinvented government," practices are commercialized. This creates opportunities for businesses to "invest themselves" in public sector operations and processes. Market players view this as a lucrative opportunity. And so it was, particularly in the domain of IT.

The neoliberal imprimatur is discernible in the emerging investment strategies and managerial values that contributed to a "reinvented government." First, taking a cue from the financial sector, new investment vehicles facilitated the privatization of OPS operations.[5] Public–private partnerships (P3s) are in essence low-risk, high-return opportunities for large commercial investors with abundant financial resources. The BTP in the social welfare sector illustrates the intricacies and contradictions of the P3 relationship. Promoted by influential state and near-state actors, the project was both large and in the public eye, and thus very revealing. This review of the project describes the market/investment misappropriation of public sector funds under the pretexts of efficiency and modernization.[6] It also illustrates the changing relationship between the state and capital, specifically "information–knowledge" capital.

Second, the rise and consolidation of the NPM regime dictated a changing attitude towards privatization among senior-level public sector executives.[7] NPM adherents advocate a market-based approach to public sector management. They view rules, regulations, and procedures as inefficient and costly. NPM theorists developed a program that de-emphasized, even ridiculed, control processes and procedures, thus "shifting the emphasis from process accountability towards a greater element of accountability in terms of results."[8] An additional component was the welcoming of business methodologies into the public sector organization and the "lessening or the removing of differences between the public and private sector."[9]

By the mid-1990s, the OPS was well positioned for IT privatization. Government ministries required new applications, and the newly elected (June 1995) Progressive Conservative (PC) government of Mike Harris welcomed privatization and "reinvented government." *The Common Sense Revolution* was the 1995 campaign document for the Ontario PCs. Along with other neoliberal sentiments, it promoted an unambiguous "way in which government and its employees do business on a day-to-day basis, because it will demand that government does business like a business."[10]

Computer Technology and the Ontario Public Service

Like virtually all large organizations in the 1970s and 1980s, the OPS had to deal with the sudden expansion of IT. Writing in 1985, Terry Russell, Deputy Minister of Revenue, argued that the IT challenge for the public service was "to achieve results in terms of increased program productivity, and to secure the funds needed to support the habit."[11]

The rapid development of IT in those decades had a profound effect on the Ontario government and its operations. As with most new technologies, there was the fear of "not keeping up." Neglect carries substantial risks, such as falling behind so that one finds oneself living outside the network. In the private sector, falling behind translates into competitive disadvantage. In the public sector, it has reputational implications, for it means a loss of credibility in the realm of "public accountability for economic and good service."[12]

The earliest record of electronic data processing in the OPS dates back to the mid-1950s and involved an early-model computer in what was then the Department of Highways.[13] By 1970, 1,300 civil servants were working in data processing. The number of computer installations increased from two to five, in the Computer Services Centre, the Health Insurance Registration Board, and the Departments of Highways, Education, and Transport.[14]

During the 1980s, there was a correlation between the integration of IT in the OPS and the general growth in digital technology. Between fiscal year 1981–82 and fiscal year 1990–91, OPS expenditures on IT increased from $132 million to

$429 million (inflation adjusted to 1989–90 dollars).[15] Between fiscal year 1978–79 and fiscal year 1989–90, expenditures on end-user computing increased from $0 to $24 million.[16] Between fiscal year 1983–84 and fiscal year 1989–90 expenditures on personal computers increased from $4.9 million to $53 million.[17]

The growth of the labour force is another indicator of IT expansion. Between fiscal years 1983–84 and 1986–87 total IT employment within the OPS increased from 1,497 to 1,556, 1,914, and 2,401 workers respectively – an annual average growth rate of 17 per cent.[18] The strongest growth was in the systems development function, where employment increased from 392 to 713, an average annual growth rate of 22 per cent.[19] In fiscal year 1981–82, the Ontario government employed 352 IT in-house person-years and 268 IT contractor person-years for a total of 620 IT person-years. By fiscal year 1986–87 the staff numbers had increased to 1,226 in-house person-years and 318 consultant person-years for a total of 1,643 IT person-years.[20] In fiscal year 1983–84 salary expenditures (inflation-adjusted to 1990 as the base year) for in-house IT civil servants were $38.8 million and expenditures for payments to IT consultants were $14.4 million. In 1989–90 those expenditures grew to $118.3 million (a 202 per cent increase) for in-house IT workers and $50.6 million (264 per cent increase) for IT consultants.[21]

A 1985 Management Board document, "Strategies for the Management of Information Technology in the Ontario," identified three Information Age periods. Between 1950 and 1965, the so-called Accounting Era, there was a focus on payroll and accounting functions. Between 1960 and 1975, the so-called Operations Era, the focus shifted to order entry, manufacturing control, and inventory. Between 1975 and 1985, the so-called Information Era, computer processing made the transition to decision support systems, telecommunications, end-user computing and electronic mail.[22]

Substantial technological development has enhanced the information/telecommunications infrastructure in more recent times. Those developments include the expanding functionality of the internet, relational database technology, and object-oriented application development platforms. For the OPS these technologies have provided the platforms for e-kiosks, public e-governence, website interaction between citizens and ministries, integration with non-government databases, and on-line applications where citizens can access their own information. In other words, algorithms can and do replace human workers (civil servants) in administrative and bureaucratic functions.

Faced with the need to modernize government processes and integrate them with the new information and telecommunications technologies, OPS managers felt compelled to acquire skills from the growing IT service industry, which included firms such as IBM, SHL Systemhouse, Andersen Consulting, and DMR Consulting. These managers faced loud and relentless calls for privatization from neoliberal policy scholars as well as from politicians and high-level government officials,. Acceding to those calls must have seemed much simpler than resisting. In any event, P3s emerged as a prevalent response.

The Business Model – Common-Purpose Procurement

As public sector services and operational systems were privatized, new capital formations intensified the penetration by the market into the economy of the state apparatus. The P3 is a specific vehicle of privatization that suited late twentieth-century circumstances in Canada: the restructured neoliberal state, the public sector fiscal crisis, capital's need for new investment venues, the declining capacity of government to build and maintain technical infrastructure, and the growth of the management, accounting, and IT industries. Common purpose procurement (CPP) is one version of that vehicle.

According to CPP guidelines, the public sector and the private sector partners each contribute resources that are acknowledged, quantified, and tracked in a cost pool. Theoretically, each partner shares equally the risks of realizing (or not realizing) the project's potential to produce value. Each partner accesses benefits that are mutually recognized and tracked in a benefit pool. A benefit is a value that has been created as a result of the new infrastructure or innovation, such as software.[23] If an organizational efficiency or reduced cost is recognized as a result of the new information system, then it becomes a part of the benefit pool. After the benefits are quantified and attributed to the work of the appropriate partners, the ratio of the contributions by each party is calculated and the benefit is distributed between the two parties in accordance with that ratio.[24] For example, if the benefit is determined, attributed, and calculated to be $1 million and the amounts to the cost pool are 80 per cent from the private consortium or corporation and 20 per cent from the government ministry, then the former receives $800,000 and the later receives $200,000 from the benefit pool.

Compared to more traditional forms of procurement, this approach is a deeper application of the market principles and practices adopted by public sector managers. The traditional procurement method is a buyer/seller relationship in which the costs, time lines, and expectations are known by both parties. A contract describes a price for a specific product or expenditure of labour for a specific period of time. In the public sector context, the government seeks the most efficient, skilled, and cost-efficient provider for the design, construction, or maintenance of an infrastructure project.

This approach was described in the January 1997 agreement between the Ministry of Community and Social Services and Andersen Consulting for the design, construction, and implementation of the BTP. It was expected that

> both parties are entering into this Agreement on the understanding that all costs incurred by them in carrying out the Project and other amounts to which they may be entitled hereunder are to be paid from savings generated from the Project, and that while both Parties expect that savings will be achieved, there are no guarantees and neither party will be paid for any services or other costs incurred in connection with the Project until such time as benefits accrue.[25]

The benefit calculation is based on the generation and the realization of value. The difficulties lie, of course, in calculating the quantity of savings and attributing the share of savings to the correct party. In a complex government function, efficiency does not easily translate into a dollar figure. The savings resulting from fewer welfare recipients and reduced social assistance benefits might be calculable, but their attribution is problematic. Critics challenged the feasibility of objectively untangling government policy – which was to reduce social assistance rates and the number of recipients – from the administration of that policy.[26]

In 1985, Terry Russell astutely observed that "dependence on technology is a risky and expensive business."[27] This dependency is exacerbated by CPP, a model that invariably leads to a greater dependence on outside agents for technical skills and knowledge, as well as increased risk and expense.

The Business Transformation Project – Ontario Adopts CPP

In 1996 the Ministry of Community and Social Services (the Ministry) initiated the BTP (the "Project") to develop new business processes and technologies to facilitate the transformation of the Family Benefit and General Welfare Assistance programs into the Ontario Works Program and the Ontario Disability Support Program.

The Ministry finalized a CPP relationship with Andersen/Accenture on 27 January 1997 to re-engineer the IT and business systems that administered Ontario's social assistance programs. The purpose of this re-engineering project was to "develop and implement the business processes and technologies inherent in the new social assistance system that was to be put in place through the Business Transformation Project."[28]

The "Project" was conducted in the context of a legislative and policy overhaul of social assistance in Ontario. IT applications are designed and implemented within their organizational and/or ideological framework. The "Project" was a product of several features of neoliberalism and NPM: the commercialization of state processes, privatization, the restructuring of the state apparatus as a venue for capital investment, and increased precarity for the indigent as a result of a less generous and more intrusive welfare regime.

Thus, three components of neoliberalism were evident in this restructuring of the social assistance regime in Ontario. First, welfare costs were reduced by lowering social assistance rates. The Ontario government reduced social assistance by 21.6 per cent in June 1995, within two months of taking office.[29] Second, market discipline was introduced to the social assistance regime by making work and/or training a prerequisite for collecting social assistance.[30] Third, and most relevant to this study, the privatization model of CPP was utilized to redesign the IT component of social assistance delivery.

An examination of that software reveals much about the priorities and values of the Common Sense Revolution. Software applications indirectly and digitally enforce how a workplace is managed, how a business is operated, and how a social program is administered. The "Project" had features that reflected the politics of the Ontario government. In the context of this study, the systems analysts and programmers received their instructions from their employer, Andersen/Accenture. The CPP arrangement with the MCSS included financial incentives to reduce the size of the welfare bill.

Art Daniels and Bonnie Ewart were Assistant Deputy Ministers who had responsibility for the "Project." They acknowledged the intersection between software, program administration, and social policy: "The system has enhanced case management capabilities to improve current practices and streamline work for staff. The rules are built right into the system, ensuring consistent application. Enhanced eligibility and payment features will make tracking overpayments/arrears easier and ensure eligibility decisions are made more quickly and with greater accuracy."[31]

New object-oriented and Web-enabled IT application platforms had the capacity to include enhanced business functions in the software applications, allowing the "Project" to be designed with policy reforms that reduced social assistance costs by enforcing eligibility, entry, benefit, and longevity requirements. When the "Project" software application was brought into production in January 2002 it had enhanced operational features: a centralized database for direct access and update, a two-step intake process, interfaces with third-party databases for verification, interactive voice response, and streamlined case management. Two central features of the BTP application were the Consolidated Verification Process (CVP) and Change Reporting (CR). The CVP consolidated the financial review of social assistance applicants by verifying information from third-party sources; such as banks and credit agencies. CR changed the approach to reviewing case files from time-based to priority-based. The stated objectives of both were to reduce fraud and improve efficiency and accuracy. According to social policy analysts Dean Herd, Andrew Mitchell, and Ernie Lightman, the software application made things more difficult for welfare recipients. It presented "a deliberately cumbersome and complicated application process, with excessive and inappropriate requests for information, and deliberately confusing procedures."[32] For sociologist Krystle Maki, the "Project" was part of a technological assault by the state on the indigent through regulation and monitoring.[33]

Calculating the Andersen/Accenture Benefit

The "Project" was implemented incrementally between May 2001 and January 2002. In March 2002 the cost pool had total claims of $407.6 million. Andersen/Accenture's share was $253.7 million. The Ministry's claim was $153.9 million. The reported calculations in the Benefit Pool (value realized by the Ministry as a result of the "Project") produced a figure of $587.1 million, of which Andersen/Accenture received $246 million.[34]

The Anderson/Accenture claims on the cost pool were an overreach. There were severe discrepancies in charges for compensation between Ministry staff and Andersen/Accenture staff (see Table 12.1). At the same time, the Ministry's contribution to the cost pool was substantially undervalued.[35] The Ministry did not charge all of its eligible costs to project expenditures for future recovery from savings,[36] such as its $280,000 worth of programming changes to the earlier application, CIMS,[37] and the payments to other consultants for their services. Also, the Ministry did not charge for the manual review of files in Ministry offices to assess recipients' eligibility.

The 1998 Provincial Auditor's Report also pointed out that the Andersen/Accenture advantages were not limited to inflated charges for compensation and to underreporting by the Ministry. Too much of the savings realized in the provincial welfare cost reductions was credited to the "Project."[38]

Furthermore, there is no reason to believe that those inflated compensation rates were realized by the Accenture employees. In fact, the Auditor General complained that the corporations providing IT service had successfully hid their own compensation schemes behind contract privacy provisions, even though public sector salary rates are fully available to the public.[39] Also, the Auditor General reported that the partnership agreement overrode standard transparency rules in

Table 12.1. Comparison of Andersen/Accentures 1995 proposed rates with actual rates at 31 December 1997 and 1 January 2000, and with Ministry rates at 1 January 2000[40]

	Andersen/ Accenture 1995 RFP proposed hourly rates	Andersen/ Accenture December 1997 consulting rates charged per hour	Andersen/ Accenture January 2000 consulting rates charged per hour	Ministry rates January 2000
Partner/Associate Partner/ADM/ Project Director	$300–400	$530–570	$400	$75–315
Manager	$200–300	$335–472	$330	$50–180
Consultant	$150–250	$230–325	$280	$45–105
Analyst	$70–140	$105–250	$115	$35–40

Source: Auditor General of Ontario, *Annual Report* (2002), p. 263

that private contractors refused to supply information on their rates.[41] Four years later, the Auditor General's 2002 report repeated these points and questioned other aspects of the "Project." It reiterated many of its earlier criticisms: the continued advantages realized by Andersen/Accenture, the overstatement of Andersen/Accenture costs, the understatement of Ministry costs, and the overstatement of the technology's contribution to savings. The auditor also noted many technical and operational flaws in the system[42]: the payment for many out-of-scope costs to Andersen/Accenture and the weakness of technology knowledge transfer[43] from Andersen/Accenture staff to Ministry staff.[44] In a scathing critique of the "Project," the Provincial Auditor was sceptical of its contribution to the benefits realized by the "Project." Approximately 73 per cent of the benefit pool, or $427 million as at 31 March 2002, had been attributeed to the CVP. The auditor found that "its features were not being used as intended and therefore required improvements."[45]

Defending the Business Transformation Project

Government ministers, Ministry officials, and public policy academics defended the BTP on three premises: risk assumption, complexity, and the absence of required IT skills in the OPS. According to Art Daniels and Bonnie Ewart, the contract with Andersen/Accenture brought private sector knowledge of technology and experience in large-scale business redesign that the Ministry lacked.[46]

The claim of private sector knowledge and superior technological skills also arose during the hearings of the Public Accounts Committee. According to Kevin Costante, MCSS Deputy Minister (1999), the Ministry did not have the expertise or the resources. It required a private sector organization that had extensive experience providing technical and business advice around a major change such as the "Project." It also wanted a private sector partner that would share the risks, the investments, and the rewards.[47] The previous Deputy Minister (1998), Suzanne Herbert, argued that "Accenture's technical expertise in change reporting was what got us to finally implement a program that, while we knew we had to do it, we had been unsuccessful at doing it for several years."[48] Ray Hession was contracted by the Ministry to provide a third-party assessment in 1997. He acknowledged that Andersen/Accenture rates were high, "a fact obvious to anyone observing this transaction." He defended the high rates on the basis of the labour hierarchy and the quasi-monopoly of skills held by contractors and companies such as Andersen/Accenture. "Those persons do command the kind of fees that are applied here."[49]

Hession also defended the high compensation rates charged by Andersen/Accenture on the grounds of risk assumption, even "the shock (in) the differentiation between the rates in the original proposal versus those that arose in September, 1997."[50] Hession noted that the margin of profitability in consultants' rates in this industry was in the range of 25 to 35 per cent. Market logic translated into higher rates for Andersen/Accenture. According to Hession, the assumption of higher risks in 1998 meant the imposition of higher fees than those anticipated when Andersen/Accenture made its bid on the contract. Hession argued that Andersen/Accenture had the right to mitigate risk by increasing its fees.

Andersen/Accenture was "essentially banking risk in anticipation of more delay, more risk to them associated with the changes that appeared to be arising at that point, moving to different programming, different arrangements in the area of public policy, over which they have no control."[51]

Public policy scholar Sandford Borins agreed with Hession's justification for the higher rates. According to Borins, "margin banking" occurs when "the private partner earns its profit early to protect itself against future unknown risks." Like Hession, he blamed the Ontario Government for the higher risk levels and the charging of higher rates at a later date. Andersen/Accenture's reinterpretation of the contract

> ...can be seen as an attempt to minimize risk. Furthermore, Accenture would argue that, to a great extent, the risks are the result of partnering with the government. In particular, the government can delay the project if its staff are not able to perform scheduled tasks or if political decisions change the nature the task, as happened in this project. The consultant can attempt to minimize its risk in a number of ways: charging high overhead rates for its employees' time, negotiating as large a cap on payments as possible and making them immediately payable, negotiating as much of its fees as possible outside the cap.[52]

The defence of the excesses of the 'Project' was based on four points; the requirement for technological update, the lack of skills by Ministry employees, the projected savings and the need to administer the changes to social assistance, particularly Ontario Works. In December, 1998 Minister Janet Ecker argued that "the business process that supports the delivery of the welfare system is sadly out of date...and that the Ministry did not have the information technology expertise to fix the system. That's why we went through an open bidding process."[53] She argued that Common Purpose Procurement was "used by the federal Liberal government, it has been used by the New Brunswick Liberal government. It was a decision to proceed in this fashion by the previous NDP government."[54] Ecker also pointed out that "private sector companies did tend to make a profit on the work they did, otherwise they wouldn't continue in existence very much longer."[55] Minister John Baird[56] defended the 'Project' on the basis of savings. Baird cited Ray Hession as well as Hickling, Lewis and Brod "who confirmed that there are hundreds of millions of dollars of benefits to the taxpayers that will accrue as a result of the project." Baird estimated that "[we have] been able to save $66 million. By the time we're through with this project, we'll be able to save the taxpayers more than $200 million a year."[57]

That interpretation brings attention to a major difficulty with the calculation of benefits; the disentanglement of policy, economic trends and technology. Social assistance levels did substantially decrease in Ontario in the five-year period between 1998 and 2002. According to the National Council of Welfare, the number of welfare recipients in Ontario steadily decreased; from 1,091,300 in 1998 to 687,600 in 2002, about 37%.[58] Furthermore, according to data from Statistics Canada the national unemployment rate declined from 9.1% to 7.2% between 1997 and 2001. In Ontario, the unemployment rate dropped from 8.4% to 6.3% in that period, a drop that clearly diminished the requirement for social assistance.[59] The 1995 changes in social policy and the structure of federal grants for social assistance affected all provinces. It would be difficult to disentangle the decline in social assistance recipients and benefits from the complex features of the 'Project', declining unemployment rates, policy changes at the provincial level and the restructuring of grants transfers from the federal level.

Technology as Ideology

There is no question that technology provides its users with efficiencies and convenience. We produce more with less (robotics, organizational design, artificial intelligence). We write more articles in less time (word processing). We travel faster and farther (automobiles and airplanes) with more certainty (GPS). We communicate faster, wider and cheaper (skype, email, social media, Zoom, and texting). We find more information more rapidly (search engines). We shop more extensively and conveniently (eBay and Amazon).

However these efficiencies and conveniences come with costs, particularly in the deterioration of our privacy as well as in the growth of dependency. The blind faith in 'black-box' mechanisms results in over-reliance on the people and organizations with the skills and knowledge that develop and maintain these technologies. There is a long history of converting those dependencies and skills-knowledge advantages into economic and political leverage. The 'Project' described in this paper comprises one small chapter in that history.

In the late 1990s and early 2000s, Information Technology and social media corporations and consultants exercised that leverage in conduct that helped shape the future relationship between skilled digital technologists and the wider user community. Two events stand out. First, much of the world was made fearful during the late 1990s by the over-hyped Y2K bug.[60] The computer consultants and IT corporations who benefitted from the Y2K bug predicted an imminent catastrophe. According to their claims, only they can correct the bug and only with an inflated price tag.[61] Second, the Google/Facebook surveillance business model initially appeared in the aftermath of the 2000-2002 dot.com bubble burst. Google executives wanted to maintain its 'free' web search service but still required a secure revenue stream.[62] Google engineers developed surveillance software to track and store the searches of individuals producing data that became the raw material of targeted advertising. Searchers became the product.[63] Facebook adopted this business model in 2008 with the arrival of Sheryl Sandberg from Google.[64] Reckless over-spending and abandonment of oversight characterized both events. In the case of Y2K, large portions of the IT corporate and consultant sector used the threats of exaggerated embedded time bombs in their own software to drive large parts of the population into a state of fear.[65] In the Google/Facebook surveillance business model, large sectors of the population abandoned their privacy to maintain 'free' searches and social media. In both cases, the dependency relationship between citizen-users and techno-gurus and corporations was consolidated.

These technological ruses coalesced with neo-liberal ideologies in the late 20th century and early 21st century, ideologies promoted by corporate and consultant interests who stood to gain from fear and dependency. The Ontario Public Service was a prime target, as a huge largely-untapped investment gold mine.[66] The Public-Private Partnership (P3) was a promising investment vehicle that suited their objectives. Cash-starved and skills-depleted governments turned to the P3 to develop essential infrastructure. Doing otherwise was riddled with the risk of producing inferior information infrastructure and falling behind. The price of dependency seemed inconsequential in the face of that risk. Predictably the use of private corporations and consultants contributed further to the depletion of those skills.

The alignment of neo-liberal ideology, a weakened public sector, techno-dependency and an aggressive IT consultant industry sets the stage for addressing the central questions of this study. Why did managers in the Ontario Public Service privatize the development of information systems? Why did they misconstrue matters of risk, knowledge management, efficiency, dependency on external suppliers and the control of vital technological skills? Why did they delegate their management responsibility to outside contractors whose primary objectives did not include public sector responsibility or well-being?

Public Sector Administration as Ideological Battleground

The late 20th century transition to neo-liberalism had its articulation in the management of the public sector. The ideological-operational transition from Progressive Public Administration (PPA) to New Public Management (NPM) provides the background to changing attitudes towards privatization from senior level public sector managers. NPM challenged the assumptions of what political scientist Christopher Hood calls "progressive-era models of public accountability."[67] Bureaucratic controls and balances were put in place to control corruption and private-sector intrusion. "Private sector contracting leads to high-cost low-quality products because of corrupt influence or organized crime."[68] The accountability paradigm of PPA places heavy emphasis on keeping the public sector sharply distinct from the private sector with a system of procedures and rules "designed to prevent favoritism and corruption."[69] This corresponds with the growth of the social welfare state and the Keynesian demand management state of the mid twentieth century.

This PPA/NPM dichotomy had a resonance in the Integrated Justice Project, another high-priced Information Technology project. Michael Jordan, Chief Information Officer for the Ministries of Attorney General and Solicitor General and Correctional Services in the late 1990s described how the separate cultures of the two parties emerged during the planning process.[70] The corporate consortium demanded assurance that it would be adequately compensated given the risks that it was taking. The public sector party, according to Jordan, was more focused on process, accountability and governance.

Several policy analysts and scholars advocated the transition to a private sector influence in public sector management. David Osborne and Ted Gaebler promoted those principles in their influential book *Reinventing Government*. They argued that the imperative of competition enhances government operations. According to them, government officials "have discovered that when service providers must compete, they keep their costs down, respond quickly to changing demands and strive mightily to satisfy their customers."[71] Osborne and Gaebler acknowledge and applaud the "characteristic in enterprising governments as an 'investment' perspective – a habit of gauging the return on their spending as if it were an investment. This is not the way to make money; it is a way to save money. By measuring their return on investment, they understand when spending money will save them money."[72]

Osborne and Gaebler had their adherents in Canadian public policy circles. Roy Hrab described how New Public Management transformed the character of the state as a result of its relationship with capital. He argued that "the new public management is not solely concerned with more private sector involvement in the delivery of public services but also the transformation of government itself into a more business-like operational unit that is results oriented" and that "Alternative Service Delivery (ASD) planning involves private sector participation in public sector services and infrastructure provision."[73] In their 2002 book *The New Public Organization*, Sandford Borins, Kenneth Kernaghan and Brian Marson urged public sector managers to "minimize bureaucratic mechanisms and public programs by emphasizing such market mechanisms as managing demand through user fees and creating market institutions to fill gaps in the market."[74]

The potency of New Public Management ideology in the late 1990s compelled the active collaboration of high level civil servants in privatization projects, less than 20 years after their earlier counterparts expressed strong reservations about privatization.[75] A 1981 study by the Ontario Civil Service Commission,[76] "Survey: Systems Community Use of Consultants" recommended that ministries should develop plans to increase internal staffing "to achieve the ideal organization with the commitment of future Ministry cost savings because of resulting improved systems."[77] The Ontario Systems Council (OSC)[78] utilized its 1982 study, "The Systems Manpower Planning Survey," to lobby for the transfer of jobs from the unclassified service[79] and from consultants to the classified service.[80] Contrary to New Public Management and neo-liberal perspectives on private sector efficiencies, the Ontario Systems Council report argued that this de-privatization would increase productivity and savings and should be used by ministries to "help reduce the heavy backlog of new systems development facing them."[81] Clearly, the attitudes of senior public servants towards IT privatization were informed by prevailing political ideologies.

By the late 1990s, senior civil servants, cabinet ministers and public policy analysts adopted the opposite view of privatization as they expressed deference to the very high rates charged by the IT corporations in relation to public sector salaries. They argued that the private sector was assuming the bulk of the risk in infrastructure projects. Deputy Solicitor General Virginia West testified at the Public Accounts Committee that "with respect to the rates that were identified and charged by the consortium, these rates are, we think, quite reasonable and fair given the risk that the consortium is taking on."[82] Deputy Attorney General Mark Freiman described how the ministries' "goal in the negotiations is to maximize the benefit to the government and therefore to taxpayers without increasing the risk or exposure, their (service providers) goal is to minimize their risk and maximize their revenues, and they're looking for ways. We consider those ways."[83]

Private Sector (In)Efficiency

In the BTP case study, it is evident that the promised fruits of "private sector efficiency" were not delivered. If anything, privatization resulted in higher costs and the wholesale transfer of funds and skills from the cash-strapped public sector to the service-providing corporation. It is odd that the OPS adopted knowledge management (KM) policies as a template for management efficiency yet pursued a strategy of IT privatization that ran counter to those principles and efficiencies. "It involves taking a strategic approach to creating, capturing, using, organizing, sharing, preserving and maintaining information and knowledge."[84] The whole or partial surrender of methodological and technical knowledge to the corporate service providers clearly contradicts that policy, raising questions about the OPS's commitment to efficiency, as defined in its own terms.

The various incarnations of IT privatization in Ontario were manipulated by decisions made by central ministries. In the early 1980s, the Ministry of Government Services and the Treasury Board allocated sufficient funds for new information infrastructure projects, such as the Vehicle Registration Project at the Ministry of Transportation and Communications, but withheld sufficient complement to staff the projects. That discrepancy led to "body-shopping," that is, the hiring on contract of independent consultants or employees of private IT service providers to work alongside civil servants. However, by the 1990s those same central funding ministries were withholding adequate financing for huge IT infrastructure projects, such as the BTP. Given those constraints, the P3 provided a vehicle for acquiring that funding, albeit at a price. Through P3 funding arrangements, the OPS transferred to the private sector much of its capacity to develop and plan technological and organizational infrastructure. Not only did the public sector mortgage off future savings and revenue streams to the private sector party, but the private sector party was consulted in the earlier stages of the development process.[85]

After the province and the consortium signed the BTP contract in 1997, there was a three-month "planning phase" during which, according to Michael Jordan, "the ministries and consortium would establish a governance structure, the Project Management Office (PMO), develop a high-level work plan for the initiative, and prepare individual business cases for each of the projects."[86] This was a further incursion into the OPS apparatus by the private investor.[87] During the planning phase, the consortium and the ministries "jointly identify, design and implement the systems that are to achieve the desired results."[88] In other words, the private sector party participated in the development of new business processes.[89] The public sector's loss of capacity and control was exacerbated by the hiring of a consultant, at a cost of $584,000, to assist in the selection of a CPP partner for the "Project."[90] Furthermore, the OPS compromised public sector transparency in reporting to the public on expenditures and operations, raising questions about the state of public sector governance.

The Legacy of Privatization

Privatization is not simply "another way of doing business." It represents a serious disruption in the relationship between the state and capital. For much of the twentieth century the public sector has been seen and experienced as a public commons, as economic activity strictly for the sake of the public good, not for the realization of profit. Privatization entails a drift from the Keynesian welfare state regulation of capital markets towards an intrusion by capital into public sector economic activity.

IT privatization is not an "Ontario" issue. It is a Canadian issue, and it is international in scope. In 2013, the rollout of the Obamacare website was botched by Conseillers en Gestion et Informatique (CGI), a Quebec-based company. Apparently that public relations debacle did not prevent CGI from landing contracts for future public health care information projects. According to its own website,[91] CGI received contracts from British Columbia, five other provinces, the military service in the United Kingdom, and right across Europe, North America, and Australia. Other IT service companies also continue to receive lucrative contracts. Accenture won a $744 million contract from CMHC in 2020.[92] Deloitte won a $16 million contract to build the National Vaccine Management Information

Program in January 2021.[93] In 2017, Alberta Health Services signed a $459 million contract with Wisconsin-based Epic Systems Corporation.[94] In British Columbia between 1998 and 2020, expenditures on IT privatization increased tenfold from $50 million to $500 million.[95] Probably the most public debacle was the Phoenix Payroll System, a project of the Canadian public service. What started as a $70 million project in 2009 in a contract with IBM resulted in more than $1 billion in costs and $560 million in paid-out claims to employees for damages.[96]

The public sector economy is traditionally a non-market economy in which processes and products are not commodities that can be bought and sold for profit. The expanded privatization of public assets and public projects is a feature of neoliberalism. In spite of the negative impact on the public commons, public goods are readily transformed into commodities by assigning them a market value.

Political economist Ursula Huws argues that this commodification process can be regarded as kind of a "secondary primitive accumulation." In this process, activities already carried out in the paid economy for their use-value are standardized in such a way as that they can be traded for profit and appropriated by capital. This secondary form of accumulation is based on the expropriation, not just of nature or unalienated aspects of life, and not just of unpaid domestic labour, but also of the results of past struggles by workers for the redistribution of surplus-value in the form of universal public services.[97]

According to political scientist Elmar Altvater, "every good can actually become private property just by allocating proprietary rights." The privatization of public goods transforms a public service, a public good, or a public function into a commodity, a bearer of value, thus a source of profit. The power of capital to expand into all economic spheres is behind its move into state activities, including those involving internal administrative and informational activities. Altvater explains that "the prevailing capitalist tendency is the conversion of all work into work that increases surplus value."[98]

Political theorist David Harvey argues that "the conversion of public assets into private investments is a clear objective as neo-liberals are particularly assiduous in seeking the privatization of assets. The absence of clear property rights is seen as one of the greatest of all institutional barriers to economic development and the improvement of human welfare. Enclosure and the assignment of private property rights are considered the best ways to protect against the so-called 'tragedy of the commons.'" Sectors formerly run or regulated by the state must be turned over to the private sphere and be deregulated.[99]

The BTP in Ontario between 1996 and 2003 is one small yet significant component of this legacy.

Conclusion

Clearly, the BTP was not a common-purpose partnership. The objective of Anderson/Accenture was to make money. The objective of the Ministry was to develop an information system that would administer welfare reform – specifically, disentitlement, the reduction of benefits, and the introduction of market discipline through a workfare program. Ministry officials turned to the private sector to develop an information system and business procedures to achieve those results. Because of the cost/benefit structure of CPP, the private partner benefited financially from the lowering of social assistance.

If there was an unstated common purpose between the two parties, it was the further downgrading of the indigent – an economic benefit for Andersen/Accenture and a policy achievement for the Ontario government.

This account of the BTP privatization project depicts the self-fulfilment tendencies of NPM. Privatization depletes the government of technical and organizational skills. As a result, the government needs to develop and implement complex software applications without the necessary funds and resources. Risk transference to the private partners is defended, however excessive their claims may be. A clear (and expensive) indication of the strength of neoliberalism and its beneficiaries is how much they are pandered to. In his study on the BTP, David Whorley raised the "issue of differences in organizational power between public and private partners."[100]

The BTP is symptomatic of a deepening colonization of the machinery of the Ontario government by the corporate sector, based on the new relationship between capital and the state. The business sector regards the state's vast resources as a venue for low-risk investment. NPM theorists legitimize the privatization investment vehicle. In the IT sector, the technological mystique provides the background and the pretext as the public sector is compelled to develop new information/knowledge systems. After years of vilification and revenue reduction, the OPS lacks the resources, skills, and confidence to build those systems. Dependency on technology and on the firms the provide it completes the circle.

Once captivated by the skills and knowledge of the technological corporate giants, we become prey to their demands. What is inside the black box does not matter. What matters is that it works. If they tell us there is a ticking Y2K bomb in their software, we must believe them and pay them. As for the public sector managers who must build new information and governance applications, they must rely on the very high-priced skills that reside in the prestigious corporations where they migrated in previous contracts. The P3 is a system of self-fulfilment.

QUESTIONS FOR CONSIDERATION:

1. Why do neoliberal politicians and policy analysts support a market-influenced public sector?
2. How does privatization transform public services and public infrastructure?
3. Using the BTP and late-1990s social welfare policy reform as background, did the Common Sense Revolution pave the way for a "New Ontario?"
4. How did the BTP reflect and reinforce social welfare policy reform during the Mike Harris government (1995–2003)?
5. Does the public sector require the latest technological hardware and software?
6. Why would a government ministry/agency use corporate sources to construct IT infrastructure? Why would they avoid it?

NOTES

1 Before enrolling in the Canadian Studies graduate program at Trent University in 2009, the author worked for the Ontario Public Service as an IT specialist. He was also a member-activist in OPSEU for several years.

2 The Ontario government refers to the majority party or coalition that governs Ontario, formulating and implementing policy and managing the Ontario Public Service (OPS). The OPS refers to the administrative apparatus that delivers public services and public policies, by and large the several ministries.

3 Andersen Consulting was created by Arthur Andersen Associates in 1989. It became its own division within the corporation, Andersen Worldwide, operating separately from Andersen Audit. Tensions grew between the two divisions throughout the 1990s. Through an arbitration process, the two sides went their separate ways in 2000, with Andersen Consulting paying Andersen Audit $1 billion. The separation occurred about one year before Arthur Andersen was sullied with the Enron debacle. Andersen Consulting adopted the new corporate name Accenture. (Markham, pp. 204–205) By 2000, Accenture had net revenues exceeding US$9.5 billion and employed more than 70,000 IT professionals in forty-six countries. https://www.accenture.com/ca-en/accenture-timeline. The BTP contract with the Ontario government occurred during these events, starting with Andersen and continuing with Accenture. For the purposes of continuity and clarity, the name Andersen/Accenture is used throughout this chapter.

4 Modernization is an ambiguous term. It implies *progressive, improved*, and *forward-looking*. In this context and in this period, it has a different meaning. It signifies the adoption by the OPS of organizational and technical standards and practices that are deemed "current" or "up-to-date." And these "current" standards are not progressive, as we show later in the chapter.

5 After the 2008–9 financial meltdown we became aware of new and risky financial vehicles such as hedge funds, credit default swaps, and collateralized debt obligations.

6 Proponents and beneficiaries of technology have a long history of "good intentions"; collective protection (nuclear weapons), free Web search and social media access (digital surveillance), economic efficiencies (techno-induced unemployment and the gig economy), and security from technologically induced disasters (the Y2K glitch). The methods by which technical labour and skills are acquired to develop and implement public sector IT applications provide

an insight into the neoliberal influence on public sector labour markets, the public sector as an arena for low risk private investment, and the acquiescence of OPS managers to the logic of market forces.

7 Later in the chapter, we explore how senior level OPS IT executives opposed the practice of privatization as recently as the mid-1980s.
8 Christopher Hood, "The 'New Public Management' in the 1980s: Variations on a Theme" in *Accounting, Organizations and Society* 20, nos. 2–3 (1995): 93–109. This article was found in Darrin Grimsley and Mervyn K. Lewis, *The Economics of Public Private Partnerships* (Cheltenham: Edward Elgar, 2005), 94.
9 Hood, *"The 'New Public Management,'"*, 94.
10 Progressive Conservative Party of Ontario, "The Common Sense Revolution" (1994), http://www.scribd.com/doc/57099326/Common-Sense-Revolution, 16.
11 Terry Russell, "Challenges and Promises of Technological Innovations: Executive Issues," paper presented to the 18th national seminar of the Institute of Public Administration of Canada, 9 October 1985, i.
12 Information Technology Systems Steering Committee (ITSSC), "Strategies for the Management of Information Technology in the Ontario Government" (1986), 7.
13 David Rapaport, "Rewiring the State: The Privatization of Information Technology in the Ontario Public Service (1972–2003)," PhD diss., Trent University, 2015, 132.
14 Rapaport, "Rewiring the State," 132.
15 Management Board of Cabinet, "Information Technology Trends Report, 1991. Information Technology Expenditures by Ministry, 1980–1991," table 13, 18.
16 Management Board of Cabinet, "Information Technology Trends Report, 1991," 10.
17 Management Board of Cabinet, "Information Technology Trends Report, 1991," table 3, 11. (It is unclear whether these expenditures are inflation-adjusted. However, the decrease in the value of the dollar in that period would be at least partly offset by the declining costs for personal computers.)
18 Information Technology Branch of Management Board Secretariat, "Information Technology in the Ontario Government, 1985–1987" (1988), chart 3, 11.
19 "Information Technology in the Ontario Government, 1985–1987" (1988), table 4, 12.
20 "Information Technology in the Ontario Government, 1985–1987" (1988), table 12, 15.
21 "Information Technology in the Ontario Government, 1985–1987" (1988), table 7, 15.
22 Management Board of Cabinet, "Strategies for the Management of Information Technology" (1986), 1–3.
23 Clearly, it is much simpler to calculate benefits from revenue, such as in the case of the Confederation Bridge linking Prince Edward Island and New Brunswick.
24 Office of the Provincial Auditor (Ontario), 1998 Annual Report, 32.
25 Hickling Lewis and Brod Inc., "Government of Ontario Ministry of Community and Social Services; Business Transformation Project Review. Volume 1 – Summary Report to the Minister, Volume 2 – Final Report, Volume 3 – Appendices" (Ottawa, February 1999), vol. 2, p. 1.
26 Dean Herd, Andrew Mitchell, and Ernie Lightman. "Rituals of Degradation: Administration as Policy in the Ontario Works Programme," *Social Policy and Administration* (February 2005), 75.
27 Russell, "Challenges and Promises," i.
28 Office of the Provincial Auditor (Ontario), 2000 Annual Report, 259.
29 Allan Moscovitch, "Social Assistance in the New Ontario," in *Open for Business, Closed to People; Mike Harris's Ontario*, ed. Diana Ralph, André Regimbald, and Nérée St-Amand (Halifax: Fernwood Publishing, 1997), 85.
30 Moscovitch, "Social Assistance in the New Ontario," 89.

31 Arthur Daniels and Bonnie Ewart, "Transforming Ontario's Social Assistance Delivery System," *Canadian Government Executive* 1 (2002): 26.
32 Herd, Mitchell, and Lightman. "Rituals of Degradation," 76.
33 Krystle Maki, "Neoliberal Deviants and Surveillance: Welfare Recipients under the Watchful Eye of Ontario Works," *Surveillance and Society* 1–2 (2011): 52–3.
34 Office of the Provincial Auditor (Ontario), 2002 Annual Report, 35.
35 Office of the Provincial Auditor, 1998 Annual Report, 47–8.
36 Office of the Provincial Auditor, 1998 Annual Report, 34.
37 CIMS is an acronym for Comprehensive Income Maintenance System.
38 Office of the Provincial Auditor, 1998 Annual Report, 42.
39 The Integrated Justice Project was another IT P3 study that the author conducted. In 2001 the auditor requested compensation data from EDS, the private sector contractor.
40 Office of the Provincial Auditor (Ontario), 2000 Annual Report, 263.
41 In the 2002 Annual Report, the Provincial Auditor found many problems with the system as implemented. "Most service manager staff we communicated with expressed considerable dissatisfaction with the BTP, stating for example that the new system was in many respects a step back from what had been available previously and that it was essentially still a work in progress" (p. 26). "The new system did not provide service managers with accurate and reliable expenditure information" (p. 26). "The new IT system often failed to provide needed information" (p. 27). "There were unexplained errors or omissions" (p. 27). "Intake-screening units and the resultant two-step process for eligibility assessment were not meeting the anticipated objective of significantly reducing the number of lengthy in-office interviews" (p. 27). In its response, the ministry admitted that the system had been released too early. "The Ministry believes that the complex systems of this type normally require a substantial operating period in a live environment to deal with all of the complexities that are inherent in the design of such large multi-user systems" (p. 29).
42 The anticipated knowledge transfer was not sufficiently advanced, with the result that the ministry was not in a position to operate and maintain the information technology system. Instead, Accenture and other private sector consultants provided nearly all of the technical resources necessary for completing, maintaining, and operating the IT system after January 2002, at a substantial cost to the ministry. For example, Accenture services were extended from 26 January 2002 to 31 March 2002 and then to 31 May 2002 to provide technical maintenance services at an estimated cost of $5.7 million. Office of the Provincial Auditor (Ontario), 2002 Annual Report, 36.
43 Office of the Provincial Auditor (Ontario), 2002 Annual Report, 334.
44 Office of the Provincial Auditor (Ontario), 2002 Annual Report, 334.
45 Office of the Provincial Auditor, 2001 Annual Report, 84.
46 Daniels and Ewart, "Transforming Ontario's Social Assistance Delivery System," 28.
47 Standing Committee on Public Accounts, 9 December 1999, 3.
48 Standing Committee on Public Accounts, 17 December 1999, 12.
49 Standing Committee on Public Accounts, 16 December 1999, 16.
50 Standing Committee on Public Accounts, 16 December 1999, 16.
51 Standing Committee on Public Accounts, 16 December 1999, 17.
52 Sandford Borins, "Contracting and Partnerships in IT Services to Government," Report to the Panel on the Role of Government, October 2003, 34. http://www.law-lib.utoronto.ca/investing/reports/rp38.pdf.
53 *Hansard*, Ontario Legislature, 17 December 1998.
54 *Hansard*, Ontario Legislature, 17 December 1998.

55 *Hansard*, Ontario Legislature, 17 December 1998.

56 After the re-election of the Progressive Conservatives in 1999, John Baird replaced Janet Ecker as Minister of Community and Social Services.

57 *Hansard*, Ontario Legislature, 9 December 1999.

58 Those figures roughly correspond with the figures from the 2002 Auditor's Report. Between 1999–2000 and 2001–2002 (two years as opposed to five years), the number of beneficiaries in the Ontario Works program decreased from 577,983 to 412,266 – that is, by about 29 per cent. In the same period, the money expenditures for Ontario Works decreased from $1.75 billion to $1.37 billion – by about 22 per cent. Oddly enough, the administrative costs, where one would expect to see savings from the BTP, remained roughly the same, falling from $172 million to $171 million.

59 Statistics Canada, "Annual Average Unemployment Rate, Canada and the Provinces, 1976–2017," January 2018, http://www.stats.gov.nl.ca/statistics/Labour/PDF/UnempRate.pdf.

60 David Rapaport, "We've been had by Y2K doomsayers," *Toronto Star*, 10 January 2000, A11; "Doomsday Profits," *This Magazine*, May–June 1999, 15–17.

61 It is estimated that Canadian private and public enterprises spent about $15 billion on the "Y2K fix." "According to John Gantz – chief research officer at the highly regarded US analyst International Data Corp. – Canada spent more than $15 billion (US$10 billion) in the past three years on the problem" (David-Robert Loblaw, "You got conned and I told you so," *Globe and Mail*, 6 January 2000). "Some analysts are harsher about what they saw as overly generous spending, however, International Data Corp. (IDC) estimates that IS worldwide overspent by some US$70 billion. 'We spent too much on contingency, which takes in staffing and preplanning, as well as on actual remediation which I am calling the "hype tax,"' says John Gantz, chief research officer and team leader for IDCs Project Magellan Y2K analysis. Gantz adds that 'Y2K took on a life of its own through politicians, the media, and consultants.'" (Eve Epstein and Ed Scannell, "Did IS Spend Too Much on Y2K?" *IT World Canada*, 30 January 2000).

62 Shoshana Zuboff, *The Age of Surveillance Capitalism* (New York: Public Affairs, 2019), 89–91.

63 Zuboff, *The Age of Surveillance Capitalism*, 71.

64 Zuboff, *The Age of Surveillance Capitalism*, 92.

65 The threat related to the size of the year field. Until the mid-1990s, information project managers saved money by truncating two bytes from the year field. Thus, 1993 was represented as "93." The first two digits were assumed to be 19. That became a problem in the year 2000, when that configuration led to results where 1993 was later than 2000.

66 According to the 2017–18 public accounts, Ontario had $93 billion in financial assets and $154.3 billion in annual expenditures. https://www.ontario.ca/page/public-accounts-2017-18-annual-report.

67 Hood, "The 'New Public Management,'" 93.

68 Hood, "The 'New Public Management,'" 93.

69 Hood, "The 'New Public Management,'" 93–4. This transition, according to Hood, represented "a new conception of accountability, since it reflected high trust in the market and private business methods and low trust in public servants and professionals."

70 Michael Jordan, "Ontario's Integrated Justice Project: Profile of a Complex Partnership Agreement," in *Canadian Public Administration* 42, no. 1 (Spring 1999): 34.

71 David Osborne and Ted Gaebler, *Reinventing Government: How the Entrepreneurial Spirit Is Transforming the Public Sector* (New York: Addison-Wesley, 1992), 79.

72 Osborne and Gaebler, *Reinventing Government*, 205.

73 Roy Hrab, "Private Delivery of Public Services: Public Private Partnerships and Contracting-Out," report to the Panel on the Role of Government, January 2004, 14.

74 Kenneth Kernaghan, Brian Marson, and Sandford Borins, *The New Public Organization*, monographs on Canadian Public Administration, no. 24 (Toronto: Institute of Public Administration of Canada, 2000), 17–18.
75 Rapaport, “Rewiring the State,” 159–62.
76 The Civil Service Commission (CSC) was the central human resources body in the Ontario government.
77 Civil Service Commission (CSC), “The Systems Community Use of Consultants” (1981), 6–7.
78 The Ontario Systems Council (OSC), founded in 1981, was an inter-ministry committee that included directors responsible for the IT management function in each ministry of government.
79 Unclassified staff employees are civil servants hired on fixed-term contracts with few benefits.
80 OSC, “The Systems Community Use of Consultants,” 6.
81 OSC, “The Systems Manpower Planning Survey” (1982), 6–7.
82 Standing Committee on Public Accounts (Ontario), *Minutes*, 27 February 2002.
83 Standing Committee on Public Accounts (Ontario), *Minutes*, 27 February 2002.
84 “Knowledge Management in the Ontario Public Sector – A Direction Setting Paper” (March 2002), p. 4 http://www.ontla.on.ca/library/repository/mon/13000/258956.pdf.
85 This observation corresponds with the findings of Ontario’s Auditor General: “We noted that the tangible costs (such as construction, financing, legal services, engineering services and project management services) were estimated to be nearly $8 billion higher than they were estimated to be if the projects were contracted out and managed by the public sector” (Ontario Auditor General, 2014 Annual Report, 197).
86 Jordan, “Ontario’s Integrated Justice Project,” 37.
87 It also meant a deepening involvement in public policy by the private sector. When doing research in New Brunswick, Baar observed that while planning justice integration, “they were also discussing fundamental issues of the mission of the court system and figuring out ways to drive that mission, led by Andersen.” Rapaport, “Rewiring the State,” 263.
88 Office of the Provincial Auditor, 2001 Annual Report, 71.
89 Alon Peled argued that IT vendors were becoming more influential in the design of public sector operational and management processes. The IJP joint planning phase is an example of the how IT vendors “play an increasingly influential role in shaping the agenda of public IT projects.” Alon Peled “The Politics of Outsourcing: Bureaucrats, Vendors, and Public Information (IT) Projects,” *Information Infrastructure and Policy* 6 (2000).
90 Office of the Provincial Auditor, 2001 Annual Report, 87.
91 https://www.cgi.com/en/health.
92 https://www.cmhc-schl.gc.ca.
93 https://www.canada.ca/en/public-services-procurement/services/procuring-vaccines-covid19.html.
94 https://edmontonjournal.com/news/local-news/alberta-health-services-signs-459-million-deal-for-massive-new-technology-system.
95 https://blog.cleverelephant.ca/*2020/11/bc*-it-outsourcing-201920.html.
96 Beatrice Paez, “Ottawa Spent Over $560 Million on Damages Over the Phoenix Pay System, Records Show,” *Globe and Mail*, 20 December 2021.
97 Ursula Huws, “The New Gold Rush: The New Multinationals and the Commodification of Public Sector Work,” *Work Organization, Labour, and Globalization* 2, no. 2 (Autumn 2008), 1.
98 Elmar Altvater, “What Happens When Public Goods Are Privatized?,” *Studies in Political Economy* 74 (Autumn 2004): 45–57.
99 David Harvey, *A Brief History of Neoliberalism* (New York: Oxford University Press, 2005), 65.
100 David Whorley, “The Andersen-ComSoc Affair: Partnerships and the Public Interest,” *Canadian Public Administration* 44, no. 3: 323.

Part III

FAMILY

CHAPTER THIRTEEN

Families, Institutions, and the State in Late Nineteenth-Century Ontario

EDGAR-ANDRÉ MONTIGNY

Just as the state has enacted major changes in the social welfare system during the last fifty years, so the second half of the nineteenth century also witnessed a significant transformation in poor-relief policies. During this period the Ontario government came to accept a great deal of responsibility for the care of the ill, the insane, the destitute, and the dependent aged. For the most part, the government focused on providing institutional forms of care, often purposely eliminating all alternatives. By the end of the nineteenth century, however, these policies had backfired, as the absence of alternatives created an ever-increasing demand for institutional care that forced the government to re-evaluate its commitment to the various groups of dependent people who sought relief.

Rather than attempting to re-establish alternative forms of care, the government decided simply to force families to care for their dependent members. The result was a campaign to reduce the financial burden represented by social welfare responsibilities, such as institutional care, by blaming increasing costs on irresponsible families who refused to carry out their care-giving obligations. Although these policies applied to a wide variety of dependent populations, the dependent aged and their families were the most affected by changes in the way assistance was offered. By the end of the century the aged were the focus of most policy discussions. For this reason, policies affecting the dependent aged will be used as a case study to illustrate the impact of late nineteenth-century developments in Ontario's provincial welfare environment on the dependent populations who required assistance and their families.

Until the last decades of the nineteenth century, most Ontarians who required public assistance received local outdoor relief. This assistance consisted of donations of cash or of food, fuel, or clothing, provided in their own home through a combination of the informal charity of neighbours and more formal contributions from the local municipal or township council. Since most of the communities providing this relief possessed only limited resources, these outdoor relief systems were far from ideal. The assistance was rarely sufficient to do more than keep a person alive, but the system was flexible. Both the community and the local government generally understood that although families should have the primary responsibility for caring for their dependent members, particularly the aged, there was a definite limit to how much the community could expect a family to do. In most instances the community was willing to assist families with their care-giving obligations, mainly to ensure that they were able to continue in their task.

By the end of the nineteenth century these communal relief systems had, for the most part, ceased to function. While population growth and migration may have weakened community bonds, it appears that the demise of local communal relief systems was due mainly to provincial policy changes that favoured, promoted, and even enforced a shift towards institutional modes of care. Although the full impact of this shift would not be felt until after Confederation, the legislative framework that allowed for it began to develop in 1837.

Before 1837 there were no institutional modes of relief to turn to. By mid-century, even, only Toronto and Kingston were served by institutions that accepted aged people and were capable of housing more than a handful of people.[1] Twenty years later, there were still fewer than twenty private charitable homes and only sixty-one public institutions in the province; of the latter, fifty-three were prisons. It was not until the 1880s that institutional care became the standard form of public assistance available for the aged. The opening of the Toronto House of Industry in 1837 and the Toronto Lunatic Asylum in 1838 had marked the first steps in a process that eventually eliminated outdoor relief, emphasized the notion that the aged were properly a familial as opposed to a community responsibility, and forced the aged poor who could not be supported by kin to segregate themselves from their communities in order to receive public assistance.[2]

A prime motive behind the initial construction of institutions for the care of the poor and disabled was cost. In the 1830s, massive immigration, combined with economic upheavals and transformations, contributed to a substantial rise in unemployment and poverty in the province. The cost of providing relief to the masses of needy people escalated beyond the means of the private charity organizations that had previously managed to care for these people.[3] District magistrates also found that they lacked the funds to distribute outdoor relief – such as pensions or grants – to all the aged and needy persons who petitioned them for aid.[4] It was in this environment of fiscal desperation that the provincial government found itself compelled to assume responsibility for the destitute.[5]

The government could have provided financial assistance to private charities and local district and municipal councils, allowing them to continue providing outdoor relief to the poor and to people who were caring for the ill and the aged. Instead, the provincial authorities decided to focus poor-relief efforts on establishing and encouraging the use of institutions. This shift, Richard Splane elaborates, was largely due to the strength of the movement towards institutional care – and away from outdoor relief – that was gaining ascendancy on both sides of the Atlantic.[6] Moreover, as the incidence of destitution increased, so too did popular distrust of the poor.[7] As has frequently been explained, in the nineteenth century, poverty and misfortune had come to be blamed on personal faults. Hence, charity organizations felt not only that generous assistance would harm the poor but also that the poor would take advantage of any assistance that was too easily available.

After 1837, private charities increasingly came to rely on government funding, and municipal and district councils found themselves unable to cope with the demands for assistance they received. Under these circumstances the provincial government established a spiralling degree of control over public assistance for the poor.[8] As more control over poor-relief policy was placed in the hands of the government, institutions began to dominate larger segments of the poor-relief landscape.

Legislation, such as the 1838 House of Industry Act, placed the authority over institutions in the hands of the province, thus reducing the influence of local authorities over poor-relief decisions.[9] After 1834, various municipal incorporation acts defined the responsibilities of town councils towards the poor solely in terms of institutional care, and in some cases specifically limited the provision of poor relief to that type of care.[10] In addition, the 1849 Municipal Incorporation Act, while it granted some authority relating to poor relief to county councils, restricted municipal powers by putting in question the right of municipalities to tax themselves for the support of the poor.[11] Together, these actions effectively removed control of poor-relief efforts from local authorities. Henceforth, the poor were increasingly subjected to the dictates of provincial policy.[12]

The province, meanwhile, refused to acknowledge any responsibility for outdoor relief, even after 1871, when the government had ample revenues to fund such activities.[13] Instead, it chose to limit spending to the construction of provincial institutions, such as asylums, and to assist private charity groups that emphasized institutional care.[14] In fact, the inspector of prisons and public charities, J.W. Langmuir, declared that communal relief systems promoted ineffectual "unsystematic charity." He advocated the elimination of outdoor relief as a means of encouraging the construction of county houses of industry, which he felt should assume the burdens of municipal poor relief.[15]

The government formalized its dedication to institutional care in 1874 with the passing of the Charity Aid Act, which focused provincial funding for private charity organizations on those that provided institutional relief. In a move that put municipal outdoor relief efforts at a distinct disadvantage, provincial assistance was, in most cases, allotted solely on the basis of the number of people resident in any given charitable institution. Institutions were not eligible to receive funding for any people they decided to assist outside the establishment.[16] As one report noted, "outdoor-relief seems to go for nothing, and the government assistance is given exclusively on the number of permanent paupers assisted. The more permanent these are so much greater the public help!"[17] This trend was of particular significance to the aged. One 1879 report declared that of the applicants for outdoor relief in Toronto, a majority of the women were beyond middle age and nearly all the men were old and infirm.[18] It was clear that any reduction in outdoor relief payments would affect the aged more severely than any other group and force them, more than any other group, into institutions.

Although provincial policies were increasingly obliging aged people in need of public assistance to enter institutions, few institutions were constructed specifically for the elderly. At the same time, specialized facilities were established for other groups, such as children and women.[19] As the size of the aged population in Ontario grew rapidly, and at a much faster rate than the number of beds in public institutions, most non-specialized institutions, such as Houses of Industry, "swiftly found themselves depositaries for the decaying and the decrepit."[20]

Local authorities, meanwhile, could do little to combat the trend towards institutionalization. Mary Stokes has outlined how municipal authorities found that, after the passing of the Municipal Corporations Act, or "Baldwin Act," in 1849, their autonomy in many areas was reduced. Increasingly municipalities came under the power of the central authorities, especially in regard to their spending. Using the powers granted to them by the Baldwin Act, provincial authorities regularly imposed new responsibilities – and expenses – on municipal authorities without offering any compensation.[21] These duties put additional pressure on municipal finances and left even less money available for discretionary spending such as on outdoor relief.

With little influence and limited finances, the counties and municipalities of the province found themselves less able to distribute funds within local communities either to help people care for those who could not care for themselves or to provide pensions that would enable people, many of them aged, to remain independent. As non-institutional relief received no support from provincial authorities, county and municipal councils were forced to seek cost-saving methods of assisting the poor. In this regard, Langmuir and other provincial officials promoted institutional relief as being more effective and less costly than outdoor relief. Hence, the goal of reducing municipal poor-relief spending became a strong catalyst for constructing institutions.

Although some council members supported the construction of houses of industry because they genuinely believed the poor would be better cared for in an institution, most focused their arguments on the possibility that "establishing a Poor House would be a great saving to the county."[22] Almost all the surviving municipal material on houses of industry is concerned with the costs of running the institutions, not the quality of care being given to the residents. In the counties of Kent, Leeds and Grenville, and Lanark, for instance, most house of industry correspondence was concerned with calculating how much each municipality owed the county council for housing indigents, and with expelling paupers from municipalities that did not contribute to the institution's expenses.[23] Caring for the poor became a second priority to ensuring that all "unjust impositions on this charity" were avoided.[24]

It is evident that municipalities envisaged institutional relief as a replacement for, rather than a compliment to, outdoor relief. Municipalities frequently reduced their spending on outdoor relief drastically once institutional forms of relief were made available. In Brantford, for example, both the county council and the municipal council distributed funds for outdoor poor relief. Once municipal funds were diverted towards maintaining a house of industry, however, local assistance to groups providing outdoor poor relief was reduced or halted. As the *Brantford Courier* reported, the construction of the house of industry would "remove the Ladies Aid Society from any further responsibility in the matter of charitable donations, at least as far as the city grant is concerned."[25] Once the Ladies Aid Society municipal grant was eliminated, the society was no longer able to assist the local poor by distributing outdoor relief. As a result, people previously being supported in their own homes were forced to enter the newly constructed house of industry.

Two investigations of municipal poor relief were carried out in 1874 and 1888. These reports indicated that the number of people assisted by municipal relief declined between the two dates, despite the massive population growth experienced in most of the province.[26] In addition, reports of the sums local county councils gave to each pauper during the same period reveal a general trend towards smaller disbursements. While the provincial average for outdoor relief payments was $10 per head in 1874,[27] once a house of industry was opened in 1883, Welland County officials usually granted no more than $6 in aid to any one person.[28] Other reports suggest that by the 1880s, most municipalities distributed between $3 and $8 to each person on their charity list.

It also appears that certain councils were less willing to provide aid to people who were caring for others. In Lanark County in 1862, for instance, five people received between $20 and $76 each as compensation for caring for indigent or insane individuals.[29] By the 1880s there is little record of similar payments being made. These changes were certainly related to the establishment of county houses of industry, most of which were constructed after 1874. Although the information available from newspaper reports and municipal records is far from conclusive, the existing evidence suggests that the amounts given as outdoor relief to the poor were most likely to decrease in localities that had recently constructed some type of institution to care for the poor.

Lincoln County, for instance, paid between $5 and $10 a month in outdoor relief to each person on its destitute and insane charity list. In this manner the county council distributed an average of $1078.65 a year on outdoor relief between 1882 and 1886. In 1887, however, the council spent only $381 on poor relief, and after 1888, spending fell to less than $100 a year.[30] The main reason for this drastic drop in outdoor relief payments was the opening of the Lincoln County House of Industry in January 1887. Between 1884 and 1887, council was assisting between fourteen and twenty people a year. Between 1888 and 1891 it assisted only one (see Table 13.1). With the opening of a local institution, Lincoln County's recipients of poor relief were cut off from local relief payments, and no new names were added to the list.

In effect, the county ceased to distribute outdoor relief once the house of industry was constructed. And, because the house of industry was the only source of public assistance available to them after 1887, people requiring support had no choice but to enter the institution. Although the existing records list most persons entering the institution only as "an indigent," Mrs Bowman, Elizabeth Howell, and Mrs Spears, who were receiving outdoor relief before 1887, were listed as having been sent to the house of industry between January and June 1887.[31] It is likely that several of the other "indigents" were also people formerly on the outdoor relief list.

The house of industry was expensive to build, but the institution's daily maintenance did not cost the county much more than it had previously been spending on outdoor relief. It also allowed the county to support a few more people. According to the 1891 census, the institution housed twenty-one people. More significant, however, while the province limited the amount the county could spend on outdoor relief by refusing to offer provincial grants for such activities, the county received a $4,000 legislative grant in 1891 to assist it with the expenses of maintaining the poor in an institution.[32] Financially, institutionalizing the poor made a great deal of sense for Lincoln County. Little mention is made, however, of the quality of care people received in an institution that was constructed specifically to save money.

Table 13.1 Outdoor relief payments in Lincoln County between 1882 and 1891

	1882		1884		1885		1887		1891	
Recipient	Jan.	June	Jan.	June	Jan.	June	Jan.	June	Jan.	June
Terryberry						*				
Caugh										
Shelley										
Isaubacker										
Burghart										
Gregory										
Howell										
Simmerman										
Bowmann										
Spears										
Cook										
Wilcox										
Finn										
Wilkinson										
Dolan										
Mellow										
Slough										
Turl										
Schwabb							*			
Osbourne										

Source: AO, RG 21, Municipal Records, Lincoln County Clerk, Treasurer's Letterbook: see expenses for Insane and Destitute, 1884–91.
Notes: ▬ length of time person was receiving outdoor relief.
* died.

As municipalities provided less assistance for the non-institutionalized poor, and as people caring for the elderly found it more difficult to receive assistance from their local municipalities, it became increasingly difficult for aged persons to remain in their own homes and for other people to provide care for them. Although municipalities never completely halted outdoor relief payments, evidence indicates that the portion of the population assisted by such funds declined drastically during the last quarter of the century. As a result, outdoor relief became a less viable means of support for the aged.[33]

This process was exacerbated by the fact that the immediate impact of the government's refusal to recognize outdoor relief as a legitimate subject of provincial support was to encourage the construction of new institutions at the expense of local communal relief systems. There were only four publicly assisted charity establishments in 1866, but thirty-three in 1893. By the end of the century this number had risen to nearly one hundred.[34] Since municipalities reduced or even eliminated their outdoor relief efforts once an institution was established nearby, each additional institution led to a further reduction in the amount of outdoor assistance available to the aged poor and their families. Basically, the provincial government's insistence on putting all public funds into institutional care effectively eliminated outdoor relief as an option for anyone needing more than temporary aid.[35] The disappearance of outdoor aid forced many persons who required long-term assistance, which was often the case with the elderly, to enter institutions.

Although anti-outdoor-relief policies in Ontario were not enforced as brutally as those in other jurisdictions, such as England and some US states, the provincial government's refusal to assist people outside institutions still forced many aged people to enter houses of industry, houses of refuge, or old age homes. The insistence that institutions were the only way to provide public assistance to the needy increased the number of people requiring institutional care by eliminating other viable options.[36] It also created undue hardships for many poor people and their families because, although the provincial policies eliminated most alternative forms of relief, the government failed to provide sufficient institutional facilities to accommodate all the people who needed care.

While government policies directed all those in need of assistance towards institutions, the province did little more than encourage counties to provide adequate facilities to accommodate all those in need. Often outdoor relief was eliminated before anyone could ensure that the people who had formerly been assisted in this manner could be accommodated in an institution. In some municipalities, for instance, outdoor relief had been limited to people requiring temporary or emergency assistance before a house of industry had been erected to care for those individuals who needed more long-term support.[37]

Once again this problem developed largely because of provincial funding policies. Although the province agreed to assist establishments that provided institutional care for the poor, it did not, until 1890, provide funds to assist counties with the cost of constructing institutions. Houses of industry saved counties money in the long run, but they were usually expensive to construct. Lincoln County, for example, spent almost $28,000 over a four-year period to construct its house of industry and prepare it to receive residents.[38] This cost deterred many counties from establishing a house of industry, while others reduced outdoor relief expenditures in order to accumulate funds with which to commence constructing an institution. The overall effect of these trends was to limit the amount of support available to the aged and their families outside institutions, without ensuring that institutional care expanded to keep up with the demand for care. Hence, in public institutions, there were never anywhere near the number of beds required to accommodate all the aged people who needed care.[39] As a result, the institutions that did exist were forced to adopt rigid entrance requirements and to refuse entry to anyone who did not meet the specifications.[40]

Despite restrictive admission policies, the aged came to constitute an ever increasing segment of the province's institutionalized population. Provincial policies left elderly people with nowhere else to go. Forcing the aged into institutions, however, had far more serious consequences than merely removing them from their homes and segregating them from their communities. The institutionalization of the aged population affected not only how the aged lived but also how they were perceived by institution administrators, government officials, and the public in general. Institutions focused attention on the desperate and needy elderly, thereby making the most decrepit and dependent segment of the aged population the most visible.[41] As a result, an image of the elderly as incapacitated, unproductive, and helpless was created and confirmed.[42] Thereafter, officials and administrators often implemented policies for the aged that were based on this impression.

These policies, which tended to have a significant impact on the future of many aged people and their families, rarely bore any relation to the experience and situation of the vast majority of the aged population that resided outside institutions. However, government officials, who tended to formulate policies based on what was visible to them, rarely saw the vast number of non-institutionalized aged people. They knew only the elderly who filled the rooms and corridors of the province's houses of industry and houses of refuge.

When only the institutionalized aged were considered, it appeared that a large portion of the elderly population was destitute and without families able or at least willing to care for them. Despite attempts to limit the number of aged people admitted into institutions, both the number of elderly within their walls and the portion of the institutionalized population they represented grew steadily during the final decades of the nineteenth century. It appeared to officials that there was no end to the number of aged people who needed public care. The main explanation officials could find for this increase in the number of aged people needing care was that families and communities were using institutions as a means of evading their obligations towards the aged. The fact was, however, that regardless of how many elderly people crowded into the province's institutions, they were never more than a small minority of the total aged population.

Nevertheless, it was possible for government officials to argue that families were institutionalizing the aged at an ever increasing rate during the 1890s. At the beginning of the decade, the elderly formed a minority of the population within institutions. By the end, this was no longer the case. The number of old people in institutions grew and came to form a large portion of the province's institutionalized population. The fact that the institutionalized elderly population was increasing during a period when the government was building more institutions, many specifically designed to shelter aged people, added further weight to the government's argument.

Census reports indicate that in 1891 there were 152,488 persons in Ontario who were over the age of sixty. In September of the same year, the inspector of prisons and public charities reported that there were 1,260 beds in government-funded charitable institutions likely to shelter aged people.[43] In addition, there were 3,318 beds in the various provincial asylums for the insane. Altogether, there was potential accommodation for 4,478 aged persons. Even if every one of these beds had been occupied by someone over the age of sixty, this number would have represented only 0.3 per cent of the province's total aged population.

In fact, the number of elderly people in these institutions was much smaller. At no time, for instance, did the aged constitute more than 20 per cent of the insane asylum population. Between 1888 and 1896 the elderly represented only 15 per cent of the total number of people admitted to all provincial asylums.[44] Also, as Table 13.2 shows, an 1889 investigation indicated that aged people accounted for fewer than half of the residents of the province's county houses of industry.[45] The number of old people in Ontario's institutions in 1891, then, represented no more than 2 per cent of the total aged population of the province.

Over the course of the 1890s, however, the aged population within public institutions grew to the point that by the turn of the century, the elderly constituted approximately 80 per cent of the population of Ontario's houses of refuge and 70 percent of the province's county houses of industry.[46] This increase occurred even though the decade was a period of institution building. The number of houses of refuge, county houses of industry, and other publicly funded charitable institutions in the province rose from sixty-two at the beginning of the decade to nearly one hundred in 1901. In houses of refuge alone the number of beds almost doubled, increasing from 1,260 to 2,268 (see Table 13.3). In total, provincial institutions could accommodate as many as 4,485 persons by the end of the century.[47] At the same time, almost 2,000 new beds were added to provincial asylums for the insane. This figure represented an 80 per cent increase in the number of aged people who could potentially be housed in a public institution. When the aged population of these institutions grew despite their enlarged capacity, it is not surprising that government officials concluded, at least initially, that the aged were being sent to institutions at an ever increasing rate and that the burden on the public treasury would soon become unbearable. In truth, this was not the case.

The problem was that the new accommodations in provincial institutions came nowhere near to keeping pace with the even more dramatic increase in the total number of aged people in the province. Between 1891 and 1901 the number of people over the age of sixty grew by more than 30,000, to a total of 182,735. Even

Table 13.2 Number of aged people reported as resident in houses of industry in Ontario, 1889

County	Total inmates	Aged inmates	% aged
Brant	60	unknown*	unknown*
Elgin	109	46	42.2
Lincoln	52	19	36.6
Norfolk	75	19	25.3
Middlesex	127	60	47.2
Waterloo	118	72	61.1
Welland	59	35	59.3
Wellington	77	54	70.1
York	157	78	49.7
Total	774*	383	49.4

*Brant was not included in the total calculations.
Source: *Ontario Sessional Paper*, no. 61, 1889.

Table 13.3 Number of beds available in Ontario's houses of refuge, 1889–99

Year	Total number of beds
1889	1,260
1891	1,349
1893	1,706
1895	1,917
1897	2,120
1899	2,268

Source: AO, *Annual Report*, 1889–99, "Report of the Inspector of Prisons and Public Charities upon Houses of Refuge."

though the number of beds increased during the 1890s, provincial institutions could still shelter no more than 3 per cent of Ontario's aged population.

Thus, while officials blamed the ever increasing numbers of old people located in public institutions on the willingness of families to abandon the aged, the portion of the total aged population being sent to institutions changed little between 1891 and 1901. Notwithstanding government reports, even if the aged had filled every bed in every institution, the vast majority of them would never have seen the inside of one of these places. Rather than any deterioration of the sense of familial responsibility towards the aged, a rough estimate indicates that for every aged individual in an institution, there were at least thirty-three others being cared for by kin or living on their own.

Nevertheless, in a manner that would be echoed a century later, Ontario officials acted on the assumption that aged people were being institutionalized needlessly. They argued that "the number of aged and infirm people who can work very little or not at all is not a large one. The number of those of this class who have no friends to support them," and hence may become candidates for institutionalization, "is still smaller."[48] While this may have been true, the government assumed that anyone who had "friends," a term that referred to relatives as well as non-related people, was not a candidate for institutionalization. Thus, even the minority of the aged population that sought the shelter of institutions because they truly needed assistance often found that restrictive admission policies denied them access to care. If one could not enter an institution, there were, by the 1890s, few alternative forms of care available. One observer commented that it was often so difficult to obtain admission to a house of industry that it "was easier for an aged infirm pauper to get into jail than into [an] institution."[49]

It was common, for instance, for institutions to adopt policies that denied access to institutions to any person from outside the region served by the establishment. People who lived in counties that had no house of industry were left with no place to go. Institutions also demanded that residents be easy to care for and that they behave appropriately. These requirements affected the aged more severely than others because the elderly frequently suffered from illnesses or senility, which made them difficult to care for or troublesome. As one house of industry inspector pointed out, the aged residents were "in many cases most trying patients."[50]

It was the aged with kin, however, who suffered the most from the fact that, in attempting to limit the cost of maintaining people in public institutions, government officials tried to reduce the number of elderly persons eligible for institutional care. As a result, institutional administrators expressed the view that the aged were not proper candidates for institutions. Instead, it was argued, they should be cared for by their families.[51] In a manner that reflected the new emphasis on the self-supporting family and the increased responsibility that late nineteenth-century society placed on individual families with regard to the care of dependent individuals, officials began to argue that if public shelters were made accessible, they would "take away ... the filial obligation for the support of aged parents which is the main bond of family solidarity."[52]

In the name of supporting familial responsibilities, institution officials often tried to locate relatives in order to force them to take responsibility for their aged kin. Often when relatives were discovered, inmates were discharged into their care as they were no longer seen to be fit candidates for public charity. This was the case with one destitute old woman in Ottawa who had found refuge in the Protestant Orphans' Home. As Lorna McLean explains, the woman had lived in the home for one year when it was discovered that she had two sons to support her. She was dismissed and sent to her children.[53] Unlike communal support networks, which recognized that families were not always able to care for an aged relative without assistance, institutional caregivers demanded that families look after their aged regardless of their financial ability. These tactics ignored the fact that a person whose relatives were able or willing to provide care would probably not have arrived at the institution.

One could argue that the government officials could not possibly have been unaware of the inaccuracy of their statements. Surely they should have realized that the very economic crisis that was causing bureaucrats to advocate cost-cutting measures was also having a major impact on the working class. As David and Rosemary Gagan explain, during the 1890s, working-class incomes and standards of living fell, causing individual and familial distress.[54] The government itself reported in 1895 that, "owing to the general depression in business and consequent hard times during the past years, the number of paupers has greatly increased."[55] The same downturn certainly had an impact on families' ability to care for dependent relatives.

The government appears to have ignored these facts. Legislators and bureaucrats rarely understood that many families, especially among the working class, lacked the physical or financial resources required to care for an aged relative. Government officials, for the most part, belonged to elite families, and they tended to base their ideas about family care on the situation found in their own homes. As with many of the traditional views of family life in the past, the ideal image of family care for the aged was the reality only for wealthy families. This image included a large family that was able to "easily manage" the care of an infirm, ill, or senile older person because several kin were available to help with those relatives who required assistance. Also, unlike the majority of the population, the wealthy could provide care for ill kin without worrying about the financial strain such actions might place on the family.

It could also be argued that, despite their personal biases, government officials could not ignore the needs of working-class voters. It appears, however, that the working class could be effectively ignored by bureaucrats and legislators alike. Universal manhood suffrage was a recent innovation in Ontario, Oliver Mowat having made the reform only in 1888. Despite this increased voting power, as well as the activities of working-class political movements, it appears that the interests of working men were systematically neglected by Liberals and Conservatives alike. The Knights of Labor tried to elect working-class men to the legislature to ensure that it would "take some interest in the welfare of the class,"[56] but this working-class political movement was organized in only a few locations and was never very successful. By 1894 the Knights were described as "devastated."[57] Although the activities of the some working-class political groups forced Conservatives and Liberals to pass certain pieces of labour legislation, they achieved little with regard to improvements in social policy or social spending.

Ignoring both the circumstances and the needs of the dependent elderly and their working-class families, the government instead pursued policies that were more in line with the views of middle-class reformers. They emphasized the theory of the ideal family and were also concerned with moral, urban, and social reform. In almost all their activities, these reformers displayed a distinct lack of understanding or sympathy for the poor. When working-class families failed to live up to middle-class notions of acceptable behaviour or to carry out what the reformers felt were their proper responsibilities and obligations, many reformers, instead of reconsidering their assumptions, advocated the use of state intervention to force the lower classes to conform to the reformers' ideals.[58]

In the realm of caregiving for the dependent aged, government policy-makers appear to have accepted the basic premise of the reformers' arguments, perhaps because it was a convenient justification for cost-cutting measures. Social spending, which represented 32.4 per cent of provincial expenditures in 1893, made up only 14.7 per cent of spending by 1911.[59] Since over 70 per cent of the social welfare budget consisted of expenditures on institutions, especially mental hospitals and government-funded charitable institutions such as county houses of industry and houses of refuge, these cuts could not help but affect the availability and quality of institutional care for the aged. To justify these cuts the government argued it would be better for everyone if families carried a larger share of the burden. In making this demand on families, however, the state was enforcing a notion of the ideal family that was completely beyond the capacities of most of the families that would be affected by government social policies or institutional regulations. It was also based on a distorted image of the past. Institutional adminstrators ignored the fact that families that may previously have been able to provide care for the aged, largely because they were assisted by their community, were no longer able to do so because their communities could not assist them. Provincial policies had worked to eliminate municipal outdoor relief for the poor and aged, and this reduced the effectiveness of the communal support networks that had accompanied these formal relief systems. Institutional care was established to replace community relief, but various fiscal restraints, combined with ideologies of familial responsibilities, prevented many needy aged people from gaining access to these institutions. Large numbers of elderly people were left dependent on relatives who were totally unable to care for them. Hence, the combination of the province's preference for institutional care and the emergence of an ideology that emphasized the self-supporting family left many aged people with no form of support. These casualties of "the great social transformation" usually found themselves destitute and homeless. As one late nineteenth-century Canadian social commentator noted, "we build large buildings to accommodate unfortunates, but we initiate no system whereby the aged and the needy will be able to live without begging."[60] When begging failed, many homeless old people found themselves imprisoned in local jails.

Nineteenth-century laws in Ontario permitted county magistrates to confine homeless old people in the local jail as vagrants. In earlier decades the aged formed only a small portion of jail inmates; by the later decades of the century it was clear that, in many jails, elderly vagrants comprised a large portion of the inmates. The increase in the number of old people in jails was almost certainly a direct consequence of two trends: provincial policies that limited public relief for the aged to institutional care, and an increasing emphasis on familial responsibility for the aged that limited the access of the elderly to institutions.

In the 1890s, determining the boundary between state responsibilities and family obligations towards the aged became a key element in provincial policies concerning the institutionalization and support of Ontario's elderly people. Basically, the government faced a situation that was very similar to the problem facing the province's legislators today: how to deal with a rapid increase in the demand for institutional accommodation for the province's aged population during a period of fiscal restraint. The nineteenth-century solution to this problem was to blame the situation on the irresponsibility of families. The government insisted that the increasing number of aged people in institutions was obvious evidence that families were shirking their duties and attempting to force on the state responsibilities that properly belonged to the family. In response, the government simply restricted the admission of old people to institutions and declared that the care of the aged was a family obligation. In defining the boundaries between family obligations and state responsibilities in this manner, the Ontario government argued that, before the creation of provincially funded institutions, the aged were the sole responsibility of their families. It was not unreasonable, therefore, in a time of fiscal crisis, for the state to request that families once again assume the responsibilities they had formerly carried out:

> In fact, the provincial government was doing more than merely returning to the family those responsibilities that it had previously carried out. Traditionally, rather than being solely a family responsibility, the aged had been viewed as a legitimate concern of the entire community. Friends, neighbours, and members of the community in general assisted families in the performance of their caring functions. When the Ontario government argued that the care of the aged was the obligation of the family,

> it was, in fact, attempting to redefine the boundary between state responsibilities and family obligations in a manner that placed a far greater share of responsibility on the family than had previously been the case.

Defining the care of the elderly in this manner, however, allowed the government to justify its refusal to increase public expenditures on institutional accommodation for the dependent aged. By promoting an image of families shirking their duties and foisting their aged on the state, the government generated sympathy for policies that were really intended to reduce the state's responsibility for the poor and reduce social welfare spending. Similarly, the high levels of poverty, destitution, and dependency reported among Ontario's elderly population at the end of the last century were often the result of changes in government policy and the large-scale transfer of the state's responsibility for the aged to the family. Turning government responsibilities into family obligations may have reduced social welfare expenditures, but these policies often ignored the fact that families were rarely able to bear the degree of responsibility now placed on them. The result was widespread suffering among both the dependent aged population and their families.

QUESTIONS FOR CONSIDERATION:

1. What was local outdoor relief in Ontario in the late nineteenth century?
2. How did the aged fit into Ontario's institutions according to Montigny?
3. How did the state treat the aged by the end of the nineteenth century, in terms of institutional care?
4. Were families able to meet the needs of the aging population in need of care in these times?
5. By the end of the nineteenth century, provincial institutions could no longer accommodate the aged? Why?
6. Compare and contrast Ontario's welfare state in the late nineteenth century with Struthers's description of it in the early twenty-first century.

NOTES

1 Lorna McLean, "Single Again: Widow's Work in the Urban Family Economy, Ottawa, 1871," *Ontario History* 83, no. 2 (1991): 127.

2 Allan Irving, "The Master Principle of Administering Relief: Jeremy Bentham, Sir Francis Bond Head, and the Establishment of the Principle of Less Eligibility in Upper Canada," *Canadian Review of Social Policy* 23 (1989): 16–17; see also Rainer Baehre, "Paupers and Poor Relief in Upper Canada," *Historical Papers* (1981): 79.

3 Baehre, "Paupers and Poor Relief," 59.

4 See David Murray, "The Cold Hand of Charity: The Court of Quarter Sessions and Poor Relief in the Niagara District, 1828–1841," *Canadian Law in History Conference* (Carleton University, June 1987): 201–38; and Ruth Bleasdale, "Class Conflict on the Canals of Upper Canada in the 1840s," *Labour/Le Travailleur* 7 (1981): 14.
5 For evidence of a similar financial crisis in local poor relief in the US, see Raymond Mohl, "Three Centuries of American Public Welfare, 1600–1932," *Current History* 65 (1973): 8.
6 Richard Splane, *Social Welfare in Ontario, 1793–1893* (Toronto: University of Toronto Press, 1965), 70.
7 See Joan Underhill Hannon, "Poor Relief in Antebellum New York State: The Rise and Decline of the Poorhouse," *Explorations in Economic History* 22 (1985): 234.
8 For reference to this process in England and Europe, see J.S. Zainaldin and P.L. Tyor, "Asylums and Society: An Approach to Industrial Change," *Journal of Social History* 13 (1979–80): 40.
9 Baeher, "Paupers and Poor Relief," 75.
10 Splane, *Social Welfare in Ontario*, 72, 74.
11 Splane, *Social Welfare in Ontario*, 74.
12 Elizabeth Wallace, "The Origin of the Social Welfare State in Canada, 1867–1900," *Canadian Journal of Economics and Political Science* 16 (1950): 384; see also Philip Lee and A.C. Benjamin, "Intergovernmental Relations: Historical and Contemporary Perspectives," in *Fiscal Austerity and Aging: Shifting Governmental Responsibility for the Elderly*, ed. Carroll Estes and R. Newcomer (London: Sage, 1983), 60.
13 Splane, *Social Welfare in Ontario*, 12.
14 Kenneth Bryden, *Old Age Pensions and Policy Making in Canada* (Montreal and Kingston: McGill–Queen's University Press, 1974), 22.
15 Splane, *Social Welfare in Ontario*, 109.
16 Splane, *Social Welfare in Ontario*, 104; see also Carole Haber, *Beyond Sixty-Five: The Dilemma of Old Age in America's Past* (Cambridge: Cambridge University Press, 1983), 85.
17 City of Toronto Archives (CTA), SC 35, series H, "Report on Asylums and Hospitals," *Globe*, 6 February 1877.
18 "The Charity System," *Globe*, 24 December 1879.
19 Stormi Stewart, "The Elderly Poor in Rural Ontario: Inmates of the Wellington County House of Industry, 1877–1907," *Journal of the Canadian Historical Association* (Charlottetown, 1992), 224.
20 Andrew Scull, *Museums of Madness: The Social Organization of Insanity in Nineteenth-Century England* (London: Allen Lane, 1979), 40.
21 See Mary Stokes, "Local Government in the Shadow of the Law: The Municipal Corporation as Legal Actor in Canada West/Ontario, 1850–1870" (unpublished paper, University of Western Ontario, 1987), esp. 28–32 and n70; see also Stokes, "Petitions to the Legislative Assembly of Ontario from Local Governments, 1867–77: A Case Study in Legislative Participation," *Law and History Review* 11, no. 1 (1993): 169, 176.
22 Archives of Ontario (AO), RG 21, Municipal Records, Ontario County Clippings Album, June 1878.
23 AO, RG 21, Municipal Records, series F-1886, Raleigh Township, House of Industry Reports; RG 21, Municipal Records, Lanark County, House of Industry Management Board Minutes; RG 21, Municipal Records, series F-1740, Leeds and Grenville, January 1893; RG 21, Municipal Records, series F-1740, box 16, file 4, Leeds and Grenville, 1857.
24 AO, RG 21, series F-1740, 1883, file 111B, Leeds and Grenville.
25 "Ladies Aid Society," *Brantford Courier*, 19 January 1887.
26 Splane, *Social Welfare in Ontario*, 109.
27 Splane, *Social Welfare in Ontario*, 109.

28 See *Newmarket Era*, March–April 1883; *Brantford Daily Courier*, 20 December 1888; in the fall of 1887, the Burford Town Council gave out $123, an average of $5 per person.
29 *Perth Courier*, 7 January 1862.
30 AO, RG 21, Municipal Records, Lincoln County, Clerk Treasurer's Letterbook: see payments for Destitute and Insane.
31 Ibid.: see expenses for the Industrial Home, 166, 466, and 468.
32 Ibid., 1882–93; House of Industry, Expense Book.
33 This trend was discovered in Philadelphia by Haber, *Beyond Sixty-Five*, 85; for England, see Zainaldin and Tyor, "Asylums and Society," 40.
34 Splane, *Social Welfare in Ontario*, 84.
35 CTA, SC 35, series H, *Globe*, 12 October 1877.
36 Andrew Scull, "A Convenient Place to Get Rid of Inconvenient People: The Victorian Lunatic Asylum," in *Buildings and Society*, ed. A.D. King (London: Routledge and Kegan Paul, 1980), 39; see also J.B. Williamson, "Old Age Relief Policies prior to 1900: The Trend Towards Restrictiveness," *American Journal of Economics and Sociology* 43, no. 3 (1984): 369–84; and Benjamin Klenbaner, "Poverty and Relief in American Thought," *Social Services Review* 38 (1964): 399.
37 AO, RG 21, Municipal Records, Ontario County, Newsclippings Album, June 1877.
38 AO, RG 21, Municipal Records, Lincoln County, Clerk Treasurer's Letterbook.
39 Bryden, *Old Age Pensions and Policy Making in Canada*, 35.
40 Stewart, "The Elderly Poor in Rural Ontario," 35.
41 Stephen Katz, "Alarmist Demographics: Power, Knowledge, and the Elderly Population," *Journal of Aging Studies* 6, no 3 (1992): 213.
42 Carole Haber, "The Old Folks at Home: The Development of Institutional Care for the Aged in Nineteenth-Century Philadelphia," *Pennsylvania Magazine of History and Biography* 110, no. 2 (1977): 249; see also Haber, *Beyond Sixty-Five*, 126.
43 See AO, Annual Report of the Inspector of Prisons and Charities for the Province of Ontario (Annual Report), 1891. Beds in institutions such as orphanages, lying-in hospitals, Magdalene asylums, schools for the deaf and blind, and reformatories were excluded from this total, given that they were unlikely to house older individuals.
44 Annual Report, 1897.
45 See *Ontario Sessional Papers*, no. 61, 1889.
46 See Annual Report, "On Houses of Refuge for the Province of Ontario," 1896; and D.C. Park and J.D. Wood, "Poor Relief and the County House of Refuge System in Ontario, 1880–1911," *Journal of Historical Geography* 18, no. 4 (1992): 446.
47 Annual Report, 1901.
48 CTA, SC 35, series H, "Provision for the Poor," *Globe*, 20 October 1877.
49 "Remodel It," *Evening Star*, 20 September 1897.
50 AO, RG 21, Municipal Records, series F-1551, Brant County, Correspondence, 2 January 1905.
51 See Ann Shola Orloff, *The Politics of Pensions* (Madison: University of Wisconsin Press, 1993), 163–6, for an example of how this sentiment became embedded in relief practices. See also Diane Matters, "Public Welfare Vancouver Style, 1910–20," *Journal of Canadian Studies* 14, no. 1 (1979): 11.
52 Judith Husbeck, *Old and Obsolete: Age Discrimination and the American Worker, 1860–1920* (New York: Garland Press, 1989), 170.
53 McLean, "Single Again," 144.

54 David Gagan and Rosemary Gagan, "Working Class Standards of Living in Late-Victorian Urban Ontario: A Review of the Miscellaneous Evidence on the Quality of Material Life," *Journal of the Canadian Historical Association* (1990): 180.

55 *Ontario Sessional Papers*, no. 11, "27th Annual Report on the Common Gaol, Prisons and Reformatories," 1895, xii.

56 Gregory Kealey and Brian Palmer, *Dreaming of What Might Be: The Knights of Labor in Ontario, 1880–1900* (Toronto: New Hogtown Press, 1987), 206.

57 Kealey and Palmer, *Dreaming of What Might Be*, 247.

58 See Marianna Valverde, *The Age of Light, Soap, and Water: Moral Reform in English Canada, 1885–1925* (Toronto: McClelland and Stewart, 1991), introduction.

59 Allan Moscovitch and Glenn Drover, "Social Expenditures and the Welfare State: The Canadian Experience in Historical Perspective," in *The Benevolent State: The Growth of Welfare in Canada*, ed. Allan Moscovitch and Jim Albert (Toronto: Garamond Press, 1987), 18–19.

60 Norman Patterson, "Canadian People, A Criticism," *Canadian Magazine* 12 (1899): 135.

CHAPTER FOURTEEN

"A barren cupboard at home": Ontario Families Confront the Premiers during the Great Depression, 1929–39

LARA CAMPBELL

On 3 October 1933, Mr. T. Frith of Pembroke, Ontario, wrote his fourth of six letters to Premier George Henry. Unemployed and supporting a family, he unsuccessfully petitioned Henry for a job:

> I am getting fed up with everything. It looks strange to me men that never did anything for the Government can be holding down permanent jobs and the likes of me face poverty ... I would just like too [*sic*] know how you would like it yourself if you fought 3 1/2 years for your Government ... do you think you would be getting a fair deal if they wouldn't give you a little work to keep your wife and family.[1]

Unemployed citizens of Ontario wrote thousands of similar letters to Premiers George Henry and Mitchell Hepburn during the Great Depression. In 1931, an estimated 18 per cent of wage earners in the province were officially unemployed, and by 1935 in some cities between 33 and 45 per cent of the population relied on relief.[2] At the beginning of the Depression, social welfare programs in Ontario were under provincial jurisdiction and limited in scope, consisting mainly of Mothers' Allowance, Workmen's Compensation, and a means-tested federal Old Age Pension. With no system of unemployment insurance, unemployment relief in the 1930s was a poorly resourced and complex tripartite system funded by the federal and provincial governments and administered by the municipalities. Until 1932, the federal government funded public works projects. But Prime Minister R.B. Bennett was preoccupied with preventing deficits, and the expense of public works convinced him to transition to a system of federal transfer grants for direct relief. This system continued, albeit with increased federal control over protocols, under the Liberal government of William Lyon Mackenzie King.[3] As a result of the belief that generous social welfare would undermine the work ethic, the unemployed were expected to be destitute in order to quality for relief. Relief payments were managed differently in each municipality across the province and could be paid in cash, kind, or vouchers.[4] Relief policies prioritized married men, leaving unemployed women to rely on private charity or family support, and unemployed unmarried men on the federally funded relief camps scattered across the country and the province.[5]

In response to high unemployment and inadequate relief policies, many Ontario citizens wrote directly to the premiers of Ontario. Some letters consist of criticisms of government policy, complaints against relief recipients, or economic solutions to the Depression, but most are requests from unemployed, white, working-class men and women for employment or financial aid. The only Canadian study looking at similar sources is *The Wretched of Canada*, Michael Bliss and L.M. Grayson's collection of letters to Prime Minister R.B. Bennett published in 1974. The auth"rs note that these letters were written by those whose lives were "a single-minded struggle for survival" and show that Canadians "had too much discipline, too much individualism ... too little political sophistication to fight back in a radical protest against a whole economic and social system."[6] Some letters were indeed desperate pleas for help, but they are better understood as a form of expressive politics – an attempt to engage public officials, participate in political dialogue, and assert the right to a public voice.[7] The rich historiography of the Canadian welfare state has been crucial in tracing the origins and functions of social welfare, but a focus on political institutions can overlook what Eric Strikwerda calls the "resistance and agency" of unemployed people and relief recipients, who played an important role in welfare state development.[8] Taking these letters seriously challenges the assumption that political engagement is best understood by looking for mass public protest or engagement in formal political parties. Most unemployed people in Ontario were involved in neither, but they spoke back to local and provincial authorities and developed complex understandings of entitlement and worth in order to demand more from the state.

Letter writers believed that as citizens, they and their families had a right to economic security. As people attempted to influence government policy and make claims on the state, they engaged in the work of defining citizenship, both its meaning and its limits.[9] A proper citizen had a strong work ethic, ideally was married and raising a family, fulfilled normative gender roles, and was white and of Anglo-Canadian background. Letter writers explicitly used the language of citizenship, a powerful word connoting "respect, rights, and dignity," to argue that the government should take the problems of unemployment and poverty seriously.[10] Echoing what T.H. Marshall defines as "social citizenship," writers understood themselves as members of a larger community who were entitled to claim a central place in the social and economic order and to make demands on the state for economic security and comfort.[11]

Linda Gordon and Nancy Fraser argue that social welfare policy is based on the principles of contract and charity. They define charity as a handout symbolizing dependence, or "a gift on which the recipient had no claim," whereas a contract is associated with rights and dignity.[12] Feminist theorists and historians have argued that this opposition between contract and charity is a gendered one that creates a two-tiered welfare state intended to uphold the traditional family model of the male breadwinner and the dependent female homemaker. Programs that serve a mainly female constituency, such as Mothers' Allowance, more closely resemble charity-based programs because they are low-paying, stigmatizing, and based on the applicant meeting a standard of moral propriety. Programs that are based on male patterns of labour force participation, such as Workmen's Compensation and Unemployment Insurance, are contract-based, less stigmatizing, and more generous.[13] These tensions between charity and contract are encountered throughout most social welfare programs and policies in Canada. But instead of thinking about charity and contract as dichotomous or binary categories, it is more productive to see them as existing on a spectrum of entitlement: where a particular claimant fits themselves (or others), or where they are situated by the state, is mediated by a range of factors, including gender, marital status, race, and nationality. It is important to remember that even programs aimed at the "most deserving" incorporate concerns over upholding the work ethic and preventing the "undeserving" from receiving aid.[14] Furthermore, social welfare programs developed in this period were restricted to "British subjects" and excluded many racialized groups from eligibility. Recent immigrants who became dependent on public relief could be deported by the federal government. Indigenous people with status under the Indian Act could apply for relief, but their eligibility was determined directly by Indian Agents rather than by municipal or provincial regulations. Many of these exclusions continued into the post-war period and were incorporated into social welfare programs that claimed to be "universal." Whether social welfare should be temporary and minimal, or a "guarantee of a decent standard of living, economic security and honorable entitlement" remains a topic of debate in twenty-first-century policy development.[15]

Drawing on ideas about what constitutes expressive political engagement, along with emotional histories of pride and shame, this chapter argues that letters written by breadwinners, mothers, veterans, and Canadians of British background found the gendered duties of respectable manhood and womanhood, the value of hard work, and patriotic service to the nation to be powerful ways of understanding their relationship to one another and to the state. It is important to think about the "voice" that letter writers adopted as they engaged with public officials, paying attention to the style and expression used to make an argument, demand, or authoritative assertion.[16] While some of the language is deferential and rests on traditional values of service and duty, it also incorporates newly developing ideas about entitlement to non-stigmatizing and state-sponsored welfare. These letters show us that disenfranchised people believed they had a right to challenge governmental failure and claim entitlement to jobs and economic security, and that they were neither submissive nor accepting of poverty and unemployment. The thousands of letters received by federal and provincial governments demanding that the state protect its citizens, along with ongoing relief protests and other forms of unrest, helped shift the government towards a more interventionist and rights-based welfare state, albeit one that was fraught with tension about the limits of entitlement and that never adequately redistributed wealth.[17] A broad consensus of public opinion slowly developed around the belief that the shame and stigma of charity-based unemployed relief no longer remained acceptable.

Feeling Human: Men and Unemployment

Mass unemployment – both currently and in the 1930s – was an economic problem with profound social and gendered repercussions. Men's status and sense of dignity has long been intricately bound together with paid labour and the ability to work.[18] In the 1930s, having a job was understood as crucial to feeling fully human, and a central way for men – especially married men – to embody the hegemonic cultural ideas regarding responsible masculine citizenship, pride, and self-worth.[19] Because the stereotype of the lazy, unemployed worker persisted in this period, unemployed men carefully pointed out their strong work ethic, their desire to stay active rather than "idle," and their willingness to perform any type of labour for pay.[20] It is "not the ambition of any red-blooded human being," wrote H. Foate to Hepburn, "to spend his best years living on charity."[21] In contrast to the pride associated with work, unemployment and the spectre of relief evoked feelings of shame: both exposed men's dependence and placed them "out of place" in relation to the cultural expectations of manhood.[22] "I haven't asked for any relief of any kind yet," wrote one man to Premier Henry in 1933. "If I had to do that it would break my heart, all I want is some work to make my own Living."[23] When men wrote the premiers about their broken hearts, they were expressing the magnitude of loss, fear, and shame that accompanied unemployment: the way they deeply felt the "blow" to their pride brought on by the inability to "make their own way" and support their families; the instability and dependence that came from poverty and "living on the charity of others"; the overwhelming sadness that came from pretending "everything is fine" and hiding joblessness and debt from their loved ones.[24] The "emotional regimes" of a given period are described by historian William Reddy as powerful systems that valorize, uphold, and reinforce social norms. [25] The language of pride and shame was so deeply felt because of the long-standing cultural association of masculinity with self-reliance, breadwinning, and pride of work.

Individual emotions of shame were shaped by these cultural ideals of masculinity, but they also took on meaning within a relief system designed to differentiate between the deserving and undeserving poor. Policies were shaped by the assumption that generous social welfare would encourage men to claim benefits they did not "deserve." Ontario relief recipients were expected by municipal authorities to give up so-called luxuries, a common expectation in shame-based and stigmatizing social policies throughout the twentieth century: items such as liquor permits, telephones, radios, and cars all had to be relinquished.[26] Cities found ways to remind relief recipients that they could not be trusted to be honest about their need, and to ensure they remembered they were under public surveillance. Some cities symbolically criminalized men on relief by forcing them to register at the local police station or requiring them to take an oath before officials, testifying to their unemployed status. In 1932, the city council in the Northern Ontario town of Timmins voted to publish the names and addresses of relief recipients in the newspaper each month.[27] Most relief applicants were carefully scrutinized by investigators, who were known to search food cupboards to ensure that families were actually hungry, and they were compelled to demonstrate they did not have excessive amounts of food, fuel, or clothing.[28] But relief recipients were also judged by members of their own communities, who observed their behaviour and activities and threatened to report them to city council or the provincial government.[29] Relief was particularly stigmatizing because it was linked to receiving charity and was associated with feminine "weakness" and dependence in contrast to the masculine resilience associated with work. Reports from social service agencies and family court records in Ontario bear out the gendered tensions that developed when unemployed men went on relief and, in many municipalities, were subject to investigations by white-collar female relief workers.[30]

As much as unemployment was felt as a loss of status and relief experienced as shameful, these feelings were tempered by the powerful sense of masculine entitlement to work. Men did not feel"that it was shameful to remind the government of its responsibility to help them find work, consistently reminding the government they were "entitled, deserving and in dire need of work."[31] The state, men declared, had an obligation to help them fulfil their manly duties, as it would "lift a man up to be given work instead off [*sic*] charity."[32] The commonly used phrase "no fault of their own" resonated so strongly in the Depression because it allowed men to interpret unemployment as a condition imposed by a mass economic breakdown rather than solely as a personal failure. Unemployment is a persistent feature of modern capitalism, but surveys from the early 1930s suggest it was experienced by a wider range of men, including those who had once enjoyed some degree of economic security, as the Depression continued and they "exhausted" all other means of support.[33] Both men and women believed that as breadwinners, married men were most entitled to and deserving of paid employment.[34] Men articulated their demands for jobs through a discourse of independent breadwinner status, claiming that they had never before needed help, and insisting that they desired employment rather than relief. As one man pointed out, "I love to work ... but, if I work or run the race, I want to win some sort of prize."[35] The ideal prize was a family wage that was high enough to allow a man to support a family, including a dependent wife and children. The family wage ideal crossed class and political divides and was a powerful value shared by working men, organized labour, and middle-class social reformers.[36] For married men, masculinity and self-respect were linked closely with the right to work and the ability to support family dependents. Even though a family wage was only a reality for a minority of male workers, the belief that a husband and father was the main contributor to the family economy remained a powerful ideal. As one unemployed man stated: "I respectfuly request that the Government will give me the opportunity to work ... and provide fully all that is needed for the support of my wife and child ... for whose welfare, both the Government and myself are legally and morally responsible."[37]

These values were underpinned by relief and employment policies across Ontario, which gave priority to married men and excluded both unmarried men and most women from relief. These exclusions, however, ignored a more complicated reality: unmarried men and women were often responsible for supporting parents, siblings, or members of an extended family, and many widowed or separated women were household heads in desperate need for work or relief.[38]

Men argued for entitlement on the basis of their experience and identity as men, but these rights were articulated not just from their economic position as a breadwinner and provider. Men's rights as wage earners drew strength and power from their role as husbands and fathers, and their letters referred to the emotional trauma they suffered when they failed to meet the expectation of being a good provider. By the interwar period, fathers were expected to remain the main breadwinners but also to take on more active and involved roles with children.[39] Although most keenly expressed by middle-class experts, these idealized norms of compassionate and loving fatherhood were valued among workers as well, who saw the role of fathering and the duty of breadwinning as crucial to the survival of the working-class family unit.[40] Mass male unemployment provoked a powerful individual and collective emotional response. To see one's children hungry was a visible and painful reminder of a father's failure as a provider, and a psychological challenge to the duties associated with respectable fatherhood.[41] Men feared for the health and well-being of their wives and their children, worried about the potential separation of their families, and struggled mightily to support a wide range of family members, including children, parents, and siblings. They shared some of their deepest fears with the premiers, telling them they were writing through "tears" and were sick with anxiety and fear of showing their loved ones "how much pain I am in and how bad I feel."[42] They feared the loss of their homes and worried that their children would be placed in institutional care.[43] Family court records from this period are replete with fathers whose families came under the purview of the court system when they kept their children home from school because they were ashamed by their inadequate clothing and their lack of shoes.[44]

These individual feelings of failure, sadness, or despair could become motivators of collective action and were understood by state authorities as a potential threat to a social order that could no longer reward men for fulfilling the expected roles of husband, father, and provider. "You can readily understand a hungry man," claimed Sam Harris, president of the Navy League, "especially if he has children, is dangerous. Holdups, robberies, purse-snatchings, porch-climbings, and other things, might easily happen."[45] Men drew on their role as fathers not just to ask for work, but to demand it as men and as fathers: to remind the government that the stability of the state and the security of the family were intricately bound together. "It will be a strong man patriotically who this winter will drown out the cries of his children for bread with the strains of The Maple Leaf Forever," claimed one unemployed veteran.[46] Another unemployed man told Hepburn: "We hear our little ones crying for many things that they cannot have under this wave of charity, they do not get enough to eat and they have to starve and suffer these evictions ... and see Bailiffs throwing their home on the street their toys and Belongings can you wonder why men are clamering [*sic*] for a Revolution."[47]

These reminders to the state were not just rhetorical flourishes empty of material meaning. The Ontario government, for example, expected municipalities to require married men to "work" for even meagre amounts of direct relief, and the public nature of that work exposed them to the judgment of the wider community.[48] But what in some circumstances was experienced as shame could in others be interpreted as an injustice best addressed through collective action.[49] In some Ontario communities with high levels of unemployment organizing, such as Oshawa, Guelph, Long Branch, and North and East York, anger at the injustice of unemployment and at the low maximum relief rates set by the provincial government was collectively turned against municipal and provincial authorities. Organized unemployed called for relief strikes, occupied relief and council offices with their families, and occasionally undertook symbolic "hostage takings" of municipal councillors or relief officials to demand increased relief rates, better-quality food, or more choices in relief vouchers.[50] That these events were covered with a degree of sympathy by local media suggests that such demands had widespread support, especially as the Depression wore on with seemingly no end in sight. The argument that the state's fundamental responsibility was to protect families from instability created a powerful demand for more expansive, state-supported social welfare. Certainly, the development of post-war social welfare programs can be interpreted as part of the Cold War project to bolster heterosexual family life and to introduce a level of stability that would protect the state from socialist pressure. The powerful rhetoric of post-war welfare programs, and Unemployment Insurance and Family Allowance, were rooted in the demands of Depression-era families for their right to protection by the state.[51]

Keeping Body and Soul Together: Militant Mothers

Women wrote to the premiers as frequently as men, but the basis of their arguments for entitlement differed. While men consistently referred to their status as breadwinners, women were viewed primarily as wives and mothers – dependents of men – who had no rightful claim to paid labour, especially when male unemployment was so high.[52] But women spoke through the language of rights and entitlement even though such rights were not based on their position in the market economy. As wives and mothers, they demanded help on behalf of their husbands' and families' well-being and independence, and like men, they viewed the family as a self-supporting unit that "ideally was free from dependence on charity. They were careful to point out the respectable status of their families and their husbands' strong work ethic. "We want work not charity" was the refrain from women as much as unemployed men.[53] When Mrs. Alice Bouton wrote to Henry to criticize his unemployment policies, she expected him to provide "work to keep us human"; by this, she meant a job for her husband so that he could support her and their large family.[54] Women made indirect claims on the state rooted in their position as wife, mother, and dependent, asking for jobs on behalf of their husbands and aid for their children in order to maintain the pride and security of the family.[55] "My husband feels terrible he loves his family, is willing to work hard," wrote a mother of seven whose university-educated husband lost his job as a salesman. Her husband, and many other men, she claimed, were "people who have always paid their way people unaccustomed to hardship [and] are losing everything they ever worked for through no fault of theirs."[56] Male breadwinners claimed a more direct form of entitlement predicated on a broad public consensus around their right to paid employment. But women found ways to argue for their right to economic security even within the framework of a familial status that defined them primarily as dependents.[57]

Although the family wage ideal excluded women from an inherent right to paid labour, women drew on the rights associated with it to criticize the impact of inadequate unemployment and relief policies. As one woman wrote: "It is almost winter and our men have had no work for ages and we have no winter clothes and no prospects of any my own children have no clothes ... Its work we want not relief. We don't our living [*sic*] for nothing we want work and lots of it."[58] Women insisted on their children's need for adequate food, clothing, schoolbooks, and medication, reminding the premiers that their husbands required jobs to provide these necessities. The Depression drove home the disparity between idealized prescriptions for motherhood and the reality of taking care of a family on a limited budget. "The situation we mothers are up against," wrote Mrs. Wallace Gow to Henry, was kitchens with "barren cupboards" and husbands with empty "lunch pales [*sic*]."[59] The pride many women felt in their ability to "make do" – to stretch low wages and creatively care for their families – was increasingly challenged as the 1930s wore on, as hunger pressed closer, and as household budgets were pushed to the limit.[60] As women's ability to manage households grew increasingly constrained, they politicized the rhetoric associated with the family wage and its accompanying obligations of motherhood.[61] A letter signed by the "mothers of Sturgeon Falls" illustrates women's ability to make collective demands on the state as wives and mothers:

> There are many fathers without work, some with only three days a week. Fathers have these young, unemployed men to care for … As a father, Hon. Sir, you will understand the situation, we mothers are up against, who have our young sons on our hands, who cannot get employment ... the people will need relief money, or some

means given by the Government that the people may have a way of living to keep body and soul together.[62]

This rhetorical framing was powerful in part because of the cultural weight and emotional norms associated with caregiving and motherhood. But this language was also powerful because married women had few options to make their case for economic security outside of heterosexual marriage and family units. Men in Ontario were considered the household head and responsible for the family's economic support and survival. Most municipal policies excluded a woman from applying for relief unless she was a widow or could prove that she had been legally "deserted" by her husband. And even in cases of marital separation or desertion, before women could receive relief, they were expected to prove to officials that they had searched for their husbands and attempted to force them to provide support or apply for relief on their behalf.[63]

Reflecting how economic desperation could turn the shame of unemployment into broader demands and collective action, wives and mothers sometimes expected men to protest against the unemployment that made it difficult to manage the household. One woman from Welland observed "there are millions of men driven to being red. A man can stand a good deal but when his wife and children suffer if he is a man he becomes desperate."[64] This rhetoric was in the tradition of "militant mothering," in which mothers demanded more work and better social welfare to support husbands.[65] When men protested against low wages or inadequate relief, their wives clearly framed those actions within the proper responsibilities of manhood. After the arrest of Stratford relief strikers in 1936, one of many wives wrote to Hepburn in protest against the state's actions: "Surely it "is no crime to ask for more food that our children may not suffer from malnutrition."[66] Another wife asked the attorney general and the premier, "Why should our children and I be denied having a good husband and father in our home just because he protested against the low standard of relief?"[67] The powerful belief that real men provided for a family regardless of the cost echoes the chants of Long Branch mothers who urged male relief workers to go on strike by exhorting them to "be men" and to "stand by their families."[68] The arguments made by women on behalf of their families were rooted in deeply gendered roles, but their actions demonstrate that they did not see themselves as passive victims.

Women with husbands could make claims on the government based on the powerful demand of a family wage. Women who were deserted or widowed also used the language of entitlement to claim the right to Mothers' Allowance. By the 1920s, many provinces in Canada had introduced an allowance or pension intended to provide support for mothers without male breadwinners, although eligibility requirements differed across provincial boundaries. Letters indicate that many women understood Mothers' Allowance as a form of entitlement, adopting the language of contract to clothe their claims in a discourse of rights that validated their needs as legitimate entitlements tied to motherhood.[69] This argument was grounded in the demands for a pension or an allowance that had emerged as first-wave feminists earlier in the century had criticized women's dependence on men. "To raise a future Canadian in the way he should be raised," claimed one widow, "is an important and full time job, enough responsibility for any woman however strong, without the added burden of trying to find a job."[70] Women drew on the gendered expectations of womanhood to legitimate their requests and to demand recognition, arguing that the state owed them support in return for fulfilling their roles as mothers.[71] A deserted wife whose remarriage disqualified her from a veteran's pension drew on her status as a mother and the language of service used by veterans, claiming, "at the same time after I have struggled to raise my boys up to manhood the Government would expect my boys to step out and do their share to protect the country should a war break out; that go [*sic*] to show how much respect the Government has for the citizens of the country."[72] Women protested when allowances were cut off or denied, contacted local Mothers' Allowance Boards, and wrote to politicians. "Why do innocent children have to suffer the loss of a good home," asked one woman, "when we are Canadians, and our parents before us."[73] While not always successful, their determination indicates that women were serious in attempting to force the state to recognize their maternal concerns and duties.

Programs like Mothers' Allowance emerged from coalitions built by Christian reformers, women's organizations, suffragists, and occasionally union leaders, but there was little agreement about how generous such a program should be. Some feminist activists – and often the women themselves who applied for a pension – had hoped for a pension that would acknowledge women's household and mothering duties with a wage high enough to support them and their children without having to take on low-paid work. But all provinces set allowance amounts far too low to support a family, fearing that generous benefits would encourage women to abandon their marriages. Such programs were also designed to differentiate between the deserving and undeserving and to exclude those who did not meet certain requirements. Ontario's program was restrictive, ensuring that the allowance did not go to women who had children outside of marriage, were divorced, or had only one child. Recipients had to be "a fit and proper person," and either be a British subject or the wife/widow of one. The program excluded many racialized women, and while Indigenous women with status under the federal Indian Act were technically eligible, they were subject to decisions made by local Indian Agents.[74] And even if the limited payment received was welcome, the program regulated women's intimate lives by making their eligibility dependent on meeting high standards of moral propriety and respectability, including proper housekeeping standards and clean and well-behaved children. Sexual standards were of particular concern to investigators, and many women were cut off from the allowance after being accused of immorality.[75] But even those recipients who were accused of impropriety drew on the rhetoric of those reformers who had originally envisioned the allowance as a payment that recognized women's important reproductive labour.[76] And by drawing on their status within the Anglo-Canadian community, women could strengthen and bolster their claims. A woman accused of moral impropriety for keeping a male boarder in her home unsuccessfully protested the removal of her allowance by claiming, "I am a member of the Church of England and a conservative and I am trying to bring my children up right."[77] In some cases, however, being a good mother was enough to maintain the allowance, even in the face of sexual scandal. A woman from Toronto, whose application for Mothers' Allowance was rejected because she had two children by a man who turned out to be a bigamist, appealed successfully, saying: "I am a Canadian girl born and raised in Toronto and I am a Mother. I think I am deserving of that allowance."[78] Like most women who wrote to the premiers, single mothers believed that they and their children were entitled to economic and family security.

All these mothering claims were strengthened by the enfranchisement of white settler women who were British subjects. Such women had won the provincial vote in Ontario in 1917, and suffrage allowed them to participate more widely in the political sphere, voice opposition to the government, demand political accountability, and threaten to withhold their vote in the next election. As one woman admonished Henry after writing him three times in vain, there was "one vote here the last time and will be three this time if i get no help i give none."[79] As Linda Gordon points out, when women made such demands they were rejecting charity, "inventing rights," and claiming the status of rightful citizen.[80] Their demands for respectability and security should be recognized as a crucial factor in transforming state obligations for social welfare.

Respectable Citizens of "Canadian Birth"

Letter writers used the discourse of national identity to place themselves, along with the politicians they were addressing, within a collective, albeit narrowly defined, Canadian identity. If a nation is an "imagined community," then it is crucial to understand how conceptions of national belonging were imagined and expressed at the popular level.[81] Anyone who was white and of British heritage was a true Canadian and was demonstrably worthy of financial aid and economic justice. Those who were "Canadian by Birth" and more specifically, of British Anglo-Canadian heritage, were seen as truly deserving citizens of Canada.[82] To letter writers, the United Empire Loyalists and the early pioneers symbolized the belief in an organic community in which generations of Canadian settlers were linked together in the industrious labour of building up the Canadian nation. An unemployed man on the verge of foreclosure wrote to Henry to ask for help in saving his family's home: "My wife is a Canadian of three generations back and myself I am forty-five years in Canada a British subject at that."[83] United Empire Loyalist "stock" was a signifier of status to both men and women, and both Conservative and Liberal supporters.[84] One woman explicitly linked the Hepburn government with "pioneer British stock" from "the Stirring days of Alexander McKenzie."[85] Women also drew on their status as members of the Anglo-Canadian community to argue for greater recognition and entitlement, and for a stronger position on the spectrum of charity and contract. This reflected the language and work of women's organizations in the period, which also harnessed women's claims to greater rights and recognition to their role in building and contributing to a white settler society.[86] Genealogy was a calling card and a signifier of status. "I am no foreigner," wrote a widow who was facing foreclosure. "I was born in Ontario from parents that [were] also born in Ontario. My grandfather was a U. E. L. my grandparents on my mothers side were Irish. My husband was also a good Canadian born in Canada from English blood."[87] Another woman wrote: "Are we not true, loyal Canadians from the same descent as your wife Mrs. Henry. Her ancestry [*sic*] Laura Secord was mine also as well as Sir Allen McNab and the other faithful early settlers."[88] Mothers who had been deserted could call on their Anglo-Canadian background to more forcefully argue their status of respectability and right to economic security. A woman who was turned down for Mothers' Allowance wrote to Henry to complain: "We are respectable citizens of Canada and have been for generations back. I am bringing up my family deasent and respectabel [*sic*] and educating them the best I can ... I feel I have been dealt out of my rights by some-one who thinks it there [*sic*] duty to save government money."[89]

Anglo-Canadian identity was a powerful way for the unemployed to claim respectability and to make demands for economic justice. But the narrow definition of a true Canadian excluded the non-Canadian born and "foreigners" who were not of British background, and who were less able to demand the benefits claimed by those considered full citizens.[90] "Is there a chance," asked one unemployed man, “for a good honest Canadian Citizen to make an honest living for himself and Family ... Why do our Governments ... permit our own Canadians to be shut out and all classes of foreigners placed in their positions.”[91] Writers complained with bitterness and hostility that “foreigners” were taking away Canadians’ rightful place in the labour force and stealing potential opportunities. As one unemployed woman stated: “It is impossible for a single man, during the last five years, to have any hope of marriage ... It is the foreigner and the Jew who are taking our trades and work from us, who can afford to marry and start a home.”[92] While letter writers imagined that the “other” was unfairly taking work or welfare more rightfully belonging to certain Canadians, in reality, a range of racial and ethnic exclusions were already encoded into social welfare policy. Municipalities generally excluded unnaturalized immigrants – mainly from Europe – from accessing relief and public works projects, and the federal government deported over 14,000 such immigrants between 1931 and 1933.[93] Indigenous men and women with status under the Indian Act were considered the responsibility of the federal government and were subject to the authority of the Department of Indian Affairs. Indian Agents were responsible for assessing, administering, and monitoring applicants’ eligibility for social welfare programs, and they often refused adequate support based on racialized assumptions that Indigenous people did not “need” as much monetary support as did those of Anglo-Canadian backgrounds.[94] This long-standing racism, settler colonialism, and xenophobia crossed ideological, class, and gender lines and underpinned some of the most powerful Depression-era demands for economic security.

In the public imagination, the fear of immigrant “foreigners” was also associated with the fear of communist protest against capitalism.[95] Letter writers used the rhetoric of “British justice” to set criticism of the government and claims for entitlement apart from more radical critiques of the economic and political system, although the distinction between radical critiques and “British justice” was often deliberately ambiguous. “I don’t want any Czar of Russia methods in what I have always been taught was a free Canada for Canadians,” claimed an unemployed miner from Cobalt. “But in my case it is far from being a free country ... I do not want you to think I am a Red or an agitator, but I do feel that I have been very unfairly dealt with.”[96] Many individuals wrote to say they were neither communist agitators nor radicals, just ordinary people who desired “British justice,” which they defined variously as “the Right to work in a man’s own country,” to receive a living wage, and to provide for a wife and family, as well as the freedom to criticize government relief and policy measures and to receive priority for jobs if a veteran or Canadian born.[97] Using the threat of commun“sm or “turning red” in ”heir “etters was a way for writ”rs to express the depth ”f their concerns about economic conditions. An unemployed veteran told Henry in 1”31, “I am no extremist or radical,” but “starvation breeds revolution,” particularly when “my children” are receiving less nourishment than I received while in a Soviet prison ”n Moscow.”[98] A woman with an unemployed husband and a sick child who proudly claimed U.E.L. descent asked Henry, “Do you wonder in the face of such suffering that people become radicals?”[99] This rhetorical twist – which asserted that the letter writer was *not* radical while simultaneously claiming that poverty and suffering might inspire them to become so – amounted to a serious critique of the government's profound failure. And this rhetoric held some political weight in the 1930s, as the communist-led Workers Unity League succeeded in organizing some unemployed men, the socialist Co-operative Commonwealth Federation (CCF) emerged as a new political force, and increasingly militant language “gained acceptance” among working-class and unemployed people, even if they did not identify specifically as socialist.[100]

It was First World War veterans and their families who were most powerfully positioned to draw on notions of British justice, respectability, and the language of sacrifice and service. Front-line service was reserved for men, and veterans' sense that they embodied the highest ideals of manly service and patriotism, combined with a masculine entitlement to employment, was a powerful way to set their demands above other claims on the state.[101] Letters from unemployed veterans carefully pointed out their years of service and duty, claiming that patriotic loyalty was the duty of the soldier but that in return, the government had an ongoing moral obligation to protect and support them. Unemployed veterans felt abandoned by a government that was reluctant to offer them special status in recognition of their sacrifices. “It certainly does not make me feel very nice,” claimed one unemployed man, “to think I helped to defend a country that will not help me in times when I and my family need it badly.”[102] Veterans' associations complained to the government that veterans' dismissals from jobs were contrary to “British justice” and that employers should give returned men preference for employment above all other men.[103] One veterans' group protested the arrests of Etobicoke relief strikers since some of the men were vets “who at the country's call willingly went through hell, believing they were fighting for Justice, Peace and Freedom and now when they dare Fight for even a miseryable [*sic*] existence for themselves and their wives and Families you have them thrown into prison cells.”[104] Access to employment and to economic security, veterans claimed, were entitlements they had earned overseas while proving themselves worthy Canadian men and loyal citizens.

Veterans' criticisms of the government in the 1930s were rooted in their collective interwar protest against inadequate government compensation, poor retraining programs, inadequate pensions for disabled soldiers, and unfair differentials in pensions based on rank.[105] They made these claims for compensation, Desmond Morton argues, on the basis of "moral entitlement."[106] Veterans' feelings of anger and bitterness grew stronger as the economic crisis deepened and many were unable to find work or perform the manual labour required for recipients of direct relief. "I would have been better to have never come back than to go through what I am going through now," one veteran bitterly told Premier Henry.[107] They repeatedly reminded governments that it was "unfair" and unjust that those who had served their country suffered from unemployment while "men that never did anything for the Government can be holding down permanent jobs."[108] Veterans argued that their service to the nation had not ended with war, nor had the government's obligation to support them. They pointed to the economic sacrifices made by years of low soldier wages and lost job promotions, the emotional sacrifices caused by family separations, and the physical and psychological suffering related to injury and disability. All of these sacrifices made it difficult for veterans to find and keep work, perform relief work, or rely on savings to weather high levels of unemployment.[109] Their fulfilment of the masculine call to sacrifice deserved special recognition particularly when high unemployment made it increasingly difficult for them to support their families. "When MEN were needed to save our nation," claimed the Canadian Legion, "the boys responded to the call unselfishly, upholding the best traditions of our Empire. They gave their all. Promises of Freedom and Security have been broken or forgotten."[110] The discourse of sacrifice and duty combined with the privilege associated with the role of breadwinner was a powerful argument for veterans' right to employment. One veteran with an ill wife and four children reminded Henry that it was soldiers who had "wallowed in the mud of Flanders," and it was they who deserved "a chance to make a few dollars and keep the Respectability of ourselves and our families."[111]

As veterans organized, their associations built on criticisms of poor post-war re-establishment and called for a range of special programs and policies, including preferential hiring in the civil service, preferential access to public works projects, and higher subsidies for job retraining. The Ontario Provincial Command of the Legion called for increased taxation to help fund specialized programs as well as universal state-funded social welfare programs to benefit veterans and the unemployed more generally, including unemployment, old age, and medical insurance.[112] Legion members and leaders argued that the paltry pensions for veterans who had suffered war-related injury or disability came nowhere near to compensating for the "pre-aging" and "burnt-out" conditions that made unemployment a vicious reality for ex-soldiers.[113] And after discovering that veterans with small disability pensions were ineligible for municipal relief, the Legion successfully advocated for relief top-ups, which the federally commissioned Hyndman report recommended be referred to with the less stigmatizing term "unemployment assistance."[114]

In claiming that their sacrifices for the nation had not ended with the war, veterans and their families made demands for justice that linked the suffering of the past with the suffering of the present. As one father reminded Henry, "We thought that when two of our boys went overseas, that they went to protect our home."[115] But veterans and their families were also able to link the past with the future in order to make claims on the government. Their wartime service had protected the home and the nation, and the future security of the country rested on the willingness of the state to adequately honour and reward soldiers for their services. One mother reminded Henry that "if this country ever has to fight again it can call on my eight boys to protect it well you cannot expect them to protect homes they haven't got."[116] Future soldiers were the same young men who were currently unemployed and unable to fulfil the basic duties of citizenship. Their families reminded the government that success in future international conflicts depended on the willingness of young men to enlist, and in return, they expected protection on the home front in times of economic crisis.

Conclusion

In the process of writing to the premiers, men and women established their needs as legitimate political concerns and participated in a debate about how those needs should be properly met.[117] Using the language of rights and entitlement, letter writers attempted to link their demands to the dignity associated with the principle of contract, claiming that economic security and stability should be provided in return for service to the state. They made their demands and criticisms on a basis of duties, obligations, and moral values, including a willingness to work, proper gender roles, and respectable behaviour. This discourse was a powerful one, but it existed within what were accepted hierarchies of gender, ethnicity and race, and marital status. Expanded government obligation for social welfare was never imagined as something that would completely eradicate economic inequality, and many people were excluded from the definition of a fully entitled and deserving citizen. The assertions by letter writers that they were entitled citizens who had fulfilled certain duties implied that others had failed to meet them.[118]

While recognizing that the emerging welfare state was never intended to fully redistribute wealth, the post-war welfare state was still an important shift in policy that recognized a right to a certain minimum level of income. Post-war programs such as unemployment insurance and family allowances and, later, universal old age security and health insurance, were non-means-tested social programs that, at minimum, "have been crucial breakthroughs in the fight against poverty and insecurity, and have helped to create a sense of social rights linked to national citizenship."[119] Within a limited range of discursive possibilities, writers were imagining and demanding a positive vision of a society in which citizens could expect protection from capitalist instability and mass unemployment. In Depression-era Canada, the demands of unemployed men and women for a reciprocal relationship between citizen and state should be understood as one important factor in the transition to an expanded post-war social welfare state.

QUESTIONS FOR CONSIDERATION:

1. What does Campbell mean when she uses the term "top-down approach?"
2. How did the letters written by women differ from the ones written by men?
3. Discuss how Campbell characterizes the treatment of veterans following the First World War. How did this contribute to what was happening in the 1930s?
4. The "personal is political" is an oft-used phrase. How does it apply in this chapter?
5. Campbell asks readers to think about ethnicity and identity. How were these concepts applied to the policies that Campbell explores in the chapter?
6. Campbell argues that the efforts of these unemployed men and women in the 1930s contributed positively to the development of the expanded post-war welfare state. Discuss.

NOTES

1 Archives of Ontario (AO), RG 3-8, G.S. Henry Papers, MS 1759, File: Department of Public Works, Mr. T.F. to Henry, 9 October 1933.

2 John T. Saywell, "'Just call me Mitch': The Life of Mitchell F. Hepburn (Toronto: University of Toronto Press, 1991), 84, James Struthers, *The Limits of Affluence: Welfare in Ontario, 1920-1970* (Toronto: University of Toronto Press, 1994), 92.

3 For a close analysis of the relationship of municipalities to the federal government, see Eric Strikwerda, *The Wages of Relief: Cities and the Unemployed in Prairie Canada, 1929–30* (Edmonton: Athabasca University Press, 2013).

4 See James Struthers, *No Fault of their Own: Unemployment and the Canadian Welfare State, 1914–1941* (Toronto: University of Toronto Press, 1983); and Dennis Guest, *The Emergence of Social Security in Canada* (Vancouver: UBC Press, 1985), 84–5.

5 Laurel Sefton MacDowell, "Relief Camp Workers in Ontario during the Great Depression of the 1930s," *Canadian Historical Review* 76, no. 2 (June 1995): 205–28; Lorne Brown, *When Freedom Was Lost: The Unemployed, The Agitator, and the State* (Montreal: Black Rose), 1987.

6 Michael Bliss and L.M. Grayson, *The Wretched of Canada: Letters to R.B. Bennett, 1930–1935* (Toronto: University of Toronto Press, 1971), xxv. For similar American collections, see Gerald Markowitz and David Rosner, *Slaves of the Depression: Workers' Letters about Life on the Job* (Ithaca: Cornell University Press, 1987); and Elena C. Green, *Looking for the New Deal: Florida Women's Letters during the Great Depression* (Columbia: University of South Carolina Press, 2007). Green argues that most letters did not see requests for jobs or aid as charity but rather as earned entitlements. Green, *Looking for the New Deal*, 4

7 Shirley Tillotson has found similar sets of letters to federal officials regarding tax policy, and argues they are both records of how individuals implored, protested, and pushed back against government, and "conversations" that worked out what it meant to be a citizen with a right to a political voice. Tillotson, *Give and Take: The Citizen-Taxpayer and the Rise of Canadian Democracy* (Vancouver: UBC Press, 2017), 7–8.

8 Eric Strikwerda, *The Wages of Relief*, 7. The history of the welfare state has been well-documented in Canada, especially the influence of government, business, religion, and political parties. For a recent synthesis of welfare state development see Alvin Finkel, *Social Policy and Practice in Canada: A History* (Waterloo: Wilfrid Laurier University Press, 2006); see also Raymond B. Blake, Penny E. Bryden, and J. Frank Stein, *The Welfare State in Canada: Past, Present, and Future* (Concord: Irwin, 1997). On the intersection of business, religion, philanthropy, and/or state formation with welfare state policy, see Finkel, *Business and Social Reform in the Thirties* (Toronto: James Lorimer, 1979); Allan Moscovitch and J. Albert, *The Benevolent State: The Growth of Welfare in Canada* (Toronto: Garamond Press, 1987); Struthers, *No Fault of their Own* and *The Limits of Affluence*; Penney E. Bryden, *Planners and Politicians: Liberal Politics and Social Policy, 1957–1968* (Montreal and Kingston: McGill–Queen University Press, 1997); Doug Owram, *The Government Generation: Canadian Intellectuals and the State* (Toronto: University of Toronto Press, 1986); Michiel Horn, *The League for Social Reconstruction* (Toronto: University of Toronto Press, 1980); Larry Glassford, *Reaction and Reform: The Politics of the Conservative Party under R.B. Bennett, 1927–1938* (Toronto: University of Toronto Press, 1992); Walter Young, *Anatomy of a Party: The National CCF, 1932–61* (Toronto: University of Toronto Press, 1969); and Nancy Christie and Michael Gauvreau, *A Full-Orbed Christianity: The Protestant Churches and Social Welfare in Canada, 1900–1940* (Montreal and Kingston: McGill–Queen's University Press 1996). For discussions on grassroots activism and citizen participation in welfare state development, see Frances Fox Piven and Richard A. Cloward, *Regulating the Poor: The Functions of Public Welfare*, 2nd ed. (New York: Vintage Books, 1993). In Canada, see Shirley Tillotson, *Contributing Citizens: Modern Charitable Fundraising and the Making of the Welfare State, 1920–1966* (Vancouver: UBC Press, 2008); Dominique Marshall, "The Language of Children's Rights, the Formation of the Welfare State, and the Democratic Experience of Poor Families in Quebec, 1940–55," *Canadian Historical Review* 78, no 3 (September 1997); 409–439; and Shirley Tillotson, "Citizen Participation in the Welfare State: An Experiment, 1945–57," *Canadian Historical Review* 75, no. 4 (December 1994): 511–42.

9 Linda Gordon, *Pitied but Not Entitled: Single Mothers and the History of Welfare, 1890–1935* (Cambridge, MA: Harvard University Press, 1994), 274.

10 Nancy Fraser and Linda Gordon, "Contract versus Charity: Why Is There No Social Citizenship in the United States?" *Socialist Review* 22, no. 3 (July–September 1992): 45.

11 T.H. Marshall argues that social citizenship ranges from the "right to a modicum of economic welfare and security to the right to share in the social heritage and to live the life of a civilized being according to the standards prevailing in the society." Marshall, *Citizenship and Social*

Class (London: Pluto Press, 1992), 6. For a critique of Marshall's typology, see Gordon and Fraser, "Contract versus Charity," 48–56; and Carol Pateman, *The Disorder of Women: Democracy, Feminism, and Political Theory* (Stanford: Stanford University Press, 1989), 184–5.

12 Fraser and Gordon, "Contract versus Charity," 55–9. Carole Pateman argues this is fundamentally rooted in the liberal right of male citizens to own property and control their labour power. Pateman, *Disorder of Women*.

13 Struthers, *Limits of Affluence*, 19–49; Patricia Evans, "Divided Citizenship? Gender, Income Security, and the Welfare State," in *Women and the Canadian Welfare State*, ed. Evans and Gerda R. Wekerle (Toronto: University of Toronto Press, 1997), 91–116; Margaret Little, "The Blurring of Boundaries: Private and Public Welfare for Single Mothers in Ontario," *Studies in Political Economy* 47 (Summer 1995): 89–109; Jane Ursel, *Private Lives, Public Policy: 100 Years of State Intervention in the Family* (Toronto: Women's Press, 1992); Ruth Roach Pierson, "Gender and the Unemployment Insurance Debates in Canada," *Labour/Le Travail* 25 (Spring 1990): 77–103; Dominique Jean, "Family Allowances and Family Autonomy: Quebec Families Encounter the Welfare State, 1945–1955," in *Canadian Family History: Selected Readings*, ed. Bettina Bradbury (Toronto: Copp Clark Pitman, 1992), 401–41; Annalee Golz, "Family Matters: The Canadian Family and the State in Postwar Canada," *left history* 1, no. 2 (1993): 9–50. For the US, see Barbara Nelson, "Origins of the Two-Channel Welfare State: Workmen's Compensation and Mothers' Aid," in *Women, the State and Welfare*, ed. Linda Gordon (Madison: University of Wisconsin Press, 1990); Ann Shorla Orloff, "Gender and the Social Rights of Citizenship: The Comparative Analysis of Gender Relations and Welfare States," *American Sociological Review* 58 (1993): 303–28; and Mimi Abramovitz, *Regulating the Lives of Women: Social Welfare Policy from Colonial Times to the Present* (Boston: South End Press, 1988).

14 James Struthers argues that the principle of less eligibility was written into unemployment insurance by making benefits lower than market-based wage rates and favouring those with steady, full-time employment. Struthers, *No Fault of their Own*, 211–12. See also Pierson, "Gender and the Unemployment Insurance Debates"; and Guest, *The Emergence of Social Security*, 146–7.

15 Fraser and Gordon, "Contract versus Charity," 48. For an example of how this discourse played out in debates over work incentives and unemployment benefits during the 2020 COVID-19 pandemic, see "Ottawa Must Remove Disincentives to Return to Work," Fraser Institute, 14 May 2020, https://www.fraserinstitute.org/blogs/ottawa-must-remove-disincentives-to-return-to-work.

16 Literary scholar Mary Chapman argues for careful attention to how campaigns of the politically disenfranchised utilized voice as a form of political self-expression, an assertion of the right to speak, and a particular form or literary style. Mary Chapman, *Making Noise, Making News: Suffrage Print Culture and U.S. Modernism* (New York: Oxford University Press, 2014).

17 See Craig Jenkins and Barbara G. Brents, "Social Protest, Hegemonic Competition, and Social Reform: A Political Struggle Interpretation of the Origins of the American Welfare State," *American Sociological Review* 54 (December 1989): 891–909; Saywell, *"Just Call Me Mitch,"* 265–6; and Gordon, *Pitied but Not Entitled*, 241–251.

18 On the male breadwinner ideal, see Eric Strikwerda, "'Married Men Should, I Feel, Be Treated Differently': Work, Relief, and Unemployed Men on the Urban Canadian Prairie," *left history* 12, no. 1 (2007): 30–51; Cynthia Comacchio, "A Postscript for Father: Defining a New Fatherhood in Interwar Canada," *Canadian Historical Review* 78, no. 3 (September 1997): 305–408; Comacchio, *The Infinite Bonds of Family: Domesticity in Canada, 1850–1940* (Toronto: University of Toronto Press, 1999); Robert Griswold, *Fatherhood in America: A History* (New

York: Basic Books, 1993); Joy Parr, *The Gender of Breadwinners: Women, Men, and Change in Two Industrial Towns, 1880–1950* (Toronto: University of Toronto Press 1990); Suzanne Morton, *Ideal Surroundings: Domestic Life in a Working-Class Suburb in the 1920s* (Toronto: University of Toronto Press, 1995); Ava Baron, "On Looking at Men: Masculinity and the Making of a Gendered Working-Class History," in *Feminists Revision History*, ed. Ann-Louise Shapiro (New Brunswick: Rutgers University Press, 1994): 236–7; and Ava Baron, ed., *Work Engendered: Toward a New History of American Labor* (Ithaca: Cornell University Press, 1991).

19 See essays in Robert Rutherdale and Peter Gossage, *Making Men, Making History: Canadian Masculinities across Time and Space* (Vancouver: UBC Press, 2018); and R.W. Connell and James W. Messerschmidt, "Hegemonic Masculinity: Rethinking the Concept," *Gender and Society* 19, no. 6 (2005): 829–59.

20 *Porcupine Advance*, 12 January 1932.

21 Henry Papers, MS 1760, file: Relief Asked For, Harold Foate to Henry, 18 January 1933.

22 Elspeth Probyn, *Blush: Faces of Shame* (Minneapolis: University of Minnesota Press, 2005), 38. See also Sally Alexander, "Men's Fears and Women's Work: Responses to Unemployment in London between the Wars," *Gender and History* 12, no. 2 (200): 401–24.

23 Henry Papers, MS 1759, file: Department of Public Works, East Block, Russel Morris to Henry, 24 June 1933. Memoirs and oral histories often comment on the humiliation and sense of degradation that accepting relief brought to unemployed men. See also Barry Broadfoot, *Ten Lost Years: The Lost Years, 1929–1939: Memories of Canadians Who Survived the Depression* (Toronto: Doubleday, 1973); and Robert Collins, *You Had to Be There: An Intimate Portrait of the Generation That Survived the Depression, Won the War, and Reinvented Canada* (Toronto: McClelland and Stewart, 1997).

24 AO, Hepburn Papers, box 225, file: Hepburn, personal, no. 6, Mr Herbert T. to Hepburn, 14 August 1934; box 247, file: Public Works Department, George Wilson to Hepburn, 1935.

25 William Reddy, *The Navigation of Feeling: A Framework for the History of Emotions* (Cambridge and New York: Cambridge University Press, 2001). Emotions history provides a powerful way of understanding both individual and collective feelings. See Eric Reiter, *Wounded Feelings: Litigating Emotions in Quebec, 1870–1950* (Toronto: University of Toronto Press, 2019); and Rob Boddice, "The Affective Turn: Historicizing the Emotions," in *Psychology and History: Interdisciplinary Explorations* (Cambridge: Cambridge University Press, 2014): 147–65.

26 See <full cite pls> Campbell, *Respectable Citizens*, 61, 217n23; and Margaret Little, "'Manhunts and Bingo Blabs: The Moral Regulation of Ontario Single Mothers," *Canadian Journal of Sociology* 19, no. 2 (1994): 233–47.

27 North Bay debated forcing unemployed men to register and take an oath: *North Bay Nugget*, 13 January 1932. In Fort William, unemployed men registered at the police court building: Thunder Bay Archives, series 4, 124, box 209, file: Labor Situation, 1929–30. On Timmins, see *Porcupine Advance*, 31 March 1932.

28 *Child and Family Welfare* 1, no. 2 (1934), 50; Campbell, *Respectable Citizens*, 215n27.

29 One storeowner in East York offered to keep track of his customers and report them when they bought beer, gasoline, or movie tickets. Residents in Sudbury wrote letters to their city councillors to report their neighbours for the same. AO, Hepburn Papers, box 190, file: Public Welfare Department, general, no. 2, Frank Hitchings, Clover Leaf Grocery to Hepburn, 15 August 1935; *Porcupine Advance*, 11 August 1932.

30 In some municipalities, relief investigators were unemployed men, while in others, they were dominated by women. In response to complaints by men on relief, some city councils hired additional male supervisors to oversee female "visitors." Campbell, *Respectable Citizens*, 62–3.

"Relief recipients," claimed one man to Henry, were "forced to answer the regulation 137 questions to obtain relief and <became?> become the object of curious official investigating old maids," Henry Papers, MS 1759, file: Public Works, J. Frise to Henry, 12 December 1933. An investigation in Ottawa in 1934 suggested that women workers be replaced by "competent male investigators" unless the family was headed by a woman. See F.A. Matatall and Hector Menard, *Report on the Cost of Relief and Its Administration in the City of Ottawa*, 16 July 1934. Held in AO, RG 29-74, Ontario Department of Public Welfare, J.S. Band Files, file: 74-1-58, Reports and Surveys, box 7. In 1936, Ottawa fired forty female social workers and replaced them with eleven "male detectives": see Struthers, *No Fault of Their Own*, 149. See similar reports in Ruth Shonle Cavan and Katherine Howland Ranck, *The Family and the Depression: A Study of One Hundred Chicago Families* (Freeport: Books for Libraries Press, 1969), 159. On the shift from a casework approach to supposedly "objective" approaches to unemployment, see Nancy Christie, *Engendering the State: Family, Work, and Welfare in Canada* (Toronto: University of Toronto Press, 2000), 200–1.

31 Henry Papers, MS 1759, file: Department of Public Works, Mr. G.D to Henry, 20 July 1933.

32 Henry Papers, MS 1752, file: Department of Public Works, Mr. S.J. to Henry, 11 May 1932.

33 Harry Cassidy, *Unemployment and Relief in Ontario, 1929–1932* (Toronto: Dent, 1932), 41, 48. On unemployment in the nineteenth century, see Peter Baskerville and Eric Sager, *Unwilling Idlers: The Urban Unemployed and Their Families in Late Victorian Canada* (Toronto: University of Toronto Press, 1988).

34 Margaret Hobbs, "Gendering Work and Welfare: Women's Relationship to Wage-Work and Social Policy in Canada during the Great Depression" (unpublished PhD diss., University of Toronto, 1995); "Rethinking Antifeminism in the 1930s: Gender Crisis or Workplace Justice? A Response to Alice Kessler-Harris," *Gender and History* 5, no. 1 (Spring 1993), 4–15; and Lois Scharf, *To Work and to Wed: Female Employment, Feminism, and the Great Depression* (Westport: Greenwood Press, 1980).

35 Henry Papers, MS 1755, file: Legislation, mortgage, Mr. R.H. to Henry, 7 January 1932.

36 Tarah Brookfield, *Our Voices Must Be Heard: Women and the Vote in Ontario*, (Vancouver: UBC Press, 2018); 120–5; Ruth Frager, *Sweatshop Strife: Class, Ethnicity, and Gender in the Jewish Labour Movement of Toronto, 1900–1939* (Toronto: University of Toronto Press, 1992); Martha May, "Bread before Roses: American Workingmen, Labor Unions, and the Family Wage," in *Women, Work and Protest: A Century of U.S. Women's Labour History*, ed. Ruth Milkman (Boston: Routledge and Kegan Paul, 1985), 1–21.

37 Henry Papers, MS 1759, file: Department of Public Works, T.H.G. to Henry, 3 October 1933.

38 See Katrina Srigley, *Breadwinning Daughters: Young Working Women in a Depression-Era City, 1929–1939* (Toronto: University of Toronto Press, 2010); Margaret Hobbs, "Equality and Difference: Feminism and the Defence of Women Workers during the Depression," *Labour/Le Travail* 32, no. 4 (1993): 201–23.

39 Morton, *Ideal Surroundings*, 72; Parr, *Gender of Breadwinners*, 82. Cynthia Comacchio argues that breadwinning encompassed the emotional ideals of "fatherly devotion" and "paternal protection" as well as material provision. See Comacchio, "A Postscript for Father," 395. Robert Rutherdale argues that fathers have historically been more than income earners in their families. See Rutherdale, "Fatherhood and Masculine Domesticity during the Baby Boom: Consumption and Leisure in Advertising and Life Stories," in *Family Matters: Papers in Post-Confederation Canadian Family History*, ed. Lori Chambers and Edgar-André Montigny (Toronto: Canadian Scholars' Press), 310; Rutherdale, "Three Faces of Fatherhood as a Masculine Category: Tyrants, Teachers, and Workaholics as 'Responsible Family Men' during

Canada's Baby Boom," in *What Is Masculinity? Historical Dynamics from Antiquity to the Contemporary World*, ed. John H. Arnold and Sean Brady (Basingstoke: Palgrave Macmillan, 2011; and Peter Gossage, "Celebrating the Family Man: From Father's Day to La Fête des Pères, 1910–60," *Making Men, Making History*, 385–408.

40 See Ron Rothbart, "Homes Are What Any Strike Is About: Immigrant Labour and Family Wage," *Journal of Social History* 23, no. 2 (1989): 267–84; Jane Humphries, "The Working Class Family, Women's Liberation, and Class Struggle: The Case of Nineteenth Century British History," *Review of Radical Political Economies* 9, no, 3 (1997): 25–40; and Mary Blewett, "Manhood and the Market: The Politics of Gender and Class among the Textile Workers of Fall River, Massachusetts, 1870–1880," in *Work Engendered*, 92–113.

41 Michael Roper and John Tosh argue that male power is continually "contested and transformed," partly because financial self-sufficiency has always been hard to achieve. Roper and Tosh, *Manful Assertions: Masculinities in Britain Since 1800* (London: Routledge, 1991), 18. See also Mark Carnes and Clyde Griffen, eds., *Meanings for Manhood: Constructions of Masculinity in Victorian America* (Chicago: University of Chicago Press, 1990).

42 Henry Papers, MS 1745, file: Relief Asked For, Mr. A.E. Owen to Henry, 6 June 1931; AO, Hepburn Papers, box 247, file: Public Works Department, George Wilson to Hepburn, 1935.

43 Henry Papers, MS 1744, file: Positions, General, June 1931 to January 1932, D.G. Firth to Henry, 16 and 17 September 1931; Henry Papers, MS 1761, file: Soldier's Aid Commission, Grant MacMillan to Henry, 30 June 1933.

44 For example, see AO, RG 22-1333, Carleton County Juvenile and Family Court, Adult Case Files, box 62, 1936.

45 Henry Papers, MS 1757, file: Navy League, Sam Harris, President, Navy League of Canada to Henry, 27 March 1933.

46 Henry Papers, MS 1747, file: Unemployment Relief #3, Lieut. W.J.O. to Henry, 8 October 1931.

47 AO, RG 3 series 9, M.F. Hepburn Papers, #180, file: Unemployment Relief #2, L.W. to Hepburn, 24 June 1934.

48 The province required men receiving direct relief to do work "equivalent to the amount of relief given" in return. AO, RG 29-74, J.S. Band Files, box 9, Relief Memoranda, file: Official Memoranda, "Memorandum as to Direct Relief," December 1933.

49 See Jeff Goodwin, James M. Jasper, and Francesca Polletta, *Passionate Politics: Emotions and Social Movements* (Chicago: University of Chicago Press, 2001). For a recent exploration of emotions in collective organizing against oppression, see Rosemary Hennessy, *Fires on the Border: The Passionate Politics of Labor Organizing on the Mexican Frontera* (Minneapolis: University of Minnesota Press, 2013).

50 For unemployed organizing in this period, see Patricia V. Schulz, *The East York Workers' Association: A Response to the Great Depression* (Toronto: New Hogtown Press, 1975); John Manley, "'Starve, Be Damned!' Communists and Canada's Urban Unemployed, 1929–39," *Canadian Historical Review*, 79, no. 3 (September 1998): 466–91; Bryan Palmer, *Toronto's Poor: A Rebellious History* (Toronto: Between the Lines, 2016); and Campbell, *Respectable Citizens*, 156–7. Regarding the protests recorded by the Department of Labour, for example, almost half of relief strikes in Ontario involved domestic concerns such as adequate and good-quality food, proper children's clothing, and more comfortable housing. See Library and Archives Canada (LAC), RG 27, Department of Labour, Strikes and Lockout Files. Ontario relief maximums were set out in the Campbell Report of 1932 and readjusted as the province formulated increases based on rising food costs. See Wallace Campbell, Chair, Advisory Committee on Direct Relief, "Report on Provincial Policy in Administrative Methods in the Province of

Ontario" (Ontario: King's Printer, 1932); and Dorothy King, "Unemployment Aid and Direct Relief," in *Canada's Employment Problem*, ed. Lothar Richtar (Toronto: Macmillan, 1939): 100. The provincial government increased supervision of municipalities where protests had increased relief rates over the maximum ceilings. In 1936, Minister of Public Welfare David Croll imposed additional property taxes to punish municipalities that offered relief above the maximum amount. Struthers, *Limits of Affluence*, 93–6.

51 For an analytical approach to understanding the post-war period, see Magda Fahrni and Robert Rutherdale, *Creating Postwar Canada: Community, Diversity, and Dissent, 1945–1975* (Vancouver: UBC Press, 2008); Annalee Golz, "Family Matters"; and Jennifer Stephen, *Pick One Intelligent Girl: Employability, Domesticity, and the Gendered of Canada's Welfare State, 1939–1947* (Toronto: University of Toronto Press, 2007).

52 Pierson, "Gender and the Unemployment Insurance Debates"; Pateman, *The Disorder of Women*, 182–5, 192–5.

53 AO, RG 3, series 9, Hepburn Papers, #180, file: Unemployment Relief #2, Mrs. M.G. to Hepburn, 27 July 34.

54 Henry Papers, NS 1744, file: Positions, General, June 1931 to January 1932, Mrs. Alice Boulton to Henry, 27 June 1931.

55 Evans, "Divided Citizenship," 91, 95.

56 Henry Papers, MS 1745, file: Relief, asked for, Mrs. W.A. Rowland to Henry, 1 October 1931.

57 See Linda Gordon, *Heroes of Their Own Lives: The Politics and History of Family Violence, 1880–1960* (New York: Penguin, 1988).

58 AO, RG 3, series 9, Hepburn Papers, #180, file: Unemployment Relief, Mrs. W.H. to Hepburn, 1934.

59 Henry Papers, MS 1747, file: Unemployment Relief, no. 3, 9 September 1931, Mrs. Wallace Gow to Henry.

60 Denyse Baillargeon; *Making Do: Women, Family, and Home in Montreal during the Great Depression*, trans. Yvonne Lein (Waterloo: Wilfrid Laurier University Press, 1999); Laura Hollingsworth and Vappu Tyyska, "The Hidden Producers: Women's Household Production during the Great Depression," *Critical Sociology* 15, no. 3 (1988): 3–27.

61 See Lara Campbell, "Respectable Citizens of Canada: Gender, Maternalism, and the Welfare State in the Great Depression," in *Maternalism Reconsidered: Mothers and Method in Twentieth-Century History*, ed. Rebecca Plant et al. (Oxford and New York: Berghahn Press, 2012), 99–120; and Lois Rita Helmbold, "Beyond the Family Economy: Black and White Working-Class Women during the Great Depression," *Feminist Studies* 13, no. 3 (Fall 1987): 629–49.

62 MS 1747, Henry Papers, file: Unemployment relief #3, Mrs. W.G. on behalf of the mothers of Sturgeon Falls, 29 September 1931.

63 Campbell, *Respectable Citizens*, 82.

64 AO, RG 3-10, Hepburn Papers, #250, file: Comments on unemployment relief, 29 July 1935.

65 See Joan Sangster, *Dreams of Equality: Women on the Canadian Left, 1920–1950* (Toronto: McClelland and Stewart 1989); Irene Howard, "The Mothers' Council of Vancouver: Holding the Fort for the Unemployed, 1935–38," *BC Studies* 69–70 (Spring–Summer 1988), 249–87; and Annelise Orleck, "'We Are That Mythical Thing Called the Public': Militant Housewives during the Great Depression," *Feminist Studies* 1 (Spring 1993): 147–72.

66 AO, RG 3-10, Hepburn Papers, #203, file: Provincial Secretary's Department, Mrs. J.J. to Hepburn, 14 May 1936.

67 AO, RG 3-10, Hepburn Papers, #203, file: Provincial Secretary's Department, Mrs. L.M. to Hepburn, 10 May 1936.

68 LAC, RG 27, box 57, vol. 375, 1935.

69 See Lisa Pasolli, *Working Mothers and the Child Care Dilemma: A History of British Columbia* (Vancouver: UBC Press, 2015); <full cite pls> Little, *No Car, No Radio, No Liquor Permit*; <first name?> Little, "Claiming a Unique Place: The Introduction of Mothers' Pensions in British Columbia," in *Rethinking Canada: The Promise of Women's History*, ed. Veronica Strong-Boag and Anita Clair Fellman (Toronto: Oxford University Press 1993), 285–303; Strong-Boag,"Wages for Housework: Mothers' Allowance and the Beginning of Social Security in Canada," *Journal of Canadian Studies* 14 (1979–80): <pages?>

70 AO, RG 3-10, Hepburn Papers, #190, file: Public Welfare Department, Mothers' Allowance, Mrs. R.H. to Hepburn, 21 February 1935. Quoted in Struthers, *Limits of Affluence*, 99.

71 Recent literature has argued that the welfare state can provide a potential escape route for women from dependence on individual men by providing a direct relationship to the state. See Pateman, *The Disorder of Women*, 196; Evans, "Divided Citizenship," 95; Gordon, "What Does Welfare Regulate?" *Social Research* 55, no. 4 (Winter 1988): 609–630; and Orloff, "Gender and the Social Rights of Citizenship," 305.

72 AO, RG 3, series 9, Hepburn Papers, #180, file: Unemployment Relief #2, Mrs. J.W. to Hepburn, 6 September 1934.

73 Henry Papers, MS 1745, file: Relief: asked for, Mrs. C.G. to Henry, 9 June 1931. See also Mothers' Allowance files in MS 1742, Henry Papers, 1931, and MS 1757, Henry Papers, 1933.

74 Little, *No Car, No Radio*, 66.

75 Little, "The Blurring of Boundaries;" Struthers, *Limits of Affluence*, 43.

76 Struthers, *Limits of Affluence*, 48.

77 Henry Papers, MS 1742, file: Mothers' Allowance Commission, Mrs. C.C. to Henry, 30 October 1931.

78 Henry Papers, MS 1757, file: Mothers' Allowances Commission, Mrs. R.C. to Henry, 5 March 1933.

79 Henry Papers, MS 1736, file: Agricultural Development Board, Mrs. A. S. to Henry, 26 August 1931. On women's political citizenship in Ontario, see Brookfield, *Our Voices Must Be Heard*, 188–90.

80 Gordon, *Pitied but Not Entitled*, 627.

81 Benedict Anderson, *Imagined Communities: Reflections on the Origins and Spread of Nationalism* (London: Verso, 1983). On women, race, and settler-colonialism see Jennifer Henderson, *Settler Feminism and Race Making in Canada* (Toronto: University of Toronto Press, 2003); and Lykke de la Cour, "Eugenics, Race, and Canada's First-Wave Feminists: Dis/Abling the Debates," *Atlantis* 38, no. 2 (2017): 176–90. On Britishness in settler societies see Cecilia Morgan, *Building Better Britains: Settler Societies in the British World, 1783–1920* (Toronto: University of Toronto Press, 2016). On national identity in the period see Carl Berger, *The Writing of Canadian History: Aspects of English Canadian Historical Writing since 1900* (Toronto: University of Toronto Press, 1986); and Mary Vipond, "Nationalism and Nativism: The Native Sons of Canada in the 1930s," *Canadian Review of Studies in Nationalism* 9, no. 1 (Spring 1982): 81–95.

82 Henry Papers, MS 1761, file: Soldiers' Aid Commission, Mr. E.L. to Henry, 14 January 1933.

83 Henry Papers, MS 1762, file: Unemployment Relief #1, Mr. T.H. to Henry, 7 August 1933.

84 On Loyalist myths see Cecilia Morgan, "History, Nation, and Empire: Gender and Southern Ontario Historical Societies, 1890–1920s," *Canadian Historical Review* 82, no. 3 (2001): 500–17; and Carl Berger, *The Sense of Power: Studies in the Ideas of Canadian Imperialism* (Toronto: University of Toronto Press, 1970), 99–101. On British and colonial identities see Angela

Wollacott, "'*To Try her Fortune in London*': *Australian Women, Colonialism, and Modernity* (New York: Oxford University Press, 2001), 142–3.

85 AO, RG 3-10, Hepburn Papers, #225, file: M.F. Hepburn, private #3, Miss M.E.M. to Hepburn, 3 July 1934.

86 See Nancy Forestell and Maureen Moynagh, "Unsettling Imperial Ties: Rethinking Suffrage in the Context of Settler Colonialism in Canada," in *Suffragette to Homesteader: Exploring One Woman's Memoir of Life in England and Canada*, ed. Emily van der Meulen (Halifax: Fernwood, 2018), 126–42; Antoinette Burton, *Burdens of History: British Feminists, Indian Women, and Imperial Culture, 1865–1915* (Chapel Hill: University of North Carolina Press, 1994); and Ann Curthoys, "Identity Crisis: Colonialism, Nation, and Gender in Australian History," *Gender and History* 5, no. 2 (Summer 1993): 165–76.

87 Henry Papers, MS 1750, file: Mothers' Allowances Commission, Mrs. S.B.S. to Henry, 24 February 1932.

88 Henry Papers, MS 1760, file: Relief, asked for, Mrs. C.R.C. to Henry, 2 August 1933.

89 Papers, MS 1745, file: Relief, asked for, Mrs. A.H.M., 29 December 1931.

90 Although it is difficult to assess the exact ethnic background of letter writers, a careful study of the letters reveals few non-Anglo names. However, some may have been Anglicized and others may not have explicitly placed themselves within a particular community. See Laura Tabili, *We Ask for British Justice: Workers and Racial Difference in Late Imperial Britain* (Ithaca: Cornell University Press, 1994): 4–15, for analysis of how subordinated groups could use tropes of British "fair play" to claim equality. See Tillotson, *Give and Take*, for how "foreigners" were marked as "other" in tax discussions, 130–3.

91 Henry Papers, MS 1744, file: Positions, general, Mr. B.C. to Henry, 19 November 1931.

92 Henry Papers, MS 1750, file: Mothers' Allowances Commission, Miss A.M. to Henry, 26 August 1932.

93 Barbara Roberts, *Whence They Came: Deportation from Canada, 1900–1935* (Ottawa: University of Ottawa Press, 1988), 160–9; Brown, *When Freedom Was Lost*, 37; M.C. Urquhart, *Historical Statistics of Canada*, 29, series A 342-7 (Toronto: Macmillan, 1965).

94 Robin Jarvis Brownlie, *A Fatherly Eye: Indian Agents, Government Power, and Aboriginal Resistance in Ontario, 1918–1939* (Toronto: Oxford University Press, 2003); Brownlie, "'Better Citizens Than Lots of White Men: First Nations Enfranchisement – An Ontario Case Study, 1918–40," *Canadian Historical Review* 87, no. 1 (2006): 29–52; Strikwerda, *Wages of Relief*, 62n24.

95 Donald Avery, *"Dangerous Foreigners": European Immigrant Workers and Labour Radicalism in Canada, 1896–1932* (Toronto: McClelland and Stewart, 1979); Avery, *Reluctant Host: Canada's Response to Immigrant Workers, 1896–1994* (Toronto: McClelland and Stewart, 1995).

96 Henry Papers, MS 1760, file: Relief, asked for, Mr. H.L.S. to Henry, 26 July 1933.

97 Henry Papers, MS 1760, file: Relief, asked for, Mr. H.L.S. to Henry, 26 July 1933; Campbell, *Respectable Citizens*, 174–83

98 Henry Papers, MS 1747, file: Unemployment Relief #7, Lieut. W.J.O. to Henry, 8 October 1931.

99 Henry Papers, MS 1762, file: Unemployment Relief: homeowners, Mrs. K.H. to Henry, 21 July 1933.

100 Manley, "'Starve, Be Damned."

101 Marlene Epp, "Heroes or Yellow Bellies? Masculinity and the Conscientious Objector," *Journal of Mennonite Studies* 17 (1990) <pages?>; Amy J. Shaw, *Crisis of Conscience: Conscientious Objection in Canada during the First World War* (Vancouver: UBC Press, 2009); Mark Moss, *Manliness and Militarism: Educating Young Boys in Ontario for War* (Toronto: University of Toronto Press, 2001); Mike O'Brien, "Manhood and the Militia Myth: Masculinity, Class, and Militarism in Ontario, 1902–14," *Labour/Le Travail* 42 (Fall 1998): 115–41.

102 AO, RG 3, series 9, Hepburn Papers, #180, file: Unemployment Relief #1, Mr. W.K. to Hepburn, 17 December 1934.

103 See letters in AO, RG 3-10, Hepburn Papers, #171, File: B.E.S.L., 1934.

104 104

105 Desmond Morton, "The Canadian Veterans' Heritage from the Great War," in *The Veterans Charter and Post-World War II Canada*, <city/publisher/year?> 22–3; Morton, "'Noblest and Best': Retraining Canada's War Disabled 1915–23," *Journal of Canadian Studies* 16, nos. 3–4 (Fall–Winter 1991): 75–85; Mark Humphries, "'War's Long Shadow': Masculinity, Medicine, and the Gendered Politics of Trauma, 1914–1939," *Canadian Historical Review* 91, no. 3 (September 2010): 503–31; Humphries, *A Weary Road: Shell Shock in the Canadian Expeditionary Force, 1914–1918* (Toronto: University of Toronto Press, 2018).

106 Morton, "Canadian Veterans," 22.

107 Henry Papers, MS 1752, File: general correspondence, H. Vandervelde to Henry, 16 April 1932 Y, 16 April 1932.

108 Henry Papers, MS 1759, File: Department of Public Works, T. Frith to Henry, 9 October 1933; and Ibid., MS 1745, File: Returned Men, F.J. Shaw to Henry, August 1931

109 Morton, "The Canadian Veterans' Heritage," 23; Desmond Morton and Glenn Wright, *Winning the Second Battle: Canadian Veterans and the Return to Civilian Life, 1915–1930* (Toronto: University of Toronto Press, 1987), 233; Lara Campbell, "'We Who Have Wallowed in the Mud of Flanders': First World War Veterans, Unemployment, and the Development of Social Welfare in Canada, 1929–1939," *Journal of the Canadian Historical Association* 11 (2000): 125–50 at 129–30; *The Legionary* 12, no. 4 (November 1936): 25, 30; 5, no. 4 (January 1937): 13.

110 AO, RG 3, series 9, Hepburn Papers, #180, file: Unemployment Relief, Canadian Legion Unemployment Committee, B.E.S.L. Hamilton Branch to Hepburn, December 1934.

111 Henry Papers, MS 1759, file: Department of Public Works, East Block, Mr. F.K to Henry, 24 May 1933.

112 Report of the Ontario Provincial Command, Annual Convention, 1931 and 1933. By 1919, the Great War Veterans' Association advocated not just for support to veterans but for broader state policies such as public housing, a minimum wage, nationalization of primary resources, profit controls, and age, sickness and unemployment insurance. See Jeffrey A. Keshen, *Propaganda and Censorship during Canada's Great War* (Edmonton: University of Alberta Press, 1996), 204; Campbell, *Respectable Citizens*, 130–1.

113 *Legionary* 12, no. 9 (April 1937), 9; 4, no. 10 (March 1930), 5; Guest, *Emergence of Social Security in Canada*, 95.

114 Morton and Wright, *Winning the Second Battle*, 214, 218; *Legionary* 10, no. 4 (April 1935), 9; LAC, RG 27-3, vol. 187, file 614.06:6, "Unemployment of Ex-Servicemen, 1935."

115 AO, RG 3-8, Henry Papers, MS1762, file: Unemployment Relief, homeowners, Mr. H.V.W. to Henry, 8 September 1933.

116 AO, RG 3-8, Henry Papers, MS1744, file: Positions, general, Mrs. A.B. to Henry, 27 June 1931.

117 Nancy Fraser, "Struggle over Needs: Outline of a Socialist-Feminist Critical Theory of Late Capitalist Political Culture," in *Women, the State, and Welfare*, ed. Linda Gordon, 202; Tillotson, "Citizen Participation in the Welfare State"; Tillotson, *Contributing Citizens*.

118 Fraser and Gordon, "Contract versus Charity," 59.

119 Struthers, *The Limits of Affluence*, 4. Although Family Allowance benefits were never adequate, Dominique Jean argues that they "led parents to incorporate the idea of an adequate allowance into their concept of their rights as Canadians … [and] to enlarge their concepts of their rights as citizens." Jean, "Family Allowances and Family Autonomy," 430.

CHAPTER FIFTEEN

Adoption Records in Ontario: Secrecy and the Movement for Reform

VALERIE J. ANDREWS AND LORI CHAMBERS

Adoption has fascinated the public for centuries and adoption themes are prominent in fairy tales, modern literature, and film.[1] From the mid-twentieth century, questions regarding secrecy in adoption and potential adoption reunions have captivated the public imagination. This curiosity is not surprising as adoption is both complex and ethically challenging. Historically in Western societies and under Canadian law,[2] adoption has been viewed as an altruistic mechanism for "saving" unfortunate children. As Karen Dubinsky argues, "ideologies and images of rescue"[3] are foundational to adoption practice. But from what and from whom were, and are, children to be saved? What led to the secrecy and shame that have characterized adoption practices in Western cultures? In seeking answers to these questions, and to challenge this secrecy, this chapter focuses on a single jurisdiction, Ontario. As Canada's largest province, Ontario provides an excellent case study for beginning to explore the specifics of adoption law and the myths and secrecy that continue to surround adoption practice.

In this chapter we show that despite the efforts of adoption activists and reformers, the legislature and courts in Ontario have been clear on this matter. As of this writing, adoptions completed in the post–Second World War era will most likely continue to remain shrouded in shame and secrecy rather than transparency and openness. It is only by listening to the voices of the stakeholders – the mothers who surrendered their children and those who were adopted – that we can learn about the complexities and the myths surrounding adoption disclosure, and how these matters continue to impact so many people in Ontario today. The mothers from this era are an aging population, now mostly in their senior years. Many are already deceased, leaving their "shameful" secrets untold. Without mothers left to find, adoptees continue to search for half-siblings and other extended family. This makes the need for legislative reform to implement full transparency in adoption records an urgent one, as extended family members emerge as the new seekers of adoption truth in the twenty-first century.

This chapter has five sections. The first, "Brief History of Adoption," focuses on how and when adoption as we know it today came into existence in law. The second, "Adoption Mandate," examines the post-war decades during which unmarried mothers became the primary source for infants for adoption due to the stigma of their unmarried status, which in the eyes of the law and social services rendered them unfit to be mothers. In the third section, "Sealed Records and the Adoption Disclosure Registry," we describe the sealed or closed adoption records system and its impact on mothers and adoptees as well as the creation of the voluntary and provincial disclosure registry in 1978.[4] In the fourth section, "Changing Legislation and Legal Challenges," we follow the transformation of the Disclosure Registry into an active registry in 1987,[5] the creation of the Adoption Information Disclosure Act in 2005,[6] the successful court challenge to this legislation,[7] and the compromise measures enacted in 2008.[8] The final section, "The Adoption Reform Movement," outlines the major arguments of present-day adoption reformers against the closed records system, as well as the opposition to the shame and secrecy of the past that continues to be reproduced and entwined in twenty-first century legislation.

History of Adoption in Ontario

During the nineteenth century the transfer of a child was often accomplished through a guardianship executed under the Guardianship Act, enacted in 1827, which "allowed a Probate or Surrogate Court Judge to appoint an individual to safeguard the child's 'property, person and education' until maturity."[9] Under that act, natural parents retained filial attachment to the child. It was not until 1921 that adoption legislation passed in Ontario created the permanent legal transfer of a child and the severing of filial ties. From 1921, an adoption order in Ontario divested "the natural parent, guardian or person in whose custody the child ha[d] been of all legal rights in respect of such child."[10] The ties between the child and his or her natural parents were irrevocably severed, and the surrendering parent had no right to information about the child. In fact, neither the person adopted nor the natural mother had the right to obtain identifying details about the other.[11] There was some ambiguity in this regard in the legislation of 1921; however, a 1927 amendment confirmed that records would be sealed and provided that "an application for an adoption order may be heard and determined in chambers, and if the child was born out of wedlock this fact shall not appear upon the face of the adoption order."[12] As one commentator on adoption in *Chatelaine* magazine asserted approvingly in 1932, many adopted children knew nothing about their ancestry because "a good deal of trouble and expense" had been employed to "cover up the fact" of adoption.[13]

The first adoption under this new legislation was completed in July 1921 and was one of sixty-six adoptions that year.[14] During the interwar period adoption as a form of child transfer became more common, albiet still somewhat limited due to the rise of the eugenics movement, which contributed to the notion that children up for adoption might be tainted with the moral, mental, and physical weaknesses of the natural parents.[15] By the 1940s, re-emerging sociological theory related to the "blank slate" premise was applied to adoption practice. Blank slate theory suggested that the human mind was a blank slate to be written upon – that it was experience and environment that shaped a child's mind, not heredity. According to the blank slate theory, any perceived inherited intellectual or moral impediments in an infant would be erased once they were adopted.[16] Adoptions increased.

The Adoption Mandate

Until the 1970s, by far the greatest number of children adopted in Ontario had been born to unmarried mothers. Simultaneously, adopters were married couples. The heteronormative familial imperative of the immediate post-war and Cold War years generated a high demand for newborns to address the problem of infertility and create nuclear families. For example, from 1942 to 1971 total adoptions in the province were 131,301, and of these, 96,367 (73.4 per cent) involved infants born to unmarried mothers.[17] These numbers reflect the prevailing social prescription for unmarried motherhood in the post-war era—the "realistic plan," a euphemism for adoption used extensively in Ontario social work practice. This practice became embedded in the policies of the provincial government and was accomplished through Children's Aid Society (CAS) social workers, clergy, the medical community, and families. By the 1940s, a period rife with emerging psychoanalytic theories, there was a major preoccupation with what was now being called the "unwed mother." In the Victorian era such women had been constructed as "fallen" and sinful; now they were characterized as having a mental disorder. Rickie Solinger explains:

> The postwar, modern alternative claimed that illegitimacy reflected a mental not environmental or biological disorder, and was, in general a symptom of individual, treatable neuroses ... Since society reserved deeply punitive responses for unwed

> mothers, a single girl who flew in the face of certain and severe censure and became pregnant had to be sick. She had, in fact, to be pregnant on purpose. Only a truly sick person could deny reality so radically.[18]

In this context, adoption in post-war Ontario served as a social "safety valve":[19] a young mother, having become pregnant out of wedlock, would be simultaneously punished for her transgression and "rehabilitated" through the surrender of her child for adoption, leaving her "mistake" in the past. This period of adoption practice, coined the "adoption mandate" by Lori Chambers,[20] entailed thousands of young unmarried mothers in Ontario, and indeed across Canada, being coerced to surrender their (usually) first-born babies for adoption, simply because of their marital status. Valerie Andrews describes the mandate as "a process of interrelated power systems which, together with socio-cultural norms, ideals of gender heteronormativity, and emerging sociological and psychoanalytical theories, created historically unique conditions in the post WWII decades wherein the white unmarried mother was systematically separated from her baby by means of adoption."[21] Although the Universal Declaration of Human Rights, ratified by Canada in 1948, stated in Article 2 that "motherhood and childhood are entitled to special care and assistance,"[22] this did not appear to apply to the unmarried mother in Canada's post-war decades.

CASs facilitated adoptions through their control of adoption paperwork (and the selection of adoptive parents) and their discretion with regard to court proceedings initiated by unwed mothers seeking support from putative fathers.[23] Furthermore, as in other provinces, the Ontario government funded church-run "homes for unwed mothers" that were operated by the mainstream Christian churches, including Catholic, Anglican, United, Presbyterian, Salvation Army, and Evangelical. In these quasi-carceral settings, unmarried mothers were subjected to coercive systems leading to adoption. Ontario government reports and records referred to the mothers in these facilities as "inmates." Adoption rates for these "homes" were around 95 per cent.[24] This is in stark contrast to today, when unmarried mothers surrender their babies for adoption at the rate of around 2 per cent.[25]

In Ontario hospitals, unmarried mothers were subject to adoption protocols upon arrival. Adoption was the assumed practice for unmarried mothers, particularly those arriving from maternity homes. Mothers reported being subjected to verbal, physical, and psychological abuse as well as punitive treatment.[26] Unmarried mothers were segregated from married mothers. Mothers were left to labour alone. Some were overmedicated and had little or no memory of events, while others were given no medications at all. A protocol known as "clean break" meant that most babies were taken away directly from the delivery table while the mother was in the final stages of delivery – whisked away with no eye contact, which was often prevented by the use of sheets, pillows, the hiding of mirrors, and other means.[27] Some mothers reported trying to run after their babies, while others reported the use of restraints. One mother reported seeing "a little mop of dark hair poking out of the blanket" as her child was whisked away from the delivery room, never to be seen again.[28] One mother from Humewood House, a Toronto maternity home, stated that "I was not allowed to see my infant son after he was born … When other babies were wheeled into the ward for feeding, I sat alone and watched … Eventually I became hysterical with grief."[29] Another mother, who gave birth in 1964, wrote, "My head was restrained when I begged to see my baby … I never had the chance."[30] These mothers were routinely denied their right to see, hold, feed, and mother their babies. Without prior consent, mothers' breasts were bound and lactation suppressants were administered. Some mothers were told their babies had died, only to learn years later that they had been adopted. Others still do not know whether they gave birth to a boy or a girl, being told, "That is nothing to do with you."[31]

Under Ontario's 1921 Adoption Act, the guardian or parents of the child to be adopted were required to sign a consent. In the case of unmarried mothers only the mother's consent was required. In a 1937 amendment, the right of the court to dispense with consent was broadened and became "open to considerable discretion."[32] During the period of the adoption mandate, the consent was not to be signed before the seventh day after birth and the mother was afforded a twenty-one-day revocation period by law. However, there were very few cases in which the baby was returned to the unmarried mother even when the request was made within the prescribed period. Social workers, women in religious orders, and others often used high-pressure tactics to obtain consent from the unmarried mother. Mothers report that social workers often resorted to threats, fear, duress, lies, trickery, and even physical force.[33] Mothers were not provided with legal counsel, nor, in most cases, were they given a copy of any paper they signed, and many were not informed of their right to revocation. Ontario social workers routinely withheld information about mothers' rights and resources that would help them to parent, asserting that it was in the best interest of the child to be in a two-parent household. After birth, mothers returned to their communities, still in shock and traumatized, and were told to keep the birth secret. They were given no aftercare or counselling.[34] In the wider popular culture, these mothers were constructed as uncaring abandoners, unnatural mothers with no maternal sentiments who "gave away their babies."[35] They were thus condemned to a lifetime of secrecy and shame.

Unmarried mothers of the post-war era continue to be cited by successive governments and others as the reason for ongoing secrecy in adoption records. Contrary to discourse in various debates in the Ontario legislature leading to adoption disclosure, and various court proceedings, however, we could find no document on record to suggest that secrecy was promised as a right for these mothers. In fact, mothers assert the opposite was true: in order to coerce them into releasing their children, many unmarried mothers were given assurances they would see their children when the children turned eighteen.[36] Mothers were groomed for shame and secrecy by maternity home matrons, social workers, clergy, the medical community, and their own families.[37] The trauma these mothers endured and the secrets they were told to keep still prevent many mothers of the mandate from moving forward when records open or when the prospect of reunion presents itself. This is not because they were promised secrecy in adoption records. Instead, they are a traumatized group, many suffering from post-traumatic stress disorder (PTSD)[38] and other mental health issues as a result of the lifelong trauma many have suffered due to stigma, shame, harsh treatment, the often violent loss of their babies, and the effects of keeping the secret of birth from family and friends for a lifetime. A recent Senate committee in Canada looking into such adoptions has recommended that mental health professionals be educated about these issues and that mental health assistance be provided to these traumatized mothers.[39]

Sealed Records and the Adoption Disclosure Registry

Throughout the period of the adoption mandate, surrendering mothers were required to register the births of children with provincial authorities, and a registration of birth contained the child's name as given by the mother as well as, if the mother was unmarried, her surname, the date and place of birth, and the mother's name, age, marital status, and residence at the date of the child's birth. If the mother had been in a maternity home, the address of the home was recorded as her residence. In cases where the mother was married, her husband was recorded as the father, whether or not this was biologically accurate. An adoption order sometimes contained the pre-adoption surname or surname initial of the child to be adopted (usually the surname of the unmarried mother), the names of the adoptive parents, and the adopted child's post-adoption given name and surname. New birth certificates were issued for adopted children, and it is estimated that for about 60 per cent of those in Ontario who have been adopted, two registrations of birth exist: "a sealed original birth registration … and a substituted birth registration containing the post-adoption name and the particulars of the adoptive parents."[40] Even when adopted persons were able to obtain original birth certificates, such records were sparse; personal details were primarily to be found in the adoption files created by social service agencies facilitating the transfer of children. The Adoption Act, 1927, stipulated that "the papers used upon an adoption application shall be sealed up and shall not be open for inspection save upon the direction of a Judge or the Provincial Officer."[41] The circumstances under which an adoption file might be opened by a judge or provincial officer were not detailed, and much was left to the discretion of both adoption agencies and courts. Closed adoption records were based on two assumptions: that children needed to be protected from the shame of illegitimacy, and that adoptive families might be threatened by any connection to a birth parent. The secrecy provisions in Ontario adoption law were not unusual; similar systems existed in all the Canadian provinces as well as the United States, New Zealand, the United Kingdom, and Australia.[42]

In such circumstances, social workers "had the power to provide or deny access to adoption records."[43] Evidence from adoption files suggests that social workers at the CAS in Ontario were sometimes willing to reassure mothers that children had been placed in loving homes and that they were healthy and thriving (whether or not this was true), but routinely refused to release any information that might have pointed to the child's whereabouts or adoptive name. In Ontario and elsewhere, particularly in contexts in which mothers were under significant pressure to surrender, lack of knowledge about children released for adoption caused distress. As noted earlier, studies show that relinquishing mothers want to know how their children have fared in life.[44] In revealing autobiographical stories, mothers have eloquently described being "haunted by fear for their child's welfare, [and of] guilt both for abandoning their child and for continuing to love and long for him."[45] These emotions are evident in CAS adoption files. One mother, seeking information about the welfare of a child she had relinquished, asserted that "there are things that go on in your mind. You think about it. Sometimes you wonder if the child is alright."[46] Several described yearning to "know that she was ok, that she was happy, that my decision was good for her."[47] Although women who sought information from CAS might be given general reassurances that their children had been placed in good homes, they were told to get on with their lives, that they had no right to any identifying information, and that their relationships with their children had been permanently and irrevocably severed. Mothers were often told by social workers to forget about their children. One Ontario mother, a witness at the Senate hearings on the adoption mandate in Canada, told the committee, "I was told that I would eventually get married and forget about my baby. How does a mother forget her baby?"[48]

Mothers were not the only parties to adoption to question secrecy. Adoptees also informally approached the CAS for information, and adoption case files reveal that for some of them, relinquishment could raise subtle questions about belonging. For example, one child, born and adopted in 1960, started writing letters to the CAS in 1971 requesting information about her biological parents. She wrote eleven letters of inquiry between 1971 and 1977.[49] As was the case when mothers sought information, it seems that social workers were unwilling to provide identifying information about mothers to adoptees, even if there was correspondence for them from the mother in the file, or if their mother was also looking for them. These inquiries, however, did not advance to court. Those who opposed secrecy, however, became increasingly vocal as the twentieth century progressed.

In Canada, wider popular discussion about searching began with the work of Clare Marcus.[50] Marcus was born to an unmarried mother in Winnipeg in 1924 and adopted privately directly from hospital. She wrote two books, published in 1979 and 1981 respectively: *Adopted? A Canadian Guide for Adopted Adults in Search of Their Origins*, and *Who is My Mother?* She called for the creation of an adoption registry and provided advice for searching adoptees as to how to find their biological parents. She was also a founding member of Parent Finders, a group that originated in British Columbia and remains one of the leading organizations assisting those separated by adoption in the reunion process in Canada.[51]

While Marcus and activists in other jurisdictions were articulating the pain of mothers separated from their children, social science researchers were asking important questions about outcomes in adoption. David Kirk, a Canadian sociologist and adoptive parent, in a provocative book published in 1964,[52] argued that more openness was necessary in adoption. He hypothesized that adoptive children were like first-generation immigrants into their new families. This theory was described as "complacency-shattering" for those involved in adoption.[53] He "stressed the need to acknowledge that adoptive families are different from biological ones."[54] He did not, however, disparage adoption itself, emphasizing that with acknowledgment of difference adoptive families could be very happy. Other researchers asserted much more controversial findings, in particular Annette Sorosky, Reuben Baran, and Arthur Pannor,[55] who claimed that for all those involved in the adoption transaction, feelings of loss, pain, and mourning were permanent. The search movement in the 1970s based its demands on the presumed psychological needs of adopted children.[56]

The search movement gained significant public attention in a context of increased concern about children's rights in general, in particular as articulated by the UN Convention on the Rights of the Child. Article 8 of that convention (1989) explicitly articulated the child's "right to identity, including nationality, name and family relations."[57] Although such arguments were originally framed with regard to children subject to dislocation during wartime and other crises, the adoption rights movement extrapolated from this a right to identity for adopted children and found considerable public support. Moreover, demands regarding individual rights as raised by adoptees and birth mothers were "tailor-made for mass circulation magazines which were quick to exploit the melodrama inherent in adoptee searches,"[58] and this ensured wide interest in adoption and secrecy. Public discourse about adoption outcomes and the harms of secrecy undoubtedly influenced the Ontario government's decision to create a mutual consent adoption registry in 1978.

That year, by a 37–36 vote in the legislature, an Adoption Disclosure Registry was established in Ontario through a revision to its Child Welfare Act.[59] That registry worked to match adult adoptees and biological mothers (and fathers who were named in adoption documents, although this was unusual) who wished to reunite. A series of forms had to be completed and then revised and verified in order to initiate a search. Next, a social worker would attempt to make a match. A match was only possible if both parties had applied. If both had not, the applicants were entered in the registry and were told that the ministry would contact them in the event that the other party had registered. Parties were explicitly granted veto powers.[60]

Legalization and Legal Challenges

The first challenge to Ontario's closed adoption regime reached the Ontario County Court, Middlesex, and was heard by Killeen Co. Ct. J. in 1983.[61] The applicant wanted access to information about her origins, and the court had to determine what constituted "good cause" to order that files be opened. The applicant, Elizabeth Ferguson, had entered her name in the adoption registry, but the surrendering mother had not. She had tried to convince the CAS and Vital Statistics to release the information voluntarily, explaining that she had "experienced a sense of incompleteness, as if missing a piece of the puzzle of my identity." The ministry had refused to release the information on the basis that, absent the consent and registration of her mother, it could do so only "where some overriding compelling circumstances related to the health of the adoptee dictate the release of such information as a matter of policy." Killeen Co. Ct. J. expressed that he was very impressed by the applicant, who had "not attempted to colour or clog her application with dubious or tenuous medical materials aimed at establishing that she has a compelling need for the requested biological and related information. Rather, she grounds her application on the simple argument that she has a healthy and continuing 'natural curiosity' to know about her origins."

Her lawyer asserted that the "best interests of the child" should override the concerns of birth parents, although he did assert (as would many who followed) that "most birth parents -- and especially birth mothers – have given up their children for adoption in the expectation that their particular role in the adoption process will be accorded some privacy and confidentiality." The ministry, however, asserted that the voluntary adoption registry was sufficient and that the revisions of 1978 provided "a complete code on the disclosure of Ministry information about adoptees except for those rare cases – based on a 'compelling need' standard – where the court might order the release of information." Killeen Co. Ct. J. chastised the government for failing to publicize that the registry existed. He asserted that anonymity remained central to adoption and that while the "best interests of the child" test should determine the adoption itself, this doctrine had "no place in a disclosure decision: after the adoption order has been signed, the shield of secrecy erected around the adoption process demands that equal prominence be given to the interests of each of the parties to the adoption triangle." While sympathetic to Elizabeth Ferguson, therefore, he denied her request.[62] Ferguson appealed this decision, but Killeen Co. Ct. J. was upheld.[63]

In response to the *Ferguson* case, the Ontario government attempted, in 1985, to make the release of any information from adoption files illegal. The Minister of Community and Social Services (ComSoc), Frank Drea, asserted that any information could identify individuals in small communities and that therefore such information had to be carefully protected to ensure privacy. However, he was accused of wanting to reseal adoption records because his own adopted daughter was actively seeking her birth family. Public outcry "prevented the legislation from being enacted."[64] Also in 1985, ComSoc appointed a special commissioner, Dr. Ralph Garber, to make recommendations regarding the disclosure of adoption information.

While the legislature was awaiting the report of the Garber Commission, another county court in Ontario denied access to information regarding adoption. This time the request came from a mother, not an adopted adult, and the court was significantly less sympathetic than had been the case in *Ferguson*.[65] The mother had been provided with detailed, non-identifying information by the CAS to reassure her that her child was thriving in his adoptive home. In her affidavit the applicant mother described eloquently the "social pressures to which she [had been] subject in 1964 at age 20 on her pregnancy being confirmed and complain[ed] of lack of counselling as to how she could keep her baby and thrive on her own." She asserted not only that a reunion with her son would be good for her but also, echoing the rhetoric of the adoption rights movement, that contact would benefit her son. Gotlib D.C.J. disagreed, asserting that

> the applicant appears to be obsessed with making contact with her son, but … he is of university age, and may never have been curious about his natural mother, in which case any inquiry or communication will come to him as a brutal surprise. Indeed, if he is vulnerable, it could be a blow from which he might never recover. I consider that the best interests of the child come before those of the natural mother.

He also found that the applicant had registered with the Provincial Adoption Disclosure Registry and that "if the applicant's adopted son should develop any curiosity about his roots and his natural mother, he is free to register also, at which time appropriate meeting arrangements can be made."[66]

Shortly after that, Garber recommended that adult adoptees be permitted access to identifying information without the consent of the person identified, but this recommendation was not enacted by the legislature.[67] In the provincial legislature, John Sweeney, in rejecting complete openness, "asserted that the adopted adult's 'right to know' had to be balanced against the birth parents' historic right to confidentiality and privacy."[68] As a compromise measure, in 1987, amendments to the Child Welfare Act and the provisions of the Adoption Disclosure Statute Law Amendment transformed the once passive Adoption Disclosure Registry into an active search system[69] "whereby adopted persons and certain categories of birth relatives [could] be located even in the absence of registration in the passive registry." Consent would still be required, however. Under this system, instead of waiting to match parents and children once both had registered, "the registrar [would] conduct an active search for a specified second party after the first party ha[d] registered with the registry … [and] when a match [was] made on the registry, the two parties [would be] contacted by a government social worker who determine[d] if the parties g[a]ve their 'mutual consent' for the identifying information to be released and/or for contact to be made." The director also retained the right to allow disclosure "of identifying information where required for the health, safety or welfare of any individual."[70] In the months after the implementation of the new provisions, more than 4,500 requests for information were submitted, indicating significant discontent with the secrecy of adoption procedures and records.[71]

Pressure for further reform continued to mount. The most vocal advocate of reform in Ontario was Marilyn Churley, an MPP and mother who had surrendered her infant during the adoption mandate. Churley introduced private member's bills to the legislature in 1998, 2000, 2001, and 2003.[72] She proposed a system that would allow a contact veto, but not a disclosure veto.[73] Advocates of reform were successful in Ontario in 2005, when the legislature passed the Adoption Information Disclosure Act.[74] The bill was introduced on 29 March 2005 by the ComSoc minister, Sandra Pupatello. Adoptees over eighteen years of age, and birth mothers (once the children in question reached the age of nineteen), would be able to obtain copies of original birth records and adoption orders. Birth mothers and adoptees could file no-contact notices, and a mechanism was created for denying disclosure altogether, but that would require a determination by a board that the non-disclosure was necessary to prevent physical or sexual harm to the party seeking to prevent disclosure (a show cause procedure).[75] This reform was controversial and faced serious opposition in the House. In particular, the province's Information and Privacy Commissioner, Ann Cavoukian, "repeatedly criticized the retroactive nature of the bill and the consequent harmful social consequences – careers ruined, family life destroyed, privacy invaded – that she warned would occur as a result of the enactment of the Adoption Information Disclosure Act." In a context in which privacy was of increasing public concern due to the development of new means of communication, particularly the internet and the increasing use of large computer data sets by governments and other organizations, her arguments had some public support. Nonetheless, the bill passed by a vote of 68–19 and received Royal Assent on 3 November.[76] Implementation was delayed until 19 September 2006 in the interest of public education (to allow time for non-contact orders to be filed). In the interim, two Ontario court cases challenged adoption disclosure provisions. In *Marchand*,[77] an adult adoptee sought retroactive disclosure of her putative father's name and was denied access to this information. In *Cheskes*,[78] four parties challenged the provisions of the Adoption Information Disclosure Act as violating their constitutional right to privacy and were successful.

The plaintiff in *Marchand* had been adopted as an infant in 1957. By the time she sought out her birth parents, her mother was long dead, but adoption agency files contained the name of a man identified by her mother as her father. The man denied paternity both at the time of the birth and also when approached by the CAS regarding reunion, and refused to have his name released to the applicant. The CAS had released non-identifying information to her, as was permitted under legislation. She again contacted the Adoption Disclosure Registry and was given information about her mother's cause of death and place of burial.[79] The applicant then had her lawyer approach the registrar seeking disclosure of her putative father's name; disclosure was again denied.[80] During her childhood the applicant had not been told of her adoption and had been subjected to severe physical, emotional, and sexual abuse. She claimed that her life had been seriously marred by secrecy and that denial of knowledge about her putative father had deprived her "of what she describe[d] as the fundamental right to know where she c[ame] from. She argue[d] that the closing of records is profoundly damaging to adoptees as it prevents them from achieving wholeness … [and that the provisions were] in breach of … her right to liberty, security of the person pursuant to s. 7 of the *Charter*, and … her equality rights pursuant to s. 15 of the *Charter*." The attorney general countered that the Adoption Disclosure Registry was intended to balance the "competing demands of access to information and protection of privacy of those involved in an adoption."[81]

Frank J. of the Ontario Superior Court of Justice found that the "information was refused … because there was no match on the Adoption Disclosure Register and because the man denied his consent to disclosure." Frank J. held that "while there is no question that the applicant is enormously frustrated by her inability to access the name of the person identified by her birth mother as being her birth father … the evidence does not support her assertion that her life would have taken a fundamentally different course had she been allowed to openly access her birth and adoption records," and that "extensive sexual and physical abuse" and "the secrecy that informed her childhood" were problems created, not by the impugned legislation, "but rather [by] the attitude and approach of her adoptive parents." Thus there was no connection between the secrecy imposed by her family and the structural secrecy created by legislation itself.[82] The court rejected her expert evidence asserting that adopted children suffered harm because of secrecy;[83] that evidence was deemed to be biased and to ignore "recent, large, representative and methodologically sophisticated studies … that have found no significant differences between the behaviors and characteristics of matched groups of adopted children and non-adopted children." Her assertion that only the rights of the adopted child should be considered was also rejected: "while there may not be anything in writing confirming to birth parents that their privacy will not be breached, their understanding and expectation was that their confidentiality would be maintained." The court asserted that "there is no liberty right to obtain identifying information about a person who has expressly refused to consent to its disclosure." Her s. 15 claim was denied because the legislation was intended to facilitate reunions and to ameliorate the condition of adopted children and "a reasonable person, in assessing whether the scheme treated the applicant as less worthy of respect and consideration than non-adopted persons, would take this into account."[84]

Marchand appealed, but in the interim the legal environment had changed because the Adoption Information Disclosure Act was subject to constitutional challenge in the Superior Court, where it was ultimately deemed unconstitutional. On the first day of the appeal hearing, the Ontario government announced that it would not appeal the *Cheskes* decision but instead would "introduce new legislation that would let parents and children involved in past adoptions veto disclosure of information."[85] Because such an announcement was deemed likely to lead to the "return to something like the repealed Child and Family Services Act scheme," the court asserted that it was important to hear Marchand's appeal. The Court of Appeal accepted the judgment of the lower court in full: "in our view, this analysis is sound … [and] the unconditional disclosure of identifying personal information of third parties, even if they are birth parents of the claimant, without regard to the privacy and confidentiality interests of the persons identified and without regard to any serious harm that might result from disclosure … is not a principle that is vital or fundamental to our societal notion of justice." Leave to appeal to the Supreme Court of Canada was filed on 29 January 2008, submitted to the Court on 10 March 2008, and dismissed by McLachlin C.J. and Fish and Rothstein J.J. on 24 April 2008.[86] The claim that adult adoptees have a right to information about their birth parents had failed.[87]

In the interim, moreover, the rights of parties who opposed disclosure had been upheld. In *Cheskes v. Ontario*, four applicants – three adult adoptees and a putative father who denied paternity – expressed fear and anxiety about the possible implications of the Adoption Information Disclosure Act for their families, arguing that disclosure of personal information without their consent would violate their s. 7 rights to life, liberty, and security of the person. They did not oppose the idea of open adoption on a going-forward basis, but they objected to "retroactive application of the legislation." They asserted that "the opening of confidential adoption records on a retroactive basis and the removal of the consent requirement violates the applicants' right to privacy under s 7 of the *Charter* in a manner that cannot be justified under s 1. On the other hand, the right of searching adoptees or birth parents to gain access to confidential adoption information, although important and heart-felt, is not a *Charter*-protected right."

The personal reasons for opposition to the opening of records varied. Joy Cheskes had a happy adoptive family life and did not want this life disrupted by contact from birth parents. She also asserted that the proposal that a disclosure veto be obtained via a hearing violated her right to make autonomous decisions: "I do not see why I should be forced to reveal this information or go through the stress and emotional turmoil of having to divulge these feelings to a board in the hope of then being allowed to keep my personal information private." Moreover, she asserted that providing identifying information to a birth parent would have an enormous, and unwanted, impact on her family: "by disclosing my identity, I am disclosing theirs, too."[88]

Denbigh Patton was concerned about the impact of contact with a birth parent on his elderly, and very loving, adoptive parents, and asserted that the "no-contact provision would not prevent the disclosure of his identity and with that identifying information." He spoke eloquently about the process by which he had come to the decision that he did not want to have contact with his birth parents: "I am not currently willing to risk trauma to my life as it is, to my family, to my loving aging parents, to my identity. This is a weighty decision that I have carried all my adult life and will continue to ponder. But it is for me to ponder and it is I who will suffer or benefit as a consequence of this decision." He also asserted that the prospect of being exposed against his will had caused him such anxiety that he had sought medical intervention.[89]

C.M. had also grown up in a happy adoptive home and for fourteen years had known that a birth parent was avidly searching for her. She had repeatedly told the social work agency that she did not desire contact, but the searching continued, and she feared that the release of identifying information would lead to an unwanted invasion of her privacy, since her birth parent had already disregarded her clear statement that she did not want contact: "The no contact order is totally irrelevant to me, because no contact will not mean that they cannot watch me, they can't drive past my house. This person could get my name and give this to children that she has, to other friends, to relatives. It … does not provide me any comfort whatsoever … I could be stalked. She expressed feeling 'hunted' by her birth mother."[90]

The fourth applicant, D.S., had fathered a child who had subsequently been adopted. The child was the product of a brief sexual relationship, and the putative father had heard about the birth itself only when contacted by the CAS. He had denied paternity at the time, but his name was nonetheless included as the father of record. He subsequently married and had a family, only to later be contacted by a social worker asking if he would be willing to have contact with the adopted adult. He declined, stating that his wife and family were unaware of the child and subsequent adoption and that such disclosure would tear his family apart. He asserted that "this exposure would render me even more powerless, humiliated, and vulnerable."[91]

The *Cheskes* court accepted the validity of the arguments and the concerns of the applicants, noting that while the interests of searching adopted children have been the subject of public discussion, "the feelings and the fears of the 'non-searching' adoptees and birth parents who do not want to be found are no less legitimate and no less compelling," and that "the impact on their lives and those of their families is just as significant … Lives could be shattered." It may be that the segment of the adoption population identified by the court as "non-searching" in *Cheskes* supports the adoption status quo. However, although it was suggested in *Cheskes* that there have been few studies of relinquishing mothers, this is not in fact the case nor was it at the time of the court proceedings. As noted earlier in this text, there have been many studies about the impact of "relinquishment" on surrendering mothers. These reports are routinely ignored in these types of discussions and by courts.

The violation imposed by the Adoption Information Disclosure Act was deemed to be an invasion not just of documents or records, but also "of the dignity and self-worth of the individual, who enjoys the right to privacy as an essential aspect of his or her liberty in a free and democratic society"; such liberty interests included the right to make fundamental life choices without interference from the state. The court asserted that "the protection of privacy is a fundamental value in modern democracies" and noted that personal information is for that person "to communicate or retain for himself as he sees fit." The no-contact provisions and the non-disclosure provisions were also found to be inadequate to protect the needs articulated by the applicants. The court affirmed the line of cases asserting that "the right to know one's past" is not a constitutionally protected right under Canadian law but that the right to privacy is such a protected interest: "where a reasonable expectation of privacy has been established in the collection and storage of one's personal and confidential information, one should have the ability to control the dissemination of this information." Contrary to the arguments of the Ontario government, moreover, the legislation could not be saved by reference to s. 1 of the Charter as "opening adoption records on a retroactive basis is no doubt extremely important for many, but the new law cannot be said to fall within any of the extraordinary or emergency categories."[92] The court asserted that other provinces continued to endorse mutual consent provisions with regard to adoption registries such as those in Ontario that had prevailed before the passage of the Adoption Information Disclosure Act.[93] Furthermore, even the four provinces that had recently reformed their adoption information disclosure provisions allowed for disclosure vetoes without show cause procedures.[94] In this context, the Adoption Information Disclosure Act was declared null and void, and Ontario was ordered to amend its legislation.

In the wake of the *Cheskes* decision, the Ontario government announced that it would not appeal. Instead, ComSoc minister Madeleine Meilleur stated that the government would introduce new compromise legislation.[95] As a result of these reforms, under current provisions, adopted adults and birth mothers can file disclosure vetoes to protect their privacy if the adoption was finalized before 1 September 2008. Such a veto prevents the release of post-adoption information about the person who filed that veto. If the adoption was finalized after the specified date, a person can only file a no-contact notice, and this requires an appearance before a board and proof of exceptional circumstances.[96] This legislation represents an acknowledgment that adoptive relationships are not identical to those based in biology. It also respects the privacy of those who were adopted, or who released children for adoption in an era in which secrecy was practised. But it does not satisfy many searching parents and/or their adult children.

Adoption Reform Movement

As the new millennium approached and with the introduction of the internet, a worldwide community of adoption activists and reformers came together, now known as the adoption reform movement. Activists are mostly adoptees seeking adoptee rights with respect to adoption records, as well as surrendering mothers seeking justice for past adoption practices. Although current adoption practice trends towards openness, the fact remains that adoption records remain sealed or semi-sealed in all provinces in Canada. Adoption records in Nova Scotia remain completely sealed, although public consultations to open records are currently under way in that province. Quebec legislation allows only adult adopted persons to obtain information, while mothers remain unable to access documentation. In all other provinces, vetoes or contact preferences apply, leaving records only semi-open.[97] In some provinces, large fines and jail terms apply for contravening a veto or contact preference. In Ontario, the fine is $50,000 for contravening a contact preference,[98] although to date the authors are unaware of an instance in which this fine has been imposed. Adoption reformers are outraged that those separated by adoption continue to be characterized as a "criminal" or "suspect" group within society simply for desiring their own birth information, or that pertaining to the children to whom they gave birth. Activists assert that when "special laws" are created for those separated by adoption they are further stigmatized and marginalized, since there are already laws for those who harass or engage in unwanted contact with others. Furthermore, they assert that in the internet age we are inundated with unwanted contact and have the right to choose whether or not to interact with others who may initiate contact with us. It is their stance that this should also apply to those separated by adoption and that no special law with fines and jail terms is required.

For activists, the premise of transparency in adoption records is rooted in adoptee rights – in the belief that it is a basic human right to know one's origins. This idea stems in part from the UN Universal Declaration of Human Rights (1948), which states in Article 7 that "[a]ll are equal before the law and are entitled without any discrimination to equal protection of the law." Adoption reformers assert that since documentation pertaining to one's birth is available to all members of society except to those separated from their families by adoption, this constitutes a form of discrimination and a violation of human rights. As previously mentioned, adoptee rights groups also continue to cite the UN Convention on the Rights of the Child (1989). The adoption reform community contests the use of vetoes in legislation, taking the position that no individual should have the right in law to prevent another individual from receiving their own documentation pertaining to their own birth, and that the adoptee's basic human right to know their origins should supersede any right of privacy for mothers (who would still have the right to decide whether or not they wished to have relationships with any child by whom they might be contacted and who could prevent unwanted contact through existing harassment law).

In contemporary society it is no longer socially or legally acceptable to stigmatize parents and children with the stain of "illegitimacy." Reformers claim that keeping records closed perpetuates adoption myths and stereotypes and reinstitutes the status of "illegitimacy" in contemporary law – a status that is no longer relevant or appropriate since Ontario abolished illegitimacy in the Family Law Reform Act in 1980.[99] It is their contention that through such systems, the contemporary state is actively involved in maintaining the shame, secrecy, and stigma of illegitimacy as it existed in the past. Furthermore, in keeping records sealed, or subject to vetoes, the state is preserving the social secrets of a small segment of the population with all the associated administration and costs that entails. Reformers insist that it is not the role of the state to keep the social secrets of its constituents.

Activists and reformers contend that the primary stakeholders in any legislative reform to open adoption records are only those separated from a family member by adoption – natural parents, adoptees, and extended natural families. Although adoptive parents may be interested parties, they have not been separated from any family member through adoption. Furthermore, since any proposed changes in the opening of adoption records in Canada usually pertain to adopted adults who have reached the age of majority, no parent, adoptive or otherwise, has rights with respect to their adult children and their personal documentation or affairs. Therefore, adoptive parents are not deemed to be stakeholders by the adoption reform community.

As we have seen in Ontario, although the confidentiality and privacy of surrendering mothers is almost always used as the premise position by legislators when they contemplate the opening of adoption records, these stakeholders are rarely consulted. Instead, their "promised" privacy is spoken about freely by lawyers and legislators. Adoption activists, many of whom are surrendering mothers, maintain that the majority of mothers never asked for secrecy, nor were they promised it – that adoption records were not sealed primarily to protect unmarried mothers from the stigma of bearing an out-of-wedlock child. Rather, they were sealed in order to completely sever ties between the adoptee and their natal family in order to uphold the "as if born to" myth of the adoptive tie and to provide security to the newly formed adoptive relationship. According to Keith Griffith, the notion of a complete break through the sealing of records had three main components: (1) protective role – safeguard and protect the child and adoptive parents from interference; (2) constructive role – to emphasize the formation of a new relationship; and (3) destructive role – to destroy any connection with the past.[100] Unmarried mothers, who were disparaged and subject to illegal, unethical, and human rights abuses in adoption practice during the adoption mandate period, were not considered important in the adoption transaction. Care and concern for these mothers after birth was virtually non-existent. It is unlikely that the interests of the unmarried mother were strongly considered in adoption secrecy and the sealing of records. However, those interests continue to be used today as the reason to keep records sealed.

One of the myths of adoption disclosure is that reunion or a relationship follows. Some may simply wish to obtain their records and store them for their personal use, a right that adoption reformers feel strongly should be available for any mother who gave birth to a child, as well as to those who are adopted. In Ontario, adoption disclosure does not include personal information such as place of work or current address. Only name at birth, place of birth, date of birth, and mother's name and address at the time of the birth on the birth registration are revealed to searchers. Most mothers at the time of the mandate were given no paperwork at all pertaining either to the birth of their child or to the adoption. These mothers assert that they have a right to paperwork connected to any child they birthed – particularly any paperwork they may have signed, such as the original birth registration and adoption consents, documents not given to them at the time. These documents are available through the CAS that handled the adoption where such records have been maintained. New regulations under the Child, Youth and Family Services Act of 2017 that came into effect on 1 January 2020 require the CAS to provide a copy of the adoption file to the mother (with relevant third-party redactions for privacy) within thirty days of a request.[101]

Adoption reformers are also concerned that the current legislation does not allow for the names of fathers of the children of unmarried mothers to be disclosed. In many adoptions the name of the father was provided by the mother and recorded in the adoption file; in others a Declaration of Paternity may have been signed by the father and support paid. But these men did not appear on formal birth records. Under the Vital Statistics Act, until the mid-1980s unmarried mothers were prevented by legislation from naming the father on the statement of birth unless she and the father made a statutory declaration that he be named. The child was considered "illegitimate," a term not removed from the act until 1981.[102] As a result, when mothers at the time of the mandate filled out the birth registration after birth, many were told to "leave blank" the section referring to the father's name. When records were disclosed in 2009, mothers who had filled out the father's name against such advice found the name of the father blacked out, whited out, or even cut out. One mother, speaking about the altered records, felt that this was a matter of principle: "You expect that the document you signed is going to be kept intact."[103] The *Toronto Star* reported that "out of all 250,000 Ontario adoption registrations, less than 10 per cent have fathers' names on them, according to the Ministry of Government Services."[104] Although paternity can be confirmed today with the use of a DNA test, the records continue to remain sealed with respect to the identity of fathers. Secrecy also applies to extended family members. Grandmothers, siblings, cousins, and aunts continue to seek children lost to families by adoption but have no rights to disclosure under the current legislation.

The idea of maintaining secrecy in adoption is now obsolete since the introduction of the internet and DNA matching through organizations such as Ancestry and 23andMe. Adoptees and mothers alike now circumvent the secrecy of government records by searching on social media platforms such as Facebook or by obtaining DNA results for family members. This facility is important, especially for those seeking fathers, siblings, and extended family members who are not included in adoption disclosure legislation. Furthermore, those who were adopted illegally, such as the Montreal Black Market Babies[105] and others who have no provincial paperwork due to unethical adoption transactions, are now using DNA to locate their families of origin. DNA can resolve controversies surrounding identity, with or without legal change. Notwithstanding the benefits of DNA technology, reformers believe it is time to leave outdated notions of "shame" and "illegitimacy," and the myths and secrecy of the adoption mandate, in the past – and for governments to stop reinscribing these notions through contemporary legislation. After all, it is 2020s, not 1950.

QUESTIONS FOR CONSIDERATION:

1. Why were ties to natural parents severed in 1921, according to the authors?
2. What could unmarried mothers expect in hospitals in the 1960s? Why was adoption the assumed protocol?

3. In the post-war period, mothers described very different protocols than what had been promised. What was different?
4. Who is Clare Marcus? Why is she important?
5. What was the *Ferguson* case? Why is it significant in the history of adoption in Ontario?
6. After reading the chapter, why do you think adoption records remain sealed in all provinces in Canada? Do you see this changing in the future?

NOTES

1 Fiction about adoption has long been popular, with some novels achieving iconic status: L.M. Montgomery, *Anne of Green Gables* (1908); Charlotte Brontë, *Jane Eyre* (1847); Frances Hodgson Burnett, *A Little Princess* (1905); Charles Dickens, *Oliver Twist* (1837). In most novels, adoption provides wealth and opportunity for a "low-born" child, reflecting the rescue theme in adoption. Beatrice Culleton Mosionier's *In Search of April Raintree* is a harrowing account of the devastation wrought by the adoption of Indigenous children (Winnipeg: Portage and Main Press, 1983). Movies have tended to be more critical of adoption – for example, Mike Leigh's *Secrets and Lies* (1996), Micho Rutare's *Adopting Terror*, and Laurent Boileau's *Approved for Adoption*. These are but a few examples.

2 Many cultures, including Indigenous cultures in North America or Turtle Island, however, have practised what would now be referred to as open adoption, without shame or secrecy for either the birth or the adoptive family. This perspective, however, was not incorporated into adoption laws in the West when such laws were formulated in the early twentieth century.

3 Karen Dubinsky, *Babies Without Borders: Adoption and Migration across the Americas* (Toronto: University of Toronto Press, 2010), 95.

4 Ferguson Colm O'Donnell, "The Four-Sided Triangle: A Comparative Study of the Confidentiality of Adoption Records," *University of Western Ontario Law Review* 21, no. 1 (1983): 135.

5 *An Act to Amend the Child and Family Services Act* S.O. 1987.

6 *Adoption Information Disclosure Act* S.O. 2005, c. 25.

7 *Cheskes v. Ontario (Attorney General)* [2007] O.J. No 3515 (Sup. Ct.).

8 *Access to Adoption Records Act (Vital Statistics Statute Law Amendment)* S.O. 2008, c. 5.

9 Archives of Ontario (AO), Guardianship and Adoption Archives of Ontario, Research Guide 223, November 2013.

10 *Adoption Act*, c. 55, s. 10(1) (a), (b), (c), and 11(2).

11 Cindy Baldassi, "The Quest to Access Closed Adoption Files in Canada: Understanding Social Context and Legal Resistance to Change," *Canadian Journal of Family Law* 21 (2005), para. 1.

12 *Adoption Act*, s. 9 (3).

13 L.E. Lowman, "Mail Order Babies," *Chatelaine (*April 1932), 32.

14 AO, RG 29-1-RG 29-01-418-Interim Box 50, "Adoptions," 30 December 1960.

15 Lori Chambers, *A Legal History of Adoption in Ontario, 1921–2015* (Toronto: University of Toronto Press, 2016), 20. See also Valerie J. Andrews, *White Unwed Mother: The Adoption Mandate in Postwar Canada* (Demeter Press, 2018), 67.

16 Andrews, *White Unwed Mother*, 96.

17 Andrews, *White Unwed Mother*, 70.

18 Rickie Solinger, *Wake Up Little Susie: Single Pregnancy and Race before Roe v. Wade* (New York and London: Routledge, 1992), 16, 88.
19 Solinger, Rickie, *Wake Up Little Suzie*, 153.
20 Lori Chambers, *Misconceptions: Unmarried Motherhood and the Ontario Children of Unmarried Parents Act, 1921–1969* (TorontoL Osgoode Society for Canadian Legal History, 2007), 85.
21 Andrews, *White Unwed Mother*, 21.
22 See UN, Universal Declaration of Human Rights, https://www.un.org/en/universal-declaration-human-rights.
23 Chambers, *A Legal History*.
24 Andrews, *White Unwed Mother*, 166.
25 Although there is no direct comparable for Canada, data from the US suggest that by 1988 surrender rates by unmarried mothers had fallen to approximately 2 per cent <full cite pls> (Sobol, Daly, 1994:494)
26 Valerie Andrews and Art Eggleton, "Time to acknowledge the other baby scoop," *Toronto Star*, 30 October 2017.
27 Andrews and Eggleton, "Time to acknowledge."
28 Origins Canada, "Past Adoption Policies and Practices: Non-Indigenous and Indigenous Contexts," Conference with MPs and Senators, Parliament Hill, 17 May 2016.
29 See Leslie Ferenc, "Turning shame to empowerment for 100 years," *Toronto Star*, 10 April 2012, G2.
30 Ferenc, "Turning shame to empowerment."
31 Senate Standing Committee on Social Affairs, Science and Technology, Hearings, 20–2 March 2018.
32 Chambers, *A Legal History*, 26–41.
33 Senate Standing Committee on Social Affairs, March 20–2, 2018; see esp. speech from Valerie Andrews, Executive Director, Origins Canada, 20 March.
34 Senate Standing Committee, speech from Andrews, 20 March.
35 Senate Standing Committee, speech from Andrews, 20 March.
36 Monica Byrne quoted in Marilyn Churley, *Shameless: The Fight for Adoption Disclosure and the Search for my Son* (Toronto: Between the Lines, 2015), 149.
37 See Andrews, *White Unwed Mother*, 83–149.
38 Bryony Lake, "Posttraumatic Stress Disorder in Natural Mothers," MA thesis, City University, BC, June 2009.
39 Standing Senate Committee on Social Affairs, Science and Technology, "The Shame Is Ours," July 2018, 17.
40 *Cheskes v. Ontario*, at para. 15.
41 *Adoption Act*, s. 9 (3).
42 Jeanne House, "The Changing Face of Adoption: The Challenge of Open and Custom Adoption," *Canadian Family Law Quarterly* (1996): 334.
43 E. Wayne Carp, *Family Matters: Secrecy and Disclosure in the History of Adoption* (Cambridge, MA: Harvard University Press, 2000), 102, 79.
44 New Brunswick, Public consultation on opening adoption records, https://www2.gnb.ca/content/dam/gnb/Departments/sd-ds/pdf/adoption/PublicResponsePaper.pdf. See also E.Y. Deykin, L. Campbell, and P. Patti, "The Postadoption Experience of Surrendering Parents," *American Journal of Orthopsychiatry* 54, no. 2 (1984): 271–80, https://doi.org/10.1111/j.1939-0025.1984.tb01494.x See also Origins Canada Adoption Trauma Studies, https://www.originscanada.org/adoption-trauma-2/adoption-trauma-studies.

45 Kate Inglis, *Living Mistakes: Mothers Who Consented to Adoption* (Toronto: HarperCollins, 1985), 294.
46 AO, box 411-1-2-9, case 976, York, 1959.
47 AO, box 411-1-3-12, case 2066, York, 1952.
48 Eugenia Powell, Senate Standing Committee, "The Shame is Ours," 3.
49 AO, box 411-1-4-1, case 455, York, 1960.
50 Veronica Strong-Boag, *Finding Families, Finding Ourselves: English Canada Encounters Adoption from the 19th Century to the 1990s* (Toronto: Oxford University Press, 2006), 224.
51 Clare Marcus, *Adopted? A Canadian Guide for Adopted Adults in Search of Their Origins* (Vancouver: International Self-Counsel Press, 1979); Marcus, *Who Is My Mother? Birth Parents, Adoptive Parents, and Adoptees Talk about Living with Adoption and the Search for Lost Family* (Toronto: Macmillan, 1981). The movement for open adoption records was very much a North American phenomenon, and in the 1970s, in the US, a new, very vocal leader emerged in the adoption rights movement – Florence Fisher, a New York City homemaker. After a traumatic but successful search for her birth parents, Fisher founded the Adoptees' Liberty Movement Association (ALMA). <full cite pls> Carp, "Does Opening Adoption Records Have an Adverse Social Impact," 33. ALMA launched a constitutional challenge to the closed adoption record regime: *ALMA Society Inc. v. Mellon*, 601 f.2d 1238–1239 (2nd cir.) cert denied, 1101 (1986). They argued that adoptees had a fundamental right to their records, that denial of access violated the equal protection clause, and that such denial constituted inhumane treatment, which they likened to slavery. All of their arguments were rejected.
52 H. David Kirk, *Shared Fate: A Theory and Method of Adoptive Relationships* (Port Angeles and Brentwood Bay: Ben-Simon, [1964]1984). For a description of his work and its importance, see: Strong-Boag, *Finding Families, Finding Ourselves*, 132, 211, 218, 240, 243.
53 June Callwood, "Adoption Not All Hearts and Flowers," *Chatelaine*, April 1976, 108.
54 Baldassi, "The Quest to Access Closed Adoption Files in Canada," at para. 25.
55 Annette Baran, Rueben Pannor, and Arthur Sorosky, "Open Adoption," *Social Work* (March 1976), 98.
56 Carp, "Does Opening Adoption Records Have an Adverse Social Impact," 33.
57 UN Convention on the Rights of the Child, Art. 8, 20 November 1989, 28 I.L.M., 1448.
58 Carp, *Family Matters*, 159.
59 *Child Welfare Act*, S.O. 1978.
60 Marcus, *Adopted?*, 77.
61 *Ferguson v. Director of Child Welfare et al* (1983) 40 O.R. (2d) (Co. Ct.), 294.
62 *Ibid.*, at 297, 295, 301, 310, 311, 315, 317.
63 *Re Ferguson and Director of Child Welfare et al* [1983] O.J. No. 180 (C.A.).
64 Margot Lettner, "Closing the Door on Disclosure: The Adoption Records Provisions of the Child and Family Services Act, 1984" (1985) 44 *Reports of Family Law* (2d) 28 at 30. For examples of the public outcry, see Doris Anderson, "Adoption Law Will Leave Parents, Kids in Limbo," *Toronto Star*, 13 April 1985, L1; June Callwood, "Adopted People May Never Know," *Globe and Mail*, 3 May 1985, L2; and Janice Dineen, "New Adoption Law 'Retrogressive,'" *Toronto Star*, 20 May 1985, C1.
65 *Tyler v. Ont. Dist. Ct.* [1986] O.J. No. 3074 (Co. Ct).
66 *Ibid.*, at paras. 3, 2 and 4.
67 Ralph Garber, *Disclosure of Adoption Information*, Report of the Special Commissioner to the Honourable John Sweeney, Minister of Community and Social Services, Government of Ontario, November 1985.

68 *Ontario v. Marchand* [2006] O.J. No. 2387 (Sup. Ct.), at para. 10.
69 *An Act to Amend the Child and Family Services Act*, 1987.
70 Joanne Klauer, "Open Adoption Records: A Question of Empowerment," *Saskatchewan Law Review* 57 (1993), 416.
71 Nico Trocme, "Child Welfare Services," in *The State of the Child in Ontario*, ed. Richard Barnhorst and Laura C. Johnson (Toronto: Oxford University Press, 1991), 79.
72 In addition, MPPs Tony Martin, Alex Cullen, and Wayne Wettlaufer introduced bills in 1994, 1996, and 2003 respectively. See https://parentfindersottawa.ca/ontario-legislation.
73 For further details regarding Marilyn Churley, see Kris Scheuer, "Churley relives her son's adoption in tell-all book," *My Town Crier*, 28 April 2007.
74 *Adoption Information Disclosure Act*, ss. 48.1 to 48.12.
75 Anyone who violated a "no contact" notice was to be subject to criminal prosecution and fined up to $50,000. For persons who did not wish to have their identifying information disclosed, ss. 48.5 and 48.7 of the *VSA* provided that birth parents and adult adoptees could apply to the Child and Family Services Review Board ("the Board") for a "non-disclosure order." Sections 48.5 (7) and 48.7 (3) of the *VSA* required the Board to grant a non-disclosure order if it was satisfied that "because of exceptional circumstances the order is appropriate to prevent sexual harm or significant physical or emotional harm to [the adopted person or birth parent]."
76 *Hansard*, 2005, pp. 1069–74.
77 *Ontario v. Marchand* [2006] O.J. No. 2387 (Sup. Ct.).
78 *Cheskes v. Ontario*.
79 *Ontario v. Marchand*, at paras. 1, 47 and 50.
80 *Ibid.*, at para. 53. It is interesting to note that the applicant was difficult, at best, in her dealings with the registrar and other officials, comparing "them to Nazis and refus[ing] to speak to them because to do so would be 'like a Jew sitting down with Albert Speers'": at para. 65. Although the conduct of the registrar was not under review, the court found that "credible evidence is consistent with the employees and the Registrar having dealt with the applicant throughout in a responsive and professional manner in the face of what can be characterized as considerable abuse from the applicant": at para. 66.
81 *Ibid.*, at paras. 40, 41, 64, and 67.
82 *Ibid.*, at paras. 30, 70, and 74.
83 It is noteworthy that she called David Kirschner as one of her expert witnesses.
84 *Ontario v. Marchand*, at paras. 85, 96, 116 and 160.
85 *Globe and Mail*, 14 November 2007, A8.
86 *Ontario v. Marchand* [2007] O.J. No. 4440 (C.A.), at paras. 7 and 12.
87 This was further confirmed in the *Pratten* decision in British Columbia, a case involving a claim by a woman born of anonymous sperm donation that she had a right to identifying information about her donor. Pratten asserted that all children, except those born via sperm donation, know their genetic histories. This is erroneous, and the assertion of the Attorney General of British Columbia that "there is no law in B.C. guaranteeing anyone the right to know their genetic heritage and no law granting children, generally, the legal right – constitutional or otherwise – to access a parent's medical history or personal information" has significant merit. For this and other reasons, Pratten's claim was denied: *Pratten v British Columbia (AG)*, [2010] B.C.J. No 2012 (S.C.) and *Pratten v British Columbia (AG)*, [2012] B.C.J. No 2460 (C.A.). For further discussion of this case, see Lori Chambers and Heather Hillsburg, "Desperately Seeking Daddy: A Critique of *Pratten v. British Columbia (Attorney General)*", *Canadian Journal of Law and Society* 28, no. 2 (Spring 2013): 229–246.

88 *Ibid.*, at paras. 33 and 32.
89 *Ibid.*, at paras. 35, 33 and 34.
90 *Ibid.*, at paras. 41 and 43.
91 *Ibid.*, at paras. 45 and 49.
92 *Ibid.*, at paras. 65, 82, 87, 62, 84, 107, and 138.
93 These provinces, at the time of *Cheskes*, included Quebec, Nova Scotia, New Brunswick, and Prince Edward Island. *Civil Code of Quebec*, S.Q. 1991, c. 64, arts. 582-3; *Adoption Information Act*, S.N.S. 1996, c. 3, s. 19; *Family Services Act*, S.N.B. 1980, c. F-2.2, ss. 91-2; *Adoption Act*, R.S.P.E.I. 1988, c. A-4.1, s. 53.
94 *Adoption Act*, R.S.B.C. 1996, c. 5, s. 53; *Child, Youth and Family Enhancement Act*, R.S.A. 2000, c. C12, s. 74.2(4); *The Adoption Act*, C.C.S.M., c. A2, s. 112; *Adoption Act*, S.N.L. 1999, c. A-2.1, s. 50.
95 *Globe and Mail*, 14 November 2007, A8.
96 For more information see http://www.ontario.ca/en/information_bundle/adoption/111872.html.
97 For more information see adoption disclosure details for all provinces:
Newfoundland: https://www.gov.nl.ca/snl/birth/accessing-records-under-adoption-act/#limitationsofdisclosure.
Nova Scotia: https://novascotia.ca/coms/families/adoption/AdoptionDisclosure.html.
Prince Edward Island: https://www.princeedwardisland.ca/en/information/social-development-and-housing/open-adoption-records.
New Brunswick: https://www2.gnb.ca/content/gnb/en/departments/social_development/promos/adoption.html.
Quebec: https://www.quebec.ca/en/family-and-support-for-individuals/adoption/researching-information-on-your-parents-of-origin-or-your-adopted-child.
Ontario: https://www.ontario.ca/page/search-adoption-records.
Manitoba: https://www.gov.mb.ca/fs/childfam/adoption_search.html.
Saskatchewan: https://www.saskatchewan.ca/residents/births-deaths-marriages-and-divorces/births-and-adoptions/adoption/post-adoption-services.
Alberta: https://www.alberta.ca/adoption-records.aspx.
British Columbia: https://www2.gov.bc.ca/gov/content/life-events/birth-adoption/adoptions/adoption-records.
Yukon: http://www.hss.gov.yk.ca/adoption.php.
98 Province of Ontario, *Adoption Information Disclosure Act*, 2005, S.O. 2005, c. 25 – Bill 183, 56.1 (5).
99 See Family Law Reform Act, R.S.O. 1980, c. 152 s. 1(a). See also Lori Chambers, *Misconceptions: Unmarried Motherhood and the Ontario Children of Unmarried Parents Act, 1921–1969* (Toronto: University of Toronto Press, 2007), 168.
100 See Keith Griffith, *The Right to Know Who You Are: Reform of Adoption Law with Honesty, Openness, and Integrity* (Katherine W. Kimball, 1991), 6.
101 See Ontario Regulation 158/18, *Child, Youth and Family Services Act* 2017, pt. III, subs. 9.
102 Nicole Baute, "Adoptee can find mom, but not dad," *Toronto Star*, 10 December 2009.
103 Baute, "Adoptee can find mom, but not dad."
104 Baute, "Adoptee can find mom, but not dad."
105 Adam Segal, "Black Market Babies," *Maisonneuve* (Summer 2017), 26–35. See also "Gene Machine," <*This Magazine*?> *This*, January–February 2019.

Part IV

EPIDEMIOLOGIES AND ENVIRONMENTS

CHAPTER SIXTEEN

"I had a little bird, its name was Enza": Children and Adolescents in Ontario and the Spanish Flu

JAMES ONUSKO

I had a little bird,
its name was Enza.
I opened the window,
and in-flu-enza.

Children's jump rope rhyme, 1918

A little more than a century ago, children and adolescents were, as always, active participants in daily life in Ontario and around the world. When children played together, they sang and rhymed. The devastating influenza pandemic (known colloquially as the Spanish flu or Spanish Lady) that raced around the globe from 1918 through early 1920 inspired youngsters to share their voices and animate something that few of them were able to understand fully. This short rhyme helped them cope with what was happening to themselves, family, friends, and community members. This was not the first time that children had created rhyme to cope with disease and death; one of the most famous children's rhymes begins with "Ring around the rosie." While there is some debate as to its origins, it is generally accepted that it refers to the fourteenth-century Black Death (associated with the bubonic plague) that killed tens of millions of people around the world over a four-year period. The "ring" referred to the rose-coloured, round rash marks on the skin – an early sign that a person had the deadly plague. At the end of the rhyme, the children "All fall down," referencing the unimaginable illness and death that engulfed them nearly 700 years ago.

For those who experienced the 2020 coronavirus pandemic, grasping for clearer understanding and deeper meanings has been commonplace. The unknown is rarely welcomed by any of us, especially when it comes to public health and the threat of a deadly pandemic. As historians, collectively, we fix our gaze on the past, but we live in the here and now. We are also motivated by a desire to find something new, underrepresented, or comparatively ignored in the historiography of an issue, event, or subject. I am a historian of childhood, so typically, when analysing the past, I focus on young people. My focus on children, the timing of the COVID-19 pandemic, and the fact that there is so little in the historical record about Ontario's experience with the Spanish flu – especially its impact on children and adolescents – is what has prompted me to write this chapter. There is no question that Ontario's young people suffered greatly when the Spanish flu infected much of the province. As is so often the case, silences and gaps brought meaning to this episode that was so devastating to children, adolescents, and their families, not just in Ontario but throughout the world.

It is clear that there was no universal experience associated with the 1918 pandemic in Ontario. As has been noted elsewhere, people experienced the Spanish flu differently – socially, emotionally, and economically, with arguably, the heaviest impact on young children.[1] Certainly, few Ontario families escaped the Spanish flu and its effects (either directly or indirectly), yet some groups (young people, women, the poor, working-class families, and Indigenous communities) were impacted more than others; children and adolescents who died were lost permanently as loving, and loved, family members. This chapter shines a light on children and adolescents and demonstrates that statistics tell only part of any historical study. While young people were not in the age group most affected by the Spanish flu (in terms of morbidity or fatality), they were impacted in other meaningful ways. What also needs to be considered is how these patterns re-emerge, episodically; much of the mainstream coverage of the COVID-19 pandemic emphasized how young people were relatively (at least statistically) unaffected by the disease, while failing to consider the individual lives and stories behind the official statistics. Not emphasized was young people losing beloved family members, friends of all ages, community members, and other significant people in their lives.

The large majority of histories of the 1918 influenza pandemic in Canada focus on individual cities: Esyllt Jones's *Influenza 1918: Disease, Death, and Struggle in Winnipeg*; the bulk of Jones and Fahrni's *Epidemic Encounters: Influenza, Society, and Culture in Canada, 1918–1920*; and several peer-reviewed journal articles.[2] While edited collections make impressive connections between cities and larger areas, few of the other studies consider individual provinces, as this chapter does.

Further to this, is that while some of these works feature sections dedicated to young people, their experiences and voices are often a small part of the overall story, if to be found at all. That gap is addressed directly in this chapter.

As mentioned, locating sources when tracing and analysing histories of childhood is challenging. I have used newspapers (some of which contained oral histories), magazine articles, government documents from the three levels of government, and secondary sources, namely journal articles and monographs. In creating the narrative, I move from the general to the particular. I begin with the global context, and move next to the Canadian context; then, in turning to Ontario, I begin with Toronto, followed by some other major centres. I close the piece by exploring the rural experience, and, finally, concentrate on some Indigenous people's experiences in different parts of the province. Exploring pandemics in historical context is a good starting point on a path towards better understanding the Spanish flu's impact on the province's young people.

Pandemics and the Spanish Influenza in Global Context

An epidemic is defined as an unexpected and far-reaching rise in disease cases at a specific time. Typically, such rises are temporary, but that is not a universal. A pandemic is an epidemic that grows very large – beyond a community, or cluster of communities. A pandemic can be national in scope, and oftentimes it has global reach. There is no question that fear and dread mark pandemics – this is a universal quality. For centuries, until the bacteriological revolution of the late nineteenth century[3], debates raged over whether diseases were contagious or initiated by miasma – that is, by bad air caused by decaying and rotting animal and vegetable matter.[4] Though this was not understood fully in earlier times, epidemics and pandemics cannot happen without some combination of population density and mobility. Thus, the earliest large-scale outbreaks of contagion were tied to the rise of early modern states in the fourteenth century. Many of these states were parts of far-reaching trade networks and the associated intercontinental movement of merchants and crews – all contributing to the spread of disease.

Prior to the bacteriological revolution, states did respond to the threat of widespread illness and death associated with pandemics. As early as the fifteenth century, in direct response to the plague, Italian city-states established state-sponsored boards of health.[5] Centuries later, this dynamic played out again – indeed, it was one of the major consequences of the Spanish flu. Canada, for example, created the federal Department of Health in 1919 in response to the pandemic. Formal quarantining dates back to at least the fourteenth century and the bubonic plague; in later centuries, nationwide, mandated quarantines marked the cholera pandemics of the nineteenth century – these could only be enacted and enforced by a powerful central state.[6] Quarantining proved to be one of the few effective methods for combating the Spanish flu and mitigating its effects in Ontario, and elsewhere. For the most part, though, quarantining was voluntary across the province. For all the advances made in medicine and public health by the early twentieth century, there was little in the end that modern medicine could offer Ontarians (and others around the globe) as a defence in the fall of 1918.

The 1918 pandemic circled the entire globe, leaving virtually no community untouched. In terms of morbidity and mortality, it was the worst pandemic in history since the Black Death. It did not originate in Spain, but that country was neutral during the First World War, so its press was in a position to openly discuss the spread of the disease, at a time when press censorship in much of Europe, the US, and Canada was much more heavily censored.[7] We know now that there were unreported cases in several places around the world; however, the Spanish press's reports of sickness and death were the most prominent and comprehensive. This particular influenza strain was devastating, with extremely high morbidity and mortality rates. While the precise numbers will never be fully known, conservative estimates generally place the number of worldwide deaths at 20 to 50 million people. There is some thought that close to 100 million may have died from the disease in these years, although experts use 40 million as a general consensus. Also, as many as 500 million were infected by the disease – fully one third of the global population.[8] Reporting was a challenge for various reasons: censorship was imposed for the sake of morale; influenza was not a reportable disease in many jurisdictions; the First World War was still raging, so people's focus lay elsewhere; many people (especially the young) died in isolation, with the official cause of death unknown; and, most significantly, many stricken with influenza ultimately died from pneumonia and other afflictions. In this era before antibiotics, secondary bacterial infections resulted in the development of pneumonia.[9] Pneumonia was submitted as the official cause of death in millions of cases, even when the patient had first contracted influenza and *then* pneumonia, as often happened. This lack of certainty is not isolated to this particular pandemic, for there can be multiple contributing factors to death during a pandemic. In terms of the public awareness, it cannot be forgotten that in addition to the First World War, women's suffrage and prohibition were also front and centre in much of the public discourse in 1918.

A confounding feature of the Spanish flu was the fact that the microorganism that causes influenza remained unknown until 1933. British researchers determined that it was a virus now known as Influenza A.[10] Further research led to the understanding that there are three major forms of influenza – A, B, and C – all transmitted through airborne particles.[11] Influenza A turned out to be new, so the victims had no prior immunity to this particular strain. The virus needed a host to survive, which is not the case with bacterial infections. Also, viruses are significantly smaller than bacteria, which was one reason why researchers did not discover it until 1933, when more powerful microscopes were available. Because it is a viral infection, influenza spreads primarily when an infected person coughs, sneezes, or breathes out fluid droplets containing a virus that others may come into contact with through the air and sometimes on hard surfaces.[12] The majority of influenza transmission likely occurs within three feet of the infected person – therefore, social contact and interactions are critical to spreading the disease.[13] This was not fully understood in 1918, despite the important advances in public health knowledge in the late nineteenth and early twentieth centuries.

The origins of the 1918 influenza strain remain clouded; more than a century later, there is still no consensus. Given that it emerged in the spring of 1918, rumours spread in Italy that it was not even influenza, but a form of chemical warfare launched by German forces.[14] There were three recognized waves: the first began in the spring of 1918; the second, deadliest wave in the fall of 1918, which moved across the globe; and a third and final wave, somewhat milder than the others, in late 1919 and early 1920, eventually ending in the spring. The pandemic's early spread can be linked directly to the maritime transportation networks developed for the First World War and the heavy troop movements during the earliest months of the pandemic. The first known outbreak involved soldiers at Camp Funston, Kansas (a primarily rural area with intensive hog farming) on 5 March 1918. These soldiers presumably carried influenza with them to the European battlefields. The disease may have circled the globe twice before receiving wide media attention. It emerged simultaneously in Boston, Massachusetts; Brest, France; and Freetown, Sierra Leone.[15] As mentioned, it was Spanish newspapers that began the widespread reporting to the public; indeed, one of the first public figures stricken with influenza was the Spanish king, Alfonso XIII, who became gravely ill recovered, though he later recovered.[16]

The flu presented with a wide range of symptoms, complicating and hindering health professionals' diagnoses. At times, patients exhibited mild common cold symptoms, and some never developed more than these, becoming only mildly ill, and recovering within a week or even less. Others might have the cold symptoms along with a headache, a sore threat, and a high temperature. For the more severely affected, symptoms might begin as chills and aches that could take over the body, causing severe headaches, high fever, nausea, and vomiting.[17] Science journalist Alanna Mitchell notes that some people turned a strange plum-like colour and suffered from restricted breathing. For other victims, every muscle, every joint, could ache. Blood would pour from the nose. Teeth might fall out, along with hair. Vomiting and diarrhoea were common, complicated by delirium. The purplish-black colouring was linked to the lungs filling with fluid; when fingertips and toes turned this inky colour, the end was near and came swiftly; these victims fought to catch their breath only to drown in their own bodily fluids.[18] This flu could be a truly horrible way to die – another factor in why so many people in later years were unwilling to discuss the Spanish flu and its effects. Under some circumstances, the disease developed very rapidly. In the most severe cases, victims succumbed to it in less than twenty-four hours. Dr. E.A. Robertson, a physician at the Quebec City garrison, described the symptoms in a 1919 journal article:

> When first seen, the patient's face was flushed, the nostrils blocked, the tongue heavily coated with thick whitish fur at the edges with a brown centre, the lips blue, the throat dark red, the skin hot and moist, the temperature 103 or 104 degrees … As time went on, quantities of blood-stained expectoration or nearly pure dark blood was expelled, respiration became laboured, face fingers cyanosed, active delirium came on, the tongue became dry and brown, the whole surface of the body blue and the patient died from failure of respiration.[19]

The Spanish flu's mortality rate among those in the prime of life made it especially difficult to comprehend for many. The very old and the very young were less likely to die than those between twenty and forty years old. One hypothesis was that exposure in early life to an earlier, 1889–90 influenza virus may have meant increased susceptibility to severe illness and death for those later struck by the Spanish flu virus.[20] The high infection rates in this age group had not happened in earlier pandemics, which often saw the young and the elderly affected most adversely. This was disturbing on more than one level. In many countries, the young male population had already been decimated during the First World War. The women who died may have already been widowed, thus leaving their children fully orphaned. In other family circumstances, fathers were left without a partner while having to deal with the impact of the war on the home front. This might include a lack of housing, unemployment or underemployment, no social safety net (such as unemployment insurance), no universal health care, and so forth. While we continue to learn more and more about the Spanish flu, many elements remain a mystery in that the pandemic's origins, its full extent, its epidemiology, and its morbidity rates and total mortalities remain somewhat obscured. Much of this also applies to people's experiences in Canada and Ontario.

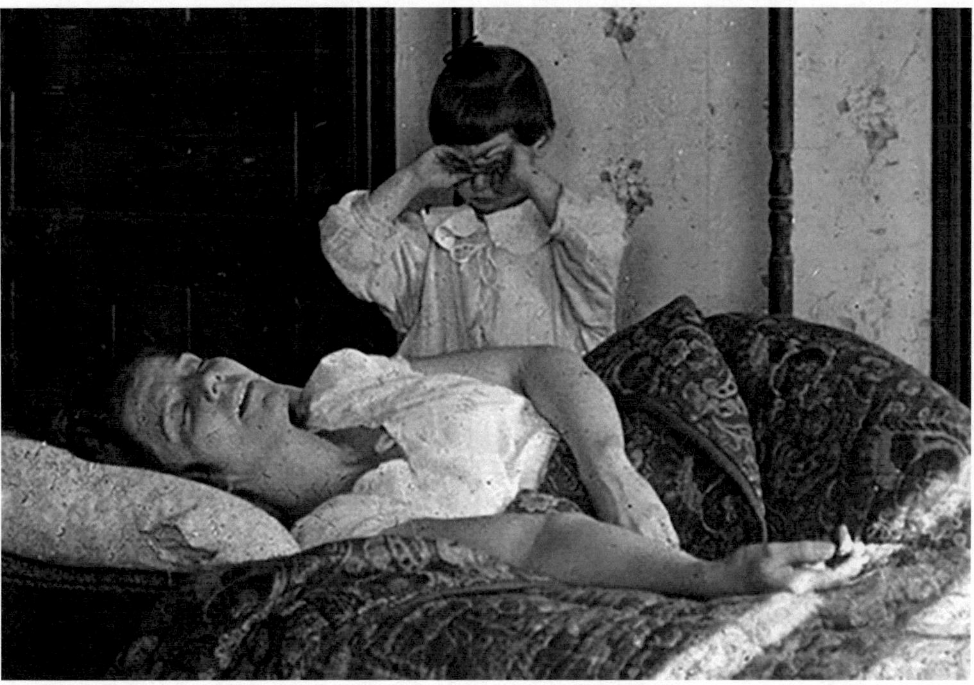

Figure 16.1. A little girl stands next to her sister.
Source: Library of Congress, Prints and Photographs Division.

Spanish Flu in Canada – An Overview

At the outset of the pandemic in 1918, Canada's population was 8.7 million.[21] More than 500,000 Canadians had served in the Canadian Expeditionary Force (CEF) during war; at least 60,000 and as many as 66,000 of them had been killed and more than 170,000 wounded. This was a staggering toll in dead and wounded and on their loved ones as well. Over 40 per cent of those who served in the CEF were Ontarians.[22] That figure is important because even though the war effort had wound down by the fall of 1918 (some of this due to the Spanish flu and its impact on troops from around the world), the effects of war continued unabated across Canada. From the fall of 1918, and over the next eighteen months, more than 50,000 Canadians succumbed to the Spanish flu. One in six Canadian households was directly affected by the pandemic.[23] No community, however remote, was spared from the disease.

The pandemic's rapid spread was tracked by Canadian journalists in September 1918 as it infected people in cities on the North American eastern seaboard.[24] The first wave in the spring of 1918 did not significantly impact Canada; it was the second wave, in the fall of 1918, after the virus had slightly mutated, that was the deadliest. The third wave, in late 1919 and early 1920, affected some parts of the country more than others and had a relatively mild impact in most of Ontario. Canadian soldiers returning from Europe played a role in spreading the virus, which was being reported in Niagara-area military camps by mid-September of 1918. Slightly later, eastern Canadian camps also reported cases. Some of these soldiers were subsequently transported to the front in Europe with the CEF. Historian Mark Humphries has demonstrated that Canadian troops spread the disease west across the country as they were transported to Vancouver to join the Siberian Expeditionary Force. This was in the weeks before the second wave broke across Canada.[25] Soldiers were not quarantined where they were stationed. At the Niagara camps, for instance, they were able to get visitors' passes to join civilian life and spend time in Niagara-on-the-Lake. Also they enjoyed free movement within the camp at recreation venues such as the Young Men's Christian Association (YMCA) tent.[26] It would not take long for the disease to take hold in the province.

The first non-military cases emerged in late September in Toronto and Montreal and were reported on 23 September 1918.[27] The medical system was unprepared for what happened next. In this era before universal health care coverage, visiting a hospital was costly and out of reach for many. Persistent nineteenth-century approaches to social welfare,[28] including "means testing" and "less eligibility," meant that the poor and the working class had little access to hospitals and private medical care. These people feared the steep medical bills and the interrogation they would face before a hospital agreed to take them in.[29] Instead, the focus was on prevention. For example, the National School Services printed an overview for North American teachers titled "Guard Against Influenza," which directed youngsters as follows: "Influenza is spread by droplets sprayed from the nose and throat. Cover each cough and sneeze with handkerchief. Avoid crowds. Get plenty of fresh air. Do not spit on the floor or on the sidewalk. Do not use common drinking cups and common towels. Avoid excessive fatigue. If taken ill, go to bed and send for a doctor. These rules apply also to colds, bronchitis pneumonia, and tuberculosis."[30]

Influenza victims, whether they lived in a city or elsewhere, received little or no medical or nursing care.[31] Even when victims could get medical care, the providers could do almost nothing to treat patients or to halt the spread of the virus. The system was already stretched thin because so many doctors and nurses were serving overseas, so even if a family could afford some form of private care, little of it was available in many locales. Many patients were treated at home, where there was no standard treatment. Alcohol was one form of pain relief, but it was in short supply because the military's needs had been prioritized and Prohibition was in effect.[32] For milder cases, most health authorities urged rest and plenty of fresh air. What might have been most helpful (for patients able to get it) was bed rest, nutritious food, and proper hydration, along with pain and fever management, ideally provided by a nurse.[33] This is the context in which children and adolescents experienced the pandemic – a time of a transition as the war approached its end.

Childhood and Adolescence in Early Twentieth-Century Ontario

"Childhood" and "adolescence" are not simply biological or demographic classifications; they are also a sociohistorical constructions. So to view either as "natural" is misleading.[34] As a category, childhood is fluid and socially dynamic, more a consequence of human choices than a cultural or biological imperative. Cultural anthropologists tell us that throughout human history, children have been viewed quite differently than adults. Just as with race and ethnicity, and gender and women, childhood has always been shaped by established agendas that are often discriminatory. Yet children and adolescents are not powerless – they can still make decisions for themselves.

The early twentieth century marked a new era for young people in Canada. In the largely rural and pre-industrial world that preceded it, work had been central in their lives, but this changed in the early twentieth century. With increasing industrialization and urbanization in the late nineteenth century, the "modern" child faced new realities. Children had once roamed the streets of larger cities, earning their living by shining shoes, selling newspapers, and engaging in other street trades; by performing small services such as running errands, opening doors, and offering street entertainment; or by begging, petty theft, or, in the most desperate cases, prostitution.[35] The fundamental shift in this period was an emerging idealization of childhood as a time of innocence, dependence, education, need for protection, and hope. This all meant that young people were increasingly set apart from the adult world. Thus, their daily activities became increasingly distinct from those of the adult world.[36]

By the early twentieth century, the most important function of most if not all families had shifted from economic production to the care of children.[37] This meant that families ceded some responsibilities to other institutions. Childhood and schooling had become closely linked, and most youngsters spent much of their waking time in public schools under state or church authority.[38] But as the pandemic illustrated about society as a whole, the ideal of personal responsibility remained a significant element in questions around welfare and the economy, trumping any proposed growth in a welfare state. Victorian "sensibilities," which emphasized individual responsibility, even in the face of broader societal or structural problems, remained deeply entrenched across North America. Historian Joseph Illick notes that by the first decade of the twentieth century, child poverty had become an issue to be confronted. In 1909, at the White House Conference on Dependent Children, national delegates argued that young people in need should be taken care of in their homes rather than in institutions.[39] Others, though, had different agendas.

The push to implement the ideal of a more protected childhood was the result of a determined struggle by a diverse coalition of educators, physicians, psychologists, union leaders, and first-wave feminists. It was supported by government action and public policy in the form of compulsory education laws and new restrictions on child labour.[40] Canada's Juvenile Delinquents Act (JDA) of 1908 was part of this modernization. That act positioned the state as a sympathetic guardian that treated the juvenile offender as a misguided child requiring care and supervision and thus as distinct from adult offenders. In English Common Law, it had been established by this time that any child under the age of seven was incapable of determining right from wrong. The JDA created a highly discretionary justice system that left police, judges, and probation officers with the latitude to do what they believed was in the juvenile's "best interests." The new, modern system meant that young people involved with the criminal justice system were, generally speaking, treated more leniently than older individuals.[41] In addition to these changes, formal education became entrenched during this era.[42]

Formal schooling was now mandatory across Canada, and for most youngsters up until grade eight, schools were tasked with greater powers. With the advent of legislated school medical inspections, starting in British Columbia in 1910 and followed by the rest of Canada, teachers were tasked with identifying signs of illness in students and reporting them to doctors.[43] This aligned well with the broader societal changes intended to establish a more protected childhood. People (other than family members) who had been given more power over children's lives, such as doctors, nurses, social workers, and teachers, now constructed children's bodies as weak and as susceptible to serious medical issues.[44] Some of this was evidence based. As Cynthia Comacchio notes in another chapter in this collection, Dr. Helen MacMurchy (1862–1953), in her work on maternal and infant health, had reported in 1909 that in Ontario nearly seven thousand of the 52,629 children born in that year had died in their first year of life.[45] Comacchio emphasizes that by late 1918, child welfare had become a joint effort of the medical profession and new agencies at the local, provincial, and federal levels.[46] Put simply, children and adolescents had become important elements in public health. By the time the pandemic reached Ontario, the Toronto School Board had moved beyond other boards and developed one of the most inclusive and widely reported school medical systems not only in the province but in the entire world.[47] Toronto, because of its sheer size, combined with its importance, uniqueness, and impact on the rest of the province, warrants a closer look.

The Pandemic and Toronto's Children

In the fall of 1918, Toronto was a predominantly white, Anglo-Saxon, Protestant city. Less than 10 per cent of residents identified as neither Canadian (equated with white in this period) nor of British origin.[48] Being a growing, quite densely populated city (population around 490,000; Ontario's was around 2.9 million),[49] Toronto was especially susceptible to the spread of the Spanish flu. As Ontario's capital city, Toronto was home to the provincial legislature, the provincial Board of Health, the University of Toronto, and the leading medical institutions; it also managed a municipal budget equivalent to that of the provincial government.[50] On the eve of the pandemic, Toronto had English-speaking Canada's leading health department, an entrenched division of communicable diseases, a city lab for testing tuberculosis and diphtheria samples, an isolation hospital, and a division of vital statistics to provide data required for public policy decision-making.[51]

The city and many of its established medical institutions and public policies could be described as progressive and cutting-edge; it is striking, then, that during the pandemic the municipal government did not take measures to quarantine travellers or local infected individuals.[52] Undoubtedly, this was in part due to how quickly and widely the pandemic struck the city. Years later, journalist Max Brathwaite of *Maclean's* detailed how the first reported death was that of a young, unnamed twelve-year-old girl from outside the city. Before leaving her home on a Wednesday, she complained of a slight cold, but her family did not think anything of it, because other family members had it too. On her trip into Toronto she experienced some chills and a severe headache. By the time the family reached Toronto she was delirious, and her mother had her admitted to Toronto General Hospital. Just two days later, on 29 September, she was dead, Ontario's first civilian casualty.[53] The Spanish flu had arrived in Toronto and claimed the province's first victim.

This tragic death of a young girl was merely the prelude to a rapid increase in cases and deaths; within just a few days, out of Toronto's 66,000 students and 1,630 teachers, more than 10,000 students and staff were sick.[54] The Toronto numbers are stunning, but other major North American cities faced even more alarming figures in terms of the direct impact on children and their families. In New York City alone, the Spanish flu orphaned more than 30,000 children in the first few weeks of its spread. New York newspapers were filled with stories of how these children had been left to fend for themselves.[55]

It is not surprising, given that public schooling was now central to young people's lives, that schools were among the first civilian spaces where the Spanish flu spread, in Toronto and elsewhere. That children are carriers of disease is now well known; but at the time – just as it is today – putting limits on touching, maintaining physical distance from others, avoiding touching one's own face, and other related best practices

Figure 16.2. Children at Victoria Park Forest School in Toronto practise blowing their noses in 1913. Source: City of Toronto Archives.

to avoid the spread of certain diseases (including influenza) did not align well with typical adolescent behaviours, and especially not with those of pre-adolescents. In the week following the death of Toronto's patient zero, schools found themselves under stress, and that was *before* Dr. Charles Hastings, the provincial health minister, officially recognized the epidemic within the City of Toronto. Schools were still operating, even though more than 1,000 teachers were out sick and part-time teachers were unable (in some cases, unwilling) to enter the classroom.[56] Given that the city had not not quarantined travellers or individuals who had contracted the Spanish flu through local spread, these teachers' actions are understandable. By 15 October, all city schools were closed; soon after, discussions began about shuttering theatres, churches, and other entertainment sites. The ensuing notice of closure from Hastings read: "Notice is hereby given that after Saturday, October 19th, 1918, all theatres, moving picture shows, and other places of amusement, including pool rooms, billiard rooms and bowling alleys, throughout the city shall be closed during the period of the influenza epidemic, and shall not be reopened until further notice. By order of the local board of health."[57]

Most people – young people in particular – were being treated at home. Meanwhile, by 8 October, Toronto Western Hospital was operating at capacity and half the nurses at Grace Hospital were ill and unable to work.[58] At the city's newest and largest hospital, Toronto General, by mid-October, almost half the 676 patients had been admitted for the Spanish flu; eighty nurses had fallen ill, and three had died.[59] Women, as always, served as primary caregivers in a host of front-line occupations and roles, both formal and informal. As the pandemic unfolded in late September and early October, teachers, most of whom were women, continued to serve in caring roles even after the schools were shut down. *The Globe* reported at the end of October:

> "I know home after home," said one teacher yesterday, "that will be absolutely without help of any kind if the teacher who is at present acting as a housekeeper, cook and nurse is taken away." "It will involve dreadful hardship, and possibly death, if the teachers are taken from their V.A.D. work," said another who had three families under her charge, all the other members of which are down with influenza or just recovering from pneumonia. "There seems to be an extraordinary lack of realization of the extent of the disease and how badly off for help so many hundreds of even well-to-do people are. As for the conditions among the poor they are still appalling. I am speaking for several of my fellow teachers, and they all say that they feel if they are withdrawn from the cases they are now nursing the consequences will be disastrous."[60]

Teachers pointed out how social class was a major contributor to families' and individuals' experiences. Some families were left wholly untouched by the Spanish flu. If one was poor, evading the disease was much more difficult. Living in more densely populated areas, having to continue to work during the pandemic, and struggling for basic necessities like food all made it more difficult to avoid the Spanish flu. Also, many working-class neighbourhoods in larger cities like Toronto and Ottawa were near train stations; soldiers and other travellers brought the disease with them to these places and congregated around them rather than in upscale neighbourhoods, which were more shielded. Settlement workers in Toronto observed that the poor were so severely affected that they were unable to provide needed help to their neighbours – a breach of typical community practice.[61] Toronto's citizens rallied, though, and young people were an important part of the response. Concerned residents asked for donations of food, money and volunteer time, and the Boy Scouts were tasked with delivering food to houses with suffering patients.[62]

Contemporary reports make it clear that there was a differentiated response to the public health orders. Some people may have been expressing their personal agency; others may have simply been coping with the pandemic as best they could. There were anti-vaccination groups who organized rallies objecting to Dr. Hastings's dynamic leadership and his demand for mandatory vaccinations.[63] In one letter to the editor of the *Globe*, a concerned Torontonian wrote:

Table 16.1. Male and female proportionate mortality for Spanish influenza in Toronto, 1 September to 31 December 1918[64]

Age	Male	Male mortality (%)	Female	Female mortality (%)
Under 1	54	5	47	5
1–4	83	7	102	10
5–9	28	3	36	4
10–14	16	1	26	3
15–19	83	7	53	5

"Schools closed, churches closed, concerts canceled, meetings postponed indefinitely, theatres closed, movies closed, all by order of the Medical Health Officer … but note this – The Toronto Railway Company's unspeakable cars travel the streets with every window closed; packed morning, noon, and night to suffocation, with a swaying mass of girls, women, and men … it is any wonder the plague spreads?"[65]

Toronto mortality rates were clustered, quite distinctly, by age. One study details the increased infant and perinatal mortality rates and complications that can be linked directly to influenza: 1,350 pregnant women who suffered from the Spanish flu and abortion, stillbirth, and premature labour happened in 26 percent of women without pneumonia and 52 percent with pneumonia sequella.[66] The toll on pregnant women and their families in Toronto adds yet another layer of tragedy.

Although Toronto's children and adolescents were at the centre of the pandemic, youth in other cities in the province were not spared by any measure.

The Flu in Other Major Ontario Centres

Children and adolescents in other Ontario cities did not escape the pandemic, which also reached Hamilton, Ottawa, and Windsor. One of the earliest-hit cities, not just in Ontario but in Canada, was Hamilton, where the Spanish flu appeared in late September, with several cases at the Royal Air Force Camp in the city's west end.[67] Hamilton is quite close to the Niagara region, so it almost certainly arrived in the city from the military camps there. Hamilton's children and adolescents were not immediately affected, if one goes by school attendance records,[68] but this would change in October. On 5 October, headlines in the *Hamilton Spectator* blared that "Spanish Influenza Epidemic is Serious" and that a "Physician and Four Others Died in Few Hours."[69] By 16 October, schools and theatres had been closed, church services cancelled, and store hours shortened. Streetcars continued to operate, but only with the windows rolled down.[70]

Shortened store hours were meant to curb young people's activities as stores were very popular places for them when they were not in school, making them an ideal site for spreading influenza.[71]

The Hamilton school closures generated controversy: some argued that children would be better off in school as the epidemic peaked because they would be given the latest and best information on how to combat the Spanish flu and would receive better care than they might otherwise.[72] While some strides had been made in public health awareness, by this time schools were the primary site for educating youngsters in public health. The inherent tension (schools as potentially dangerous, yet also providing essential public health information) proved difficult to navigate, for the only real defence from influenza was to isolate oneself from those who had the disease. Opening schools prematurely almost certainly would have led to further spread of the disease, not only among students but also from students to family members and the community at large. Schools were closed for much of the last part of 1918 and then intermittently in early 1919 as the pandemic's effects ebbed and flowed. Despite the closures, there were seventy-four influenza-related deaths among children in Hamilton. Seven of the victims had family members who died from the flu, many of whom were siblings; the death of a parent tended to occur a matter of days before the death of the child.[73] In one tragic case in Hamilton, an entire family passed away on 27 March 1919 – the husband, the wife, and their stillborn son.[74] The families and their children who suffered most were those living in lower-income neighbourhoods, specifically the primarily industrial and working-class northern areas.[75]

Young people fell victim to the Spanish flu in other cities as well. In Ottawa, in the fall of 1918, 28 per cent of those who died were younger than eighteen.[76] As elsewhere, the Board of Health recognized the public health risks and attempted to mitigate transmission through closures. Schools, churches, theatres, pubs, pool halls, and bowling alleys, many of which were frequented by young people, were shuttered just after Thanksgiving in the nation's capital. Again, as was the case in other centres, some members of the public argued forcefully that if schools were closed, many children would be primarily in the streets, unprotected from the disease.

The Ottawa closures remained in place until the middle of November. It is estimated that 200 children and adolescents were orphaned in the city: some were taken in by family members, others entered orphanages.[77] In either case, their family patterns were disrupted permanently. The pandemic did not put a full stop to children performing certain duties. In Ottawa, as a public service, Boy Scouts delivered warning pamphlets with information about the dangers of the flu to every

Figure 16.3. Ballinahinch estate in Hamilton with nurses, physicians, and young patients in the fall of 1918. Source: Hamilton Public Library Special Collections.

home in the city.[78] In other parts of the province, children and adolescents were impacted directly.

Windsor's young people also found themselves affected by the pandemic. In that city, school-aged children were instructed to receive vaccinations,[79] but these had little impact. As we have seen, public health officials believed, incorrectly, that they were treating a bacterial infection, not a virus. The homes of those diagnosed with the influenza were never placed under quarantine in Windsor, but the mayor did issue a month-long ban in October on public gatherings, including at schools, churches, theatres, and dance halls.[80] G.R. Cruikshank, Windsor's medical officer, adopted a no-nonsense approach, dramatically comparing sick people who ignored quarantine orders to Canada's First World War enemy, Germany. "Anyone who goes into a crowded streetcar and coughs is worse than the German Kaiser," Cruikshank told the local Chamber of Commerce, and "any child that goes to school is worse than any German atrocity."[81] Schools, emptied of children and teachers, along with church basements, became temporary kitchens where volunteers made food baskets for home delivery for needy community members.[82] These community responses, in centres both small and large, must be seen as a defining element across the province. Population density made children and adolescents in Ontario's larger centres especially susceptible to the Spanish flu, but rural children and adolescents were also adversely affected.

Effects on Rural Children and Adolescents

Rural populations have not been a common focus of study in pandemic histories. Larger population centres often yield more records, and historical traces are more readily available there than in rural areas. Yet there is some limited information regarding the pandemic and its impact on children and adolescents in rural Ontario. One often finds anecdotal accounts of young people helping with chores on neighbouring farms where one or more family members were ill with the Spanish flu; some of this was happening already, with young men from across the province having enlisted to fight in the war and therefore unavailable for farmwork.

One teenager, Jack McAuliffe, who worked for a timber company on the Pickerel River in Northern Ontario, was called out to help in the camp kitchen when the Spanish flu came to his remote lumber camp:

> They sent me out to the roothouse. I had to peel nearly three bushels of potatoes and three-quarters of a bushel of carrots … By then I had the flu but it was mild, only a lot of barking and coughing. The roothouse was cool and damp, not the best place to be. Some of us decided to quit. We walked out from Camp 2, and they put us across ESS Narrows in a rowboat. We had dinner at Cole's Mill (Lost Channel) and the first thing they asked us was, "Did any of you have the flu?" We said, "no," which wasn't true. I was coughing like hell, and the guys said, "Jack, quit your coughing or we'll get nothing to eat here!" They said, "Just sit down out there, and we'll tell you when dinner is ready." Anyway, we walked that day, from Camp 2 (the CPR station at) Pakesly. That was over 20 miles.[83]

This indicates the lengths some young people went to, in remote areas of the province, to stay employed and to meet their basic needs. It required some skills that may have put others' health in jeopardy, but the actions are understandable in the context of the deadly pandemic. This was a fight for survival – to somehow get beyond the immediate threat of disease. The Spanish flu touched other smaller communities in the province, with young people often at the centre of tragedy.

In Huron County, as reported in the *Huron Signal*, Earl Strong of Howick, just eighteen years old, was the first confirmed influenza fatality, on 1 October. Just over a week later, readers were informed that "Goderich is suffering from an epidemic of influenza."[84] The schools were closed for the next month, and students were only allowed to return if they had a medical "certificate" declaring that their home had been free from the Spanish flu for at least two weeks. The disease cut a wide swath through Huron County, with no age group left unaffected. The youngest victim was Thelma Armstrong of Goderich; she was just one day old.[85]

Some rural Ontarians, seeking scapegoats, blamed the pandemic's spread on the war, along with race and ethnicity. Stephen Thornton of the *Wellington Advertiser* noted that in some churches in Waterloo County, the disease was attributed to divine judgment – that is, it was a punishment wrought on the region's large German population. This reminds us how influential the church was in some Ontarians' lives.

School closures in rural Ontario were uneven. In Eramosa and West Garafraxa, officials closed their schools, and most service clubs and volunteer groups cancelled meetings and gatherings; meanwhile, Fergus and Elora did *not* close their schools. At a school board meeting in Fergus, Dr. Armstrong, the leading public health official, told the committee members that influenza seldom struck young children and that there was no pressing need to shut down the public school – "Flu is not a child's disease, and is not carried by them." His observations did not convince everyone. Attendance at public and high schools fell below 75 per cent at the end of October, when the flu peaked. The provincial government had left most local policies and regulations to local decision-makers. The thinking in some of these centres was that while it made sense to close smaller schools in rural areas, children would congregate elsewhere, regardless of school closures.

In Salem, Mrs. Arthur Shafer came down with influenza in the final days of her pregnancy; she gave birth on 26 December 2018, and died three days later, two hours after the newborn child, leaving three children under nine. To add to the tragedy, Shafer's middle child died of the flu on 3 January 1919, five days after his mother.[86]

The flu pandemic reached parts of Northern Ontario at slightly later dates. The first victim in Kenora died in late October. Pandemic historians Marion and Scanlon note that during the second wave, sixty-six deaths were recorded in the Kenora region. Fourteen of these – around 20 per cent – were of children under five; others included a seventeen-year-old boy, a fifteen-year-old girl, and a ten-year-old (gender not noted). In Kenora, as in nearly every part of the province, the high cost of private health care meant that most flu victims remained at home, under the care of family and friends. Charles Bobbington Holland, two years old, and fifteen-year-old Rose Caron were taken to an emergency hospital set up at the local library, where they both died; the local Board of Health did not send bills (which would have been $1.50 per day) to the Caron or Holland families. Schools had been shut in late 1918 and remained closed in the area until February 1919 – longer than in many jurisdictions. When the smaller, third wave hit in the winter of 1919–20, most of those who succumbed to it were very young or relatively old.[87] This reminds us that during the pandemic, it was not always the twenty- to forty-year-old group that was hit hardest. Notably, Kingston was Ontario's only city to offer free hospital care during the pandemic. In practical terms, for many, quarantining meant that individuals died in isolation; however, as in many places, humanity and compassion showed themselves in many of these small communities.

Another Northern Ontario family was devastated by the disease. Leonard Foucault shared a family oral history told to him years earlier by his grandmother Rose. As detailed in the *Sudbury Star*, Leonard's grandfather Leopold (Sam) Foucault and grandmother Rose lived in a house by the Spanish River. By January 1919, Rose, three months pregnant, found herself caring for her husband Sam and two young children, Florence and Ernest, who were all sick. As was common in many communities, a black square cloth had to be put in the window to warn people not to enter because the house was quarantined. Leonard recalled his grandmother Rose telling him that it was very difficult for her as she had to do all the work by herself. "She had to take care of the house and farm, pump water, heat it on a wood stove, prepare food, feed the chickens and the horse, milk the cow, split wood, wash clothes in a tub all the while taking care of Sam and the two children," said Leonard.[88]

Tragically, in the early morning hours of 13 January 1919, Ernest died. Sam was still very ill, so Rose went out to the barn and built a small coffin for her seven-month-old baby son. She harnessed the horse to the wagon and, with little Florence beside her, took the coffin containing the tiny body of Ernest to the cemetery. As best she could, she lowered the coffin into the grave that had been prepared; then she said some prayers and returned home. The next day, twenty-one-month-old Florence passed away. Rose had to go through the same process as she had with Ernest. She intimated to family in later years that she was grateful for all the people who came by to check on her and especially for the support of her local priest, Father Brennan. Sam fully recovered from the virus, and on 7 June 1919, Rose gave birth to a boy they named Leo, who survived and in adulthood served as Espanola's mayor for seventeen years.[89] Yet another example of a family that was changed permanently by the pandemic. Indigenous children and adolescents, most of whom in this period lived in rural and often remote parts of Ontario, were also impacted by the Spanish flu.

Effects upon Indigenous Children

The Spanish flu killed nearly 4 per cent of Canada's Indigenous people. In Ontario, out of an Indigenous population of 26,411, there were 622 deaths, which meant the mortality rate was four times the non-Indigenous average in the country.[90] By 1918, the Residential School system was well entrenched.[91] The Spanish River School in Northern Ontario provides an example of the absolute horror that some Indigenous children and adolescents experienced during the pandemic.

The Spanish River School was located between the Serpent River and the Sagamok First Nation on Lake Huron's north shore, roughly 120 kilometres west of Sudbury.[92] The pandemic exacerbated the deplorable conditions that marked the Residential School experience. While the numbers are not entirely clear, historian Mark Humphries estimates that the real mortality rate at the school was nearly 9 per cent: 16 students of the 178 in attendance died.[93] Poor sanitation, overcrowding, overwork, and very poor nutrition, along with physical and emotional abuse, all combined to make the schools exceedingly unhealthy.[94] Yet none of this was out of context with previous policy, which was characterized by starvation, oppression, abuse, and deceit perpetrated by the federal government, some churches, and other organizations.[95]

The Beausoleil First Nation, in Simcoe County, was another site of tragedy and loss, as recounted by Laurie Leclair in the *Anishinabek News*. On 16 October 1918, John Sunday lost three of his children: Kathleen, eighteen, Dave, twenty, and Willie, twenty-two, had lived their entire short lives on Christian Island. John, fifty-two and a father of eight, was given the heartbreaking task of reporting his children's deaths to the authorities. Only the day before, Jerry Monague had lost his two sons, Edward and Jonas, who left young families behind. Beausoleil Island First Nation suffered greatly. In October alone, the community lost forty-seven individuals to the virus. The 1917 Indian Department Census reported a band membership of 317. The death of forty-seven individuals the following year represented a staggering loss of 15 per cent of its population.[96] These events were hardly isolated: population loss due to disease and state-driven starvation had marked settler–Indigenous relations episodically following first contact.[97]

The federal health care system for "Status Indians" had developed in a patchwork fashion at the end of the nineteenth century and remained in place in 1918.[98] That system had shifted from protecting Indigenous lives to safeguarding settler-invader lives.[99] By legislation, school-aged Indigenous people were expected to be in Residential Schools. As a result, sick children, already worn down and severely weakened by poor nutrition, abuse, and unsuitable work, continued to contract diseases like tuberculosis and then influenza in the fall of 1918.[100] As historians Esyllt Jones and James Daschuk have noted, from the Indigenous perspective, the Spanish flu was simply one more disease the settler-invaders had brought with them from Europe, like measles and smallpox.[101]

In the upper Ottawa Valley, the people in Algonquin settlements by 1918 had already suffered waves of disease: measles, influenza, smallpox, tuberculosis, typhoid, and scrofula.[102] Yet some families in that area were able to withstand the ravages of the Spanish flu, demonstrating that quarantining and social distancing could work in some Indigenous communities. The current Wolf Lake Chief Lisa Robinson recalled: "There was one family where the mother refused to let her children out, even after it seemed liked the pandemic had waned … Other people did venture outside, even those who had recovered from the Spanish flu, but they were all soon felled … and this woman kept her children in and they survived that second round."[103] The numbers of victims in Indigenous communities, just as in non-Indigenous communities, were almost certainly underreported. Deaths could go unregistered, and the death toll from the pandemic (especially the third wave) may have been higher for the Six Nations community,[104] among other communities.

The Spanish flu could compound underlying health conditions. Previous bouts of tuberculosis would have weakened the health of many young Indigenous people. Indigenous communities were disproportionately affected by the Spanish flu, and most lacked the resources and support to cope with it. Some residential schools did begin to instruct Indigenous girls in basic nursing skills so that they could help their communities, but that training was limited at best.[105] Despite the systemic problems, some young Indigenous women became fully trained nurses following the pandemic,. A nursing shortage in Canada arising from the First World War, high tuberculosis rates among Indigenous people, and public concerns related to the 1918 influenza pandemic all contributed to conditions that allowed for a small social experiment in Ontario, where a few Indigenous girls gained access to formal nursing training.[106] While it was a limited step forward, it was a positive step, nonetheless.

Conclusion

One of the most striking things about the Spanish flu pandemic is the comparative lack of documentation available today, not just in Ontario but around the world. Yet research on the disease has shown for some time that influenza survivors did not forget it.[107] Families, and especially children and adolescents, were affected by the pandemic for years after it ended. One New Zealander recalled how it affected some of his young classmates: "At the school, when we're in the class, and that, some of my friends whose parents had passed away would all of a sudden start their crying, and the teacher would have to console them later."[108]

Pandemic historians Marion and Scanlon argue that this pandemic, deadly as it was for so many, has been relatively overlooked because it did not fit the preferred narrative of heroic or glorious death.[109] I think some of the silence can be explained by the fact that disease – in particular, childhood disease – was more common in those times. Childhood vaccinations, on a widespread scale, remained decades away. Napanee resident Margaret Rivers, a survivor of the influenza pandemic, remembers the "In Quarantine" signs that were conspicuously posted on the front door of her childhood home in Pembroke. "I can hardly recall a time when there wasn't a quarantine sign on our door," she recalls.[110] So while those signs were prevalent mainly during the Spanish flu, they were relatively common, before and after, in Margaret's home. "I was the only sick one in the family, and I had it all, or so it seemed. Name a disease and I probably had it as a child." She laughs as she continues recollecting. "I was born with convulsions; I was shaking so horribly they didn't think I'd live. Later on, I came down with whooping cough, measles, mumps – pretty much every serious disease going."[111]

The pandemic led to the creation of a national public health office in 1919 that sought to formalize partnerships among the three levels of government in Canada. It also established that public health was a national concern and a joint responsibility. The pandemic prompted many communities to come together, often for the sake of its youngest and most vulnerable members. It is vital to remember that the pandemic years were also marked by selflessness, generosity, kindness, and love within communities. We have seen how, almost overnight, in some instances, fathers, mothers, and children died, creating widows and widowers as well as orphans. These traumas, on the heels of a demoralizing war, sapped public attention and resources.[112] This also explains some of the silence surrounding the pandemic – a tribute to its colossal destructive power, the shocking number of people it killed, and the collective inability to name and to represent mortality on a global scale.[113] The press and all levels of government did not show great concern for the young people, along with their families, who had to face devastating losses.[114] The interwar years would prove to be uneven, at best, for the children and adolescents who survived the Spanish flu. Just a decade later, these young people would face the Great Depression, which brought unemployment, homelessness, poverty, and more sorrow for millions in Ontario.

Ontario's young people suffered greatly while the Spanish flu ravaged the province. Children and adolescents were permanently affected not only individually but as loving, and loved, family members. The Spanish flu has never left us since its devastating arrival more than 100 years ago. Descendants of the virus still infect us each winter, but they are milder forms. It is a near certainty that most if not all of us had a relative – a great grandmother, a grandfather, a great aunt, or a distant cousin – who fell ill with the Spanish flu. We often fail to consider how families can be affected over time, even generations later, in that family trees are permanently changed by infectious disease,[115] especially one as overwhelming and widespread as the Spanish flu. Ontario families were changed forever, and the event leaves all of us to ponder *what might have been.*

QUESTIONS FOR CONSIDERATION:

1. What does the author mean when he says, "People experienced the Spanish flu differently – socially, emotionally, and economically." Do you believe this continues to apply during pandemics today?
2. What is a pandemic? How does it differ from an epidemic?
3. How would you describe the care that most Spanish flu patients received in 1918? What were the major contributing factors to this level of care?
4. Who was the Spanish flu's first civilian victim in the province? Describe what happened to her.
5. Do you agree with the province's official response to the pandemic – especially in how it impacted young people?
6. Onusko argues that women and young people were impacted disproportionately by the pandemic. Do you agree or disagree?
7. There were some long-term effects on young people, according to Onusko. What were these long-term effects?

NOTES

1 Ellie Vance, "The Spanish Flu Pandemic of 1918," *The Thetean* 48, no. 1 (2019): 20.
2 One notable exception in terms of a macro focus is Mark Osborne Humphries, *The Last Plague: Spanish Influenza and the Politics of Health in Canada* (Toronto: University of Toronto Press, 2013).
3 This was the nineteenth-century development, over several decades and in many different parts of the world, that saw the widespread acceptance of the germ theory of disease.
4 Christian W. McMillen, *Pandemics: A Very Short Introduction* (London: Oxford University Press, 2016), 5.
5 McMillen, *Pandemics*.
6 McMillen, *Pandemics*.

7 For further discussion of why it was called the "Spanish" flu, see "Why was the 1918–19 pandemic that killed 50 million people known as 'Spanish Flu'?," *HistoryExtra*, 19 March 2020, https://www.historyextra.com/period/first-world-war/why-was-spanish-flu-pandemic-known-called-that-where-did-name-come-from-spain-myth-coronavirus-covid-19-name.

8 This is discussed in several articles and books. For one of the more succinct discussions see Jefferey K. Taubenberger, "The Origin and Virulence of the 1918 'Spanish' Influenza Virus," *Proceedings of the American Philosophical Society* 150, (2006): 86–112.

9 Magda Farhni and Esyllt Jones, eds., *Epidemic Encounters* (Vancouver: UBC Press, 2012), 4.

10 Esyllt Jones, *Influenza 1918: Disease, Death, and Struggle in Winnipeg* (Toronto: University of Toronto Press), 15.

11 Jones, *Influenza 1918.*

12 Laura M. Glass and Robert J. Glass, "Social Contact Networks for the Spread of Pandemic Influenza in Children and Teenagers," *BMP Public Health* 61, no. 8 (2008): 2.

13 Glass and Glass, "Social Contact Networks."

14 McMillen, *Pandemics*, 89.

15 McMillen, *Pandemics*, 90.

16 Antony Trill et al., "The 1918 'Spanish Flu' in Spain," *Clinical Infectious Diseases* 47 (September 2008): 669.

17 Fahrni and Jones, *Epidemic Encounters*, 4.

18 Alanna Mitchell, "The Outbreak and Its Aftermath," *Canadian Geographic*, 23 August 2018, https://www.canadiangeographic.ca/article/outbreak-and-its-aftermath.

19 Dr. E.A. Robertson, *Canadian Medical Association Journal* 50 (February 1919).

20 A. Gagnon et al., "Age Specific Mortality During the 1918 Influenza Pandemic," *Plos One* 8, no. 8 (August 2013): 2.

21 Census of Canada, 1921.

22 It is important to note and understand that thousands of these Ontarians, although residents of the province during the First World War, were British-born. Their sympathies, in many instances, lay with Britain and the Crown.

23 Mike Clare, "Commemorating the Forgotten Plague through the Classroom," *Activehistory.ca*, 31 January 2018, https://activehistory.ca/2018/01/commemorating-the-forgotten-plague-through-the-classroom.

24 Fahrni and Jones, *Epidemic Encounters*, 4. It is important to note that while there was heavy censorship, the pandemic did not go completely unreported; some headlines emerged, especially in late October, at a time when the war was winding to its close.

25 For further reading on the spread as well as a comprehensive look at the pandemic, especially in the context of public health, see Humphries, *The Last Plague.*

26 "The Spanish Influenza," Niagara Falls Museums, https://niagarafallsmuseums.ca/discover-our-history/history-notes/the-spanish-influenza.

27 Fahrni and Jones, *Epidemic Encounters*, 5.

28 For further reading on the development of the welfare state in both Ontario and Canada, see James Struthers, *No Fault of Their Own: Unemployment and the Canadian Welfare state, 1914–1941* (Toronto: University of Toronto Press, 1983); and Alvin Finkel, *Social Policy and Practice in Canada: A History* (Waterloo: Wilfrid Laurier University Press, 2006).

29 D.A. Herring and E. Korol, "The North–South Divide: Social Inequality and Mortality from the 1918 Influenza Pandemic in Hamilton, Ontario," in *Epidemic Encounters*, ed. Fahrni and Jones, 7.

30 "Guard against Influenza," *National School Services*, 15 October 1918, https://archive.org/details/nationalschoolse01unituoft/page/50/mode/2up.

31 Herring and Korol, "The North–South Divide," 7.

32 Susan Goldenberg, "Killer Flu," *Canada's History*, 11 September 2018, https://www.canadashistory.ca/explore/arts-culture-society/killer-flu. Further to this, it should be noted that Prohibition was on consumption, not on production. It was experienced unevenly across the country as different provinces enforced laws with varying success. While the provinces controlled sales and consumption, the Canadian government was responsible for the making and trading of alcohol. By early 1919, Quebec rejected prohibition outright and became known as a "sinkhole."

33 Fahrni and Jones, *Epidemic Encounters*, 7.

34 Joy Parr, ed., *Childhood and Family in Canadian History* (Toronto: McClelland and Stewart, 1982), 8.

35 Robert McIntosh, "Constructing the Child: New Approaches to the History of Childhood in Canada," *Acadiensis* 28, no. 2 (Spring 1999): 126.

36 McIntosh, "Constructing the Child," 127.

37 Neil Sutherland, *Children in English Canadian Society* (Toronto: University of Toronto Press, 1976), 27.

38 Parr, *Childhood and Family in Canadian History*, 14.

39 Joseph E. Illick, *American Childhoods* (Philadelphia: University of Pennsylvania Press, 2002), 132.

40 Steven Mintz, *A History of American Childhood* (Cambridge, MA: Belknap Press, 2006), 153.

41 For a very good overview of the history of delinquency in this era, see D. Owen Carrigan, *Juvenile Delinquency in Canada* (University Park: Pennsylvania State University Press, 1998).

42 For further reading, see Neil Sutherland, *Growing Up: Childhood in English Canada from the Great War to the Age of Television* (Toronto: University of Toronto Press, 2002).

43 Mona Gleason, *Small Matters: Canadian Children in Sickness and Health* (Montreal and Kingston: McGill–Queen's University Press, 2013), 177.

44 Gleason, *Small Matters*, 192.

45 Cynthia R. Comacchio, "'By Every Means in our Power': Maternal and Child Welfare in Ontario, 1900–1945" in *Ontario since Confederation: A Reader*, ed. Edgar-André Montigny and Lori Chambers (Toronto: University of Toronto Press, 2000), 169.

46 Comacchio, "'By Every Means in our Power,'" 171.

47 Sutherland, *Children in English Canadian Society*, 47.

48 MacDougall, "Toronto's Health Department in Action: Influenza in 2018 and SARS in 2003," in *Epidemic Encounters*, ed. Fahrni and Jones, 226.

49 Census of Canada, 1921.

50 MacDougall, "Toronto's Health Department," 226.

51 MacDougall, "Toronto's Health Department," 229.

52 D. Ann Herring, ed., *Anatomy of a Pandemic* (Hamilton: Anthropology Publications, 2006), 109.

53 Max Brathwaite, "The Year of the Killer Flu," *Maclean's*, 1 February 1953, https://archive.macleans.ca/article/1953/2/1/the-year-of-the-killer-flu.

54 MacDougall, "Toronto's Health Department," 230.

55 Vance, "The Spanish Flu Pandemic of 1918," 21, 22.

56 Fuller and Vizcardo, "Children, School, Influenza," 112.

57 "Spanish Flu," Cathedral Church of St. James, https://stjamescathedral.ca/about/archives-museum/spanish-flu.

58 MacDougall, "Toronto's Health Department," 230.

59 MacDougall, "Toronto's Health Department."
60 *Globe*, 31 October 1918, 10.
61 MacDougall, "Toronto's Health Department," 234.
62 MacDougall, "Toronto's Health Department."
63 MacDougall, "Toronto's Health Department."
64 Slonim, "'Send only your serious cases,'" 86.
65 "Letter to the Editor," *Globe*, 28 October 1918.
66 Karen Slonim, "'Send only your serious cases': Delivering Flu to Toronto: An Anthropological Analysis of the 1918–19 Influenza Epidemic in Toronto, Ontario, Canada" (PhD diss., University of Missouri, 2010), 84.
67 Herring & Korol, "The North-South Divide," 99.
68 Fuller and Vizcardo, "Children, School, Influenza," 167.
69 "Spanish influenza epidemic is serious," *Hamilton Spectator*, 5 October 1918.
70 Mark McNeil, "The day the pandemic came to Hamilton," *Hamilton Spectator*, 26 Oct 2018, https://www.thespec.com/news/hamilton-region/2018/10/26/the-day-the-pandemic-came-to-hamilton.html.
71 Melanie Murken, "Everyday Life in the Third Wave: Social Response to Public Health Policies in Hamilton," in *Recurrence and Resilience: The Third Wave of the 1918–19 Influenza Pandemic in Hamilton* <full cite pls> (Eds.) D. Ann Herring and Sally Carraher (Hamilton: Anthropology Publications, n.d.), https://macsphere.mcmaster.ca/bitstream/11375/14364/1/fulltext.pdf, 147.
72 Murken, "Everyday Life in the Third Wave," 149.
73 Kirsty Bond, "The Plight of the Children," in <full cite pls> *Anatomy of a Pandemic*, ed. D. Ann Herring, 84.
74 Wright, "Mother & Infant Mortality During the Third Wave," in Herring and Caraher., 71.
75 Herring and Korol, "The North–South Divide," 107.
76 Bruce Deachman, "A century ago, the Spanish lady came to Ottawa, claiming more than 500 lives," *Ottawa Citizen*, 8 December 2018, https://ottawacitizen.com/news/local-news/a-century-ago-the-spanish-lady-came-to-ottawa-claiming-more-than-500-lives.
77 Deachman, "A century ago."
78 Deachman, "A century ago."
79 Windsor Public Library, "Spanish Flu Pandemic," 2016, https://www.windsorpubliclibrary.com/?page_id=63184. Connaught laboratories, operating in Toronto since 1914, developed a vaccine, which was distributed not only in Ontario but across Canada via the provincial health ministry. No claims of effectiveness were made, and while it didn't help anyone, it did not harm anyone either.
80 Windsor Public Library, "Spanish Flu Pandemic."
81 Jamie Bradburn, "When the Spanish flu came to Ontario," *TVO*, 15 February 2018, https://www.tvo.org/article/when-the-spanish-flu-came-to-ontario.
82 Bradburn, "When the Spanish flu came to Ontario."
83 "Spanish flu of 1918 ravaged remote lumber camps," *Huntsville Forester*, 30 June 2006, https://www.muskokaregion.com/news-story/3611228-spanish-flu-of-1918-ravaged-remote-lumber-camps.
84 David Yates, "The 'Spanish' influenza in Huron County, 1918," *Goderich Signal-Star*, 13 March 2020, https://www.goderichsignalstar.com/opinion/columnists/the-spanish-influenza-in-huron-county-1918-2.
85 Yates, "The 'Spanish' influenza."

86 Stephen Thorning, "Flu epidemic peaked locally in November 1918," *Wellington Advertiser*, 25 March 2020, https://www.wellingtonadvertiser.com/flu-epidemic-peaked-locally-in-november-1918-2.
87 Nicole Marion and Joseph Scanlon, "Mass Death and Mass Illness in an Isolated Canadian Town," *Mortality* 16, no. 4 (November 2011): 333–8.
88 Patricia Drohan, "The pandemic of 1918–1920 and one Espanola family's loss," *Sudbury Star*, 30 April 2020, https://www.theobserver.ca/news/local-news/the-pandemic-of-1918-1920-and-one-espanola-familys-loss/wcm/d4b65b35-87c4-42c1-84a7-f8da439992b8.
89 Drohan, "The pandemic of 1918–1920."
90 Humphries, *The Last Plague*, 127, 128.
91 For further reading, see Truth and Reconciliation Commission of Canada, *They Came for the Children: Canada, Aboriginal Peoples, and the Residential Schools* (2012); Robert Carney, "Aboriginal Residential Schools before Confederation: The Early Experience," *Historical Studies: Canadian Catholic Historical Association* 61 (1995), 13–40; John S. Milloy, *A National Crime: The Canadian Government and the Residential School System, 1879 to 1986* (1999); J.R. Miller, *Residential Schools and Reconciliation: Canada Confronts Its History* (2017).; and J.R. Miller, Shingwauk's Vision: *A History of Native Residential Schools* (1996).
92 Humphries, *The Last Plague*, 128.
93 Humphries, *The Last Plague*, 129.
94 Humphries, *The Last Plague*.
95 See John S. Milloy, *A National Crime: The Canadian Government and he Residential School System, 1879 to 1986* (Winnipeg: University of Manitoba Press, 20117); and J.R. Miller, *Residential Schools and Reconciliation: Canada Confronts Its History* (Toronto: University of Toronto Press, 2017).
96 Laurie Leclair, "Remembering Beausoleil's Spanish flu epidemic of 1918," *Anishinabek News*, 19 November 2014, http://anishinabeknews.ca/2014/11/19/remembering-beausoleils-spanish-flu-epidemic-of-1918.
97 For further reading, see James Daschuk, *Clearing the Plains: Disease, Politics Of Starvation, and the Loss of Indigenous Life* (Regina: University of Regina Press, 2013).
98 Mary-Ellen Kelm, "What Kind of Government Is This?" *Defining Moments Canada*, 2018, https://definingmomentscanada.ca/wp-content/uploads/2018/06/First_Peoples.pdf.
99 Kelm, "What Kind of Government Is This?"
100 Kelm, "What Kind of Government Is This?"
101 Esyllt Jones, "What Is Forgotten?: Influenza's Reverberations in Post-War Canada," *Active History*, 30 January 2018, http://activehistory.ca/2018/01/what-is-forgotten-influenzas-reverberations-in-post-war-canada.
102 Jorge Barrera, "Epidemics and Resilience," *CBC News* 10 May 2020, https://newsinteractives.cbc.ca/longform/algonquin-epidemics.
103 Barrera, "Epidemics and Resilience."
104 Jean A. Thompson, "Haudenosaunee Dying: Influenza Deaths amongst the Six Nations," in Herring and Carraher, 77.
105 Cynthia Toman, "'My Chance Has Come at Last!,'" *Native Studies Review* 19 no. 2 (2010): 106.
106 Toman, "'My Chance Has Come at Last!,'" 95.
107 Jones, "What is Forgotten?"
108 "Kids Coping – The 1918 Influenza Pandemic," *New Zealand History*, https://nzhistory.govt.nz/media/sound/kids-coping-the-1918-flu-pandemic.

109 Nicole Marion and Joseph Scanlon, "Mass Death and Mass Illness in an Isolated Canadian Town," *Mortality* 16, no. 4, 325–42 at 339.

110 Patrick Kennedy, "Napanee woman who survived Spanish flu remembers 'In Quarantine' signs," *Kingston Whig Standard*, 28 March 2020, https://www.thewhig.com/opinion/columnists/napanee-woman-who-survived-spanish-flu-remembers-in-quarantine-signs.

111 Kennedy, "Napanee woman who survived Spanish flu."

112 Fisher, *Envisioning Disease, Gender, and War* (New York: Palgrave Macmillan, 2012), 6.

113 Fisher, *Envisioning Disease, Gender, and War*, 7

114 Jones, *Influenza 1918*, 171.

115 Children's Hospital of Philadelphia, "Parents PACK Personal Stories – Influenza," https://www.chop.edu/centers-programs/parents-pack/personal-stories/influenza.

CHAPTER SEVENTEEN

From Polluted Periphery to Vital Green Corridor: Toronto's Don River Valley, 1793–1989

JENNIFER BONNELL

For the people who live there, Toronto is less a lakefront city than a city of ravines. For those who live in the northern neighbourhoods, the lakefront is a distant place; by contrast, the forested, forking ravines of three major river valleys (from west to east, the Humber, the Don, and the Rouge) reach into all corners of the city. The publicly managed conservation areas within these watersheds form a well-used recreational network for cyclists and pedestrians, birdwatchers and weekend picnickers (not to mention bats, raccoons, and coyotes) (see map 17.1).

But this wasn't always so. One hundred fifty years ago, the city's ravines – especially the Don River Valley on what was then the city's eastern edge – were viewed as polluted and dangerous spaces to avoid rather than destinations to seek out. Revitalizing Toronto's urban river valleys took time and effort, something Ontario's provincial government has been quick to forget in its 2019 directives to delete funding for education and public engagement from the budgets of the conservation authorities that own and manage many of Toronto's ravine lands.[1]

Forgotten in these cost-cutting measures, for example, are the efforts by the Task Force to Bring Back the Don, a citizen advisory committee formed in the late 1980s to facilitate public access to the deindustrializing landscapes of the Lower Don by removing chain-link fences and constructing pedestrian bridges. Through wetland construction initiatives, river clean-up days, and annual events like Paddle the Don, citizens' groups and conservation authorities have attracted volunteers and broader publics to come to know the Don Valley's landscapes and work for their protection. Forgotten, too, are the efforts of an earlier generation of conservationists, who propounded the idea that the city's urban river valleys were vital green "lungs" offering Torontonians opportunities for reflection and recreation.

This chapter explores the decades-long transformation in how Torontonians perceive and experience their ravine lands, with a focus on the city's long-maligned and only recently revalued Don River Valley. From its headwaters north of the city in the Oak Ridges Moraine to its outlet 38 kilometres south in Lake Ontario, the Don flows through one of the most heavily urbanized watersheds in Canada. While some of the valley's bottom lands are now protected parkland, close to 90 per cent of the lands within the river's catchment area have been developed for residential, commercial, or industrial uses.[2] Environmental historians often work with long time frames to better understand the origins of thorny environmental problems in the present as well as the changes in human economies, technologies, and ideas about environment that have exacerbated or mitigated those problems over time. In this chapter, an understanding of twentieth-century developments within the Don Valley – specifically, the competing perceptions of the valley held by urban conservationists and developers of the Don Valley Parkway – requires that we appreciate the perceptions of possibility and risk that developed around valley environments one hundred years earlier. This account begins, then, in the early nineteenth century, when ideas about the hidden dangers of the river's marshy lower reaches shaped the future development of the city. The lower river was associated with danger and disease, and decades later, this would propel its industrial transformation.

Perceptions of the Lower Don as an unhealthy and uncivilized environment reflect a broader tendency to categorize urban environments, and urban peripheries especially, as problematic spaces to be improved through industrialization and development. For late nineteenth- and twentieth-century North Americans, nature was "out there" – in cottage country, in provincial and national parks, in wild spaces outside the city. Cities were by definition artificial environments where nature – at least, nature worth caring about – did not reside. This perception of cities as unnatural was shared by an earlier generation of environmental historians, who directed their energies to histories of wilderness preservation and wildlife protection in environments distant from the cities where they lived. Not until the early 1990s would environmental historians begin to turn their attention to environments closer to home, to nature within the city and the history of its transformation to serve human ends. Ignoring environments close to home, they argued, reinforced problematic boundaries between nature and culture and neglected questions of environmental justice (exposure to environmental risk and access to environmental amenities like green space) in our cities and towns.[3]

This chapter draws upon the writings of these earlier historians to recognize the Don River Valley as an environment worthy of attention: a place that different groups of people over time struggled with and sought solace within, manipulated and worked to protect. Neither fully natural nor fully artificial, it was (and remains) a place that shaped the development of the city in significant ways. From the mosquito-infested marsh at its mouth to the occasionally devastating floods it wrought upon valley landowners, to the large quantities of silt and debris it washed into Toronto's harbour, the river was an active participant in the city's development. The valley's geography, with its steep ravine walls and wide plateaux, was even more influential, at once a formidable barrier to the eastward expansion of the city and an enabling corridor for transportation and urban growth.

This chapter examines the origins of the urban conservation movement that developed to protect Toronto's Don River Valley beginning in the 1940s. As changes in transportation and manufacturing technology saw the relocation or closure of many industries along the waterfront and the river corridor, a new generation of Ontario writers, artists, and conservationists began to reimagine the Don Valley and other urban ravines as iconic Toronto landscapes worthy of protection. By the 1950s, Ontario's embrace of watershed-level conservation, prompted in part by the effects of Hurricane Hazel on southern Ontario, had brought recognition of the vital role of river valleys as drainage corridors in times of flooding and established a system of valley parklands.[4]

Characterizations of the valley as a dangerous place in need of improvement would surface again, however, in the muted debates that surrounded the construction of the Don Valley Parkway in the early 1960s. As development transformed valley landscapes and their significance within the broader metropolitan region, the construction of the parkway illuminated conflicting visions of the Don: would it be a valuable corridor for transportation, or a cherished place for recreation and reflection?

By the late 1960s and 1970s, a new generation of Toronto-based environmental activists working to raise awareness about water quality in the Great Lakes seized upon the deplorable condition of the Don as a potent local example of all that had gone wrong and of the potential for renewal. Unlike the urban conservationists who preceded them, Ontario environmentalists in the 1960s and 1970s employed theatrical tactics to raise public awareness about more systemic problems, such as pollution and ecosystem degradation.[5] The chapter ends in 1989, with the creation of the Task Force to Bring Back the Don and the rise of a more diverse group of citizen activists who concentrated their efforts on enabling public access to the river valley as a means of generating awareness of and protection for a cherished urban green space. Their efforts contributed to changing public perceptions of the valley as a degraded but ultimately salvageable natural system and fuelled initiatives to reimagine the Don as Toronto's urban wilderness.

This study of the transformation of a single watershed in the evolving city of Toronto illuminates broader trends in the history of the relationship between Ontarians and the natural environments upon which they depend. In it, we can see the power of colonial visions for settlement based on the exploitation of natural resources, and the blindness of those visions to the particularities and risks of local environments. We can see the long reach of perceptions of danger and disorder in determinations of which places would become "sacrifice zones" to industrial development in the late nineteenth and early twentieth centuries. And we can see the ways in which groups with conflicting visions articulated the values, and the liabilities, of those environments in shaping the futures they imagined. This layered history of human uses and perceptions of environment is written into the landscape of places like the Don River Valley.

Creating a Polluted Periphery

Scanning the waterfront on a reconnaissance expedition in the spring of 1793, Upper Canada's first Lieutenant Governor John Graves Simcoe saw in the sheltered curve of the east end of Toronto Bay and its tributary streams a landscape of possibility. He noted the harbour's natural defences and its potential to supply the future settlement with lumber. "At the Bottom of the Harbour," he reported to acting colonial administrator Alured Clarke in May 1793, "there is a Situation admirably adapted for a Naval Arsenal and Dock Yard, and there flows into the Harbour a River the Banks of which are covered with excellent Timber."[6] Satisfied with the area's potential, Simcoe had his surveyor lay out a plot for the future town of York immediately to the west of the mouth of the Don, at the foot of today's Parliament Street. He reserved a large area for military purposes at the west end of the harbour, and at the east end, between the townsite and the Don River, set aside four hundred acres for future government buildings. Four years later, the capital's first parliament buildings stood just west of the "Government Park" on the eastern lakeshore.[7]

In the early years of European settlement, the Don River Valley held considerable value as an integral part of Simcoe's imagined future for the colony. Anchoring a vision of nature transformed in Britain's image – in place of vast forests and wetland wastes, there would be a compact urban settlement supported by a grid of surrounding farms, woodlots, and industries – the valley served the economic aspirations of the colony. As the site of the fledgling farms and country estates of the elite, it also fulfilled important social and political functions of the colonial project. Military officers and favoured officials in Simcoe's inner circle received generous farm lots to the north and east of his town plot. Proximity to the Don River appears to have been

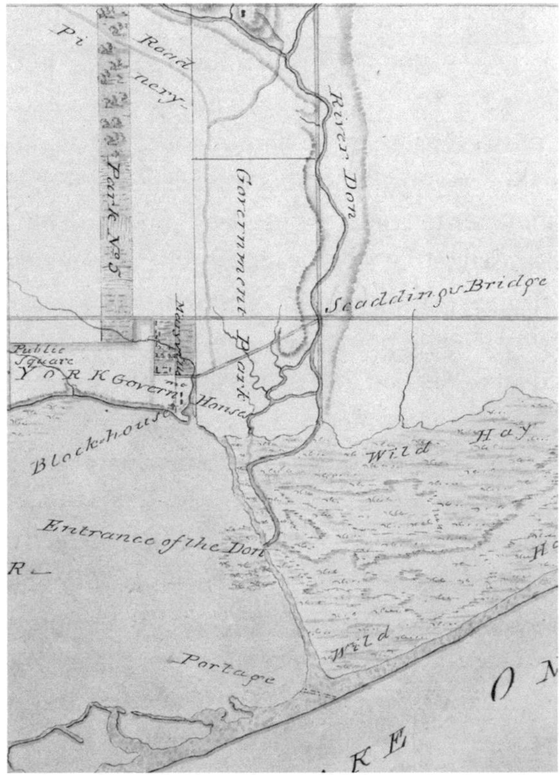

Figure 17.1. The town of York and Government Park reserve, 1802. The Government Park reserve runs along the west side of the river, with the "Governmt House" [*sic*], or parliament buildings, indicated northwest of the river mouth. Ashbridge's Bay Marsh appears southeast of the river mouth. Source: Detail from William Chewett, P*lan of 916 1/4 Acres, in the Township of York in Upper Canada*, 1802, Toronto Public Library, MS1889.1.6.

a significant consideration in these awards. Lots running east of Yonge Street and north of Bloor, for example, were laid out east and west "to equalize the river frontage."[8] Simcoe himself claimed a 200-acre parcel on the west side of the river, north of the government reserve. He awarded the 250-acre parcel opposite him, on the east side of the river, to his secretary, John Scadding, and the lot north of him to George Playter, a respected military captain. For many grantees, holdings along the Don complemented already valuable properties closer to town. They could dabble with farming along the flats of the river, with little pressure to create viable operations. Some, like Scadding, farmed their holdings with relative success.[9] Others chose instead to erect lavish suburban mansions on their lands overlooking the valley. This was particularly true west of the river along Yonge and Davenport Streets, where country estates such as Rosedale prevailed until mid-century and beyond.

Agricultural settlement and country estates, modest or otherwise, were just one component of the colonial vision for the Don River Valley. Another was the promise the valley held as a site for industrial activities. In the "excellent timber" that covered the banks of the Don near the harbour, and the stands of straight white pine farther upriver, Simcoe saw ship masts to replenish naval fleets in the event of war, and accessible lumber to construct needed homes and buildings for the new capital. Rich clay deposits in the lower valley promised raw material for potteries and brickworks. Fish and riparian wildlife offered ready sources of sustenance, and the flow of the river itself could power future milling operations.[10]

The valley provided, as Simcoe had anticipated. At the peak of water-powered milling in 1860, the watershed supported more than fifty mills producing paper, lumber, flour, and wool. Most of these operations congregated along the upper reaches of the river, where gradients were steeper and flow rates faster.

What Simcoe failed to anticipate, however, during his brief stay at York, was the influence of the wide, shallow marsh stretching south and east of the river mouth on the health of York's future inhabitants. Each summer, residents of the developing town suffered through bouts of what they called "lake fever" or "ague." Characterized by alternating symptoms of severe fever and shaking chills, the ague was an almost inevitable, if rarely fatal, aspect of life in Upper Canada in the late eighteenth and early nineteenth centuries.[11] Now understood as a strain of malaria, a disease spread by the bite of the *Anopheles* mosquito, at the time the ague was thought to result from inhaling "bad air" (hence mal/aria). In a letter to a former employer in Quebec City in September 1801, Toronto printer John Bennett wrote:

> I am just recovering from a severe fit of fever and ague which confined me to bed for ten days past – no body [*sic*] can escape it who pretends to live here … There is a marsh about [half] a mile from where I live from which a thick fog arises every morning – people attribute [the fever] in great measure to that and to the low and uncultivated state of the Country.[12]

Gases produced by decomposing organic matter took on the ominous label of "miasmas" –disease-producing vapours – and the places where such organic matter accumulated, such as swamps and wetlands, became places to fear, avoid, and, best yet, destroy through drainage and fill.

Before the discovery of the malaria parasite in 1880 and the subsequent discovery that it was transmitted by mosquitoes, place itself bore the mantle of disease risk. Certain environments were considered more "unhealthy" than others. In 1803, for

Figure 17.2. D.C. Grose, *Taylor Brothers Paper Mill on the Don River,* c. 1860. The mill was located on the east side of the river near Pottery Road.
Source: Toronto Public Library, Historical Pictures Collection, B 3-27c.

example, Isaac Brock reported in a letter to military secretary James Green that the soldiers quartered in the Block House at the mouth of the Don "are falling ill of the Ague and Fever in great numbers," while the garrison at the west end of town "continues in perfect health." The evidence confirmed his suspicions about the environment around the lower river, "[shewing] plainly that the character given of the situation of the Block House is … well founded."[13] A quarter century later, in 1830, petitioners to the Upper Canadian legislature pointed to the "inconvenience and unhealthiness" of the site of the recently burned Parliament House, located at the foot of Parliament Street just west of the Don marshes, in their call for new parliament buildings to be constructed near the lieutenant governor's residence in New Town (west of the original town plot). "No person having a regard to health would select [the site near the marsh] for a residence," they argued. "The untenanted State of houses adjoining the said Marsh, confirm them in this opinion."[14] Simcoe's vision of a secure and prosperous settlement at the east end of Toronto Bay had been dashed.

Historian Conevery Bolton Valencius provided useful context for this notion of "unhealthy" landscapes in her 2002 monograph *The Health of the Country*. For nineteenth-century Americans, Valencius reminds us, "the environment [did not stop] at the seeming boundary of the skin." Instead, "the surrounding world seeped into [one's] every pore, creating states of health that were as much environmental as they were personal."[15] Elevated sites with fresh, circulating air were considered salubrious; low, marshy areas where air and water alike were thought to stagnate were considered unhealthy and malevolent.[16] Miasmas "entered the body as breath or fluid, and they operated within it just as they did within terrain. They carried the environment's imbalance, disturbance, or putrefaction into the depths of the body, expressing within the individual the sickly tendencies of the locale."[17] For Brock's soldiers and the petitioners to the Upper Canadian parliament, then, the marshlands around the mouth of the Don were inherently unhealthy.

Ironically, despite mistaken theories about the origin of disease, fears of miasma were not entirely misplaced. Brock's observations about the disproportionate frequency of ague among soldiers at the eastern blockhouse corroborate other anecdotal sources in suggesting that malaria cases were more numerous in areas adjacent to the marsh.[18] Indeed, the slow-moving waters of the Don marshes would have served as an excellent breeding ground for mosquitoes, and efforts made to avoid these "unhealthy places" and to shut out the dangerous "night air" often had the effect of shutting out mosquitoes as well. Even before significant industrial development in the area, the marshes of the lower river were experienced, and imagined, as a diseased landscape.

Not surprisingly, perceptions of unhealthiness had significant implications for the area's development. In an 1833 letter to Viscount Goderich, Secretary of State for the Colonies, Lieutenant Governor John Colborne explained that the westward expansion of the city was the only reasonable option: "the Eastern part of the Town is affected by the effluvia of the marshes of the Don, and the rapid increase in the population requires that the Town should be extended towards the Westward, the most salubrious and convenient site."[19] Toronto did, indeed, "lean west" in the decades that followed, pulling away from the site of the original town plot near the mouth of the Don. Parliament moved to new and more fashionable quarters in the west end of town (at Front and John Streets) in 1832, escalating with its relocation the desirability of west-end real estate (and the corresponding undesirability of the east end).[20] When the city incorporated in 1834, the lower river came to represent an official margin, its curving course forming the eastern border of the city between Bloor and Queen Streets. The largely undeveloped area between Parliament Street and the Lower Don was further marginalized by its placement within the city liberties, an ambiguous administrative status that meant residents neither enjoyed full city rights and services nor paid full city taxes. From 1834 until the abolishment of the liberties in 1859, the Lower Don occupied an urban margin, both within the everyday experience of the city's residents and in the official sphere of city maps and jurisdictional boundaries.[21] An urban periphery had been created, a designation that would become even more pronounced as industrial activities further transformed the valley in the late nineteenth century.

As perceptions of unhealthiness and poor agricultural potential dampened the desirability of valley landholdings in the 1830s and 1840s, and the status of the valley as an urban periphery solidified, new land uses began to take hold. While water-powered mills continued to congregate along the upper branches of the river in this period, the lower river took on new significance as an attractive site for factories producing a broader array of goods after 1850. The arrival of the Grand Trunk's east–west rail line across the Toronto waterfront in 1856 drew tanneries, breweries, foundries, and, later, meat packing plants, soap factories, and oil refineries to the lower reaches of the river and the river mouth. With them came working-class housing, from isolated cottages in the early years to ethnic and mixed-origin neighbourhoods such as Cabbagetown, Corktown, and Riverside in the late nineteenth century.

These early firms attracted others, creating constellations of mutually supportive operations. Soapworks in the lower valley, for example, took advantage of local supplies of tallow from nearby animal processing plants, while tanneries produced the leather belts used for power transmission in early factories and mills. In the 1860s and 1870s, widespread adoption of steam power stimulated industrial expansion across the city. The existence of a growing industrial hub on the Lower Don, with its established benefits of affordable land and convenient rail and shipping access, provided the foundation for further industrial growth. The 1880s and 1890s would see greater expansion still, with the infusion of state funds to straighten the river and create new industrial lands. By the turn of the century, the lower reaches of the river and the river mouth had been transformed into a built environment especially conducive to industrial production.

An area vilified as "diseased" since the early nineteenth century came to be understood in this period as a providential site for industrial development. As the editors of the *Toronto World* reasoned, on 8 May 1884, "every city that has manufacturing industries has a district set apart therefor, and the Don is the district that nature and expedience have set apart for Toronto. It is not frequented by the fastidious, it possesses excellent railway and shipping accommodations, the land is cheap, there is good accommodation for working people, and it is accessible to the business centres by the street cars."[22]

Figure 17.3. Bird's-eye view of the Lower Don River, 1893. Note the oil refineries to the right (east) of the bend in the river and the marsh stretching south and east of the river mouth. The stockyards of William Davies Co. pork packing plant, one of several abbatoirs in the area, is visible in the centre of the image, north of the bend.
Source: Detail from Barclay, Clark and Co, *City of Toronto,* 1893, Toronto Public Library, Historical Pictures Collection, 916-2-1.

The consequence of these changes was a grossly polluted waterway. It is important to remember, too, that this was a small river – a river you could throw a stone over. The effects of pollutants would have been more pronounced, and more rapid, than in other more sizeable urban-industrial waterways like the St. Lawrence or the Allegheny. For most industrial operations along the Don, the river offered a convenient disposal site for industrial wastes. Animal carcasses, lime from tanning operations, corrosive lye from soap works, and industrial by-products such as gasoline all found their way into the river. Organic wastes such as animal offal and manure put heavy stress on the river's supply of dissolved oxygen, a vital ingredient for the maintenance of aquatic life and the decomposition of wastes. In limited quantities, organic wastes will be broken down by microorganisms present in river water. As tanneries, breweries, and other industries multiplied along the lower river in the latter half of the nineteenth century, however, the river's ability to assimilate these wastes would have been seriously compromised.[23] Sewage pollution added to the cocktail. Sewage disposal in the river was largely incidental until the 1880s and 1890s, when the city extended the sewer system to the east and ran several outfalls into the Don. Consumption of land around the river mouth also removed porous wetlands, further reducing the river's capacity to process wastes.

By the 1880s, the Lower Don was widely perceived as an "objectionable stream" and as a persistent threat to public health. Years of waste disposal by local industries and municipal authorities, combined with changes in the river's hydrology caused by deforestation, soil erosion, and water diversion for agricultural and industrial purposes, contributed to highly polluted conditions in the slow-moving, serpentine reaches of the lower river and the wide swath of marshland at its mouth. An article in the *Toronto Mail* on 20 March 1894 described the lower river as a "pestilential channel" whose waters had taken on "a yellowish green colour, and a slimy, soup-like consistency." Perceptions that the valley was a polluted and unhealthy space built upon others that had been in place since the early 1800s.

The Don Valley Conservation Movement

Running counter to these perceptions of the Don as a providential site for industry, and as a polluted and dangerous space at the edge of the city, were notions of the valley as an urban green space to be protected and cherished. Visions of the valley as a cherished place are present in the earliest written records. Elizabeth Simcoe's use of the valley in the 1790s as a retreat in times of illness, and a destination for picnicking parties in summer, is an early expression of this broader trend. Travelling up the Don by sleigh in winter or through the woods in summer, Simcoe hosted picnics for friends on a promontory overlooking the valley, sketched local wildlife and scenes along the river, and retreated to a modest cottage with her children when they took ill. A retreat from political life, it was also a retreat *to* the healing and inspiring environment provided by the height of land and the impressive views of the valley below. She wrote on 18 April 1796: "Francis has not been well. We therefore set off to [Castle] Frank today to change the air intending to pass some days there." And two days later: "the Porticos here are delightful pleasant & the Room cool from its height & the thickness of the logs of which the House is built, the Mountain Tea berries in great perfection. Francis is much better & busy in planting Currant bushes & Peach Trees."[24]

One hundred fifty years later, in the 1940s, writers, artists, and conservationists found similar value in the valley landscapes – particularly in the still largely rural landscapes north of Bloor Street – as fragments of "wildness" in the city that had the potential to rejuvenate harried urban minds and bodies. The most prominent champion of the Don Valley as a vital urban green space was Charles Sauriol. A vocal advocate for valley conservation from the 1940s on, Sauriol was also a seasonal cottager in the valley. Every summer his family packed up and moved from their Toronto home near Broadview and Danforth Avenues to a cottage near the Forks of the Don, just a few kilometres away. They summered there every summer for forty-one years, between 1927 and 1968. Over those decades, Sauriol planted an extensive vegetable garden and orchard, tended honeybees, and engaged in reforestation efforts on his valley holdings, which he expanded in the 1930s and 1940s.

Sauriol makes a compelling subject for study in part because he left behind a rich record of his life experiences. He wrote six books about his experiences as a conservationist, an apiarist, and a cottager in the Don Valley, along with numerous unpublished manuscripts, and he kept a diary throughout his life; clearly, he found it meaningful to document his experiences. He was a less elegant writer than John Muir or Aldo Leopold, Ernest Thompson Seton or Roderick Haig Brown, and his focus was on a place perhaps less compelling than Yosemite or the wilds of British Columbia. As a result, his work never received the recognition that other conservationist-writers enjoyed in this period. Most of his books are today out of print, and his name is unfamiliar to most Torontonians outside of local history and environmental advocacy circles. His influence survives, however, in the physical landscape of valley parklands, including the Charles Sauriol Conservation Reserve created in the east valley in 1989 and a number of other protected areas he had a hand in creating across the province.

In the spring of 1947, as residential and commercial development began to encroach on the valley, Sauriol and two conservation-minded colleagues formed the Don Valley Conservation Association (DVCA). The DVCA's 300-plus members worked to protect the valley's resources and to inform the public that a wilderness on their doorstep was being threatened. Nature walks, annual tree-planting days, and automobile tours of the watershed emphasized the still "wild and serene" Don Valley as a "green buttress" to the growing city below it. A contemporary of the better-resourced Don Valley Conservation Authority (which confusingly adopted the same acronym), the association was propelled almost entirely by the energy of its founders and the support of its members.[25] Like similar efforts in other North American centres at the time – notably, American urbanist William Whyte's efforts to protect the Brandywine Valley outside Philadelphia, and Congressman John Seiberling's campaign to protect the Cuyahoga Valley near Cleveland – the DVCA emphasized conservation, aesthetic amenities, and outdoor recreation in its efforts to protect the Don.[26] Sauriol was well connected to conservation advocates locally, and he drew upon established tropes of conservation and wilderness preservation in advancing his campaign.

Some of the DVCA's earliest initiatives involved efforts to control public behaviour in nature. Incensed by "despoilers of the beautiful," Sauriol and his colleagues set out to curb such "menaces to conservation" as "the shooting of songbirds, ducks

Figure 17.4. Unidentified Don Valley Conservation Association member with tree conservation signs, Don Valley, 1947.
Source: City of Toronto Archives, fonds 4, series 81, file 73.

[and] pheasants, the setting of grass fires, [and] the hacking of trees by juveniles." In 1947 they established a citizens' patrol of the valley to protect trees from the hatchets of young boys and rare wildflowers from the enthusiasm of their admirers. That same year, an Easter week "Save the Valley" campaign proved especially successful in "uproot[ing] vandalism." Visits to schools and Scout groups informed children about the benefits of non-intrusive nature study, and collaboration with the local police saw the seizure of "18 axes, 7 bayonets and a few butcher knives" from would-be valley vandals.[27] Besides cultivating respect for the non-human world, the DVCA propounded an understanding of nature as a place in which humans played no part, except as contemplative visitors or caring stewards. By proscribing certain behaviours and promoting others, they aligned themselves with their counterparts in wilderness conservation; for them, nature was a static entity that, bounded and regulated, could be protected from human interference.[28] This ideological shift

from private enjoyment to the regulated public use of nature would have deeply personal consequences for Sauriol in the years to come.

In 1951, Sauriol launched the DVCA–East York (DVCA-EY) branch's quarterly magazine, *The Cardinal*. Written and produced entirely by Sauriol with modest financial assistance from the DVCA-EY, the magazine contained a mixture of short articles on valley history, fictional stories emphasizing the moral righteousness of nature stewardship, news about conservation activities, and educational "conversations" between the DVCA mascots, Canny and Candid Cardinal. Sauriol wrote in his inaugural Spring 1951 issue: "[p]ersons residing in the Toronto metropolitan area have at their disposal a … bower of natural beauty which is the envy of many other cities: *The Cardinal* will endeavour to make … the streams, woodlands, birds and flowers at your door … mean more to you than ever before."[29] Between 1951 and 1962, annual steam locomotive trips through the valley capitalized on a general public nostalgia for train touring.[30] These "Conservation Specials" brought considerable exposure to the DVCA cause, attracting an average of eight hundred passengers each year.[31] The DVCA continued to provide a grassroots voice for valley conservation into the early 1960s, when rapid environmental change and a shifting social and cultural landscape gave rise to new strategies.

Conservation activities in the valley received a boost from an unexpected source in the early morning of 16 October 1954. A tropical storm originally projected to dissipate over southern Ontario suddenly reintensified, pounding Toronto with winds that reached 110 kilometres per hour. From his home on Hillside Drive overlooking the valley, Sauriol watched through the night as heavy rain and winds transformed the Don into a rushing torrent with an astonishing capacity for destruction. "The quiet of the night," he wrote, "was shaken by the reverberations of huge floating trees pounding objects in their path; the water was littered with fast-moving objects scarcely discernible in the darkness."[32] In the space of forty-eight hours, Hurricane Hazel dumped 285 millimetres of rain in the Toronto area, washing out bridges and roads across the city and taking eighty-one lives across southern Ontario. In Toronto alone, more than 1,800 people were left homeless, and damage across the province was estimated at roughly $100 million (about $1 billion today). Although no lives were lost in the Don Valley, two cars and their occupants were swept into the river.[33]

The storm and its consequences had long-term implications for conservation initiatives in the valley and across the city. As the city rebuilt over the winter of 1954–55, it did so with a new awareness of the significance of valley lands as natural drainage channels for flood waters.[34] In 1957, four Toronto-area conservation authorities, including the Don, amalgamated to form the Metropolitan Toronto and Region Conservation Authority (MTRCA), to enable greater coordination between

Figure 17.5. Cover plate, *The Cardinal*, 1st ed., Spring 1951.
Source: City of Toronto Archives, fonds 4, series 104, file 14.

jurisdictions in regulating the use of urban watersheds. The MTRCA was given the power to acquire valley lands for flood control and recreation purposes, with important implications for the future of the Don Valley.

Conflicting Visions: The Valley and the Road

Ultimately, Sauriol's efforts to see the valley recognized as a cherished urban *place* ran up against more powerful visions of the valley as a *corridor* for transportation and development. The construction of the Don Valley Parkway (DVP) in the early 1960s radically transformed valley landscapes, laying a ribbon of pavement along the valley bottom and demolishing hills and other landforms. It also had deeply personal ramifications for Sauriol, in that it brought about the expropriation of his valley landholdings and the demolition of his beloved family cottage.

The DVP brought to fruition half a century of visions for the valley as a high-speed transportation corridor, building upon its function as a rail corridor since the 1880s. Constructed between 1958 and 1967, the DVP was a signature development of North America's first metropolitan government. It was also the vision of a man synonymous with that government from 1953 to 1962: Metro Toronto's founding chair, Frederick Gardiner. Possessed with what his biographer called an "unalloyed fascination" with multilane highways, Gardiner was a tenacious promoter of the

DVP as a vital component of a larger network of urban expressways serving the metropolitan region.[35] The DVP was an ideal flagship project for the metropolitan government, for it would relieve congestion in the downtown core and carry automobile traffic efficiently to the city's rapidly expanding suburban districts.

Metro Council approved plans for the parkway in 1956; work began on its southern reaches two years later. The road would run directly through Sauriol's orchard and the site of his cottage, "wiping out," he wrote bitterly in 1956, "the work of 30 years."[36] In 1961, workmen pulled down the Sauriols' cherished cottage. The road right of way left Sauriol and his family with a portion of their original holdings, including an older cottage previously owned by the De Grassi family on the west side of the river. Restored after Hurricane Hazel as the headquarters of Sauriol's DVCA, the De Grassi cottage provided an opportunity to regroup and start over. Demonstrating great pluck, Sauriol and his family packed their possessions and moved across the river. By 1964 construction was completed from the Gardiner Expressway north to Bloor Street; the parkway reached its end-point at Highway 401 in 1967 (and would be continued as Highway 404 in the 1970s and 1980s).

For Gardiner, the parkway represented the best use of a blighted and underdeveloped space. Addressing the inaugural meeting of Metro Council in January 1960, Gardiner asked, "Who remembers the Don Valley north of … the Prince Edward Viaduct which so recently was a swale and a jungle until the bulldozers tore the whole countryside apart and put it together again into what in a few months will be the Don Valley Parkway and the Bayview Extension?"[37] In conjunction with plans to transform the surrounding valley lands into landscaped parks and recreational amenities, the road would act as a civilizing force to convert an unruly, dangerous landscape into a pleasing scenic backdrop. For Gardiner, and for many Toronto residents in this period, the DVP represented the best use of a natural corridor through the city. The history of the valley as a corridor for the movement of people and goods, by water and later by rail, preordained its transformation as a modern transportation corridor.

In the broader context of expressway development in Toronto, the parkway was noteworthy for the strong consensus in favour of it. Unlike the Spadina Expressway, plans for which were ultimately cancelled in the early 1970s following heated public opposition, the DVP was a relatively "friction-free" development: few homes stood in its way, and few people objected. As the consulting engineers had predicted, the project would pose little threat to property values and would require only limited expropriation of private lands because it would be running through a largely undeveloped valley. Furthermore, the general popularity of the car, and expressways, in this period, guaranteed the project a good reception. Although the shine was by then beginning to come off expressway projects in the US (San Francisco's freeway

Figure 17.6. Grading on the Don Valley Parkway at Don Mills Road, facing east, November 1959. The remains of Tumper's Hill are visible in the background.
Source: City of Toronto Archives, fonds 220, series 3, file 116, item ES13-187.

revolt of the late 1950s was perhaps most notable in this regard), traffic congestion in Toronto and the city's relative lack of experience with urban expressway development created favourable conditions for public support.

It seems that the public, rather than questioning the DVP project, wanted to see it built *faster*. Among Torontonians on the city's east side, the noise of heavy transport vehicles on their streets and mounting congestion problems on major thoroughfares prompted demands that the plan for a limited-access highway through the valley be expedited.[38] Suburban development in the northern reaches of the city provided further impetus. North York's Don Mills development, with a population of 7,000 in 1955, planned to accommodate another 25,000 people over the following five years, which threatened to strain heavily congested traffic arteries still further.[39] The parkway's planners estimated that the road would reduce travel time from the proposed suburbs northeast of the city from sixty to twenty minutes.

Clearly, Sauriol's opposition to the DVP was a voice in the wilderness. As he recalled in a 1992 interview with the *Toronto Star*, "there just weren't many people arguing against it, but in building it, they took ... away some irreplaceable things."[40] *Toronto Star* columnist Ron Haggart was among the few who commented on the changes wrought by the parkway construction. Writing the day before the first section of the parkway opened on 31 August 1961, he lamented the loss of Sugar Loaf Hill, which had been the inspiration for Ernest Thompson Seton's 1898 children's classic *Wild Animals I Have Known*. Dump trucks had reduced the hill to 1.25 million cubic metres of earth, carrying away a place known and beloved by "three generations of schoolboys."[41] Gardiner dismissed such minority sentiment with characteristic terseness. "I'll tell you what the Don Valley was," he reputedly told a Metro Council member who lamented the loss of the Don woods near Castle Frank. "The Don Valley was a place to murder little boys, that's what it was."[42] The collective memory of the valley as an unsavoury, somehow deviant place played an important role in mobilizing public support and ultimately transforming the landscape.

For Gardiner, viewing the completion of the roadway from retirement, the DVP was a monumental achievement and an essential component of a network of infrastructure that would support the development of the metropolitan region. The second component (and, it turned out, the last) of a proposed network of urban expressways, it enabled the northeastern expansion of the city: the road drove development just as much as development drove the road.

For Sauriol, the DVP brought heartache and ultimately an end to his years as a cottager in the valley. In 1968, the MTRCA expropriated his second cottage property as part of a broader floodplain acquisition strategy. In the aftermath of Hurricane Hazel, it had become abundantly clear that the city's river valleys were vital drainage corridors. In the years that followed, the MTRCA began acquiring floodplain lands in the valley bottoms with the goal of protecting them. Sauriol – who sat on the MTRCA board – had become a victim of his own success.

The loss of Sauriol's De Grassi cottage in 1968 brought to end his forty-plus years of summering in the Don Valley. Over the decades, Sauriol had seen the valley evolve from a border zone of farms and woodlands into an increasingly threatened green corridor. The loss of his cottage to conservation initiatives of his own making reflected a recurrent tension in Sauriol's life between private nature appreciation and the public good, as well as a similar tension, frequently observed in parks historiography, between the desire to create a space for human recreation and the desire to preserve a wilderness devoid of human influences.

The construction of the DVP between 1958 and 1966 marked a turning point in the history of the Don Valley. The significance of the valley had shifted: no longer was it the polluted periphery of a nineteenth-century city; now it was a vital transportation corridor through the centre of a large metropolitan region. The valley's historical role as a corridor for the movement of people and goods lay the foundations for that transformation. The DVP was, in effect, the grandest elaboration of this persistent theme in the history of the relationship between the river, the valley, and the evolving city. Following the line of least geographical resistance, the parkway transformed the valley from a barrier to east–west movement and eastward development into a corridor that facilitated movement throughout the metropolitan region. Today, the DVP has become synonymous with the valley itself. References to "the Don Valley" on the radio are shorthand for the DVP: the place has become the road. For most Torontonians, the view through the windshield on their daily commute is their only contact with the river valley.

Yet Sauriol's efforts were not completely in vain. In the years after Hurricane Hazel, the Don Valley was "revalued" as a recreational landscape. Between 1957 and 1994, around 15 per cent of the Don watershed came under the protection of the MTRCA floodplains program.[43] At the same time, the Municipality of Metropolitan Toronto began a massive overhaul of the city's aging sewage infrastructure. Between 1956 and 1965, Metro removed five overburdened sewage treatment plants from the Don watershed. These developments had implications not only for the river's water quality but also for the newly created valley parklands, which had once been unbearable to visit because of the sewage stench. The removal of upstream plants contributed to a change in public perceptions of urban ravines. Once viewed as inaccessible wastelands and barriers to development – obstacles to be bridged or filled – these rugged valley landscapes were increasingly recognized as urban amenities, vital green corridors through the heart of the city.[44]

Bringing Back the Don

As environmental awareness in Canadian society gained momentum through the 1960s, a new generation of activists turned their attention to the condition of the Don and its relationship with the city. As Samuel Hays has concluded for the American context, a key difference between the environmental movement of the 1960s and 1970s and its pre-war predecessors was the broad popular support it achieved.[45] Public concern for the environment stemmed in part from the gravity of ongoing problems, including, in the urban context, air and water pollution, issues of consumption and waste, and the shrinking availability of what was then termed "open space." American historian Adam Rome argues that the origins of post-war environmentalism lay in the loss of meadows, forests, and children's play areas close to home: "The desire to preserve wilderness was ... [only] the most visible part of a much larger concern about the destructive sprawl of urban civilization."[46] For Torontonians, such concerns came to focus increasingly on the Don. By the late 1960s, the river had emerged as a potent symbol of environmental degradation and mismanagement.

Despite major improvements in sewage treatment and disposal following Hurricane Hazel, the Don remained dangerously polluted. Local industries continued to discharge harmful effluents into the sewage system, and combined sewers in the older parts of Toronto, including most of the Lower Don, continued to overflow during periods of heavy rain, sending raw sewage and other pollutants into the river. Fecal coliform levels soared as high as 61 million counts per 100 ml in the late 1960s, 25,000 times the safe swimming level of 2,400 counts.[47] Also, the river had become increasingly inaccessible to Toronto residents, especially in its lower reaches. The construction of the Don Valley Parkway and other arterial roads in the late 1950s and early 1960s had cemented perceptions that the Lower Don was an urban wasteland criss-crossed with rail and road arteries and littered with abandoned industrial buildings, road salt storage sites, and equipment storage yards. Fences erected along the freeways made public access to the lower river valley very difficult, further sealing the fate of the Don as out of sight, out of mind.

Sauriol's approach to conservation, which combined public education about the wonders of Toronto's "back yard wilderness" with efforts to shame offenders, was joined in the late 1960s by a new and more playful brand of activism. In November 1969, an ad hoc group of University of Toronto professors and students organized under the name of Pollution Probe brought the plight of the Don to public attention.[48] Declaring the river "dead" as a result of years of pollution and detrimental development, Probe members led a 100-car cavalcade, including a hearse, from the university grounds to a funeral ceremony on the river north of the Bloor Street Viaduct. Funeral organizer Martin Daly detailed for a crowd of about 200 the history of abuses to the river, while a student dressed as eighteenth-century writer and artist Elizabeth Simcoe played the role of the river's widow, weeping as she read excerpts from her diary describing a river once teeming with salmon and waterfowl. As subway passengers looked on from the viaduct above, Daly concluded the event by tossing a wreath into the river. "And now," he announced to the mourners, "we await the resurrection."[49]

Pollution Probe's tactics were connected to broader trends in environmental activism at the time. For example, groups like Greenpeace (established 1971) employed guerrilla theatre, stunt work, and other unconventional techniques to capture public attention and bring a sense of urgency to their cause.[50] Close to mind for many observers would have been the June 1969 oil fire on the Cuyahoga River in Cleveland, brought to international attention by *Time* magazine in the summer of 1969.[51] The funeral for the Don received widespread media coverage and fuelled new demands from individuals and community-based organizations for a cleaner and more accessible Don River. Sauriol's response was dismissive: "All of my associations with the Don were reasonable and rational," he wrote in 1991, aligning himself with an earlier generation of sober conservationists. "I avoided such misfits in common sense as the burial held for the Don, complete with coffins and mourners."[52] Yet Pollution Probe's message reiterated what long-established groups such as the Toronto Field Naturalists (and Sauriol's own DVCA, defunct since the early 1960s) had been saying for years: the Don had the potential to be a vibrant green space in the heart of the city, a refuge for wildlife and a destination for recreation, and it was worthy of protection. Unlike earlier groups, however, which struggled to deliver their message to a largely uninterested public, Pollution Probe spoke for a new generation that refused to accept environmental degradation as an inevitable consequence of development.

The 1969 funeral was followed by a brief surge of interest in the Don, and a 1971 campaign by the Ontario Water Resources Commission to reduce phosphates in Ontario waterways succeeded in raising oxygen levels in the Don and improving aquatic habitat.[53] In the summer of the same year, college students hired for the MTRCA's "Don Patrol" removed more than 200 tons of litter from the river and surrounding valley. It wasn't until the late 1980s, however, that heightened public concern for the environment generated new and sustained visions for a restored river environment.

In September 1989, Sauriol's beloved East Don Valley received protection as a nature reserve within the Toronto Parks system. Sauriol recalled the dedication as "the most rewarding, significant day in [his] long career as a conservationist."[54] Named in his honour, the Charles Sauriol Conservation Reserve stretched from the Forks northeast to Eglinton Avenue, encompassing sixty-seven hectares of signature valley lands. Fittingly, it commemorated both his lifelong commitment to valley conservation and a valley landscape mostly lost. Later that fall, Sauriol received the Order of Canada for his life's work of protecting natural spaces in Canada.

The year 1989 also marked a turning point in citizens' efforts to revitalize the Don. In February, Toronto City Council responded to concerns from local residents' associations by endorsing a recommendation "that the Don River and its related recreation and wildlife areas be made fully useable, accessible and safe for the people of Toronto no later than the year 2001."[55] Two months later, *Toronto* magazine hosted a day-long public forum on the future of the Don at the Ontario Science Centre. Attended by about 500 people, the forum represented a watershed in public awareness about the Don. Later that spring, the newly created Task Force to Bring Back the Don presented a vision for a clean, green, and accessible Don – a resurrection, of sorts, of a long neglected urban river. Between its establishment and its disbandment by Mayor Rob Ford's cost-cutting administration in 2010, thousands of Task Force volunteers planted tens of thousands of trees, shrubs, and wildflowers in the Lower Don Valley, removed many tons of garbage and debris, and threw their collective muscle behind forty restoration projects throughout the central and lower valley.[56] The slow process of deindustrialization had created space for new possibilities. By the time of Sauriol's death in 1995, the river had re-emerged as a symbol of urban health – specifically, the health of the relationship between urban residents and the natural environment on which they depend.

Conclusion

In the more than two centuries since 1793, the Don slipped in the eyes of Toronto's civic leaders from a place of relative importance – a place fit enough to host the province's first parliament buildings – to a place widely perceived, by the mid-nineteenth century, as polluted, dangerous, and disease-ridden. As we have seen, the foul odours and polluted waters resulting from the Lower Don's designation as a "space apart" were for many observers the price of prosperity, and the price of keeping other parts of the city more habitable. Less appreciated as a source of natural resources, the river valley nevertheless continued to serve as a vital component of the city's economy in its role as a sink for municipal and industrial wastes.

The "recentring" of the valley in the mid-twentieth century as a metropolitan corridor running through the middle of a larger region, rather than the edge of the old city, contributed to yet another shift in perceptions. More Torontonians than ever before experienced the valley on their daily commute to the city centre. Viewed through the windshield, the valley's brilliant fall foliage and lush summer greenery helped put to rest perceptions of the valley as a dangerous, polluted underworld. Ontario's mid-century adoption of watershed-based conservation enabled citizen activists and local conservation authorities to protect valley environments and improve public awareness in ways that further fuelled this transition. Although still polluted in its lower reaches, the river valley today is nevertheless valued as one of Toronto's iconic landscapes.

Sauriol and the activists and citizens' groups who followed contributed to this sea change in thinking about spaces like the Don River Valley. In the work of the Task Force especially, an emphasis on public access and education as an avenue to protection led to the creation of a huge constituency of valley users.[57] Efforts to protect the Don, furthermore, were transferred to other Ontario environments. Sauriol, for example, applied his brand of conservation to two decades of work protecting Ontario and Canadian landscapes with the Nature Conservancy of Canada. And as Ryan O'Connor has shown in his work on Ontario environmentalism, the lessons learned from efforts to protect local environments like the Don River Valley were absorbed into broader campaigns for pollution control and water quality improvement across Ontario's Great Lakes region.[58]

Threats to Toronto's beloved ravines will continue to come from invasive species, climate change, and short-sighted government administrations.[59] And those threats will demand that this constituency of ravine enthusiasts, so deliberately created, take action to ensure their protection. Whether or not valley users will respond with the noise and urgency required will put to the test the beliefs of an earlier generation of conservationists that people will fight to defend the places they love.

QUESTIONS FOR CONSIDERATION:

1. Why does Bonnell posit that the Don Valley is neither "fully natural nor fully artificial"?
2. Why was the Don Valley considered valuable in the late eighteenth century?
3. What is miasma? Why was it significant in the nineteenth century?
4. What effects did growth and industrialization have on the Don Valley in the nineteenth century?
5. Bonnell describes a tension between "corridor" and "place" that runs throughout the valley's history. Explain.
6. Describe the Don Valley Conservation Movement in your own words. How impactful was it?

NOTES

1 Robert Benzie and May Warren, "Ford government urges winding down of conservation programs to conserve cash," *Toronto Star*, 20 August 2019, https://www.thestar.com/politics/provincial/2019/08/20/ontario-government-urges-winding-down-of-conservation-programs-to-conserve-cash.html.

2 Over the past two hundred years, almost all of the significant wetlands within the watershed have been drained or filled to support urban development. The six tributaries of the lower river have mostly disappeared, buried by fill or encased in sewage infrastructure.

3 Martin Melosi and Joel Tarr were among the first historians to explore questions of environment in the urban context, and pollution and water quality in particular. See, for example, Martin V. Melosi, *Pollution and Reform in American Cities, 1870–1930* (Austin: University of Texas Press, 1980); and Joel Tarr, *The Search for the Ultimate Sink: Urban Pollution in Historical Perspective* (Akron: University of Akron Press, 1996). On the value of including cities in the study of environmental history, see Melosi, "The Place of the City in Environmental History," *Environmental History Review* 17, no. 1 (1993): 1–23; William Cronon, "The Trouble with Wilderness; or, Getting Back to the Wrong Nature," in *Uncommon Ground: Rethinking the Human Place in Nature*, edited by William Cronon, 69–90 (New York: W.W. Norton, 1996); and Jenny Price, "Remaking American Environmentalism: On the Banks of the L.A. River," *Environmental History* 13, no. 3 (2008): 536–55. An early and influential work in the now-extensive environmental justice literature is Andrew Hurley's *Environmental Inequalities: Class, Race, and Industrial Pollution in Gary, Indiana, 1945–1980* (Chapel Hill: University of North Carolina Press, 1995).

4 The Ontario Conservation Authorities Act of 1946 enabled Toronto to partner with neighbouring municipalities to create conservation authorities for each of its watersheds. Of all the Canadian provinces, only Saskatchewan rivals Ontario for the age and longevity of its watershed conservation agencies (enabled by legislation in 1949). Only in Ontario, furthermore, have these agencies had an urban as well as a rural focus since their origins in the 1940s. Other provinces followed Ontario's example, adopting some form of watershed management, including basin-specific watershed boards, in urban and rural areas between the 1970s and the early 2000s. For an in-depth account of the role of planners in Toronto's history of watershed management, see Richard White, *Planning Toronto: The Planners, The Plans, Their Legacies, 1940–80* (Vancouverâ€¯: UBC Press, 2016).

5 See Ryan O'Connor's *The First Green Wave: Pollution Probe and the Origins of Environmental Activism in Ontario* (Vancouver: UBC Press, 2015) for a detailed analysis of Ontario environmentalism in this period.

6 Lieutenant Governor John Graves Simcoe to Major General Alured Clarke, 31 May 1793, reprinted in Edith G. Firth, *The Town of York, 1793–1815: A Collection of Documents of Early Toronto* (Toronto: Champlain Society, 1962), 4.

7 Graeme Mercer Adam, Charles Pelham Mulvany, and Christopher Blackett Robinson, *History of Toronto and County of York* (Toronto: C. Blackett Robinson, 1885), 211.

8 Ontario Department of Planning and Development, "Don Valley Conservation Report" (Toronto: Ontario Department of Planning and Development, 1950), pt. 1, 34.

9 In these early years, time limits for settlement duties weren't strictly enforced, allowing for many absentee landowners. John Ross Robertson, *Robertson's Landmarks of Toronto: A Collection of Historical Sketches of the Old Town of York from 1792 Until 1833, and of Toronto from 1834 to 1893* (Toronto: J. Ross Robertson, 1894), Vol. VI, 194–5.

10 Simcoe to Clarke, 31 May 1793, in Firth, *The Town of York, 1793–1815*, 4.

11 The strain of malaria prevalent in early nineteenth-century southern Ontario was less deadly than its tropical cousins. As James L.A. Webb concludes, malaria lasted only a few generations in North America. The "principal and characteristic disease of the North American agricultural frontier," malarial infections receded as crop cover stabilized disturbed, logged-over soils and habitat for mosquito-breeding shrunk. Webb, *Humanity's*

Burden: A Global History of Malaria (Cambridge and New York: Cambridge University Press, 2009), 5–6, 88–9.

12 John Bennett to John Neilson, 18 September 1801, in Firth, *The Town of York, 1793–1815*, 242. In 1911, for example, the *Encyclopedia Britannica* defined malaria as "an Italian colloquial word (from mala, bad, and aria, air), introduced into English medical literature by MacCulloch (1827) as a substitute for the more restricted "marsh miasm." The term was "generally applied to the definite unhealthy condition of body known by a variety of names, such as ague, intermittent (and remittent) fever, marsh fever, jungle fever, hill feve, 'fever of the country' and 'fever and ague'" https://en.wikisource.org/wiki/1911_Encyclop%C3%A6dia_Britannica/Malaria.

13 Isaac Brock to James Green, 29 July 1803, in Firth, *The Town of York, 1793–1815*, 72.

14 Petition of Inhabitants of York, 11 February 1830, in Firth, *The Town of York, 1793–1815*, 30-31.

15 Conevery Bolton Valencius, *The Health of the Country: How American Settlers Understood Themselves and Their Land* (New York: Basic Books, 2002), 12.

16 Valencius, *The Health of the Country*, 89–90.

17 Valencius, *The Health of the Country*, 110–14. See also Martin V. Melosi, *The Sanitary City: Urban Infrastructure in America from Colonial Times to the Present* (Baltimore: Johns Hopkins University Press, 2000); Melosi, *Effluent America: Cities, Industry, Energy, and the Environment* (Pittsburgh: University of Pittsburgh Press, 2001), 225–37; and Tarr, *The Search for the Ultimate Sink*, 342–43.

18 See also "Toronto General Hospital," *Upper Canada Journal of Medical, Surgical, and Physical Science* 3, no. 2 (1853): 69–77.

19 Lieutenant Governor John Colborne to Viscount Goderich, 23 January 1833, in Firth, *The Town of York, 1793–1815*, 31–3.

20 Frederick H. Armstrong, *A City in the Making: Progress, People, and Perils in Victorian Toronto* (Toronto: Dundurn Press, 1988), 17.

21 Isobel K. Ganton, "Development between Parliament Street and the Don River, 1793–1884," 1974, City of Toronto Archives (hereafter CTA), fonds 92, Papers and Theses Collection, item 347, 35. The liberties stretched east of the river in a thin band from Queen Street south to the lakeshore all the way east to the east end of Ashbridge's Bay. Like other suburban areas around the city, development here was slower and more sporadic than in the more desirable and (marginally) better serviced areas of the centre and tended to concentrate along central access routes. Only by satisfying certain population and assessed property qualifications could areas within the liberties receive full city membership as annexations to existing wards or as wards of their own. In 1859 the liberties were abolished entirely, bringing full city rights and responsibilities to the suburban area west of the Don and east of the river south of Queen. The area of the "Don marshes" – south of King Street and west of the river – was left out of the 1859 incorporations, likely because of the area's long-established reputation for insalubriousness.

22 *Toronto World*, "The smell at the Don," 8 May 1884.

23 Theodore Steinberg, *Nature Incorporated: Industrialization and the Waters of New England* (Cambridge and New York: Cambridge University Press, 1991), 209.

24 Steinberg, *Nature Incorporated*, 177.

25 Don Valley Conservation Association (DVCA), *The Cardinal*, Fall 1954, Charles Sauriol fonds, file 14, series 104, fonds 4, CTA.

26 On William Whyte, see Adam Rome, *The Bulldozer in the Countryside: Suburban Sprawl and the Rise of American Environmentalism* (New York: Cambridge University Press, 2001), 119–52. John Seiberling's work as a conservationist is documented in Daniel Nelson, *A Passion for the Land: John F. Seiberling and the Environmental Movement* (Kent: Kent State University Press, 2009).

27 Charles Sauriol, “Beginnings of the Don Valley Conservation Association,” *The Cardinal*, Spring 1954, Charles Sauriol fonds, file 14, series 104, fonds 4, CTA; Sauriol, *Trails of the Don* (Orillia: Hemlock Press, 1992), 268–9.

28 On the exclusionary effects of the twentieth-century conservation policies in the US and Canada, see Karl Jacoby, *Crimes against Nature: Squatters, Poachers, Thieves, and the Hidden History of American Conservation* (Berkeley: University of California Press, 2001); Tina Loo, *States of Nature: Conserving Canada's Wildlife in the Twentieth Century* (Vancouver: UBC Press, 2007); and John Sandlos, *Hunters at the Margin: Native People and Wildlife Conservation in the Northwest Territories* (Vancouver: UBC Press, 2007).

29 DVCA, “The Cardinal,” 1951, 56, Charles Sauriol fonds, file 14, series 104, fonds 4, CTA. In 1949 the DVCA reorganized into three regional branches within the Don watershed, Sauriol taking up the leadership of the East York branch (DVCA-EY).

30 John R. Stilgoe, *Metropolitan Corridor: Railroads and the American Scene* (New Haven: Yale University Press, 1983), esp. ch. 13.

31 Sauriol, *Tales of the Don* (Toronto: Natural Heritage/Natural History, 1984); Sauriol, “Beginnings of the Don Valley Conservation Association.”

32 Sauriol, *Trails of the Don*, 282.

33 Toronto and Region Conservation Authority (TRCA), “Hurricane Hazel 60 Years Later,” http://www.hurricanehazel.ca; Jim Gifford and Mike Filey, *Hurricane Hazel: Canada's Storm of the Century* (Toronto: Dundurn Press, 2004).

34 While Hazel can be credited with tipping the balance towards watershed conservation in southern Ontario, and greatly accelerating plans for the acquisition of valley lands, floodplain protection had been a subject of discussion among conservation-minded planners and scientists for a number of years before the storm hit. The City Planning Board's 1943 *Master Plan for the City of Toronto and Environs*, for example, proposed (unsuccessfully) to protect the Don and Humber river valleys from “encroachment and vandalism” by incorporating them within a U-shaped green belt linked by a low-speed “drive-way.” Toronto City Planning Board, *The Master Plan for the City of Toronto and Environs*, 31 December 1943. See also White, *Planning Toronto*, ch. 1.

35 Timothy J. Colton, *Big Daddy: Frederick G. Gardiner and the Building of Metropolitan Toronto* (Toronto: University of Toronto Press, 1980), 62.

36 Charles Sauriol, *Remembering the Don: A Rare Record of Earlier Times within the Don River Valley* (Toronto: Consolidated Amethyst Communications, 1981), 138.

37 Frederick Goldwin Gardiner, “The Face of the City Has Changed. An Address to the Inaugural Meeting of the Metropolitan Council,” 12 January 1960, 4.

38 “Urge Don Valley Parkway to relieve east traffic,” *Toronto Daily Star*, 18 May 1954; “Woman raps mayor for ‘pious talk,’” *Toronto Daily Star*, 13 February 1957.

39 Lee Belland, “Six-lane road in valley will link expressway with Toronto arteries,” *Toronto Daily Star*, 4 October 1955.

40 Belland, “Six-lane road in valley.”

41 Ron Haggart, “Ernest Thompson Seton and the new parkway,” *Toronto Daily Star*, 30 August 1961.

42 Michael Smith, “Love it or hate it, Parkway's 25 years old,” *Toronto Star*, 13 August 1986.

43 Metropolitan Toronto and Region Conservation Authority, “Plan for Flood Control and Water Conservation” (Woodridge: MTRCA, 1959); Toronto and Region Conservation Authority (TRCA), "The History of Flood Control in the TRCA," https://trca.ca/conservation/flood-risk-management.

44 Thanks to Toronto historian Richard White for this insight.

45 Samuel P. Hays, *Beauty, Health, and Permanence: Environmental Politics in the United States, 1955–1985* (Cambridge: Cambridge University Press, 1987).
46 Rome, *The Bulldozer in the Countryside*, 7–8.
47 Thomas Claridge, "Pollution Probe mourns for beloved, dead Don," *Globe and Mail*, 17 November 1969, 1.
48 For more on the history of Pollution Probe and its influence on environmental politics in Ontario, see Ryan O'Connor, *The First Green Wave: Pollution Probe and the Origins of Environmental Activism in Ontario* (Vancouver: UBC Press, 2015).
49 "Mock rites mourn death of Don River killed by pollution," *Toronto Star*, 17 November 1969, 21; Claridge, "Pollution Probe."
50 Robert Gottlieb, *Forcing the Spring: The Transformation of the American Environmental Movement* (Washington, D.C.: Island Press, 2005), 252–3.
51 "The Price of Optimism," *Time*, 1 August 1969, http://content.time.com/time/magazine/article/0,9171,901182,00.html. For an insightful analysis of changes in the public perception of fires on the Cuyahoga, see David Stradling and Richard Stradling, "Perceptions of the Burning River: Deindustrialization and Cleveland's Cuyahoga River," *Environmental History* 13, no. 3 (2008): 515–35.
52 Charles Sauriol, *Green Footsteps: Recollections of a Grassroots Conservationist* (Toronto: Hemlock Press, 1991), 21.
53 Toronto Area Watershed Management Study and Paul Theil Associates Ltd., *Strategy for Improvement of Don River Water Quality: Summary Report* (Toronto: Queen's Printer, 1989), 4.
54 Sauriol, *Green Footsteps*, 279.
55 Toronto City Council Proceedings, 23 February 1989, cited in Mark J. Wilson (Chair of the Task Force to Bring Back the Don 1991–98), "How Did the Task Force to Bring Back the Don Get Started?," https://web.archive.org/web/20040606185147/http://www.toronto.ca/don/faq.htm.
56 A number of other citizen-led groups have since formed to address concerns about habitat degradation, access, and pollution in the watershed. See Jennifer Bonnell, "Bringing Back the Don: Sixty Years of Community Action," in *HtO: Toronto's Water from Lake Iroquois to Lost Rivers to Low-flow Toilets*, ed. Wayne Reeves and Christina Palassio (Toronto: Coach House Books, 2008), 266–83.
57 Shawn Micallef, "Conservation authorities make Ontario liveable: We need to defend them," *Toronto Star*, 30 August 2019, https://www.thestar.com/opinion/contributors/2019/08/30/conservation-authorities-make-ontario-livable-we-need-to-defend-them.html.
58 See ch. 3, "Building an Environmental Community," in O'Connor's *The First Green Wave*.
59 The City of Toronto's 2017 *Toronto Ravine Strategy* itemizes some of these threats to city ravine spaces and the protections needed to support their long-term resilience: https://www.toronto.ca/city-government/accountability-operations-customer-service/long-term-vision-plans-and-strategies/ravine-strategy.

CHAPTER EIGHTEEN

Ontario and a Changing Climate

MARK WINFIELD AND COLLEEN KAISER

Climate change has been described as "perhaps the most profound challenge ever to have confronted human social, political, and economic systems … as the stakes are massive, the risks and politics bitter and complicated, the psychology puzzling, the impacts devastating, the interactions with other environmental and non-environmental issues running in many directions."[1]

For Ontario, climate change presents an environmental challenge unlike any ever faced by the province before. Earlier environmental issues, like acid rain in the 1970s and 1980s, and water pollution from the pulp and paper sector in the 1990s, required regulatory and policy responses that were focused on specific sectors and facilities. The achievement of major emissions reductions did not require significant restructuring of the province's economy.[2] In contrast, an effective response to climate change will require systemic changes throughout the province. Significant changes will be needed in industry, buildings, transportation and urban form, agriculture, and natural resources management, among other sectors, to transition away from the use of fossil fuels and towards low-carbon energy sources. The province will have to adapt to the impacts of an already changing climate at the same time.

The province's approach to the issue of climate change, from the time of the emergence of a global scientific consensus around the problem and its causes in the late 1980s, has been notable for its inconsistency. At times the province has shown relatively strong positive leadership on the issue. Under the Liberal governments of Dalton McGuinty and Kathleen Wynne, for example, Ontario collaborated closely with other provinces and even US states to construct policy responses despite the absence of federal leadership on the issue. In other instances, the province has tended towards disengagement and – most recently, under the premiership of Doug Ford – outright hostility to significant action on the issue.

Ontario's behaviour on climate change policy has been driven by several factors. Structural economic changes, particularly an accelerating transition from an industrial to a more knowledge- and service-based economy, have left some regions of the province in significant economic decline and distress and thus sensitive to pressures for further structural economic changes. This is especially the case when such changes involve increases to already rising energy costs. These sensitivities were exploited very successfully by the Progressive Conservative campaign in the 2018 provincial election, highlighting the challenges of implementing low-carbon transition strategies in times of significant economic change.

Ontario serves as an important case study in other aspects of climate change policy. The province's industrial emissions of greenhouse gases have declined significantly since the early 1990s. Growth in emissions is now concentrated in sectors like transportation and buildings. These sectors are by their nature difficult to affect through conventional climate change policies such as carbon pricing. Instead, they will require complex combinations of price signals, infrastructure investments, regulatory tools ranging from land-use planning rules to energy efficiency standards, capacity building, and education for provincial agencies, municipalities, and communities to achieve significant emission reductions. It remains to be seen whether the province will be able to develop, implement, and sustain such strategies in practical or political terms.

This chapter begins with a discussion of the science of climate change and the specific implications of a changing climate for Ontario. It goes on to provide an overview of the evolution of climate change policy in the province, from the recognition of the issue in the late 1980s through to the dismantling of many of the province's climate change policies following the 2018 provincial election, including the province's shifting relationship with the federal government on the issue. The chapter concludes with a discussion of the challenges associated with the relatively distributed nature of greenhouse gas emissions in Ontario, compared with provinces where emissions are concentrated among a small number of industrial facilities and sectors, and the prospects for future action on climate change.

A Changing Global Climate

The physical basis of the climate change problem is well understood. Solar radiation penetrates the earth's atmosphere easily, but the thermal radiation emitted upwards from the earth does not. Certain gases, known as greenhouse gases (GHGs), including carbon dioxide, methane, and nitrous oxide, when present in the atmosphere, are extremely effective at absorbing this thermal infrared radiation, which contributes to the warming of the atmosphere.[3] Increased concentrations of GHGs in the atmosphere reinforce the absorption and re-emission of infrared radiation to the earth, resulting in rising atmospheric temperatures.[4]

A defining event in modern climate change science was the World Conference on the Changing Atmosphere, held in Toronto in 1988, which led to the creation of the UN Environment Programme (UNEP), sponsored Intergovernmental Panel on Climate Change (IPCC).[5] The IPCC's recent assessment reports have concluded that

> anthropogenic greenhouse gas emissions have increased since the pre-industrial era, driven largely by economic and population growth, and are now higher than ever. This has led to atmospheric concentrations of carbon dioxide, methane and nitrous oxide that are unprecedented in at least the last 800,000 years. Their effects, together with those of other anthropogenic drivers, have been detected throughout the climate system and are extremely likely to have been the dominant cause of the observed warming since the mid-20th century ...[6]
>
> Warming of the climate system is unequivocal, and since the 1950s, many of the observed changes are unprecedented over decades to millennia. The atmosphere and ocean have warmed, the amounts of snow and ice have diminished, and sea level has risen.[7]

It has been estimated that without any effective efforts to reduce GHG emissions, GHG concentrations could rise from their current levels of 400 ppm CO2e to 700–900 ppm CO2e by the end of the century and continue to rise thereafter, potentially generating up to 5°C warming by the end of the century.[8] Even under scenarios of 2–3°C warming, the social, economic, and environmental impacts of climate change are projected to be significant, including:[9] melting glaciers increasing flood risk during wet seasons and reduced dry season water supplies for one-sixth of the global population; declining crop yields that leave hundreds of millions unable to produce a sufficient amount of food; ocean acidification, with adverse impacts on marine ecosystems and fish stocks; increases in deaths due to vector-borne diseases, malnutrition, and heat stress; and an increasing threat to the world's ecosystems, resulting in the extinction of as many as 40 per cent of all species.

There are also concerns about the potential for climate change processes to destabilize the global atmosphere in unpredictable ways.

The IPCC has projected that to prevent "dangerous" climate change (i.e., >2°C average temperature increases), CO_2 emissions will need to decline by about 25 per cent by 2030 relative to 2010 levels and reach net zero around 2070.[10] The most recent IPCC reports have emphasized that limiting warming to 1.5°C may be necessary to prevent catastrophic impacts.[11] To achieve that target, anthropogenic CO_2 emissions will need to decline by about 45 per cent from 2010 levels by 2030 and achieve net zero around 2050.[12] Given that fossil fuels currently provide more than 80 per cent of the world's primary energy, the achievement of such reductions will require major structural shifts in global patterns of energy use.[13]

The emerging scientific consensus around climate change has prompted a series of global agreements intended to address the problem – agreements in which Canada has been a central, if not always constructive,[14] participant. The 1992 UN Framework Convention on Climate Change established a goal of stabilizing emissions at 1990 levels by the year 2000. Under the succeeding 1997 Kyoto Protocol, Canada's federal government committed to a 6 per cent reduction in emissions relative to 1990 by the protocol's first (2008–12) commitment period. The election of President Barack Obama in the US, and that country's re-engagement with global climate negotiations, led to the 2009 Copenhagen Accord, under which Canada abandoned its Kyoto commitments, choosing instead to move in lockstep with the US. That meant adopting a new reduction target of a 17 per cent by 2020 relative to 2005 – a substantial retreat from the Kyoto targets.[15]

Under the most recent international accord, the 2015 Paris Agreement, Canada committed itself to a 30 per cent reduction in its emissions, relative to 2005, by 2030. The IPCC and others have highlighted that none of the international agreements have succeeded in actually reducing GHG emissions.[16] The cumulative impact of the individual country commitments made under the Paris Agreement still falls well short of what is required to meet that agreement's goal, which is to limit global warming to less than 2°C.[17]

As Figure 18.1 indicates, Canada has made some marginal progress in reducing its GHG emissions, although the reductions have fallen far short of its international commitments. Except in Ontario, such gains have been largely the result of changing economic conditions, resulting in restructuring, rather than specific policy interventions by Canadian governments.

As shown in Figure 18.2, Ontario now holds second place in Canada, after Alberta, among the provinces in terms of total GHG emissions. The province saw a substantial drop in its emissions between 2005 and 2017, due to a combination of the phase-out of coal-fired electricity generation and restructuring within the manufacturing sector.

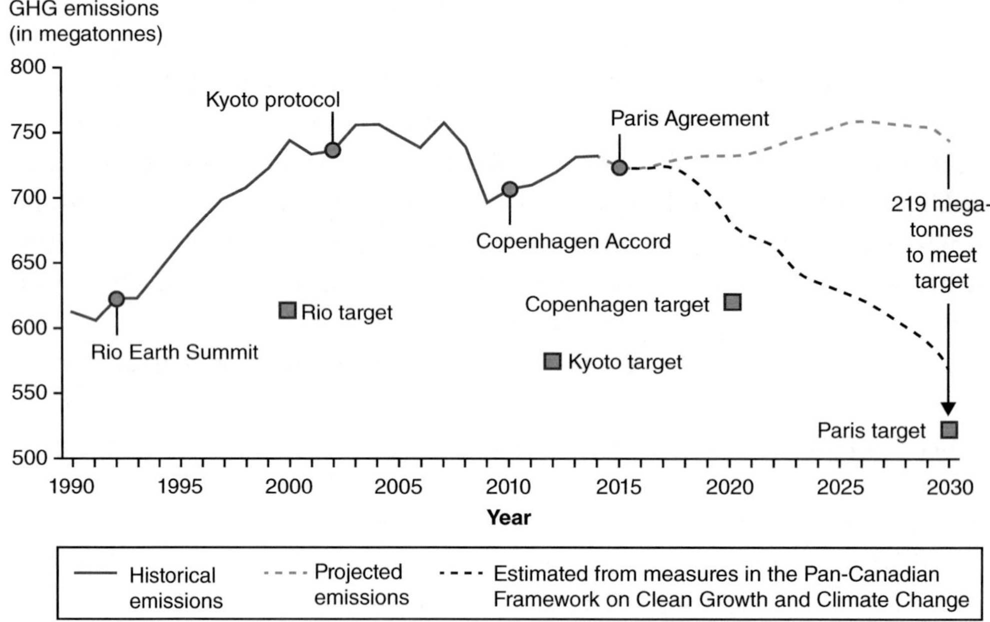

Figure 18.1. Canadian GHG emissions and international commitments.[18]

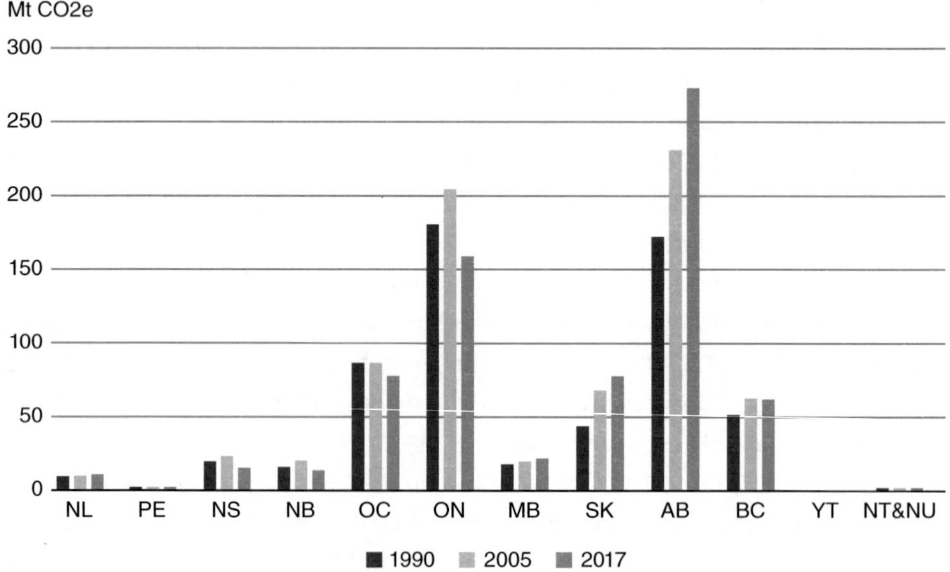

Figure 18.2. GHG emissions by province, 1990–2017.[19]

Climate change Impacts in Ontario

The potential impacts of climate change at a regional level within Canada have been understood through modelling, with increasing levels of detail since the mid-1990s. A defining feature of the past decade has been growing recognition in Ontario, and elsewhere, that these impacts have moved from the realm of theory to that of lived experience.[20]

The most visible manifestations of the impacts of climate change in Ontario have been in the form of extreme weather events, reflecting an increasingly unstable climate. Examples have included ice storms, like the one experienced in Toronto in 2013, and intense precipitation events resulting in flooding, such as the one seen in the Muskoka and Ottawa River watersheds in the spring of 2019.[21] Among other things, these events have done significant damage to infrastructure designed to withstand the most significant storm events experienced over the previous century (the 100-year standard). That infrastructure is now being confronted with weather events beyond its design envelope. The deterioration of infrastructure is now accelerating as a result of unanticipated weather stresses.

In addition, there are potentially synergistic relationships between climate change and air quality, leading to smog and heat episodes of increased frequency and intensity. Business-as-usual projections for southern Ontario, for example, indicate a future of summers defined by thirty to forty "oppressive" days (i.e., with high heat, humidity, and smog), with significant adverse impacts on human health, especially for vulnerable populations.[22] Additional public health concerns are emerging as a result of the expanded range for disease vectors traditionally limited by cold winters. This may well lead to the increasing occurrence of illnesses not normally seen in Ontario, such as West Nile virus, hantavirus, and Lyme disease.[23]

Agriculture is seen to be at increased risk due to drought, pests, disease, and climate variability.[24] Wildlife, including fish, will be placed at risk due to habitat loss, heat stress, and the increased presence of invasive species whose range had heretofore been limited by colder winters. There will be intensified risks from insect pests and forest fires.[25] Even with increases in annual average precipitation, increased evaporation and evapotranspiration due to higher temperatures may lead to overall lower water levels. These may interfere with navigation and shipping, as well as hydroelectricity generation. In the far north, shorter and warmer winters may degrade winter ice road networks that are vital to remote northern communities.[26]

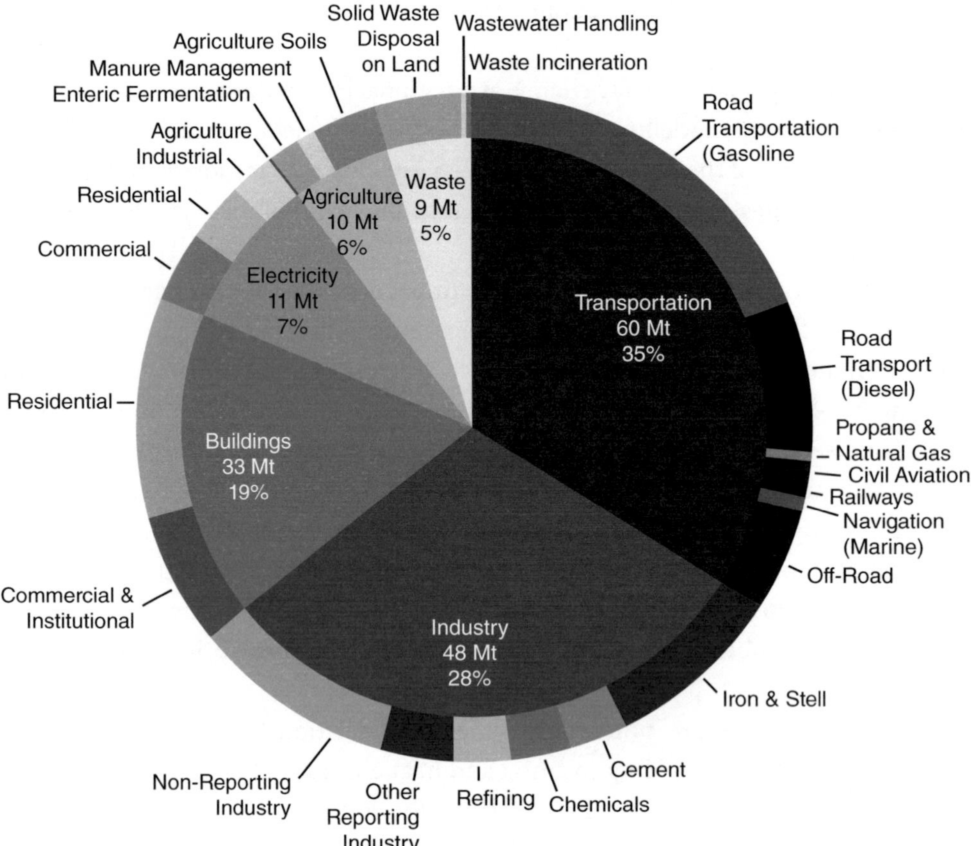

Figure 18.3. Ontario GHG emissions in 2013, by sector.[27]

Climate Change Policy in Ontario

As shown in Figure 18.3, Ontario's GHG emissions are relatively concentrated in a few specific sectors. The key sources of emissions include fossil fuel use for road transportation, residential, commercial, and institutional building space and water heating, and manufacturing and resource processing.

The province's emission profile does give it some potential advantages in responding to the challenge of climate change relative to other Canadian provinces. Although there is still some oil and gas production in southwestern Ontario, the province is not a major fossil fuel producer. Rather, it relies on imported fossil fuels, principally oil and natural gas from western Canada, for transportation and space and water heating, industrial uses, and some electricity generation.

Thus, addressing climate change by reducing GHG emissions through reductions in fossil fuel use is not perceived as an inherent threat to the province's existing economic structure, as it would be for the major fossil-fuel producing and exporting provinces like Alberta and Saskatchewan.[28] In fact, reductions in imported fossil fuel use through efficiency gains, changes in transportation patterns and modes (e.g., transit and active transportation vs. automobiles), and fuel switching could be economically advantageous for the province. This situation potentially positions Ontario in its somewhat traditional moderating role in Confederation between the "carbon" provinces like Alberta and Saskatchewan, whose economies depend heavily on carbon-intensive fossil fuel extraction and export, and lower-carbon provinces, like BC, Manitoba, and Quebec, which have substantial hydroelectric resources.[29]

Climate change emerged as a significant public policy issue in the mid- to late 1990s. Around the same time in southern Ontario, major public health concerns came to the forefront regarding air quality (i.e., smog). There were, and continue to be, significant overlaps in the major sources of smog and GHG emissions in the province. These sources include automobile-based passenger transportation (a consequence of urban sprawl in the Greater Toronto Area), the use of fossil fuels (coal and natural gas) to generate electricity, industrial activities, and the use of natural gas for building space and water heating. This also meant, however, there was significant potential for mutually reinforcing benefits in the province's responses to both climate change and smog problems.

In Alberta and Saskatchewan, growth in GHG emissions has been strongly concentrated in the oil and gas sector. By contrast, economic restructuring in Ontario, principally in the form of a shift from manufacturing to information- and service-based activities,[30] has meant that industrial GHG emissions outside of electricity generation have declined significantly (by around 25 per cent relative to 1990) without significant environmental or climate change policy interventions. As shown in Figure 18.4, growth in GHG emissions has been largely come from passenger and freight transportation, and residential and commercial buildings.

The Evolution of Climate Change Policy in Ontario

The first serious consideration of the implications of climate change for Ontario came from the September 1992 report of the Ontario Round Table on the Environment and the Economy. The Peterson government had established the multi-stakeholder round table in 1988 as part of Canada's overall response to

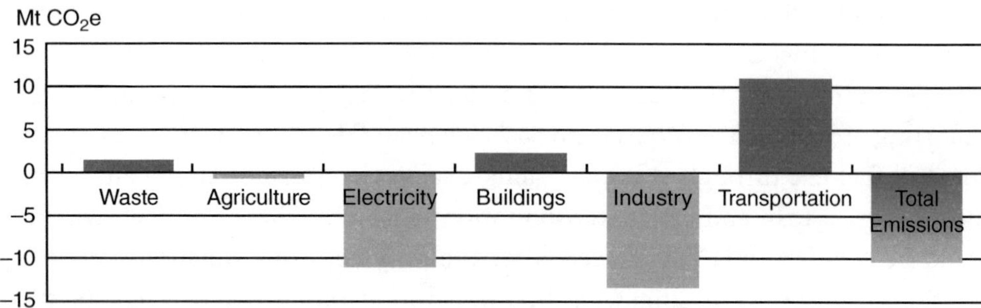

Figure 18.4. Long-term changes in Ontario emissions, 1990–2012, by sector.[31]

the 1987 recommendations of the World Commission on Environment and Development (aka the Bruntland Commission). That commission had introduced the concept of sustainable development, which sought to integrate environmental and economic decision-making.[32]

The incoming New Democratic Party (NDP) government, elected in 1990 and led by Bob Rae, had asked the round table to address, for the first time, the issue of global climate change in the Ontario context. Reflecting a federal–provincial consensus at the time, Canada committed itself to stabilizing its GHG emissions at 1990 levels by 2000 through the UN Framework Convention on Climate Change, which was adopted at the 1992 Rio Conference. Ontario's round table recommended that in addition to meeting that stabilization target, the province reduce its emissions by 20 per cent by 2005 and by between 70 and 80 per cent by 2030.[33]

In April 1994, the province's Minister of Environment and Energy formally embraced the goal of stabilizing GHG emissions by 2000, with a longer-term target of a 20 per cent reduction.[34] Two months later, the Legislative Assembly endorsed a federal commitment to reduce GHG emissions by 20 per cent relative to 1988 by 2005.[35] No other specific actions were taken on climate change. However, the NDP government did implement major reforms to the province's land-use planning system, emphasizing more compact and transit-supportive urban development patterns.[36] Those themes would later come to be understood as essential to reducing transportation-related emissions of GHGs and smog precursors.

The Rae government had brought about the first stirrings of action around climate change in Ontario; however, the potential for more substantive movement came to an abrupt halt with the defeat of the NDP government by Mike Harris's Progressive Conservative Party in June 1995. The Harris government was elected based on an avowedly neoliberal "Common Sense Revolution" platform. The new government embarked on an aggressive agenda of budget cuts, which included rewriting the province's environmental and natural resources legislation. This led to a lost decade in terms of climate change policies.

One of the Harris government's immediate targets was the Rae government's reforms to the land-use planning system, which had been intended to control urban sprawl and promote transit-supportive urban development. At the same time, the province's transportation policy shifted its focus from public transit to a major expansion of the provincial highway network in the GTA. That strategy seemed virtually guaranteed to induce automobile-dependent long-distance commuting patterns and their accompanying emissions of GHGs and smog precursors.

Even more catalytic events followed. In July 1997, an external review raised significant concerns about the maintenance and safety of Ontario's nuclear power plants. In response, Ontario Hydro adopted a Nuclear Asset Optimization Plan (NAOP), under which the seven oldest of the utility's twenty power reactors were taken out of service for repair and overhaul. Ontario Hydro would rely, in the interim, on its coal-fired generating facilities (Lakeview [Mississauga], Nanticoke, Lambton, Thunder Bay, and Atikokan) to replace the power supplies lost through the temporary decommissioning of nuclear units at the Bruce and Pickering facilities. The result, predictably, was major increases in emissions of smog and acid rain precursors, heavy metals, and greenhouse gases from these facilities. Between 1995 and 2001, their greenhouse gas emissions increased by a factor of 2.3, and their emissions of the smog and acid rain precursors, sulphur dioxide and nitrogen oxide, doubled and increased by a factor of 1.7, respectively.[37] By 2001 the five coal-fired generating facilities accounted for around 20 per cent of the province's total GHG emissions.[38]

At the national level, the Harris government aligned itself closely with its ideological counterpart, Alberta premier Ralph Klein's PC government, in opposition to Ottawa's efforts to ratify the UN's Kyoto Protocol.[39] Ontario seems not to have entertained the possibility that its interests in formulating a national climate change policy might be different from those of a province whose economy was grounded in fossil fuel extraction and export.

Yet the Harris government's actions laid the foundations for the land-use, transportation, and energy policies of its successors. In the late stages of the Harris government, the perception – indeed, the reality – that automobile-dependent urban development was out of control, and was having a deleterious impact on natural heritage and high-value agricultural lands around Toronto, set in motion discussions about transit-supportive, "smart" urban growth.[40] At the same time, the health impacts of deteriorating air quality resulting from greater automobile traffic and the effects of the NAOP were being highlighted with increasing vigour by the Ontario Medical Association and public health officials. In the 2003 provincial election, a phase-out of coal-fired electricity generation – which would have major impacts on both air quality and GHG emissions – would be a feature (albeit on different timelines) of the platforms of all three major parties.[41]

The election resulted in a majority Liberal government, led by Dalton McGuinty. There had been no mention of climate change per se in the Liberals' 2003 platform. However, action on transit and land-use planning, and a commitment to phase out coal-fired electricity by 2007, did figure prominently.[42] In 2004, reflecting a more cooperative intergovernmental approach on the climate file, Ontario signed a bilateral agreement with the federal government, now led by Liberal prime minister Paul Martin, that provided financial support for the phase-out of coal-fired electricity.[43]

The most significant environmental initiative of the first stages of the McGuinty government was a series of planning reforms adopted in 2005–6 that created a Greenbelt and Growth Plan for the Greater Golden Horseshoe region surrounding Toronto. There was also a broader revision of the province's planning policies. The reforms were motivated primarily by concerns about urban sprawl and traffic congestion. The overall approach emphasized more compact development, "complete" mixed-use communities, and transit and other non-automobile-based transportation options,[44] all of which was consistent with the notion of low-carbon urban forms and would ultimately be linked to the province's later climate strategies.

The McGuinty government's interest in the climate change file intensified with the arrival of the Conservative minority federal government led by Stephen Harper in January 2006. The new government, with its political base in western Canada, had a strong desire to back away from previous Liberal government commitments under the Kyoto Protocol to reduce Canada's GHG emissions by 6 per cent relative to 1990 by the first (2008–12) commitment period under the protocol.[45] Ontario announced its own "Go Green" climate change plan in June 2007.[46] The plan committed the province to reducing its GHG emissions to 6 per cent below 1990 levels by 2014, 15 per cent by 2020, and 80 per cent by 2050. The centrepiece of the plan was the existing commitment to phase out coal-fired electricity generation,[47] which at the time accounted for 25 per cent of the province's electricity supply; that commitment was supplemented by significant investments in public transit and a cap-and-trade system for other large industrial sources. The plan acknowledged that these measures alone would not be sufficient for the province to meet its targets.[48]

At the same time, the province began to build alliances around climate change with other provincial and state governments in North America. Ontario announced its decision to join British Columbia, Manitoba, and Quebec as a partner in the

Western Climate Initiative (WCI). The WCI, which emerged in February 2007, was initially a partnership between the states of California, Arizona, New Mexico, Oregon, and Washington, and focused on the development of common GHG emission reduction targets (a 15 per cent reduction relative to 2005 levels by 2020) and the creation of a regional cap-and-trade system for GHGs.[49] The following month, Ontario announced that it intended to join northeastern states in a second regional initiative, the Regional Greenhouse Gas Initiative.[50]

Several factors drove the province's participation in these initiatives. There was seen to be a need to create markets large enough for cap-and-trade systems to be viable. Ontario was also concerned about the potential distributional impacts of the Harper government's approach to climate change, which was seen to favour the western oil and gas industry at the expense of manufacturing in eastern Canada.[51] In this context, both Ontario and Quebec saw potential advantages in locking into the WCI system, the most evolved initiative in the US and one that was likely to have a strong influence on any overall North American GHG emission regime. In addition, with a provincial election looming in the fall of 2007, there could be political advantages to running against the federal Conservatives' weak record on climate change at a time of strong public concern about the environment in general and climate change in particular.[52]

The October 2007 election rewarded the McGuinty government with a second majority government. The Liberals' 2007 platform had committed them to carry through on their climate plan, with a coal phase-out to be completed by 2014. But the fall 2008 global financial crisis profoundly disrupted the government's plans. Among other things, the financial collapse triggered a further crisis in the North American automaking industry. As a result, the province's economy lost nearly 250,000 jobs between the fall of 2008 and the spring of 2009.

Picking up on signals from the incoming Obama administration in the US, the province made strong moves to link its economic recovery strategy to environmental sustainability, particularly in the form of the 2009 Green Energy and Green Economy Act (GEGEA). That act provided, among other things, the authority for a feed-in tariff (FIT) mechanism, similar to those employed in Germany, Spain, and Denmark, for low-impact renewable energy sources. FIT mechanisms pay the owners and operators of renewable energy projects a guaranteed fixed price for the electricity produced by their facilities.[53] It was hoped that the FIT program, in addition to supporting the phase-out of coal-fired electricity through the development of renewable energy sources, would prompt the development of a renewable energy technology manufacturing and services sector in the province. It was expected that this would help replace some of the manufacturing jobs lost during the 2008 economic downturn.[54]

The GEGEA prompted major debates over the cost of the FIT program and the approval process established for renewable energy projects by the legislation.[55] In tandem with several competitive request-for-proposal processes, the legislation did facilitate a substantial increase in renewable energy capacity in the province. From a starting point of virtually zero in 2005, around 5500 MW of wind and 2600 MW of solar PV capacity had been installed by the end of 2018.[56]

The Liberals' 2011 election platform had been very thin on new commitments related to the environment, energy, and natural resources. Its principal environmental elements had been a vague proposal to expand the GGH Greenbelt – an option recycled from the party's 2007 document – and the phase-out of coal-fired electricity. The Liberals emerged from the election just short of a majority government (a "major minority" in Premier McGuinty's words).

Electricity issues plagued McGuinty's final term in office, particularly around the cancellation of proposed gas-fired electricity plants in Oakville[57] and Mississauga in the run-up to the 2011 election. The legislative opposition's pursuit of that latter issue, in the context of the minority legislature produced by the October 2011 election, was central to McGuinty's decision in October 2012 to prorogue the legislature and announce his intention to resign.[58] In the face of these difficulties, the province's ongoing weak economic performance, and the withdrawal of any serious threat of federal action on GHG emissions,[59] the government did not move forward with the implementation of the WCI GHG cap-and-trade system. It had initially been scheduled for launch in 2012.

Kathleen Wynne succeeded McGuinty as Liberal leader in February 2013. Wynne's leadership platform had included several specific environmental components, largely carried over from the McGuinty era. These included completing the coal phase-out by the end of 2014 and continuing investments in public transit. There were also references to improving the efficiency of water and waste-water infrastructure and enhancing energy conservation and recycling rates.[60]

A major retreat from the McGuinty government's high-profile green energy initiatives began to materialize early in Wynne's term in office. A moratorium was placed on the controversial Green Energy Act FIT program in March 2012. In May 2013, the FIT program was terminated for large projects (greater than 500kw) in favour of competitive bidding processes. There were no commitments to any additional renewable energy supplies beyond 2018.[61]

The phase-out of coal-fired electricity was completed in April 2014,[62] reducing provincial emissions by 17 per cent. This is widely regarded as the largest single

GHG emission reduction initiative taken in North America to date.[63] The phase-out was facilitated by a combination of energy efficiency measures, continuing declines in electricity demand, the construction of new gas-fired generating facilities, new renewable energy sources, and the return to service of some of the nuclear facilities taken out of service through the NAOP.[64]

The June 2014 election resulted in an unexpected majority government for Premier Wynne's Liberals. Despite a focus on energy and electricity issues in the run-up to the election, environmental questions were not perceived as having a significant impact on the outcome. The Liberals were the only one of the three other major parties to say anything at all about climate change, and even they simply reiterated their existing commitment to their 2020 targets.[65]

In practice, action on climate change emerged as the main environmental theme of Wynne's majority government. In February 2015, the province released a discussion paper indicating its intention to put a price on carbon, potentially in conjunction with Quebec's cap-and-trade system for greenhouse gas emissions, in place since January 2013.[66]

A Climate Change Strategy was released in November 2015, setting out the government's vision to 2050 for how it would grow a resilient low-carbon society and economy. Carbon pricing was to be the cornerstone of the government's plans.[67] The strategy committed the province to develop a more detailed five-year climate change plan outlining specific commitments and initiatives to meet interim and long-term emission reduction targets.[68]

The Climate Change Mitigation and Low Carbon Economy Act (2016)[69] was passed in May 2016. The legislation provided an overall framework for addressing climate change in Ontario and established targets for GHG reductions. These were set at 15 per cent below 1990 levels for 2020, 37 per cent by 2030, and 80 per cent for 2050.[70]

The central element of the government's approach to GHG mitigation was to proceed, beginning in 2017, with the introduction of the cap-and-trade system, as had first been proposed as part of the WCI activities in 2007. Proceeds from the program were to be directed towards a new fund, the Greenhouse Gas Reduction Account, which would support activities and projects for reducing GHG emissions.[71] The 2016 legislation also required the development of a comprehensive climate change action plan and provided a framework for reviewing and revising GHG reduction targets.

Under the cap-and-trade program, caps were established for emissions allowances for the first compliance period (2017–20), as well as dates for subsequent three-year compliance periods. There were three types of participants under the program: (1) mandatory participants, including facilities emitting more than 25,000 tonnes of CO2 per year, fuel suppliers selling more than 200 litres of fuel per year, and electricity importers; (2) voluntary participants, who could choose to opt into the program and who emitted between 10,000 and 25,000 tonnes of CO2 per year; and (3) market participants, who could opt into trading in the carbon market. A November 2017 revision to the program allowed the province to link its carbon market with those of California and Quebec through the WCI. The first joint auction was held in February 2018.[72]

For the initial (2017–20) compliance period, eligible capped participants (i.e., virtually all industrial facilities), except for fuel suppliers/distributors, electricity importers, and most electricity generators, were provided free allowances as a "transitional measure."[73] With the large final emitters being given allowances for free, most of the early revenue generated from the system came from allowances purchased by transportation and heating fuel distributors. These costs were generally passed through directly to consumers. The result, at least initially, was a de facto carbon tax on heating and transportation fuels. Given California's dominant position in the Ontario–Quebec–California carbon market, it acted as the price setter, with a carbon allowance cost of approximately US$15/ton.[74] In Ontario, carbon allowance auctions were expected to generate between $1.5 and $2 billion per year in revenues during the program's initial phase.[75]

As required by the Climate Change Mitigation and Low Carbon Economy Act (2016), the provincial government released its Climate Change Action Plan in June 2016.[76] In addition to initiatives meant to ensure that the short-term (2020) emission reduction target was met, the plan set a mid-term 2030 target that focused on buildings as well as a shift to a lower-carbon transportation system.[77] In support of these directions, the plan referenced land-use planning changes to promote active transportation and transit expansion. It also contained initiatives to promote the diffusion of cleaner (i.e., hybrid and electric) vehicles. The objective was for these vehicles to make up 5 per cent of sales by 2020.

With respect to buildings, key initiatives included incentives to install and retrofit clean energy systems and new rules to increase the energy efficiency of new buildings. A "green bank" was created to help businesses and homeowners pay for energy-efficient technologies, help businesses adopt lower-carbon technologies, and intensify efforts to support low-carbon innovation, research, and development.[78] C$375 million was dedicated to cleantech research and development.[79] A Municipal GHG Challenge Fund was established to help municipalities fund plans and projects that would result in emission reductions. In addition, a Green Ontario

Fund was established as a not-for-profit government agency to help homeowners and businesses meet the costs of energy-saving retrofits and installations.[80]

The election in June 2018 of a Progressive Conservative government, led by Doug Ford, resulted in a dramatic shift in government orientation with regard to climate change. Although the impact of the cap-and-trade system on the election outcome is a matter of debate,[81] the new government, elected based in part on promises to reduce short-term energy costs to consumers, moved quickly to dismantle the previous government's climate change strategy.

Almost immediately after being elected, the Ford government withdrew Ontario from the WCI and moved to cancel the cap-and-trade program.[82] The province's flagship climate legislation, the Climate Change Mitigation and Low Carbon Economy Act (2016), was repealed in November 2018. The new government also moved to cancel all of the programs that would have been funded through cap-and-trade revenues, including those related to electric and hydrogen vehicles, building retrofits, and municipal climate change action. The cancellation of the final round of 738 new, mostly municipal, community, or First Nations-led renewable energy projects was announced in July 2018.[83] The province's "Conservation First" framework for electricity conservation was cancelled in March 2019.[84]

The Ford government's initiatives affecting climate change extended well beyond the immediate dimensions of climate and energy policy. Its amendments to land-use legislation and the GGH growth plan significantly weakened the 2006–17 policies as they related to intensification, density, and the promotion of public transit and supportive urban design. If these changes remain in place, they will likely encourage low-density sprawl and embed automobile-dependent commuting patterns more deeply.[85]

The new government's approach to climate change placed it in direct conflict with the federal Liberal government, led by Justin Trudeau, elected in 2015. The Liberal government was elected in part based on commitments to substantive action on climate change.[86] Under the terms of the December 2016 Pan-Canadian Framework for Green Growth and Climate Change (PCF), the Federal Greenhouse Gas Pollution Pricing Act (2018) had provided for a federal carbon backstop price, to be applied in provinces that did not introduce carbon pricing systems of their own. The Wynne government had been a key signatory to the Pan-Canadian Framework. Under the terms of the PCF, it was accepted that any federal carbon-pricing backstop would not apply in Ontario as a result of the implementation of the province's cap-and-trade system.[87]

With the termination of the cap-and-trade system by the Ford government, the federal government made it clear that it would be implementing the backstop federal carbon price in Ontario, beginning 1 April 2019.[88] That price, set to start at $20/tonne CO2e in 2019, and rising to $50/tonne by 2022, has two components: a charge on heating and transportation fuels, and an output-based pricing system for large (>50,000 tonnes/yr) industrial emitters.[89] The Ford government joined Saskatchewan and Alberta in launching a legal challenge against the federal carbon pricing regime for provinces that did not implement systems of their own. In August 2019, the Ontario Court of Appeal found the federal government's backstop carbon pricing regime constitutionally sound.[90]. A notice of appeal of the Court of Appeal's findings was subsequently submitted to the Supreme Court of Canada by Ontario, Saskatchewan, and Alberta.[91]

In addition to the lost revenue due to its cancellation of the cap-and-trade system, the province may also be denied its $420 million share of the federal Low Carbon Economy Fund.[92] The fund was established by the federal government to encourage provincial participation in the PCF.[93]

In an effort to forestall the imposition of a federal backstop carbon price, the Ford government released a "Made-in-Ontario " environment plan in December 2018.[94] The plan did recognize the significance of the climate change problem as well as the need to address its impacts on the province. Considerable attention was paid within the plan to the need to adapt to climate change at the provincial and local levels.

At the same time, the plan significantly weakened the province's GHG emission reduction goals, to the point – by some interpretations – that they were one third[95] as ambitious as those put forward by the previous government. The plan referred to a regulatory framework for industrial emitters, but this was not fully articulated. In July 2019, the province submitted a proposed framework for industrial sources, seeking an exemption from the federal OBPS. The province's plan was widely regarded as substantially weaker than the federal requirements.[96]

The plan had some progressive provisions, most of which, however, were carried over from the previous Liberal Climate Change Action Plan. These elements included changes to land-use planning rules to take climate change into account, the development of municipal energy and climate change plans, and commitments to consider climate change in government decision-making. There was also a strong emphasis on energy efficiency and conservation. However, an analysis of the plan tabled in December 2019 by the Auditor General and the Environmental Commissioner of Ontario concluded that little had been done to implement the plan and that even if there were implementation efforts, it was unlikely that the plan would meet even the province's reduced GHG emission reduction targets.[97]

Analysis and Discussion: Shifting Landscapes, Institutions, Discourses and Societal Forces

A number of factors have shaped Ontario's approach to climate change. Some flow from the province's changing economic structure, specifically the accelerating transition from an industrial to a more knowledge- and service-based economy. [98] Others relate to shifting relationships with the federal government and the injection of new ideas, discourses, and societal actors into the climate change policy landscape.

As noted in the introduction, the province has moved from recognizing the existence of climate change and projecting its potential impacts in the 1990s, to actually seeing those impacts in the 2010s in various forms, including extreme weather events, floods, damage to infrastructure, the emergence of new health threats, and stresses on water resources, wildlife, forests, and agriculture.

The situation has produced complicated political and economic dynamics around climate change. Industrial emissions have declined significantly since the early 1990s. Yet emissions have continued to grow in sectors such as transportation and buildings, which are difficult to decarbonize. Buildings involve long-term capital stocks, and progress on transportation-related emissions may require significant investments to change urban forms and provide lower-carbon transportation alternatives such as transit networks and electric vehicles. Carbon pricing, on its own, is unlikely to be effective for reducing these sources of emissions.

This was particularly the case in Ontario, where the initial carbon price for industrial emitters under the 2017–18 system was effectively zero due to the distribution of free allowances. While the program applied to heating and transportation fuels, the initial price for allowances for these fuels, when flowed through into gasoline prices and consumers' gas bills, amounted to an estimated 4.3 cents/litre for gasoline and $5 per month in household natural gas costs.[99] This was likely far too low to affect consumer behaviour significantly. A carbon price would have to be raised to levels far beyond the realm of political acceptability to affect consumer behaviour significantly in areas such as transportation and buildings.[100]

In Ontario's case, while carbon pricing via the cap-and-trade system was the most prominent element of the 2016 plan, it may not have been its most important operational component in terms of reducing GHG emissions. Instead, the primary function of the cap-and-trade system in the 2016 plan may have been to generate revenue to finance investments in low-carbon transitions in the building and transportation sectors. Reflecting this underlying primary function, cap-and-trade systems with low implicit prices are increasingly referred to as "cap and invest" systems in North America.[101]

In Ontario, such an approach makes a certain amount of sense, as the two sectors driving the growth of emissions (transportation and buildings) are very difficult to affect through carbon pricing alone. Regulatory tools such as standards and codes for appliances, buildings, and vehicle fleets, and changes in land-use planning rules, are also likely to play central roles in addressing these sectors. Importantly, all of these measures require substantial governmental capacity to develop and implement.

In Ontario's case, "complementary" climate change policies emerged as more important to the province's strategy than the "core"[102] climate policy element of carbon pricing. The risk with such an approach is that political decision-makers may be tempted to invest carbon pricing revenues in politically attractive projects rather than effective climate change mitigation and adaptation measures. Mechanisms to address those risks were never fully developed prior to the 2018 provincial election.

From the recognition of the climate change problem in the late 1980s up to the June 2018 election, the province enjoyed a fairly high level of autonomy around climate policy, with limited direct federal pressure for action. Canadian provinces enjoy strong jurisdictional clout with regard to climate change mitigation and adaptation. They have authority over public and private land use, road transportation and public transit, natural resource management, electricity systems, and municipal governments, as well as a widely accepted capacity to regulate GHG emissions and to price carbon if they choose to do so.[103] The direct federal role in Ontario, through the Chrétien and Martin governments, was limited mainly to providing financial incentives for provincial cooperation on climate change.[104]

That said, the province's initial engagement with the WCI was at least in part intended to counter moves viewed as potentially hostile to the province's interests by the Conservative federal government led by Stephen Harper. Engagement with the WCI also strengthened Ontario's alignment with other provinces, particularly BC and Quebec, which were moving forward on the climate change file, even in the absence of significant federal action. Up to the 2018 provincial election, the Wynne government allied Ontario with the Trudeau federal government (elected in 2015) and with other provinces, at the time including then NDP-led Alberta, in advancing carbon pricing through the 2016 Pan-Canadian Framework on Green Growth and Climate Change.

In contrast, the post-2018 election situation has introduced an extraordinary level of conflict between the federal government and Ontario around climate change. The outcome of the October 2019 federal election in Ontario was widely interpreted as a major defeat for the Ford government around the issue of carbon pricing, and its handling of the climate change question more generally.[105]

Although some Ontario municipalities have shown great leadership with regard to prioritizing action on climate change, capacity remains very limited, and supportive policy measures at the provincial level were only established very late in the province's climate change policy process.[106] The 2016 Climate Change Action Plan did include substantial amendments to the Municipal Act, the Planning Act, and Greater Golden Horseshoe Growth Plan, emphasizing climate change mitigation as well as adaptation through land-use and transportation planning. The plan also made provisions for substantial financial support to municipalities for energy and climate change plan development and implementation. The legislative and planning policy changes have survived the Wynne/Ford transition. However, the funding mechanisms for municipal action were terminated with the cap-and-trade system.[107]

Climate change as a public policy issue has evolved from its recognition within the scientific community to more mainstream awareness, particularly since the mid-2000s. The past few years have seen stronger connections being made between climate change and its visible and lived impacts (floods, forest fires) in Ontario, Canada, and internationally, including in the media. The 2018 wildfires in northern and central Ontario and the 2019 floods in many parts of the province strongly reinforced these connections.[108] A 2019 poll following the release of the Ontario PC climate change plan found that 89 per cent of Ontarians said they were very or somewhat concerned about climate change.[109] The situation has been described as "a new normal in terms of the level of interest in this issue, and the policy choices that governments make around it."[110]

In general, the Liberal administrations of Peterson, McGuinty, and Wynne, as well as Bob Rae's NDP government, employed ecological modernist frames[111] around environmental, energy, and climate change issues. These emphasized win–win (economy–environment) outcomes when discussing transitioning to a low-carbon and more sustainable economy. Health framings were also widely utilized, proving very effective in building support for closing the province's coal-fired power plants over the objections of major institutional actors in the electricity sector and the province's major industrial electricity consumers.[112]

In contrast, incoming PC Premier Ford framed the previous government's climate change policies as a liberal elitist project and a justification for expanding government. Action on climate change was characterized as disconnected from the real needs of "the people." Cap-and-trade was portrayed simply as a government tax grab. The legislation to repeal the cap-and-trade system was presented as providing "relief" from high energy costs, to which the carbon pricing system, along with the renewable energy FIT program, was a contributor.[113] Because the Wynne government failed to focus on the broader vision (i.e., it focused too much on the mechanics), the program did not resonate with voters, who were concerned about making ends meet and being able to pay their hydro bills.

In institutional terms, the speed with which much of Ontario's climate change governance regime was dismantled highlighted the vulnerability of emergent climate governance regimes. The core element of the regime, the cap-and-trade system, was in place for a little more than a year, and free allowances had been given to industrial emitters as part of the initial compliance phase. With little industrial investment in the system, there was minimal pushback when it was repealed. The situation might have been quite different had the cap-and-trade system, and the programs financed through it, been in place for a longer time.

The longer-term landscape is potentially more hopeful. The Ford government's right-wing populist approach has become deeply unpopular, suggesting that the 2018 election may have been an aberration flowing from an unpopular premier and an insufficiently appealing alternative offered by the NDP.[114] The spring 2019 floods, August 2019 Ontario Court of Appeal's finding in favour of the constitutionality of the federal backstop carbon pricing system, gas-pump stickers blaming the federal carbon pricing backstop for higher gas prices (which wouldn't stick to the pumps),[115] the October 2019 federal Liberal success in Ontario,[116] and the December 2019–January 2020 Australian wildfires,[117] all seemed to be converging to place Premier Ford on the wrong side of history on the climate change file.

Conclusions: The Path Forward on Climate Change?

The 2018 provincial election brought about a dramatic shift in direction in the province's approach to the climate change issue. The province had engaged with the issue incrementally from 1990 onwards. Still, movement on implementing a comprehensive climate change strategy did not occur until the late stages of the Wynne government. The core elements of that strategy, particularly the cap-and-trade system and the portfolio of programs to be funded through it, were swiftly dismantled by the incoming Ford government.

Where the province goes from there is an open question. The physical realities of the impacts of climate change have become more difficult to ignore, and the public salience of the issue has grown substantially over the past two years. Municipalities, which are confronted directly with the health, environmental, and infrastructural impacts of climate change, have become increasingly engaged in community energy and climate change planning, regardless of the province's direction.

Some form of carbon pricing seems likely to continue in the province as long as a moderately progressive federal government remains in power.[118] The technological means for low-carbon transitions, from electric vehicles to advanced grid management, renewable energy, and energy storage technologies, are largely available, with improving technical performance and falling costs. These factors have the potential to reinforce a long-term low-carbon trajectory for the province.

At the same time, significant challenges remain. Decision-making around major infrastructure projects, particularly in relation to electricity and transportation, has become deeply politicized. The situation carries with it significant risks of embedding pathways that do not align with climate change mitigation and adaptation goals. The Ford government's weakening of land-use rules around urban development seems likely to encourage sprawl and embed automobile-dependent commuting patterns more deeply than ever, making the mitigation of transportation-related emissions even more challenging.

The province's electricity system has been the source of Ontario's largest gains in terms of GHG emission reductions through the phase-out of coal-fired electricity generation. However, the system is about to become much more carbon-intensive as nuclear power plants are permanently or temporarily decommissioned, and their output likely replaced with newly built natural gas-fired generation.[119] Broader discussions about the role of natural gas in a low-carbon transition in a province where it provides an overwhelming majority of building space and water heating services, and a significant degree of energy system resiliency, are only beginning.

Whatever the outcome of the 2022 provincial election, it seems likely that climate change will remain a central issue in the province's political and policy life.

QUESTIONS FOR CONSIDERATION:

1. Describe climate change in your own words.
2. What are three major, projected social, economic, and environmental impacts of climate change?
3. What have been some of the major consequences of climate change in post-2000 Ontario?
4. What effect did the Common Sense Revolution have on climate change policy in Ontario?
5. What is a cap-and-trade system? Why is it important?
6. How have federal–provincial relations affected climate change policy in Ontario since 2010?

NOTES

1 J. Dryzek, R. Norgaaed, and David Schlosberg. "Climate Change and Society: Approaches and Responses," in *The Oxford Handbook of Climate Change and Society*, ed. Dryzek, Norgaard, and Scholsberg (Oxford: Oxford University Press, 2011), 3.

2 A total of eight facilities constituted the principal sources of acid rain: five coal-fired power plants owned by Ontario Hydro; the Inco and Falconbridge nickel smelters in Sudbury; and the Algoma Steel plant in Sault Ste. Marie. On the acid rain and pulp and paper issues generally, see M. Winfield, *Blue-Green Province: The Environment and the Political Economy of Ontario* (Vancouver: UBC Press 2012), 40–90.

3 Robert Ristinen and Jack Kraushaar, *Energy and the Environment* (John Wiley and Sons, Inc., 2006), 332.

4 Charles Pearson. *Economics and the Challenge of Global Warming* (Cambridge: Cambridge University Press, 2011).

5 Libby Robin, Sverker Sorlin, and Paul Warde, eds. *The Future of Nature: Documents of Global Change* (New Haven: Yale University Press, 2013).

6 Intergovernmental Panel on Climate Change (IPCC), *Climate Change 2014 Synthesis Report: Summary for Policymakers* (Geneva: IPCC, 2014), https://archive.ipcc.ch/pdf/assessment-report/ar5/syr/AR5_SYR_FINAL_SPM.pdf.

7 IPCC, *2014 Assessment Report: Summary for Policy Makers*, 1.1.

8 IPCC, *2014* Assessment Report, *Summary for Policy Makers*, 2.2.

9 N. Stern, *The Economics of Climate Change* (Cambridge: Cambridge University Press, 2006), 65.

10 IPCC, *Global Warming of 1.5°C: Summary for Policy Makers* (Geneva: IPCC, 2018), ch.1., https://www.ipcc.ch/sr15.

11 IPCC, *Global Warming of 1.5°C, SPM.*

12 IPCC, *Global Warming of 1.5°C, SPM*, C.1.

13 Stern, *Economics of Climate Change.*

14 M. Winfield and V. Scanga, "International Climate Change Policy in the Harper Era," in *Canadian Foreign Policy in the Harper Era*, ed. P. McKenna (Toronto: University of Toronto Press). In Press.

15 M. Winfield and D. Macdonald, "Federalism and Canadian Climate Change Policy," in *Canadian Federalism: Performance, Effectiveness, and Legitimacy*, 3rd ed., ed. G. Skogstad and H. Bakvis (Toronto: Oxford University Press, 2012).

16 C. Kaiser, "State Steering in Polycentric Governance Systems: Climate Policy Integration in Ontario and California's Transportation Sectors" (PhD diss., York University, 2020), ch. 3.

17 See for example, Toon Vandyck, Kimon Keramidas, Bert Saveyn, Alban Kitous, and Zoi Vrontisi. "A Global Stocktake of the Paris Pledges: Implications for Energy Systems and Economy," *Global Environmental Change* 41 (2016): 46–63, 10.1016/j.gloenvcha.2016.08.006.

18 Commissioner for the Environment and Sustainable Development, *Report 1-Progress on Reducing Greenhouse Gases-Environment and Climate Change Canada* (Ottawa: Supply and Services Canada, 2017), www.oag-bvg.gc.ca/internet/English/parl_cesd_201710_01_e_42489.html.

19 Environment and Climate Change Canada (ECCC), "Greenhouse gas emissions," https://www.canada.ca/en/environment-climate-change/services/environmental-indicators/greenhouse-gas-emissions.html.

20 Environmental Commissioner of Ontario (ECO), *2015 Climate Change Progress Report* (Toronto: ECO, 2015), http://docs.assets.eco.on.ca/reports/climate-change/2015/2015-GHG.pdf.

21 M. Rabson, "Ford links floods to climate change, says situation 'just rips your heart out,'" *Canadian Press*, 26 April 2019, https://www.ctvnews.ca/canada/ford-links-floods-to-climate-change-says-situation-just-rips-your-heart-out-1.4396432.

22 ECO, *Facing Climate Change: 2016 Greenhouse Gas Progress Report* (Toronto: ECO 2016), 29, http://docs.assets.eco.on.ca/reports/climate-change/2016/2016-Annual-GHG-Report-EN.pdf

23 ECO, *2016 Greenhouse Gas Progress Report*, 30.

24 ECO, *Feeling the Heat: 2015 Greenhouse Gas Progress Report* (Toronto: ECO, 2015), 5, http://docs.assets.eco.on.ca/reports/climate-change/2015/2015-GHG.pdf.

25 ECO, *Facing Climate Change*, 30.

26 ECO, *Feeling the Heat*, 6.

27 ECCC, *National Inventory Report 1990–2014: Greenhouse Gas Sources and Sinks in Canada*, pt. 3, table A11-12, (2016), 55, cited in ECO, *Facing Climate Change*, figure 2.

28 ECCC, "Greenhouse Gas Emissions: Regional and Economic Sectors," https://www.canada.ca/en/environment-climate-change/services/environmental-indicators/greenhouse-gas-emissions.html.

29 See, generally, D. Macdonald, *Carbon Province, Hydro Province: The Challenge of Canadian Energy and Climate Change Federalism* (Toronto: University of Toronto Press, 2020).

30 Ontario Ministry of Finance, *Ontario's Long-Term Report on the Economy*. (Toronto: Queen's Printer, 2017), http://www.fin.gov.on.ca/en/economy/ltr/2017/ltr2017.pdf.

31 Ontario Ministry of Environment and Climate Change, *Ontario's Climate Change Update 2014* (Toronto: Queen's Printer, 2014), https://www.ontario.ca/page/ontarios-climate-change-update-2014.

32 Winfield, *Blue-Green Province*, 57.

33 Ontario Round Table on the Environment and Economy, *Report: Restructuring for Sustainability* (Toronto: ORTEE 2992), xiv–xvi.

34 Memorandum to members of the externalities collaborative, Ministry of Environment and Energy, 22 April 1994.

35 *Legislative Debates*, 9 June 1994, 6757, 6772

36 Winfield, *Blue-Green*, 80–3.

37 Winfield, *Blue-Green*, 111–12.

38 See Melissa Harris, Marisa Beck, and Ivetta Gerasimchuk, *The End of Coal: Ontario's Coal Phase-Out* (Winnipeg: International Institute for Sustainable Development, 2015), 12, https://www.iisd.org/library/end-coal-ontarios-coal-phase-out.

39 Winfield and Macdonald, "Federalism and Canadian Climate Change Policy."

40 C. Kaiser, "State Steering in Polycentric Governance Systems."

41 Winfield, *Blue-Green*, 156–7.

42 See Ontario Liberal Party, *Growing Strong Communities* (Toronto: OLP, 2002).

43 See Ontario Ministry of Finance, *2007 Ontario Budget*, http://www.fin.gov.on.ca

44 Winfield, *Blue-Green*, 158–63.

45 D. Macdonald, "The Failure of Canadian Climate Change Policy: Veto Power, Absent Leadership, and Institutional Weakness," in *Canadian Environmental Policy and Politics*, 3rd ed., ed. Debora VanNijnatten and Robert Boardman, 152–66.

46 Ontario Ministry of the Environment, *Go Green – Ontario's Action Plan on Climate Change* (Toronto: Queen's Printer, 2007).

47 C. Kaiser, “Decarbonizing Road Transportation in Ontario” (working paper, Joint Clean Climate Transportation Research Partnership, 2018), https://jcctrp.org/wp-content/uploads/2018/11/JCCTRP_Working-Paper-2018-1_Ontario_Nov28_Final.pdf.
48 See ECO, *Finding a Vision for Change: Annual Greenhouse Gas Progress Report 2008/09* (Toronto: December 2009). See also Pembina Institute, *Highlights of Provincial Greenhouse Gas Reduction Plans* (Drayton Valley, AB, August 2009).
49 www.westernclimateinitaitive.org.
50 Winfield, *Blue-Green*, 173.
51 I. Urquhart, “Don’t look to premiers for leadership,” *Toronto Star*, 10 August 2007.
52 K. Howlett, “McGuinty plans to target Green vote,” *Globe and Mail*, 1 January 2007.
53 Pembina Institute, *Fact Sheet: How Feed-I Tariffs Maximize the Benefits of Renewable Energy* (Calgary: Pembina Institute, n.d.), https://www.pembina.org/reports/feed-in-tariffs-factsheet.pdf.
54 M. Winfield, “Ontario’s Green Energy and Green Economy Act as an Industrial Development Strategy,” in *Work and the Challenge of Climate Change: Canadian and International Perspectives*, ed. S. McBride and C. Carla Lipsig-Mummé (Kingston and Montreal: McGill–Queen’s University Press, 2015).
55 M. Winfield and B. Dolter, "Energy, Economic, and Environmental Discourses and their Policy Impact: The Case of Ontario’s Green Energy and Green Economy Act," *Energy Policy* 68 (May 2014): 423–35, https://doi.org/10.1016/j.enpol.2014.01.039.
56 Independent Electricity System Operator (IESO), *Ontario’s Supply Mix*, http://www.ieso.ca/en/Learn/Ontario-Supply-Mix/Ontario-Energy-Capacity.
57 J. Jenkins and A. Artuso, “Cancelled Oakville gas plant to be moved to Napanee,” *St. Catharines Standard*, 24 September 2012.
58 K. Howlett, A. Morrow, and P. Waldie, “Ontario premier Dalton McGuinty resigns,” *Globe and Mail*, 15 October 2012.
59 See D. Macdonald, “Climate Change Policy,” in *Canadian Environmental Policy and Politics: The Challenges of Austerity and Ambivalence*, 4th ed., ed. Debora VanNijnatten (Toronto: Oxford, 2015), 220–34.
60 M. Winfield, “Environmental Policy: Greening the Province from the Dynasty to Wynne,” in *Government and Politics of Ontario*, 6th ed., ed. J. Malloy and C. Collier (Toronto: University of Toronto Press, 2016).
61 Ontario Ministry of Energy, “Ontario Working with Communities to Secure Clean Energy Future” [news release], 30 May 2013.
62 Government of Ontario, “The End of Coal,” https://www.ontario.ca/page/end-coal.
63 Sarah Petrevan, “Ontario’s coal phaseout in perspective,” *Clean Energy Canada*, 17 January 2017, http://cleanenergycanada.org/ontarios-coal-phaseout-perspective.
64 See Harris, Beck, and Gerasimchuk, *The End of Coal*. See also Winfield and MacWhirter, “The Search for Sustainability in Ontario Electricity Policy.”
65 Winfield, “Greening the Province.”
66 Ministry of Environment and Climate Change, Re: *EBR Posting 012-3452 Ontario Climate Change Discussion Paper* (Toronto: Queen’s Printer, 2015).
67 Kaiser, “Decarbonizing Road Transportation in Ontario,” 7.
68 Government of Ontario, *Ontario’s Climate Change Strategy* (Toronto: Queen’s Printer, 2016), https://dr6j45jk9xcmk.cloudfront.net/documents/4928/climate-change-strategy-en.pdf.
69 Climate Change Mitigation and Low-Carbon Economy Act, S.O. 2016, c. 7 (https://www.canlii.org/en/on/laws/stat/so-2016-c-7/latest/so-2016-c-7.html, last accessed 7 April, 2024).

70 Climate Change Mitigation and Low-Carbon Economy Act, S.O. 2016, c 7, s.6.
71 Government of Ontario, "Cap and trade: program overview," https://www.ontario.ca/page/cap-and-trade-program-overviewed, cited in Kaiser, "State Steering in Polycentric Governance Systems," 86.
72 Ontario, "Cap and trade: program overview," cited in Kaiser, "Decarbonizing Road Transportation in Ontario" 10.
73 Ontario, "Cap and trade: program overview," cited in Kaiser, "Decarbonizing Road Transportation in Ontario," 10.
74 J. Larson, "The footprint of US carbon pricing plans" (New York: Rhodium Group, 2018), https://rhg.com/research/the-footprint-of-us-carbon-pricing-plans.
75 Financial Accountability Office of Ontario, *Cap and Trade: A Financial Review of the Decision to Cancel the Cap and Trade Program* (Toronto: Queen's Printer 2018), https://www.fao-on.org/web/default/files/publications/ending%20cap%20and%20trade%20oct%202018/Cap%20and%20Trade.pdf.
76 Office of the Premier, "Ontario releases new climate change ction Plpan: Plan charts course to an innovative, low-carbon economy," 8 June 2016, https://news.ontario.ca/opo/en/2016/06/ontario-releases-new-climate-change-actionplan.html.
77 Government of Ontario, *Ontario's Five Year Climate Change Action Plan: 2016–2020* (Toronto: Queen's Printer, 2016), http://www.applications.ene.gov.on.ca/ccap/products/CCAP_ENGLISH.pdf cited in Kaiser, "Decarbonizing Road Transportation in Ontario."
78 Ontario, *Five Year Climate Change Action Plan*, cited in Kaiser, "State Steering in Polycentric Governance Systems," 88.
79 A. Morrow and G. Keenan, "Ontario to spend $7-billion on sweeping climate change Plan," *Globe and Mail*, 16 May 2016, https://beta.theglobeandmail.com/news/national/ontario-to-spend-7-billion-in-sweepingclimate-change, cited in Kaiser, "Decarbonizing Road Transportation in Ontario," 12.
80 Ontario, *Five-Year Climate Change Action Plan*.
81 Erick Lachapelle and Simon Kiss, "Opposition to Carbon Pricing and Right-Wing Populism: Ontario's 2018 General Election," *Environmental Politics* 28, no. 5 (2019): 970–6, 10.1080/09644016.2019.1608659. See also M. Winfield, "Environmental positions show divisions among Ontario Parties," *Hamilton Spectator*, 4 June 2018.
82 Office of the Premier Designate, "Premier-designate Doug Ford announces an end to Ontario's cap-and-trade carbon tax," 15 June 2018, https://news.ontario.ca/opd/en/2018/06/premier-designate-doug-ford-announces-an-end-toontarios-cap-and-trade-carbon-tax.html.
83 Ministry of Energy, "Backgrounder: Ontario reducing costs by centralizing and refocusing conservation programs," 21 March 2019, https://news.ontario.ca/mndmf/en/2019/03/ontario-reducing-costs-by-centralizing-and-refocusing-conservation-programs.html.
84 Ontario Ministry of Energy, Northern Development and Mines, "Backgrounder: Ontario reducing costs by centralizing and refocusing conservation programs," 21 May 2019, https://news.ontario.ca/mndmf/en/2019/03/ontario-reducing-costs-by-centralizing-and-refocusing-conservation-programs.html.
85 S. Novakovic, "Ontario's growth plan changes: The end of smart growth?" *Urban Toronto*, 22 January 2019, https://urbantoronto.ca/news/2019/01/ontarios-growth-plan-changes-end-smart-growth.
86 Liberal Party of Canada, *A New Plan for a Strong Middle Class* (2015), ch. 3, https://www.liberal.ca/wp-content/uploads/2015/10/New-plan-for-a-strong-middle-class.pdf.
87 Winfield and Macdonald, "Federalism and Canadian Climate Change Policy."

88 Government of Canada, "Ontario and pollution pricing," 7 May 2019, https://www.canada.ca/en/environment-climate-change/services/climate-change/pricing-pollution.

89 Environment and Climate Change Canada, *Technical Paper on Carbon Pricing Backstop* (2017), https://www.canada.ca/en/services/environment/weather/climatechange/technical-paper-federal-carbon-pricing-backstop.html.

90 Reference *re Greenhouse Gas Pollution Pricing Act*, 2019 ONCA 544.

91 J. Keller, "Ontario files appeal with Supreme Court in fight against federal carbon tax," *Globe and Mail* 28 August 2019, https://www.theglobeandmail.com/canada/articleontario-files-appeal-with-supreme-court-in-fight-against-federal, cited in Kaiser, "State Steering in Polycentric Governance Systems," 119.

92 Kaiser, "State Steering in Polycentric Governance Systems," 119.

93 S. Wechsler, "Trudeau government reviewing $420 million in transfer payments to Ontario after Doug Ford begins 'orderly wind-down' of green programs," *Canada's National Observer*, 3 July 2018, https://www.nationalobserver.com/2018/07/03/news/trudeaugovernment-reviewing-420-million-transfer-payments-ontario-after-doug-ford.

94 Ontario Ministry of Environment, Conservation and Parks, *A Made-in-Ontario Environment Plan* (Toronto: Queen's Printer, 2018), https://www.ontario.ca/page/made-in-ontario-environment-plan.

95 See Office of the Auditor General of Ontario/Environmental Commissioner of Ontario, *2019 Annual Report*, vol. 2: *Reports on the Environment* (2019), ch. 3, http://www.auditor.on.ca/en/content/annualreports/arreports/en19/2019AR_v2_en_web.pdf.

96 Isabelle Turcotte, Jan Gorski, and Brianne Riehl, *Carbon Emissions: Who Makes Big Polluters Pay: A Comparison of Provincial and Federal Industrial Carbon Pricing Systems for Industrial Emitters* (Calgary: Pembina Institute, 2019), https://www.pembina.org/pub/carbon-emissions-who-makes-big-polluters-pay.

97 Auditor General of Ontario/Environmental Commissioner of Ontario, *2019 Annual Report*, vol. 2, ch. 3.

98 Ontario Ministry of Finance, *Ontario's Long-Term Report on the Economy*.

99 Government of Ontario, *Cap and Trade in Ontario*, https://www.ontario.ca/page/cap-and-trade-ontario.

100 See Mark Jaccard, Mikela Hein, and Tiffany Vass, *Is Win–Win Possible? Can Canada's Government Achieve Its Paris Commitment … and Get Re-elected?* (Burnaby: Energy and Materials Research Group, Simon Fraser University, 2016), http://rem-main.rem.sfu.ca/papers/jaccard/Jaccard-Hein-Vass%20CdnClimatePol%20EMRG-REM-SFU%20Sep%2020%202016.pdf.

101 Karen Glitman, *Cap-and-Invest: A Review of Policy, Design and Models and Their Applicability in Vermont* (San Diego: Center for Sustainable Energy, 2019), https://energycenter.org/sites/default/files/docs/nav/resources/2019-04_Cap-and-Invest-A-Review_Report.pdf; Transportation Climate Initiative, *Cap-and-Invest Program to Reduce Pollution* (2019), https://www.transportationandclimate.org/sites/default/files/TCICap-and-Invest 101_0.pdf.

102 Ann E. Carlson, "Designing Effective Climate Policy: Cap-and-Trade and Complementary Policies," *Harvard Journal on Legislation* 49, no. 2 (Summer 2012): 207–48, https://heinonline.org/HOL/P?h=hein.journals/hjl49&i=215.

103 Bryan P. Schwartz, *Legal Opinion on the Constitutionality of the Federal Carbon Pricing Benchmark and Backstop Proposals* (2017), 15–16, https://www.gov.mb.ca/asset_library/en/climatechange/federal_carbon_pricing_benchmark_backstop_proposals.pdf.

104 Winfield and Macdonald, "Federalism and Canadian Climate Change Policy."

105 Philippe J. Fournier, "A 338Canada analysis: Where the Conservatives lost," *McLean's*, 27 October 2019, https://www.macleans.ca/politics/ottawa/a-338canada-analysis-where-the-conservatives-lost. See also K. Brooks, "Climate Action and the Environment Won – That's the Big Take Away from the 2019 Federal Election," *Environmental Defense*, 23 October 2019, https://environmentaldefence.ca/2019/10/23/climate-action-environment-won-thats-big-take-away-2019-federal-election.

106 Kaiser, "State Steering in Polycentric Governance Systems"; M. Winfield, S. Wyse, and S. Harbinson, "Enabling community energy planning? Polycentricity, governance frameworks, and community energy planning in Canada" (working paper, York University Sustainable Energy Initiative, 2020), https://sei.info.yorku.ca/files/2020/01/Community-Energy-Planning-paper-January-15-2020-for-Posting-1-1.pdf?x10807.

107 Winfield, Wyse, and Harbinson, "Enabling community energy planning?"; Kaiser, "State Steering in Polycentric Governance Systems."

108 Rabson, "Ford links floods to climate change."

109 A. Jones, "Internal poll finds voters have negative opinion of PCs environmental Policies," *CBC News*, 31 March 2019, https://www.cbc.ca/news/canada/toronto/ontarioenvironment-ford-poll-climate-carbon-tax-1.5079010.

110 B. Anderson and D. Coletto, "Trump Attracts Most Canadians' Attention; Jobs, Climate Change and Khadr Hot Button Issues," *Abacus Data*, 21 July 2017, https://abacusdata.ca/trump-attracts-most-canadians-attentionjobs-climate-change-khadr-hot-button-issues.

111 J. Drysek, *The Politics of Earth: Environmental Discourses* (Oxford: Oxford University Press, 2013), 162–80.

112 Harris, Beck, and Gerasimchuk, *The End of Coal*; Winfield and MacWhirter, "The Search for Sustainability."

113 Office of the Premier Designate, "Premier-Designate Doug Ford announces an end to Ontario's cap-and-trade carbon tax," 15 June 2018, https://news.ontario.ca/opd/en/2018/06/premier-designate-doug-ford-announces-an-end-toontarios-cap-and-trade-carbon-tax.html.

114 M. Winfield, "Will the Ford era lead to a political realignment in Ontario?" *Policy Options* (May 2019), https://policyoptions.irpp.org/magazines/may-2019/will-the-ford-era-lead-to-a-political-realignment-in-ontario.

115 R. Benzie, "It seems the Ontario government's gas-pump stickers aren't sticky enough," *Toronto Star*, 12 September 2019, https://www.thestar.com/politics/provincial/2019/09/12/it-seems-the-ontario-governments-gas-pump-stickers-arent-sticky-enough.html.

116 Philippe J. Fournier, "A 338Canada analysis: Where the Conservatives lost," *Maclean's*, 27 October 2019, https://www.macleans.ca/politics/ottawa/a-338canada-analysis-where-the-conservatives-lost.

117 "Australia bushfires factcheck: Are this year's fires unprecedented?," *The Guardian*, 22 November 2019, https://www.theguardian.com/australia-news/2019/nov/22/australia-bushfires-factcheck-are-this-years-fires-unprecedented.

118 *Reference re Greenhouse Gas Pollution Pricing Act*, 2019 ONCA 544; *Reference re Greenhouse Gas Pollution Pricing Act*, 2019 SKCA 40.

119 IESO, *The IESO's Annual Planning Outlook in Six Graphs* (2020), http://www.ieso.ca/Powering-Tomorrow/Data/The-IESOs-Annual-Planning-Outlook-in-Six-Graphs.

Part V

THE STATE AND WELFARE

CHAPTER NINETEEN

"By every means in our power": Child and Maternal Welfare in Ontario, 1914–40[1]

CYNTHIA R. COMACCHIO

What could bring the importance of viable public health structures into the popular consciousness more than a global pandemic of horrifying proportions? The novel coronavirus, officially SARS 2 COVID-19, struck China in late December 2019. By early March 2020, when the World Health Organization (WHO) officially declared it a pandemic, most nations had been visited by this twenty-first-century plague. Many went into "lockdown," a state-mandated self-isolation or "shelter at home" order, that shuttered socio-economic structures abruptly and for an indefinite period of time. The world-historic event that is COVID-19 blindsided the "advanced" capitalist nations of Western Europe and North America. Governments reeled, fumbled, grasped at all plausible solutions – and not a few implausible ones – and at times faltered gravely as cases and casualties soared.[2]

Around the world for decades, there have been clawbacks to state health and welfare programs, reflecting late twentieth-century neoliberal politics. Yet Canadians, for their part, have largely remained committed to the Medicare system established in the late 1960s.[3] Health and welfare programs across all three levels of government, though definitely worn down, have not been disempowered to the same extent as in other hard-struck capitalist democracies. Where private medical insurance has triumphed over state provision, as in the US, the human toll from COVID-19 has been especially high in terms of illness and mortality.[4]

In many ways, but by no means all (thanks to medical advances and the fact that most nations currently have some sort of health and welfare safety net), the COVID-19 pandemic resembles the Spanish influenza epidemic that shook the world just as the First World War ended a century ago.[5] However important their influence, that war and that pandemic were not the sole determinants of state-run and -regulated public health systems in Canada. Most urban municipalities, a smaller number of rural and outpost districts, and each province, established boards of health when they entered Confederation. By 1920, many of these boards had been formalized into departments headed by medical officers of health (albeit many on a part-time basis) who were trained physicians. The larger and better-organized urban departments also contracted medical specialists for consultative purposes, and most employed at least one trained nurse to carry the public health message into homes.[6]

Nonetheless, war and influenza impressed upon governments, social leaders of all stripes, and the burgeoning social reform movement that the nation's future was contingent "as never before" on the health and welfare of *all* its citizens, not just those who could pay. Under the BNA Act, health and welfare were under the purview of the provinces. But calls for a federal health department – something for which the Canadian Medical Association had long been calling – had generated enough public support by 1919 for the federal government to act. The Dominion Council of Health was established as an advisory body, on which sat representatives from each provincial health department and appointed delegates from rural and urban women's groups, labour and agriculture organizations, and the health professions. It was mandated to cooperate with provincial, territorial, and other health authorities "with a view to the coordination of the efforts proposed or made for preserving and improving the public health, the conservation of child life, and the promotion of child welfare."[7] Its commitment to child welfare was reinforced in 1920, when a separate Child Welfare Division was created under the direction of Dr. Helen MacMurchy; this was followed by a new Council on Child Welfare (later the Canadian Welfare Council), with Ottawa social worker Charlotte Whitton in charge. All nationally organized agencies engaged in any aspect of child welfare work were represented on the council, a voluntary body that received some federal funding for its educational services. By the Second World War, this quasi-state agency had become the nation's paramount social service tribunal.[8] The health and welfare of the Indigenous population, notably Status Indians on reserves, remained in the hands of federally appointed Indian Agents, who did notoriously little to help their charges.[9]

This chapter discusses how the development of a modern public health system in Canada, shaped by war and pandemic, owed much to growing concerns about the nation's children. Children embody the future, and anxieties about their condition and prospects were strongly reflected in reformist thought at the time. Child welfare was viewed as a "social problem," and was at the top of a long list of "moral" problems,

Figure 19.1. The "infant/child soldier" was a popular trope during the Great War. The popular "ladies' magazine," *Everywoman's World*, featured a child in military uniform and pose, in this instance also bearing the imperial flag, in honour of the fiftieth anniversary of Confederation. Source: *Everywoman's World*, Confederation.

which meant that addressing it promised to solve many others.[10] Child welfare advocates took to heart what they saw as a critical relationship between children and nations. The public saw children as the foremost victims of the "war to end all wars," and their plight led directly to the founding of international organizations such as the League of Nations and Save the Children.[11] Moreover, mass death both at the war front and among civilian populations generated a strong movement towards pronatalism as essential to reconstruction. Infant and child mortality, and consequently maternal health, were in the forefront of public consciousness and reform campaigns at a time when so many fathers and future fathers had been killed in the war. Saving "infant soldiers" and guiding their mothers through safe pregnancies and childbirth were fundamental to the new federal department's mandate.[12]

The development of a systematized child and maternal welfare program under Ontario government auspices was an important step towards achieving the newly proclaimed national goals. Few could question the provincial department's assertion that

> it is scarcely necessary to point out the value to any country of the proper care of infant life. Not only will an immense proportion of child life be saved by suitable measures, but it is safe to predict that the physique of our people will in future years be found to have been greatly improved by the efforts in this field of preventive medicine. Viewed in the light of our present knowledge, this is probably the most promising field of public health work in this country.[13]

During the interwar years, Ontario's health department led a nationwide campaign to save mothers and children, part of a sweeping movement that dated from the beginning of "Canada's Century," heralded internationally as "The Century of the Child."[14] Although contemporary ideological and political constraints limited their achievements, Ontario public health reformers and child welfare advocates developed progressive structures and programs that reached far more infants, children, and mothers, across barriers of class, race, and region, than any previous public health endeavour. Some were foundational to the post–Second World War welfare state. Some, like well-baby and prenatal clinics, and home nurse visits, were arguably more accessible and beneficial than what is available today for many twenty-first-century mothers and children.

Infant Mortality as Social Crisis: Defining the "Problem"

As the most populous, urbanized, and industrialized of the provinces, with the largest number of medical schools, hospitals, physicians, and nurses within its boundaries, Ontario took the lead in contemporary health and welfare concerns. The Public Health Act of August 1912 strengthened provincial supervision over municipal health boards; seven district officers were appointed as full-time supervisors of public health across the province. The growing emphasis on child welfare in the overlapping reform and medical circles led to the creation of the Child Welfare Bureau (1916). The first of its kind in Canada, it represented what a modern provincial government could do on behalf of public health and welfare. Obliged to operate within wartime budgetary restraints, however, the bureau's work was actually limited to sending one nurse across the province with its "Child Welfare Special," a specially outfitted exhibition clinic on wheels. "Demonstration" work was performed in hopes of convincing resident medical practitioners to become involved in local voluntary clinics and to encourage local governments to hire their own nurses.[15] In 1920, the province became the first in Canada to establish a specialized

Division of Maternal and Child Hygiene in its health department, already held to be the Canadian exemplar of modern public health systems.[16]

Also important was the key role of the province's child welfare advocates, most of them Toronto-based. Dr. Helen MacMurchy was a physician, health activist, and avowed eugenicist; she was also the first woman faculty member in the University of Toronto's obstetrics department, the first city "inspector of the feebleminded" (1906–19), author of the Ontario Board of Health's critical series of infant mortality reports (1910–13), and the first chief of the federal health department's Child Welfare Division. All of this ideally positioned her to issue this nationwide call to arms: "To glorify, dignify, and purify motherhood, by every means in our power."[17] Her intensive involvement at all government levels ensured that much of the campaign's early twentieth-century story was Ontario-based. Like MacMurchy, Toronto's Dr. Alan Brown was an official consultant to the municipal, provincial, and federal governments and to various other governments and agencies outside Ontario. A pre-eminent Canadian pediatrician in his day (albeit there were few of those), he became the campaign's unofficial "grandmaster." Brown was appointed physician-in-chief at the Hospital for Sick Children in 1919. The nation's first pediatric hospital attained international stature during the interwar years, thanks in large part to Brown's leadership.[18] When the province's new Division of Maternal and Child Hygiene became operative, his appointment as pediatric consultant was widely applauded. He was involved from the start in devising and effecting its strategies and personally oversaw the training of nurses and other division officers.[19] Much of the pediatric research integral to the campaign's goals, and most of the childrearing educational literature it distributed, emanated from Toronto and Ottawa, published and circulated exclusively by the provincial and federal child welfare divisions. MacMurchy and Brown played a major role in in all these efforts into the post–Second World War years.

Some settler families, especially rural residents, northern and prairie homesteaders, and urban immigrants, faced the persistent problems of isolation and inaccessibility due to geography, finances, and cultural and linguistic differences. The distance to medical (or any) assistance was often exacerbated by weather extremes that aggravated illness and made it difficult or impossible to get medical care. The threats associated with childhood diseases, and even with the "ordinary" female experiences of pregnancy and childbirth, were barely mitigated by the onward march of medical science: rural and outpost areas and reserves were seriously underserviced by doctors, trained nurses, and midwives.[20] Many families had to rely on the skills and knowledge of women – mothers, grandmothers, and neighbours – who held a store of "home remedies," handed down generationally, often transported from "the old country." A public health nurse visiting a "foreign" home in Northern Ontario was horrified to find an eight-month-old baby, suffering from pneumonia, with bags of chopped onions on its chest and back and tied to its feet. Chest plasters made of onions, garlic, and mustard seed were common for all ages, and herbal teas were given even to infants and toddlers to calm them and ease their coughs.[21] Indigenous neighbours offered their own traditional remedies and practices based on their in-depth knowledge of local herbs and plants.[22] All such remedies were deemed "superstition" by health professionals and dismissed as evidence of an abiding ignorance rooted in class and racial inferiority. From a public health perspective, it was argued, "nationalities more closely resembling British, and coming from a similar stock, and having had a closely similar environment, present the least problem."[23] Yet a profound belief in the value of a proper education delivered by the proper sources allowed some room for an optimism that, if racist in itself, tended to soften racial determinism.

Even where medical assistance was available, this was a time when doctors were paid on a "fee for service" basis and that fee often constituted more than a day's wages for male household heads. Thus, poverty and the racialization that often went with it also affected health and health care. Congested, crowded, ill-ventilated homes furthered the spread of airborne diseases. Much of the period's appalling infant mortality was caused by contaminated food, milk, and water, which led to mass contagion. It is estimated that at the turn of the century, "cholera infantum" (gastroenteritis) and common respiratory diseases carried off as many as 10 per cent of the nation's children under five years of age – and double that proportion, possibly one in five, of infants in the "dangerous" first twelve months of life.

Progress was evident by 1920, as vaccinations and antitoxins for such historic scourges as diphtheria became more widely available, yet respiratory and contagious diseases still accounted for nearly 23 per cent of all infant deaths, with diarrhoea and enteritis accounting for another 18 per cent.[24] Diseases thought to have been vanquished sometimes returned: the smallpox vaccine had been available since the late nineteenth century, yet an epidemic of it swept Windsor, Ontario, in 1924, affecting children most of all.[25]

Public health professionals realized that ill health and lack of medical care disproportionately affected the poor. Many expectant mothers saw a doctor only at childbirth, if then, and infants and children saw one only when they were very ill (and frequently past saving). For the working poor, medical attendance was often a last resort for any family member. Medical fees stretched middle-class household budgets as well, especially when children were young and vulnerable to the so-called childhood diseases that infested schools and neighbourhoods. A 1908 survey conducted by municipal public health nurses in Toronto suggested how much class mattered: on Eastern Avenue, a working-class district with a large number of the recent immigrants, the death rate for infants was 250 per thousand births, whereas

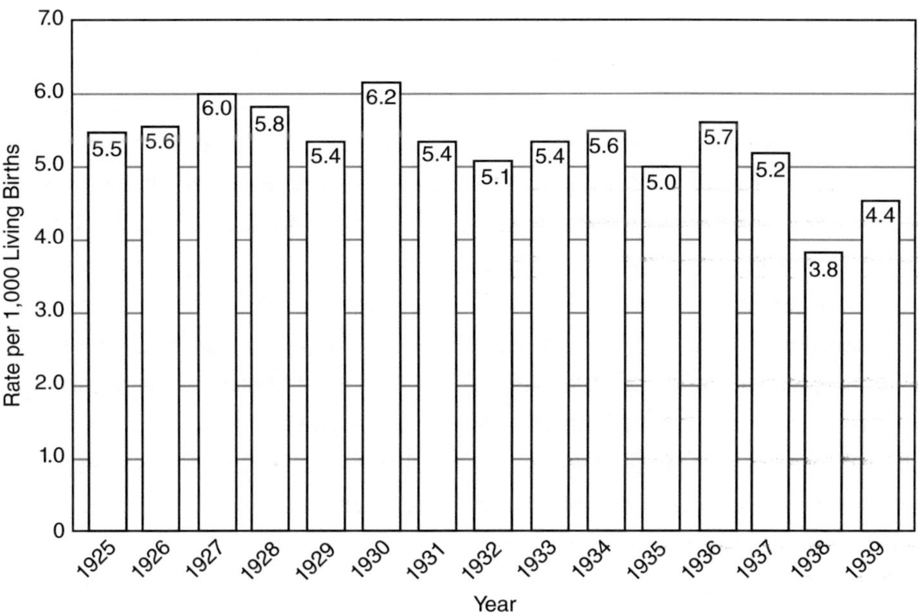

Figure 19.2. Infant mortality in Ontario, 1925–39.
Source: Ontario, Department of Health, *Annual Report* (1940).

in affluent Rosedale, it was 113.4 per thousand. While both figures are shocking, the poor area clearly suffered double the losses of the wealthier one.[26] Statistics such as these underscored that this was a class-defined mortality, afflicting primarily the ill-fed, ill-housed, and often recently arrived families of workers.

The Ontario government commissioned MacMurchy to provide the first statistical account of the extent and nature of the province's infant mortality. She published her first report in 1910, with revised editions in the subsequent two years. The reports galvanized child welfare advocates across the nation, providing a seemingly scientific (although largely impressionistic and moralistic) platform for a concerted child-saving campaign. The first report revealed that death had claimed 6,932 children under one year in the nation's wealthiest province in 1909 – more than 10 per cent of the 52,629 children born that year. Toronto alone suffered 230 deaths per thousand live births. Although those deaths were associated primarily with intestinal diseases, she emphasized that this mortality stemmed from a range of societal causes. Foremost were ignorance, poverty, and inadequate medical assistance. She concluded that only "national action, government action, collective action, not individual action, can save the baby."[27] As the first systematic, large-scale surveys of the matter, MacMurchy's reports set the tone and approach for the ensuing national campaign.

Public urgency about this huge waste of promising young lives was heightened by influential pseudoscientific theories, especially the distortion of Darwinian evolution known as eugenics. Early twentieth-century eugenicists, many of them members the educated middle class, sounded dire warnings about the imminent degeneration – even devolution – of Canadian society owing to ill-advised marriages and unconsidered reproduction, ill-informed childrearing practices, and the reckless intermingling of "the races" as a result of unprecedented immigration. The high casualties of war – some 60,000 "future fathers of the race" had been lost – magnified concerns about "race suicide" and the depletion of "the better stock" with whom white Anglo-Celtic middle-class Canadians identified. Recognizing the enormity of the problem, which threatened the social order, the reformers (who came from that strata) looked to the state to intervene in the process of social reproduction.[28] Contemporary critics understood reproduction in its broader social as well as its vital biological terms: it meant the "proper" socialization, physical maintenance, and emotional nurture of all family members. The traditional family, ever more so in these unsettled modern times, would play a crucial political role to ensure that healthy children were trained to model citizenship, the model entirely reproducing their own class and race-based ideals. Discounting the environmental and subjective components of health – factors that all too often hinged on economics – early twentieth-century doctors looked to explain infant and maternal mortality as a "failure of motherhood." Just as MacMurchy's reports made "ignorance" the primary cause, the physician-led child welfare campaign assumed that all mothers, especially those "marked" by racial and class inferiority, needed education, supervision, and regulation. Science and technology were visibly restructuring the world. In this future-oriented milieu, childhood had to be reconfigured to meet evolving social needs and aspirations. "Improper," inferior, and outmoded childrearing practices were major contributors to pending social degeneration.[29]

All-too-common intestinal maladies were the primary killers of infants, and this suggested the most promising and practical approach, given that medicine remained far more effective at prevention than care until the advent of antibiotic therapy during the Second World War. Doctors contended that most intestinal illnesses, often called "summer complaints" because their incidence peaked during that season, were directly attributable to the spreading practice of bottle-feeding. More and more women, they charged, were shirking their maternal – and "patriotic" – breastfeeding duties. If they did not yet know precisely why artificially fed infants were dying from intestinal infections or how to isolate the specific organisms, doctors were convinced of the link between infant feeding and infant death, especially in poor households. Few children in those households enjoyed regular medical supervision, and their mothers were thought to be particularly remiss about hygiene and sanitation. True improvement called for the kind of education and supervision that only medical professionals could provide. The "problem" thus defined was best approached through public education, attempts to regulate the milk supply, and the voluntary efforts by organized women that exemplified their maternal feminism: pure milk dispensaries, well-baby clinics, and home visits.[30]

These early voluntarist programs spread gradually through Ontario towns and cities during the war years. By 1920, as federal and provincial governments modernized and restructured their public health services, they found themselves being eclipsed by state public health agencies. The former, however, remained the campaign's hallmark services, because they exemplified state intervention in ways that upheld medical dominance. In deference to the medical hierarchy and fee-for-service model, these services were exclusively diagnostic. Even when doctors participated voluntarily, all patients were referred to private physicians for treatment. Many families lacked private physicians and thus were unable to follow up. But professional livelihoods and authority were left untouched. No doubt most parents were grateful for any measure of assistance, especially if they could not pay a doctor, and the health department's visiting nurses, local and provincial, were often warmly welcomed.[31] But the best intentions of child welfare advocates and public health reformers could do little to modify the entrenched "Canadian" middle-class perspective that found ignorance, filth, and parental – especially maternal – negligence endemic on struggling farms and in the congested homes of the working poor.

Fighting for "the Infant Soldier": War and Reconstruction

The First World War renewed public commitment to "regeneration" through reform, especially where the besieged family was concerned. Canadians who witnessed the federal government's management of the war economy, including such "philanthropic" programs as the maintenance of soldiers' dependents, were impressed by the peacetime possibilities that state intervention might offer.[32] The sociocultural and economic changes in the war's aftermath further opened the gates to a "scientific" mode of childrearing meant to serve a complex set of social relations. The war's exceedingly high casualties, along with public disenchantment with "tradition" in this newly modern age, transformed the child welfare movement's leadership. As Dr. Alan Brown declared, echoing the views of many other child welfare advocates,

> it is for us, here, highly to resolve that for every life given on these fields, for every body warped or maimed, a thousand young lives shall be raised into fuller freedom

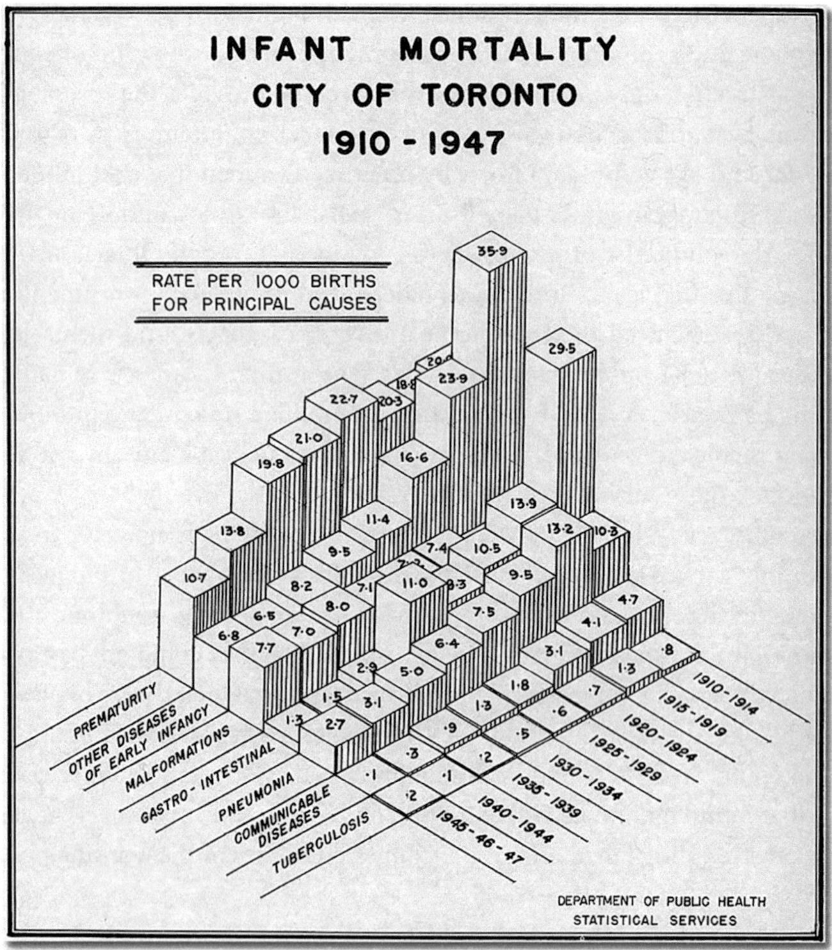

Figure 19.3. Infant mortality graph, Toronto, 1910–47. The graph shows the slow but steady decline in infant deaths as the so-called "diseases of childhood" diminished; note especially the drop in gastro-intestinal diseases, the foremost preventable fatality, from 29.5 to 1.3 per 1000 live births. Source: Toronto, Department of Public Health, Annual Statement 1947; Series 365, File 75.

> and health on this side of the ocean; that for every life sacrificed a thousand children shall have straighter, stronger, freer bodies, and straighter, stronger, freer spirits. This should be our living memorial to the men who died in the cause of democracy.[33]

The earlier female volunteers gave way to modern credentialed experts, most of whom were men. An insistent caste of such experts, drawn from child-focused disciplines but largely from medicine, elbowed its way ahead of parents, teachers, nurses, and volunteers to head the child-saving campaign. With its cultural emphasis on the "new" and the modern, the 1920s gave rise to a science of childrearing, a project in human engineering that appealed to increasing numbers of would-be progressives in Canada and across the Western world. Science would provide the best response to Ellen Key's plea to progressive reformers, on behalf of all children everywhere, to give their welfare utmost priority. The First World War thus transformed a loose coalition of reformers into a focused campaign under professional direction and, increasingly, state control. The key issue was maternal ignorance; the solution, education and supervision by health professionals; and the principal instrument, the state.

Integral to the Ontario government's reconstruction plans, the Division of Public Health Nursing was incorporated with that of Maternal and Child Hygiene in 1921, on the premise that the campaign's goals would be best attained through an extensive public health nursing network focused on "teaching health in homes, clinics and schools." Nurses specially trained in maternal and child welfare were sent in pairs to the farthest reaches of the province. Although there was no fixed plan, the aim was to have the nurses provide three months' demonstration in each locality. The new Division of Health Education was devoted entirely to promoting preventive measures through literature, exhibits, films, radio talks, and special lectures. By 1925, school health services had been removed from the Department of Education and folded into the Division of Maternal and Child Hygiene. In its first five years, that division took charge of the needs of Ontario mothers and children from conception through puberty, reinforcing the campaign's ideal that "the first point in any scheme for public health is emphasis on intelligent maternity ... children can grow up only once."[34]

Widely considered the prototype for municipal child welfare work, Toronto's post-war efforts were unrivalled anywhere in Canada. The city's Hospital for Sick Children played a far-reaching role in both the provincial and the national campaigns, thanks largely to its physician-in-chief, the indomitable Alan Brown. He had been directing Toronto's Division of Child Hygiene since 1914; once he became chief of the hospital in 1919, it was a simple matter to link clinic work throughout the city with the hospital. All milk dispensed at clinics was pasteurized in the hospital's laboratory. All doctors and nurses staffing the twenty-eight clinics established between the wars were trained and supervised through the hospital. By the early 1920s, Brown was child health consultant to the School of Hygiene at the University of Toronto and to the federal and provincial health departments, "thus enabling," in his own words, "practically all phases of children's work and problems to be guided from the children's hospital." Toronto also provided the best prenatal supervision in the province. The city's general hospitals opened prenatal clinics in the early 1920s, and the municipal board sent twenty special nurses on home visits to expectant and new mothers.[35]

Having pledged themselves to preserve infant life, doctors committed themselves to greater involvement in the physiological and emotional aspects of maternity. MacMurchy's influence again made itself felt. Her 1928 report for the federal government, *Maternal Mortality in Canada*, confirmed that Canada had the fourth-highest rate among the nineteen nations that could provide similar statistics. Ontario's rate, 5.6 per thousand, slightly exceeded the national rate. Doctors surmised that women's diffidence about prenatal care was the major impediment to be overcome by public education. With her characteristic bluntness, MacMurchy pointed out that "only 190 of the 1,532 dead Mothers had Pre-Natal Care."[36] A 1933 study conducted by the province's Division of Maternal and Child Hygiene confirmed the harsh realities. Despite all the advances in obstetrics, the establishment of prenatal clinics, the growing trend towards hospital births, and intensifying education campaigns, the five years between 1927 and 1931 showed no decline in maternal deaths: 17.7 per cent of all deaths among women 20 to 39 years of age resulted directly from pregnancy and childbirth, which made childbirth second only to tuberculosis as the cause of death for this age group. Thirty-seven per cent of those who perished had received no medical care during pregnancy; an additional 11 per cent had received "inadequate" care. Deaths were actually higher (5.7 per thousand live births) in hospital than in home deliveries (2.3 per thousand live births), and in urban than in rural areas. Professing themselves befuddled by the disappointing results, doctors offered no remedies beyond the further development of obstetric specialization.[37]

Only four of the 334 deaths recorded involved midwife deliveries. MacMurchy's follow-up national survey, dramatically titled *Need Our Mothers Die?* (1935), acknowledged that trained and licensed midwives were key players in the United Kingdom, several American states, and much of Europe. Canadian doctors recognized widwives as a factor in those places' lower rates, but they had been outlawed in Ontario in 1875, thanks to pressure from organized medicine.[38] The majority of births before the Second World War took place at home, with an estimated 40 per cent unattended by trained medical professionals. Women's organizations resolutely petitioned governments to permit midwife training and employment. Doctors just as resolutely battled against it. The CMA and its provincial bodies unequivocally opposed the licensing of midwives until 1988.[39]

Contemporary class, race, and gender constructions, rather than any truly scientific assessment of the health problems of parturient women, inextricably linked child and maternal welfare.[40] Modernizing motherhood appeared the best approach to producing healthy children who would adapt readily to the modern order and realize its splendid potential for the nation. Ultimately, doctors' ambivalence about the extent of their own responsibility for maternal mortality, their embrace of the all-encompassing "maternal ignorance" explanation, their resolute abhorrence of trained midwives, and their dread of "Bolshevist medicine" made the campaign's crucial prenatal aspects the least developed of all strategies. Attempts were made to improve obstetrical training and to provide a modicum of free prenatal supervision by nurses; but all the while, doctors protected their authority and earnings by means of the education panacea.[41]

Notwithstanding important federal initiatives immediately after the First World War, the primary responsibility for public health remained in provincial hands. Rhetoric aside, the federal government sidestepped accountability for creating, maintaining, or directing health care programs beyond committing itself to restricted lump-sum funding. Meanwhile, the expanding health and welfare needs of an increasingly industrial, urban, and multicultural society created an imbalance between the provincial and local governments' responsibilities and their ability to fund needed services. The publicity campaign waged by successive Ontario governments gradually persuaded a number of municipalities to take up child welfare and public health nursing work on a permanent basis. The overall results were disappointing. In 1921, the first year of organized provincial demonstration work, twenty-four municipalities had public health nurses and child welfare clinics; by 1938, the number had increased only to thirty-six, not including the twenty-eight clinics boasted by the city of Toronto. Although many municipalities declared their support for child welfare projects, most of them lacked the budgets to participate.[42]

The state's role was given much rhetorical significance in child welfare circles, but it was always cautiously defined. Governments at all levels gradually expanded their efforts during the interwar years, but their involvement centred on administration and direction of educational measures. Child welfare advocates never interpreted their favourite emblem of the child as national asset to mean direct state responsibility for the health of mothers and children. It meant, rather, a new obligation on the part of mothers regarding their duty to the nation; as MacMurchy insisted, the Canadian mother was nothing less than "the first Servant of the State."[43] Maternal education fit its proponents' status and outlook. It allowed doctors greater scope for their professional authority while protecting their livelihoods. It upheld traditional feminine roles at a time when enfranchisement and new education and employment opportunities challenged those constructs, decreeing motherhood to be a "national duty" and "a profession of the highest order." As doctors argued, "intelligent motherhood alone can give to the infant that which neither wealth nor state nor yet science can offer with equal benefit to mother or child."[44] The goal of modernizing motherhood dictated both the campaign's direction and its measures throughout its course. In a wider sense, it shaped new relationships between doctors and mothers, mothers and children, and, ultimately, women, the family, and the state.

Raising Baby by the Book: Educating Mothers

The response to the social/moral crisis signified by infant and maternal mortality was a maternalism depicted as regenerative while operating in a fundamentally regulatory manner. Medicine and the state would see that mothers were "educated" – trained, upgraded, truly reformed – so that families could meet the needs of modern industrial society while preserving their traditional form and relationships. Those who accepted their national duty would help minimize the "inefficiency and waste" that their children's poor health signified. Once their health was assured, they could "manage" them along the path to a healthy, productive, and useful adulthood. The state simply aimed "to see that the rights of the children are not ignored and that the mothers have the opportunity given them of learning how best to rear their children." The result would be the modern Canada that every progressive Canadian should aspire to live in, a nation that would take its rightful place in the post-war world order.[45]

In contrast to the philosophical, pedagogical, and often religious literature that had long informed its readers about childrearing, the modern version was turned out by medical professionals, and increasingly by pediatric specialists, as well as by psychologists, educators, and social workers, all of them with expertise in the new field of child development. Despite the scant, and often erroneous, science behind many of their theories, modern experts articulated concepts of childhood that would shape policies well into the twentieth century. The life course was a series of age-defined, interconnected stages, each critical in its own right and requiring its own mode of governance. And no stage was more critical than early childhood, an idea that underpinned Sigmund Freud's psychoanalytic theories, which were increasingly popularized after the war.[46]

The language of scientific childrearing openly reflected industrial trends, both in mechanized production and in such regulatory strategies as American engineer Frederick Winslow Taylor's "scientific management." Based on time-motion studies, Taylorist principles were applied to industrial production to heighten worker efficiency. Taylorism, however, made its influence felt in many areas far removed from the factory, including the home and the nursery. Experts embraced mechanistic conceptions of mind and body. The infant was likened to "a little machine." Clocks became the most important tools in infant care and early childhood training. Furthered by a rising mass media, these ideas encouraged the spread of practices attuned to new standards for evaluating, shaping, and regulating childrearing. Although prescriptive, the new standards were also normative, in that they looked to establish "norms" while measuring how some children deviated from them.

Much of the new science of childrearing emanated from Western Europe and the US, but Canadian experts were apprised of, and actively contributed to, the expanding knowledge base. Pre-eminent among these experts were three Toronto practitioners, all US-educated, who worked in different fields but shared an uncompromising commitment to "the normal child." Dr. Peter Sandiford trained generations of teachers over more than a quarter century at the University of Toronto's esteemed Ontario College of Education; his manuals for teacher education were adopted across Canada. He was a committed eugenicist and the chief advocate of racialized IQ testing, with dire results for the minority schoolchildren thus assessed. Psychologist Dr. William Emet Blatz, who also had a medical degree, inaugurated the experimental St. George Nursery School at the University of Toronto (later the Institute of Child Study) in 1926. On his own, and with his colleague Helen McMurchie Bott, Blatz produced internationally regarded studies of child behaviour, beginning with *Parents and the Pre-School Child* (1928). He also trained several generations of child development experts and teachers.[47] The ubiquitous Brown, the "father of Canadian pediatrics," set down his core principles in *The Normal Child: Its Care and Feeding* (1923), the original "made in Canada" childrearing manual, a bestseller reissued in several editions. Its simple title encapsulates the experts' shared premise: that the "normal child" could be "made" by applying science to childrearing.[48] All three participated in contemporary child welfare and public health reform programs, but Brown's pediatric training, experience, and inclination to take charge made him the most influential. Brown's influence spread widely and quickly through the state and academic networks of the time. During the interwar years, it was difficult to read or experience anything having to do with child health and welfare that did not bear Brown's imprint.[49]

Sandiford, Brown, and Blatz strived to establish science as the only viable foundation for the socialization of normal children, hence the ideal citizens of the future.[50] They absorbed the mechanistic language of their times: Sandiford contended that "all mental action" was based in "physical equipment," Brown likened the infant to "a little machine," and Blatz saw "the kitchen timepiece" as the key instrument in early childhood training.[51] The classroom, the nursery school, the doctor's examining room, the psychologist's office, the public health clinic, and the hospital – and ideally the home – were laboratories for their observation and assessment of children. The experts set more precise regulations and higher standards for the various phases of modern childhood, which they vociferously promoted as superior to the traditional childhood directed by "ignorant" parents. The mid-century years would give rise to a generation of parents and children trained "by the book" – so long as the experts wrote it.

The campaign's true "foot soldiers" were the public health nurses. More than most doctors, nurses had direct contact with mothers and children. Given the persistent, and insistent, medical hierarchy of the time, the relationship between doctors (almost exclusively male) and nurses (exclusively female) was a major point of contention. Nurses were to deliver the message while respecting the strictures defining medical territory. Doctors recognized that nurses were the essential liaison between mothers and medicine, but nurses and mothers were to be subordinate and obedient to their command; both were to follow doctors' orders. Nowhere was this more critical than in the matter of infant feeding.[52] Since the turn of the century, mothers of all social backgrounds had increasingly adopted bottle-feeding, despite medical admonitions against it, which became increasingly strident as the links between bottle-feeding and infant death were made clearer. While promoting breastfeeding, doctors took control of artificial feeding by insisting that only they could devise the correct formula, individually calculated, to ensure infant health. Until the advent of commercially prepared, medically sanctioned, government-regulated canned formula in the 1950s, the correct recipe for homemade formula was exclusively dispensed by doctors' prescription.

Because so many mothers enjoyed no more regular medical supervision than that provided by nurses in clinics and home visits, they made up their own unhealthy and frequently contaminated concoctions of unpasteurized cow's milk with unsterilized water and sugar. Some nurses felt compelled to provide unauthorized instructions for making adequate formula, and otherwise took steps beyond weighing and "checking" babies and urging physician consultation. Doctors' anxieties about such transgressions prompted frequent charges against "overstepping" nurses, to the point that the Division of Maternal and Child Hygiene need to constantly reassure doctors that the scope and function of public health nurses were carefully delimited and closely monitored. Nursing director Mary Power recognized that "in spite of the fact that both workers, public health nurses and practising physicians, are seeking the same goal by parallel roads, there exists in some places a lack of sympathy between the two groups which I am convinced is based on misunderstanding."[53] Nurses often felt that their child welfare victories had been won in spite of doctors, not with their support. They were "angels without wings," subject to exacting standards without the necessary resources, as well as to undue criticism, "often captious."[54] This was more than a problem of appropriate doctor–nurse relations, or even gender relations circumscribed by the period's patriarchal ideas: the conflict also stemmed from the clash between the medical autonomy signified by private practice and the perceived state encroachment that public health services represented to many doctors.

An abundant state-published advice literature, written largely by doctors, circulated widely during the interwar years. It was produced by medical professionals, new health and welfare agencies at all levels of government, and in conjunction with private insurance companies and voluntary health and social service organizations. The mass media ensured its pervasiveness: it was disseminated in the advice columns and "women's pages" of magazines and newspapers, in government-produced radio shows and short films, through mothers and "little mothers" (i.e., young girls') classes in settlement houses, by public health nurses holding "demonstrations" at baby clinics, in homes, at women's organization meetings, and at local fairs and festivals, including the annual Canadian National Exhibition. "Management," an almost solely masculine endeavour, was the core concept. Modern motherhood was infused with the spirit of industry, with its unrelenting demands for regularity, repetition, scheduling, systematization, discipline, and productivity, so as to effectively transform each child – it was hoped – into a "little machine," the modern prototype, the best of all possible citizens. The literature was at once advisory and propagandistic. It strived to establish doctors as maternal mentors, to associate maternalism with national interest, and to reformulate motherhood – and, consequently, childhood.[55] Science and state lent the weight of their combined authority to social constructions depicting the ideal mother, the ideal child, and ideal family relationships. Despite some attempts to make the literature more relevant to mothers on far-flung prairie homesteads and northern outposts and First Nations reserves, its embedded central Canadian, urban, white, middle-class biases shone through.[56]

While conceding the limits of education, and despite Depression-era constraints on all government spending, child welfare workers believed that their efforts were having a definite impact on their target audience by the close of the 1930s. Nurses observed that "we are dependent upon a public which is becoming increasingly more interested and better informed."[57] The press, too, sensed that parenthood and childhood were in transition. For some, the changes were not altogether positive, notwithstanding that more children were surviving the fraught early years. Even the more privileged children, critics worried, free from the need to earn, were now spending their childhood in rigorous training for greater things than simple play would allow: "most children nowadays ... never are children at all." Modern motherhood made childhood an intensely specialized and "managed" event.[58]

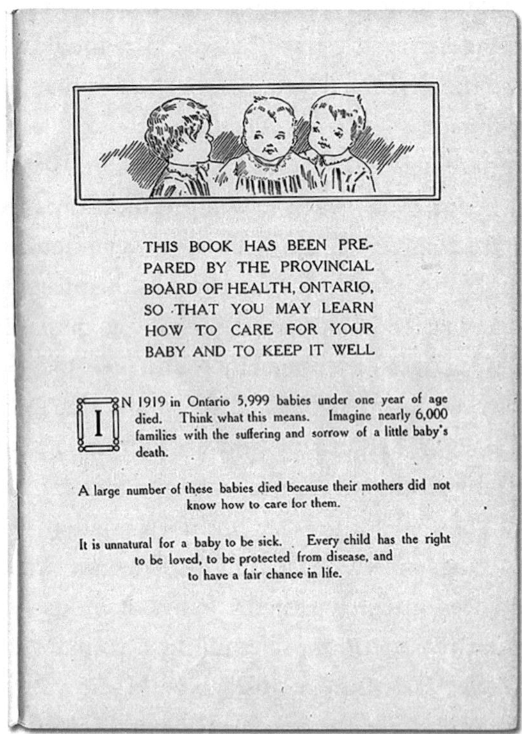
THIS BOOK HAS BEEN PREPARED BY THE PROVINCIAL BOARD OF HEALTH, ONTARIO, SO THAT YOU MAY LEARN HOW TO CARE FOR YOUR BABY AND TO KEEP IT WELL

IN 1919 in Ontario 5,999 babies under one year of age died. Think what this means. Imagine nearly 6,000 families with the suffering and sorrow of a little baby's death.

A large number of these babies died because their mothers did not know how to care for them.

It is unnatural for a baby to be sick. Every child has the right to be loved, to be protected from disease, and to have a fair chance in life.

Figure 19.4. Inside page from *The Baby*, 1920. Variations on this simple manual were published and circulated, free of charge, from 1914 through the 1950s.
Source: Ontario, Public Health Nursing Branch, Reference Code RG 10-30-A-1-3.

"What of *my* children?": The Campaign's Limitations

Contemporary assessments of the infant mortality problem regurgitated a complicated and confused logic that recognized the link between poverty and ill health but refused to see poverty itself as the primary cause. They also gave little thought to the actual costs of fee-for-service health care, which shifted regular medical supervision – exactly what they so vehemently promoted – from many families' reach. A 1918 Dominion Bureau of Statistics survey found that 46 per cent of the labour force of seven major industries earned less than $20 per week; a doctor's attention cost at least $5, not including drugs and dental care. Costs for medical attendance at childbirth ranged from $15 to $25 – a full week's wages for many breadwinners. The CMA consistently maintained that, compared with other professional incomes, the average medical income was "not excessive." Yet the 1920s were years of unprecedented medical affluence. The association's own study of two

Ontario districts served by 500 doctors reported that their average gross annual income from 1925 to 1930 was $6,262.78, comparing favourably with the $1,024 average annual earnings of industrial workers.[59] Organized medicine was profoundly opposed to anything resembling "state medicine," which was seen as a direct threat to professional autonomy and personal livelihood and emblematic of the "Bolshevism" that so frightened the Western world after the Russian Revolution. The profession's official stance did not waver throughout these years, even when, during the bleak Depression years, they could not deny the need for sort form of state medicine and the consequences of not providing it.

The politicization of child welfare made state medicine an increasingly important component of organized labour platforms. Labour commentators contended that the child welfare problem was systemic: under "a properly organized social system," children "with bodies ruined by lack of food and attention" would not exist. Workers were urged "to look at the deaths which are preventable and yet go on, and ask yourself is it worth wearing out the only life you have in bolstering a thoroughly rotten system, which exists for the benefit of the few?" Only by realizing their collective power could workers "forever abolish the specter of dread which now haunts every working-class mother."[60] In 1932, the Women's Canadian Labour Council passed a resolution supporting "the principle and practice of state medicine." The United Women's Educational Federation of Ontario and the United Farm Women passed similar resolutions and sent delegations to lobby municipal and provincial governments to "get measures through in the interests of women and children."[61]

Health inequalities were nowhere more apparent than in rural and outpost districts. The primitive outpost conditions of northern frontier communities, the so-called New Ontario, aggravated both health problems and access to care. The province established a skeleton framework of public health services for its sparsely populated regions in the 1920s, but only ten municipalities in all Ontario in 1936 had a full-time medical officer of health. Of a population of 3.6 million, only one third lived in areas where public health services had adequate direction.[62] Even in the more populous south, rural areas benefited from medical programs only to the degree that they were near an urban centre. In much of "new" Ontario, recent settlement meant there was little municipal organization. The few existing municipalities there could not finance child welfare efforts, and meanwhile, the federal and provincial governments were mired in a jurisdictional impasse. For many families outside the cities and larger towns, health care proved to be the scarcest resource of all. Organized medicine was so concerned about the scarcity of doctors in rural and northern districts that it repeatedly urged the provincial government to place and maintain recent medical graduates in these areas. The CMA's pleas went unheeded. Beyond conferring with

Ontario health officials, encouraging discussion in the Dominion Council of Health, and publishing some modified advice literature, the federal government took little action.[63] Throughout the interwar years, at least half the province lacked public health programs. While provincial administrators ascribed municipal reluctance to invest in public health to popular ignorance and false economy, the reports of local medical officers repeatedly underscored financial constraints as the reason.[64]

As they always had, volunteer groups attempted to fill the void where official agencies were unwilling or unable to provide medical services. The Red Cross Hospital-on-Wheels operated in Northern Ontario's most isolated districts. The first of these outpost centres opened at Wilberforce in 1921; there were twenty-nine centres by 1940. Red Cross nurses provided prenatal supervision and attended confinements when no doctor was available.[65] MacMurchy acknowledged the vital obstetrical work performed by Red Cross Outpost and Victorian Order (VON) nurses in remote communities. She refused to identify them as midwives, however, portraying them as nurses performing emergency deliveries on those rare occasions when a doctor was absent.[66] The conditions in which the Red Cross Outpost Hospitals functioned meant that nurses probably delivered the majority of babies born in their districts. The VON also delivered babies frequently, although they, too, were never sanctioned to do so.

It was often difficult to reach the neediest mothers. The problem of geographic isolation was compounded by their poverty and their burden of daily work. In her summary of conditions in the Thunder Bay district in 1922, a provincial nurse reported that the area's young women were typically in poor physical condition, with sorry results for their children's health and welfare. Referring specifically to the "entire lack of obstetrical care" in the area, she pointed out that "there have been many who have had six or seven children without proper care and are beginning to realize that many of their ailments and suffering have been caused by their lack." North Bay's district health officer observed that home visiting was "unsatisfactory" because of the poverty that prevented mothers from putting the nurses' recommendations into practice.[67] In North Hastings County in 1925, years before the Depression's onslaught, a nurse noted that "stagnation of industry, lack of education, bad housing, overcrowding, immorality, intermarrying and the many evils which follow in its train are some of the most outstanding problems of the district and are the direct result of isolation and poverty." Coupled with this was "the daily struggle for a mere existence on land so rocky that in some localities, farming is practically impossible." The nurses' moral sensibilities may have been offended by what they saw in some impoverished homes, but they were sensitive to the desperation of these people and to the magnitude of their daily struggle. They understood that destitution did not provide fertile ground for health education. Diagnoses of health problems and recommendations for treatment were futile for those who lacked the ways and means to obtain remedies. Under these circumstances, the nurses felt, there simply was "not much use in going back." Lessons in healthful living were best concentrated "on the small number who might be taught and helped."[68] More than any of the campaign's other participants, the nurses who took its precepts directly to families were forced to confront its limitations. For some poor families, their assistance was simply too little, too late. An expectant mother in Thessalon lost two daughters to bronchitis in one week. As the nurse recounted, "she had not had the doctor as she cannot afford it ... it seemed very hard losing the two children so near together. It was a pathetic sight to see the little body wrapped in a sheet lying on a wooden bench in the corner with a lamp burning at the head and a piece of new-patched quilt on the wall to improve the place and the mother's thanks for the help that we had been to her was very touching."[69]

In 1928 the United Farm Women of Ontario tried to politicize medical care for women and children in isolated areas by petitioning the federal and provincial governments. They stressed that "the chief cause of our appalling death rate of mothers at childbirth is economic, the remedy of which is slow." To address "this calamity," they supported public education and improved medical training and obstetrics, but they also called for maternity insurance and state placement and subsidization of doctors.[70] But the only request on behalf of rural mothers and children answered by the state was an enhanced commitment to health education. Attempts to make advice literature more relevant to rural and outpost mothers actually confirmed both the extent of their need and the state's unwillingness to meet it. A new "supplement" to MacMurchy's *Canadian Mother's Book* advised isolated women on "what to do if baby arrives before the doctor does." It must have been small consolation to anxious expectant mothers for whom this impending arrival was little more than fantasy. The few physicians settled in these districts were at times leery of attending to poor families, who might at best offer a couple of chickens in payment--especially during the Depression, when their own incomes were also declining.[71]

The economic collapse naturally made matters worse for families already on the margins. Identifying herself only as "A Worried Expectant Mother," a woman from Wabewawa in Northern Ontario wrote a heart-wrenching letter to the federal health department in 1932. She assured officials that she was not writing to beg food or clothing, "though I am in need of both." The imminent delivery of her sixth child was the "thing that worries me the most." At the age of twenty-five, she had already borne five children in as many years, all without medical help, at great cost to her health and with much risk to the infants. No doctor would come to her isolated homestead for less than $25, a sum far beyond her family's means. "It is a tragic thing," she concluded, "that the mothers of the land must suffer."[72] Similar plaintive stories from other parts of Canada are stark testimony to the connections between

Figure 19.5. Children lined up to receive their needles at a public health immunization clinic in the District of Algoma, 1932.
Source: Ontario, Ministry of Health, Reference Code RG 10-30-2, 2.15.3.

material circumstances and health. Poverty prevented the seeking of medical help and also kept parents from obtaining the necessary remedies. A 1930 department survey of twelve Ontario cities indicated that inability to pay delayed follow-up medical attention by a year or more in 45.5 per cent of cases.[73]

As efforts to subsume the Division of Child and Maternal Welfare within the federal health department commenced in the late 1930s – another Depression-induced measure – even the free information services were threatened. A Northern Ontario woman was unstinting in her criticism of what she regarded as the government's callous disregard for the nation's mothers and children:

> The government is a poor blind and horribly ignorant affair that is too busy with the petty details of its today to think of the nation of tomorrow ... if you were a bunch of real statesmen and nationbuilders rather than a scraggly bunch of cheap politicians you would be thinking of building the nation some backbone for its future ... do the doctors boss you or do you boss the doctors? Isn't it possible for you to pass a law saying that every doctor must examine every maternity patient before they are paid by them. You are in a position to allow clever young people to have healthy clever babies and a foundation for a grand new nation. What are you going to do about it?[74]

Women raised their children within specific material circumstances that defined their options, regardless of the "rightness" of any amount of advice or instruction provided by clinics, nurse visits, and, especially, heaps of prescriptive literature. In the depths of the Depression, "A Canadian Mother" aptly described the situation in Chatelaine, the nation's foremost "ladies' magazine." Struggling to raise five young children on relief with only two quarts of milk per week permitted, she was nonetheless the hapless recipient "of more free advice than any mortal on earth."[75]

In 1932, as the Depression deepened, the Ontario government's public health staff conducted a field survey of "the effectiveness of child health services." They confirmed that everywhere they visited, parents were very interested in the well-being of their children, and that publications, clinics, and nurse visits were increasingly reaching them. In qualitative terms, however, such services remained seriously deficient. In many Ontario towns, nothing was carried out on any systematic basis.[76] The findings persuaded the provincial government to set up a permanent rural health unit for the impoverished eastern counties of Stormont, Glengarry, Prescott, and Russell. It would emphasize child and maternal welfare work. Two thirds of the funds for the Eastern Ontario Health Unit would be contributed by the municipalities involved, and one third by the province. This centralization of child and maternal welfare efforts represented progress compared to the earlier, haphazard demonstration work, but it did not expand the scope or educational nature of that work. The unit's directors quickly conceded, as had the nurses many years before, that material deprivation made any such efforts without free services ultimately fruitless.[77] Only when the market failed doctors as much as other working Canadians did they invoke state responsibility for health care, and then only as an emergency relief measure. It was estimated that nearly 3 million Canadians were "medically indigent" by 1935. Managed by the Ontario Medical Association, the system implemented in the province that year was the largest organization of medical relief services in Canada, serving about 50,000 people per month. Once economic pressures affected their largely middle-class clientele, and consequently their own earnings, the resolutely anti-state medical profession was prepared to deliver medical care to many Ontario families who could not have afforded it in better times.[78]

As such stories demonstrate, educating mothers in scientific childrearing was far from easy. But education inspired both professional support and popular faith in an age of scientific advances and seeming progress. Education also corresponded to middle-class aspirations for reforming Canadian families. It enhanced a specific professional status while protecting the system. It fit well with the welfare ideology prevailing in state circles. Its comparatively low cost speaks for itself as a motivating factor. Despite unquestionably good intentions – to save mothers and babies

– issues of authority, control, and responsibility circumscribed campaign efforts and confirmed for many, participants and clients alike, that education, no matter how modern and scientific, could not be the foremost remedy.

Conclusion: Outcomes and Prospects

Several trends in public health advocacy during the interwar years held particular implications for infants and children. First, reformist language made children "national assets," hence state interests rather than merely those of the private family. The welfare of all children, therefore, was inarguably important to the modern nation-building project. Especially after the First World War, the state's critical "investment" in children equated the "best interests of the child" with those of the nation. The second trend derived from this newly politicized view of children, and, of necessity, their mothers: modern child welfare demanded a maternal education that only modern experts could provide. Consequently, the social and political status of professionals, especially in medicine, also expanded. To persuade mothers of their need for guidance and supervision – effectively, regulation – the state supported science with policy, legislation, and limited funding. The marriage of the modern state and modern science would modernize motherhood to make healthy children for a prosperous modern Canada.

To that marvellous end, experts began to play an unprecedented part in the historically private relations of parents (especially mothers) and children, with the equally unprecedented support of state agencies, some created precisely for that purpose. A combination of practical concerns with new thinking about children, braced by scientific advances, strengthened the popular appeal of such new approaches. This was by no means a linear process. The modernization of the parent–child relationship was mediated by the retention of those cultural patterns that parents found personally significant. If most mothers shared concerns for their children's health and an interest in learning how to ensure it, those most vulnerable – according to the doctors' own classifications of what constituted such vulnerability, deemed "ignorance" – were also least satisfied with the means undertaken to meet their needs.

The massive reorganization necessitated by Canada's participation in the Second World War meant that governments at every level directed all resources to the war effort. This world war, too, the second in little more than a generation, proved an important breakthrough for public health and child welfare. By its close, most Ontario towns were served by some form of public health nursing. More county health units were created in unorganized rural and outpost districts. Clinic and visiting nurse services continued, expanding into municipalities just acquiring their own public health organizations. Their function was educational, as always, but a 1946 amendment to the Public Health Act allowed each expectant mother one free complete prenatal medical examination by a physician of her choice. In 1950 the proportion of free prenatal examinations in relation to live births was 60 per cent. Maternal deaths in Ontario reached an all-time low in 1946 of 1.64 per cent, with the infant death rate falling to 18.8 per thousand live births.[79] While there was still a long way to go, Ontario families at mid-century enjoyed far more health care options than ever before.

Lessons learned from the Depression experience, full-scale state intervention for the war effort, and public pressure about post-war reconstruction plans together pushed and pulled the nation towards the welfare state. Canadians who suffered through the 1930s with inadequate state assistance were not going to sacrifice themselves and their children to another war unless money could be found to better their lives in its aftermath.[80] As such, Mackenzie King's Liberal government was at last prepared to consider coherent social security legislation. In 1943, McGill University social scientist Leonard Marsh presented his *Report on Social Security for Canada* to the House of Commons Committee on Reconstruction and Rehabilitation. The Marsh Report attempted to establish a justifiable social minimum for all Canadians and asserted that children "should have an unequivocal place in social security policy." After much criticism and consternation, the Family Allowances Act was passed in 1944, the first universal welfare legislation based on citizenship rights, and fundamentally for children's benefit. Produced the same year, Dr. J.J. Heagerty's comprehensive recommendations for both insurance and public health grants were jettisoned when the provincial and federal governments were unable to agree on fiscal terms.[81] Nor was organized medicine in favour. Despite their experiences during the Depression, the majority of doctors insisted that state control of health care would undermine its quality and consequently people's health. Hospital insurance measures would await the economic affluence and "baby boom" of the 1950s; Medicare would become another Liberal government project some twenty years later. For all its shortcomings, Mackenzie King's reconstruction package introduced social policies concerned with minimum entitlements for all, replacing moral judgment and "means tests" with the notion of citizenship rights that underpins the modern welfare state.

The Second World War was a watershed in the history of North American children, the portal to a more child-centred society than Canadians had ever before known. A half century of public concern and measured state involvement in child and maternal welfare was intensified by short-term reconstruction pressures and widening Cold War anxieties. These years heralded a period of relative prosperity that improved the material situation of many children, a crucial factor in improving health and welfare. Roughly a century after the original "cult of domesticity," more Canadians could approximate the Victorian ideal of the male breadwinner family. The "baby boom" seemed to affirm Canadians' belief in family. Children were now seen to be possessed of inalienable rights that applied to them *as children*.[82] A half century of interventions by experts and the state had reconfigured the meaning of child welfare, hence the cultures of motherhood and of childhood.

Despite repeated attempts to dismantle, or at least diminish, public health and welfare programs in recent years, what remains is resilient. We have coped with the unprecedented crisis that is COVID-19 without catastrophic outcomes. But the true health and welfare impacts on mothers, infants, and children have yet to be calculated. Relevant state agencies such as the Provincial Council for Maternal and Child Health (2008) issued detailed protocols for the care and treatment of pregnant and parturient women during an indeterminate time of health care rationalization due to the crisis. Medical researchers conducting limited studies have found that the stillbirth rate rose during the pandemic's first and most dangerous months. And mothers themselves, for whom fear, anxiety, and isolation are the historic traits of even "ordinary" experiences of pregnancy, parturition, and childrearing, are feeling the very special stresses of performing their role in unsettled times.[83] The situation may be unprecedented, the worries likely more than most contemporary Canadian women have had to confront. But this was the all too common lot of many mothers in the early twentieth century, and the spark that ignited Ontario's campaign to save mothers and babies. If the current crisis has proven anything, it is that investment in public health is never wasted: it may become a matter of outright survival, for individuals and nations alike. As we pick up the pieces in whatever post-COVID Canada will look like, we must attack the inexcusable and shockingly high infant mortality statistics that nakedly expose our historic neglect of First Nations, Inuit, and Métis mothers and children.[84]

QUESTIONS FOR CONSIDERATION:

1. What were some of the key developments in the early twentieth century in Ontario's public health system?
2. What were the major findings of Dr. Helen MacMurchy's reports, first published in 1910?
3. According to Comacchio, how did the First World War contribute to significant changes in public health associated with children?

4. Why was Toronto considered "the prototype for municipal child welfare work" following the First World War?
5. Describe the "modern" approach to childrearing following the First World War. How did it differ from earlier approaches?
6. What effect did the Great Depression have on child and maternal welfare in Ontario?
7. What were the major trends in public health advocacy during these years?

NOTES

1 I would like to thank this volume's editors, Dimitry Anastakis and James Onusko, for the opportunity to substantially revise and update the original chapter published in 2000. And especially for their patience and compassion about the travails of doing so in the time of COVID-19.

2 World Health Organization (WHO), "Naming the Coronavirus Disease (COVID-19) and the Virus That Causes It," https://www.who.int/emergencies/diseases/novel-coronavirus-2019/technical-guidance/naming-the-coronavirus-disease-(covid-2019)-and-the-virus-that-causes-it (n.d.).

3 The National Medical Care Insurance Act was passed in the House of Commons on 8 December 1966 (taking effect in 1968) by a vote of 177 to 2. Government of Canada, *Healthy Canadians: A Federal Report on Comparable Health Indicators* (2008), found 82.5 per cent "very satisfied" or "somewhat satisfied" with health care services. A Nanos poll commissioned by the Canadian Health Coalition (2009) found that 86.2 per cent supported continued public provision. See André Picard, "Transforming Medicine: Canadians Back 'Public Solutions' to Improve Care, Poll Finds," *Globe and Mail*, 12 August 2009, A15; and Picard, "The Lose–Lose Issue for Politicians: Canadians Love Their Medicare," *Globe and Mail*, 16 September 2015, A15.

4 As of 13 July 2020, there were 107,843 cases in Canada, with 8,788 deaths; see *Global News*, "Coronavirus Tracker," https://globalnews.ca/news/6649164/canada-coronavirus-cases. For the period 15 January to 12 July, there were 36,839 confirmed cases of COVID-19 in Ontario; total deaths were 2,722, of which 1,730 were in long-term care homes. Government of Ontario, "How Ontario Is Responding to COVID-19," https://www.ontario.ca/page/ how-ontario-is-responding-covid-19. As of 13 July 2020, WHO reported 12.8 million cases and 566,654 deaths globally; WHO, Situation Report 175, https://www.who.int/ emergencies/diseases/novel-coronavirus-2019/situation-reports. For the same period, cases reported in the US were 3,236,130, with 134,572 deaths: Statista, "Total Number of Cases and Deaths from Coronavirus (COVID-19) in the United States as of July 12, 2020," https://www.statista.com/ statistics/1101932/coronavirus-covid19-cases-and-deaths-number-us-americans.

5 In Ontario alone, the official estimate of death was "upwards of 10,000" for the 1918–19 wave; see Ontario Board of Health, *Annual Report* (1920), 43. The board became the Department of Health in 1924. See Mark Humphries, *The Last Plague: Spanish Influenza and the Politics of Public Health in Canada* (Toronto: University of Toronto Press, 2013), esp. ch. 9, 149–70; Esyllt W. Jones and Magdalena Fahrni, eds., *Epidemic Encounters: Influenza, Society, and Culture in Canada, 1918–20* (Vancouver: UBC Press, 2012); Esylitt W. Jones, *Influenza 1918: Disease, Death, and Struggle in Winnipeg* (Toronto: University of Toronto Press, 2007).

6 Ontario Board of Health, *Annual Report* (1920), 30.

7 Canada, pt. II, s. 9, The Department of Health Act, 1919; see "The Federal Health Bill," *Public Health Journal* 10, no. 4 (April 1919): 179–81. Early commentaries on the need for a federal department include: "A Dominion Minister of Health" [Editorial], *Canada Lancet* 37, no. 1 (January 1903): 243; and "The Lives of the People" [Editorial], *Public Health Journal* 7 (July 1913), 422–3; see also Humphries, *The Last Plague*, 149–70. *Public Health Journal* changed names several times, becoming *Canadian Public Health Journal* (1929–42), and currently *Canadian Journal of Public Health / Revue Canadienne de Santé Publique.*

8 Dominion Department of Health, *Report of the Deputy Minister* (1922), 22. The federal department's first deputy minister, Dr. John A. Amyot, was a veteran director of the Ontario health department; Ontario Board of Health, *Annual Report* (1920), 46. "Child Welfare Activities in Canada" [Editorial], *Canadian Medical Association Journal* 11, no. 5 (November 1921): 396. <first name?> Helen MacMurchy provides her own overview of the division's work in MacMurchy, "The Division of Child Welfare: Department of Pensions and National Health," *Public Health Journal* 19, no. 11 (November 1928): 514–21. The Department for Soldiers' Civil Re-establishment was integrated into the federal department to form the Department of Pensions and National Health in June 1928. The Canadian Council on Child Welfare, which received $10,000 annually in federal funding, became the Council on Child and Family Welfare (1931), then the Canadian Welfare Council (1935). See P.T. Rooke and R.L. Schnell, *No Bleeding Heart: Charlotte Whitton, a Feminist on the Right* (Vancouver: UBC Press, 1987), 93–4; and Cynthia R. Comacchio, *Nations Are Built of Babies: Saving Ontario's Mothers and Children, 1900–1940* (Montreal and Kingston: McGill–Queen's University Press, 1993): 96, 100–1.

9 Brenda Elias, "Moving Beyond the Historical Quagmire of Measuring Infant Mortality for the First Nations Population in Canada," *Social Science and Medicine* 123 (2014): 125–32. Elias (127–8) points out that, because Indian Agents were originally responsible for birth and death registration, and relied on pay and census lists, infant mortality rates were highly unreliable because deaths of children born before payment and enumeration were not recorded. From 1908, the Ontario's Births, Marriages and Deaths Act (8 Edwin. VII, c. 28, s. 3) applied "to land reserved for the Indians," but accuracy and reliability remained problematic until at least 1950. See also J. Smylie, D. Fell, and A. Ohlsson, "A Review of Aboriginal Infant Mortality Rates in Canada: Striking and Persistent Aboriginal/Non-Aboriginal Inequalities," *Canadian Public Health Association Journal* 101, no. 2 (February 2010): 143–8.

10 Comacchio, *Nations Are Built of Babies*, 43–51; Neil Sutherland, *Children in English Canadian Society: Framing the 20th Century Consensus*, 2nd ed. (Waterloo: Wilfrid Laurier University Press, 2001), esp. ch. 4, 56–70; Xiaobei Chen, *Tending the Gardens of Citizenship: Child Saving in Toronto, 1880s–1920s* (Toronto: University of Toronto Press, 2005). See also Denise Baillargeon, *Babies for the Nation: The Medicalization of Motherhood in Quebec,1910–1970*, transl. Donald Wilson (Waterloo: Wilfrid Laurier University Press, 2009); and Amy Kaler, *Baby Trouble in the Last Best West: Making New People in Alberta, 1905–1939* (Toronto: University of Toronto Press, 2017). On doctors in reform campaigns, see Angus McLaren, *Our Own Master Race: Eugenics in Canada, 1885–1945* (Toronto: McClelland and Stewart, 1990), 8, 28–9; and Mariana Valverde, *The Age of Light, Soap, and Water: Moral Reform in English Canada*, 1885–1925, 2nd ed. (Toronto: University of Toronto Press, 2008).

11 Dominique Marshall, "Humanitarian Sympathy for Children in Times of War and the History of Children's Rights, 1919–1959," in *Children and War: A Historical Anthology*, ed. James Marten (New York: NYU Press, 2002):184–99. In 1919, Eglantyne Jebb founded the Save the Children Fund in London, England, the first organized global movement for children; see Linda Mahood,

Feminism and Voluntary Action: Eglantyne Jebb and Save the Children, 1876–1928 (New York: Palgrave Macmillan, 2009).

12 Cynthia Comacchio Abeele, "'The Infant Soldier': The Great War and the Medical Campaign for Child Welfare," *Canadian Bulletin of Medical History* 5 (1988): 99–119; Deborah Dwork, *War Is Good for Babies and Other Young Children: A History of the Infant and Child Welfare Movement in England* (London: Tavistock, 1987); Comacchio, *Nations Are Built of Babies*, 54-6.

13 Ontario Board of Health, *Annual Report* (1920), 46.

14 In 1900, Swedish social activist Ellen Key published her book, translated into English by that title: Ellen Key, *Century of the Child* (New York: G.P. Putnam, 1909). It was issued in eleven languages; see Krista Lindenmeyer and B. Sandin, "National Citizenship and Early Policies Shaping 'The Century of the Child' in Sweden and the United States," *Journal of the History of Childhood and Youth* 1, no. 1 (2008): 50–62; and Shurlee Swain and Margot Hillel, eds., *Child, Nation, Race, and Empire: Child Rescue Discourse, England, Canada, and Australia, 1850–1915* (Manchester: Manchester University Press, 2010).

15 Ontario Board of Health, *Annual Report* (1919), 37–42.

16 Ontario Board of Health, *Annual Report* (1920), 28–30.

17 McLaren, *Our Own Master Race*, 30; Dianne Dodd, "Advice to Parents: The Blue Books, Helen MacMurchy, MD, and the Federal Department of Health, 1920–34," *Canadian Bulletin of Medical History* 8 (1991): 203–30; Dodd, "Helen MacMurchy: Popular Midwifery and Maternity Services for Canadian Pioneer Women," in *Caring and Curing: Historical Perspectives on Women and Healing in Canada*, ed. Dianne Dodd and Debora Gorham (Ottawa: University of Ottawa Press, 1994), 135–61. There is no extant full-length biography, but see the biographical sketch by Dodd, "Helen MacMurchy," in *The Oxford Companion to Canadian History*, ed. Gerald Hallowell, https://www-oxfordreference.com.

18 Brown received his postgraduate training in pediatrics under the renowned American pediatrician Dr. L. Emmett Holt at the Babies' Hospital of New York; he was consultant to the Toronto Board of Health and the federal and provincial Divisions of Maternal and Child Hygiene; physician-in-chief at Toronto's Hospital for Sick Children, 1920–50; and chair of the Department of Pediatrics, School of Medicine, University of Toronto. He was one of the founders of the Canadian Society for the Study of Diseases of Children (1922), later the Canadian Pediatric Society. The only book-length biography is A.B. Kingsmill, *Dr. Alan Brown: Portrait of a Tyrant* (Toronto: Fitzhenry and Whiteside, 1995).

19 Ontario Board of Health, *Annual Report* (1920), 46.

20 Comacchio Abeele, "'The Mothers of the Land Must Suffer': Child and Maternal Welfare in Rural and Outpost Ontario, 1918–1940," *Ontario History* 80 (September 1988): 183–205; Sandra Rollings-Magnusson, "Flax Seed, Goose Grease, and Gun Powder," *Journal of Family History* 33, no. 4 (2008): 388–410 at 394.

21 Archives of Ontario, RG 62, F-2, vol. 488, Field Reports, G. Bastedo, "Public Health Work in the Thunder Bay District," 19 September 1922; Ontario Department of Health, *Annual Report*, 1927, 70. See also Dr. E. Morgan, "Some Traditional Beliefs Encountered in the Practice of Paediatrics," *Canadian Medical Association Journal (CMAJ)* 24, no. 12 (1934): 666.

22 Rollings-Magnusson, "Flax Seed, Goose Grease, and Gun Powder," 396; see also Mona Gleason, *Small Matters: Canadian Children in Sickness and Health, 1900–1940* (Montreal and Kingston: McGill–Queen's University Press, 2014), esp. 46–84; and Comacchio, *Nations Are Built of Babies*, 210.

23 F.W. Jackson, "Racial Origin in Relation to Public Health Activities," *Canadian Public Health Journal* (*CPHJ*) 22, no. 6 (June 1931): 316.

24 Ontario Board of Health, *Annual Report* (1922), 12–13. The reportable diseases were smallpox, scarlet fever, diphtheria, measles, whooping cough, typhoid, tuberculosis, infantile paralysis, and cerebrospinal meningitis. In 1932, communicable diseases were still responsible for 600 deaths annually in Ontario, concentrated in the under-ten age group; see M.A. Ross, "The Mortality in Ontario of Four Communicable Diseases of Childhood," *CPHJ* 23, no. 7 (1932): 340.

25 "Smallpox is Still a Menace" [Editorial], *Canadian Journal of Public Health* 41, no. 4 (April 1950): 171–2. See the overview by Neil Sutherland, "North American Perspectives on the History of Child Health in the Twentieth Century," in *Healing the World's Children: Interdisciplinary Perspectives on Child Health in the Twentieth Century*, ed. Cynthia Comacchio, Janet Golden and George Weisz (Montreal and Kingston: McGill–Queen's University Press, 2008), 18–49.

26 Eunice Dyke, RN, "Sickness and Poverty," *Public Health Journal* 10, no. 6 (June 1919): 287–90. Dyke became Superintendent of Public Health Nurses shortly after joining the Toronto public health department in 1911; Marion Royce, *Eunice Dyke: Health Care Pioneer* (Toronto: Dundurn, 1983).

27 Dr. Helen MacMurchy, *Infant Mortality: First Special Report* (Toronto: Ontario Sessional Papers, no. 66, 1910), 17. Two subsequent reports were published in 1911 and 1912.

28 Dr. P.H. Bryce, "The Scope of a Federal Department of Health," *CMAJ* 10, no. 1 (1920): 3; Dr A. Meyer, "The Right to Marry: What Can a Democratic Civilization Do about Heredity and Child Welfare?," *Canadian Journal of Mental Hygiene (CJMH)* 1, no. 2 (1919): 145; Dr. Helen MacMurchy, "The Parent's Plea," *CJMH* 1, no. 3 (1919): 211. See also MacMurchy's reports for the Ontario government, "The Feeble-Minded in Ontario," in Ontario, *Sessional Papers* (Toronto: King's Printer, 1907–15); and MacMurchy, *Sterilization? Birth Control?* (Toronto: King's Printer, 1934). All these texts use blatant class and race arguments to explain perceived social degeneration. See McLaren, *Our Own Master Race*; Erika Dyck, *Facing Eugenics: Reproduction, Sterilization, and the Politics of Choice* (Toronto: University of Toronto Press, 2013); and Dyck, "History of Eugenics Revisited," *Canadian Bulletin of Medical History* 31, no. 1 (2014): 7–16.

29 Charges of maternal ignorance and negligence run rampant through the medical and social service journals: "Save the Children" [Editorial], *Canada Lancet* 40, no. 10 (1907): 934; "The Health of the Child" [Editorial], *CMAJ* 2, no. 7, (1912): 704; Dr. B.F. Royer, "Child Welfare," *CPHJ* 12, no. 8 (1921): 293; Dr. Helen MacMurchy, "A Safety League for Mothers," *Social Welfare* 13, no. 9 (1931): 184.

30 Dr. A. Brown, "Infant and Child Welfare Work," *CPHJ* 9, no. 4 (1918): 149; A.W. Coone, "The Child as an Asset," *Social Welfare* 1, no. 2 (1918): 38; and Dr. P.H. Bryce, "Infant Mortality and Disease," *Social Welfare* 1, no. 6 (1919): 133. Support for maternal education as the best solution also rose steadily: S.M. Carr-Harris, RN, "Reasons for Parental Education," *The Canadian Nurse* 22, no. 6 (1926): 312–14; A. Mackay, "Caring for the Children," *Maclean's* (15 August 1928), 25; Dr. E.K. Clarke, "Community Responsibility for Habit Training in Children," *Social Welfare* 13, no. 11 (1931): 228; K.W. Gorrie, "Parent Education and Social Work," *Canadian Child and Family Welfare* 11, no. 5 (1936): 33–4. See also Veronica Strong-Boag, "Intruders in the Nursery: Childcare Professionals Reshape the Years One to Five," in *Childhood and Family in Canadian History*, ed. Joy Parr (Toronto: McClelland and Stewart, 1982), 160–9; Harley D. Dickinson, "Scientific Parenthood: The Mental Hygiene Movement and the Reform of Canadian Families, 1925–1950," *Journal of Comparative Family Studies* 24, no. 3 (1993): 387–40; Katherine Arnup, *Education for Motherhood: Advice for Mothers in Twentieth-Century Canada* (Toronto: University of Toronto Press, 1994).

31 LAC, MG 28, I 10, vol. 35, file 168, Letters to the Canadian Welfare Council, from Norwich, Ontario, 25 August 1933; London, 21 August 1933; Rainy River, 1 April 1929. Similar grateful

sentiments are expressed in letters from Toronto, September 1933; and Kapuskasing, 16 December 1935. Although various government reports remark on the great number of mothers' letters sent to the council, few seem to have survived.

32 Dr. Alan Brown, "Child Health," *Journal of Public Health* 11, no. 2 (February 1920): 49. The war context is further developed in Abeele, "The Infant Soldier"; see also Dwork, *War is Good for Babies.*

33 Brown, "Child Health," 49.

34 Archives of Ontario (AO), RG 10, 30–A-L, box 11, file 11.3, typescript, undated, unsigned, "Maternal and Child Hygiene." Each of the eight public health nurses was paired with a Red Cross nurse and sent to a district for a three- to six-month tour. See also Ontario Board of Health, *Annual Report* (1921): 171; and Ontario Board of Health, *Annual Report* (1922), Report of Associate Director Beryl Knox, 177≠-9.

35 Brown, "Child Health," 53; George Smith, "The Result of Three Years' Work," *Public Health Journal* 9, no. 7 (1918): 310–14 at 313; E.M. Forsythe, "Child Welfare Clinics," *CPHJ* 9, no. 4 (1918): 170. By the end of the period the city employed ninety-six nurses.

36 Dr. Helen MacMurchy, *Maternal Mortality in Canada* (Ottawa: F.A. Acland, 1928), 61.

37 Dr. J.T. Phair and Dr. A.H. Sellers, "A Study of Maternal Deaths in the Province of Ontario," *CPHJ* 25, no. 12 (December 1934): 563–79. Phair was Director of Ontario's Division of Maternal and Child Hygiene.

38 Dr. Helen MacMurchy, *Need Our Mothers Die?* (Ottawa: Canadian Welfare Council, 1935), 5; Gwenith Siobhan Cross, "'A Midwife at Every Confinement': Midwifery and Medicalized Childbirth in Ontario and Britain, 1920–1950," *Canadian Bulletin of Medical History* 31, no. 1 (2014): 148; Judith Bender Zelmanovits, "'Midwife Preferred': Maternity Care in Outpost Nursing Stations in Northern Canada, 1945–1988," in *Women, Health, and Nation: Canada and the United States Since 1945*, ed. Georgina Feldberg, Molly Ladd-Taylor, Alison Li, and Kathryn McPherson (Montreal and Kingston: McGill–Queen's University Press, 2003), 161–88.

39 Cross, "A Midwife at Every Confinement," 149–51; Dr. H.E. Young and Dr. J.T. Phair, "Maternal Mortality in Canada," *CPHJ* 19, no. 3 (February 1928): 135; Dr. G. Fleming, "The Future of Maternal Welfare in Canada," Dominion Council of Health, *Report of the 26th Meeting* (June 1933), 3–4; Dianne Dodd, "Helen MacMurchy," 135–61; Kristin Burnett, "Obscured Obstetrics: Indigenous Midwives in Western Canada," in *Recollecting: Lives of Aboriginal Women of the Canadian Northwest and Borderlands*, ed. Sarah Carter and Patricia McCormack (Edmonton: Athabasca University Press, 2011), 157, 169–70; Wendy Mitchinson, *Giving Birth in Canada: 1900–1950* (Toronto: University of Toronto Press, 2002), 91; Cheryl Krasnick Warsh, *Prescribed Norms: Women and Health in Canada and the United States Since 1800* (Toronto: University of Toronto Press, 2010), esp. 80–115.

40 MacMurchy's most explicit statement of the link can be found in "The Relation between Maternal Mortality and Infant Mortality," *Public Health Journal* 16, no. 8 (August 1925): 379–82.

41 Dr. W.W. Chipman, "Problems of Obstetrical Practice," *CMAJ* 13, no. 6 (June 1923): 379–80; Dr. Grant Fleming, "The Future of Maternal Welfare," *CMAJ* 9, no. 2 (August 1933):162; Dr. J.T. Phair, "Radio Talk," *CPHJ* 18, no. 3 (March 1927): 133; "Preliminary Trends," *Canadian Welfare Summary* 15, no. 5 (May 1940): 55.

42 Ontario Board of Health, *Annual Report* (1922), 177–9; AO, RG 62, 1-f-1-b, box 473, Correspondence, "List of Municipalities Employing Public Health Nurses."

43 Dr. Helen MacMurchy, *The Canadian Mother's Book* (Ottawa: King's Printer, 1936), preface.

44 "Infant Mortality" [Editorial], *CPHJ* 6, no. 10 (October 1915): 510.

45 Dr. Helen MacMurchy, "The Baby's Father," *CPHJ* 9, no. 7 (July 1918): 315.

46 The classic recapitulationist text is G.S. Hall, *Adolescence: Its Psychology and Its Relation to Physiology, Anthropology, Sociology, Sex, Crime, Religion, and Education* (New York: D. Appleton, 1904). Hall was a founder of child psychology and a leading figure in the child study movement; see D. Ross, *G. Stanley Hall: The Psychologist as Prophet* (Chicago: University of Chicago Press, 1983), 332–3. See also Howard P. Chudacoff, *How Old Are You? Age Consciousness in American Culture* (Princeton: Princeton University Press, 1989), esp. 65–91; Teresa R. Richardson, *The Century of the Child: The Mental Hygiene Movement and Social Policy in the United States and Canada* (Albany: SUNY Press, 1989); and Dickinson, "Scientific Parenthood," 160-69.

47 William E. Blatz and Helen McMurchie Bott, *Parents and the Pre-School Child* (New York: W. Morrow, 1928). See also Theodore Michael Christou, *Progressive Education: Revisioning and Reframing Ontario's Public Schools, 1919–1942* (Toronto; University of Toronto Press, 2012), esp. 70–5; and Cynthia Comacchio, "Dr. William Emet Blatz," *The Oxford Companion to Canadian History* (Toronto: Oxford University Press, 2004).

48 Dr. Alan Brown, *The Normal Child: Its Care and Feeding* (Toronto: McClelland and Stewart, 1923); it was in its third edition by 1932; final edition, 1954.

49 Dorothy Sangster, "Alan Brown of Sick Kids," *Maclean's* (1 September 1952), 12; Dr. J.H. Ebbs, "Alan Brown, the Man," *CMAJ* 113 (September 1975): 557; Veronica Strong-Boag, *The New Day Recalled: Lives of Girls and Women in English Canada* (Toronto: Copp Clark Pitman, 1988), 168–9.

50 Sandiford's major work was *The Mental and Physical Life of School Children* (London: Longmans, Green and Company, 1913); there were four editions, the final one published in 1922. He was on the University of Toronto faculty for twenty-eight years, established the Canadian Council for Educational Research, and authored numerous research studies, books, and "textbooks internationally used." See "In Memoriam: Peter Sandiford," *Journal of Higher Education* 12, no. 9 (December 1941): 496. See also McLaren, *Their Own Master Race*, 61-3; Christou, *Progressive Education*, 17, 108; and Jason Ellis, *A Class By Themselves? The Origins of Special Education in Toronto and Beyond* (Toronto: University of Toronto Press, 2019), esp. 75–99.

51 Sandiford, *The Mental and Physical Life*, 3; Brown, *The Normal Child* (1926), 5; Blatz and Bott, *Parents and the Preschool Child*, 28.

52 AO, Pamphlet Collection, Dr. J.T. Phair, "Report of a Survey of the Services Extended by the Health Department of the City of Toronto," December 1943, 2; AO, 16383, 3–14, Ontario Welfare Council, *Annual Report* (1930), "Report of the Child Welfare Committee," 5–7; Dr. A.M. Jeffery, "The Private Physician Looks at Public Health Nursing," *CPHJ* 23, no. 10 (1932): 459–60.

53 Mary Power, "The Scope of the Public Health Nurse," Division of Maternal and Child Hygiene and Public Health Nursing, *Bulletin* (September–October 1924), 20.

54 B.E. Harris, "The Public Health Nurse Looks at Herself," *CPHJ* 23, no. 10 (1932): 467. See also Kathryn McPherson, *Bedside Matters: The Transformation of Canadian Nursing* (Toronto: Oxford University Press, 1996); and Meryn Stuart, "Shifting Professional Boundaries: Gender Conflict in Public Health, 1920–1925," in *Caring and Curing*, ed. Dodd and Gorham, 49–70.

55 The federal government's Division of Child and Maternal Welfare produced MacMurchy's series of seventeen *Little Blue Books* and various editions of her *The Canadian Mother's Book*, as well as the council's *The Canadian Mother and Child* and a series of newsletters titled *Prenatal Letters, Postnatal Letters*, and *Preschool Letters*. The *Letters* series circulated, with various updates, throughout the 1920s and 1930s, reaching an estimated one-quarter of all Canadian mothers; *The Canadian Mother and Child* remains in publication today. Advice manuals included Brown, *The Normal Child*, and Dr. F.F. Tisdall, *The Home Care of the Infant and Child* (New York: Harper, 1931). Brown and Tisdall, Canada's foremost pediatricians during this period, were colleagues at the Hospital for Sick Children; with Dr. T.H. Drake, they created Pablum.

See Dodd, "Advice to Parents," 203–30; Cross, "A Midwife at Every Confinement," 150–1; and Comacchio, *Nations Are Built of Babies*, esp. chs. 5 and 6.

56 Dodd, "Advice to Parents," 223–4; Cynthia Comacchio Abeele, "'The Mothers of the Land Must Suffer': Child and Maternal Welfare in Rural and Outpost Ontario, 1918-1940," *Ontario History* 80, no. 3 (September 1988): 183–205.

57 Toronto City Hall Archives, RG 11, box 1, file 1, Historical Material on Maternal and Child Health, A. Thomson, "Changing Practices in Public Health Nursing," undated manuscript, 1930s, 1.

58 "Leave Jack and Jill Alone," *Canadian Congress Journal* 10, no. 1 (1931): 41; [An Average Mother], "Psychology Does Not Always Work," *National Home Monthly* (December 1932), 54–5; Enid Griffis, "Who's Boss in Your Home?," *National Home Monthly* (March 1933), 55.

59 "Changes in the Cost of Living in Canada from 1913–1937," *Labour Gazette* (June 193), 819–21; CMA, *Annual Report* (1934), 62; David Naylor, *Private Practice, Public Payment: Canadian Medicine and the Politics of Health Insurance, 1911–1966* (Montreal and Kingston: McGill-Queen's University Press, 1986), 47.

60 J. Farrant, "What of My Children?," *Canadian Trade Unionist*, 30 August 1932.

61 "Women Urge State Medicine," *Canadian Trade Unionist*, 29 February 1932; "Women Are Needed in the Labour Movement," *The People's Cause*, 27 April 1926.

62 National Committee for Mental Hygiene, *A Study of the Distribution of Medical Care and Public Health in Canada* (Ottawa: Department of National Health, 1939), 82; Dr. D.R. McClenahan, "Observations on Rural Public Health Work in Ontario," *CPHJ* 23, no. 4 (1932): 170–1; Meryn Stuart, "Ideology and Experience: Public Health Nursing and the Ontario Rural Child Welfare Project, 1920–25," *Canadian Bulletin of Medical History* 6 (1989): 111–31; Abeele, "The Mothers of the Land Must Suffer,"183–205.

63 CMA, *Annual Report* (1931), 324; *Annual Report* (1933), 415; "Go Rural Young Man" [Editorial], *The Canadian Doctor* 5, no. 5 (1939): 21–6; House of Commons, *Debates* (3 March 1930), 223; D. Mickleborough, "Health Services Outside the City," *Social Welfare* 14, no. 6 (1933): 197.

64 Ontario Department of Health, *Annual Report* (1927), 24; *Study of the Distribution of Medical Care*, 84.

65 CMA, *Annual Report* (1934), 34; AO, RG 10, 30–A-3, box 16, Public Health Nursing Field Reports, Apsley file, June 1935; [An Ontario Outpost Nurse], "Experiences in a Red Cross Outpost," *The Canadian Nurse* 22, no. 2 (1926): 76–7; W.F. Marshall, "The Red Cross Outposts," *The Canadian Nurse* 26, no. 3 (1930): 128–30.

66 MacMurchy, *Need Our Mothers Die?*, 5; Cross, "'A Midwife at Every Confinement,'" 148; Zelmanovits, "'Midwife Preferred,'" 161–88.

67 AO, RG 62, F-2, vol. 488, Field Reports, G. Bastedo, "Public Health Work in the Thunder Bay District," 19 September 1922.

68 AO, RG 10, 30-A-1, box 1, Field Reports, E. Corbman, Hastings County file, 17 March 1925, 1–5; RG 62, F-2, vol. 488, Field Reports, G. Bastedo, "Thunder Bay District," 3.

69 AO, RG 62, f-2, box 488, Field Reports, I.J. Grenville, Report of Visit to Thessalon, December 1920–March 1921.

70 Department of Pensions and National Health, *Annual Report* (1928–9), 126.

71 Dr. Helen MacMurchy, *Supplement to the Canadian Mother's Book* (Ottawa: King's Printer, 1923), 139; Dr. W. Woolner, "Medical Economics in Rural Districts of Ontario," *CMAJ* 24, no. 3 (1934): 307; Dr. W.E. Park, "Rural Medical Relief," *CMAJ* 24, no. 4 (1934): 438; Dodd, "Helen MacMurchy," 139. Dodd points out that the cover page is inscribed with "For Distribution by Doctors and Nurses Only," signifying that it was not intended for regular circulation to mothers.

72 LAC, RG 29, vol. 991, file 499-3-2, pt. 2, Canadian Welfare Council, letter to Minister of Health, signed "A Worried Expectant Mother," Wawbewawa, Ontario, 10 July 1935.

73 Dr. J.T. Phair, "Effectiveness of Child Health Programs in Ontario by Survey Methods," *American Journal of Public Health* 30, no. 1 (1933): 127.

74 LAC, MG 28, I 10, vol. 35, file 168, Letters to the Canadian Welfare Council, RG 29, vol. 991, file 499-3-2, pt. 3, Canadian Welfare Council, from Sudbury, 8 January 1937. No reply was found.

75 "I Am a Canadian Mother," *Chatelaine* (April 1933), 18, 74, cited in Dodd, "Advice to Mothers," 121. A number of letters from dissatisfied mothers to the federal government's Division of Child and Maternal Welfare and the Canadian Welfare Council, especially during the Depression, similarly called for real medical care, not just advice; see Comacchio, *Nations Are Built of Babies*, 209–11.

76 AO, RG 10, 30–A-1, box 7, file 7, Division of Maternal and Child Hygiene and Public Health Nursing, Annual Report (1933), Dr. J.T. Phair, Director, and Edna Moore, Chief Public Health Nurse, "A Survey of the Effectiveness of Child Welfare Measures," 3.

77 AO, RG 10, 30-A-3, box 3, Eastern Health Unit file, "Varied Activities of Health Unit in 1937," newspaper clipping, unknown source; *Report on Child Welfare Work in the Eastern Ontario Health Unit* (1937), 1.

78 Canada, House of Commons, *Debates* (25 January 1935), 204; League for Social Reconstruction Research Committee, *Social Planning for Canada* (Toronto: T. Nelson, 1935), 390.

79 Ontario, Department of Health, *Annual Report* (1950), 6, 79–81; the department's *Annual Report* (1982) summarizes advances in public health during the 1940s and 1950s.

80 See the views expressed by organized labour in "What of the Future?" [Editorial], *Labour Press* (Oshawa), 9 February 1939; see also the satirical poem by Berton Brady, "Owed to the Future," *Labour Leader* (Oshawa), 16 June 1938.

81 Many of these ideas were proposed in A.E. Grauer, *Public Health: A Study Prepared for the Royal Commission on Dominion–Provincial Relations* (Ottawa: King's Printer, 1939). See Dennis Guest, *The Emergence of Social Security in Canada*, 3rd ed. (Vancouver: UBC Press, 1997), 149–50.

82 Marshall, "Humanitarian Sympathy for Children," 184–99; Jane Helleiner, "'The Right Kind of Children': Childhood, Gender and 'Race' in Canadian Postwar Political Discourse," *Anthropologica* 43, no. 2 (2001): 143–52.

83 Ontario Department of Health and Long-Term Care, Provincial Council for Maternal and Child Health, *Maternal-Neonatal COVID-19 General Guideline*, 30 April 2020 (Toronto: PCMCH, 2020), 23 pp., https://www.pcmch.on.ca/wp-content/uploads/2020/05/MatNeo-COVID-19-Guide_V4.pdf. The limited study was conducted at St. George's University Hospital, London, UK: see Asma Khalil, Peter von Dadelszen, Tim Draycott, Austin Ugwumadu, Pat O'Brien, and Laura Magee, "Change in the Incidence of Stillbirth and Preterm Delivery During the COVID-19 Pandemic," *Journal of the American Medical Association* (online), 10 July 2020: 10.1001/jama.2020.12746. The incidence of stillbirth was significantly higher during the early pandemic period [9.31 per 1,000 births] than pre-pandemic [2.38 per 1,000 births]. On women's experiences, see Sarah MacMillan, "Covid-19 an Added Stress for Sudbury Woman Preparing to Give Birth," *CBC News*, 6 April 2020, https://www.cbc.ca/news/canada/sudbur/sudbury-covid-19-pregnancy-1.5519433.

84 The current (2019) rate in Canada is 3.7 per 1,000 live births; for Inuit the rate is 3.9 times higher than the national rate; for First Nations, it is 2.3 times higher, and for Métis, 1.9 times higher; see https://www.canada.ca/en/public-health/services/publications/science-research-data/inequalities-infant-mortality-infographic.html.

CHAPTER TWENTY

The Birch Battles: Day Care and the Welfare State in 1970s Ontario

LISA PASOLLI

In late 1974, officials in Ontario's Ministry of Community and Social Services (ComSoc) were circulating a draft of a document called "A Philosophical Approach to Day Care Services." The ministry's decision to develop such a document was a sign of the times. The rapid growth in the numbers of working mothers in the province, as well as the rising tide of feminist consciousness that argued that those mothers deserved more and better access to day care, raised urgent questions about Ontario's responsibilities in the child care arena. Unsurprisingly, then, the philosophical statement was effectively a long list of queries. Should day care be "child-focused" and concerned with the "developmental experience" of preschool children, or should it "primarily be seen as a support for working mothers?" For that matter, "are the needs of parents and children compatible?" Should day care be universally available, or targeted to those with financial or social need? If subsidies are offered, how much of the cost should they cover and who should be eligible? Officials questioned whether day care was the best use of government funds. Would it be more desirable, they asked, to create programs such as "pensions for housewives" and allow mothers to stay home to care for their young children? "To what extent," the draft asked, "should government be responsible for the provision of day care for the children of working mothers? Is it legitimate to spend public funds to free women to work? Do women have a *right* to work at the expense of publicly funded day care?"[1]

It is not entirely clear whether the philosophical statement made it past the draft stage, or what kind of impact it had within the ministry. The importance of this document, however, lies in the fact that these questions were even being asked. That the provincial government was seriously considering its responsibilities to working mothers and their children represented a significant departure from decades of policy that had treated day care as an afterthought and considered it a residual service for "needy" families. This draft statement, in other words, was symbolic of the shift taking place in Ontario's child care landscape in the early 1970s. For the first time since the Second World War – when the province, sharing the cost with the federal government, had temporarily established a publicly funded day nursery program for mothers working in war industries – Ontario was being forced to grapple seriously with its approach to day care policy. Working mothers and child care advocates, drawing on the energy and theorizing of what is usually referred to as the "second wave" of feminism,[2] had begun to call on the provincial government to work towards a universal day care program that would buttress mothers' rights to workplace equality and young children's rights to quality care. For the sake of a fair and equitable society, they said, it was time to leave behind the idea that the care of children was solely a private and familial responsibility, and to create social policy that recognized care as a public good.

There is much that could be said about the ways in which feminist advocacy and activism permanently recast Ontario child care politics in the late 1960s and early 1970s. As a way to illustrate the broader contours of this era, however, this chapter narrows in on a series of events that unfolded in 1974–75. In the spring of 1974, the Provincial Secretary of Social Development Margaret Birch, a cabinet member in Premier William (Bill) Davis's Progressive Conservative government, proposed a series of day care reforms. The Birch proposals, as they became known, would have changed some of the regulations of the Day Nurseries Act, provincial legislation that had been in force since 1946. These seemingly small regulatory changes would in fact have had significant consequences for day care services in the province. Birch proposed to relax the standards around staff/child ratios, staff qualifications, and physical infrastructure requirements regarding fire safety and kitchen facilities. Such changes, she said, would make day care services more cost-effective, thus promoting a much-needed expansion of services across the province. But day care workers, parents, municipal social service officials, feminist activists, and many others with a vested interested in Ontario child care were appalled at Birch's plan. In response, a campaign was launched by a remarkable coalition of advocates, who organized petitions, rallies, educationals, and other initiatives to fight the Birch proposals. The public outcry was intense enough that the ComSoc minister, René Brunelle, appointed an Advisory Council on Day Care to take stock of the provincial approach to day care policy. For these activists, and for the members of the Advisory Council, what was at stake in the Birch battles was far more than regulatory details. Advocates argued that the proposed reforms threatened the quality and safety of day care services and that they would provide the most benefit to commercial and for-profit day care. They viewed the Birch proposals as linked to the government's privatization agenda and warned that the changes would lodge the care of children even more deeply within the familial and market spheres, thus contributing to women's subordination. Fighting the Birch proposals, then, was about insisting that day care be delivered as a high-quality public service in recognition of the rights of children and their working mothers.[3]

As a defining moment in Ontario child care politics, the Birch battles also illuminate crucial elements in the evolution of the provincial welfare state in the post-war period. Like Lara Campbell's chapter on unemployment relief in the Great Depression, this chapter sees the origins, implementation, and administration of social welfare programs as reflections of "social citizenship," which British political theorist T.H. Marshall defined as encompassing the rights to economic well-being and security.[4] Put another way, social citizenship was about who had access to the *care* provided by social welfare programs. As political scientists Jane Jenson and Mariette Sineau explain, welfare programs might "redistribute the risk of differential needs for care" (as with family policies meant to assist with the costs of raising children), improve the quality of care (as with regulating service providers), or "reduce dependence and sustain autonomy" (as with pensions for the elderly).[5] Social welfare programs, in other words, are fundamentally about redistributing care among states, markets, communities, and families so that all citizens are able to live, as Marshall said, "the life of a civilized being according to the standards prevailing in the society."[6]

Campbell's analysis and James Struthers's more general history of welfare policy in chapter 23 make the crucial point that social citizenship has always been contested. Ontarians' abilities to make claims on the state depended on their gender, marital status, nationality, and race, as well as on how, in particular historical contexts, those categories shaped ideas about deservedness and entitlement. If we think about social citizenship as a matter of access to and redistribution of care, it is particularly important to apply a gender lens. After all, the work of caring, especially of children but also of the aged, the ill, and people with disabilities, has been (and continues to be) considered women's responsibility, something they are expected to perform as unpaid labour. Such expectations very often act as barriers to women's access to educational and job opportunities, and gendered assumptions about motherhood and care also follow women into the paid labour force, where they are treated as second-class workers. Feminist theorists argue, therefore, that making care a public good – recognizing its value and using the welfare state to ensure it is more equally shared between women, men, communities, and society – is one of the crucial levers for ensuring women's equality.[7]

What gender-equitable care policy actually looks like in practice, however, is a matter of much debate. In the history of social welfare in Ontario, attempts to redistribute care have had mixed results at best. Take, for example, the history of Ontario Mothers' Allowances. Introduced in 1920 as the province's first income assistance program, mothers' allowances provided widowed mothers with a modest monthly cheque in recognition of the importance of their care work in the home. But the program was fraught with contradictions, as James Struthers's and Margaret Little's work has shown.[8] On the one hand, the allowances had the potential to recast mothers' care work as a basis for social citizenship alongside the more readily accepted social rights afforded to male breadwinners.[9] On the other hand, the receipt of an allowance placed mothers in a "moral relationship with government," one laden with conditions about proper feminine behaviour. The imperatives of welfare delivery in the early twentieth century also said that dependency was to be avoided at all costs, so mothers were encouraged to take on part-time work to supplement the allowance and maintain their work ethic.[10] In other words, public recognition of mothers' caregiving was tenuous and came with patriarchal strings attached. This experiment in redistributing care resources, while it did offer a welcome measure of financial relief to (some) widowed mothers, did not result in a fully realized version of social citizenship for women.

The social and economic context in which the Birch battles unfolded was very different from the one that had given rise to mothers' allowances in 1920, but the essential policy question remained the same. Was there a role for the state in providing for and redistributing the care of young children? And if so, how should that care be organized to best ensure security and well-being for those children, their mothers, and other family members? With mothers' allowances, the answer was to provide money to allow mothers to care for their children at home. While proposals for that kind of maternalist policy approach did not disappear,[11] a different set of circumstances in the 1960s and 1970s gave rise to demands that care be redistributed by means of a publicly funded, accessible, and high-quality child care system that would allow mothers to engage in meaningful employment. For one thing, working motherhood was becoming the norm.[12] While women's labour force participation grew steadily from the Second World War, in the 1960s what was particularly notable was the number of mothers taking up paid work. By 1973, 40 per cent of women with children were in the paid labour force, and those numbers were only rising. The growth of day care services had not kept up, however: most of those mothers had trouble accessing reliable and high-quality care, which meant they faced constant worries about the well-being of their children and were sacrificing (or being denied) opportunities for higher-paying and full-time jobs because of inadequate care arrangements.[13] At the same time, as Struthers's chapter outlines, single mothers were swelling the ranks of welfare recipients, and their lack of access to day care made it difficult for them to escape from poverty. For feminists, a public approach to child care offered a solution to these intertwined problems.

Day care advocates, though, were up against the still-powerful societal belief that the care of young children belonged in the home – that if a mother "chose" to work then she ought to rely on family or make private arrangements to pay for babysitting. In the early 1970s, resistance to day care policy was also part of a more general call for restraints on welfare spending. Struthers explains that the backdrop for understanding social welfare policy in this era was "deteriorating economies, ballooning budget deficits, and a growing backlash against the expanding army of dependent poor."[14] The Birch battles were thus fraught with questions about welfare entitlement, gender, care, and social citizenship.

For all of these reasons, and because of the remarkable degree of public engagement around an issue that was usually pushed to the periphery of social policy debates, the Birch battles deserve to be untangled from the broader history of day care in Ontario. In this chapter, the focus is on the public debate about day care, so newspapers, transcripts of debates in the Legislative Assembly, and the archival records of advocacy groups comprise much of the primary source material. Another important source is the records of the Advisory Council on Day Care, which began meeting regularly in August 1974. Although its mandate was somewhat vague, the council members worked hard to collect views on day care from around the province, and their archival records therefore provide insight into the perspectives of individual parents, day care and social service groups, and various bureaucrats with knowledge of the provincial day care bureaucracy (the Philosophical Statement, for example, was presented to the Advisory Council by officials from ComSoc). Taken together, these sources reveal a wide-ranging opposition to the Birch proposals that united sometimes unlikely allies. In the bigger picture, they show that the Birch battles, at their core, hinged on the question of whether the care of working mothers' young children was a private responsibility or a public one.

Background to the Birch Battles: Day Care as Welfare

Feminists in the late 1960s and 1970s viewed a publicly funded universal child care program as a social citizenship right. However, they were up against a longstanding belief that day care was a targeted and residual service for the poor and "needy." Day care programs had existed in Ontario since the nineteenth century, but they operated on the margins of social policy. Most services were charitable and were run by religious organizations, motivated by pity for impoverished working mothers who had been driven into the labour force by economic desperation.[15] This approach prevailed for the first decades of the twentieth century, until the explosion of women's paid employment in the Second World War between 1939 and 1945 disrupted people's assumptions about day care. To facilitate mothers' wartime employment, the federal government in Ottawa introduced the Dominion–Provincial Wartime Day Nurseries Agreement (WDNA) and offered to share the costs with the provinces to set up public child care programs. Aside from Ontario, the only other province to take the federal government up on its offer was Quebec. Ontario went the furthest, however, establishing twenty-eight day nurseries (for preschool-aged children) and dozens of before- and after-school programs. The widespread acceptance of working motherhood and Ontario's embrace of the WDNA seemed to offer the potential to radically rethink public responsibility for child care and perhaps even to make it a permanent part of the post-war social policy landscape. The respectability of child care in Ontario was bolstered by the fact that Dr. William Blatz and his colleagues at the University of Toronto's Institute of Child Study played a central role in establishing WDNA guidelines and nursery programming.[16] From the federal government's perspective, however, the WDNA was an emergency measure that was only appropriate for the duration of the war. Ottawa announced the end of the program at the end of 1945 and cut off funding in April 1946. The decision to terminate the WDNA was rooted in the belief that the care of children was still, fundamentally, the responsibility of mothers – and that, in the post-war years, the best place for mothers was in their homes caring for their young children. In that sense, the cancellation of the WDNA was linked to the broader imperatives of post-war social welfare policy, which was driven by assumptions that society worked best when designed around families with a male breadwinner and a female homemaker.[17]

This gendered policy framework, however, did not necessarily reflect the reality for Ontario families. Reliable access to high-quality day care services had made a profound difference in the lives of many working mothers, and the short-lived experiment in wartime care shifted the terrain of child care politics. One survey of 542 Toronto mothers who had used day nurseries during the war revealed that all but fifty-eight of them "intended to continue working indefinitely," in most cases because they simply needed the money.[18] When Ottawa's funding was withdrawn, many of those mothers and their allies organized a campaign to save the day nurseries. They established the Day Nurseries and Day Care Parents Association in 1946 and for the following five years lobbied the provincial and municipal governments to sustain support for day nursery services. And they were fairly successful: historical sociologist Susan Prentice, who has documented the efforts of the Parents Association, shows that their efforts persuaded the City of Toronto to maintain or open twelve day nurseries and three day care centres. More importantly, Prentice credits pressure from the Parents Association with convincing the province to pass the 1946 Day Nurseries Act. Besides establishing licensing and regulatory standards, the act provided for cost sharing of day nursery services between the province and municipalities, an arrangement that was unique in Canada.[19]

The Day Nurseries Act created the possibility that municipalities and the province could work together to set up publicly funded child care services, but in reality, the take-up was limited in the 1940s and 1950s. The province, Prentice shows, was a "grudging supporter of child care" and wanted to keep the services it funded as narrow and targeted as possible. Even in the context of new legislation and funding arrangements, the assumption remained that day care was for "needy" mothers in need of social rehabilitation. City officials in Toronto, for example, monitored the users of day nurseries closely to ensure that they were "deserving" candidates for admission, which usually meant making judgments about the legitimacy of mothers' employment – that is, that they were working out of "need" rather than selfishness.[20] Nursery school and kindergarten programs expanded during the 1950s and 1960s, but such programs were mostly about part-day enrichment and school preparation for middle-class families and were not necessarily useful for working parents. The care of the young children of working mothers was largely still considered to be a residual and welfare-oriented service.[21]

The welfare logic of day care in Ontario was reinforced in the mid-1960s when federal funding once again became available through the Canada Assistance Plan (CAP). Part of Ottawa's "War on Poverty," the CAP was meant to consolidate spending on public assistance and expand cost-sharing to programs such as mothers' allowances, child welfare, and social administration, previously areas of exclusive provincial responsibility.[22] Although day care was not one of Ottawa's priorities, many provinces, Ontario included, used CAP funding to establish and expand provincial day care subsidy programs.[23] There were strict conditions on how CAP funds could be spent, however, so this new injection of day care funding was restricted to those in need or likely to become in need. This meant that in Ontario, funding was delivered directly to families deemed eligible by a needs test; the focus of public spending was on solving individual family poverty rather than supporting day care programs and services. In other words, funding for day care remained within the framework of welfare.[24] The new funding arrangements to which CAP gave rise did result in a modest expansion of day care spaces in Ontario, since municipalities' share of funding was reduced from 50 per cent to 20 per centt. The number of day care services grew even more after 1972, when changes to CAP extended shareable costs beyond salaries to "all costs applicable to the provision of day care services."[25] Even then, however, the number of day care spaces in the province fell far short of the need, and the welfare orientation continued to define the still-limited public provision of child care in Ontario.

Feminism and the Changing Politics of Day Care

Such was the state of affairs that Premier Bill Davis inherited when he took office in October 1971. Davis was the fourth in a consecutive line of Progressive Conservative premiers, following George Drew (1943–49), Leslie Frost (1949–61), and John Robarts (1961–71). He was the last in what historians refer to as the "Tory dynasty" that lasted until 1985, one in which the Conservatives "adroitly and continuously recast themselves to match Ontario's changing needs, composition, and outlook." Davis's government is often characterized as "Red Tory," meaning that it was conservative but embraced elements of reformism. Political scientist Cheryl Collier suggests that Davis's government was pragmatic rather than ideological and that it "balanced both progressive and conservative approaches" to meet prevailing public opinion.[26]

Davis's attentiveness to public opinion meant that he could not ignore the demands of the feminist movement, which had emerged as a powerful societal force by the time he took office in 1971. His biographer, Claire Hoy, notes that Davis was "uncomfortable personally" with women stepping outside the bounds of traditional expectations, but he recognized that his party had to take women's issues "seriously."[27] Feminist activism, protest, and advocacy had transformed politics in virtually every arena by the early 1970s, and this had put day care on the public agenda.[28] Perhaps the most powerful symbol of this shift in day care politics was the 1970 report of the Royal Commission on the Status of Women, which called on the federal government to establish a national Day Care Act as an essential ingredient of women's equality.[29] Unwilling to wait for government policy to catch up, however, grassroots feminist organizations around the country were also taking matters into their own hands by creating community-based child care services. University campuses, in particular, were hotspots for action. At the University of Toronto in 1969, for example, a group of women's liberationists occupied a house at 12 Sussex Drive and established the Campus Cooperative Community Daycare. Their occupation led the following year to a sit-in at Simcoe Hall – where the university president's office is located – to demand financial support and guarantee of space for on-campus day care. In 1972, another occupation – this one of the campus Meteorological Observatory – was sparked by demands for even more day care spaces; in tandem with this were protracted conflicts with the province about licensing, staff training, and physical regulations.[30] Campus activism had ripple effects that were felt throughout Toronto; those involved in the occupations went on form the Daycare Organizing Committee in 1972, which had a broad mandate to push for free universal child care and also provided practical advice to community groups in Toronto looking to set up day care services.[31]

This grassroots action in Toronto is just one example of the feminist child care initiatives that were widespread and dynamic throughout Ontario in the late 1960s and early 1970s. Drawing on feminist theory that saw women's place in the private, patriarchal nuclear family as the source of their oppression, groups of women (and men) prioritized day care as a way to collectively provide care and thus free women for work and education. They established childcare cooperatives, organized community-based centres, and launched educational campaigns.[32] In addition to providing on-the-ground services at a time when day care needs were urgent, feminists came to realize that they needed to "get involved with the state."[33] Many families relied on a provincial subsidy to be able to afford day care, but that subsidy was an inadequate solution to the widespread lack of access to high-quality care services. Subsidies to low-income parents, advocates said, did nothing to increase the number or quality of day care spaces in the province. They insisted that it was time for the province to move beyond the welfare model and beyond the societal belief that caring for children was a private, familial, or market responsibility. For feminists, the care of young children was a matter of public importance, especially in terms of ensuring women's full and equal participation in education, paid work, and society.

Fighting the Birch Proposals: Debating Public and Private Day Care in Ontario, 1974–75

The demands of the women's movement meant that Davis could not ignore day care, though it was far from a priority in the first years of his administration. Nevertheless, he recognized the urgent need for more day care spaces in the province. Even with the growth facilitated by CAP funding, mothers faced crisis-level shortages of reliable day care spots. Estimates from the early 1970s suggested there were only enough spaces for about 20 per cent of children who needed them, and fewer than half of those were subsidized.[34] Accordingly, the Davis administration's first foray into day care policy focused on capital grants. Through an initiative called "Project Day Care," the province provided 100 per cent capital funding to municipalities and Indian Bands looking to establish day care centres. It is significant that Project Day Care was launched as part of an "economic stimulation" program for the winter of 1971–72, signalling that for Davis the building of day care spaces was just as much (if not more) about providing work in tough economic times as it was about enhancing child care provision.[35] Davis also oversaw amendments to the Day Nurseries Act that allowed provincial funding to be used to purchase services in family day homes and allowed associations that provided services to children with intellectual disabilities to be eligible for capital grants and subsidies comparable to those provided to municipalities and Indian Bands. By the end of 1973 the capital funding program had resulted in only 2,850 new spaces, barely making a dent in the need. Davis's critics contended that the approval rates for applications under Project Day Care were puzzlingly low.[36] Child care shortages remained a desperate issue for many working families.

Under increasing pressure, in early 1974 Davis initiated another round of day care reform. By that time, he was also undertaking a significant government reorganization that included the creation of ComSoc, which would be responsible for day care policy.[37] Davis also created the non-departmental cabinet position of Provincial Secretary for Social Development, a position meant to coordinate activities across several ministries, and appointed Margaret Birch, the MPP for Scarborough East, to the role. Birch had become Ontario's first female cabinet minister when Davis appointed her a Minister without Portfolio in 1972 and placed her at the head of the new Youth Secretariat. As the coordinating provincial secretary for social welfare services, Birch placed an ambitious program for day care reform and expansion high on her agenda.

On 4 June 1974, Birch outlined her proposed reforms in the legislature, explaining that they were prompted by "changes in our society, especially the growing participation by women in the labour force."[38] The government planned to spend an additional $15 million in 1974–75, which almost doubled the total provincial day care budget and was expected to result in 3,000 new spaces. Of that, $10 million was earmarked for capital expenditures, with a focus on renovations rather than new construction. Just under $5 million would be spent on enhancing day care access for – in order of priority – children with disabilities, and children in low-income families and Indigenous children. Just as important were the regulatory reforms Birch announced. First were changes to staffing requirements: no longer would supervisors be required to have professional qualifications. Instead, Birch explained, the emphasis would be on "individual competence and experience." Birch also proposed to remove some care arrangements from the oversight of the Day Nurseries Act, namely parent-provided care of five or more children. The second set of reforms pertained to staff/child ratios: for all age groups, Birch proposed significant changes to the mandated ratios that would result in more children per staff member. The third area of reform relaxed the requirements for physical spaces: centres would now be allowed to operate without kitchens (as long as catering was provided), and licensing would be offered to centres above the first three stories of a building (which was about fire safety).[39]

Birch explained that the revised regulations were practical measures designed to get more day care spaces established more quickly, since strict regulations "hindered the development of day-care centres."[40] The reforms, she said, would remove bureaucratic red tape and allow centres to operate more "economically." Since staff costs were by far the biggest line in day care services' budgets, the government expected significant cost savings to result from relaxing the regulations around professional qualifications and ratios. For centres that cared for children under eighteen months, Birch suggested that the new ratios could save up to 20 per cent in staff costs.[41] But there was also an ideological element to her proposals. Birch framed these reforms as part of a shift in the "practices of government" with respect to day care, one that eschewed government overreach into the sector. Put simply, the Birch proposals were about reinforcing private responsibility for the care of children. The Davis government's day care program was "an important change in emphasis within the social policy field," Birch explained, representing

> a change away from high-cost institutionalized services, controlled entirely by the government and financed entirely by the tax-payer; a change toward more decentralized and diverse services, supported in part by the government by involving much more voluntary action by citizens and backed up by programmes that will provide individual citizens of Ontario with the resources they need to purchase services for themselves.[42]

In this formula, government responsibility for day care would extend only to individuals in need, not to a monopolistic public program. Birch was clear: "We will not establish a system of 'free' universal daycare across Ontario." Such a system, she said, would be too expensive. Moreover, it would compromise parents' rights. For Birch, the right to which parents were entitled was not a publicly funded child care program, as feminist activists proposed, but the right "to choose for themselves the kind of care their children will receive."[43]

The Birch proposals sparked immediate outrage. In the legislature, members of both the opposition Liberals and the New Democratic Party (NDP) – and especially NDP Leader Stephen Lewis, long an advocate for public day care – decried the reforms as a betrayal of parents and day care workers. With very few exceptions, the press was critical of Birch's plans, especially in smaller cities already struggling to maintain decent standards and spaces.[44] Most significantly, though, opposition to the Birch proposals "galvanized" a broad spectrum of the day care community into a powerful movement.[45] Individual day care workers as well as the professional organizations that represented them, parents, feminist groups, municipal social service officials, social workers, and social service agencies were united in broad opposition to the proposals. As child care scholar Luc Turgeon explains, these alliances represented "perhaps one of the most important moments in the history of Canada's child-care movement because it brought together groups that … were often at odds."[46] Anti-Birch forces included, for example, influential early childhood professionals like Dorothy Millichamp and Mary Northway (professors at the University of Toronto's Institute of Child Study and, in Millichamp's case, a long-serving public servant in the Day Nurseries Branch), who had dedicated their careers to high-quality day care services but preferred half-day nursery programs for child development rather than prioritizing the needs of working mothers.[47] They fought alongside groups like the Revolutionary Marxist Group, which viewed day care as a "class issue and a women's issue" and insisted on free, twenty-four-hour, publicly funded day care as a necessity and a right for working families.[48] Despite their very different views of the scope and purpose of day care, both worried that Birch was taking the province in the wrong direction.

The broader day care community launched itself into action within a few days of Birch's announcement. A group calling themselves the Committee in Opposition to Revisions in the Day Nurseries Act, for example, which included the Association of Early Childhood Educators of Ontario (AECEO), purchased newspaper space to condemn the proposals and gathered more than 5,000 names for a petition, which was tabled by Liberal leader Robert Nixon on 20 June.[49] By early July, a Toronto coalition of twenty-two day cares and social service agencies called the Group for Daycare Reform (which had existed pre-Birch and was organized by people who had also been involved with the Day Care Organizing Committee, the group that had grown out of campus cooperative activism) was holding public meetings attended by several hundred people. By the end of the summer, these groups and many more had coalesced into the Day Care Reform Action Alliance.[50] After unsatisfactory meetings with the Deputy ComSoc Minister as well as with Birch, and after being stood up by René Brunelle at a meeting he had scheduled for them, the alliance decided that conversations with government officials were futile and instead focused on petitions, pickets, flyers, mailouts, newsletters, and public "educationals."[51]

The high point of their resistance was a rally and march in Toronto in September, which drew supporters from as far away as Sarnia, Ottawa, and the reserve day care on Walpole Island.[52] The demonstration drew 1,000 marchers, including, as keynote speaker, the progressive activist June Callwood, who spoke on "women's rights to universal day care." The participants claimed that it was the largest "women's issues" demonstration ever held in Toronto and certainly the largest gathering of day care advocates since the end of the Second World War.[53] The chorus of anti-Birch forces by that point included the Ontario Welfare Council, the Early Childhood Education Committee of the Ontario Teachers' Federation, the Toronto Children's Aid Society, and too many other day care centres and social service agencies to count.[54] Notably, however, members of the alliance were disappointed about the lack of support from unions and especially from liberal feminists. For example, Laura Sabia, the chair of the Ontario Status of Women Council and one of the key figures who had convinced the federal government to establish the Royal Commission on the Status of Women, suggested that activists should not interfere with the promised $15 million in new funding.[55]

For the advocacy community, the problems with the Birch proposals started with the threat they posed to the quality and safety of day care services. Efforts at cost-effectiveness, critics said, should not come at the expense of children's well-being. The AECEO deemed the new ratios and weaker staff qualification requirements an "incomprehensible" risk to children's "safety, educational benefit, and mental health" that flew in face of fifty years of research.[56] Concerns about quality were also at the heart of the Day Care Reform Action Alliance's message; they contended that in setting up a choice between quantity and quality Birch was playing a "false and dangerous" game. The expansion of day care services was counterproductive, they said, if such services did not include a safe and healthy environment and stimulating programming that allowed children to have sustained individual attention from caregivers. Birch's proposals put all of those things at risk.[57]

If the Birch proposals flew so baldly in the face of best practices and nationally accepted standards, from where had they originated?[58] The lack of transparency was another main area of concern for the anti-Birch forces. Under pressure in the legislature, particularly from the NDP's Stephen Lewis, Birch eventually explained that her proposals stemmed from the report of a two-year task force on the care and education of young children. But she also insisted – and in this, she was supported by Premier Davis – that this report was confidential.[59] Birch eventually relented and publicly identified the members of the task force, but that raised even more suspicion: one of those she named was Elsie Stapleford, the long-serving and highly respected director of the Day Nurseries Branch, who had recently been made a "special consultant" when the reorganization of ComSoc eliminated her position.[60] Stapleford denied her involvement, and Birch was forced to admit that she was not actually a task force member but "did make a contribution at various stages on different work study groups."[61] Even worse for Birch, Stapleford, who refrained from commenting publicly, was widely reported to oppose the proposals.[62] Her private correspondence with the Director of the Children's Services Bureau confirmed that she considered the changes to ratios to be "positively dangerous."[63]

All of Birch's hedging and obfuscation only reinforced what her critics suspected, which was that commercial interests had exerted the most influence over her reform agenda. Commercial and for-profit day cares, many pointed out, stood to benefit from the proposals. Lower staff costs meant higher profits. Speculation was rampant that John Christiansen, a former Minister of Welfare in Manitoba's PC government in the early 1960s, and president of the commercial child care chain Mini-Skools, had met with the task force to press for relaxed regulations.[64] Christiansen downplayed the meeting and denied discussing ratios – as did both Birch and Brunelle – but the anti-Birch forces were not convinced. Adding fuel to the fire, it turned out that the program director of Mini-Skools was one of the few pro-Birch voices in the extensive media coverage that unfolded through the summer and fall of 1974.[65] One activist's account of the battles indicated that the task force report had actually been leaked to members of the day care community, helping "substantiate the belief that the Ontario government's policy changes were in response to commercial interests not to their concern for children."[66] The controversy over Christiansen's role was more than just backroom gossip. For the anti-Birch forces, opening the door to more commercial and for-profit services was a profound betrayal of the Ontario day care community and of children and families more broadly. The care of children, they argued, was not a profit-making enterprise. Birch could dress up her reforms in the language of decentralization, choice, diversity of services, and warnings about "institutionalizing" children, but this was simply rhetoric that obscured a move to privatization. As one reporter put it, day care was a "vital public service," and in failing to treat it as such, the Davis government had "seriously sidestepped its own responsibility."[67]

While the mobilization against the Birch proposals gained steam throughout the summer and fall of 1974, Minister Brunelle attempted to diffuse the outrage by appointing an Advisory Council on Day Care. An eleven-member committee that included representatives from the AECEO, Curve Lake Indian Band, the Status of Women Council, and several social agencies, the council was asked to investigate and provide advice to the government on Birch's proposals. At least, that is what its members thought they were doing. As their work got under way in the fall of 1974, their actual mandate became a matter of some debate. From the outside, advocates wondered if the council was simply going to rubber-stamp Birch's proposals, or if Brunelle was actually displeased with Birch and hoped to withdraw her proposals under the cover of the council's recommendations.[68] Over the course of the council discussions, members remained unclear whether they were specifically examining the Birch reforms or more broadly considering the entire day care situation in the province. If it was the former, the council was continually frustrated by Birch's refusal to meet with them or to provide the background research on which she had based her recommendations.[69] In an attempt to cover all their bases, in its first progress report on January 1975 the council declared support for the "general intent" of Birch's goal to expand day care services but urged prudence in regulatory changes. Specifically, they called for a pause on any discussion of ratios and suggested that, above all, much more time and attention needed to go into studying and assessing the province's day care needs.[70]

In the early months of 1975, the Advisory Council attempted to do as much of that assessment as possible. As they consulted with the day care community around the province, it became clear to them that taking on day care reform was not simply a matter of whether or not to endorse Birch's proposals. The problems with access to and affordability of day care could not be solved with some regulatory adjustments and a bit of capital funding. For example, relaxed staff/child ratios in day care centres were meaningless in rural areas, where scattered populations and seasonal work made in-home care a much more suitable option.[71] Members of the council visited day care services on reserves and heard from communities that debates about staff training programs were incidental to their main concern, which was the pressing need for Indigenous day care workers, whose qualifications could not be captured by a "piece of paper."[72] And what about the needs of shift workers? And those who worked on weekends? What about emergency drop-in services? And programs focused on children's enrichment needs? What about mothers who considered longer maternity leave and shorter working hours to be the solution to their care dilemmas?[73] The council heard about the challenges and complexities of families' child care arrangements and came to see that moving that care into the public realm called for a nuanced approach.

The Second Progress Report, accordingly, covered a range of issues, which included the need to bolster private-home day care programs and to ensure that all areas of the province were covered by a fully staffed roster of provincial day care counsellors. But those recommendations (and others) were overshadowed by the council's clear condemnation of the Birch proposals. Their second report insisted that all staff should have recognized qualifications, that volunteers should not be considered in staff complements, and that ratios should not be tampered with.[74] The report was welcomed by the day care community, but, with an election approaching in the fall of 1975, it seemed to make Brunelle nervous.[75] Despite receiving the report from the council in the summer and despite council chair Anne Barstow insisting that it be released as soon as possible, Brunelle delayed its release until 18

September, Election Day.[76] The Day Care Reform Action Alliance tried to make day care a priority during the campaign, but they were running out of money and hampered with internal disagreements about strategy.[77] The election of a PC minority took the wind out of the advocacy sails and also spelled the end of the Advisory Council's work. The new ComSoc Minister, Jake Taylor requested the final report in January 1976, forcing the council to cut short their work without providing the "systematic overview of day care services" and "the development of planning policy for government" they had hoped to deliver.[78] Their work ended with a whimper rather than the bang for which they had hoped.

Conclusion: The Victories and Limits of Day Care Advocacy

In several respects, day care advocates were able to claim a victory in the Birch battles. First and foremost, the proposed changes were never implemented. Effective advocacy protected the existing standards around quality and safety. The defeat of the Birch proposals, then, arrested the expansion of commercial and for-profit child care, a win that scholars suggest has had significant long-term implications for Ontario child care policy. Without the 1970s mobilization, there might have been decades of unchecked growth in the commercial and for-profit child care sector.[79] To be sure, this was far from a wholesale victory. As Susan Prentice has shown, subsequent PC governments came under pressure from groups like the Association of Day Care Operators of Ontario (which had been founded by Mini-Skools representatives) to take a "pro-business approach" to commercial day care, with the result that auspice debates have animated Ontario child care politics since the 1980s.[80] That said, anti-Birch advocacy helped establish the principle that day care in Ontario is a public good that should not be downloaded to the private sector. Political scientist Rianne Mahon has argued that 1970s anti-Birch activism created space in Toronto's municipal social policy, for example, to develop a public child care program built on citizenship rights rather than a residualist welfare approach; and Luc Turgeon draws a line from the Birch battles to the establishment in 2010 of full-day learning programs for four- and five-year olds.[81] It is significant that even today the provincial and municipal policy architecture sustains a higher proportion of not-for-profit spaces in the province, including publicly operated ones.[82] Years of evidence have shown, moreover, that not-for-profit and publicly operated care is of higher quality, which was one of the key messages of the anti-Birch forces.[83]

From one perspective, then, the Birch battles point to the power of grassroots action to shape social policy. Much like Lara Campbell's letter writers, who defined their Depression-era needs as "legitimate political concerns" – as rights within the social welfare state – the anti-Birch forces turned their need for a collective approach to child care into a political issue that continues to reverberate in the provincial as well as federal and municipal policy arenas. They not only stopped the proposed reforms in their tracks but also provoked a provincial response that included the Advisory Council on Day Care and reflection within the Davis government about their approach to working mothers and day care services. Moreover, the day care community not only defended that care as a public good but also made it an issue of gender equality, thus injecting a crucial feminist thread into child care politics. It was significant that advocates framed Birch's proposals not just as a threat to quality and safety but also as "anti-woman."[84] Without the anti-Birch mobilization, it is difficult to say how long it might have taken the provincial government to even consider whether women had a "right to work at the expense of publicly funded day care," as the Philosophical Statement asked.

From another perspective, though, the Birch battles demonstrate the limits of day care advocacy. Put simply, the Davis government answered a firm "no" to the question of whether day care was a right of social citizenship for women. Davis's decision to walk back the Birch reforms was the bare minimum he could have done in terms of day care policy. He certainly made no moves towards policy that separated day care from its welfare-based approach, nor did he come to see the care of working mothers' children as, fundamentally, a public and collective responsibility. Cheryl Collier, who has studied the relationship between Ontario governments and women's movements, argues that the Davis government did not act meaningfully on any women's issues throughout its fourteen years in power.[85] The widespread and very public unpopularity of the Birch proposals may have spurred Davis, who had a reputation for "govern[ing] by polls," to walk back the proposed reforms in much the same way that he cancelled the controversial Spadina Expressway (a proposed freeway linking Highway 401 to downtown Toronto) in response to grassroots opposition from neighbourhood groups.[86] But cancelling plans that were roundly criticized by a broad coalition of the day care community, and that earned his government much condemnation in the press, was a far cry from adopting new policy that represented a meaningful, rights-based approach to child care.

Finally, the Birch battles point us towards reflection on the opportunities and limitations embedded in the history of the child care movement itself. Child care advocacy is complex. It has to take into account lobbying of federal, provincial, and local governments. Historically, it has had to contend with the reframing of child care as "a women's issue, a children's issue and a family issue."[87] Shifting emphasis on early childhood development, anti-poverty initiatives, and the economic case for child care has changed the contexts of day care debates over the years.[88] Child care advocates have to reckon with the rights of day care workers, the need for culturally diverse services, the need to address regional, rural, and urban differences, and the fact that commercial and for-profit services still occupy an important place in service delivery. Child care advocacy is also woven into broader conversations about the redistribution of care to support women's equality, which includes policies such as maternity leave and support for stay-at-home mothers that contain echoes of the maternalist policy of mothers' allowances from the early twentieth century. There are many interests to represent, in other words. The success of the anti-Birch forces lay in the fact that they represented a remarkable coalition of parents, workers, feminists, social service agencies, welfare organizations, public servants, and even small-scale commercial operators, all united around a clear goal. That the Day Care Reform Action Alliance dissolved so quickly in the aftermath of the Birch battles reminds us, however, of the fragility of such coalitions. Divisions within the alliance hampered the effectiveness of day care advocacy, and it would be several years before advocates regrouped in 1979 into the broadly based Action Daycare, which became the Ontario Coalition for Better Child Care in 1981.[89] Effective child care advocacy still requires, as it did in the early 1970s, navigating the challenges of working within "mainstream" ideas about child care while challenging deeply rooted government ambivalence towards working mothers.

Contained within the Birch battles, then, were all of the complexities and opportunities of a much longer history of day care in Ontario. In the end, though, Ontario's approach to child care policy remains a patchwork designed to achieve anti-poverty, educational, and developmental goals but one in which those goals lack coordination and in which parents and especially mothers are still considered the most responsible for arranging and paying for child care services.[90] In Ontario, as in most of the rest of Canada, child care is a "market system" funded primarily through parent fees.[91] It is, put simply, still firmly associated with the private sphere. It continues to be true that leaving care to the private, family, and market spheres places an uneven burden on women.[92] The COVID-19 crisis has laid bare just how much of the responsibility for care continues to rest with women and the extent to which caregiving responsibility impedes women's economic security and well-being. Job losses in the heavily female service sector, school closures that have resulted in the need to home-school, the shutdown of child care centres, increased elder care burdens – all of these pandemic consequences have led to the lowest level of women's labour force participation in three decades.[93] As the country comes to terms with the profound and long-term effects of the pandemic, feminist policy analysts, scholars, and activists insist that building public capacity for caregiving – and chiefly, establishing a national, universal, high-quality child care system – will be the key to economic and social recovery.[94] As the pandemic has demonstrated, the stakes are high for women. Whether governments take action, and whether Canadians will emerge from the current crisis with a new collective and public understanding of care, remains to be seen.

QUESTIONS FOR CONSIDERATION:

1. Pasolli is clear on child care being a public good. Do you agree or disagree?
2. Describe the "work of caring?" Why is it important? Who typically performs this work?
3. What was Project Day Care? Was it successful?
4. Outline the Birch proposals. What were the highlights?
5. Who opposed the Birch proposals? Why did they oppose them?
6. Why does Pasolli argue that day care advocates could claim a victory in the Birch battles?

NOTES

1 Emphasis in original. Archives of Ontario (AO), "A Philosophical Approach to Day Care Services," undated (circulated December 1974), file "General Policy 1974/75," box B133988, RG 29-42 Advisory Council on Day Care Files (1974–76). Throughout this chapter I use "day care" and "child care" interchangeably to refer to the non-parental care of children. Day care was the more common term in the 1970s, while child care is the preferred term today.

2 Historians of feminism have increasingly begun to suggest that the "wave" metaphor is, as Joan Sangster puts it, "outmoded." Feminism was present in the "first wave" (typically identified by suffrage campaigns) and again in "second wave" (typically identified as the activism of the 1960s–70s). While there were certainly "upsurges" in the currents at different historical moments, the wave metaphor runs the risk of oversimplifying the sustained and dynamic history of feminisms throughout the twentieth century. See Joan Sangster, "Radical Ruptures: Feminism, Labor, and the Left in the Long Sixties in Canada," *American Review of Canadian Studies* 40, no. 1 (March 2010): 2.

3 Scholars have provided brief accounts of the Birch episode: see Cheryl Noël Collier, "Governments and Women's Movements: Explaining Child Care and Anti-Violence Policy in Ontario and British Columbia, 1970–2000" (PhD diss., University of Toronto, 2006), ch. 4; Rianne Mahon, "Child Care as Citizenship Right? Toronto in the 1970s and 1980s," *Canadian Historical Review* 86, no. 2 (June 2005): 294–95; Susan Prentice, "'Kids are not for profit': The Politics of Childcare," in *Social Movements/Social Change: The Politics and Practice of Organizing*, ed. Frank Cunningham et al. (Toronto: Between the Lines, 1988), 111–14; Susan Prentice, "The Business of Child Care: The Issue of Auspice," in *Early Childhood Care and Education in Canada*, ed. Larry Prochner and Nina Howe (Vancouver: UBC Press, 2000), 284–6; and Luc Turgeon, "Activists, Policy Sedimentation, and Policy Change: The Case of Early Childhood Education in Ontario," *Journal of Canadian Studies* 48, no. 2 (Spring 2014): 234–6. For a general overview of child care politics in post-war Canada, see Alvin Finkel, "Even the Little Children Cooperated: Family Strategies, Childcare Discourse, and Social Welfare Debates 1945–75," *Labour/Le Travail* 36 (Fall 1995): 91–118; and Annis May Timpson, *Driven Apart: Women's Employment Equality and Child Care in Canadian Public Policy* (Vancouver: UBC Press, 2002).

4 T.H. Marshall, "Citizenship and Social Class," in *Class, Citizenship, and Social Development: Essays by T.H. Marshall* (Westport: Greenwood Press, 1964).
5 Jane Jenson and Mariette Sineau, "The Care Dimension in Welfare State Redesign," in *Who Cares? Women's Work, Childcare, and Welfare State Redesign*, ed. Jenson and Sineau (Toronto: University of Toronto Press, 2001), 7.
6 Marshall, "Citizenship and Social Class," 72; Julia S. O'Connor, Ann Shola Orloff, and Sheila Shaver, *States, Markets, Families: Gender, Liberalism, and Social Policy in Australia, Canada, Great Britain, and the United States* (Cambridge: Cambridge University Press, 1999).
7 There is a vast feminist literature on care, gender, and the welfare state. See, for example, Sonya Michel and Rianne Mahon, eds., *Child Care Policy at the Crossroads: Gender and Welfare State Restructuring* (New York: Routledge, 2002).
8 See chapter 1 of James Struthers, *The Limits of Affluence: Welfare in Ontario, 1920–1970* (Toronto: University of Toronto Press, 1994); and Margaret Jane Hillyard Little, *No Car, No Radio, No Liquor Permit: The Moral Regulation of Single Mothers in Ontario, 1920–1997* (Toronto: Oxford University Press, 1998).
9 On worker-citizenship, mother-citizenship, and the welfare state, see Margaret Hillyard Little, "Claiming a Unique Place: The Introduction of Mothers' Pensions in B.C.," *BC Studies* 105–6 (Spring–Summer 1995): 80–102.
10 Struthers, *The Limits of Affluence*, 20.
11 The "Wages for Housework" movement of the 1970s, for example, drew attention to the exploitation of women's domestic labour and called for that labour to be paid. See Louise Toupin, *Wages for Housework: A History of an International Feminist Movement, 1972–77*, trans. Käthe Roth (Vancouver: UBC Press and Pluto Books, 2018).
12 For a more general discussion of women and work in the post-war years, see Joan Sangster, *Transforming Labour: Women and Work in Postwar Canada* (Toronto: University of Toronto Press, 2010).
13 Michael Krashinsky, *Day Care and Public Policy in Ontario* (Toronto: University of Toronto Press, for the Ontario Economic Council, 1977), 8.
14 Struthers, *The Limits of Affluence*, 275; Wendy McKeen, "Seen but Not Heard: The Construction of 'Welfare Mothers' in Canada's Late 1960s/Early 1970s 'War on Poverty,'" *Canadian Woman Studies* 29, no. 3 (Spring 2012): 109.
15 Larry Prochner, "A History of Early Education and Child Care in Canada, 1820–1966," in *Early Childhood Care and Education in Canada*, ed. Larry Prochner and Nina Howe (Vancouver: UBC Press, 2000), 11–65.
16 Larry Prochner, "'Share their care Mrs. Warworker': Wartime Day Nurseries in Ontario and Quebec, 1942–1945," *Canadian Journal of Research in Early Childhood Education* 5, no. 1 (1996): 115–26; Mary J. Wright, "Toronto's Institute of Child Study and the Teachings of W.E. Blatz," in *Early Childhood Care and Education in Canada*, ed. Prochner and Nina Howe, 96–114.
17 Lisa Pasolli, "'I ask you, Mr. Mitchell, is the emergency over?': Debating Day Nurseries in the Second World War," *Canadian Historical Review* 96, no. 1 (March 2015): 1–31; Ruth Roach Pierson, *"They're still women after all": The Second World War and Canadian Womanhood* (Toronto: McClelland and Stewart, 1986). There is a broad and important historiography about the gendering of the post-war Canadian welfare state. As a start, see Nancy Christie, *Engendering the State: Family, Work, and Welfare in Canada* (Toronto: University of Toronto Press, 2000); and Jennifer Stephen, *Pick One Intelligent Girl: Employability, Domesticity, and the Gendering of Canada's Welfare State, 1939–1947* (Toronto: University of Toronto Press, 2010).
18 Pasolli, "'I ask you, Mr. Mitchell,'" 25.

19 For a fuller discussion of the Day Nurseries and Day Care Parents Association, including the red-baiting that undermined their work, see Susan Prentice, "Workers, Mothers, Reds: Toronto's Postwar Daycare Fight," *Studies in Political Economy* 30, no. 1 (1989): 115–41; and Susan Prentice, "Theorizing Political Difference in Toronto's Postwar Child Care Movement," Occasional Paper no. 8 (Toronto: Childcare Resource and Research Unit, 1996).
20 Prentice, "Theorizing Political Difference," 11-13.
21 Prochner, "A History," 54–62.
22 Struthers, *Limits of Affluence*, 233–5.
23 Dana Hanson (researcher), "The Canada Assistance Plan and Day Care," prepared for LAC, Task Force on Child Care, 1984, file 1320-3 pt. 1, box 56, Acc. 1999-00341-1, RG 106 Status of Women Canada.
24 Rianne Mahon, "The Never-Ending Story: The Struggle for Universal Child Care Policy in the 1970s," *Canadian Historical Review* 81, no. 4 (December 2000): 595–9.
25 AO, John Heywood, *Facts and Figures on Day Care in Ontario* (Ministry of Community and Social Services, Children's Services Bureau, April 1975), file "Facts and Figures on Day Care in Ontario 1975," box B133988, RG 29-42.
26 Collier, "Governments and Women's Movements," 56.
27 Claire Hoy, *Bill Davis: A Biography* (Toronto: Methuen, 1985), 232.
28 As a starting point for the history of the women's movement in Canada, see Nancy Adamson, Linda Briskin, and Margaret McPhail, *Feminist Organizing for Change: The Contemporary Women's Movement in Canada* (Toronto: Oxford University Press, 1988).
29 Florence Bird, *Report of the Royal Commission on the Status of Women* (Ottawa, 1970).
30 Katherine Clare Simon, "'Not just somebody's mother': University Campus Daycare Co-operatives in British Columbia and Ontario, 1960s to 1970s," (unpublished, 2019).
31 University of Ottawa Archives and Special Collections (UOASC), Day Care Organizing Committee, "Tiptoe through the Tulips: Setting Up Co-operative Daycare Centres," n.d., file 22, box 20, collection 10-001 Canadian Women's Movement Archives (CWMA).
32 Judy Rebick, *Ten Thousand Roses: The Making of a Feminist Revolution* (Toronto: Penguin, 2005), 59–68.
33 Rebick, *Ten Thousand Roses*, 65.
34 Heywood, *Facts and Figures*, 38.
35 Heywood, *Facts and Figures*, 20.
36 Heywood, *Facts and Figures*, 16–24.
37 Nancy Cooper, "New day-care plans catch Social Services officials by surprise," *Globe and Mail*, 11 June 1974, 12.
38 Ontario, *Official Report of Debates: Legislative Assembly of Ontario* (4 June 1974), 2819 (Hon. M. Birch) (hereafter *Legislative Debates*).
39 *Legislative Debates*, 4 June 1974, 2819–26 (Hon. M. Birch). Another useful summary of Birch's reforms is AO, Gladys De Schepper, "New legislation to lower child care standards," *Toronto Citizen* (2–22 August 1974), 10, in file "Clippings 1974," box B144958, RG 29-42, [hereafter "clippings file."]
40 Rosemary Spiers, "$28 million budgeted for Ontario day care," *Toronto Star*, 5 June 1974, A2, in clippings file.
41 *Legislative Debates*, 4 June 1974, 2824 (Hon. M. Birch).
42 *Legislative Debates*, 4 June 1974, 2820 (Hon. M. Birch).
43 *Legislative Debates*, 4 June 1974, 2821 (Hon. M. Birch).
44 "A day care policy that suits no one," *Windsor Star*, 18 September 1974; Cathy Hawkins, "Day care proposal called 'dangerous,'" *Oakville Daily Journal Record*, 6 June 1974, both in clippings file.

45 Collier, "Governments and Women's Movements," 88; Prentice, "'Kids are not for profit,'" 111.
46 Turgeon, "Activists," 235.
47 Cited in Prentice, "Theorizing Political Difference," 5.
48 UOASC, Dorothy Knight and Ruth Taillon (Revolutionary Marxist Group), "An Alternative Strategy," n.d., file 23, box 20, collection 10-001 CWMA.
49 "A Giant Step Backwards for Children in Ontario!," n.d.; Nancy Cooper, "5,300 petition against changes proposed for Day Nurseries Act," *Globe and Mail*, 21 June 1974, 12, in clippings file.
50 "Day care reformers to protest changes," *Toronto Star*, 30 August 1974, in clippings file.
51 UOASC, "Good Day Care," n.d., in file 23, box 20, collection 10-001 CWMA.
52 "Birch heckled on day-care reform," *Globe and Mail*, 16 September 1974, in clippings file.
53 UOASC, Sandy Steinecker, untitled, n.d., file 23, box 20, collection 10-001 CWMA. Although this document does not have a title or a date, it is clearly an insider's account of the work of the Day Care Reform Action Alliance.
54 *Legislative Debates*, 28 October 1974, 4482 (E. Martel).
55 Steinecker, untitled, 9.
56 "Group opposes changes in day nursery rules," *Toronto Star*, 7 June 1974, in clippings file.
57 The Day Care Reform Action Alliance, "Meeting Ontario Day Care Needs: Prepared for Consideration by Members of the Ontario Legislature," September 1974, https://riseup feministarchive.ca/wp-content/uploads/DCRAA-Brief-MeetingOntarioNeeds-1974.OCR_.pdf.
58 It was widely noted that the ratios Birch proposed were significantly lower than those recommended by the Canadian Council on Social Development as well as child welfare agencies in the US and UK. AO, E.M. Stapleford (Special Consultant on Early Childhood Education) to J.K. Macdonald (Director, Children's Services Bureau), 7 June 1974, file "General Policy 1974/75," box B133988.
59 *Legislative Debates*, 11 June 1974, 3105 (S. Lewis).
60 "Profits for day-care business not part of new ratios: Brunelle," *Globe and Mail*, 14 June 1974, in clippings file.
61 *Legislative Debates*, 30 October 1974, 4599 (Hon. M. Birch).
62 Peter Mosher, "Day-care changes please no one but money-men," *Globe and Mail*, 15 June 1974, in clippings file.
63 Stapleford to Macdonald, 7 June 1974.
64 *Legislative Debates*, 11 June 1974, 3104-06 (S. Lewis); Linda McQuaig, "Day-care task force was lobbied, official says," *Globe and Mail*, 26 June 1974, in clippings file.
65 "Study on day care won't be made public," *Globe and Mail*, 12 June 1974, in clippings file.
66 Steinecker, untitled, 6.
67 De Schepper, "New legislation to lower child care standards."
68 *Legislative Debates*, 27 June 1974, 3846 (S. Lewis); Steinecker, untitled, 7.
69 AO, Advisory Council on Day Care, "Goals and Concerns of Council," 13 August 1974, file "Terms of Reference (Advisory Council) 1974/75," box B133988, RG 29-42.
70 Advisory Council on Day Care, "Progress Report," December 1974, file "Advisory Council's First Report Jan. 1975," box B133988, RG 29-42, AO.
71 Advisory Council on Day Care, "Members' Confidential Record of Meeting Held on February 17th and 18th/75," and "Members Confidential Record of Meeting Held on January 27th and 28th/75," in file "Advisory Council on Day Care Discussion Notes – Term I (Aug 7 74 to June 24 75)," box B133988, RG 29-42, AO.

72 AO, Advisory Council on Day Care, "Visit of Advisory Council on Day Care to Essex, Kent, and Lambton Counties," 25–26 March 1975, in file "Advisory Council on Day Care Discussion Notes – Term I (Aug 7 74 to June 24 75)," box B133988, RG 29-42; AO, Julie Fels (Lakehead Social Planning Council) to Hon. James Taylor (Minister of Community and Social Services), 25 November 1975, file "Responses to Progress Report II," B133988, RG 29-42.

73 AO, Advisory Council on Day Care, "Members' Confidential Record of Meeting Held on November 7th and 8th/74," in file "Advisory Council on Day Care Discussion Notes – Term I (Aug 7 74 to June 24 75)," box B133988, RG 29-42.

74 AO, Advisory Council on Day Care, "Progress Report II," June 1975, in file "Advisory Council – Second Report June 1975," box B133989, RG 29-42.

75 AO, Kathleen Gallagher-Ross (Faculty, Early Childhood Education, Centennial College) to Anne Barstow, 26 September 1975, file "Responses to Progress Report II," B133988, RG 29-42.

76 See the correspondence, memos, and clippings from late August and early September 1975 in AO, file "Advisory Council – Second Report June 1975," B133989, RG 29-42.

77 Steinecker, untitled, 29.

78 AO, Advisory Council on Day Care, "Third Report," June 1976, in file "Spare Copies – Third Report Final Draft," box B133989, RG 29-42.

79 Turgeon, "Activists, Policy Sedimentation, and Policy Change," 242; Mahon, "Child Care as Citizenship Right?," 295, citing Kyle.

80 Prentice, "The Business of Child Care," 284–5.

81 Mahon, "Child Care as Citizenship Right?"; Rianne Mahon, "Challenging National Regimes from Below: Toronto Child-Care Politics," *Politics and Gender* 3 (2007): 55–78; Turgeon, "Activists, Policy Sedimentation, and Policy Change."

82 Martha Friendly et al., *Early Childhood Education and Care in Canada 2016* (Toronto: Childcare Resource and Research Unit, 2018), 64.

83 Gordon Cleveland and Michael Krashinsky, "The Nonprofit Advantage: Producing Quality in Thick and Thin Child Care Markets," *Journal of Policy Analysis and Management* 28, no. 3 (Summer 2009): 440–62.

84 Steinecker, untitled, 22.

85 Collier, "Governments and Women's Movements," 55–8.

86 Hoy, *Bill Davis*, 221.

87 Susan Prentice, "Introduction: Changing Child Care: Looking Back, Moving Forward," in *Changing Child Care: Five Decades of Child Care Advocacy and Policy in Canada*, ed. Susan Prentice (Halifax: Fernwood, 2001), 23.

88 Linda White, "From Ideal to Pragmatic Politics: National Child Care Advocacy Groups in the 1980s and 1990s," in *Changing Child Care*, 97–111.

89 White, "From Ideal to Pragmatic Politics," 100.

90 White, "From Ideal to Pragmatic Politics," 100.

91 Friendly et al., *Early Childhood Education and Care in Canada 2016*, ix–xii.e.

92 Including women who work in child care centres, many of them racialized, who subsidize private operations through their low wages. See Jane Beach, *Overview of Child Care Wages 2000–2010* (Child Care Human Resources Sector Council, January 2013).

93 Pamela Jeffery, "Decades of progress on gender equality in the workplace at risk of vanishing," *Globe and Mail*, 2 August 2020.

94 Kate Bezanson et al., "From Stabilization to Stimulus and Beyond: A Roadmap to Social and Economic Recovery," 6 April 2020, https://drive.google.com/file/d/1jplKknjy9ON_ItnbEtQTxW602AKTIhqJ/view.

CHAPTER TWENTY-ONE

Intolerable Harm: Demanding Mental Health Services for Franco-Ontarian Youth Prior to the Montfort Hospital Crisis[1]

MATHIEU ARSENAULT AND MARCEL MARTEL

On 27 March 1984, a Franco-Ontarian mother from the Ottawa region wrote to provincial Liberal MPP Don Boudria exposing the difficulties her son was facing in his efforts to obtain psychiatric services in French.[2] Clearly frustrated and feeling quite powerless, she agreed to entrust her child to the Quebec health system in order for him to receive adequate treatment in a mental health centre in Hull. This letter is not exceptional. On the contrary, this is one among many that have been sent to MPPs. The letters attest to activism by individuals who are seeking mental health care in French. By demanding the right to speak out and go beyond specific cases, petitioners also manifested a form of collective activism. For minority francophone groups, access to services in one's own language and the training of professionals fluent in French were vital issues.

This chapter examines the language aspects of mental health services in Ontario, particularly for youth. For a long time, the province of Ontario based its actions on the principle that in matters of health, the language in which patients were treated was of little concern. The situation changed thanks to the strong activism of the Franco-Ontarian community, which, according to the 1971 census, made up 6.3 per cent of Ontario's population; ten years later, that percentage had decreased and stabilized at 5.5 per cent.[3] However, it was not until the matter of French-language high schools was settled in the 1960s that the question of mental health became a public issue. Before 1968, the provincial government did not fund high schools for Franco-Ontarians. If parents wanted their children to receive their education in French, they had to send them to private schools. Preoccupied by national unity and the claim by the Royal Commission on Bilingualism and Biculturalism in 1965 that

Canada was going through its greatest crisis, one that threatened its future, Premier John Robarts came to accept that the grievances of French-speaking Ontarians should be addressed. The time had come to implement policies that would promote the French language in Ontario. Thus, he decided to provide funding to French-language schools until grade thirteen. This political decision was an important victory for Franco-Ontarians, after several decades of lobbying. Franco-Ontarian leaders could now focus their attention on other issues, such as mental health care.

In his survey of access to mental health care in French, Matthew Hayday credits the Association canadienne-française de l'Ontario (ACFO) with forcing the Ontario government to act. Hayday writes that progress was slow between 1970 and 1986; the hostility towards institutional bilingualism and Franco-Ontarians that marked those years made the government cautious. In the tense political environment following the election of the Parti Québécois in Quebec in 1976, some people interpreted that caution as a lack of leadership.[4] Linda Cardinal, for her part, credits the Franco-Ontarian community, and especially women's groups, with forcing the province to act after the French Language Services Act[5] was passed in 1986.[6] Various studies have emphasized the efforts of the community; however, they do not, except for an article by Marie-Claude Thifault, Marie Lebel, Isabelle Perrault, and Martin Desmeules, deal with mental health services.[7]

Numerous studies attest to the mobilization of Franco-Ontarians around the issue of health. This has given rise to a considerable number of academic publications.[8] The present chapter focuses on a specific aspect of that activism: young people's vulnerability because of their age and, in the case of Franco-Ontarians, their belonging to a language minority. After the 1970s, access to mental health services for francophone youth was a cornerstone demand by the community as it set out to influence provincial policy towards francophones. These young people stood out as the "minority" subject *par excellence* as they experienced what it meant to belong to a language minority. Minority children and youth, after all, were even more vulnerable when they were unable to receive treatment in their own language. That they were "second-class citizens" in this situation was intolerable. So young people became both the subject of francophone demands and the source of mobilizing arguments that fed social activism. Many studies have stressed women's activism, and indeed, women did not hesitate to exploit the special ties between mothers and children. Maternal instinct, that unique proclivity of mothers to safeguard and nurture their children, does much to explain how they mobilized around issues such as education and French immersion,[9] unemployment during the Great Depression,[10] the dangers of drugs,[11] and children's well-being against the backdrop of the Cold War.[12]

This chapter demonstrates that the rhetoric about youth was not solely a female concern, but was shared by many social agents who hoped to speed up the implementation of services in French. The dearth of adequate services in French was presented as a failure on the part of the government to respond to the ideal put forward by Confederation. The election of René Lévesque' PQ in 1976 produced a shock wave that reached other provincial politicians; that young Franco-Ontarians were needing to seek treatment in Quebec seemed profoundly unfair.

This chapter has three parts, all touching on vulnerable children. The first part examines the efforts of the Liberal and NDP opposition parties in Ontario's provincial Legislature. Those parties contended that the government's failure to ensure that Franco-Ontarians – especially the youngest and most vulnerable – were receiving what they needed to thrive was handing ammunition to Quebec sovereigntists. The 1981 language crisis at the Children's Hospital of Eastern Ontario (CHEO), analysed in the second part, reveals that interest groups and individuals also began demanding that Ontario improve its youth mental health services in French. However, the pressure they exerted ran up against the hostility of the anglophone administrators of health care facilities, as well as the policy of "bilingualism in small steps" of the Ontario government, which refused to act with regard to hospitals. Faced with the snail-like pace of provincial action, the ACFO supported the nomination of francophones to those hospital boards whose responsibility it was to craft bilingual policies. The chapter concludes with a discussion of the citizen action that ensued. The issue of access to mental health care in French occupied the Canadian Mental Health Association (CMHA), which called on Franco-Ontarians to mobilize and send letters of protest to the provincial Minister of Health.

Access to Mental Health Care in French for Children: A National Issue

Access to mental health care in French for the Franco-Ontarian minority first arose as a political issue in the 1970s. It was part of the struggle to counter linguistic assimilation. Franco-Ontarians mobilized their resources to develop institutions for themselves in which French would be the working language. At the same time, they pressed the province to allocate resources so that the community would have access to an array of services in French. In response to the pressure exerted by the ACFO, the Ontario government established a working group, led by Dr. Jacques Dubois, to investigate the range of health care services available to Franco-Ontarians. The resulting report, tabled in 1976, in its chapter devoted to "exceptional children," pointed to the unfair treatment of francophone children in a system designed to respond to the needs of the anglophone majority. Dubois found it incredible that because they spoke a language other than English, these young people faced often insurmountable challenges.[13] With regard to mental health, they had to contend with serious communication problems. When patients spoke French, health professionals did not understand them, and this seriously affected their ability to make diagnoses and propose suitable treatments. Moreover, because they had to speak English in hospitals where that was the dominant language, these young people risked being assimilated. According to the report, "hospitalized Francophones become anglicized and subsequently experience other difficulties on returning to their family environment."[14]

When there was no immediate response to the report from the Minister of Health, opposition MPPs raised the issue in the legislature. The Liberal MPP for Ottawa East, Albert Roy, declared that treating patients suffering from psychiatric problems while ignoring communication difficulties showed a lack of humanity. Furthermore, the problem was much more serious in the case of young Franco-Ontarians. Commenting on the services offered at the Ottawa children's hospital, Roy took a stand against the inability of health facilities to respond to the basic needs of the young people in his region: "You're bringing children in there, and yet the doctor or some of these specialists – 12 out of 12 of these specialists can't speak French … When you get with children it becomes a problem to communicate. How can you treat them if there is some difficulty in communicating with them?"[15] The situation was also unsatisfactory in Northern Ontario. Before the Dubois report was even tabled, research by the French-Language Health Services Task Force emphasized that the Northeastern Regional Mental Health Centre in Timmins had serious language problems.[16] In fact, the only psychiatrist available to serve a population of 100,000 people was an anglophone.[17] New Democrat MPP Charles "Bud" Jackson Wildman emphasized that the situation was of concern in the Algoma region:

> Imagine the problems of a francophone if he has a psychological or psychiatric problem, wants to get treated and can't speak the same language as the practitioner; how on earth is that dealt with? If you're a francophone from Dubreuilville in my riding and you go to Sault Ste. Marie for treatment you're pretty well out of luck. You're probably a lot more likely to get treatment if you can speak Italian than you are if you can speak French.[18]

The NDP MPP for Cochrane South, William Herman Ferrier, presented the absence of appropriate care for francophones as an injustice that threatened the existence of psychiatric treatment. Commenting on the absence of French-speaking psychiatrists and personnel in hospitals like the one in Brockville, which nevertheless admitted francophone patients, he found it offensive that hospitals were facilitating the assimilation of young Franco-Ontarians: "The statement was made that for a francophone to enter the Ontario Hospital system was like taking an immersion course in English. That's a terrible indictment, when we're supposed to be showing good faith to our minority group and providing some leadership in this country."[19]

The debate over the absence of mental health care in French for children and youth was conducted in the tense political atmosphere brought about by the election of a PQ government in Quebec. This created a sense of urgency, in that the situation of Franco-Ontarians was now being talked about as a national unity issue. Thus, when Liberal MPP Albert Roy pressed the government to acknowledge its responsibilities towards Franco-Ontarians, he declared: "I don't want to start sabre-rattling and say if the people in Quebec feel the way they do and if they vote the way they do, it is because they feel that they can only keep their culture and exist as French-Canadians in the province of Quebec."[20]

For Roy, developing adequate health services in French was fundamental to demonstrating Ontarians' sincere commitment to Canada: "The best evidence that the system works is to show that minorities in this province can exist as Canadians and can keep their culture and their language."[21] NDP MPP W.H. Ferrier demanded that the government act instead of criticizing Quebec, a province that was doing much more than Ontario with regard to providing health services for its language minority.[22] However, the argument linking the provision of health services in French to the future of the country came up against the reality on the ground. Whereas the Dubois Report emphasized that it was because the "Ministry recognizes the problems of the cultural and linguistic ambience [that it] grants financial support to the institutionalization of Francophones in Quebec,"[23] the fact that some fifteen adolescents from southeastern Ontario and a number of others from the northeast were housed in health centres in Rouyn-Noranda and Montreal seemed inconceivable. That these young Franco-Ontarians were being treated in Quebec became a powerful symbol of the inaction and negligence of the Ontario government.

In 1981, the issue gave rise to another debate in the legislature. The NDP MPP for Scarborough West, Richard Frank Johnston, was angry that some thirty young Franco-Ontarians were being treated at the Maison Rouyn-Noranda because they were unable to receive services in their own language in Ontario. He called on James Francis Drea, the new Minister of Community and Social Services, to explain why young francophones suffering from mental health problems were being cast aside: "Does [the Minister] have a double standard for northern children as compared with southern children and for French-speaking children versus English-speaking children? If not, how does he explain that there are no group homes for French-speaking children north of Sudbury in this province?"[24]

The minister admitted there was a lack of French-language services in child mental health care. Community and Social Services had announced in 1978 that it was investing $700,000 to establish a mental health program in French for the children of Prescott and Russell Counties,[25] and it had announced the opening of a mental health facility for children in Ottawa slated for January 1982, yet, as Johnston pointed out, twenty-five young Franco-Ontarians were still being treated at the Maison Rouyn-Noranda. Surprisingly, the patients were not all from Northern Ontario, which pointed to the lack of services in the province as a whole. The minister responded that the opening of a bilingual mental health facility for children in North Bay, slated for March 1982, would help ensure that before long, young Franco-Ontarians would be receiving treatment in their own language. Regarding northeastern Ontario, Drea claimed there was a lack of available professional resources to treat francophone children suffering from mental illnesses. He averred that while waiting for personnel to become available, "we would be extremely foolish to not send children from Cochrane South and so forth over to Rouyn rather than bring them down to Sudbury."[26] Notwithstanding the minister's remarks, it seems that efforts to improve the provision of mental health services for young Franco-Ontarians from the north were being made largely by Quebec. Referring to the plan of the director of the Maison Rouyn-Noranda to establish a facility in the Timmins region to treat young people in their own community, Johnston again called on the Minister of Community and Social Services to state his intentions regarding the provision of care to the children of northeastern Ontario.[27] It seemed as if the minister was in no hurry to allocate the resources required to respond to their needs.[28]

Faced with the gaps in child mental health services in French raised by the Northeastern Ontario Mental Health Study of 1981, notably in the Dubreuilville region, Sudbury, and the Algoma and Cochrane districts,[29] the Minister of Health, Larry Grossman, acknowledged the importance of finding a solution to the dearth of psychiatrists in the north.[30] The North Bay Psychiatric Hospital was at the centre of a pilot project in 1982 for planning services in French. Dr. André Côté, the newly appointed coordinator for mental health services in French, had been assigned by the Minister of Health to draw up a plan to recruit francophone psychiatrists to eastern and northeastern Ontario.[31] A team of six bilingual psychiatrists from McGill University was formed to offer ambulatory services one day a month in Mattawa, Sturgeon Falls, Timmins, and Sudbury, where children's psychiatric treatment was concentrated.[32]

Notwithstanding some improvements, at the time the French Language Services Act was passed in 1986, it was still viewed as a persistent government failure that young Franco-Ontarians were having to seek treatment in Rouyn-Noranda.[33] As for language planning policy in the area of health, which prioritized language training and the recruitment of bilingual personnel, results were minimal. Since the tabling of the Dubois Report in 1976, the Ontario government had shown little inclination to intervene in hospitals. When the language crisis arose at the CHEO, its tardiness was widely perceived as simple neglect.

Language Crisis at the CHEO: A Matter of Internal Politics?

Opened in Ottawa in 1974, the psychiatric unit at the CHEO soon found itself in a language maelstrom, attesting to the government's half-heartedness when it came to improving services in French. In 1978, a bilingualism committee was formed "spontaneously" by a group of francophone employees who were frustrated "about certain flagrant inadequacies in the services provided in French at the Hospital."[34] The committee, led by Carole St-Aubin, criticized the hospital administrators for their reluctance to deal with language issues and submitted the "Parlons-nous" report to the CHEO board of directors in 1981. That report, which caught the attention of the francophone media and social players in the Ottawa region, stressed "that the principle of offering services in French at the Hospital is in line with current political developments in the province."[35] The policy of increasing the provision of services in French announced by the Robarts government in 1968, and renewed by William G. Davis in 1971, suggested a degree of progress. But despite political directives and the Dubois Report, provision of health services to the francophone population remained inadequate. The committee pointed especially to the very small number of francophone representatives in the CHEO administration,[36] as well as to the lack of bilingual specialist doctors. The report was critical with regard to the hospital. The authors denounced the hostile climate within the hospital, where, "on several occasions, during their work, members of the Committee had seen anglophone employees call Francophones mentally defective simply because they could not communicate in English."[37] On other occasions, "a head of department urged the Francophones on his staff to introduce from time to time [a] few sentences in English when they spoke to each other."[38] Pointing out the presence everywhere of "an Anglophone stronghold mentality,"[39] the committee members accused the CHEO of contributing to the assimilation of francophones. The regional ACFO quickly became involved in the matter, denouncing the inertia of the CHEO regarding "the intolerable situation imposed on young francophone users of the hospital." The absence of French was unfair, because "it was not the role of young patients who were little able to communicate to suffer further because of the negligence of a board of directors insensitive to the wrongs caused by the monolingual nature of its services."[40]

Claiming to be anxious to offer bilingual services, the hospital administration acknowledged the gaps in the services offered in French.[41] Nevertheless, it did not fail to criticize the message and the methods of the Bilingualism Committee. The director of social services, Airdrie Thompson-Guppy, even accused the committee of wanting to impose "francophone domination" within the institution. She added that "the francophone mentality" in the hospital created an atmosphere hostile to dialogue and that the issue of cultural assimilation was "a philosophical fantasy." Her verdict on the "Parlons-nous" report was unequivocal: "I want to say that eight, idealistic, impatient employees have managed to get away with being insubordinate to their superior, have violated the press code, have misused work hours, and have ripped apart a very special and effective philosophy of our hospital because they are French. And because they are French, our hands seem to be tied by politics."[42]

In a telegram to Dennis Timbrell, the Minister of Health, dated 26 June 1981, the ACFO in Ottawa-Carleton pressed the minister to force the CHEO to investigate bilingualism. It also demanded that the hospital administration dissociate itself from Thompson-Guppy's remarks, which were considered an example "of hate literature towards Francophones."[43] The response to ACFO, which was signed by Premier William G. Davis himself, was not very convincing. In a poorly translated letter, Davis repeated the main points of the government's bilingualism policy and reiterated his support to francophones. He also, however, admitted that he was powerless to act on the problems at the CHEO, viewing them as an internal matter arising from a misunderstanding among employees. And he stressed that the Minister of Health lacked the authority to impose sanctions on hospitals. The premier stated that "the government is and will always be at the service of [F]ranco-[O]ntarians,"[44] but did little to conceal his reluctance to intervene in the management of health services in French.

Despite the controversy stirred up by the "Parlons-nous" report, and the subsequent creation of the Advisory Committee on Bilingualism, the development of francophone services at the CHEO was not a priority for the hospital administration. The members of the Bilingualism Committee at the root of the controversy soon questioned the relevance of the new committee the hospital had created, stressing that its president "gave very low priority to the whole issue of bilingual services in this house."[45] The staff, patients, and interest groups fighting for improvement in French services at the CHEO ran up against the hostility of the management and board of directors responsible for developing services in French. But they had learned an important lesson: the problem would not be solved by the Minister of Health, nor even by the premier.

The crisis in French-language health services at the CHEO marked a turning point for the francophone social actors involved, especially in organizations like the Ottawa-Carleton ACFO. The local association took complete stock of the problem of underrepresentation of francophones on hospital boards – a problem that had been raised by the ACFO in Timmins in 1979.[46] In a similar vein, the regional Social Planning Council published a report on "Services in French in Ottawa-Carleton Hospitals," which maintained that the inadequacy of services in French stemmed from "poor communication between Anglophone hospital administrators and the francophone community."[47] Taking the measure of the "serious unease with regard to services in French"[48] at the CHEO, the Committee for French Language Services of the Social Planning Council made the question of mental health services for children and "leadership" in the francophone community priority issues for 1982. Similarly, the Ottawa-Carleton ACFO reminded the Ministry of Health that francophone representation in centres of power such as steering committees constituted a priority.[49] At the same time, the Canadian Mental Health Association (CMHA) began to take serious notice of the needs of the francophone population, thanks to the arrival of the former director of the Ottawa-Carleton ACFO, Suzanne Bédard, as a mental health community worker in 1982. The CMHA maintained there was an urgent need to establish mental health services in French and hire health professionals.[50] Its annual report of 1982 stressed the importance of placing "greater emphasis on the needs of the francophone population in matters of mental health."[51] Bédard was aware that the lack of francophone professionals and social actors was a barrier to improving mental health services; she also contended that to improve French-language services, francophone professional elites in policy-making circles would have to be brought on board.[52]

Having first been raised by a group of employees, the issue of French-language services at the CHEO evolved into a genuine language crisis. As a consequence of the intransigence of the board of directors and the inaction of the government, the affair migrated beyond the bounds of the hospital. While the government hesitated to intervene, citing difficulties in recruiting qualified francophone employees in order to justify the *status quo*, the regional ACFO and the CMHA came to realize that if the problem of lack of services in French was going to be solved, it was essential for a francophone voice to be heard in the centres of power.

"A chorus of voices needs to be raised": Citizen Action of Parents et amis des malades mentaux

In the spring of 1982, the CMHA tabled its report: *A Matter of Urgency: The Psychiatrically Disabled in the Ottawa-Carleton Community*. Although the issue of services in French was not mentioned, the report was an important step, for it encouraged citizen involvement: "A chorus of voices needs to be raised for the psychiatrically disabled."[53] It seems that members of the Association des parents et amis des malades mentaux de la région d'Ottawa (APAMM) heard that call, for a number of them took up their pens to write to the Minister of Health, Larry Grossman, between April and July 1982. Whereas anglophones dealt specifically with the issues referred to in the report – notably accommodation and long-term care – and pressed the minister to implement some of its recommendations, francophones demonstrated much more personal concerns. Some of the letters in French, such as the one sent to the minister by the mother of a schizophrenic son on 26 April 1982, did indeed confine themselves to relatively cryptic support for the "29 recommendations drawn up by Anne Louise Parker." But most of these letters dealt with specific problems faced by Franco-Ontarians in the area of mental health. A number of letter writers viewed their participation in the French chapter of APAMM as a source of legitimacy that lent weight to their requests. When an Ottawa woman wrote to Grossman in July 1982, she built her symbolic capital on her experience with the association: "I would like to tell you about my interest in Canadian Mental health & APAMM. In the more than twenty years that I have been a member of this association, what disappoints me the most is the lack of services in French in psychiatry … I speak not only for myself but more for people with mental health issues and especially family members who are involved."[54]

Another Ottawa resident mentioned her long years of membership in the APAMM, as well as her husband's. She attempted to show how serious she was by emphasizing that her letter was more than just a personal opinion. In the very first line, she mentioned that she was interested in those suffering from psychic disabilities, "like many others," and she ended by pointing out that her letter was not an isolated effort: "I do not wish to go into further detail in this letter of which I believe you must have had many others of this kind."[55] Nevertheless, the document was not really addressing the CMHA report.

The two letters mentioned above deplore the lack of mental health services: "I believe there is a great need for a Mental [*sic*] hospital like the one in Brockville here [in] Ottawa, in order to have our patients closer to us, to help them [to] function better."[56] The letters also evoked the need for services in French: "I refer especially to the urgent need to group francophone patients together in sections of the hospital and community services and also have francophone personnel to help them."[57]

In other instances, legitimacy was conferred by personal experience. In a letter to the minister dated 30 April 1982, a mother of six children described the difficult history of her "exceptional"[58] son. Stressing that his transfer to the psychiatric hospital in Brockville, for want of a place to treat him in Ottawa, "was an experience he did not need," she asked Grossman to act. Although the writer did not associate herself directly with APAMM, she referred to the title of the report when she wrote: "I beg you Sir, do everything you possibly can *there is as urgent need*." And she ended the letter with a vague reference to the report's conclusions about financing, which she combined with what was, in her opinion, the most urgent need in the area of mental health: "There are many families suffering because of the lack of help. Especially having a French Hospital and the [recommendation] and no. 25 on grants." She then pleaded for services for the Franco-Ontarian community: "I thank you for your attention to *us* and may God guide you in your work."[59] In another letter, the female writer claimed her right to speak as a "patient suffering from psychiatric problems." This helped lend special credibility to her story. Adopting a personal tone, she described how the lack of services in French had affected her:

> I have already been hospitalized at the Royal Hospital but was offended not to have French people. All the staff were English. I have already been admitted to Montfort Hospital but there are practically no beds and we often have to stay home and our health deteriorates. I would like there to [be] professional people who would visit us & comfort us when we are depressed. I would like there to be follow-up plans for when we leave the hospital to support us. I hope that one day, we will benefit from a francophone hospital to serve Ottawa & Gloucester.[60]

Inadequate access to mental health care was the theme of the letter from a mother whose daughter "suffered a great deal from mental health for over twenty-five years" before committing suicide "for want of anyone who could have helped her." The mother then broached the subject of services in French, emphasizing the problems she had accessing the resources of Montfort Hospital. She wrote that at the time she was seeking help for her daughter, the psychiatrist answered that according to "the most recent law passed by the government, the person in question had to be suicidal, or wanting to kill another person," to be admitted. Reminding the minister of his responsibilities, and particularly the fatal consequences of government policies, she exclaimed: "and this has been the result." Alluding to the appalling situation in which "these poor people" found themselves, she ended her letter by endorsing "strongly the twenty-nine recommendations"[61] of the CMHA.

A volunteer working in a hospital in eastern Ontario unambiguously co-opted the CMHA report with the aim of promoting access to mental health care in French. In his letter to the minister, he commended the report, which he described as "a special study of the association of relatives and friends of the mentally ill." Despite his discomfort at demanding "special attention with regard to the problems of mental health patients" because he lived in Quebec, he nevertheless specified that he "knows people who are unfortunately disadvantaged when it comes to psychiatric care because of a language 'blockade' of staff appointed to psychiatric units." He ended his letter by begging the minister to implement the recommendations of the report "for the well-being of our fellow citizens of Ontario." It is worth noting that he viewed the APAMM as a group that "aims above all to obtain for the mentally ill a service offered by francophone staff."[62] Clearly, members of the French section of the association had succeeded in co-opting the report, using the symbolic capital of the ACSM to promote better access to mental health care for Franco-Ontarians in the Ottawa-Carleton region.

The letter-writing campaign showed that citizens of the Ottawa region believed that politicians could solve the problems they faced. Yet the government did not deem the situation in the region to be inadequate. Replying to a female resident who complained about the lack of French-language psychiatric services, Grossman stated:

> The Montfort Hospital, the Ottawa General Hospital and the Royal Ottawa Hospital all provide services in French to adults. The Ontario Hospital for children and adolescents and the department for children and adolescents of the Royal Ottawa Hospital also offer similar services. With the possible exception of long-term hospitalization, which is rarely necessary these days, any French-speaking person applying to receive psychiatric care could obtain help in the Ottawa region.[63]

The minister's words did not reflect reality. Treatment for children was inadequate at the Royal Hospital, to the point that the unit, which suffered from a chronic lack of specialists and staff able to speak French, had to be temporarily handed over to the Ottawa-Carleton Youth Services Bureau in 1983.[64] A letter from a woman resident of Lefaivre to MPP Don Boudria on 27 March 1984 described the difficulties of "obtaining help in the Ottawa region." She emphasized that it was a shame to have to "run after interpreters" to obtain services in French in the emergency department. She was frustrated by the monolingualism of psychiatric services:

> Well, at the moment my boy has problems he ends up in psychiatry. <u>This is ridiculous</u>. My child <u>cannot</u> communicate with the children they are <u>all</u> English [including] the staff. Let's say 10 people who work there <u>1</u> or <u>2</u> speak French. How do you treat a child in psychiatry if he is not served in his language frankly as a parent I am fed up … I'm

> not saying that the English staff are not good carers. (No). I'm complaining about the language. At the moment I'm waiting for my child to be taken to Hull Pierre Janet, because of the language, but it's been a week since he's had any treatment it's only English and I'm frustrated, and my child even more so … I hope there will be some changes, not just for me, but for the others who've told me that [they] are scared to write to avoid problems. I only want us to understand each other in our language.[65]

In referring this letter to Keith Norton, the Minister of Health, Boudria stressed the difficulties experienced by this twelve-year-old boy: "Once again, I am unfortunately obliged to write to you about services offered in French at the Children's Hospital of Eastern Ontario … The situation would be unacceptable in any hospital, but in a 'bilingual' hospital, providing services to children, I find the situation shameful."[66]

Here, as elsewhere, the image of the child is mobilized as an aggravating factor in an already unacceptable situation, thus suggesting the urgent need for action. Like the letter sent to Grossman in the spring of 1982, this one is signed by "a frustrated mother," thus speaking to the difficulties in accessing mental health care in French. A decade after the Dubois Report was tabled, young Franco-Ontarians were still suffering from a lack of adequate treatment, or even no treatment at all, because it was impossible for them to communicate with the medical staff. The Ottawa-Carleton Regional District Health Council accurately summed up the general feeling when it wrote, in its 1981–82 report, that "many members of the francophone community believe that great strides are needed, where tiny steps have been taken."[67]

These accounts singled out the problem of access to mental health services in French. They described a desire to force politicians to intervene in order to solve an urgent problem. They were human dramas presented in language tinged with anger and frustration. Who could remain indifferent, especially when mothers took the time to write and describe the dramas they had lived through? Those letters also allow us to put the enthusiasm of the Assistant Deputy Community and Social Services Minister, John Burkus, in perspective. Commenting on the services provided for young Franco-Ontarians in his address to the Ottawa-Carleton Social Planning Council in 1985, he argued that "in every respect ... we now have a model program of mental health services for francophone children in this sector."[68] Despite the founding of the francophone residential facility Renaissance in 1984, followed by the passing of the French Language Services Act 1986, the crisis caused by the announcement of the closure of the Montfort Hospital in 1997 shook the community. While progress since the tabling of the Dubois Report was relatively modest, notably in the north, the disappearance of the only hospital providing a psychiatric program in French raised the spectre of a step backward.[69] Mobilization of the community and decisions of the courts would guarantee a future for the Montfort Hospital. Although the government granted new human and financial resources to that hospital, it did so especially in order to allow it to pursue its work in training medical staff who used French as a working language.

Conclusion

The issue of youth mental health services was a crucial aspect of the battle for access to health care in French in Ontario. A symbol *par excellence* of the minority figure, young Franco-Ontarians allowed politicians, the population, and interest groups in the province to denounce vigorously the injustices to which they were being subjected in matters of mental health, a situation that English-speaking youth did not have to face. The national political context of the 1970s encouraged the opposition in Queen's Park to instrumentalize the issue, and accordingly, they denounced the Ontario government's inability to ensure its francophone minority population the means to flourish. In the same way, ACFO criticized the indifference of the boards of health centres to their obligation to implement bilingual services, pointing out that it was not the responsibility of children to suffer further because of their inability to communicate with medical staff. Similarly, it was the vulnerable figure of the child that prompted members of the Franco-Ontarian community to write to the Minister of Health.

This analysis of the opinions expressed by Ontario's francophones regarding mental health services illustrates the challenge of forcing the province to allocate adequate resources to the sector. One argument put forward was the vulnerable situation of young people. In general, these young francophones did not act directly, and their voices can only be heard through parents, workers, and activists. This statement may be surprising, since young people have long been politically active. They challenged education, uninspiring school curricula, and conservative social values during the 1960s. More recently, they have denounced ongoing tuition increases and the lack of action on environmental and climate change issues. However, the research material used for this chapter indicates otherwise. The young adults at the forefront of these social and political changes just mentioned are not representative of the youth portrayed during the campaign to improve French mental health services. On the contrary, it was the "adults" – the mothers, politicians, health professionals, ACFO militants, and other organizations – who built up a picture of the young Franco-Ontarian as an innocent child who must be protected against unjust treatment by the state and presented it as a political issue to be addressed. These "adults" believed that their arguments and actions would be strong enough to force the government, and especially politicians, to take action.

After all, who could remain indifferent when faced with letters from mothers describing the problems their children faced in obtaining adequate treatment, especially when these children were in crisis? Who could ignore the opinions of health professionals and militants in organizations devoted to mental health and those of the ACFO, which documented the inadequate nature of the mental health services and the sometimes dramatic consequences to which they gave rise?

Yet the reality that children and youth were unable to receive mental health care was not enough to speed up the implementation of mental health services by the Ontario government. Government action was characterized by slowness. This case exemplifies the classic problem of making choices in the allocation of limited government resources when a multitude of needs are at hand. Franco-Ontarians tried to direct these limited resources towards meeting their needs, as their letters, reports, and other forms of mobilization show. The government's slowness was also explained by the complexity of mental health policy. The needs expressed by Franco-Ontarians required the province to act on many fronts: training medical staff able to speak French, hiring and retaining those staff in hospitals, and actively offering services in French in hospitals, while also meeting the demand for these services by patients and their support networks. In allocating resources to deal with the various aspects of providing mental health services in French, the province discovered its own limits, as it had to work with teaching institutions regarding training, hospitals regarding provision of care, and organizations regarding patient support when they left hospital. All these social actors also demanded resources and intervened in the debate on mental health services in French. For them, young people were only one of many client groups.

QUESTIONS FOR CONSIDERATION:

1. How did Franco-Ontarian people mobilize over the issue of health services for youth?
2. What tactics and approaches were successful or unsuccessful in shifting the political dynamic around this issue? How did each of the political parties view the matter, and what did they do?
3. How would you describe the attitude of the Ontario government towards minority-language health services for youth?
4. Can you comment on how these issues have changed for francophone youth health services in Ontario since the events described in this article?

NOTES

1 Research for this chapter was funded with a grant from the Canadian Institutes of Health Research (CIHR) for the project led by Marie-Claude Thifault titled "Déhospitalisation

psychiatrique et accès aux services de santé mentale : regards croisés Ontario-Québec, 1950–2012" (126100). The project was undertaken as part of the research program of the Chaire de recherche sur la francophonie canadienne en santé. The research for this chapter is based on a journal article that appeared in *Minorités linguistiques et société/Linguistic Minorities and Society* 9 (2018): 55–73. We thank Lin Burman for the translation and the journal editors for giving us permission to reuse our journal article. We have made changes based on comments from the editors of this collection.

2 Letter to Don Boudria, 27 March 1984, Centre for Research on French Canadian Culture (CRFCC), fonds Don Boudria, P366/2/51, file P366-2/51/6 Health.

3 Jean-Pierre Corbeil and Sylvie Lafreniere, *Portrait des minorités de langue officielle au Canada : les francophones de l'Ontario* (Ottawa, Statistique Canada, 2010), 11.

4 Matthew Hayday, "'Pas de problème': The Development of French-Language Health Services in Ontario, 1968–86," *Ontario History* 94, no. 2 (2002): 183–200.

5 *French Language Services Act*, LRO 1990, c. F32.

6 Linda Cardinal in collaboration with Caroline Andrew and Michèle Kérisit, *Chroniques d'une vie politique mouvementée : l'Ontario francophone de 1986 à 1996* (Ottawa : Le Nordir, 2001).

7 Marie-Claude Thifault, Marie Lebel, Isabelle Perreault, and Martin Desmeules, "Regards croisés Ontario-Québec : les services de soins de santé mentale des communautés de langue officielle en situation minoritaire de 1950 à nos jours," *Reflets : revue d'intervention sociale et communautaire*, vol. 18, no. 2 (2012): 122–39.

8 Stéphane Savard and Jérôme Boivin (dir.), *De la représentation à la manifestation : groupes de pression et enjeux politiques au Québec, XIXe et XXe siècles*, Québec, Septentrion, 2014; Miriam Smith, *A Civil Society? Collective Actors in Canadian Political Life* (Peterborough, Broadview Press, 2005); Suzanne Staggenborg, *Social Movements*, 2nd ed. (Toronto, Oxford University Press, [2007]2012).

9 Matthew Hayday, *So They Want Us to Learn French: Promoting and Opposing Bilingualism in English-Speaking Canada* (Vancouver: UBC Press, 2015).

10 Lara Campbell, *Respectable Citizens: Gender, Family, and Unemployment in Ontario's Great Depression* (Toronto, University of Toronto Press, 2009).

11 Marcel Martel, *Not This Time: Canadians, Public Policy and the Marijuana Question, 1961–1975* (Toronto: University of Toronto Press, 2006).

12 Tarah Brookfield, *Cold War Comforts: Canadian Women, Child Safety, and Global Insecurity, 1945–1975* (Waterloo: Wilfrid Laurier University Press, 2012).

13 Jacques Dubois, *Pas de problème : rapport du Comité d'action sur les services de santé en langue française* (Toronto, Ministère de la santé, 1976), 38.

14 Dubois, *Pas de problème*, 43.

15 Ontario, *Legislature of Ontario Debates*, 30 November 1976, 5242.

16 Archives of Ontario AO, [Unknown newspaper], "Language problem at Northeastern found in study," 29 December 1975, RG 0-67, Provincial Psychiatric Hospitals Administration files, B282736, Northeastern file – Newspaper Clippings on Closure.

17 Ontario, *Legislature of Ontario Debates*, 6 November 1979, 4257.

18 Ontario, *Legislature of Ontario Debates*, 14 May 1979, 1905.

19 Ontario, *Legislature of Ontario Debates*, 2 December 1976, 5325.

20 Ontario, *Legislature of Ontario Debates*, 30 November 1976, 5242.

21 Ontario, *Legislature of Ontario Debates*, 30 November 1976, 5242.

22 Ontario, *Legislature of Ontario Debates*, 2 December 1976, 5325.

23 Dubois, *Pas de problème*, 45.

24 Ontario, *Legislature of Ontario Debates*, 22 June 1981, 1876.

25 AO, Ontario Council of Health, *Report of Committee on Mental Health Services in Ontario "Agenda for Action,"* June 1979, 296, RG 10-67, B313962, file Ontario Council of Health – Report of Committee on Mental Health Services in Ontario.
26 Ontario, *Legislature of Ontario Debates*, 6 April 1982, 613.
27 Ontario, *Legislature of Ontario Debates*, 6 April 1982, 614.
28 Ontario, *Legislature of Ontario Debates*, 6 April 1982, 617.
29 AO, Mark Shuparski (coordinator), *Northeastern Ontario Mental Health Study*, April 1981, 121–2, 130–3, 150, RG 10-67, B206137.
30 AO, Statement by the Hon. Larry Grossman, Minister of Health, to the Standing Committee on Social Development, communiqué, November 1982, RG 10-67, B347627, Minister's Releases file.
31 AO, Letter from the administration of the North Bay Psychiatric Hospital to the acting executive director of the Royal Ottawa Hospital, RG 10-67, B373275, North Bay Psych. Hosp. General Hospital file 1982–88.
32 AO, Ministry of Health, "French Language Services to Northeastern Ontario," RG 10-67, B336347, file 2211-2 – North Bay Psych. Hosp. General Hospital Admin. etc., file no. 2; AO, Ministry of Health, "North Bay Psychiatric Hospital 'A Mental Health Resource for Northeastern Ontario,'" RG10-67, B137574, file North Bay Psychiatric Hospital Information Summary and Program Description.
33 See remarks by R.F. Johnston, Ontario, *Legislature of Ontario Debates*, 15 May 1990, 1225.
34 Comité pour le bilinguisme, "Parlons-nous : un rapport sur les services en langue française de l'HEEO," Ottawa, March 1981, 2, CRFCC, fonds ACFO, C2/94, file C2[6]/94/8, C2[6] I 14,14,14 Santé Hôpital pour enfants de l'est de l'Ontario, 1981 à 1983.
35 Comité pour le bilinguisme, "Parlons-nous," Ottawa, March 1981, 1, CRFCC, fonds ACFO, C2/94, file C2[6]/94/8.
36 According to the committee, barely four members of the board of directors out of twenty-seven are francophone. Comité pour le bilinguisme, "Parlons-nous," Ottawa, March 1981, 5. The administrators affirm for their part that twelve members of the board are bilingual. "Bilingualism at C.H.E.O", communiqué, 24 June 1981, CRFCC, fonds ACFO, C2/94, file C2[6]/94/9, C2[6] I 14,14,14 Santé Hôpital pour enfants de l'est de l'Ontario, 1981 à 1983.
37 Comité pour le bilinguisme, "Parlons-nous," Ottawa, March 1981, 6, CRFCC, fonds ACFO, C2/94, file C2[6]/94/8.
38 Comité pour le bilinguisme, "Parlons-nous," Ottawa, March 1981, 6, CRFCC, fonds ACFO, C2/94, file C2[6]/94/8.
39 Comité pour le bilinguisme, "Parlons-nous," Ottawa, March 1981, 7, CRFCC, fonds ACFO, C2/94, file C2[6]/94/8.
40 Communiqué de l'ACFO du 9 juin 1981, CRFCC, fonds ACFO, C2/94, fonds C2[6]/94/9.
41 « Bilinguism at the C.H.E.O », communiqué, 24 June 1981, CRCCF, fonds ACFO, C2/94, file C2[6]/94/9.
42 Letter from Airdrie Thompson-Guppy to David Gowing, President of the Hospital for Children of Eastern Ontario, 22 June 1981, CRFCC, fonds ACFO, C2/94,file C2[6]/94/9.
43 Telegram from ACFO in Ottawa-Carleton to the minister Dennis Timbrell, 26 June 1981, CRFCC, fonds ACFO, C2/94, file C2[6]/94/9.
44 Letter from William G. Davis, Premier, to ACFO in Ottawa-Carleton, 7 August 1981, CRFCC, fonds ACFO, C2/94, file C2[6]/94/9.
45 Réponse au communiqué de presse "Le bilinguisme à l'H.E.E.O.," 24 August 1981, CRFCC, fonds ACFO, C2/94, file C2[6]/94/9.
46 Ontario, *Legislature of Ontario Debates*, 6 November 1979, 4257.

47 Conseil de planification sociale d'Ottawa-Carleton, "Services en français dans les hôpitaux d'Ottawa-Carleton," June 1980, CRFCC, fonds ACFO, C2/93, file C2[6]/93/21, C2[6] I 14,14,1 Santé généralités, 1981 à 1984, 1987.
48 Extrait du rapport annuel du Conseil de planification sociale d'Ottawa-Carleton de 1981 à 1982, "Comité des services en français," CRFCC, fonds ACFO, C2/94, file C2[6]/94/25, C2[6] I 14,15,6 Services sociaux et communautaires, Centre de planification sociale d'Ottawa-Carleton, 1981–89.
49 Letter from ACFO to Darwin J. Kealey, assistant deputy minister, Ministry of Health, 23 August 1982, CRFCC, fonds ACFO, C2/93,file C2[6]/93/21.
50 Letter from the Canadian Mental Health Association to ACFO in Ottawa-Carleton, 20 March 1984, CRFCC, fonds ACFO, C2/83, file C2[6]/83/3 C2[6] I 13,28,8 Pouvoir décisionnel, Hôpitaux et services de santé, Assocation Canadienne pour la santé mentale, section d'Ottawa-Carleton.
51 Canadian Mental Health Association, Ottawa-Carleton branch, 29th Annual Report, 8 March 1983, CRFCC, fonds ACFO, C2/83, file C2[6]/83/3.
52 Letter to Jefferey R. Allan, ACFO in Ottawa-Carleton, 20 March 1984, CRFCC, fonds ACFO, C2/83, file C2[6]/83/3.
53 Anne Louise Parker and Louise Rosborough, *A Matter of Urgency: The Psychiatrically Disabled in the Ottawa-Carleton Community*, Ottawa, Canadian Mental Health Association, Ottawa-Carleton branch, 1982, 72.
54 Letter to Larry Grossman, Minister of Health, 29 July 1982, AO, RG 10-67, B344559, file Public Inquiries – Community Mental Health.
55 AO, letter to Larry Grossman, Minister of Health, 28 May 1982, AO, RG 10-67, B344559.
56 AO, letter to Larry Grossman, Minister of Health, 29 July 1982, RG 10-67, B344559.
57 AO, letter to Larry Grossman, Minister of Health, 28 May 1982, RG 10-67, B344559.
58 AO, letter to Larry Grossman, Minister of Health, 30 April 1982, RG 10-67, B344559.
59 AO, letter to Larry Grossman, Minister of Health, 30 April 1982, RG 10-67, B344559 (our emphasis).
60 AO, letter to Larry Grossman, Minister of Health, 20 May 1982, RG 10-67, B344559.
61 AO, letter to Larry Grossman, Minister of Health, 2 June 1982, RG 10-67, B344559.
62 AO, letter to Larry Grossman, Minister of Health, 4 May 1982, RG 10-67, B344559.
63 AO, letter to Larry Grossman, Minister of Health, 9 August 1982, RG 10-67, B344559.
64 Allocution prononcée par M. John Burkus, sous-ministre adjoint, Division de l'élaboration des politiques et des programmes, ministère des Services sociaux et communautaires, devant le Conseil de planification sociale d'Ottawa-Carleton, 4 mars 1985, CFRCC, fonds ACFO, C2/94, file C2[6]/94/13, C2[6] I 14,14,18 Santé professionnels francophones dans le domaine de la santé, 1982–85.
65 Letter to Don Boudria, 27 March 1984, CRFCC, fonds Don Boudria P366/2/51 (underlined in the original).
66 Letter from Don Boudria to Keith Norton, Minister of Health, 9 April 1984, CRFCC, fonds Don Boudria P366/2/51.
67 "Revue 1981–1982," Conseil de santé pour le district regional Ottawa-Carleton, CRFCC, fonds ACFO, C2/83, file C2[6]/83/10 C2[6] I 13,28,15 Pouvoir décisionnel, Hôpitaux et services de santé, Conseil de santé pour le district regional Ottawa-Carleton, décembre [1983?] à janvier [1984?].
68 Allocution prononcée par John Burkus, sous-ministre adjoint, Division de l'élaboration des politiques et des programmes, ministère des Services sociaux et communautaires, devant le Conseil de planification sociale d'Ottawa-Carleton, 4 mars 1985, CRFCC, fonds ACFO, C2/94, file C2[6]/94/13.
69 Open letter from Don Boudria to Duncan Sinclair, President of the Health Services Restructuring Commission, 4 April 1997, CRFCC, fonds Don Boudria, P366-1/131/006.

CHAPTER TWENTY-TWO

A Disability History of Ontario from Confederation to the Coronavirus Pandemic, 1867–2022

GEOFFREY REAUME

This chapter traces many of the initiatives undertaken by governments affecting disabled people in Ontario, as well as the rising influence of disability advocates over government policies during the decades discussed here. Disabled people have long had an impact on the policies as well as the attitudes that have shaped their lives and have, in turn, shaped Ontario's civil society for the better. Given that this chapter covers one and half centuries, it is inevitable that much will be left out of this brief survey. And as will become apparent, there is much we still do not know about disability history in Ontario (and in Canada more generally), given how new the field is. We are fortunate, though, that enough material is available to make a chapter like this possible, thanks to scholars and activists in Canada and around the world who have written so much already from a variety of perspectives, from within and outside the growing field of critical disability studies.[1] This overview of one Canadian province fits within the broader historiography that seeks to understand disability from a critical perspective based on the lives and experiences of disabled people. While the actual words of disabled people are not usually present in this history, their historical presence as sentient human beings is of paramount importance in understanding the past that is being written about. Thus, no attempt is made here to try to see "both sides" – disabled and non-disabled – for example, when addressing the history of institutionalization. The goal here is to try to understand the histories of disabled people in Ontario, prioritizing their position in that history above all else, however complicated a task that may be. With very few exceptions, almost all of the documentation is from already published work – secondary sources – rather than from original or primary sources. As such, this chapter is as much a survey of existing published work on Ontario's disability history, as it is an overview of the topic itself. I will not be interpretating historical studies; instead, I will be borrowing historical details from those studies that provide scope and context to the unfolding past. As I hope will become apparent in this survey, however many differences there are and always have been among disabled people, there is also much that brings them together. The pages that follow focus on the broader historical forces that have impacted disabled people in Ontario since 1867.

Disabled people, like everyone else during the different time periods examined here, were significantly affected in their everyday lives by broader political, social, and economic developments, such as wars and civil rights protest movements. So this chapter is divided into eras, all of which are interconnected, given the legacies that succeeding generations have at various times learned from, forgotten, built upon, dismantled, uncovered anew, or were baffled about. History is seldom tidy, and disability history is no exception. I start with the first five decades of disability history in Ontario after Confederation, 1867–1914, a time of large-scale institutionalization during which what we now call disability began to be defined. The section that follows covers the decades of and between the two world wars, 1914–45, during which disabled people's place in society began to be reconsidered, in large part because of the impact of wars and economic depression, a time when only limited state support for some disabled people was offered in the community. The third section covers the post-war years, 1945–70, the time of the rise of the Canadian welfare state, when social and economic aid for disabled people became far more widespread. The section after that, covering 1970–95, discusses the impact of disabled people's activism on social policies and public consciousness, when widespread civil rights activism built on the work of earlier generations of activists and their allies.

The final section of this chapter, covering 1995–2022, makes it clear that progress for disabled people has not been linear. During those years, provincial and federal governments retreated from the post-1945 welfare state, causing enormous hardships that disabled people and allies continue to resist as this is being written. Overall, the history of disability in Ontario since Confederation reflects shifts in policy initiatives, from those that have sought to impose practices by governmental directive from above, to those in which disabled people demand to have their voices heard regarding decisions affecting their lives. That struggle is far from over.

Disability in Ontario from Confederation to the First World War, 1867–1914

The half century between Confederation and the First World War saw the expansion in Ontario of pre–welfare state institutions for disabled people: some of these places were coercive and confining, such as mental institutions, while others set out to provide education and industrial training, albeit limited in scope. It was also a period when questions about who was disabled and why, and what should be done with people so defined, came into sharper focus than in the past. In the decades after Confederation, "disability" was grouped among a collection of terms, most of which are now considered offensive: crippled, feeble-minded, deaf and dumb, lunatic, insane, spastic, and assorted terms related to gender, such as hysteric. Only a few terms from this period are today considered acceptable by disabled people, blind, deaf, and epileptic being the most obvious. Importantly, many of the people described in this chapter as "disabled" did not identify as such.

Two points need to be stressed in describing disability during the post-Confederation decades. First, there was no universally defined category of disability in North America: the very notion was in the process of being "invented," as Sarah F. Rose has described in her book on this topic about the US.[2] In Canada, diagnostic terms related to insanity were highly disputed among practising physicians. One doctor at the Toronto Asylum for the Insane complained in 1897 that the "intolerable evil of many names makes psychiatry the ridicule of the outside profession."[3] If doctors who were directly involved in developing terminology around what constituted a particular disability were not clear about what these terms meant, the wider public would have been even more confused. Not until the first decades of the twentieth century, especially in the 1930s, were clearer classification systems around disability formulated in Ontario as rehabilitation programs for wounded veterans made their mark and related efforts to medically systematize physical, mental, and sensory differences had a gradual impact on terminology.[4] Moreover, most of the people whose lives are now categorized as disabled were living in the community. Mirroring developments in the US at this time, places of confinement for some disabled people significantly increased in number in Ontario in the post-Confederation decades, specifically for those deemed insane or feeble-minded.[5]

The creation of large-scale public institutions in Ontario and Quebec was influenced by similar developments in the US and the UK, for state and medical officials in Canada had been in regular contact with Anglo-American asylum promoters since before Confederation.[6] For other groups of disabled people in Canada, educational facilities were now being founded, modelled less on asylums (which were highly stigmatized) and more on the residential schools for deaf and blind people that were by then appearing in the US and Europe.[7] Thus, in pre–welfare state late nineteenth-century Ontario, the beginnings of state intervention in the lives of some disabled people was evident, with growing numbers of public asylums for people deemed mentally incompetent, as well as increased state support for the education and industrial training of people with sensory disabilities. But while institutionalization had started, and was expanding, it was not yet widespread, and disabled people in all categories continued to live in the community with family members.[8] Meanwhile, some government agencies were beginning to institutionalize children deemed "backward" in "reformatories." Many disabled children would be horrifically abused in these punitive environments, while some people who became disabled as they grew old (and whose families did not or could not support them) died in insane asylums.[9] For example, the Asylum for the Insane in London, Ontario, opened in 1870, recorded 457 people confined shortly after its first months of operation.[10] By 1900, this same institution recorded more than twice that number: 1,008 people were reported confined behind its walls.[11] Thus, while not all disabled people were sent to institutions, more of them were than ever before.

The situation for disabled people in the community during this period has received much less attention than drawn by people confined in asylums or resident in educational facilities. There is evidence that "wandering fools" – mentally disabled people who had no family to support them – were "still very much a part of the rural landscape" around the mid-nineteenth century, when only a few mental institutions existed in Ontario.[12] By the end of the nineteenth century, however, Ontario had six large-scale public insane asylums, with the result that more and more people who might have been accepted by their local community as homeless mentally disabled people, or at least allowed to continue to live in that community, were instead confined in institutions.[13] The opening of provincially run public insane asylums in Toronto (1841), London (1870), Kingston (1876), Hamilton (1876), Mimico (1892), and Brockville (1894), along with a few branch asylums, indicates the widespread expansion of facilities to confine and control populations deemed "deviant" at a time of increasing industrialization, urbanization, immigration, and social dislocation, with the attendant social stresses that arose during this period of tumultuous change.[14] The increasing focus on populations considered unproductive and mentally incapable also led to the founding in Orillia of an asylum for people labelled "feeble-minded," in 1876.

Provincial figures from 1900 show that 5,152 people were confined in Ontario's seven public institutions for people with mental disabilities. Of these, 654 were confined in the Orillia asylum for people with intellectual disabilities and 4,498 in six public asylums for people with mental health disabilities.[15] These facilities were a public expression of the increasing desire to confine large numbers of people with mental disabilities in large-scale institutions, which, instead of providing the caring, therapeutic retreat their proponents claimed to offer, became warehouses of despair. They quickly filled to capacity, and abuse within their walls was rife. The "therapy" they offered consisted of unpaid labour for the mass of poor inmates, which ironically, undercut the notion that disabled people were an economic burden on society, given that the inmates contributed vast amounts of work to the internal economy of institutions.[16] Yet notwithstanding this intensification of institution-building, some disabled people – including mentally disabled people, as well as people with physical and sensory disabilities – continued to live in the community, and others were sent to institutions for disabled people for short-term treatment or education rather than long-term confinement.

In disability historiography, the asylum looms far larger than the community when it comes to understanding what actually happened to mentally disabled people during this period, whether in Ontario or elsewhere.[17] This is not surprising, given the scale of institutionalization during this period. It also means that, practically speaking, there are far more sources immediately available about people who lived and died in state-run institutions than there are for those in the wider community. Similarly, more information is accessible about the lives of people with sensory disabilities who were in educational facilities for the blind and deaf during this period. A privately run school for the blind existed as early as the 1860s. The province's first publicly funded institution for blind people opened in Brantford in 1872; the first public facility for the education for deaf children had opened in Belleville two years earlier.[18] While schools in both places provided education based on the wider public school system during this period, the emphasis was on making people with sensory disabilities work at jobs specific to their disability. Historian Vanessa Warne notes in regard to blind students during this time: "A group understood as characterized by unusual tactile skill and manual dexterity was also understood as a group best suited to manual labour – to the making of brushes, brooms, mattresses, and chairs."[19]

There was opposition to this practice from blind people themselves; in 1896, E.B.F. Robinson criticized the absence of a focus on the intellectual abilities of blind people by sighted educators, who instead streamed them into work as low-paid labourers.[20] Whatever the differences between and among people with different types of disabilities, the common feature of their existence in the late nineteenth and early twentieth centuries was that they were generally considered incapable of productive labour in capitalist society and were thus a burden on society. Provincial officials in Ontario made inmates of mental institutions do vast amounts of unpaid labour, all the while claiming that these labourers were unreliable or second-rate compared to non-disabled workers, even when their own annual reports provided evidence to the contrary. Superintendents openly boasted of the amount of money they saved the province by making asylum inmates work for no pay.[21]

While people in mental institutions toiled as cheap labour, deaf and blind youth were expected to view the work they were trained for as a form of "civic duty" to earn their citizenship status in a rapidly industrializing society; their integration into the economy was deemed essential if they wished to avoid being viewed as a burden.[22] To be a disabled worker during this period meant having one's work downgraded as of less value than that of people who were not disabled. Perhaps the clearest example of this involved workers who became disabled on the job and who still lived in the community. Little research has been published about injured workers in nineteenth-century Ontario; however, Dustin Galer's study of late nineteenth-century fraternal insurance associations in the province demonstrates how working-class men who became impaired on the job had extremely limited access to compensation, for their worth was calculated away by employers until they became destitute.[23] However, this idea that once-able-bodied people were no longer of much value was not uniformly shared by all sectors of society at the time; in particular, it was not shared by family members, as historian Edgar-André Montigny has shown in regard to how older men and women were cared for by lower- and middle-class families. Only when they could no longer support these people at home did families try to admit relatives to asylums. The provincial government responded to this by accusing family members of not taking care of their relatives, while enacting policies to cut back on such admissions through austerity measures so as to reduce state costs for supporting poor older people in public institutions. As Montigny has documented, by the late nineteenth century in Ontario, "families were often forced to shoulder the entire burden of care alone; provincial policies dictated that only in exceptional circumstances were aged people with relatives eligible for public support, which was usually provided in the form of institutional accommodation."[24]

By the early twentieth century, the situation of disabled people in Ontario was decidedly bleak: large-scale mental institutions had quickly filled to capacity and had become places where people were warehoused in prison-like settings, with little in the way of beneficial treatment beyond exploitative unpaid work under the guise of therapy. For still others, the province sought to cut costs in another way, by leaving it up to most families to care for older disabled relatives at their own expense. For people with sensory disabilities, education and training began to be offered as a publicly funded option in the 1870s, but the employment prospects for these people were negligible and based on negative stereotypes about what to expect, or not to expect, from them. As will be seen in the next section, injured white male workers were the only disabled group for whom prospects seem to have improved by 1914: a limited amount of income support was agreed upon by the provincial government at a time when state intervention to assist larger numbers of disabled people waxed and waned between war and peace.

From the First World War to the Second World War, 1914–1945

The colossal social and economic changes wrought by industrialization and urbanization in Ontario prior to 1914 were amplified considerably by the upheaval caused by the First World War, its aftermath, and the Second World War. The impact on disabled people was significant in many ways but also incremental, depending on who is being discussed. Changes, aside from those already described, were unfolding prior to the outbreak of war in the summer of 1914. Baby steps toward a provincial Workmen's Compensation Act (WCA) began in 1910 with the appointment by Premier James Whitney's Conservative government of William Meredith to head a royal commission on this issue; that commission led to the introduction of the WCA in 1914 and its passage the following year. The act was intended to address the plight of injured workers and their families, though in doing so it excluded as much as it included. A decades-long struggle ensued for the remainder of the twentieth century over who should be eligible for compensation and how much.[25] While urban male workers disabled on the job were included from the start, farmworkers were excluded. So were most women, largely because of the places where they were most likely to be employed: domestic service, "textile work in sweatshops, office work, education and health."[26] Labour studies scholar Robert Storey observes that "the WCA, by incorporating women almost solely as dependents, reinforced the dominant gendered assumptions regarding women workers' ephemeral relationships to the labour market. Moreover … it was legislation aimed almost exclusively at the white male working class body."[27] Disabled women workers and disabled racialized workers of both sexes would continue to struggle for inclusion in compensation benefits for decades to come.

One further development during the interwar period was the passage in 1931 of the Ontario Blind Workmen's Compensation Act, which was intended to encourage the employment of visually impaired workers by limiting employers' liability for injuries sustained on the job, while ensuring that blind workers continued to be compensated.[28] The 1931 act, which would be replaced by the 1980s with human rights legislation, was passed at a time when blind men had very few employment prospects, and blind women even fewer, except in low-paying workshops where the focus was on tactile skills, such as broom making. These workshops had been operating in Canada since the late 1800s and seldom led to better-paying work in the mainstream economy, for sighted employers were opposed to hiring blind people.[29]

State support for disabled people in the community was significantly impacted by the First World War, at least when it came to veterans. This was evident with the first federal disability pension, enacted in 1916 by Robert Borden's Conservative government for war veterans and their dependents, though it was left to medical officials to verify claims.[30] This legislation was a breakthrough for state-mandated income supports for disabled people, but it was highly restricted in terms eligibility and compensation. Generally speaking, state support for disabled soldiers was sporadic and inconsistent: an initial spurt of assistance during and immediately after the war was followed by "years of struggle," in the words of military historian Serge Marc Durflinger, who describes how blind Canadian veterans fought, alongside other disabled veterans, to protect their pensions from cutbacks during the Great Depression.[31] It was largely thanks to the advocacy efforts of blind ex-soldiers through organizations they founded – most notably the Canadian National Institute for the Blind, established in 1918 – that their situation was not even worse; along with fellow legion members, disabled veterans kept up the pressure on federal and provincial governments to address their needs. Nevertheless, the federal government's miserly funding of rehabilitation and pension programs, which rejected the vast majority of disabled veterans who applied, underscores the desperate situation in which ex-soldiers from low-income backgrounds found themselves, in Ontario and elsewhere during the interwar years.[32]

The First World War also led to the establishment of veterans' health care facilities in various parts of the country, including in Ontario. Obviously, disabled veterans needed these facilities. The provision of federally run veterans' hospitals in the province during and after the First World War included the founding of the Dominion Orthopaedic Hospital for physically disabled veterans in Toronto, which by 1916 housed an artificial limb shop where disabled veterans were employed making supportive devices for fellow soldiers.[33] The first-person accounts of physically disabled veterans from this period are few, but among those that do exist is a letter from William P., who became paraplegic a few days before the end of the war due to a bullet wound. Unlike most First World War veterans with spinal cord injuries (whose life expectancy was two years after injury, due to bladder infection), he lived for several decades after 1918. This included a period as a patient at the Orthopaedic Hospital before he moved back to a farm near Sault Ste. Marie, from where, nearly thirty years later, he wrote: "any place I can't go with my wheelchair, such as up steps, I have to be carried. I drive my own car which is fixed up to operate all by hand."[34] William was fortunate to have survived as long as he did and to have had some mobility, given that collapsible wheelchairs were little available until after 1945.[35] In addition to the hospital for physically disabled veterans where William was a patient, there were veterans' psychiatric hospitals in London and Cobourg: the former was a permanent institution for veterans; the latter served as a military mental hospital for three years until 1920, after which it reverted to civilian use.[36]

Mental hospital treatment of disabled soldiers, many of them suffering from shell shock, was being offered at a time when eugenics exerted an especially powerful influence on medical diagnoses as well as social policies towards disabled people. As Kandace Bogaert notes, some medical officials at the Cobourg hospital sought to blame the hereditary background of mentally impaired soldiers for their state of mind, rather than war trauma.[37] Ontario never had a eugenically inspired sexual sterilization law on the books; even so, an unknown number of sterilizations were carried out in the province.[38] Furthermore, eugenics ideas and practices were loudly promoted in Ontario by medical officials like C.K. Clarke, a psychiatrist, and Helen MacMurchy, a renowned doctor and school inspector. They were aided by the Toronto-based Canadian National Committee on Mental Hygiene (later the Canadian Mental Health Association), established in 1918, and the Eugenics Society of Canada, founded in 1930.[39] Support for eugenics was widespread among Ontario's political and medical establishment, which viewed it as a form of social control and as a way to reduce expenditures for disabled people, most of whom were deemed to be of lower social and economic value. In a 1936 speech, Herbert Bruce, the province's lieutenant governor, lauded Nazi Germany's sterilization campaign against disabled people, whom he labelled "misfits." Bruce's views were publicly endorsed by, among others, the head of the Children's Aid Society.[40] Others, however, opposed such views, especially the Catholic Church, which had significant influence in Ontario and Quebec, unlike in western Canada. As a result, sterilization was never "officially" approved by the Ontario legislature. Sterilizations were instead done unofficially, on mentally disabled people, without public scrutiny in Ontario until at least the late 1970s.[41] It took even longer than that for eugenically oriented educational statutes to be overturned in the province.

During the interwar years, eugenics was at the height of its public influence in Ontario, and this had a significant, and highly negative, impact on the public education of disabled youth. As historian Jason Ellis has poignantly observed, in the first decades of the twentieth century, eugenics "went to school."[42] Eugenicists in 1914 Ontario were behind the passing of an act that barred children deemed mentally incapable from attending regular public schools, as they had been legally able to do since 1910. Such children were instead expected to be educated by their parents, if they had the resources to do so; otherwise – and likely especially for poor families – they were to be sent to prison-like institutions for people labelled feeble-minded.[43] Not until the last two decades of the twentieth century were these disastrous laws repealed so that certain categories of mentally disabled students were no longer deliberately excluded from the province's publicly funded classrooms.[44] The people targeted by eugenics promoters in Ontario, as elsewhere, whether in schools, in mental institutions, or in the wider community, were those deemed "feeble-minded," a catch-all term that included people considered deviant, with real or presumed mental disabilities. For them – and especially for young women of childbearing years – confinement prevented them from having children. This practice had the same effect as sterilization – it stopped disabled people from procreating.[45] The policies carried out between 1914 and 1945 cemented, for the rest of the twentieth century, systematic efforts to stigmatize people with intellectual disabilities and deliberately exclude them from communities across the province. This was a social policy disaster that did incalculable harm to those directly affected.

While the exclusion of certain disabled people from education was being enforced, another form of exclusion was proceeding apace. Immigrants with disabilities were also being cast out as part of the eugenics agenda. They had been a focus of attention since the late nineteenth century, when new immigrants began surging into the country, particularly from eastern and southern Europe. Around this time, people with certain physical and/or mental disabilities were targeted for exclusion.[46] While immigration was primarily a federal jurisdiction, officials in Ontario were also involved in enabling and expediting the deportation of immigrants deemed feeble-minded, insane, or having physical disabilities, such as being mute or epileptic.[47] As historian Valentina Capurri has documented, during a 1928 debate in the House of Commons an MP from British Columbia favourably quoted the superintendent of an Ontario asylum for people deemed "insane, feeble-minded and epileptic"; this doctor had complained in testimony a few years earlier about admissions to his hospital:

> The proportion of the foreign born was 32 percent. Many of the foreign born were from southern and eastern Europe ... Very few of this class have any means, but become public paupers to be supported by the taxpayers of Ontario. One wonders, when dealing with this subject, how long such an immigration policy should continue, and why the people of Ontario should be taxed to maintain such an alien element who rarely become permanent assets but are simply floating liabilities.[48]

Xenophobia towards racial and ethnic minorities in white, Anglo-Saxon–dominated English Canada during this period combined with prejudice towards disabled people made Ontario, and other Canadian provinces, an unwelcome place for foreign-born immigrants who had various forms of impairment.

Prejudice against physical and racial difference led to a different form of public attention for disabled people in Ontario during this period – the freak show. As Jane Nicholas has shown, people with bodies or skin colour different from the majority white able-bodied population came to be exoticized and voyeuristically stared at, such as at the Canadian National Exhibition (CNE) in Toronto. This dehumanized the people on display, whether they were Indigenous Canadians or physically disabled children.[49] Though the agency of people who were exhibited in such shows is important to consider, attendees' ogling at freak shows in places like local fairs was rendered still more impactful by the increasing social and economic isolation of large numbers of disabled people in a society that stigmatized visible differences. To be visibly disabled in Ontario was to be stared at as truly different. Visibly disabled people were not generally seen in the workplace, schoolroom, or local community, so to see "freaks," you had to go to a carnival.

There were, of course, disabled people who were not held up to public stares as overtly as at freak shows, most notably veterans, though othering still took place. So let us return to where we left off earlier: the effort to make certain disabled people "pay their way" in a capitalist society so as not to become dependent on the state. As Roy Hanes, a scholar of social work, has shown in regard to the Ontario Society for Crippled Children between 1920 and 1940, Rotary Clubs, whose members were local white businessmen, utilized their private businesses and political contacts to provide support services on behalf of visibly disabled children. The aim was to try to ensure that physically disabled children – in this case boys – would not become a provincial "burden" as adults. Rotarians, most of whom "viewed crippled children as pitiable creatures who were … less human than 'normal' children," viewed their community work as a public service, in that they were giving visibly disabled children supports to enable them to integrate themselves later on in life into the economic mainstream.[50] This was based on individualistic ideas about pulling oneself up by one's own bootstraps after getting some initial support at an early stage in life. Rotarians, however, did not consider the vast structural, physical, social, and economic barriers that the disabled children they sponsored had to contend with when seeking employment as adults.

During the Second World War, a federally commissioned report on social security was issued by economist Leonard Marsh in 1943. That report recognized the structural barriers that prevented disabled people from finding and keeping work. To address this issue, Marsh called for a disability insurance program as a way to provide income security for disabled Canadians.[51] These wartime proposals would be acted upon in the post-war years federally and provincially, including in Ontario, as the next section will discuss. By the end of the Second World War, except for Workmen's Compensation, the only other provincially initiated disability income support in Ontario was the extension of publicly paid medical coverage in 1942 to individuals who received pensions due to old age, blindness, or the mother's allowance.[52]

State intervention was also significant in public perceptions of a "new" disability. Polio, which can lead to temporary muscle weakness, full or partial body paralysis, and, in some cases, death, was especially prominent in Ontario from the 1920s to the 1950s. In those decades, it primarily affected children. Since polio was caused by a virus, quarantine measures were regularly instituted in parts of Canada, including Ontario; this meant closing public facilities, such as swimming pools, parks, and movie theatres, especially in the summer. Historian Christopher Rutty has pointed out, however, that "polio's dramatic threat and associated paralysis striking otherwise healthy middle-class children was more significant for its public management than its actual prevalence relative to other, more deadly, diseases of the period."[53] In some years the number of people who had polio was especially high, such as in 1937, when Ontario recorded "a total of 2,546 cases, at a case rate of 70 per 100,000, and [polio] claimed 119 lives," which "came as a major shock" to the province.[54] Generally, however, the numbers of people with polio were lower in most years. Not until the late 1950s and early 1960s, when polio vaccines became publicly available, did this disability, largely viewed as public health threat, recede as a topic of widespread concern, though polio survivors continued to struggle for supports long afterwards.

Overall, the years 1914–45 saw some incremental change for disabled people in regard to state intervention, notably for injured workers, though even that was quite restricted in terms of gender, race, and material benefits. This was a period of continuing challenges for disabled people in Ontario whether in the form of eugenics campaigns that targeted specific groups of disabled people, or immigration restrictions. Veterans were the one group of disabled people who were held in high public regard, because of their war service, but even here, one has to distinguish between physically disabled and mentally disabled veterans; the latter group experienced greater prejudice, particularly when it came to receiving or maintaining a pension after the war.[55] As will become evident in the next section, the following decades began to witness more of an effort to challenge many of these prejudices. That effort came from disabled people themselves.

The Growth of the Welfare State, 1945–1970

The growth of the welfare state after 1945 included increased state support for disabled people outside of long-term institutional confinement or education. This was most apparent soon after the end of the war in the field of rehabilitation. Federal and provincial governments cooperated in the immediate post-war years when advancing supports for physically disabled people to reintegrate into the community. This was initially geared towards supporting disabled Second World War veterans in a more just manner than had been done for disabled veterans after the First World War, which had engendered much bitterness.[56] In Toronto, the founding in 1945 of Lyndhurst Lodge for spinal cord–injured soldiers was spearheaded by veterans working with doctors who specialized in this field. This was essential for addressing the long-term needs of physically disabled soldiers and, eventually, civilians, including those with spinal cord injuries and with polio. The Canadian Paraplegic Association (CPA), which was founded in Toronto by spinal cord–injured soldiers at the end of the war, was particularly prominent in establishing these supports.[57] As with the blind soldiers who founded the CNIB in the final year of the First World War, returned soldiers with spinal cord injuries engaged in advocacy with their peers through the newly founded CPA to influence government policy, first towards disabled veterans and then towards physically disabled people more generally. In this they were successful: the Ontario government played an important role in the late 1940s in making the transition from rehabilitation services focused on ex-soldiers to broadening rehabilitation for civilians. Ontario's Progressive Conservative government under George Drew provided the funding to keep Lyndhurst open and ensure that civilians would receive the same supports for decades to come.[58]

The improved efforts to reintegrate veterans with physical and sensory disabilities after 1945 had a significant impact on civilians with similar disabilities, in that services originally intended for veterans were expanded to the wider civilian population more than ever before. As well, the legacy of how some disabled veterans, notably blind ex-soldiers, had built up a positive image of their abilities during the interwar period was added to in the post-1945 period as more visibly disabled people sought to reintegrate into the Canadian mainstream.[59] With the passage of the federal Disabled Persons Act (DPA) in 1954, Ontario, along with all other provinces, split the cost with the federal government of providing an income for "permanently and totally disabled" adults between eighteen to sixty-five, so long as the recipient underwent a means test and was not receiving other state financial supports.[60] As with the DPA, federal and provincial governments agreed to split the costs in the 1961 Vocational Rehabilitation of Disabled Persons Act. This legislation was designed to support the employment prospects of physically and mentally disabled people through various rehabilitation services.[61] This was a follow-up from the efforts to get disabled veterans back into the job market after 1945.

While the ideal of getting disabled people regular employment – and thus not be viewed as a long-term public "burden" – was considered a positive outcome of an increasingly interventionist state, the stark reality was different. Jobs were difficult to find, and disabled people being viewed as a "burden" in an inaccessible world was hardly conducive to reintegration for those who had to endure this prejudice. A 1962 survey of 931 spinal cord–injured people who had gone through rehabilitation at Ontario's Lyndhurst Lodge found that only 51.5 per cent were known to be employed.[62] Not the least problem was finding accessible employment for physically disabled job hunters. Travelling to and from work was not easy for someone who had mobility impairments in a world in which steps were everywhere, from public transportation to places of work and education. Even if employers were willing to hire disabled applicants, the daily commute and access to buildings posed a major obstacle. Thus, the built environment, along with social prejudices, made employment far more challenging for disabled people than for the able-bodied. For people with mental disabilities, employment prospects were particularly bleak. Parents of people labelled mentally retarded established community workshops with support from the Ontario and local governments beginning in 1955. By the late 1960s, there were ninety workshops for disabled Ontarians, sixty-three of which were for people defined as mentally handicapped.[63] Technically, disabled people who toiled in workshops were not actual employees under the provincial labour code, as they were categorized as being rehabilitated for work, a process that could last for years. Disabled people did do genuine work in workshops during this period; however, they received a mere pittance; by the early 1970s, disabled workshop labourers in Ontario were being paid between three and eleven cents an hour.[64] As will be seen in the next section, exploitative conditions like this would lead to protests in the decades to come.

For most mentally disabled people who lived in Ontario's institutions, the burgeoning welfare state between 1945 and 1970 did little to liberate them from confinement. While there were calls for the deinstitutionalization of some people with intellectual disabilities and increasing attention was being paid to the wretched conditions in places like Orillia – thanks in part to concerned journalists like Pierre Berton – the impact of this wider public interest would be felt largely in later decades.[65] For most people with intellectual disabilities already confined in one of the eleven institutions designated for them in Ontario in the two and a half decades after the Second World War (eventually increasing to sixteen institutions by 1976), life was bleak, traumatic, and utterly isolated from the wider world.[66] Violence inflicted on inmates was common, and there were documented cases of disabled inmates quite literally being killed by staff. Historian Katharine Viscardis how shown how there was a "conspiracy of silence and culture of denial" that lasted for decades, as with the murder of eighteen-year-old Indigenous youth Albert Morrison in 1954 by a staff member at Orillia.[67] As historian Carolyn Fast has poignantly observed, the writings of institutional survivor Peter Park show "that institutions were, for inmates, not homes (or even treatment centres) but prisons, and that those confined within them were frequently confused about the reasons why."[68] Disability scholars Madeline Burghardt and Victoria Freeman have documented the trauma inflicted on individuals with intellectual disabilities who were imprisoned in such places, as well as the guilt and conflict endured by their families across the generations.[69] During this period when the standard medical advice was to incarcerate mentally disabled children in long-term facilities, there were also parents, and in some cases grandparents, who cared for their intellectually disabled children at home and did not send them to institutions. It was people from this group, along with some parents of children who were already institutionalized, who founded the Parents Council for Retarded Children in 1948. In the coming decades, it would evolve into an advocacy group for community living, albeit with plenty of internal divisions along the way.[70] While often criticized in later years for not representing the voices of disabled people, parents' groups such as this one that spread around Ontario and Canada during the 1950s and 1960s were among the earliest to advocate for community supports for their disabled children, and thus for deinstitutionalization. It would take decades of work for these advocates to bring about real change for people with intellectual disabilities. Finally, by 2009, all such places of confinement were closed in Ontario in favour of community living.[71] The seeds for these changes were being planted during the immediate post-war decades.

For people in psychiatric institutions, calls for deinstitutionalization grew apace in the 1960s for much the same reasons as just described – the abuse and dehumanization of people in prison-like institutions had come to light. However, as Harvey Simmons has shown for this decade, the decline in the number of people in Ontario's psychiatric hospitals was not a result of discharges into community support programs (few of which existed); rather, it was due to large numbers of people being sent to residential units *within* the same mental hospitals. Transfers to those units were then recorded as discharges, even though they were not.[72] Even when people actually did leave Ontario's psychiatric hospitals, there was little planning or coordination, and little thought was given to what would happen to them next.

Simmons contends that "if by deinstitutionalisation we mean a clear-cut policy directed towards reducing the population of provincial psychiatric hospitals and establishing community services to receive discharged patients, then no such policy ever existed in Ontario."[73] Not until the next century would this change.

Institutions like the ones just discussed were notorious for the abuses that went on in them. In abusive institutions of another kind – Indian residential schools – disabling experiments were conducted on Indigenous people from 1948 to 1952. As Ian Mosby has documented, federally sponsored nutrition experiments were carried out on malnourished Indigenous children without informed consent at six residential schools across Canada, including in Ontario, as part of a diet-changing assimilation policy to gauge the impact of insufficient nourishment on children's development.[74] That such unethical experiments were conducted on hungry children isolated from their home and culture reflected the broader history of how Aboriginal Canadians' health, and thus disabilities, were an area of scant regard for officials in Ontario and elsewhere. Officials were fully aware of the catastrophic conditions their colonial policies had created; in the early 1940s, the Indian Affairs Department had noted that death rates from tuberculosis overall were "ten to thirty times higher [for Indigenous Canadians] than among the white population."[75] Similarly, state authorities knew about the deadly impact of residential schools in Ontario and throughout Canada, as has been documented by the Truth and Reconciliation Commission, which stated that

> thousands of Aboriginal children died in residential schools. They were killed by relentless waves of epidemics – tuberculosis and a host of other infectious diseases that swept repeatedly through the institutions. Those children did not have to die. The spread of disease was fed and facilitated by crowded living conditions at the schools, along with a lethal combination of substandard sanitation, poor nutrition, and an appallingly low quality of medical care.[76]

The decades-long perpetuation of abusive, violent conditions in state-supported institutions for Indigenous Canadians, as well as among disabled people confined in provincial facilities, reflects the arrogance of state officials at both the federal and provincial levels, who thought they were unaccountable to the most marginalized in society. Unfortunately, they were in fact unaccountable. In the late 1960s, protests against other types of oppression, including racism, as well as civil rights and anti-war struggles, were joined by disability activists who also wanted a better world. In Ontario in 1967, a Toronto-based group formed called the Action League for the Physically Handicapped Advancement, or ALPHA. Its members included Bill Owen, who had paraplegia and went on to teach English at Ryerson Polytechnic (now Toronto Metropolitan University). One of the issues ALPHA spoke out about was the lack of accessible ramps on Toronto's streets. They argued that these ramps were needed everywhere, for people who use wheelchairs had the same right as anyone else to access their own community. An older organization, the Canadian Paraplegic Association, did not at the time agree with this community-wide approach to accessibility; even so, the City of Toronto passed a by-law in June 1970 stipulating that its sidewalks were to be gradually made accessible for wheelchair users in the city. That new policy, initiated by ALPHA, would have a positive impact for countless disabled and non-disabled people in the years to come.[77]

With the founding of the welfare state in post-war Canada, public policy and the daily lives of disabled people in Ontario began to change. Disabled people were still a largely marginalized group who were continuously "struggling for social citizenship," as Michael Prince has noted.[78] This struggle for societal inclusion, exemplified by parents' groups advocacy for community services for their intellectually disabled children and especially by disability activists like those involved in ALPHA, intensified significantly in the latter part of the twentieth century and beyond. As will be discussed in the final two sections of this chapter, more disabled people than ever before were influencing public debates around their place in society, and they continue to do so to this day.

Disability Activism and Rights Advocacy, 1970–1995

In 1970, the federal government, with provincial cooperation, began to implement the Canada Pension Plan–Disability benefit (CPP-D), the most far-reaching measure of the welfare state to this point for people with what were deemed permanent and full disabilities. Unlike other pensions, CPP-D had no age limit, and it covered both physical and mental disabilities. It was intended to move away from stigmatizing notions of state support for people who could not work. It was also designed as income security, higher than other CPP benefits, for people deemed to be "severely" disabled along with their dependents.[79] For the first time, Canadian disability policy was moving towards a broader notion of rights and entitlements, something that disabled people themselves were advocating in Ontario, as elsewhere. By the 1970s, disability activists were reframing public interpretations of disability: no longer was it to be determined through a medical lens that focused on the individual adjusting to an able-bodied world; instead, disability would be understood as caused by a world of inaccessible structures, practices, and attitudes.[80] It was a time of paradigm shifts: disability activists were arguing for greater rights and entitlements, encapsulated in the slogan "Nothing about us without us!"[81]

In recounting this past, histories of disability activism have tended to focus on major population centres; it is essential, though, to underscore that disability activism was taking root in rural and urban areas throughout the province. As disability scholar Ulysses Patola has documented, there was significant, decades-long activism among people with physical and sensory disabilities in Thunder Bay and northwestern Ontario. In 1972 in that region, Handicapped Action Group Incorporated (HAGI) began advocating for physically accessible transportation, housing, and built environments.[82] By this time, organizations of disabled people demanding greater accessibility and civil rights had taken root throughout Canada and indeed the entire world.[83] HAGI raised issues around physical accessibility in the wider community and pressured politicians in Thunder Bay to improve facilities and services, only to be challenged in the 1990s by more radical groups like Persons United for Self-Help (aka PUSH Northwest), who advocated for a more diverse leadership in place of the white men who had long dominated disability activism in the region.[84]

DisAbled Women's Network, or DAWN, was founded in Winnipeg in 1985 and was soon active in Ontario as well. They were among a number of new disability rights groups that sought to broaden representation beyond the older, male-dominated service organizations founded in the first half of the twentieth century.[85] That these newer groups were in tension with some of the more established organizations is perhaps best exemplified in Ontario by the emergence in 1975 of the Blind Organization of Ontario with Self-Help Tactics, or BOOST, which challenged the CNIB in myriad ways. This new group protested against the CNIB for running workshops where blind people worked for poor wages, which led to a strike in the late 1970s.[86] BOOST also called for the CNIB to "be phased out in ten years and replaced by provincial, government-run commissions of the blind."[87] This challenge to the CNIB's authority within the blind community was, for some people, a radical departure, and conflicts arose within BOOST about how to proceed. This led to the newer group's decline in the 1980s; some accused the older organization of deliberately undermining the newer, more militant group.[88] Internal dissension also played a role in parent-run groups, which during the 1970s and 1980s faced splits over whether institutions for people with intellectual disabilities should be closed.[89] The campaign to close these institutions was significantly aided by People First, an organization run by people with intellectual disabilities. It was founded in British Columbia in 1974 and had groups in Ontario by the end of the decade; the first provincial conference in 1981 attracted 650 people.[90] For six years, People First members challenged the name of the parents' group, the Ontario Association for the Mentally Retarded (part of the national organization), pointing to its prejudicial impact on their lives. Finally, in 1985, the name was changed to Community Living Ontario, which it retains to this day.[91] This name change had a huge positive impact for mentally disabled people, who had endured derisive name calling all their lives; that would not end any time soon, but the name change would also change attitudes among the public.

The term "community living" was intended to underscore that disabled people from all backgrounds should not be shut away in institutions; rather, they should live in local neighbourhoods like everyone else. The Independent Living (IL) movement, founded in California during the 1960s, had reached Ontario by 1982, when the first IL facility opened in Kitchener-Waterloo. There, physically disabled people were able to live in their own apartments with their autonomy respected, and educational resources and other supports were made available to them.[92] Justin Clark, for example, won the legal right to live out in the community after spending most of his life since the age of two in an institution for people with developmental disabilities in Smiths Falls, Ontario. Clark, twenty-one, had cerebral palsy and wanted to move in with friends in Ottawa, but his father opposed this and sought to have him declared mentally incompetent. Instead, with the support of disability lawyers and advocates, a judge found him mentally competent, and in 1982 he was allowed to leave the institution to live in the community, where he has resided for nearly forty years.[93] This was an individual victory for Clark and a collective victory for disabled people in the long struggle to close down institutions – a struggle that would last into the next century, as noted earlier.[94]

Activism among people deemed "mad" in Ontario started in the mid- to late 1970s. The Ontario Mental Patients Association (later named On Our Own) was the first such group to take root, in 1977. OOO and similar groups sometimes sought to form cross-disability alliances to fight a common cause, most notably through the Coalition on Human Rights for the Handicapped. In 1980 that group, which included representatives of people with physical, mental, and sensory disabilities, successfully opposed the Ontario government's exclusion of people defined as mentally handicapped from protection against discrimination under the new provincial Human Rights Code.[95] A year later, another group of cross-disability activists successfully pressured the federal Liberal government under Pierre Trudeau to make sure people with mental disabilities were included as protected along with all other categories of disability in the new *Canadian Charter of Rights and Freedoms*, which was signed into law in 1982.[96] Provincial funding for legal aid clinics in Ontario in the 1970s and 1980s was especially important as a means to expand disability rights. The Advocacy Resource Centre for the Handicapped (ARCH) joined other disability activists in the community to advocate for people in mental institutions to have the right to vote in Ontario municipal and provincial elections; they achieved that right in 1985.[97] Several years later, after further court challenges, the same right was extended to federal elections, but it was not until 1992 that physically accessible polling booths were guaranteed by law.[98] During this same period in Ontario, two prominent activists in the disability community were elected to public office: David Reville, the first public ex-psychiatric patient elected to Toronto City Council, was elected to the provincial legislature in 1985; and in 1990, Gary Malkowski was elected as an Ontario MPP, which made him the first Deaf legislator in Canada.[99] It is also significant that in 1990, the same year that Malkowski was elected, Deaf activists organized a "Deaf Ontario Now" campaign, which called for the official recognition of American Sign Language (ASL) as the language of the Deaf community, support for ASL interpretation in the public school system, the preservation of three Provincial Schools for the Deaf, and the hiring of more Deaf teachers, administrators, and professionals.[100]

Collectively, this activism had a significant impact on public perceptions, as well as on the inclusion of disabled people in civil society in Ontario between the 1970s and the 1990s. Even so, disabled people continued to be marginalized with regard to employment and educational opportunities. Perhaps this was most evident in the widespread protests in the early 1990s over the exploitative working conditions in sheltered workshops in Ontario, criticisms that dated from the early 1970s. By the 1990s many sheltered workshops had been closed, though some still exist for people with intellectual disabilities.[101] As austerity measures were introduced by provincial governments, particularly after 1995, when Mike Harris's Conservative government was elected, draconian cuts to social services were felt across the board. At the same time, the federal Liberal government under Jean Chrétien was enacting similar policies.[102] These were bleak years for many disabled people, but there was also resistance to these policies, as will be seen in the final section of this chapter.

Austerity and Activism, 1995–2022

As Canadian federal and provincial governments of all political persuasions sought to reduce welfare state expenditures in the name of austerity throughout the 1990s and well into the twenty-first century, disabled people experienced renewed efforts by policy-makers to remove some of them from social assistance rolls. In Ontario, some aspects of this policy led to provincial governments funding businesses run by disabled people, partly as an alternative to disreputable sheltered workshops and partly in an effort to get smaller businesses involved in hiring disabled people. These developments – very much a consequence of decades-old criticisms about the lack of employment of disabled people – led to increased funding by the Ontario government of disability-related businesses. A prime example of such a program was the Consumer/Survivor Development Initiative (later called the Ontario Peer Development Initiative), which was originally funded by the provincial NDP government under Bob Rae beginning in 1991 and which continued under Progressive Conservative and Liberal governments well into the twenty-first century.[103] By 2008 there were sixty businesses operated by psychiatric survivors and consumers in Ontario, partly a result of efforts at "creating meaningful jobs for survivors" while reducing hospital admissions.[104] These businesses reflected mainstream economic policies by successive Ontario governments aimed at disabled people generally and, in this case, at psychiatric patients in particular: "A partnership between peer support organizations and hospitals to take care of people being discharged from care also has been shown to reduce an estimated $12.2 million worth of hospital days in a group of less than 200 people."[105] It was therefore part of the deinstitutionalization process, which involved efforts to reduce state expenditures on disabled people. Some activists criticized this policy as part of the neoliberal downsizing of government support for people with disabilities.

These businesses did provide an entry point for some disabled people to find work in the community at a time when their employment prospects in the mainstream economy remained poor at best. Yet for most disabled people, struggles to find work at a living wage, rather than precarious employment or no job at all, remain the norm even today. Compounding this has been a disability benefit system that penalizes disabled people who find work and then have to worry about losing their hard-to-get benefits in an unstable job market. Around 17 per cent of disabled people in early twenty-first-century Canada do not look for work because of this dilemma – get a job, lose benefits if the wages are too high, then lose the job and be stuck with no benefits.[106] Provincial disability benefits, known as the Family Benefits Allowance until the name was changed in 1997 to the Ontario Disability Support Program, were capped so that people who earned a good wage lost their benefits.[107] Thus, while public policy had by now advanced beyond a charity model, structural problems remained.

So too did structural and attitudinal problems, which persisted for disabled people who had been discharged from large-scale institutions. As noted earlier, the last of the prison-like facilities for people with intellectual disabilities was closed in Ontario in 2009. The provincial Liberal government under Kathleen Wynne apologized in 2013 to the survivors of these institutions for the horrific abuse they had endured. But another sort of abuse persists in communities, which have often been less than welcoming to ex-inmates of institutions for people with developmental and psychiatric disabilities: minimum separation distance by-laws enacted by municipalities. As Chava Finkler has shown, in recent decades, as more and more neighbourhood group homes and other communal settings have been opened for people with disabilities, citizens' ratepayers groups and local politicians have promoted discriminatory laws to keep disabled people at a distance and to reduce their visibility to neighbours.[108] Community integration has thus been far from successful as a result of some neighbourhoods' social exclusionary policies towards disabled people. As well, group homes can replicate some of the oppressive conditions that existed in larger institutions, conditions that include intense surveillance by staff as well as, sometimes, violence. Natalie Spagnuolo and Kory Earle note that "in 2009, a stunning 53 lives were lost in Ontario group homes for people with intellectual disabilities."[109] Deinstitutionalization is not past history in this province.

As a result of the long history of discrimination towards disabled Canadians from racialized backgrounds, advocates have worked to establish supports that avoid a white, Eurocentric model and are instead run for and by racialized people. For example, Across Boundaries was founded in Toronto in 1995 after advocacy efforts by the Ethno-Racial Disabled Persons Coalition of Ontario, or ERDCO, which was formed to address racism and provide alternative sources of support for disabled people of colour.[110] At the same time, the killing by the police of racialized disabled people, particularly people with mental health disabilities in Ontario, has led to decades-long organizing by disability activists and the communities directly affected to try to stop these attacks and address the combined lethal impact of racism and ableism that continues into the 2020s.[111] Tensions within the disability rights community, many of whose leaders are white, have raised questions about how relevant disability activism has been to people from outside the majority racial population. In northwestern Ontario, disability activists in HAGI have been engaged in advocacy efforts since 1972, but white members of that group made no serious efforts to reach out to Indigenous communities until the early 2000s. For example, they neglected people living on nearby Indigenous lands that HAGI leaders characterized as "far away" or in the "far north" even when reserves were "adjacent to the south of Thunder Bay."[112] Ulysses Patola has documented how some white disability leaders kept Indigenous communities at a physical and mental distance (quite literally) owing to cultural prejudices rooted in Canadian colonial history, thus alienating Indigenous people with disabilities from a well-known local disability group. Such prejudice left "indigenous [people with disabilities] on the periphery of an accessible region."[113]

Efforts to broaden representation within the disability rights movement in Ontario have included attempts to engage more communities through events such as Mad Pride and Disability Pride celebrations, which began in the 1990s and continued into the early 2000s, with mixed results.[114] These efforts grew, in part, out of attempts by disability activists to address systemic racism, sexism, and ableism both in the wider community and within the disability community itself. A radical approach to addressing structural barriers in recent years for disabled people in Ontario is perhaps best illustrated by the response to provincial disability legislation. In 1995, the Ontarians with Disabilities Act Committee began to advocate for a law similar to the Americans with Disabilities Act of 1990. After a decade of organizing, this cross-disability network of activists succeeded in getting legislation passed in the province; the 2001 Ontarians with Disabilities Act, widely viewed as inadequate, was replaced in 2005 by the Accessibility for Ontarians with Disabilities Act (AODA).[115] Aimed at making Ontario fully accessible by 2025, the act was criticized by activists outside of the original organizing committee as phasing in accessibility provisions over two decades – some people pointed out that they might be dead by then. It was also seen as ineffective in realizing its ultimate goals, regardless of timeline. This criticism is based on its lack of enforcement mechanisms as well as jurisdictional problems in removing barriers for disabled people whether they are seeking work, education, health services, or public transportation or visiting local businesses.[116] Disability Action Movement Now, or DAMN 2025, expressed the frustration of some disabled people, arguing that the AODA "is little more than paper" and more likely to benefit already privileged disabled people rather than the mass of poor, economically marginalized members of the community.[117] At the same time, disability activists in Ontario deserve praise for their unrelenting efforts to pressure reluctant governments to do what needs to be done to make the province more accessible than ever before. In January 2022, the AODA Alliance issued a statement on the third anniversary of a 2019 independent report to the provincial Conservative government of Doug Ford. That report stated that "progress towards Ontario becoming accessible to 2.6 million people with disabilities was 'glacial', and that Ontario remains full of 'soul-crushing barriers' impeding people with disabilities." Though the Ford government pledged to support implementation when elected in 2018, AODA advocates criticized the its record in 2022 as "abysmal. It initiated a few slow, halting, and inadequate actions on accessibility. However, on balance, it made things worse for people with disabilities."[118] One hundred fifty-five years after becoming a province, Ontario remains largely inaccessible to huge numbers of disabled people.

Conclusion

As Ontario entered the third decade of the twenty-first century, the province and the entire world was confronted with the coronavirus pandemic, which posed particular dangers for disabled people. Reports of rationing of medical supplies, such as life-saving ventilators, for disabled patients in intensive care, and the horrifying tally of dead in long-term care homes for elderly citizens, many of which house disabled people, have led advocates in the early 2020s to call for safeguards to protect the rights of disabled people at a time of public health crisis.[119] That these calls need to be made, in Ontario and further afield, shows how far we still have to go in ensuring people that with disabilities are treated the same as everyone else. The history of disability in Ontario since Confederation teaches us how very long it takes to change policies and attitudes for the better when it comes to social supports for people with physical, mental, and sensory impairments, whether in an emergency situation or in daily living. That there are now a significant number of disabled people advocating for public supports for all is a sign that the danger of going back to the bleak days of large-scale institutionalization and community segregation appears to be remote. If history teaches us anything, however, it is that progress is both elusive and can be reversed. The extent to which integration of, and accessibility for, disabled people in the wider community will proceed or regress is impossible to predict. One thing that is certain is that the struggles recounted in this chapter will continue for generations to come, with past history building upon future challenges.

DEDICATION

This chapter is dedicated to the memory of my brother, Daniel Reaume (1958–2016).

QUESTIONS FOR CONSIDERATION:

1. Where did most disabled people in Ontario live during the second half of the nineteenth and early twentieth centuries? How and why did this begin to change for some groups of disabled people?
2. How was work by people with physical, sensory, and mental disabilities viewed since the nineteenth century, both inside institutions and outside in the community?
3. How have disabled people's organizations influenced public policy in Ontario beginning with veterans' groups during the first half of the 1900s and wider civil society activism since the mid-twentieth century?
4. What forms of discrimination have existed between and among disabled people in Ontario since Confederation? How have some disabled people been historically more advantaged than others when it comes to obtaining state supports?
5. What impact did the post-1945 growth of the welfare state have on different groups of disabled people in Ontario?
6. How have disabled people and allies challenged attitudes and practices about their place in Ontario since 1867? What are some of the ongoing historical inequities affecting disabled people that need to be addressed in the twenty-first century?

NOTES

1 Readers who would like to explore the field of critical disability studies in Canada can visit an open access journal that has been publishing regularly since 2012: *Canadian Journal of Disability Studies*, https://cjds.uwaterloo.ca/index.php/cjds.
2 Sarah F. Rose, *No Right to Be Idle: The Invention of Disability, 1840s–1930s* (Chapel Hill: University of North Carolina Press), 13.
3 Ezra H. Stafford, "Some Clinical Aspects of Mental Disease," *Canadian Journal of Medicine and Surgery* 1, no. 4 (April 1897): 159–60.
4 Ruby Heap, "'Salvaging War's Waste': The University of Toronto and the 'Physical Reconstruction' of Disabled Soldiers during the First World War," in *Ontario since Confederation: A Reader*, ed. Edgar-André Montigny and Lori Chambers (Toronto: University of Toronto Press, 2000): 214–34; Geoffrey Reaume, "Lunatic to Patient to Person: Nomenclature in Psychiatric History and the Influence of Patients' Activism in North America," *International Journal of Law and Psychiatry* 25, no. 4 (July–August, 2002): 410–11; Jason Ellis, *A Class by Themselves? The Origins of Special Education in Toronto and Beyond* (Toronto: University of Toronto Press, 2019), 95.
5 John Radford and Deborah Carter Park, "A Convenient Means of Riddance: Institutionalization of People Diagnosed as 'Mentally Deficient' in Ontario, 1876–1934," *Health and Canadian Society* 1,no. 2: 369–92; Geoffrey Reaume, "Patients at Work: Insane Asylum Inmate Labour in Ontario, 1841–1900," in *Mental Health and Canadian Society: Historical Perspectives*, ed. James Moran and David Wright, eds.,. Montreal/Kingston: McGill-Queen's University Press, 2006: 69-96. For developments in the United States during this period, see: Kim Nielsen, *A Disability History of the United States*, Chapter 5, "*I am disabled, and must go at something else besides hard labor*: The Institutionalization of Disability, 1865–1890" (Boston: Beacon Press, 2012).
6 James Moran, *Committed to the State Asylum: Insanity and Society in Nineteenth-Century Quebec and Ontario* (Montreal and Kingston: McGill–Queen's University Press, 2000), 20, 22.
7 Euclid Herie, *Journey to Independence: Blindness – the Canadian Story* (Toronto: Dundurn Press), 24.
8 Moran, *Committed to the State Asylum*, 113–15, 140.
9 Caroline E.M. Carrington-Decker, "Remembering the Boys," in *Untold Stories: A Canadian Disability History Reader*, ed. Nancy Hansen, Roy Hanes and Diane Driedger (Toronto: Canadian Scholars' Press, 2018), 110–20; Edgar-André Montigny, *Foisted upon the Government? State Responsibilities, Family Obligations, and the Care of the Dependent Aged in Late Nineteenth-Century Ontario* (Montreal and Kingston: McGill–Queen's University Press, 1997), 82–129. See also Veronica Strong-Boag, "Children of Adversity: Disabilities and Child Welfare in Canada from the Nineteenth to the Twenty-First Century," *Journal of Family History* 32, no. 4 (October 2007), 413–32.
10 Archives of Ontario (AO), "Annual Report of the Inspector of Asylums, Prisons and Public Charities" [London Asylum report], 1870–71, 73.
11 AO, "The Report of the Inspector of Lunatic and Idiot Asylums, Table No. 1," [London Asylum column], 1900, xvi.
12 Moran, *Committed to the State Asylum*, 122.
13 Geoffrey Reaume, *Remembrance of Patients Past: Patient Life at the Toronto Hospital for the Insane, 1870–1940* (Toronto: Oxford University Press, 2000), 47–9, 50–1.
14 Reaume, "Patients at Work," 78, 81.
15 AO, "The Report of the Inspector of Lunatic and Idiot Asylums, Table No. 1," 1900, xvii.

16 Rose, *No Right to Be Idle*, 27–36, 73–90; Reaume, *Remembrance of Patients Past*, 133–80.

17 Kim Nielsen, *A Disability History of the United States* (Boston: Beacon Press, 2012), 69–75, 88, 92; Geoffrey Reaume, "From the Perspectives of Mad People," in *The Routledge History of Madness and Mental Health*, ed. Greg Eghigian (London: Routledge, 2017), 282–5; Geoffrey Reaume, "The Place of Mad People and Disabled People in Canadian Historiography: Surveys, Biographies, and Specialized Fields," *Journal of the Canadian Historical Association* 28, no. 1 (2017), 296–9.

18 Herie, *Journey to Independence*, 26; Alessandra Iozzo-Duval, "The Education of 'Good' and 'Useful' Citizens: Work, Disability, and d/Deaf Citizenship at the Ontario Institution for the Education of the Deaf, 1892–1902," in *Untold Stories*, ed. Hansen, Hanes and Driedger, 68.

19 Vanessa Warne, "'Blindness Clears the Way': E.B.F. Robinson's *The True Sphere of the Blind* (1896)," in *Untold Stories*, ed. Hansen, Hanes and Driedger, 58.

20 Warne, "'Blindness Clears the Way,'" 59.

21 Reaume, *Remembrance of Patients Past*, 145–7.

22 Iozzo-Duval, "The Education of 'Good' and 'Useful' Citizens, 79–80.

23 Dustin Galer, "A Friend in Need or a Business Indeed?: Disabled Bodies and Fraternalism in Victorian Ontario," *Labour/Le Travail* 66 (Fall 2010): 936.

24 Montigny, *Foisted upon the Government?*, 88. See also Edgar-André Montigny, "Families, Institutions, and the State in Late-Nineteenth-Century Ontario," in *Ontario since Confederation*, ed. Montigny and Chambers (Toronto: University of Toronto Press, 2000), 74–93.

25 Alvin Finkel, *Social Policy and Practice in Canada: A History* (Waterloo: Wilfrid Laurier University Press, 2006), 83–84.

26 Robert Storey, "From Invisibility to Equality? Women Workers and the Gendering of Workers' Compensation in Ontario, 1900–2005," *Labour/Le Travail* 64 (Fall 2009): 83.

27 Storey, "From Invisibility to Equality?," 83.

28 Herie, *Journey to Independence*, 117.

29 Herie, *Journey to Independence*, 104–8.

30 Michael Prince, *Struggling for Social Citizenship: Disabled Canadians, Income Security, and Prime Ministerial Eras* (Montreal and Kingston: McGill–Queen's University Press, 2016), 67–8.

31 Serge Marc Durflinger, *Veterans with a Vision: Canada's War Blinded in Peace and War* (Vancouver: UBC Press, 2010), 137–40.

32 Finkel, *Social Policy and Practice in Canada*, 98.

33 Geoffrey Reaume, *Lyndhurst: Canada's First Rehabilitation Centre for People with Spinal Cord Injuries, 1945–1998* (Montreal and Kingston: McGill-Queen's University Press, 2007), 11.

34 Reaume, *Lyndhurst*.

35 Mary Tremblay, "Going Back to Civvy Street: A Historical Account of the Impact of the Everest and Jennings Wheelchair for Canadian World War II Veterans with Spinal Cord Injury," *Disability and Society* 11, no. 2 (1996): 149–69.

36 Kandace Bogaert, "'Due to His Abnormal Mental State': Exploring Accounts of Suicide among First World War Veterans Treated at the Ontario Military Hospital at Cobourg, 1919–1946." *Histoire Sociale/Social History* 51, no. 103 (May 2018): 99–123.

37 Bogaert, "'Due to His Abnormal Mental State,'" 112.

38 Angus McLaren, *Our Own Master Race: Eugenics in Canada, 1885–1945* (Toronto: McClelland and Stewart, 1990), 163.

39 McLaren, *Our Own Master Race*, 107–26.

40 McLaren, *Our Own Master Race*, 122, 205n87.

41 McLaren, *Our Own Master Race*, 169.
42 Jason Ellis, *A Class by Themselves? The Origins of Special Education in Toronto and Beyond* (Toronto: University of Toronto Press, 2019), 11–51.
43 Ellis, *A Class by Themselves?*, 47; Ellis, "Early Educational Exclusion: 'Idiotic' and 'Imbecilic' Children, Their Families, and the Toronto Public School System, 1914–50," *Canadian Historical Review* 98, no. 3 (September 2017): 483–504.
44 Ellis, *A Class by Themselves?*, 208–9.
45 Constance Backhouse, "'Pleasing Appearance . . . Only Adds to the Danger': The 1930 Insanity Hearing of Violet Hypatia Bowyer," *Canadian Journal of Women and the Law* 17, no. 1 (2005): 1–3; McLaren, *Our Own Master Race*, 168.
46 Ena Chadha, "'Mentally Defectives' Not Welcome: Mental Disability in Canadian Immigration Law, 1859–1927," *Disability Studies Quarterly* 28, no. 1 (Winter 2008), n.p.
47 Chadha, "'Mentally Defectives' Not Welcome'"; Natalie Spagnuolo, "Defining Dependency, Constructing Curability: The Deportation of 'Feebleminded' Patients from the Toronto Asylum, 1920–1925," *Histoire Sociale/Social History* 49, no. 98 (2016): 125–53.
48 Valentina Capurri, *Not Good Enough for Canada: Canadian Public Discourses around Issues of Inadmissibility for Potential Immigrants with Diseases and/or Disabilities, 1902–2002* (Toronto: University of Toronto Press, 2020), 38–9.
49 Jane Nicholas, *Canadian Carnival Freaks and the Extraordinary Body, 1900–1970s* (Toronto: University of Toronto Press, 2018), 39, 66, 140–8; 152, 166–7.
50 Roy Hanes, "Service Clubs and the Emergence of Societies for Crippled Children in Canada: The Rise of the Ontario Society for Crippled Children, 1920–1940," in *Untold Stories*, ed. Hansen, Hanes and Driedger, 152.
51 Prince, *Struggling for Social Citizenship*, 73–6.
52 Prince, *Struggling for Social Citizenship*, 72n3.
53 Christopher J. Rutty, "The Middle-Class Plague: Epidemic Polio and the Canadian State, 1936–37," *Canadian Bulletin of Medical History* 13, no. 2 (1996): 278.
54 Rutty, "The Middle-Class Plague," 287.
55 Mark Humphries, "War's Long Shadow: Masculinity, Medicine, and the Gendered Politics of Trauma, 1914–1939," *Canadian Historical Review* 91, no. 3 (September 2010): 503–31.
56 Jeff Keshen, "Getting It Right the Second Time Around: The Reintegration of Canadian Veterans of World War 2," in *The Veterans Charter and Post-World War II Canada*, ed. Peter Neary and J.L. Granatstein (Montreal and Kingston: McGill–Queen's University Press, 1998), 62–84.
57 Reaume, *Lyndhurst*, 54–55.
58 Reaume, *Lyndhurst*, 68.
59 Durflinger, *Veterans with a Vision*, 182.
60 Prince, *Struggling for Social Citizenship*, 83–4.
61 Prince, *Struggling for Social Citizenship*, 87.
62 Reaume, *Lyndhurst*, 104,
63 Vera C. Pletsch, *Not Wanted in the Classroom: Parent Associations and the Education of Trainable Retarded Children in Ontario, 1947–1969* (London: Althouse Press, 1997), 41–5; Geoffrey Reaume, "No Profits, Just a Pittance: Work, Compensation, and People Defined as Mentally Disabled in Ontario, 1964–1990," in *Mental Retardation in America: A Historical Reader*, ed. Steven Noll and James W. Trent Jr. (New York: NYU Press, 2004), 468–9.
64 Reaume, "No Profits," 469–70.
65 Finkel, *Social Policy and Practice in Canada*, 183-84; Victoria Freeman, *A World without Martha: A Memoir of Sisters, Disability, and Difference* (Vancouver: Purich Books, 2019),

111–12; Pierre Burton, “Huronia: Pierre Berton Warned Us 50 Years Ago,” *Toronto Star*, 20 September 2013, https://www.thestar.com/news/insight/2013/09/20/huronia_pierre_berton_warned_us_50_years_ago.html.

66 For a list and dates of Ontario’s provincial institutions where people with intellectual disabilities were confined, see https://www.mcss.gov.on.ca/en/dshistory/firstInstitution/list_institutions.aspx. For an overview of this history, including summary information on various provincial institutions that are now closed, see Ivan Brown and John P. Radford, “The Growth and Decline of Institutions for People with Developmental Disabilities in Ontario: 1876–2009,” *Developmental Disabilities* 21, no. 2 (2015): 7–27.

67 Katharine Maye Viscardis, “The History and Legacy of the ‘Orillia Asylum for Idiots’: Children’s Experiences of Institutional Violence” (PhD diss., Trent University, 2020), 1–2, 167–87; 269–330 at 269.

68 Carolyn Fast, “The Un-Making of Difference: The Winding Road of Deinstitutionalization in Ontario, 1960–2018” (MA thesis, Department of History, Brock University, 2020), 52.

69 Madeline Burghardt, *Broken: Institutional Families and the Construction of Intellectual Disability* (Montreal and Kingston: McGill–Queen’s University Press, 2018); Freeman, *A World Without Martha.*

70 Melanie Panitch, *Disability, Mothers, and Organization: Accidental Activists* (New York: Routledge, 2008), 36–7.

71 Brown and Radford, “The Growth and Decline of Institutions”; https://www.mcss.gov.on.ca/en/dshistory/firstInstitution/list_institutions.aspx.

72 Harvey G. Simmons, *Unbalanced: Mental Health Policy in Ontario, 1930–1989* (Toronto: Wall and Thompson, 1990), 158–9.

73 Simmons, *Unbalanced*, 160.

74 Ian Mosby, “Administering Colonial Science: Nutrition Research and Human Biomedical Experimentation in Aboriginal Communities and Residential Schools, 1942–1952,” *Histoire Sociale/Social History* 46, no. 91 (May 2013): 159.

75 Truth and Reconciliation Commission of Canada (TRC), “Health: 1940–2000,” in *The Final Report of the Truth and Reconciliation Commission of Canada*: vol. 1: *Canada’s Residential Schools: The History, Part 2, 1939 to 2000* (Montreal and Kingston: McGill–Queen’s University Press, 2015), 194.

76 TRC, “An Attack on Aboriginal Health: The Marks and the Memories.” in *Final Report*, vol. 5: *The Legacy* (Montreal and Kingston: McGill–Queen’s University Press, 2015), 139.

77 Reaume, *Lyndhurst*, 140.

78 Prince, *Struggling for Social Citizenship.*

79 Prince, *Struggling for Social Citizenship*, 99–107.

80 Sharon Barnartt and Richard Scotch, *Disability Protests: Contentious Politics, 1970–1999* (Washington, D.C.: Gallaudet University Press, 2000); April D’Aubin, “The Council of Canadians with Disabilities: A Voice of Our Own, 1976–2012,” in *Untold Stories*, ed. Hansen, Hanes and Driedger, 248–51.

81 James Charlton, *Nothing about Us without Us: Disability Oppression and Empowerment* (Berkeley: University of California Press, 2000).

82 Ulysses Patola, *“Get the Disabled out of Their Closets”: Disability Activism in the City of Thunder Bay and Northwestern Ontario, 1972–1990s* (PhD diss., University of Manitoba, 2019), 75, 160–94, 309–79.

83 It needs to be stressed that disability activists were engaged far afield from North America and Western Europe before the 1970s, although this is the period when the most sustained

activism began, continuing until now. See, for example, Fikru Negash Gebrekidan, "Disability Rights Activism in Kenya, 1959–1964: History from Below," *African Studies Review* 55, no. 3 (December 2012): 103–22; Gildas Brégain, "An Entangled Perspective on Disability History: The Disability Protests in Argentina, Brazil, and Spain, 1968–1982," in *The Imperfect Historian: Disability Histories in Europe*, ed. Sebastian Barsch, Anne Klein, and Peter Verstraeten (Bern: Peter Lang, 2013); and Sharon N. Barnartt, "Social Movement Diffusion? The Case of Disability Protests in the US and Canada," *Disability Studies Quarterly* 28, no. 1 (Winter 2008).

84 Patola, *"Get the Disabled out of Their Closets,"* 426–35.

85 Joanne Doucette, "The DisAbled Women's Network: A Fragile Success," in *Women and Social Change: Feminist Activism in Canada*, ed. Jeri Dawn Wine and Janice Ristock (Toronto: James Lorimer, 1991), 221–35.

86 Dustin Galer, *Working towards Equity: Disability Rights Activism and Employment in Late Twentieth-Century Canada* (Toronto: University of Toronto Preess, 2018), 87.

87 Dave Greenfield, "The Organizations That Tried: Predecessors of the AEBC" (Alliance for Equality of Blind Canadians, 2011), http://www.blindcanadians.ca/publications/cbm/32/organizations-tried-predecessors-aebc.

88 Greenfield, "The Organizations That Tried." When the author was on a research trip to Kenora, Ontario, in 1999, there was a BOOST group active there, which I was told was the only one left in Ontario.

89 Panitch, *Disability, Mothers, and Organization*, 101–25.

90 Bruce Kappel, "A History of People First in Canada," in *New Voices: Self-Advocacy by People with Disabilities*, ed. Gunnar Dybwad and Hank Bersani Jr. (Cambridge, MA: Brookline Books, 1996), 99.

91 Kappel, "A History of People First in Canada," 108–9.

92 John Lord, *Impact: Changing the Way We View Disability – The History, Perspective, and Vision of the Independent Living Movement in Canada* (Ottawa: Independent Living Canada, 2010), 41–2.

93 Panitch, *Disability, Mothers, and Organization*, 123; Marilou McPhedran, "The Habeas Corpus of Justin Clark," in *Untold Stories*, ed. Hansen, Hanes, and Driedger, 282–93.

94 Regarding the campaign to close institutions and human rights work by and with people with intellectual disabilities, see Sue Hutton, Peter Park, Martin Levine, Shay Johnson, and Kosha Bramesfeld, "Self-Advocacy from the Ashes of the Institution," *Canadian Journal of Disability Studies* 6, no. 3 (2017): 30–59.

95 Geoffrey Reaume, "Consumer/Survivor Movement in Promoting Patients' Rights in Ontario, 1977 to Present," in *Mental Health and Patients' Rights in Ontario: Yesterday, Today, and Tomorrow* – 20th Anniversary Special Report, May 2003, Psychiatric Patient Advocate Office (Toronto: Queen's Printer, 2003), 51; Gary Malkowski, "Struggles, Challenges, and Accomplishments of Deaf, Deafened, and Hard of Hearing People," in *Honouring the Past, Shaping the Future: 25 Years of Progress in Mental Health Advocacy and Rights Protection*, Psychiatric Patient Advocate Office, 25th Anniversary Report (Toronto: Queen's Printer, 2008), 63. For a discussion of mad activists' alliance-building efforts in Ontario during this period, see Reaume, "Mad Activists and the Left in Ontario, 1970s–2000," in *Voices in the History of Madness: Personal and Professional Perspectives on Mental Health and Illnesss*, ed. Rob Ellis, Sarah Kendal and Steven Taylor(Cham: Palgrave Macmillan, 2021), 307–32.

96 Yvonne Peters, "From Charity to Equality: Canadians with Disabilities Take Their Rightful Place in Canada's Constitution," in *Making Equality: History of Advocacy and Persons with Disabilities in Canada*, ed. Deborah Stienstra and Aileen Wight-Felske (Concord: Captus Press, 2003), 119–36.

97 Reaume, "Consumer/Survivor Movement," 51.

98 Michael J. Prince, *Absent Citizens: Disability Politics and Policy in Canada* (Toronto: University of Toronto Press, 2009), 21.

99 David Reville was first elected to Toronto City Council in 1980. The following year he went public as having been a psychiatric patient; in 1982, he was re-elected to City Council, where he served until 1985. He was elected twice as a Member of the Provincial Parliament for a Toronto riding, in 1985 and 1987, and served in that capacity until 1990, when he did not run again for elected office. See David Reville, "Don't Spyhole Me," *Phoenix Rising* 2, no. 1 (1981). Gary Malkowski was elected as an MPP for a Toronto riding in 1990 and served until he was defeated in the 1995 election. See: "Gary Malkowski in Profile," *Abilities* (*c*. 1990–91), https://www.abilities.ca/people/sign-of-the-times. Both Reville and Malkowski were elected as members of the Ontario New Democratic Party; both were active in the Mad and Deaf communities, respectively, before, during, and after their time in public office.

100 "Deaf Ontario Now" (1990) was inspired in part by "Deaf President Now" (1988), at Gallaudet University in Washington, D.C, where a student-led strike won its demand that the university hire the first Deaf president in its history. See: "Deaf Ontario Now – Yesterday, Today and Tomorrow" (video, 2010), https://www.youtube.com/watch?v=TsFGLKCY_qU. See also James Roots, "Deaf Education and Advocacy – A Short History of the Canadian Association of the Deaf," in *Making Equality: History of Advocacy and Persons with Disabilities in Canada*, ed. Deborah Stienstra and Aileen Wight-Felske (Concord: Captus Press, 2003). I would like to thank Samuella Johnson, York University Critical Disability Studies PhD student, for bringing to my attention the history of and documentation about Deaf Ontario Now. It needs to be noted that not all Deaf people identify as disabled. Culturally Deaf people argue that they are a linguistic minority with their own history and language, rather than a disabled group, and choose to identify as capital "D" Deaf.

101 Galer, *Working towards Equity*, 107–8, 115–17, 123–7; Reaume, "No Profits, Just a Pittance," 482–5.

102 Douglas James Nesbitt, "Days of Action: Ontario's Extra-Parliamentary Opposition to the Common Sense Revolution, 1995–1998" (PhD diss., Queen's University, 2018), http://hdl.handle.net/1974/24271. For a broader discussion of austerity measures in Ontario under both Conservative and Liberal provincial governments since 1995, see Greg Albo and Bryan Evans, eds., *Divided Province: Ontario Politics in the Age of Neoliberalism* (Montreal and Kingston: McGill–Queen's University Press, 2019).

103 Joel E. Johnson, Barbara Frampton, Raymond Cheng, and Shawn Lauzon, "From the Exception to the Expected: OPDI and Consumer/Survivor Organizations in Ontario Today," in *Honouring the Past, Shaping the Future*, 86–8.

104 Johnson et al., "From the Exception to the Expected," 87.

105 Johnson et al., "From the Exception to the Expected."

106 Megan A. Rusciano, "Towards Full Inclusion: Addressing the Issue of Income Inequality for People with Disabilities in Canada," in *Disabling Barriers: Social Movements, Disability History, and the Law*, ed. Ravi Malhotra and Benjamin Isitt (Vancouver: UBC Press, 2017), 162–4.

107 Rusciano, "Towards Full Inclusion," 166, 167, 180.

108 Lilith "Chava" Finkler, "'They should not be allowed to do this to the homeless and mentally ill': Minimum Separation Distance Bylaws Reconsidered," in *Mad Matters: A Critical Reader in Canadian Mad Studies*, ed. Brenda LeFrancois, Robert Menzies, and Geoffrey Reaume (Toronto: Canadian Scholars' Press, 2013), 221–38.

109 Natalie Spagnuolo and Kory Earle, "Freeing our people: Updates from the long road to deinstitutionalization," *Canadian Centre for Policy Alternatives* (4 July 2017), https://www

.policyalternatives.ca/publications/monitor/freeing-our-people-updates-long-road -deinstitutionalization.

110 Galer, *Working towards Equity*, 99–100; Aseefa Sarang and Kwame McKenzie, "Access to Mental Health Services and Supports for Racialized Groups," in *Honouring the Past, Shaping the Future*, 146–8.

111 Ahmad Saidullah, Geoffrey Reaume, and Judith Bell, *Saving Lives: Alternatives to the Use of Lethal Force by Police*, Report of a Conference Held in Toronto, 23–4 June 2000, Urban Alliance on Race Relations, Queen Street Patients Council, 2002; Tracy Mack, "The Mad and the Bad: The Lethal Use of Force against Mad People by Toronto Police," *Critical Disability Discourse* 6 (2014): 7–52; CBC News, "Family identifies man, 62, who was shot and killed by police in Mississauga as SIU investigates: Ejaz Ahmed Choudry, who family members say suffered from schizophrenia, died in his apartment on Saturday," 21 June 2020, https://www.cbc.ca/news /canada/toronto/siu-police-shooting-mississauga-1.5621243.

112 Patola, *"Get the Disabled out of Their Closets,"* 436, 437, 444.

113 Patola, *"Get the Disabled out of Their Closets,"* 439–42, 445–7 at 447.

114 Melissa Graham and Kevin Jackson, "Divided No More: The Toronto Disability Pride March and the Challenges of Inclusive Organizing," in *Mobilizing Metaphor: Art, Culture, and Disability Activism in Canada*, ed. Christine Kelly and Michael Orsini (Vancouver: UBC Press, 2016): 279-288.

115 David Lepofsky, "The Long, Arduous Road to a Barrier-Free Ontario for People with Disabilities: The History of the Ontarians with Disabilities Act," *National Journal of Constitutional Law* 15 (2004): 125–33; Malkowski, "Struggles, Challenges and Accomplishments," 63.

116 Galer, *Working towards Equity*," 8, 201.

117 Graham and Jackson, "Divided No More," 283–5 at 285.

118 "Press Release - Today is The Ford Government's Troubling Three Year Anniversary of Inaction On the Onley Report, Which Had Urged Bold New Action on Accessibility for 2.6 Million Ontarians with Disabilities," Accessibility for Ontarians with Disability Act Alliance (January 31, 2022), web site accessed on February 20, 2022: https://www.aodaalliance.org/whats-new /today-is-the-ford-governments-troubling-three-year-anniversary-of-inaction-on-the-onley -report-which-had-urged-bold-new-action-on-accessibility-for-2-6-million-ontarians-with -disabilities/

119 "Open Letter from Major Disability Organizations Calling on the Ontario Government to Ensure Persons are not Deprioritized from Accessing Critical Care Because of their Disability" [Press release], ARCH Disability Law Centre, 8 April 2020, https://archdisabilitylaw.ca/press -release-open-letter-from-major-disability-organizations-calling-on-the-ontario-government -to-ensure-persons-are-not-deprioritized-from-accessing-critical-care-because-of-their -disability; "ARCH Bulletin on COVID-19: Ontario Health's Clinical Triage Protocol for Major Surge in COVID Pandemic," ARCH Disability Law Centre, 14 May 2020, https:// archdisabilitylaw.ca/resource/arch-bulletin-on-covid-19-ontario-health-clinical-triage -protocol/; "ARCH Bulletin on COVID-19: June 15: Province issues Recommendations to Allow Visitors in Hospitals, but Fails to Address Rights of Persons with Disabilities," ARCH Disability Law Centre, 15 June 2020), https://archdisabilitylaw.ca/new-arch-bulletin-on -covid-19-province-issues-recommendations-to-allow-visitors-in-hospitals; "A Deeply Troubling Issue of Life and Death — An Independent Report on Ontario's Seriously-Flawed Plans for Rationing or 'Triage' of Critical Medical Care If COVID-19 Overwhelms Ontario Hospitals" [Press release], Accessibility for Ontarians with Disability Act Alliance,

25 February 2021, https://www.aodaalliance.org/whats-new/a-deeply-troubling-issue-of-life-and-death-an-independent-report-on-ontarios-seriously-flawed-plans-for-rationing-or-triage-of-critical-medical-care-if-covid-19-overwhelms-ontario-hospitals; Hilary K. Brown, Sudipta Saha, Timothy C.Y. Chan, Angela M. Cheung, Michael Fralick, Marzyeh Ghassemi, Margaret Herridge, Janice Kwan, Shail Rawal, Laura Rosella, Terence Tang, Adina Weinerman, Yona Lunsky, Fahad Razak, and Amol A. Verma, "Outcomes in Patients with and without Disability Admitted to Hospital with COVID-19: A Retrospective Cohort Study," *Canadian Medical Association Journal* 194, no. 4 (2022): E112-E121; Dave Yasvinski, "Adults with Disabilities Bearing Brunt of COVID-19: Study," *Healthing: Inspiring Canadians to Live Better*, 31 January 2022), https://www.healthing.ca/diseases-and-conditions/coronavirus/adults-with-disabilities-bearing-brunt-of-covid-19-study.

CHAPTER TWENTY-THREE

Welfare to Workfare to Basic Income: Poverty and the "Dependency Debate" in Ontario, from the 1930s to 2020

JAMES STRUTHERS

In the spring of 1995, Mike Harris's Progressive Conservative Party won a surprise victory in the Ontario provincial election by making welfare reform the most visceral issue of the campaign.[1] Vowing to "break the cycle of dependency" that he claimed trapped welfare families in poverty, Harris told Ontario's voters that, if elected, his government would give social assistance recipients "a reason to get out of bed in the morning." A PC government would cut allowances by 25 per cent and impose "mandatory work-for-welfare requirements" on all the able-bodied. Those who refused to participate would "lose their benefits entirely."[2] Harris's ability to capitalize on a groundswell of public dissatisfaction with the welfare system caught most media commentators and Bob Rae's New Democratic Party government by surprise. Ontario's total welfare caseload had more than tripled between 1981 and 1994, rising from 4 per cent to over 12 per cent of the population, or one out of every eight Ontarians. Annual welfare spending had jumped from less than $2 billion to more than $6.2 billion over the same period. The driving force behind this explosion, according to Harris, was not recession or economic restructuring, but overly generous welfare benefits that had lured the working poor into chronic dependency. "The system is broken," he argued. "It needs fixing, not tinkering."[3] Harris's adroit cultivation of a populist welfare backlash played a decisive role in the PCs' come-from-behind election victory.[4]

On taking power, the Harris government immediately slashed welfare benefits by 21.6 per cent. One year later it unveiled Ontario Works, a new mandatory work-for-welfare regime modelled on US state precedents in New Jersey, Michigan, and Wisconsin, whose goal was to have all employable welfare clients, including single mothers, enrolled in compulsory training, job search, or community work placement schemes by the end of 1998. The "current welfare system encourages indolence," Minister of Community and Social Services David Tsubouchi told the legislature in justifying the new scheme. Ontario Works, in contrast, would "demand responsible behavior and individual initiative from people on welfare. For many … this will be the first time they have had any obligation to work, or even look for work."[5]

Before the Harris victory, welfare had not been a major issue in an Ontario provincial election since the Great Depression. Why did it re-emerge so forcefully six decades later? To what extent have concerns about "welfare dependency" always surrounded policy debates around social assistance, and in what ways has the discourse been different for men as opposed to women? Why were compulsory work tests abolished in the early 1960s, and why were they restored in the 1990s? To what extent did the creation of Ontario Works represent a symbolic and controversial turning point within the Canadian welfare state? This chapter will attempt to place workfare in context by examining previous cycles of welfare reform and dependency debates in Ontario since the 1930s, ending with a discussion of the failed experiment between 2017 and early 2018 to test whether welfare could be replaced altogether through the guarantee of a basic income.

Moral panic around the work ethic during the Great Depression provides the closest parallel to the turbulent welfare politics of the 1990s and the heated contemporary debates around the efficacy of a basic income as a policy response to mass unemployment arising from the 2020 COVID-19 pandemic. It was during the economic crisis of the 1930s that the structure of our welfare bureaucracy first took shape.[6] Then, as now, Ontarians found themselves confronted by exploding welfare caseloads, persistent high levels of unemployment, and intense debates over what should be the core goals of public assistance to those in need.

One common response was to blame the unemployed for preferring relief to work, and to demand compulsory work on municipal, provincial, and federal projects as a condition for receiving assistance. "Cheating is rampant … [on] direct relief," Ontario's Minister of Public Works David Croll declared in the autumn of 1934, at a time when Canada's jobless rate stood at almost 22 per cent. Too many of the able-bodied were "being given rations, shelter, and clothing … without being required to make any return," a policy that was "detrimental to anyone's morale." Newly elected Liberal premier Mitch Hepburn agreed. "There's a growing impression among the taxpayers of this province that they are being drained of their money to provide a living for idlers," he told the legislature within a year of coming to power, adding, "There's a growing demand for a halt on rising relief costs." Arguing that "something for nothing is a dangerous creed," Croll and Hepburn demanded that local welfare departments require all able-bodied married men to perform work in municipal woodyards or on other city projects as a condition for maintaining their families' eligibility for assistance. Since 1933, single unemployed men were being sent to federal defence department relief camps to perform compulsory work in exchange for their room, board, and a daily twenty-cent "allowance." The "moral purpose" of these camps, government officials argued, was to cure a "state of mind diseased by … compulsory idleness" by abolishing the men's "mental attitude that assistance from the State was their inherent right."[7]

Croll's department also rolled back welfare rates by 14 per cent in more than thirty Ontario communities where it believed local councils were paying benefits that were too generous. In defence of the cuts, senior department officials argued that "relief allowances are so close to the amount that can be earned by laborers on full-time work that the wage earners' point of view becomes important. What incentive is there for them to work?" Despite strikes, occupations of local welfare offices, "hunger marches," and frequent demonstrations by organizations of the unemployed between 1934 and 1936, Hepburn and Croll stuck to their slogan "Relief for workers, nothing for shirkers." For the remainder of the Depression, work tests and surprise home visits to families – "to purge exploiters and cheaters" from relief caseloads – remained features of provincial and municipal welfare administration across Ontario.[8]

Welfare did not disappear as a political issue during the 1940s, even though wartime full employment had shrunk relief caseloads to only a fraction of their Depression levels. Throughout the war years, welfare was largely restricted to widows or deserted mothers with children, as well as disabled elderly men and women who were still too young to collect a means-tested old age pension.[9] The able-bodied jobless after 1941 were simply cut off relief; however, workers could now become eligible for benefits under the new national unemployment insurance scheme launched that same year.

The war experience provided fertile ground for welfare reform. Detailed research on basic minimum living costs by social planning bodies such as the Toronto Welfare Council proved extremely effective in generating widespread publicity around the glaring inadequacy of provincial and local relief allowances, first formulated during the hard times of the Great Depression. In an era when prices and wages were subjected to stringent wartime regulations, and more than one third of the men volunteering to join the armed forces had been rejected because of poor health, the dangerously low living standards of individuals and families on social assistance were hard to justify. Coordinated pressure from women's organizations, social workers, and nutritionists helped to convince first the City of Toronto, and subsequently the provincial government by 1944, to adopt scientific nutritional standards for pricing welfare food allowances across Ontario.[10] Also, women on mothers' allowances received a 20 per cent hike in benefits, the first increase since the program was launched in 1920. By 1945 they would also be getting monthly family allowance payments ranging from $5 to $8 from the federal government for each of their children. These two policy changes between 1943 and 1945 almost doubled the monthly incomes of many mothers on social assistance, notwithstanding their increased opportunities to gain earnings from part-time work.[11]

Full employment, along with a wartime political climate emphasizing the values of social solidarity, sacrifice, and post-war reconstruction, briefly transformed the context of welfare politics in Ontario, a change signalled most dramatically by the near victory of the socialist Co-operative Commonwealth Federation (CCF) in the 1943 provincial election. Demands for work tests and moral alarm over relief dependency, so prevalent during the 1930s, eased once the exceptionally tight labour market of the Second World War put virtually everyone who wanted a job into paid employment. The new PC administration of George Drew, elected on a "22 point program" of social reform, appointed a social worker, Burne Heise, as Deputy Minister of Public Works. Over the next three years Heise enlisted the help of Ontario social work leaders to develop a plan for comprehensive welfare reform. Through the creation of regional welfare units across Ontario, staffed by trained social workers, Heise planned to bring an end to "aimless policies … guided by local whims … or financial expediency," so that welfare clients, no matter where they lived, would receive "proper standards of aid."[12]

Heise's vision for a modernized and consolidated welfare system for Ontario was short-lived. The Provincial Treasurer, Leslie Frost, warned Drew that any assistance scheme not based on social insurance had a tendency "to instill into our people the feeling that the country owes them a living." In a 1946 cabinet shuffle, Drew appointed a new welfare minister, W.A. Goodfellow, a former rural reeve who believed that post-war social policy reform was moving too fast. "People are losing their spirit of independence … and the will to do for themselves," he warned, "[They] are only kidding themselves if they think they can get something for nothing." Across Ontario, particularly in rural areas, where taxes and welfare benefits were kept as low as possible, local politicians quickly mobilized strong opposition against Heise's plan to regionalize welfare services. As the treasurer of the Ontario Municipal Association reminded a 1947 conference of provincial social workers, the "primary responsibility" of local officials was "to those whom they represent and not to the underprivileged." By 1949, when Frost replaced Drew as Ontario's premier, the brief, war-inspired cycle of welfare reform was all but dead. Heise was forced to resign as deputy welfare minister, and his ambitious plan to standardize Ontario's welfare services remained stillborn. His successor, James Band, had been a relief inspector in the 1930s despite having no social work training and had carefully worked his way through the ranks of the provincial welfare department by developing a reputation for vigorously policing local welfare costs. As deputy minister, Band would dominate the formation of provincial welfare policy for the next two decades.[13]

Ontario's prolonged economic boom throughout most of the 1950s pushed issues of poverty and welfare into the background. In Toronto, shelter allowances for welfare clients between 1951 and 1961 remained effectively frozen at ceilings set in 1951, despite a 60 per cent jump in the cost of living. Maximum food allowances grew by only 30 per cent. By 1961, according to detailed calculations made by the Toronto Social Planning Council, a mother-led family on welfare with three children was receiving less than half the monthly income needed to reach a basic standard of adequacy. Single people on welfare received only 29 per cent of the council's recommended minimum monthly budget.[14] With annual unemployment rates remaining below 3 per cent, concerns about welfare dependency and the erosion of the work ethic were minimal, especially since the able-bodied jobless remained ineligible for social assistance. In the field of welfare, attention focused on the rehabilitation of "problem families" through social casework and the incremental expansion of program eligibility to include wider categories of those in need.

Two groups claimed the most attention. The first was single mothers. Since the late 1940s, Ontario's mothers' allowance program had undergone a process of incremental liberalization. In 1946, women deserted by their husbands for one year (instead of three) gained eligibility for benefits, and in 1951, divorced mothers in need were also included. But the most symbolic policy shift occurred in 1956, when unwed mothers were finally brought into the program. Since the inception of mothers' allowances in 1920, the key criterion for determining benefit eligibility had been that women be "fit and proper persons," a condition interpreted to exclude all mothers who had conceived children outside marriage. Although some advocates for mothers' pensions had never accepted a double standard that punished needy children for the marital status of their parents, most women's groups and social workers, before the 1950s, agreed with the Toronto Social Planning Council's statement that "plac[ing] the unmarried mother in the same status as the married or widowed mother [would] tend to lower standards rather than raise them."[15]

Three trends converged by the mid-1950s to undercut such moralizing distinctions. The first was the growing demand from municipal authorities that the costs of caring for illegitimate children be shifted from local taxpayers, who financed the largest share of the work of foster homes and Children's Aid Societies, to the provincial government, which had exclusive responsibility for mothers' allowances. Toronto's mayor argued in the 1940s that many unmarried mothers were "just as capable ... of giving their children good care" as foster parents, whose support, through the CAS, was a "heavy cost to the municipality." Also, by the mid-1950s the dominance of psychiatric theory among social workers employed in child welfare agencies had eroded earlier moral distinctions around who was or was not a "fit and proper person." Viewing this matter through the lens of casework, social workers argued that unwed motherhood should be seen "not ... merely as a sex experience and a violation of the moral code of the community, but as a symptom of behavior expressing the needs of the individual." Through therapeutic adjustment and with ongoing financial support, some of these women could be rehabilitated to become caring parents. Perhaps the most persuasive argument was simply that illegitimacy rates across Ontario in the 1950s were steadily declining, as was the overall mothers' allowance caseload.[16] Consequently, the cost of adding unwed mothers to the program was expected to be negligible. "We have to go slowly," argued Ontario's welfare minister Louis Cecile when this symbolic change was made in 1956. "We don't want to encourage this kind of conduct, but we ought to encourage a mother to bring up her own child."[17]

Employable men, who had been denied welfare benefits since the end of the Depression, were the second group to gain eligibility, in 1957. Single mothers were not expected to seek full-time employment; able-bodied jobless men were, and the problem of what to do about them, when they were ineligible for federal unemployment insurance benefits, revived a different moral debate around welfare rights and the work ethic. About one third of Ontario's unemployed during the 1950s were recent immigrants, workers in seasonal industries not covered under the Unemployment Insurance (UI) program, or people who had exhausted their insurance benefits through prolonged joblessness. Although their numbers were not large during these years of prosperity, their plight was desperate. The federal, provincial, and local governments were not willing to assume any legal responsibility for their care. As a result, their survival, particularly during the difficult winter months, was dependent on intermittent help from friends, family members, or private charities. Toronto officials reported that many of the married jobless in these years were "deserting their families so that the women and children could go on straight relief." Soup kitchens and hostels during winter months were "full to overflowing," and heads of families simply could not understand why they should not have either work or assistance. Since many of these men were recent immigrants, they also shared a "frantic fear of deportation."[18]

The Ontario government, and other provincial governments, argued that since Ottawa had assumed constitutional responsibility for unemployment insurance in 1940, the care of all the able-bodied jobless was a federal problem. Queen's Park wished "to have nothing to do with unemployment relief." The federal government of Louis St. Laurent replied that its primary responsibility to the jobless was limited to those who had paid UI premiums. Payments for unemployment relief would resume "only when the problem reached emergency proportions," something that clearly had not occurred during the 1950s.[19]

This impasse was finally broken in 1955, when the Canadian Welfare Council threatened to organize a national conference on unemployment to publicize the plight of the thousands of unemployed trapped outside the federal UI scheme. When most of the provinces indicated they were willing to attend, the St. Laurent government avoided political embarrassment by agreeing to resume negotiations with the provinces on a shared-cost unemployment relief scheme provided that the council called off its plans for a national conference. A year later, St. Laurent's administration passed the Unemployment Assistance Act, which, for the first time since 1941, restored federal funding for employables on provincial and local welfare.[20]

Ontario delayed entering into the new federal unemployment assistance program until 1957, when the PC government of John Diefenbaker agreed to share half the costs for *all* clients on general welfare, not simply the able-bodied, a policy change that would prove critical in the years ahead. Nonetheless, Frost's administration reinstated eligibility for welfare to employables only with reluctance, arguing that it did not wish to "revert to the dole system of the thirties." A preferable solution, W.A. Goodfellow argued, would be to allow local governments "to put a person on relief work rather than on relief and still qualify for Federal aid." Unless there were some work requirements, officials pointed out, providing relief to able-bodied men could upset the delicate relationship between welfare and wage rates for low-income workers. When medical care and family allowances were factored in, the maximum welfare allowance for men with families was already higher than what many low-wage earners could make, and most men were "reluctant to accept employment unless it would afford a higher income than Public Assistance."[21]

In 1956, when the Unemployment Assistance Act was passed, the Canadian economy was still booming, and federal officials did not expect the scheme's costs to amount to more than $13 million a year. However, the so-called Diefenbaker recession struck Canada in 1958, and the effects of that cyclical and structural downturn would persist until the early spring of 1962. Annual unemployment rates shot up to 7 per cent, more than double the levels prevailing throughout most of the

1950s. With the return of significant levels of unemployment came a 150 per cent increase in welfare caseloads, soon to be followed by renewed calls for bringing back compulsory work requirements for the able-bodied jobless.

Ottawa's Unemployment Assistance Act was silent on the question of workfare. Indeed, it contained almost no regulations on welfare standards whatsoever; it simply provided 50 per cent federal funding for all local and provincial direct relief spending. It remained up to Ontario's municipalities to decide what conditions they wished to attach to help the able-bodied applying for social assistance. By 1959 many had begun to reinstate work tests. In Chippewa, just south of Niagara Falls, women on general welfare assistance were put to work washing the windows and cleaning the floors of the town hall for sixteen hours each month. Scarborough divided the monthly welfare payments of its employables by an hourly rate of $1.55 and demanded that they work it off through eight-hour days "clearing … brush from undeveloped township land." London's mayor told Ontario's premier that the men in his city liked to work off their assistance because "it took the stigma out of welfare and helped them to retain their self-respect." The Ontario Welfare Officers' Association claimed that "the threat of work stimulates people to find other support than welfare."[22]

Workfare's most powerful advocate in the province was deputy welfare minister James Band, who had perfected such systems during his years as a roving provincial relief inspector during the Great Depression. "There are many services that can be performed by recipients in return for the assistance granted which do not greatly affect the stream of economic life in the community," Band told federal officials in justifying the return of workfare to Ontario. "Most of these projects are basically work tests of a temporary nature such as cutting wood … road work, brushing, and other projects of this type." Such tasks kept the jobless "usefully occupied … without prejudice to anyone."[23]

To his great surprise, Band discovered that in much of Ontario, and within the federal government itself, the idea of workfare was no longer acceptable. Unlike in the 1930s, Ontario by 1960 had a strong trade union movement that, after two decades of high employment and Keynesian economic thinking, viewed unemployment as a national economic problem, not a test of moral character for the jobless. Ontario's unions demanded extended UI benefits and job creation projects with real wages to combat the recession, not the return of punitive practices, which, as the National Union of Public Employees argued, would "create unemployment for regular municipal employees."[24]

Equally significant was the changed climate of public opinion, reflected in newspaper editorials about workfare across the province. "Older citizens," the *Belleville*

Intelligencer reminded its readers, "will remember the 'make-work' schemes of the Depression, the devices by which relief recipients were required to 'earn' the meagre aid received but which so often robbed this work of all dignity because it served no useful social purpose ... Lacking such a purpose, enforced labour comes very near to being a punishment for poverty." When a local alderman in Peterborough recommended bringing back work tests, the *Peterborough Examiner* argued that giving in to such demands would allow "penny-pinching municipalities to exploit those on welfare as a cheap source of labour for municipal projects." It was a "sure way to bring back the workhouse." The *Toronto Star* best summed up the way in which two decades of post-war affluence had changed public thinking about workfare by the early 1960s. "Our wealthy society has the obligation to provide [the unemployed] with work at a living wage. Failing this, it has the obligation to support them and their families decently – not in exchange for forced labour, not as a matter of charity, but simply as a matter of right."[25]

Any possibility that workfare might make a comeback during the Diefenbaker recession was put to rest by federal officials in Ottawa. Indeed, Canada's auditor general, not usually a friend of social reform, singled out Ontario's workfare schemes as an example of gross fiscal mismanagement within federal financing of the Unemployment Assistance Act, whose costs had ballooned to more than $200 million by the early 1960s. Federal funding provided through this legislation was intended solely to relieve the jobless, not to subsidize cheap labour for municipal improvement schemes, the auditor general argued. Social work officials within the federal Department of National Health and Welfare detested the idea of workfare as a "return to Old Poor Law concepts" that reflected a "punitive approach to relief recipients." Now, seizing on the auditor general's critique, they informed the Ontario government that local communities implementing workfare would be ineligible for 50 per cent federal cost sharing. "Being requested to join a work gang may be physically and emotionally more damaging than being without employment," Health and Welfare administrators argued; nor would such routine labour "help the individual to obtain new skills." They also warned that senior governments would never be able to "avoid becoming enmeshed in the normal public works and 'housekeeping' programs of the municipalities if work for relief projects involving welfare funds were developed." By 1961, faced with the loss of Ottawa's largesse, Ontario had halted its brief flirtation with a return to workfare.[26]

With the election in 1963 of a federal Liberal government under Lester Pearson, who had campaigned on an activist social policy agenda,[27] welfare reform underwent its most significant cycle of expansion, culminating in the passage of the Canada Assistance Plan in 1966. A number of different factors converged during these years to push the national and provincial governments towards a broadening of welfare entitlements. The first was an unanticipated consequence of the 1956 Unemployment Assistance Act. Ottawa's willingness to finance half the costs of provincial and local general relief caseloads through this program injected a huge stream of new revenue into the field of welfare policy. In Ontario, for example, this new federal money cut local governments' share of general welfare costs in half, from 40 per cent to only 20 per cent. This meant that municipalities now had the fiscal capacity to meet a wider portion of the unmet budgetary needs of their welfare clients, especially for burgeoning shelter costs in cities like Toronto. Provincial governments also had a strong incentive to shift as many people as possible out of other categorical assistance programs – such as mothers' allowances, where there was no federal cost sharing, and old age assistance and disability allowances, where federal aid was subject to strict conditions – onto general relief caseloads, where the more open-ended terms of the Unemployment Assistance Act gave Ottawa much weaker control over provincial spending. As a consequence, general welfare costs and caseloads rose dramatically after 1958, and they would continue to grow even as the economy pulled out of its recession. By 1963, unemployment assistance was one of Ottawa's fastest-growing social policy expenditures, yet only one third of the program's clients were "unemployed" or capable of looking for work. This rapid expansion of social spending within a shared-cost program that lacked clear standards, definitions, and accounting procedures pushed federal authorities towards an entirely new legislative framework for public assistance.[28]

Welfare reform also gained great momentum when US President Lyndon Johnson declared a War on Poverty in his January 1964 State of the Union Address. America's War on Poverty, as Gareth Davies argues, "was a war born of optimism. Abundance created the conditions in which a successful campaign might be launched, while new knowledge encouraged the belief that the causes – and not merely the consequences – could be eliminated."[29] In Canada, Pearson lost little time in echoing Johnson's uplifting rhetoric by promising "the elimination of poverty among our people" in his April 1965 Speech from the Throne.[30]

Anti-poverty crusaders on both sides of the border described the poor as being trapped in a "culture of poverty" that prevented them from taking advantage of the opportunities afforded by the economic boom sweeping across North America during the 1960s. There was a "whole subculture of poverty," Ontario's NDP argued, "of people and their families … who live within the community but are not part of it and who have developed their own culture of poverty with its own conditions and its own customs." To break out of this "vicious circle," they needed more than money. More important was the provision of "individual counselling," "remedial training and retraining," and "rehabilitation services," all of which should be designed to "assist them to reestablish themselves as independent, self-reliant citizens."[31]

In some respects, this early War on Poverty discourse shared assumptions with later workfare campaigns of the 1990s. During both eras, reformers targeted the cultural values of the poor as a principal cause of poverty and viewed character rehabilitation as key to lifting individuals and families out of poverty. But unlike workfare advocates, most anti-poverty crusaders in the 1960s did not view overly generous welfare entitlements as the principal cause of dependency, particularly given the low benefit levels and narrow eligibility criteria that had surrounded welfare during the previous decade. Nor did they support compulsory work tests as a way out of the welfare system. Instead, reformers sought to liberalize the scope and benefits of government social programs to bring wider categories of the poor within reach of job counselling, skills training, and therapeutic social work intervention. As Ontario's chief economist put it during a 1965 national conference on poverty, expanding opportunity required policies designed to "lift … the growing generation out of depressed conditions [through] education, training, or mobility, thereby not only improving their human condition but adding to [their] economic productiveness as well." From this "dynamic" viewpoint, "welfare policies become consistent with growth policies."[32]

The cause of welfare reform in the 1960s also benefited from the shared social work values and training of senior officials within the federal Department of National Health and Welfare and many provincial welfare departments. Influential members of this policy-making elite had served apprenticeships with the Canadian Welfare Council before moving into government. As Rodney Haddow argues, the Canada Assistance Plan "emerged from this cooperative group of welfare officials. They reached a general consensus on reform in the [CWC] in the late 1950s, and elaborated this in direct federal–provincial negotiations from 1960 to 1964."[33]

A key tenet of this consensus was that welfare was a social right. It should be available to any Canadian citizen at a standard sufficient to support health and decency on proof of the fact, not the cause, of need.[34] In other words, older moralizing distinctions between the deserving and the undeserving poor should be jettisoned by public welfare departments in their determinations of eligibility for welfare. This belief led federal welfare officials, along with some of their provincial counterparts, to push hard for the abolition of work tests as a key condition for funding within the Canada Assistance Plan of 1966, as well as for the abolition of the old moral requirement that mothers be "fit and proper persons" if they were to qualify for mothers' allowances.[35] They were less successful, however, in achieving meaningful definitions of national minimum standards for benefit levels to be cost shared through the Canada Assistance Plan. Despite official statements that Ottawa's goal in welfare reform was to meet the poor's "basic needs … in ways that recognize and preserve [their] rights and dignity," federal policy-makers conceded privately that it was out of the question, politically, for Ottawa to define precisely what those basic needs might be. "Standards can only be decided upon locally," the Department of Finance's deputy minister insisted. It should be up to provincial governments to decide what basic level of assistance was appropriate in relation to minimum wage rates within their own borders.[36]

The main significance of the Canada Assistance Plan was that it expanded federal cost-sharing for social assistance into entirely new areas. In Ontario, local Children's Aid Societies, women and children dependent on mothers' allowances, and welfare departments hiring new staff all became eligible for 50 per cent federal subsidies for the first time. Welfare recipients also gained appeal procedures against unfavourable decisions by local authorities, establishing the principle that welfare was indeed a social right of citizenship. Older categorical boundaries separating welfare support for the elderly, the disabled, and single mothers were abolished through the consolidation of all assistance programs into either family benefits for long-term assistance or general welfare assistance for short-term support, principally for the unemployed. When the new legislation came into effect in 1967, welfare benefits in Ontario rose 15 to 20 per cent on an across-the-board basis. It was the most significant single increase since the 1940s, although individual and family benefit levels, even after this increase, ranged from 43 per cent to 66 per cent, respectively, of the minimum budget standards for adequacy recommended by the Toronto Social Planning Council.[37]

Welfare expenditures and caseloads in Ontario continued to rise throughout the remainder of the 1960s, even though the province's economy was growing at a record pace and unemployment remained below 4 per cent. Single mothers represented by far the largest share of the rising caseload. Between 1966 and 1969 the number of families led by women on family benefits more than doubled, from 10,056 to 20,428, boosting the cost of this program by over 200 per cent. By 1972 more than 33,000 mothers in the province would be collecting family benefits, compared with only 7,400 in the mid-1950s. Mother-led families on family benefits and general welfare represented one third of the province's entire welfare caseload.[38] These soaring numbers were fuelled by both liberalized eligibility requirements and rising rates of family fragmentation.

This "feminization of poverty" remained one of the most neglected features of the entire debate on welfare during the 1960s. As in the US, most of the language and program activity flowing out of Ottawa's anti-poverty initiatives in labour market training and regional development "assumed that the overwhelming majority of those who need jobs, and therefore the skills to obtain jobs, were men," even though single mothers were the fastest-growing component of the welfare budget. As a consequence, particular structural obstacles such as the absence of affordable day care, which trapped women in a life of poverty, were ignored. By 1969, Ontario had only 5,000 publicly subsidized day care spaces, at a time when the children of family benefits and general welfare recipients numbered more than 100,000. As the province's former director of general welfare assistance pointed out, "this was like hoisting a small umbrella to shelter a stadium full of people in a downpour." Across Ontario, only 15 per cent of mothers on family benefits reported any part-time earnings, and women were staying on social assistance twice as long as men. Yet officials refused to see the provision of subsidized day care as an urgent need for women who wished to escape poverty. According to Louis Cecile, the province's welfare minister for most of the 1960s, it was the desire of too many mothers to combine "employment and homemaking [that] has contributed to many of the social problems which have to be faced and treated." Their "primary responsibility," he insisted, "[is] for family life."[39]

For women on social assistance, these arguments were hypocritical. Why did the government "pay foster mothers more money to look after youngsters than it gives to the natural mothers of these children?," asked Women Trapped in Poverty, an organization of welfare mothers, at the decade's end. "There is no recognition of our contribution to society." Echoing the origins of mothers' allowances in 1920 as a reward for "service to the state," these women insisted that natural mothers on family benefits deserved "pay for work equal to the foster mothers at least," as well as "adequate shelter for our family" and "greater opportunities and support to . upgrade our education and eventually phase out of government assistance." Instead, the level of family benefits to single mothers, as a proportion of the average Ontario family income or the Toronto Social Planning Council's minimum guide for social adequacy, remained virtually unaltered over the course of the 1960s. As Lorna Hurl concludes, over time the programme ... changed to ensure more equitable treatment of one group of sole-support ... mothers in relation to another, but not to provide greater adequacy or equality of recipients in relation to the population as a whole."[40] Thus, the War on Poverty swelled the ranks of women on family benefits but did not substantially alter their prospects for a better life.

One key group bypassed in the 1960s cycle of welfare reform was the working poor, who laboured intermittently for low wages but were unable to earn enough to bring their living standards close to or above the poverty line. Concern about the relationship between minimum wages and welfare allowances, or the work/welfare trade-off, had always been a dominant theme within Ontario and Canadian social policy. When the province's welfare benefits were enhanced after the passage of the Canada Assistance Plan, the plight of families living on minimum-wage incomes who remained ineligible for social assistance drew growing attention. A major study conducted by the Economic Council of Canada in 1968 revealed that two thirds of the poor worked at least part of the year yet could not qualify for needs-tested welfare benefits through the Canada Assistance Plan. Two years later, an influential federal study chaired by Senator David Croll revealed that more than one million Ontarians – about 13 per cent of the population – were living in poverty. "The welfare system is a hopeless failure. The matter is not even controversial," the Senate report *Poverty in Canada* concluded.[41] Ontario officials agreed that the trade-off between work and welfare had created major dilemmas in determining a decent standard of social adequacy. The province's deputy welfare minister told Croll's Senate committee:

> The problem here [is] in terms of how high the level of allowances may be. The higher they are, the greater becomes the differential between the person who works full time on low wages and the persons on public assistance … The person on public assistance begins to be in a position of marked advantage over the person working full time at low wages. If our allowances were higher … this spread would become even greater than it is at present.

As John Yaremko, Ontario's welfare minister, conceded, "our big job now is to solve the problem of how to bring up the income of a family whose head is working full time and who we call, for want of a better term, the working poor."[42]

The answer put forward by the Senate's 1970 report *Poverty in Canada*, which borrowed heavily from welfare reform proposals emanating from south of the border, was for a single Guaranteed Annual Income, financed and administered by the federal government, that would replace the complex collection of federal income security programs. The rapid economic growth and "opportunity programs" of the 1960s had largely passed over the heads of the poor, the Senate report argued. Education, economic growth, and skills training by themselves were "insufficient to break the cycle of dependency." Instead, the poor needed more money. Poverty could "be eliminated if Canadians so wish," but only through "the acceptance … of an adequate minimum income as a matter of right for all citizens." Once freed from the struggle of "meeting the basic needs of survival, [the poor] will be able to take advantage of opportunity programs which will enable them to achieve independence."[43]

Through a guaranteed annual income, all Canadians, working or otherwise, would receive a basic allowance sufficient to raise them to at least 70 per cent of the poverty line – defined by the Economic Council of Canada as the point at which an individual or family was spending 70 percent of its income on basic requirements such as food, shelter, and clothing. People would be allowed to retain a proportion of this basic allowance while working, until their earned income reached the existing poverty-line threshold for their household size. All earned income below these thresholds would be exempt from taxation. Through a combination of work and welfare, in other words, everyone would be allowed to enjoy at least a minimum standard of adequacy. Put differently, supplementing the incomes of the working poor through tax-based transfers could reduce or eliminate the discrepancy between their living standards and those of welfare clients, without punishing or humiliating families dependent on social assistance.[44]

Gareth Davies argues that these 1970s proposals for a guaranteed annual income represented a major shift "from opportunity to entitlement" in liberal thinking about poverty. At the start of the 1960s, welfare reformers and politicians who declared War on Poverty had "shared the general tendency to equate dignity with self-sufficiency." Embedded in the guaranteed income strategies of the early 1970s in both the US and Canada lay a different assumption. Dignity was now seen simply as "freedom both from hardship and stigma … independence, far from connoting self-sufficiency in the conventional sense, meant freedom from want, however achieved." As Davies concludes, this "notion of an unconditional right to income" would prove to be a tough sell.[45]

Through the Social Security Review, conducted between 1973 and 1976, Ottawa and the provinces struggled to reach agreement on some form of income supplementation or modified guaranteed income for the working poor. The federal government's 1973 Orange Paper on income security argued that Canada's existing welfare system gave the poor "too little … incentive to get off social assistance," since welfare payments were frequently "higher than what one could earn at or near the minimum wage." To get people back to work and to encourage the working poor to stay off welfare, the Orange Paper advocated a "general income supplementation plan … to provide them with an incentive to keep on working rather than giving up and living on social aid."[46]

After almost four years of federal–provincial negotiations over ways to boost the incomes of the working poor, little was accomplished. Rising unemployment and spiralling inflation during the mid-1970s provided a bad fiscal climate for launching an expensive new social program that Ottawa priced at $1 billion annually and that Ontario's treasurer estimated might cost three times as much. Quebec's wariness of any expansion of federal authority in the field of income security also created complications. But the critical opposition that destroyed any chance of success came from Ontario. Officials there had little use for the idea of a guaranteed annual income or of bringing the working poor into the framework of provincial social assistance. Ontario's veteran deputy welfare minister James Band warned the cabinet that the guaranteed income concept was "an extremely costly venture" that was "unlikely to bring us into the promised land in welfare … or in any other area." The key problem remained enforcing the work ethic. Any guarantee scheme that met standards of basic adequacy would provide few incentives to work. One that contained strong work incentives could hardly meet basic needs. "There is no simple solution to this dilemma." Supplementing the incomes of the working poor might add as many as 1.4 million Ontarians to provincial social assistance caseloads, welfare minister John Yaremko argued, and potentially serve as a magnet drawing in the poor from other provinces. Premier John Robarts worried that a guaranteed income might also "encourage … 'professional' welfare families."[47]

Throughout the four years of negotiations around the Social Security Review, Ontario's basic opposition to any widening of welfare entitlements through income supplements did not change. "Ontario cannot … support this guaranteed income scheme [which would] place another expensive burden on Canadian taxpayers," Provincial Treasurer Darcy McKeough flatly told federal officials during the final round of negotiations in 1976. As Rodney Haddow concludes in his analysis of the review, Ontario's hostility towards income supplements for the working poor, because of its scope and costs, "would make agreement virtually impossible." Instead, provincial officials began pursuing more traditional strategies for restoring the equilibrium between work and welfare. Soon after the collapse of the Social Security Review, Ontario's Provincial Secretary for Justice, Gordon Walker, began lobbying aggressively for the return of compulsory work tests for the able-bodied on social assistance. "For many able-bodied people welfare has become a right. It's almost a career choice, particularly as it can pay better than regular work," the cabinet minister argued. Canada could "correct this expensive system by introducing a workfare program to replace welfare."[48]

The conditions of the Canada Assistance Plan ruled out any return-to-work tests; other strategies, however, were employed to restore the emphasis on work. A 1974 Ontario task force recommended that mothers of young children on social assistance should be required to look for work. Another government report one year later argued that the overall proportion of the provincial budget allocated to social security should be lowered. In 1976, Ontario's welfare minister announced a new "get-tough" approach by vowing that all employables on welfare would be required to take any job that was available or be denied assistance. Most significant, the value of welfare benefits within Ontario was allowed to fall further behind the rapidly rising cost of living. In the eight years after provincial restraint policies kicked in after 1975, the purchasing power of welfare for a single person, in constant dollars, dropped by 17 per cent. By 1983 the maximum benefits paid to an Ontario mother on welfare with three children were only 57 per cent of Statistic Canada's low-income cutoff line.[49]

Over the next decade, welfare in Ontario underwent the most dramatic series of transformations since the system first emerged during the Great Depression. Welfare policy was buffeted by two severe recessions that saw unemployment in the province double from under 5 per cent to over 10 per cent of the workforce, by political upheaval that placed three different parties in power between 1985 and 1995, and by the abandonment of the Canada Assistance Plan by a national government committed to eliminating the federal deficit. Underlying all these changes was the steadily upward drift in the percentage of the Ontario population dependent on social assistance: an increase from 4 to 5 per cent in 1981, to 6.4 per cent in 1988, to a peak of 12.5 per cent – one in eight Ontarians – by 1994. That year, welfare spending accounted for 13 per cent of the total provincial budget, providing income support for almost 1.4 million people.[50]

Driving a new cycle of welfare reform, launched in the mid-1980s, was the paradox of rising welfare caseloads despite strong economic growth. An economic boom, particularly in southern Ontario, had reduced unemployment below 5 per cent, yet the provincial welfare caseload, which had spiked upwards during the 1981–82 recession, continued to climb. More people were coming onto social assistance, and they were staying on it for twice as long compared to the previous decade. In 1986, the newly elected Liberal government of David Peterson, governing in a partnership with the NDP, appointed a Social Assistance Review Committee to conduct a sweeping re-examination of the entire welfare system. *Transitions*, its 624-page final report, published two years later, contained 274 detailed recommendations for reform. In a scathing indictment, it described the province's welfare structure as lacking any "coherent set of principles and objectives." *Transitions* was the first Ontario government study to acknowledge publicly what private welfare organizations had been documenting for decades. Welfare benefits within the province "by any standard … are inadequate. They provide too little for shelter, too little for food, and too little for other necessities. Perhaps more important, they provide too little for recipients to maintain their dignity and to support the process of transition to autonomy." Basic allowances needed to be raised immediately by 10 per cent for the disabled, 17.5 per cent for single parents with two children, and 22.5 per cent for single employables, the report argued.[51]

The core theme of the study was the need to find new ways to move welfare clients back into the workforce through enhanced job training, better day care, and other transitional employment supports. In calling for a new child-based income program as well as income supplements for the working poor, *Transitions* echoed the message of many government studies completed since the Senate's report *Poverty in Canada* about the need to eliminate perverse disincentives that penalized individuals leaving welfare for low-wage work. The report also placed strong emphasis on the importance of getting single mothers – one of the fastest-growing groups within the social assistance caseload – off welfare and into paid employment. At a time when almost 60 per cent of Ontario women with pre–school-age children were active in the labour market, *Transitions*, Katherine Scott argues, articulated a vision of "greater gender-neutrality in the social assistance system." In a departure from the original premises of Ontario's mothers' allowance legislation, single mothers were no longer viewed as enjoying any special claim to state support compared to other citizens.[52]

The report's most immediate argument was that "the poor need more money." The total cost of its recommendations would be $2.1 billion a year, almost double Ontario's 1988 spending on social assistance. Despite the steep price tag, *Transitions* received a strong endorsement from Liberal social services minister John Sweeney as well as glowing reviews in the province's media, at a time when Ontario's economy was growing rapidly. It was "important to dispose of the 'myths' that people on welfare do not want to work," Sweeney argued. As one of its initial moves on welfare reform, just before the provincial election, the Peterson government raised the maximum ceiling on social allowances by 5 per cent in 1989; then in 1990 it boosted them by a further 15 per cent and 16 per cent, respectively, for a single person on General Welfare Assistance and a mother with two children on Family Benefits. NDP leader Bob Rae, the surprise winner of the 1990 election, continued the process. As head of a party with a long tradition of advocacy for a more humane welfare system, Rae increased the maximum ceilings on welfare allowances by another 14.2 per cent for a mother with two children and by 16.9 per cent for a single person on general welfare, between 1990 and 1993.[53]

The political and economic timing for these increases could not have been worse. By the fall of 1990, the Canadian economy was sliding into a deep recession that hit Ontario harder than any other province. As unemployment in the province more than doubled to over 10 per cent, welfare caseloads rocketed upwards to a peak of almost 1.4 million people in the spring of 1994, at a cost of more than $6.2 billion annually. By that year Ontario was paying welfare benefits that had increased by 33 per cent and were being paid to twice as many people as in 1989. To make matters worse, these benefits were no longer being cost shared equally with the federal government. As part of Ottawa's deficit reduction strategy, the Conservative government of Brian Mulroney placed a "cap on CAP" in 1990 that limited annual increases in its cost sharing of social assistance in Ontario, Alberta, and British Columbia (the three "have" provinces) to a maximum of 5 per cent, regardless of the actual growth in provincial welfare expenditures. In Ontario this ceiling pushed down Ottawa's share of provincial welfare spending from 50 per cent to only 28 per cent, at a total cost to the provincial treasury of $3.3 billion between 1990 and 1993. In 1995 the new federal Liberal government of Jean Chrétien went even further, announcing the abolition of the Canada Assistance Plan altogether. It would be replaced by a new block grant, the Canada Health and Social Transfer. Over the next two years this grant would reduce Ottawa's social transfers to the provinces by 23.6 per cent. The end of the Canada Assistance Plan also eliminated almost all national conditions or minimum standards attached to provincial welfare administration, including the prohibition against workfare, which dated back to 1961.[54]

As in the 1930s, a deteriorating economy and exploding social assistance costs constituted fertile ground for a "welfare backlash." Any further progress towards implementing the major recommendations of *Transitions* soon reached a dead end. In 1993 the Rae administration, claiming that the current system was "too passive," vowed to "abolish welfare as we know it" by implementing phase two of the Social Assistance Review recommendations. A new Ontario Child Income Program would be created to pay monthly income-tested benefits, administered through the tax system, to all low-income families in the province, whether or not they were on welfare. A new Ontario Adult Benefit would replace the existing general welfare and family benefit programs. Employables would be "encouraged" to participate in JobLink, a third new program designed to "help people [by providing] an employment plan … necessary to return to the labour market and to independence."[55]

Only one year later, Rae's chagrined social services minister, Tony Silipo, announced that Ottawa's "cap on CAP," combined with the ballooning provincial deficit, had killed phase two of the plans for welfare reform. "We've got a $3 billion fiscal hole that we're in because of what the federal government has done to us … How far welfare reform can go … will depend on … the federal government. Right now, we're getting a kick in the teeth." Over the next year, attitudes towards welfare clients, even within a government previously sympathetic to their plight, began to harden. Shortly after scrapping his plan to "abolish the welfare system," Silipo announced he was going to spend $40 million to create a new 270-person "anti-fraud squad" within his department. The squad would reinvestigate all welfare cases in Ontario in order to crack down on suspected welfare abuse. Welfare recipients might even be subjected to compulsory fingerprinting. Rae himself declared an "all-out war against welfare dependency," arguing that clients should "no longer be able to just cash cheques," but might soon be forced into job-training programs. "We don't want to see the creation of an underclass in this society where generation after generation after generation of people are relying on welfare." To cope with the province's budget crisis, Rae seriously contemplated a 10 per cent rollback in welfare benefits during the spring of 1994; ultimately, though, he abandoned that idea, fearing it would split his party wide open.[56] Silipo's fraud squad eventually uncovered only 1,029 cases of illegality after auditing more than 266,000 welfare files,[57] and nothing came of the NDP's musings about welfare fingerprinting, compulsory job training, or benefit rollbacks. Still, the negative rhetoric confirmed the public's growing impression that Ontario's $6.2 billion welfare system was far too generous and that it encouraged laziness, cheating, and a widening "cycle of dependency."[58]

During the 1995 provincial election, the NDP remained mostly silent on the welfare issue; by then, though, the road for Mike Harris's Common Sense Revolution had been well paved. Failure to develop an income supplement program for the working poor during the 1970s and 1980s, a deteriorating economy, Ottawa's fiscal cutbacks to the Canada Assistance Plan along with its ultimate abandonment of welfare standards, and the NDP's own policy confusion and growing frustration with the difficulties of welfare reform all made simple answers to the welfare crisis more politically attractive to voters. As in the 1930s, compelling the poor to labour in exchange for their relief re-emerged as a familiar means of reasserting the moral imperative of the work ethic within an economy increasingly unable to provide steady employment.

Between 1995 and their electoral defeat in 2003, the Ontario PCs under Mike Harris and his successor Ernie Eves sought to "break the cycle of dependency" through their signature social policy initiative, Ontario Works (OW), which emerged in 1997, two years after their Common Sense Revolution had slashed welfare rates for employable adults by 21.6 per cent. Throughout the PCs' eight years in power, OW rates remained frozen at the reduced levels established in 1995. By 2003, adjusted for inflation, OW recipients were receiving incomes 35 per cent below levels set by the NDP ten years earlier. By that year, a single adult on OW was living more than 70 per cent below Statistics Canada's low-income cutoff (LICO) compared to the much smaller 20 per cent gap that had been in place in 1993.[59] Food bank use now exploded across the province. Sixty-five per cent of food bank users were on social assistance, and 60 per cent of them were families with children. Forty per cent of the banks were forced to ration their provisions. As Graham Riches pointed out in 2002, food banks had become the "institutionalized and poor cousin of an increasingly enfeebled welfare system."[60] Between 1995 and 2004 the province's social assistance caseload plunged from 1.3 million to 672,000 through a combination of tightened eligibility requirements and ongoing economic recovery from the early 1990s recession.[61]

Apart from this collapse in welfare living standards, life for those dependent on OW changed dramatically in a number of other ways. Surveillance and moral policing of their behaviour greatly intensified within the new administrative structure of Ontario Works. Toll-free welfare "snitch lines" to report suspected fraud, contemplated briefly but never implemented by Bob Rae's NDP government, were quickly rolled out by the Harris PCs, although fewer than 1 per cent of investigations resulted in a conviction for fraud.[62] Also, "spouse-in-the house regulations," abolished by the NDP, were reinstated. throwing 10,000 women off the OW caseload for living with a man. This "heightened policing of welfare fraud … blatantly encourage[d] the public to believe that all the poor are immoral cheaters who must be constantly investigated."[63]

Also, Ontario Works contracted out its caseload management to a private consulting firm, which developed eight new computer-driven surveillance technologies, including a "voice-response" call centre that screened all initial OW applicants. The same firm also hired eligibility review officers whose job was not to prioritize need, but rather to root out fraud by looking for red flags such as "a recent move, high rental fees, a change in relationship status, [or] application to post-secondary education." Computerized personal client information was now shared widely with other government agencies. Drug-testing and frequent OW case history audits became standard practices. Any missing documents, such as credit card or bank statements going back years, could render clients ineligible. Implementing these new corporate technologies within OW "furthered the economic exploitation, stigmatization, and marginalization of Ontario's most vulnerable," leading many clients to express their experiences of welfare "as similar to incarceration because of the restrictions on their freedoms and feeling like they are being watched at all times."[64]

For mothers in need of social assistance, the most far-reaching change was a new gender-neutral "workfare" requirement: in order to "break the cycle of dependency on welfare," employable sole-support parents (overwhelmingly women) applying for social assistance would have to participate in Ontario Works as soon as their children were over the age of three. Thus they would be required to participate in "job searches, job placements, and community placements." Since 1920, Ontario governments had acknowledged the centrality of women's caregiving labour in Ontario; under the new OW regime, this was no longer the case. This dramatic change reflected "the assumption that mothers who are on social assistance do not work and therefore are not valuable, productive members of society … [and thus] are stigmatized as the 'undeserving' poor."[65]

The most telling failure of the PCs' new Ontario Works model was that it simply failed to find work for its clients or to prepare them adequately to pursue stable jobs that paid a living wage within the increasingly "precarious" Ontario economy of the twenty-first century, in which one third of low-wage workers did not earn enough to get out of poverty.[66] Workfare's core requirement was that applicants "work a maximum of seventeen hours a week in exchange for welfare." But the meaning of "work" was porous; it included temporary apprentice "employment placements," "employment support" (workshops about job searching and résumé writing), and "mandatory community placements" in volunteer organizations. A campaign by unions and the Ontario Coalition Against Poverty (OCAP) to boycott any not-for-profit charities that accepted the "compulsory voluntarism" of OW clients sharply reduced the scope for this last option in OW's early years. As a result, workfare mostly involved attendance at "job readiness" classes and workshops. As a spokesman for the protest organization Workfare Watch put it, "people are simply doing variations of things they always did." Within ten years, however, about 40 per cent of recipients would be turning to "community participation" to perform their workfare requirements, usually through unpaid volunteer activities they found on their own. Compare this to the 5 per cent who were "actually placed in a job."[67]

The transition of OW recipients from welfare to stable, adequately paid work was also unimpressive. A study of OW recipients in Toronto found that "30 percent of former OW clients who returned to work were in non-permanent jobs (temporary, casual, seasonal or contract) compared to seven percent of the labour force as a whole." Thirty-seven per cent earned less than $10 an hour, "a widely accepted benchmark for categorization as the working poor in Ontario." Seventeen per cent had returned to OW within ten months of exiting it. As the authors concluded, "workfirst" programs were based on the fallacy that personal moral failings rather than inadequate labour demand were at the root of unemployment. "The language talks of 'incentives' towards employability rather than 'barriers' to employment."[68]

In 2003, Dalton McGuinty's Liberals under the motto "Choose Change" defeated the PCs after a campaign fought primarily around increased funding for schools and hospitals, improved environmental protection, and a promise not to increase taxes. This last pledge would cripple any Liberal efforts, over the next fifteen years, to reverse the impact of the Harris social assistance cutbacks to Ontarians living in poverty. Unlike in 1995, welfare reform was not a swing issue in the election. As one pundit asked, "Where has welfare gone?"[69] Since benefits for single adults were now worth 35 per cent less than in 1993, it was an important question.

Once in office, the McGuinty Liberals promised to "treat social assistance recipients with dignity and respect," but apart from 3 per cent increases to welfare rates in each of 2004 and 2005, to compensate for inflation in those years, they did nothing to reverse the deep cuts initiated by the Conservatives in 1995, and they left the Tories' flawed "welfare-to-work strategy ... intact." In Ontario, as elsewhere, workfare was "not about creating jobs for people who don't have them; it is about creating workers for jobs that nobody wants." There was a 500,000 drop in the province's welfare caseload from the peak levels of the mid-1990s, yet the economic plight of many former recipients actually worsened.[70] The jobs they found "pay poorly and are of poor quality ... retention rates are low, job progression is lower still, and most working leavers remain in poverty."[71]

A 2008 report produced by the Ontario Association of Food Banks (OAFB) attempted for the first time to generate a detailed estimate of the "Cost of Poverty" in Ontario, as a counter-narrative to the dominant discourse, which depicted the poor themselves as a "drain" on taxpayers. The OAFB report concluded that when the social costs of increased ill health, crime, lost productivity due to joblessness and interrupted education, lower tax revenues, and the intergenerational transmission of poverty were added up, Ottawa and Queen's Park were "losing at least $10.4 billion to $13.1 billion a year in 2007 dollars, a loss equal to between 10.8 to 16.6 per cent of the provincial budget," or $2,299 to $2,895 for every Ontario household. When the private costs borne by 904,845 Ontario households in the lowest-income quintiles were added, the total economic "costs of poverty" were between $32.2 and $38.3 billion annually, or between 5.5 and 6.6 per cent of the province's GDP. The same year, that figure was confirmed by the government's own Special Committee on Poverty Reduction. "Poverty has a price-tag for all Ontarians," the OAFB report concluded.[72]

Since 1995, OCAP had been making this argument powerfully through mass protests at the provincial legislature, sit-ins at cabinet ministers' offices, organized "squats" in empty buildings to protest evictions and the lack of affordable housing, and, most successfully, through its "Raise-the-Rates" campaign, initiated in 2005, which focused on an obscure welfare regulation, the Special Diet Allowance (SDA). Under the SDA, welfare recipients were eligible for a special diet allowance of up to $250 a month if they could convince a doctor or nurse practitioner that they suffered from "one of 41 illnesses or medical conditions'" stipulated on a form.[73] OCAP advocates argued that the deep cuts in OW and ODSP rates since 1995 had created a nutritional crisis for hundreds of thousands of welfare recipients, making them "vulnerable to disease and deteriorating health." OCAP demanded that the $250 SDA maximum be extended to all 760,000 welfare recipients across the province. For a single adult on OW, receiving a maximum $585 a month in 2005, this would represent a 43 per cent boost, restoring their monthly income to the levels last provided in 1994, before the PCs took power. The mostly unknown SDA became "OCAP's wedge in a door that they wanted to open wide to Raise the Rates."[74]

Over the next five years, OCAP and its union allies, including CUPE, waged a highly effective public campaign around liberalizing eligibility for the SDA, through rallies in public parks, mass gatherings at community public health offices, and "Hunger Clinics" held on the steps of the Legislature, as well as by occupying the offices of Sandra Pupatello, McGuinty's Minister of Community and Social Services. An enraged Pupatello denounced OCAP members as "rogue advocates" who were abusing health workers and the specific medical intent of the SDA. But some doctors disagreed. As one family physician put it, "poverty is a medical condition and helping people access adequate funds to afford a nutritious diet is a medical intervention." Many others began approving maximum SDA requests for their clients receiving OW and ODSP, resulting in large increases in the program's cost. In 2002, Ontario spent only $5 million a year on the SDA. Six years later the total had risen "to almost $70 million … [and] the overall costs of operating the program had climbed from $6 million in 2001–2 to $220 million in 2009–10."[75]

OCAP ultimately failed in its goal of seeing the maximum $250 SDA added to the budget of all welfare recipients. Instead, in 2011 the Liberals implemented a "new food supplement program which greatly reduced the amount people could receive for special diet needs and tightened up the procedures that had to be followed."[76] But symbolically, OCAP's Raise the Rates campaign succeeded in shining a spotlight on the harsh reality of poverty in Ontario, which would only worsen with the onset of the 2007–8 financial crisis and subsequent recession.

The clearest evidence of the Liberals' heightened awareness of poverty as a political issue was the appointment of a special cabinet committee on Poverty Reduction in Ontario in December 2007 as a follow-up to McGuinty's October 2007 election campaign promise to "build a comprehensive poverty reduction strategy around the Ontario Child Benefit," a new income-tested tax transfer of $1,100 per child for low-income families with children, implemented in 2007.[77] The special committee's report, "Breaking the Cycle: Ontario's Poverty Reduction Strategy," was released a year later, in December 2008. Its core theme was "Kids First." The report called on the government to set "an aggressive target – reducing the number of children living in poverty by 25 percent over 5 years," which would move 90,000 children out of poverty. "The first thing to do when you want to improve something is to measure it ... Reducing poverty and improving security ... is something we can measure." The key tools would be doubling spending on the OCB to $1.3 billion a year for a guarantee of $1,310 per child, thus providing support to 1.3 million Ontario children in low-income families whether or not they were on social assistance; continuing the Liberals' strategy of gradually raising the minimum wage from $6.85 in 2003 to $10.25 an hour by 2010; allowing clients on OW to keep 50 per cent of any money they earned without losing welfare benefits; providing drug, dental, and vision benefits, already available to families on social assistance, to people exiting OW or ODSP for employment; and fully exempting earnings of welfare clients who were participating in post-secondary education.[78]

All of these recommendations flowed from earlier reports between 2004 and 2007 that had been produced by liberal and left-of-centre Ontario think tanks and advocacy organizations such as the Caledon Institute, the Canadian Policy Research Network, the Metcalf Foundation, and the Ontario Association of Food Banks, whose goal was a "workfirst" rather than "workfare" strategy that would "break down the 'welfare wall'" by "making work pay" through eliminating or sharply reducing existing disincentives for leaving social assistance for work.[79]

By focusing solely on child poverty rather than on Mike Harris's deep cuts to welfare rates, the McGuinty Liberals implicitly acknowledged arguments by policy analysts such as John Stapleton, a retired former senior official in the Ministry of Community and Services now working with the Metcalf Foundation, that "welfare programs are extremely unpopular with the public at large ... The public has largely made its decision about welfare. That decision is that it will not sustain the program." Instead, the policy goal, Stapleton argued, should be to transform Ontario Works "from a program designed to help the poorest of the poor to a program that supports transition to self-reliance."[80] Caught between the "evident popularity of the Harris assistance cuts" and their own campaign promises not to raise taxes, the Liberals had little interest in restoring social assistance rates to the peak levels reached in 1994.[81] Instead, they tried to shift the policy narrative to more popular themes such as "Kids First" and "Workfirst."

Over the next five years both of these goals were deeply compromised by the sharp economic recession that hit the world economy in 2008. Although the Liberals' "Breaking the Cycle" report appeared at the end of 2008, its origins predated the financial crisis, about which it had virtually nothing to say beyond noting that "we are living in challenging economic times."[82] The radical restructuring in the mid-1990s of Canada's national unemployment insurance program, which was replaced by a new plan of Employment Insurance, had left workers and their families deeply vulnerable to the 2008–10 recession. As a result of tightened eligibility requirements and reduced benefit duration, only one third of Ontario's jobless were able to collect EI during the recession compared to the more than 80 per cent who qualified for UI at the start of the 1990–92 economic crisis.[83] The woefully inadequate rate structure of Ontario Works was left to fill the gap, and, as John Stapleton pointed out in 2011, "it would take an increase of 55 per cent to return basic welfare rates to 1993 levels."[84]

The largest category of recipients collecting OW by 2011 (151,400) were now single adults – a "dramatic increase of 65 percent" – due to the success of new child benefit transfer programs. Persons with disabilities collecting ODSP in that year now absorbed more than 60 per cent of Ontario's social assistance costs, compared to less than one third in 1988. The new profile of the OW caseload was single, young (25–34), and increasingly male, shifting in and out of precarious, part-time work and collecting benefits "just over a third of what they would make with the most basic form of steady work" at the province's new 2010 minimum wage of $10.25 an hour. This was the lowest ratio of welfare benefits to regular minimum wage earnings in Ontario in more than thirty years.[85] At this level of poverty, did OW recipients really need to remain trapped in a program based on the premise that they needed "a reason to get out of bed in the morning"? Some Liberal cabinet members still thought so. As Diane Finlay, Ontario's Human Resources and Skills Development Minister, commented in 2009, "Our goal is to help people get back to work and to get back to work quickly in jobs that will last. We do not want to make it lucrative for them to stay home and get paid for it."[86]

In October 2012, the second instalment of the Liberals' Poverty Reduction Strategy arrived through the report "Brighter Prospects: Transforming Social Assistance in Ontario," co-authored by commissioners Frances Lankin, a key cabinet minister in Bob Rae's former NDP government, and Munir A. Sheikh, an economist and (until 2010) former head of Statistics Canada. The commission was appointed in November 2010. Its report two years later contained 108 recommendations for welfare reform.

"Brighter Prospects" began with a strong indictment of the existing OW and ODSP system:

> Across the province we heard that social assistance rates were too low to meet people's basic needs, including nutritious food and adequate housing. We also heard about the complexity of the current system. Its web of benefits and eligibility requirements results in confusion, inconsistency, an excessive administrative burden, a lack of

> transparency, and barriers to exiting social assistance to work. We heard from caseworkers who could be spending as much as 70 percent of their time just administering the rules … time they could be using … to work directly for clients to [help] them achieve their employment goals … Social assistance in Ontario must be transformed from the complex and ineffective system that it is today to a simple and effective system that can achieve its twin objectives of providing employment support and financial support.[87]

Their report was yet another call for a "workfirst" approach to welfare reform. Its key recommendation was the merger of OW and ODSP into one program "focused on ability and not on disability … [in which] all recipients would develop a Pathway to Employment Plan." Half of the more than 240 rules and directives of the existing system would be eliminated, but "the mechanisms in place to prevent and address misuse … would continue." And the basic "building block" of this unified program would be "a standard rate for all adults," varying only to reflect "regional differences in living costs across Ontario." The rate would be based on a new "Basic Measure of Adequacy" (BMA) arrived at through a "rational methodology that would help the Province achieve a balance of three objectives: adequacy of rates to cover healthy food, secure housing, and other basic necessities; fairness between social assistance recipients and low-income people who are working; and financial incentives to work." The report's major conclusion was not that welfare should be made less generous, along the lines the Common Sense Revolution; rather, it was "make work pay."[88]

However, its signature recommendation, that OW and ODSP be merged into a single program focused on enhancing the "employability" of all recipients, doomed the report's reception in the eyes of the general public and ultimately for the newly elected Liberal premier Kathleen Wynne, for it provoked a vigorous pushback from existing ODSP clients and family members, who resisted any such merger. They wanted to retain their distinctive social assistance status and benefit structure, which addressed their own special needs. The authors of "Brighter Prospects" anticipated this reaction, acknowledging that "some people with disabilities may be concerned that what they see as the more 'punitive' culture of Ontario Works will be imported into the new program." Lankin and Sheikh didn't help their case by also arguing that "there would be no difference in the requirement that recipients undertake the activities set out in their [pathway to employment] plans, and failure to do so would continue to carry the risk of reduced or cancelled financial assistance."[89]

The third instalment of the Liberals' Poverty Reduction Strategy arrived one year later through the report "Realizing Our Potential: Ontario's Poverty Reduction

Strategy, 2014–2019," overseen by Deputy Premier Deb Matthews. It was a follow-up to her 2008 "Breaking the Cycle" report, which had proclaimed the Liberals' explicit target of reducing child poverty in Ontario by 25 per cent over the five years 2008 to 2013. How well had they done? Again, the results were mixed. The goal was to lift 90,000 children out of poverty, based on LIM measurements. Instead they had "lifted 47,000 children and their families out of poverty," or about 50 per cent of their objective, for a drop in the overall Ontario child poverty rate from 15.2 to 13.6 percent, a 10 per cent rather than a 25 per cent reduction. The "Kids First" strategy put forward in "Breaking the Cycle" report had not been a smashing success. "Had the federal government done their part and the economy stayed the course, we would likely have met our target," Matthews stated. She recommitted to meeting the 25 per cent child poverty reduction target but this time gave no deadline. Her report also put forward a "new goal to end homelessness in Ontario," again with no deadline. On social assistance reform the report had little to say beyond noting that over the past decade welfare rates in Ontario had "increased by a cumulative 17.2 per cent for Ontario Works families and individuals with disabilities receiving Ontario Disability Support benefits. For single people without children receiving Ontario Works, the cumulative increase is 24.4 per cent." There were "still people of all ages living in poverty today," the report acknowledged. "For most of them, meaningful employment is the most effective and speediest way to exit poverty for good." The whole issue was "complex … and our resources are limited … Our government is committed to funding programs based on evidence."[90] Compared to "Breaking the Cycle," "Realizing our Potential," was a vague document signalling a Liberal government that had lost its focus on the poverty issue.

Critics were quick to pounce. In 2013, CUPE along with OCAP launched a "Week of Action," campaigning across the province around the slogan "No Merger of OW and ODSP." A year later the Liberals announced that they would "back off from [the] merger as a result of significant community pressure."[91] Toronto's Metcalf Foundation, meanwhile, published a report documenting the steady growth in "working poverty" in Toronto between 2000 and 2012. In 2000, working poverty in the Toronto region was 7.2 per cent. By 2012 it had jumped to 9.1 per cent. The minimum wage had increased by 37.6 per cent between 2006 and 2010 under the Liberals, but housing costs in the city had risen more quickly than that, and full-time work was less available than before:

> The fact that the slight increase in working poverty is taking place at the same time as overall employment figures are declining magnifies the significance of the increase. It points to changes within the labour market itself that are making it harder for members

> of the working poor to get ahead … [New jobs are] increasingly temporary or limited term contracts. These new jobs offer non-wage benefits and can be accompanied by irregular work schedules and earnings … This kind of work had grown by almost 50% over the last 20 years in the Greater Toronto–Hamilton area. [Changes in the labour market are] making it difficult for many people to earn enough money to stay afloat.[92]

Other researchers confirmed this analysis. A 2016 report by the Canadian Centre for Policy Alternatives focused on "Ontario's Social Assistance Poverty Gap." The "poverty gap" was the "distance between total benefit income and the poverty line" as defined by Statistics Canada. In 1989, the study argued, a single person qualifying for the equivalent of Ontario Works "faced a poverty gap of just under 40%." By 1993, as a result of the implementation of the recommendations of the 1988 *Transitions* report on social assistance reform in Ontario, the gap had been cut in half and singles on social assistance faced a poverty gap of only 20 per cent, and for other family types "the gap … disappeared entirely." By 2014, in contrast, "the gap had widened dramatically to 59%. People receiving benefits from Ontario's social assistance programs are living in a greater depth of poverty now than a generation ago." For a single adult it would take "an additional $12,301 to close the gap. For a single parent … it would take an additional $10,385 to close the gap." The 895,000 Ontarians on OW and ODSP were now "lock[ed] … into deep poverty."[93]

In 2016, two years out from the next general election, Kathleen Wynne's Liberal government clearly had come to a crossroads in helping Ontarians in need. Minimum wage increases had benefited many full-time low-wage workers but had left more than one third of workers in precarious employment and trapped in poverty. Increases to child benefits through the OCB and NCBS had made a significant difference in boosting the incomes of single-parent households. But after thirteen years in office, the Liberals had made no major modifications to the workfare-driven legacy of OW, inherited from Mike Harris's Common Sense Revolution. As a major study of the program concluded, "workfare produces neither sustained employment nor a corresponding decrease in poverty."[94] This finding was confirmed by Ontario's auditor general, who noted that since his department's last audit of the program in 2009, "the average length of time people depend on the program has nearly doubled, increasing from an average of 19 months to almost three years in 2017/18," and that "in each of the last five years, the Ontario Works program has helped only 10% to 13% of recipient cases to successfully find employment and leave the program." Compared to 2009, the cost of OW to the province had also "increased more than 55% from $1.9 billion to almost $3 billion in 2017/18."[95] The government's "workfare" or "workfirst" strategies were not working.

Wynne's response was to call for two new studies. The first, announced in her Budget Speech of March 2016, would allocate $25 million to the creation of a new three-year pilot project to "test a growing view at home and abroad that a basic income could build on the success of minimum wage policies and increases in child benefits by providing a more consistent and predictable support in the context of today's dynamic labour market".[96] Hugh Segal, a Conservative senator, former chief of staff to both Ontario Premier Bill Davis and federal Prime Minister Brian Mulroney, and a long-time advocate for basic income as a poverty reduction strategy, was invited to develop a blueprint for how such a pilot project would work.

Next, Wynne established a new Income Support Working Group on Welfare Reform, chaired by George Thomson, a former Ontario appeals court justice who had been responsible for leading the *Transitions* report on social assistance reform in 1988. Thomson's Working Group report, released in 2017, noted that "there were 1.94 million low-income persons in Ontario in 2015 … [including] 943,368 children and adults … receiving social assistance."[97] It was simply "unacceptable that so many people live in deep poverty and critical need in Ontario. It is vital that the Province establish and commit to a floor below which no one should fall."[98] But the report's recommended road for getting there was painfully slow. Ontario should "publicly commit to a Minimum Security Standard that will be achieved over a 10-year period (by 2027–28)," based initially on the low income measure (LIM) used by the earlier 2008 Poverty Reduction Strategy report, "plus an additional 30% for persons with a disability." The province should also "make social assistance simple and eliminate coercive rules and policies," as well as "rebrand the current Ontario Works … to jump-start and reinforce a positive culture of trust, collaboration and problem-solving." Current financial penalties within OW "related to employment efforts and rigid reporting requirements" should be "eliminated" in favour of a "new person-centred approach" that would "address urgent needs first (e.g. risk of homelessness)," OW and ODSP were to remain as separate, distinct programs, and asset tests were to be abolished for ODSP applicants. The welfare rate structure should guarantee that "all adults have access to a consistent level of support, regardless of living situation."[99] All these reforms, echoing many of the arguments in his earlier *Transitions* report of 1988, were long overdue and underscored just how little the Liberals had accomplished in welfare reform since taking power in 2003.

Thomson's report recommended that over the next three years (to 2020), the current standard flat rate for OW recipients be increased only to $893 a month, compared to $721 in 2017; this, in non-inflation adjusted dollars, would still leave it below the $972 established by the NDP in 1993.[100] His working group acknowledged that they "struggled with the pace at which government should bring all people out of deepest poverty, since the gap between where they are and where they need to be is so large." The reforms they recommended "in the first few years are what we see as the minimum of first steps towards a more adequate system of low-income support for working-age adults."[101] The report also revealed that "in 1990 the single social assistance rate was 70% of the minimum wage. Today, the single rate is 38% of the minimum wage" and that "single persons receiving Ontario Works and ODSP have experienced a decrease in their spending power of $315 and $302 per month respectively over the last 22 years (accounting for inflation)."[102] These figures starkly highlighted the devastation wrought by the PCs' Common Sense Revolution on families and individuals living on social assistance as well as the Liberals' failure to reverse it since coming to power in 2003.

Hugh Segal's discussion paper, laying out the framework for the Basic Income Pilot Project, was released in August 2016. In making the case for why a basic income was necessary, Segal relied heavily on earlier "Cost of Poverty" studies produced by the Ontario Association of Food Banks in 2008 and the Metcalf Foundation in 2014, as well as research behind the Ontario Poverty Reduction Strategy reports of 2008 and 2012. According to LIM measurements, "15.9 percent of Ontario adults aged 18 to 64 were living in poverty in 2014" and the federal and provincial governments were "losing between $10 and $13 billion dollars annually because of the social costs of poverty," as well as 5.5 to 6.6 per cent of GDP, due to reduced output and productivity. "Poverty hurts all of us and ... costs all of society vast amounts of money." Yet over the past quarter century, "there is probably no area of public policy, in either urban or rural Canada, where creativity and courage from governments have been less evident than on the issue of poverty faced by working age adults."[103]

Segal pointed to the success of the Guaranteed Income Supplement (GIS) in dramatically reducing poverty among seniors since its introduction in 1967, and to the success of more recent income-tested child benefits transfers such as the OCB and NCBS in lifting many low-income families with children above the poverty line. The purpose of the BI Pilot Project was "to test replacing the broad policing, control and monitoring now present in Ontario Works and the Ontario Disability Support Program, with a modestly more generous Basic Income, distributed automatically to those living below a certain threshold. Will a Basic Income reduce poverty more effectively, encourage work, reduce stigmatization, and produce better health outcomes and better life chances for recipients?"[104]

Segal's plan was to roll out eligibility for the project to the entire population in three Ontario cities, assuring them "a Basic Income (tax free) corresponding to 75 per cent of the adjusted LIM." In these communities BI would completely replace

OW and ODSP. The program was based on the premise of universality: everyone would be eligible to apply, but depending on their income, not everyone would get a monthly BI payment. For someone currently on OW, this would result in a minimum of "approximately $1350 per month, non-taxable," moving them from 45 to 75 per cent of the LIM "with an opportunity to keep partial additional income earned from participation in the labour market."[105] At $15,840, this represented more than double what they received as single adults on OW. There would also be a randomized control trial in a "major urban neighbourhood" among selected participants, to test for work incentive and other effects, including health outcomes, life and career choices, educational opportunities, food security, mobility and housing arrangements, and interactions with other social programs at various rates of "clawback." The employment effect measurement was particularly important, Segal noted, because according to current surveys, 63 per cent of Ontarians believed that a Basic Income would negatively affect the work ethic.[106]

Income currently received by existing tax-free transfer programs such as the OCB and NCBS would not be counted for purposes of implementing clawbacks. Eligibility would depend solely on an individual's age. "No other criteria should be employed." And there would be no "work test." "The core question to be answered by the evidence we seek to gain is very simple: Is there a more humane and efficient way to reduce poverty, a way that better respects the rights of those in poverty to make their own life choices, reduces stigma and growth in bureaucracy, yet produces improved outcomes in terms of work and life prospects?"[107] At the project's conclusion in three years' time, the BI would be phased out gradually. Participation would be voluntary, and it was important "that no individual be made worse off during or after the pilot as a result of participation in the pilot."[108] An advisory council of thirty-five people would oversee the project, and a Research Operations Group would run it.

The BI Pilot Project was approved by Wynne's cabinet, and launched, as anticipated, in April 2017, with some modifications. There was one "saturation site," Lindsay, Ontario, a city of 10,000, along with two other RCT sites in Hamilton and Thunder Bay. Two thousand participants were enrolled in Lindsay, one thousand in each of the other two cities. Although Segal had recommended testing several different "clawback" rates on earned incomes ranging from 75 per cent to 25 per cent, the government chose to test only one reduction rate of 50 per cent.[109] The guaranteed Basic Income was up to $17,000 a year for individuals and $24,000 a year for families, less 50 percent of any earned income.[110]

The BI Pilot Project ran for slightly more than one year, rather than the three years originally planned. In June 2018, the Wynne Liberals suffered a major defeat in the provincial election at the hands of the PCs led by Doug Ford. Despite promising during the election not to cancel the BI Pilot, the PCs did exactly that upon taking office, on the grounds that the project was "quite expensive" and was "failing." According to Ford's Minister of Children, Community and Social Services, Lisa MacLeod, "spending more money on a broken program wasn't going to help anyone … The best social program is job." MacLeod also announced that the Liberals' scheduled 3 per cent increase to welfare rates in 2018–19 would be cut in half to only 1.5 per cent, which she claimed was "compassionate."[111] Research on the BI project was stopped immediately in July 2018, but in the face of a class action lawsuit by four participants for breach of contract, the Ford government allowed all participants to continue to receive their monthly payments until 31 March 2019, so as to give them "enough time to transition."[112]

Subsequently, researchers from McMaster University surveyed more than two hundred of the participants to get their views on how their year on BI had affected their lives. The results were overwhelmingly positive. "Everyone who received basic income reported benefiting in some way … [including] improvement in their physical and mental health, labour market participation, food security, housing stability, financial status and social relationships." The most significant finding was the "noticeable impact on the use of health services" with fewer visits to health practitioners and hospital ERs. For a "significant number," the project was "transformational, fundamentally reshaping their living standards, sense of self-worth and hope for a better life." The majority who were working before the project said they kept working while getting BI, and a "common pattern was for recipients to report moving from low-paying dead-end jobs to jobs with better working conditions and with improved long-term opportunities." Eighty per cent of those surveyed said their health had improved, especially their "mental well-being." The most common report was "anxiety relief" and reduced depression, a finding particularly relevant in relation to the government's own 2019 audit of OW, which reported that 36 per cent of recipients were unable to find work due to mental health problems.

One quarter reported starting new educational training programs during the pilot. Most reported being "more motivated to find better-paying jobs. Only a few reported being less motivated. These responses dispel the view that giving individuals basic income will lead to their withdrawal from the labour market." In short, there was no evidence of a "less eligibility" effect. Participants ate more nutritious food. "No food banks for eight months. Doesn't that say it all?," as one put it. They visited the dentist more often. Pain decreased for more than half the participants. They had more time to socialize with family members and to engage in physical activities. As another respondent told the researchers, "It was very much dignifying. I was trusted for once; it felt like I could make my own decisions without having a devil and an angel on my shoulder telling me what to do. Because I know where

I am going." Another said, "Being on welfare is hugely stigmatized. Basic income gave me so much dignity … I no longer have to feel the shame of having [a] history of being on welfare." As the researchers concluded, the disbanding of the project only one third of the way through its planned trajectory was a "missed opportunity to more fully understand the effects of basic income."[113]

In January 2020, COVID-19 arrived in Canada. Two months later, as quarantines, lockdowns, and social-distancing orders were put into effect by governments, the economy nose-dived and unemployment spiked to 14 per cent, a level unseen since the Great Depression. Acknowledging the total inability of the nation's traditional social safety nets – EI and welfare – to cope with a crisis of this magnitude, the federal Liberal government of Justin Trudeau rolled out a new program – the Canada Emergency Response Benefit (CERB) – to fill the gap, paying jobless applicants up to $2,000 a month to protect living standards and avoid an explosion in poverty, particularly among those working in precarious retail sales and service sectors and the "gig" economy. CERB levels closely matched maximum monthly benefits available through EI and were more than double what was available for single adults on OW in Ontario. They were also $300 a month higher than the $17,000 BI available for a short year to participants in Ontario's BI pilot project. As of this writing, 7,800,000 Canadian workers have applied for CERB, including 75,000 Ontarians on OW who lost part-time jobs. The Ford government has allowed laid-off workers on social assistance "to keep $1,100 of the CERB on top of their provincial welfare benefits," which for a single adult on OW are only $733 a month. So far, there have been few complaints about the erosion of the work ethic. As commentators have pointed out, "CERB's eligibility requirements are less onerous than those of Employment Insurance and traditional provincial welfare and disability income-support programs," allowing millions the opportunity "of maintaining a decent income and personal dignity … after a drastic loss of income." In essence, it is a national experiment in Universal Basic Income.[114] Perhaps the one bright light of the COVID-19 crisis it that it may finally provide us with an opportunity, after more than a century of contentious debates around "less eligibility" and the work ethic, to reinvent a new way of guaranteeing the social right to a humane, non-stigmatized, and decent standard of living for citizens in need.

QUESTIONS FOR CONSIDERATION:

1. Describe "Ontario Works" in your own words.
2. Why had welfare not been a major issue during a provincial election until the Mike Harris victory?

3. Discuss the changing mindsets in the province regarding workfare. What had changed significantly over time?
4. "Welfare is a social right." Do you agree?
5. What was the Canada Assistance Plan? Why was it significant?
6. What are some of the key social costs of poverty, according to Struthers?
7. What was the Basic Income Pilot Project? What were three (3) associated effects of its implementation and subsequent cancellation?

NOTES

1 See, for example, Thomas Walkom, "Visceral issue of campaign is welfare 'reform,'" *Toronto Star*, 13 May 1995; William Walker, "Welfare watershed," *Toronto Star*, 3 June 1995; Fabrice Taylor, "Working for the welfare dollar," *Globe and Mail*, 3 June 1995.

2 James Rusk, "Harris offers fix for welfare system," *Globe and Mail*, 10 May 1995; Lisa Wright, "Harris outlines Workfare program," *Toronto Star*, 12 May 1995; Walker, "Welfare watershed."

3 Rusk, "Harris offers fix for welfare system"; Jane Gadd, "High rates were lure to welfare," *Globe and Mail*, 15 November 1995.

4 For an insightful analysis of Harris's astute use of the welfare issue during the 1995 Ontario election, see Ernie Lightman, "'It's Not a Walk in the Park': Workfare in Ontario," in *Workfare: Ideology for a New Underclass*, ed. Eric Shragge (Toronto: Garamond Press, 1997), 85–95.

5 Martin Mittelstaedt, "Ontario's welfare cuts deeper than needed," *Globe and Mail*, 30 September 1995; "Tsubouchi outlines workfare scheme," *Globe and Mail*, 7 February 1996.

6 For more details on the formation of Ontario's welfare bureaucracy during the 1930s, see James Struthers, *The Limits of Affluence: Welfare in Ontario, 1920–1970* (Toronto: University of Toronto Press, 1994), 77–116.

7 For an analysis of the work ethic imperative within federal relief camps, see James Struthers, *No Fault of Their Own: Unemployment and the Canadian Welfare State, 1914–1941* (Toronto: University of Toronto Press, 1983), 99.

8 Struthers, *The Limits of Affluence*, 91–8.

9 By 1943 only 19,000 Ontarians were collecting relief, compared to 450,000 in 1936. See Struthers, *The Limits of Affluence*, 127.

10 Toronto Welfare Council, *The Cost of Living* (Toronto, 1944); E.W. McHenry, *Report on Food Allowances for Relief Recipients in the Province of Ontario* (Toronto: Queen's Printer, 1944). On women's and social work leadership over the struggle for minimum welfare standards in Toronto during the 1940s, see Gayle Wills, *A Marriage of Convenience: Business and Social Work in Toronto, 1918–1957* (Toronto: University of Toronto Press, 1995), 80–106; and Struthers, *The Limits of Affluence*, 101-16.

11 Margaret Hillyard Little, *"No Car, No Radio, No Liquor Permit": The Moral Regulation of Single Mothers in Ontario, 1920–1993* (Toronto: Oxford University Press, 1998), 115.

12 Struthers, *The Limits of Affluence*, 130–1. Heise's main policy adviser was Harry Cassidy, director of the University of Toronto's School of Social Work. For Cassidy's ideas on welfare reform, see Cassidy, *Public Health and Welfare Reorganization in Canada* (Toronto: Ryerson Press, 1945).

13 A more extensive treatment of these events can be found in Struthers, *The Limits of Affluence*, 126–38.

14 Struthers, *The Limits of Affluence*, 191; Social Planning Council of Metropolitan Toronto, *Social Allowances in Ontario: An Historical Analysis of General Welfare Assistance and Family Benefits (with special focus on the adequacy of benefits, 1961–1976* (Toronto, 1977).

15 City of Toronto Archives, SC 40, box 168, file 4, "Interim Report of the Special Committee of the Child and Family Welfare Division Set Up to Study Survey Recommendations on Services to Unmarried Parents," May 1952. For the debate around moral regulation and eligibility criteria during the first decade of Ontario's Mothers' Allowance program, see Little, *"No Car, No Radio, No Liquor Permit,"* 32–50; and Struthers, *The Limits of Affluence*, 19–49.

16 Ontario's highest illegitimacy rate (5.2 per cent of all live births) occurred just after the war. By 1951 the illegitimacy rate was down to 3.3 per cent, and by 1960 it had dropped to 3.2 per cent, one of the lowest rates in the English-speaking world. Ontario's mothers' allowance caseload fell from 12,215 families in 1939 to 7,266 families by 1956, when unwed mothers became eligible for benefits. See Little, *"No Car, No Radio, No Liquor Permit,"* 111, 136.

17 Struthers, *The Limits of Affluence*, 159–62; see also Little, *"No Car, No Radio, No Liquor Permit,"* 120–2, 130–6.

18 Struthers, *The Limits of Affluence*, 169–73.

19 Struthers, *The Limits of Affluence*.

20 Struthers, *The Limits of Affluence*, 173–8.

21 Struthers, *The Limits of Affluence*, 149, 176.

22 Struthers, *The Limits of Affluence*, 184.

23 Struthers, *The Limits of Affluence*, 184–5.

24 Struthers, *The Limits of Affluence*, 185–6.

25 Struthers, *The Limits of Affluence*, 186.

26 Struthers, *The Limits of Affluence*, 188–9.

27 See Penny Bryden, *Planners and Politicians: Liberal Politics and Social Policy, 1957–1968* (Montreal and Kingston: McGill–Queen's University Press, 1997), 54–77.

28 Struthers, *The Limits of Affluence*, 190–1.

29 Gareth Davies, *From Opportunity to Entitlement: The Transformation and Decline of Great Society Liberalism* (Lawrence: University Press of Kansas, 1996), 39. Davies's point is captured nicely by a 20 March 1964 Toronto *Globe and Mail* editorial about Johnson's War on Poverty address, which argued, "No more than they can we be a rich country while the poor are always with us."

30 Tom Kent, *A Public Purpose: An Experience of Liberal Opposition and the Canadian Government* (Montreal and Kingston: McGill–Queen's University Press, 1988), 357.

31 Speeches by Ken Bryden and Stephen Lewis, Ontario *Hansard*, 18 March 1964, 1768–74; 14 April 1964, 2020--9. On the importance of "culture of poverty" theory for the shaping of Canadian debates on welfare reform in this period, see Struthers, *The Limits of Affluence*, 199, 212, 215, 218.

32 Struthers, *The Limits of Affluence*, 224. Or as Ontario's welfare minister, John Yaremko, argued in 1968, "We intend to lay so much stress on this social service and rehabilitation program that we will eliminate from the minds of the public the fact that there may be somebody on the maintenance rolls that shouldn't be there" (380n57).

33 Rodney Haddow, "The Poverty Policy Community in Canada's Liberal Welfare State," in *Policy Communities and Public Policy in Canada: A Structural Approach*, ed. William Coleman and Grace Skogstad (Mississauga: Copp Clark Pitman, 1990), 218. See also Haddow, *Poverty Reform in Canada, 1958–1978* (Montreal and Kingston: McGill–Queen's University Press, 1993), 66–7.

34 For early statements of this viewpoint, see Canadian Welfare Council, *Public Assistance and the Unemployed* (Ottawa, 1953); and *Social Security for Canada* (Ottawa 1958).

35 On the abolition of the "'fit and proper person' criterion in mothers' allowances," see Little, *"No Car, No Radio, No Liquor Permit,"* 142.

36 Struthers, *The Limits of Affluence*, 206–7, 234; Haddow, *Poverty Reform in Canada*, 58.

37 Struthers, *The Limits of Affluence*, 237–8; Social Planning Council of Metropolitan Toronto, *Social Allowances in Ontario*, table 6, 56.

38 Clifford Williams, *Decades of Service: A History of the Ontario Ministry of Community and Social Services, 1930–1980* (Toronto: Queen's Printer, 1984), 81; *Social Allowances in Ontario*, 31–5.

39 Diana Pearce, "Welfare Is Not for Women: Why the War on Poverty Cannot Conquer the Feminization of Poverty," in *Women, the State, and Welfare*, ed. Linda Gordon (Madison: University of Wisconsin Press, 1990), 267–71; Williams, *Decades of Service*, 81; *Social Allowances in Ontario*, 31–5; Struthers, *The Limits of Affluence*, 242–3. The divorce rate for women in Ontario jumped by almost 300 per cent over this same time period.

40 Lorna Hurl, "The Nature of Policy Dynamics: Patterns of Change and Stability in a Social Assistance Programmer," paper presented to the Fourth National Conference on Social Welfare Policy, Toronto, 24–7 October 1989, 20–1, 28.

41 Economic Council of Canada, *Fifth Annual Review* (Ottawa: 1968); Struthers, *The Limits of Affluence*, 248; Special Senate Committee, *Poverty in Canada* (Ottawa, 1970), xii–xviii.

42 Special Senate Committee on Poverty, *Proceedings of Hearings*, 25 May 1970, 14–16, 81–4.

43 Senate, *Poverty in Canada*, 169–75, xxix.

44 Senate, *Poverty in Canada*, 179–83; Struthers, *The Limits of Affluence*, 248.

45 Davies, *From Opportunity to Entitlement*, 235, 3.

46 Haddow, *Poverty Reform in Canada*, 112.

47 Struthers, *The Limits of Affluence*, 254–6.

48 Haddow, *Poverty Reform in Canada*, 146-7; Christopher Leman, *The Collapse of Welfare Reform: Political Institutions, Policy, and the Poor in Canada and the United States* (Cambridge, MA: MIT Press, 1980), 117, 128, 218.

49 Haddow, *Poverty Reform in Canada*, 146–7; Christopher Leman, *The Collapse of Welfare Reform*, 117, 128, 218; Allan Irving, "From No Poor Law to the Social Assistance Review: A History of Social Assistance in Ontario, 1791–1987," study prepared for the Ontario Social Assistance Review, July 1987, 32–6.

50 Allan Moscovitch, "Social Assistance in the New Ontario," in *Open for Business, Closed to People: Mike Harris's Ontario*, ed. Diana Ralph, André Regimbald, and Nérée St-Amand (Halifax: Fernwood, 1997), 81–3; Katherine Scott, "'The Dilemma of Liberal Citizenship: Women and Social Assistance Reform in the 1990s," *Studies in Political Economy* 50 (Summer 1996): 19, 24.

51 Ontario, *Transitions: Report of the Social Assistance Review Committee* (Toronto: Ontario Ministry of Community and Social Services, 1988), 27, 127.

52 Ontario, *Transitions*, 112–21; Scott, "The Dilemma of Liberal Citizenship," 14–17.

53 "For People on the Treadmill of Poverty," *Globe and Mail* [Editorial], 8 September 1988; Mary Gooderham, "Report urges $2.1 billion welfare increase in Ontario," *Globe and Mail*, 7 September 1988; Moscovitch, "Social Assistance in the New Ontario," 82; Scott, "The Dilemma of Liberal Citizenship," 22; Ontario, *Turning Point: New Support Programs for People with Low Incomes* (Toronto: Queen's Printer, 1993), 7; Ontario Ministry of Community and Social Services, "Ontario's Maximum Monthly Social Assistance Rates and Percentage Change for

Selected Case Types, 1981-95." These are maximum allowance ceilings assuming no other sources of income; the actual assistance paid would vary.

54 Dennis Guest, *The Emergence of Social Security in Canada*, 3rd ed. (Vancouver: UBC Press, 1997), 270–1; Ontario, *Turning Point*, 9–10; David M. Brown, "Welfare Caseloads Trends in Canada," in *Helping the Poor: A Qualified Case for "Workfare,"* ed. John Richards and Aidan Vining (Toronto: C.D. Howe Institute, 1995), figure 6, 60; Allan Moscovitch, "The Canada Health and Social Transfer," in *The Welfare State in Canada: Past, Present, and Future*, ed. Raymond B. Blake, Penny E. Bryden, and J. Frank Strain (Concord: Irwin, 1997), 110.

55 Ontario, *Turning Point*, 9, 13, 16–22.

56 Leslie Papp, "Welfare reform plan fizzling, NDP admits," *Toronto Star*, 3 March 1994; Dale Brazao, "ID card proposal attacked as degrading," *Toronto Star*, 18 February 1994; William Walker, "NDP set to root out welfare cheats," *Toronto Star*, 29 March 1994; Walker, "Welfare reliance must end Rae vows," *Toronto Star*, 7 March 1994; Walker, "NDP puts welfare cuts on the table: Explosive issue to be taken to caucus amid deficit woes," *Toronto Star*, 21 March 1994; Thomas Walkom, "Why the NDP took a step back toward the left," *Toronto Star*, 22 March 1994.

57 James Rusk, "Ontario saves $66 million by tightening up welfare," *Globe and Mail*, 27 October 1994. Ironically, as Rusk noted, "the primary source of the money saved is to get welfare recipients to claim income from other government programs to which they were entitled but of which they were not aware."

58 See, for example, "Welfare bashing," *Toronto Star* [Editorial], 3 April 1994.

59 John Stapleton, "Like Falling Off a Cliff: The Incomes of Low-Wage and Social Assistance Recipients in the 1990s," in *Finding Room: Policy Options for a Canadian Rental Housing Strategy*, ed. J. David Hulchanski and Michael Shapcott (Toronto: CUCS Press, 2004), 19; Kaylie Tiessen, "Ontario's Social Assistance Poverty Gap" (Ottawa: Canadian Centre for Policy Alternatives, May 2016), 5.

60 Graham Riches, "Food Banks and Food Security: Welfare Reform, Human Rights, and Social Policy: Lessons Lessons from Canada?," *Social Policy and Administration* 36, no. 6 (December 2002), 654, 656.

61 Linda Synder, "Workfare: Ten Years of Pickin' on the Poor," in *Canadian Social Policy: Issues and Perspectives*, ed. Anne Westhues (Waterloo: Wilfrid Laurier University Press, 2006), 319.

62 Patricia M. Evans, "(Not) Taking Account of Precarious Employment: Workfare Policies and Lone Mothers in Ontario and the UK," *Social Policy and Administration* 41, no. 1 (February 2007): 34, 38.

63 Margaret Hillyard Little, "The Leaner, Meaner Welfare Machine: The Ontario Conservative Government's Ideological and Material Attack on Single Mothers," in *Gender and Women's Studies in Canada: Critical Terrain*, ed. Margaret Helen Hobbs and Carla Rice (Toronto: Canadian Scholars' Press, 2013), 620, 628.

64 Dean Herd, "Rhetoric and Retrenchment: Ontario's 'Common Sense' Welfare Reform," *Benefits* 34, no. 10 (2002): 3-5; Krystle Maki, "Neoliberal Deviants and Surveillance: Welfare Recipients under the Watchful Eye of Ontario Works," *Surveillance and Society* 9, nos. 1–2 (2011): 52–6.

65 Julie Ann McMullin, Lorraine Davies, and Gale Cassidy, "Welfare Reform in Ontario: Tough Times in Mothers' Lives," *Canadian Public Policy* 28, no. 2 (2002): 307, 311.

66 Atkinson Charitable Foundation, *Time for a Fair Deal: Report of the Task Force on Modernizing Income Security* (Toronto: St. Christopher's House, May 2006), 11.

67 Maeve Quaid, "The Ontario Works Program – Mutiny on the Bounty," in Quaid, *Workfare: Why Good Social Policy Ideas Go Bad* (Toronto: University of Toronto Press, 2002), 172,

177–8, 184, 190; Patricia Evans, "(Not) Taking Account of Precarious Employment," 37. See also Jacinthe Michaud, "Feminist Representation(s) of Women Living on Welfare: The Case of Workfare and the Erosion of Volunteer Time," *Canadian Review of Sociology and Anthropology* 41, no. 3 (2004); and Dean Herd, Ernie Lightman, and Andrew Mitchell, "Searching for Local Local Solutions: Making Welfare Policy on the Ground in Ontario," *Journal of Progressive Human Services* 20 (2009).

68 Ernie Lightman, Andrew Mitchell, and Dean Herd, "Workfare in Toronto: More of the Same?," *Journal of Sociology and Social Welfare* 32, no. 4 (2005): 67, 71.

69 Michael Olephant, "Behind the Issues: Ontario 2003: Whatever Happened to Welfare?," Canadian Centre for Policy Alternatives, 2003.

70 Synder, "Ten Years of Pickin' on the Poor," 317, 324–5.

71 Herd, Lightman, and Mitchell, "Searching for Local Solutions," 135.

72 Nathan Laurie, Ontario Association of Food Banks, "The Cost of Poverty: An Analysis of the Economic Cost of Poverty in Ontario" (Toronto: Metcalf Foundation and the Atkinson Foundation, November 2008), 3, 7, 18; Ontario, "Breaking the Cycle: Ontario's Poverty Reduction Strategy" (Toronto: Queen's Printer, 2008), 5.

73 Bryan D. Palmer and Gaétan Héroux, *Toronto's Poor: A Rebellious History* (Toronto: Between the Lines), 401.

74 Palmer and Héroux, *Toronto's Poor*, 402.

75 Palmer and Héroux, *Toronto's Poor*, 403–11.

76 Palmer and Héroux, *Toronto's Poor*, 410.

77 Rodney Haddow, *Comparing Quebec and Ontario: Political Economy and Public Policy at the Turn of the Millenium* (Toronto: University of Toronto Press, 2015), 123.

78 Ontario, "Breaking the Cycle: Ontario's Poverty Reduction Strategy" (Toronto: Queen's Printer, 2008), 7–8, 19–20, 25, 29, 34, 41.

79 See for example, John Stapleton, "*Transitions* Revisited: Implementing the Vision," (Ottawa: Caledon Institute, 2004); Ken Battle, Michael Mendelson, and Sherri Torjman, "Towards a New Architecture for Canada's Adult Benefits" (Ottawa: Caledon Institute, 2006); Ron Saunders, "Risk and Opportunity: Creating Options for Vulnerable Workers" (Ottawa: Canadian Policy Research Network, 2006); St. Christopher's House and Toronto City Summit Alliance, "Time for a Fair Deal: Report of the Task Force on Modernizing Income Security for Working-Age Adults" (Toronto: St. Christopher's House, 2006); Stapleton, "Why Is It So Tough to Get Ahead? How Our Tangled Social Programs Pathologize the Transition to Self-Reliance," (Toronto: Metcalf Foundation, 2007); Ontario Association of Food Banks, "The Cost of Poverty: An Economic Analysis of Poverty in Ontario" (Toronto: 2008).

80 Stapleton, "Why Is It So Tough to Get Ahead?," 6, 16.

81 Haddow, *Comparing Quebec and Ontario*, 124.

82 Ontario, "Breaking the Cycle," 21.

83 Frances Lankin and Munir A. Sheikh, "Brighter Prospects: Transforming Social Assistance in Ontario" (Ontario: Queen's Printer: 2012), 110; George Campeau, *From UI to EI: Waging War on the Welfare State* (Vancouver: UBC Press, 2005), 165.

84 John Stapleton with Vass Bednar, "Trading Places: Single Adults Replace Lone Parents as the New Face of Social Assistance in Canada" (Toronto: Mowat Centre, 2011), 16.

85 Stapleton with Bednar, "Trading Places," 2, 16.

86 John Stapleton, "Close Encounters of the 'Thirties' Kind" (Ottawa: Canadian Centre for Policy Alternatives, 2009), 5.

87 Lankin and Sheikh, "Brighter Prospects," 1, 10–11.
88 Lankin and Sheikh, "Brighter Prospects," 16–18, 26.
89 Lankin and Sheikh, "Brighter Prospects," 49, 55.
90 Ontario, "Realizing Our Potential: Ontario's Poverty Reduction Strategy, 2014–2019," (Toronto: Queen's Printer, 2013), 3, 9–10, 29, 32, 39.
91 Canadian Union of Public Employees, "CUPE Ontario and the Raise the Rates Campaign" (Toronto, May 2014), 2; Laurie Monsebraaten, "Ontario nixes merger of province's two welfare programs," *Toronto Star*, 7 April 2014.
92 John Stapleton, "The Working Poor in the Toronto Region: Mapping Working Poverty in Canada's Richest City" (Toronto: Metcalf Foundation, April 2015), 10, 27, 30.
93 Kaylie Tiessen, "Ontario's Social Assistance Poverty Gap" (Ottawa: Canadian Centre for Policy Alternatives, 2016), 5–6, 8–10.
94 Sarah Pennisi and Stephanie Baker Collins, "Workfare under Ontario Works: Making Sense of Jobless Work," *Social Policy and Administration* 51, no. 7 (2017): 1314.
95 Ontario, Office of the Auditor General, "Ministry of Children, Community and Social Services, Chapter 3, Section 3.11, Ontario Works" (Toronto: Queen's Printer, 2019), 494–5.
96 Tracy Smith-Carrier and Steven Green, "Another Low Road to Basic Income? Mapping a Pragmatic Model for Adopting a Basic Income in Canada," *Basic Income Studies*, 2017, 2.
97 Ontario, "Income Security: A Roadmap for Change," Report of the Income Reform Working Group; the First Nations Income Security Reform Working Group; and the Urban Indigenous Table on Income Security Reform, 2017 (Toronto: Queen's Printer, 2017), 38.
98 Ontario, "Income Security," 2.
99 Ontario, "Income Security," 10–11.
100 Ontario, "Income Security," 17.
101 Ontario, "Income Security," 26.
102 Ontario, "Income Security," 125.
103 Hugh D. Segal, "Finding a Better Way: A Basic Income Pilot Project for Ontario, a Discussion Paper" (Toronto: Queen's Printer: August 2016), 13, 15–17.
104 Segal, "Finding a Better Way," 4.
105 Segal, "Finding a Better Way," 8.
106 Segal, "Finding a Better Way," 8–9, 42.
107 Segal, "Finding a Better Way," 63.
108 Segal, "Finding a Better Way," 7.
109 Michael Mendelson, "Lessons from Ontario's Basic Income Pilot" (Toronto: Maytree Foundation, October 2019), 12–13. Mendelson argues that Lindsay was not actually a "saturation site" because only participants who initially enrolled in 2017 could continue participating over the full three years of the pilot, rather than other individuals in the community whose incomes changed over this time period.
110 *Toronto Star*, "'I may end up homeless again': Six Ontarians talk about their life before, after and, once again, without basic income,"2 August 2018.
111 Mohammad Ferdosi, Tom McDowell, Wayne Lewchuk, and Stephanie Ross, "Southern Ontario's Basic Income Experience," (McMaster University Labour Studies, Hamilton Roundtable for Poverty Reduction, Hamilton Community Foundation, March 2020), 4; Laurie Monsebraaten and Rob Ferguson, "Ontario government scraps Basic Income pilot project, limits welfare increase to 1.5 percent," *Toronto Star*, 31 July 2018.
112 Kristin Rushowy, "Basic income pilot project to end 31 March 2019," *Toronto Star*, 31 August 2018.

113 Ferdosi et al., 4–5, 7, 9–12, 21–2, 26, 46, 60; Ontario, Office of the Auditor General, "Ministry of Children, Community and Social Services, Chapter 3, Section 3.11, Ontario Works," 494.

114 Laurie Monsebraaten, "Ontario to allow people on social assistance to keep part of emergency benefits," *Toronto Star*, 20 April 2020; Monsebraaten, "Why do provinces often confiscate federal benefits from people who clearly need them?," *Toronto Star*, 22 May 2020; David Olive, "Millions of Canadians are now collecting a state-funded income. But what happens after the pandemic ends?" *Toronto Star*, 18 April 2020; Evelyn Forget and Hugh Segal, "CERB is an unintended experiment in basic income," *Globe and Mail*, 19 April 2020.

Contributors

Carly Adams teaches and is the Director of the Centre for Oral History and Tradition at the University of Lethbridge. She is the editor of *Sport and Recreation in Canadian History.*

Dimitry Anastakis is a professor and the L.R. Wilson and R.J. Currie Chair in Canadian Business History in the Department of History and the Rotman School of Management at the University of Toronto.

Valerie J. Andrews is completing a PhD and teaches at York University. She is the author of the book, *White Unwed Mother: The Adoption Mandate in Postwar Canada.*

Mathieu Arsenault teaches at the Université de Montréal.

Rebecca Beausaert teaches at the University of Guelph and Wilfrid Laurier University. She is the author of *Pursuing Play: Women's Leisure in Small-Town Ontario, 1870–1914.*

Jennifer Bonnell teaches at York University. She is the author of the award-winning book, *Reclaiming the Don: An Environmental History of Toronto's Don River Valley.*

Penny Bryden teaches at the University of Victoria. She is the author of *Canada: A Political Biography*.

Lara Campbell teaches at Simon Fraser University. She is the author of *Respectable Citizens: Gender, Family and Unemployment in Ontario's Great Depression.*

Lori Chambers teaches at Lakehead University. She is the author of *A Legal History of Adoption in Ontario, 1921–2015.*

Cynthia R. Comacchio teaches at Wilfrid Laurier University. She is the author of *The Dominion of Youth: Adolescence and the Making of Modern Canada*, which won the prize for the best book written in Canadian history in 2008.

Afua Cooper teaches at Dalhousie University and is Chair of the Scholarly Panel on Lord Dalhousie's Relationship to Race and Slavery. She is the author of *The Hanging of Angelique: The Untold Story of Canadian Slavery and the Burning of Old Montreal.*

Peter P. Constantinou teaches at York University. He is a long-time public servant who has worked at federal and provincial levels of government in addition to his scholarly work.

Patrice Dutil teaches at Toronto Metropolitan University. He is the author of *Prime Ministerial Power in Canada: Its Origins Under Macdonald, Laurier and Borden.*

Keith R. Fleming teaches Canadian history at Western University. He is the author of *The World is Our Parish: John King Gordon, 1900–1989: An Intellectual Biography.*

Gaétan Héroux is a long time anti-poverty activist with the Ontario Coalition Against Poverty. He is the co-author, along with Bryan D. Palmer, of the award-winning book, *Toronto's Poor: A Rebellious History.*

Colleen Kaiser is a post-doctoral fellow at the Smart Property Institute. She has authored several peer-reviewed journal articles and her research interests include climate policy integration and governance regimes for low-carbon transportation.

Jean L. Manore is the Dean of Humanities at Bishop's University. She is the author of *Cross Currents: Hydroelectricity and the Engineering of Northern Ontario.*

Marcel Martel teaches at York University and holds the Avie Bennett Historica Canada Chair in Canadian History. He is the author of the book, *Canada the Good? A Short History of Vice Since 1500.*

Edgar-André Montigny is a lawyer and is the author of *Foisted upon the Government: State Responsibilities, Family Obligations, and the Care of the Dependent Aged.*

Alison Norman is Senior Historian for Crown Indigenous Relations and Northern Affairs Canada, and she is an adjunct graduate faculty member at the Frost Centre for Canadian Studies and Indigenous Studies, Trent University.

James Onusko teaches at Northern Lakes College. He is the author of *Boom Kids: Growing Up in Calgary's Suburbs, 1950-70,* which is forthcoming from Wilfrid Laurier University Press.

Bryan D. Palmer is professor emeritus as the Canada Research Chair in Canadian Studies at Trent University. He is the co-author, along with Gaétan Héroux, of the award-winning book, *Toronto's Poor: A Rebellious History.*

Lisa Pasolli teaches at Queen's University. She is the author of the award-winning book, *Working Mothers and the Child Care Dilemma: A History of British Columbia's Social Policy.*

Mona-Margaret Pon is a researcher and writer in Toronto, Ontario.

David Rapaport is an adjunct professor in the Department of Sociology at Trent University. He is the author of the book *No Justice No Peace: The 1996 OPSEU Strike Against the Harris Government in Ontario.*

Geoffrey Reaume teaches disability history at York University. He is the author of the book, *Remembrance of Patients Past: Life at the Toronto Hospital for the Insane, 1870–1940.*

James Struthers is professor emeritus at Trent University. He is the author of the book, *The Limits of Affluence: Welfare in Ontario, 1920-1970.*

Mark Winfield is a professor in the Faculty of Environmental and Urban Change at York University, and co-chair of the Faculty's Sustainable Energy Initiative. He is co-editor of *Sustainable Energy Transitions in Canada* and the author of *Blue-Green Province: The Environment and the Political Economy of Ontario.*